CAMBRIDGE LIBRARY COLLECTION

Books of enduring scholarly value

Maritime Exploration

This series includes accounts, by eye-witnesses and contemporaries, of voyages by Europeans to the Americas, Asia, Australasia and the Pacific during the colonial period. Driven by the military and commercial interests of powers including Britain, France and the Netherlands, particularly the East India Companies, these expeditions brought back a wealth of information on climate, natural resources, topography, and distant civilisations. Their detailed observations provide fascinating historical data for climatologists, ecologists and anthropologists, and the accounts of the mariners' experiences on their long and dangerous voyages are full of human interest.

History of Merchant Shipping and Ancient Commerce

The shipowner and politician William Schaw Lindsay (1816–77) combined a wealth of personal experience with a meticulous approach to research. Originally published in 1874–6, this is his authoritative four-volume history of the world of ships and maritime trade. Its coverage ranges from the legend of Noah's Ark, through ancient commerce and the colonising expeditions of the middle ages, to the progress brought about by the introduction of steam to the shipping of Lindsay's own day. Details on construction and performance sit alongside explanations of the customs and superstitions of seamen, complemented by full accounts of many important nautical events. Volume 1 encompasses shipping in the ancient world, the foundation of a royal and commercial navy in England, and tales of the Norman invasion and the Crusades to the Holy Land, ending with Christopher Columbus' voyages of discovery. Evident throughout the work are Lindsay's practical knowledge and enthusiasm for his subject.

Cambridge University Press has long been a pioneer in the reissuing of out-of-print titles from its own backlist, producing digital reprints of books that are still sought after by scholars and students but could not be reprinted economically using traditional technology. The Cambridge Library Collection extends this activity to a wider range of books which are still of importance to researchers and professionals, either for the source material they contain, or as landmarks in the history of their academic discipline.

Drawing from the world-renowned collections in the Cambridge University Library and other partner libraries, and guided by the advice of experts in each subject area, Cambridge University Press is using state-of-the-art scanning machines in its own Printing House to capture the content of each book selected for inclusion. The files are processed to give a consistently clear, crisp image, and the books finished to the high quality standard for which the Press is recognised around the world. The latest print-on-demand technology ensures that the books will remain available indefinitely, and that orders for single or multiple copies can quickly be supplied.

The Cambridge Library Collection brings back to life books of enduring scholarly value (including out-of-copyright works originally issued by other publishers) across a wide range of disciplines in the humanities and social sciences and in science and technology.

History of Merchant Shipping and Ancient Commerce

VOLUME 1

W.S. LINDSAY

CAMBRIDGE UNIVERSITY PRESS

Cambridge, New York, Melbourne, Madrid, Cape Town,
Singapore, São Paolo, Delhi, Mexico City

Published in the United States of America by Cambridge University Press, New York

www.cambridge.org
Information on this title: www.cambridge.org/9781108057622

This edition first published 1874
This digitally printed version 2013

ISBN 978-1-108-05762-2 Paperback

The original edition of this book contains a number of colour plates, which have been reproduced in black and white. Colour versions of these images can be found online at www.cambridge.org/9781108057622

HISTORY

OF

MERCHANT SHIPPING

AND

ANCIENT COMMERCE.

BY

W. S. LINDSAY.

IN FOUR VOLUMES.

VOL. I.

With numerous Illustrations.

LONDON:
SAMPSON LOW, MARSTON, LOW, AND SEARLE,
CROWN BUILDINGS, 188 FLEET STREET.
1874.

LONDON:
PRINTED BY WILLIAM CLOWES AND SONS,
STAMFORD STREET AND CHARING CROSS

PREFACE.

ALTHOUGH familiar with most subjects relating to Merchant Ships, I have found it alike necessary and desirable to look to others for aid in collecting some of the materials for this work; and I am especially indebted to my friends Mr. Vaux, F.R.S., late of the British Museum, and Sir Patrick Colquhoun, Q.C., for much valuable assistance rendered by them in connection with the two volumes now presented to the public. By combining the learning of my friends, so far as regards the records of the ships and commerce of ancient times, with my own knowledge of the subject, I am not without hope that the work may in some respects prove useful.

I am also much indebted to Mr. T. H. Farrer, of the Board of Trade, and to his assistant, Mr. Thomas Gray, of the Marine Department, for many valuable suggestions; and in thanking them for their courtesy,

I venture to express the belief that by their assistance and that of other friends I shall be able to give in the two succeeding volumes necessary to complete the work an impartial narrative of the many important events and changes which have occurred within my own time, I might say within my own experience, together with an accurate account of the ships and maritime commerce of the age in which we live.

W. S. LINDSAY.

SHEPPERTON MANOR, MIDDLESEX.

CONTENTS.

INTRODUCTORY.

CHAPTER I.

CHAPTER II.

CHAPTER III.

CHAPTER IV.

CHAPTER V.

CHAPTER VI.

CHAPTER VII.

CHAPTER VIII.

CHAPTER IX.

CHAPTER X.

CHAPTER XI.

CHAPTER XII.

CHAPTER XIII.

CHAPTER XIV.

CHAPTER XV.

CHAPTER XVI.

CHAPTER XVII.

APPENDICES.

INTRODUCTORY.

Introductory—The first attempt to float, by means of a hollowed log and raft—The Ark—Boats of skin—Earliest boats or ships—Their form—Mode of construction—Names of ships—Decorations—Launching, &c.—Master—Mate—Boatswain—St. Paul's ship—Rig and sails—Undergirders—Anchors and cables—Decks—Nautical instruments—Mariner's compass—Speed of ancient ships.

Introductory.

It is my intention to write a History of Merchant Shipping; I am not aware that there exists any work of the kind contemplated. No doubt everything relating to the vessels of ancient times has been published in one form or another, as also an account of all that is known of the maritime commerce of the Middle Ages; but this information is widely scattered, and frequently so diffused among other matters of a very different description, that considerable research is necessary to ascertain where it is to be found. I desire to remedy this inconvenience, and to furnish from those fragmentary materials a consecutive, though necessarily a condensed, account of the Merchant Shipping, Ancient and Modern, of those nations which at different periods have carried on an extensive over-sea commerce. I shall also presume to correct some errors and misapprehensions which have found their way into the writings of men who, though far more competent to undertake the work of an historian, have not had an opportunity of gaining a practical knowledge of this special subject.

It is only from Holy Writ, from the fragments in the works of heathen historians and poets, and from the sculptured monuments of the East, that information can be obtained about the vessels and commerce of very ancient times. From such sources I shall endeavour to compile, in a manner as brief as possible consistently with perspicuity, a narrative of how these vessels were constructed, manned, and navigated, separating, as far as my knowledge and experience will permit, facts from fiction, and omitting legends frequently accepted as historical truths. It can serve no good purpose to record descriptions of ships evidently the creations of romance; and, in a work professing to deal with established facts, care must be taken to admit nothing improbable unless well authenticated.

It will not be the least pleasing portion of my work to furnish, as fully as I can, a description of the manners and customs of the seamen of all nations, and, at the same time, to notice incidentally their habits, prejudices, and superstitions. To illustrate the effects produced upon maritime commerce by the laws of different nations, it will be necessary to direct attention to those legislative measures which have had a marked bearing upon its prosperity or otherwise. Towards the close of this work, the merchant vessels of our own time, the cost of construction, speed, and capacity for cargo, will be fully described, as well as the number and duties of the crew, and the expenses of management. I shall endeavour to supply every material fact connected with the business of the shipowner, which nowadays is separated from that of the merchant, so that hereafter a complaint may not be urged against me for having followed the example of other writers, and by so doing omitted interesting and instructive knowledge, simply because it was of a character hitherto considered beyond the province of the historian.

Many years have already been employed in collecting materials for this work, but hitherto time has been wanting for the study and elucidation of a subject which, from the nature of my avocations, can hardly fail to prove interesting to myself, whatever it may be to my readers. To trace the origin of navigation, and to detail the numerous steps by which the merchant vessels of the great trading nations of the world have reached their present state of perfection; to record those discoveries in science and art connected with navigation, which enable the mariner to cross the ocean without fear and with unerring certainty; to dilate upon those triumphs of man's genius and skill whereby he can bid defiance to the elements; and to enter in these pages the names of the men who have benefited mankind by their maritime discoveries, or by affording greatly increased facilities for intercourse between nations, is to me a task of the most gratifying description.

But as many of my readers may not take so lively an interest in a subject necessarily dry in its character and technical in its details, I shall endeavour to describe everything relating to shipping in clear and condensed language, so as to induce them, if possible, to accompany me in my researches; and it is to be hoped that at least the ships and commerce of the ancient Egyptians and Phœnicians, and of those nations which, like Carthage and Assyria, have long since passed away, may prove not uninteresting to the general public.

Passing from very remote ages, I purpose to examine the maritime commerce and shipping of the different nations which flourished from about the time when, on the decline of the power of Rome, the Italian Republics arose; and thence through the Middle Ages, till Spain sent forth her celebrated Armada, to the period when Great Britain, slowly but surely extending her influence upon the ocean, claimed to be "Mistress of the Seas."

Considerable space must likewise be devoted to an account of the principal institutions connected with shipping, and to the vast changes which have taken place in the over-sea carrying trade since Vasco da Gama doubled the Cape of Good Hope, and Christopher Columbus discovered a new and now mighty world to the West.

But the larger portion of this work will be devoted to the progress of Modern Shipping. Since the introduction of steam, the merchant navies of the world have increased to an enormous extent; and in comfort, beauty, and speed, the vessels of the present day immeasurably surpass those of any other period. Modern appliances in their propulsion, while altering the mode in which commercial pursuits are conducted, have also materially changed the seats and centres of maritime commerce. Changes such as these necessarily require to be fully described, and their results carefully recorded.

As the ports of Great Britain are now free to the vessels of all nations, it will be my duty to explain the nature of the navigation laws of Cromwell and of the reciprocity treaties of Huskisson, and to show how, step by step, all barriers to free navigation have been removed. The fallacy of endeavouring to enrich ourselves by the ruin of our neighbours will be exposed, and, from the experience of the past, I shall hope to inculcate lessons of use for the future.

Ample materials are to be found for the elucidation of most of these subjects, and there can be no excuse to plead, beyond my own incapacity, if I fail to produce a work which shall hereafter be useful for reference, especially with regard to the merchant vessels of modern times. Though the enterprising traders of Tyre extended their commercial intercourse to all parts of the Mediterranean and even to the Northern and the Erythræan Seas, yet her merchants, "who were princes," and her traffickers, who were "the great men of the earth," have left no records of their vast commerce, nor of the vessels which were engaged in it. No mercantile man appears to have written an account of how he conducted his trade, or given to posterity a drawing of his ship; nor, indeed, to have recorded anything relating to the great maritime state to which he belonged. Our limited knowledge of Tyre is derived therefore almost exclusively from other sources. If these early navigators had taken one-half the pains to transmit to posterity the sum of their acquired knowledge, practical and historical, which the Egyptians have done, a vast amount of information would have been added to the science of ancient navigation and commerce. Unfortunately, almost every vestige of Phœnicia has been swept away, a significant example that the most extended commerce, enjoyed by a purely trading people, cannot alone save them from eventual insignificance and oblivion.

In concluding these introductory remarks, I may be fairly permitted to indulge the hope that, from the vast stores of knowledge bequeathed to us, we may leave more lasting records of our maritime commerce than either Tyre or Carthage, and that the improved civilization and extensive colonial possessions of Great Britain may render her pre-eminence at sea and her commercial greatness much more enduring than the once celebrated maritime city of the Phœnicians, which has become "a place for the spreading of nets in the midst of the sea," and "a spoil to the nations."

The first attempt to float,

It is impossible to say who first taught man to float upon a log or an inflated skin, or who had the genius to construct the earliest raft. The exclusive honour of the discovery of navigation—which now, through the successive improvements of many ages, and the application of steam as a motive power, has arrived at its present high state of development, tending to the safety, convenience, and civilization of mankind—is too great an honour to be awarded to any single individual. Indeed it is a glory which writers alike in ancient and in modern times have declined to confer on any frail mortal like themselves. Accordingly the Libyans and the Greeks ascribed the merit of the invention to the gods. Neptune, however little in other respects may be known of this mythological personage, was not only worshipped by the ancients as the first inventor of navigation and supreme ruler of the sea, but his glory has survived the wreck of empires and the extinction of races, and the name of a heathen god is still associated with the dominion of the ocean.

by means of a hollowed log,

There is, however, no difficulty in conceiving what would give the first idea of flotation. At the period of the earliest history of man acknowledged by Christian nations, our first parents must have noticed leaves or branches of trees floating in the river "which went out of Eden to water the garden." Thus would be conceived at the creation of man the idea of a vessel or of a substance which would float and could be made useful for his wants.[1] The

[1] See a good passage in Claudian's "Rape of Proserpine," on this subject; and Virgil, Georg. i. 136.

buoyancy of the branch or trunk of a tree would suggest the means of carrying him across unfordable rivers; and there is no doubt that, long anterior to the era assigned to Noah, the first step in the art of ship-building was taken in hollowing out the log by fire, or by some rude instrument, in order to render more secure the position of any adventurous navigator. A pole or paddle might be used to propel the rude barque, but probably ages passed away without any improvement in this respect. In fact, to this day, some of the inhabitants of the Polynesian Islands have not made any greater progress in the construction of their primitive vessels; and the canoes in the Pacific, and in various parts of South America, are still formed on what is evidently the most ancient model of vessels.

and raft. While the hollow log was made to answer the purpose of a boat, a number of logs placed together would suggest the idea of a raft, for the carrying of a number of persons or animals, or of any article of greater weight than could be conveyed in a canoe across a lake or river. These, by degrees, would be improved in form, in strength, or in capacity, to suit the wants of man or the navigation for which they were intended. The ingenuity of even the rudest savages would lead them, it may be easily supposed, in course of time, to construct their raft so as to make it more easy of propulsion, and thus give to it the first form of a ship.

But it is doubtful if any progress were made in ship-building beyond the mere raft, anterior to the period assigned to the Flood; and the Ark[1] of Noah is unquestionably the first ship of which we have any notice, either in acknowledged history or in the legends of the earliest nations. As this vessel, however, has been so much a matter of controversy, some of our readers may think it well, in imitation of other modern writers, that we should omit the consideration of the subject. But the difficulties, physical and practical, surrounding it ought not to induce us to pass over altogether unnoticed the earliest recorded effort of naval architecture. This great ship is described in Scripture[2] as having been three hundred cubits in length, fifty in breadth, and thirty in height or depth—dimensions corresponding very nearly with those of the most approved models of the sailing vessels of the present day. If the cubit be taken at eighteen inches, her registered tonnage, reckoned according to the present mode of admeasurement, would not have been more than fifteen thousand tons, or considerably less than that of the *Great Eastern*.

The Ark.

But the probability is that, after all, the Ark was simply a raft of stupendous size, bearing on it a structure of the above dimensions resembling a huge warehouse, roofed in the usual manner, and built to float on the breast of a great flood, the narrative in the Bible neither suggesting nor requiring any means of propulsion.[3]

[1] Noah's Ark, B.C. 2348.

[2] Gen. vi. 15.

[3] Gen. vii. 16, 17. Cory, "Ancient Fragm.," for traditions of the Ark in various lands.

Although for years after the Flood[1] the raft may have been the only form of vessel for carrying heavy burthens, other means of flotation must soon have suggested themselves; and of these, the inflated skins of animals would seem to have prevailed the most generally and the most widely. Thus on the ancient monuments recently discovered by Mr. Layard, we find numerous representations of the Assyrians crossing a river—probably the Tigris—on inflated skins; and rafts may also be seen on which goods and men are floating down similarly supported.[2] The same practice is still in use among the present inhabitants of the country, and is also noticed as common on the Setlege by Baron Hügel, in his interesting "Travels in Cashmir."[3] Baron Hügel also speaks of baskets, suspended from ropes firmly tied to each shore, for crossing the mountain waters of the same river; while *coracles*—basket-work over which leather or prepared flannel has been stretched—may still be seen in Wales, thus enabling the inhabitants to fish, and to cross streams not

Boats of skin.

[1] The Scriptural narrative of a great flood, and of a great vessel to float upon it, has just met with a remarkable confirmation. At a meeting of the Society of Biblical Archæology, Sir Henry Rawlinson in the chair, on December 3, 1872, Mr. George Smith, of the British Museum, read a paper, giving an account of his discovery, on cuneiform tablets (part of the so-called library of Ashur-ban-i-pal, king of Nineveh), of an unquestionable account of the Deluge. The name of the king under whom this event occurred cannot as yet be deciphered, nor can anything like a certain date be assigned to it; but Sir Henry Rawlinson accepted fully the truth of Mr. Smith's decipherings. Of the inscription describing the Flood, there are fragments of three copies, containing duplicate texts.

[2] Layard, First Series. Pls. 10, 12, 13, 15, 25, 27, 28.

[3] Hügel, "Travels in Cashmir," p. 27, with a picture, p. 247.

otherwise fordable. It is also worthy of note that Pliny[1] alludes to this custom, where he states that "Even now, in British waters, vessels of vine-twigs sewn round with leather are used." Mr. Layard[2] likewise speaks of still finding on the Tigris light boats called *terradas*, constructed by the Southern Mesopotamians of twisted reeds, rendered watertight by bitumen, and often of sufficient consistency to support four or five men. As a remarkable proof of the long persistency of custom and of trade, we may add that the bitumen of Babylonia was exported to Egypt so early as the reign of Thothmes III., B.C. 1500, from the Is (now Hit) of Herodotus, where it is still abundant.

The *balza* of the western coast of South America, in use within the last hundred years, appears to have been a raft of logs of very light wood carefully fastened together, and capable of carrying occasionally as much as twenty tons.[3]

Such were probably the rude beginnings of the art of ship-building.

Earliest boats or ships.

Though it is impossible to give any authentic details of forms and means of navigation, such as those we have mentioned—remembrances as they are of pre-historic times—we need not doubt that the earliest people who practised navigation, in any sense after the manner since recognised, by ships or

[1] Pliny, vii. 57. Cf. also Lucan, Phars. iv. 131. Such vessels were called "boats sewn together," Plin. xxiv. 65; and Virgil (Æn. vi. 448) gives the same title to Charon's boat.

[2] Layard, "Nineveh and Babylon," pp. 522–524.

[3] "Relaçion historica del Viage a la America Meridional," 1748; Charnock, "Hist. Mar. Arch." i. p. 12.

boats as distinguished from rafts, were the inhabitants of the eastern coast of the Mediterranean, and, notably, the Phœnicians of Sidon and Tyre.

The Phœnicians, however, as is now admitted, were not originally inhabitants of the territory they have made famous by their commercial operations, but immigrants from the shores of the Persian Gulf, whence they carried with them the nautical tastes and knowledge they had been maturing, perhaps for centuries, to develop them in a new and enlarged sphere. Indeed, it is not unlikely that, antecedently to History, these enterprising people had made voyages even to the far-distant East, as the "Erythræan Sea" comprehended an area far wider than our Red Sea, being really, as in Herodotus,[1] what we now call the "Indian Ocean." If it be true that Jacob's blessing,[2] "Zebulun shall dwell at the haven of the sea; and he shall be for an haven of ships," is probably the earliest written document implying navigation of *any* kind, it is at the same time impossible to determine at what period that prophecy was to take place, while the occurrence of the name Zidon in the next paragraph, "His border shall be unto Zidon," might suggest the inference that the wording of this announcement, as we have it now, is of later date than Jacob himself.

Neither the Egyptians nor the Greeks have any claim to be considered among the first navigators; indeed, the former people were during their whole

[1] Herod. i. 1. [2] Gen. xlix. 13.

history averse to seafaring pursuits, and were dependent on the Phœnicians for nearly all their carrying trade, beyond what passed along their own great river, while the first Greek expedition—that of the Argonauts, to which we shall refer presently —was possibly as much a Phœnician as a Greek adventure.

In form, we may be sure that the first boats were flat-bottomed—barges for river service rather than ships for the sea. But keels must have been added as soon as ever coasting voyages commenced, or any speed was needed. In shallow waters they may have been propelled by poles, like modern punts; but oars, and at least one sail of simple construction, must have been introduced very early. **Their form.**

Passing over the exploits attributed to Perseus, Theseus, and Bellerophon, from which no facts worthy of record are deducible, it is enough to state here that in the construction of the earliest rafts or boats the axe or the adze was, probably, the only implement the builders possessed, the result of their work being doubtless of the rudest character;[1] and that the timber first employed would be that most ready at hand in the countries where such vessels were first required; though but a short time would elapse, and but little experience be needed, to insure the selection of those woods which were

[1] Homer (Od. v. 243), &c., gives some curious details of the building of the vessel of Ulysses; whence it appears that he made use of an axe, had means of cutting planks, together with a boring instrument to make holes for nails and hooks: he had also ropes, and at least one sail. His bulwark was raised higher by wickerwork, to prevent the sea dashing over.

the best for the purpose intended. Phœnicia, Cyprus, and Greece were well supplied with all the timber that could have been wanted. Hence we have early notices of the employment of the oak, the chestnut, and the cedar; while the pine, together with the alder, the ilex, and the ash, were in general use for ship-building. Many fanciful stories are told in Hesiod, Vegetius, and other writers, of the methods adopted by the ancient workmen to secure sound and durable timber; but on these we need not here dwell.

Mode of construction. It may be inferred from the passage in Homer that in his time sawn timber was not unknown; and, though nearly all the then voyages were performed by coasting from headland to headland, it is clear from other passages[1] that the navigators did even then sometimes venture out of sight of land: their vessels were, however, then, and for many years later, undecked; few representations of any ancient galleys, even on the earliest vases, having come down to us in which there is any certain indication of a deck: while Thucydides distinctly gives it as his opinion that the Homeric vessels were only large open boats.[2] The larger ones had, perhaps, a sort of half-deck, to give the people in them a little shelter. Being flat-floored and of small immersion, they as it were glided over the surface of the water, having little or no power of resistance to the action of the waves, and being, therefore, capable of very little progress except when sailing before the wind. To enable them to resist the penetrating power of

[1] Hom. Od. xii. 403, as compared xiv. 302. [2] Thucyd. ii. 13, 14.

the water, the ancients appear to have used in very early times a species of pounded sea-shells, introduced carefully into the seams and chinks between the planks—a process found to answer well for a short time; when, however, the ship strained, this caulking was liable to fall out, letting in the water as before. A somewhat similar method is described in the Transactions of the Embassy sent to China in 1792, as seen there at that time.

In later days, other methods were adopted; one of which, attributed by Pliny to the Belgæ,[1] consisted in beating pounded seeds into the fissures between the planks of vessels—a substance, he says, found to be more tenacious than glue, and more to be relied on than pitch. This is evidently the same in principle as the modern practice of caulking. In the same way we find in remote times that pitch and wax were used partly for the prevention of leakage, and partly also to preserve the planks from the sea-weeds and animalculæ with which the waters of the Mediterranean abound.[2] The discovery, too, of what is supposed to have been a galley of Trajan at the bottom of Lake Riccio shows clearly that, in Roman times, sheathing as well as caulking were used to preserve the bottoms of ships. The famous Locke,[3] alluding to this discovery, says, "Here we have caulking and sheathing together above sixteen hundred years ago; for I suppose no one can doubt that the sheet of

[1] Pliny, xvi. 158.
[2] Ovid, Metam. xi. 516, and Epist. ad Œnonen, v. 42.
[3] John Locke, "Hist. of Navigation," prefixed to Harris's "Coll. of Voyages."

lead nailed over the outside with copper nails was sheathing, and that in great perfection; the copper nails being used rather than iron, which, when once rusted in water with the working of the ship, soon lose their hold and drop out."

Names of ships.

Ships in ancient times were known by a great variety of names, most of which are descriptive of the purposes for which they were built, or of the services in which they were employed.

Omitting *triremes*, the most usual *ships of war*, the following list enumerates their chief varieties:—

Thus *olkas* was a large heavy tow-barge; *ponto*—a word of Gallic or Celtic origin[1]—a *punt*.

Gaulos, a round heavy merchant vessel, named probably so originally by the Phœnicians, and preserved to modern days in the galleon or galeass of the Middle Ages, and the *galley* of later times.

Corbitæ, slow sailing ships of burthen—so called because they carried baskets at their mast-heads. *Hippagogi*, as their name implies, carried horses. The characteristic of all these vessels was that their structure was bulky, their sides and bottom rounded from the flat, and, though not without rowers, that they were chiefly dependent on their sails.

Of a lighter class, and for greater speed, were the *scapha* (or skiff); the *acation*, or *acatus*; and the *linter*, which, though like *ratis*, often used for any kind of vessel, was more strictly a light boat or wherry.[2] Generically, merchant vessels were called

[1] Cæsar, Bell. Gall. iii. 29.

[2] Livy, iv. 21. Cæsar, Bell. Gall. i. 12. Tibull. ii. 5, 34.

mercatoriæ, or *vectoriæ*, as being the carriers of merchandise. So *piscatoriæ* were boats used for fishing.

Decorations.

The ships of the Greeks had various ornaments attached to the prow and stern, most of which were afterwards adopted by the Romans, and may even still be seen on the waters of the Mediterranean. Thus an eye painted on each sideof the prow was supposed to indicate watchfulness and to ward off ill-luck; while the prow itself terminated in the *acrostolium*, the head of an animal or bird—corresponding in principle with our figure-head. An original goose-head (technically called *cheniscus*) is still preserved in the Bibliothèque at Paris.[1] So, at a later period, St. Paul's ship had for its "ensign" the "sign of Castor and Pollux,"[2] while Ovid's ship, which bore him to the land of his exile, had a head of Minerva painted on her prow.[3]

On the stern was the *aplustre*, forming a kind of roof over the steersman, and bearing also the image of the tutelary Deity—a flag or pennon—sometimes a lantern, as may be seen on Trajan's Column, and the purple sail which, in Roman times, marked the Admiral's ship.[4] Ships, it appears, were from remote times painted with various colours. Thus Homer specifies black, red, and purple,[5] and Herodotus speaks of red paint;[6] while Plautus, in a well-known passage, classes together ships and women as equally greedy of ornament.[7] It was also, occa-

[1] Millin's "Dict. de Beaux-Arts."
[2] Acts xxviii. 11.
[3] Ovid, Trist. i. 9, 2.
[4] Pliny, xix. 5.
[5] Hom. Il. ii. 637. Od. ix. 125; xi. 124.
[6] Herod. iii. 58.
[7] Plaut. Pœn. i. 2, 6.

sionally, the custom to paint the sails with stripes of various colours.

As a rule, the names of the ships were, in ancient days, feminine, and named from celebrated women, as Nausicaa; hence Aristophanes calls them "Virgins."[1] The Romans, on the other hand, sometimes gave them masculine names.

Launching, &c.

From the earliest ages, the launch of a vessel has been attended with considerable ceremonies; frequently with feasting and bands of music, and a dedication to various deities who were supposed to watch over her safety in an especial manner. On setting sail, she was adorned with flowers and garlands indicative of future prosperity; and the special aid of Neptune, Minerva, and of the other gods invoked with solemn prayer and sacrifices for her success.[2] When large fleets started, it was usual to send the lighter vessels first, then the ships which acted as convoy, and lastly those of heavy burthen or deep draught of water. The oars, when not required, were triced up to the sides of the vessels. On the completion of the voyage, ships were generally hauled up on shore and protected from the weather; similar prayers being again offered to Nereus, Glaucus, Melicertes, and the other deities of the sea, or to Mercury, to whom the merchant and shipowner (then almost invariably identical in meaning) had specially committed their ships.[3]

Men who had escaped shipwreck felt bound to

[1] Aristoph. Equit. 1313. [2] Virg. Æn. iii. 119.
[3] Hom. Odyss. iii. 4. Anthol. vi. c. xxi. Ep. 1.

make special offerings to the gods in testimony of their gratitude; sometimes hanging up in a neighbouring temple the garment in which they had been saved,[1] or shaving their hair—a custom Petronius justly calls the last vow of men who have saved nothing but their lives.[2]

Rigid discipline was maintained on board the ships, and punishments of great severity inflicted on those who failed to keep proper ward and watch; nay, even the barbarous practice of "keel-hauling," once not uncommon in the English service, was not wholly unknown to the ancients. The crews were generally composed of two classes; the mariners, who attended to the navigation and trimming of the sails, and the rowers. These offices were usually kept distinct, the mariners being rarely, except in cases of great emergency, compelled to labour at the oars.[3]

The work of the rowers, to which we shall allude more particularly hereafter, was one of severe toil; hence, as in modern times, the music of the voice or the pipe stimulated the rowers to fresh exertion or tended to relieve the depressing monotony of their work.[4] Many ancient writers, and notably Xenophon, Polybius, and Arrian,[5] have left us interesting accounts of the way in which the rowers were trained; the practice of the Greeks and Romans, and especially that of the latter people, having been remark-

[1] Horat. Od. i. 5, 15.
[2] Petron. c. lxiii.
[3] Polyb. lib. x.
[4] Stat. Theb. v. 343. Silius, vi. 361.
[5] Xenoph. Hist. i. Polyb. lib. x. Arrian, Peripl. Mar. Eux.

able for its perfection in the execution of the most difficult manœuvres.

Master. The master or pilot, whose place was in the stern, though not himself required to steer, was expected to understand the due management of the rudder and sails, the usual course of the winds, the indications in the sky of a change of weather, and the situation of the harbours most fitting for his vessel, or of the shoals the most to be avoided.[1] He was also expected to take proper cognizance of the omens offered by the sea-fowl and fishes, with divers other phenomena, as the murmuring of the floods, the dashing of waves against the shore, and other signs believed to import changes in the weather.[2]

Mate. Next in authority to the master was the mate, whose place was at the prow of the ship, and who had charge of the tackle and of the rowers, who were placed by him on their proper seats.[3] With him was associated a third officer, whom we may call the boatswain and steward, as he gave the word to the rowers and distributed the rations.[4] There was also a fourth officer, whose especial duty it was to take heed of possible rocks or shoals, and to direct the ship at night by the aid of long poles.

Boatswain.

St Paul's ship. It is remarkable that while we have many notices of matters comparatively unimportant, no writer of antiquity has given us any intelligible account of the capacity of their ships of burthen, at least anterior to the Christian era. Nor have the speculations of

[1] Ovid. Metam. iii.

[2] Propert. lib. ii. v. 990.

[3] Xen. Œcon. v. Athen. xv.

[4] Arrian, Exp. Alex. vi.

ST. PAUL'S SHIP, FROM THE WORK BY MR. SMITH OF JORDAN HILL.

modern authors been much more successful; with the exception of Mr. Smith, of Jordan Hill. His essay "On the Voyage and Shipwreck of St. Paul," the work of a man of much practical experience in the management of sailing craft, and a yachtsman of thirty years' practice, is a really valuable contribution to the history of ancient merchant ships. Mr. Smith has tested, by modern experiences, the details furnished by St. Luke,[1] and has himself worked out the "dead reckoning" of St. Paul's ship —a feat requiring both knowledge and skill. He has also, by a diligent comparison of the representations of ancient vessels on coins, and on the marbles and paintings of Pompeii, with the scriptural account of St. Paul's ship, reproduced as perfect a drawing as we are ever likely to obtain of the Mediterranean merchant-ship at the dawn of Christianity.

St. Paul's ship must have been one of considerable size, as, besides her cargo of grain, she had on board two hundred and seventy-six souls. Moreover, as she had to make a long and, as it turned out, a boisterous voyage, she must have been completely decked, and probably had two decks from the number of passengers she carried, besides a high poop and forecastle, like the ships of two or three centuries ago, though these are not shown in the illustration; her bulwarks were formed of battens fastened horizontally across the stanchions.

Mr. Smith has collected many instances bearing upon the arrangement of different parts of ancient

[1] James Smith, "Voyage of St. Paul," pp. 147-150.

ships. Thus, from a painting at Herculaneum, said to represent the ship of Theseus, he has shown that the ancient sailors knew the use of the capstan and hawser; but it still remains a difficulty to understand how their large ships were steered, unless some machinery were used of which we have no account, to work the very large oars thrust through portholes in either quarter. Mr. Smith has also proved, from representations on the Leaning Tower of Pisa, on the Bayeux Tapestry, and on the gold nobles of Edward III., that the primitive mode of steering by one or more oars—as visible on the reliefs of Trajan's Column—prevailed as late as the fourteenth century; such rude appliances, however, could have been available only for small vessels.[1]

Rig and sails.

For a long period the rig of ancient ships was of the simplest kind—a single large square sail on the mainmast being the chief means of propulsion. In the case of large vessels there was a sort of square sail on a short mast at the stern, and a similar one at the bow; but these would be of more use in steering than in propelling. The Romans appear to have had a small triangular sail, like the Greek letter Delta (Δ), which bore the name of *suppara*, from its supposed resemblance to a woman's shift;[2] but such a sail could only have been used in fair weather.

Undergirders.

"Undergirding" a ship, as mentioned by St. Luke, is rarely practised at the present day; but implements

[1] See Smith, pp. 143–147. The same practice may be noticed on some of the English municipal seals: see below, p. 399, &c.

[2] Lucan, v. 428; Stat. vii. 32.

for that purpose—probably stream cables or hempen hawsers—would seem certainly to have been part of the occasional outfit of ancient vessels. They are mentioned as having been kept in store in the Athenian arsenals, and to have been served out for voyages known to be of unusual danger.[1]

Anchors and cables. The use of anchors was early understood, but, in Homer's time, they were simply large stones attached by ropes to the prow.[2] In after-times, much attention seems to have been paid to their construction,[3] and ships often carried several (as St. Paul's, which had four[4]). A cork float marked where the anchor was sunken;[5] and *chain* cables were sometimes used, as is noticed by Arrian in his account of the siege of Tyre by Alexander.[6] In St. Paul's case, the fact that the ship was able to anchor by the stern probably saved the lives of those on board, as otherwise she might have driven broadside on the rocks.

Decks. But though, as we have stated, the small early coasting vessels may have had no decks, the large grain-carrying ships, which performed the voyages between Alexandria and Italy, were unquestionably fully decked. In the so-called "ship of Theseus,"[7] there is a complete deck, and also what would seem to be a skylight; nor need we doubt that, in the largest and best-fitted ships, there was adequate accommodation for both men and officers. The great ships constructed by Ptolemy Philopater and Hiero

[1] Polyb. xxviii. 3. Appian, v. 91. Cf. Boeckh, Seewesen, &c., p. 134.
[2] Hom. Il. i. 436. Od. ix. 137.
[3] Pliny, vii. 209.
[4] Acts xxvii. 29.
[5] Paus. viii. 12. Pliny, xvi. 34.
[6] Arrian, Exped. Alex. ii. 21.
[7] Antichità di Ercolano, ii. l. 14.

were (as we shall see hereafter) rather "show-ships," and cannot be considered as representing the usual type of even the most sumptuous of ancient merchant vessels.

Nautical instruments.

The skilled mariners of ancient days determined their latitude by means still in use, but their instruments were very inferior. The gnomon, in some form or other, was their most common instrument for measuring the length of the sun's shadow at noon on different days and in different places. We know from Herodotus,[1] that this instrument was of great antiquity—indeed, he ascribes the invention of it to the Babylonians; but the report of Arrian to the Emperor Hadrian[2] of his shipwreck implies that there were other instruments besides this on board. Pytheas, the first known navigator of the North Sea, is said to have determined the summer solstice at Marseilles by observing the proportion of the shadow of the gnomon.[3] Further, Eratosthenes drew a parallel of latitude through Gibraltar, Rhodes, and Lycia to India; while Hipparchus made the first map, on the principle of "Mercator's Projection," by transferring the celestial latitudes and longitudes to the terrestrial globe. On the other hand, Ptolemy erred so far in his calculation of the longitude, that he placed China 60° nearer Europe than it really is, and thus led Columbus to fancy the distance he had to traverse to the New World was just so much less. It must not, however, be forgotten that Aristotle,

[1] Herod. ii. 109. [2] Arrian, Peripl. Mar. Eux.
[3] Strabo, ii. 8.

centuries before him, when reasoning from the assumed sphericity of the earth, was really the first to point out that the west coast of Spain was the fittest point of departure for India.

The latitudes were reckoned in *stadia* from the Equator to Syracuse, the stadium being about two hundred and one yards and one foot. The determination of the longitude was, however, a far more difficult problem; as the only phenomena whereby men could readily determine the distance between any two places, viz. eclipses of the moon, would have been of no practical value in calculating a ship's position at sea; moreover, it would not be easy to secure certainty in such observations, nor could they easily be repeated. Hence the ancients were led to depend either on actual survey, or on the vague information obtainable from the reckonings of sailors, or on the itineraries of travellers. We need not, therefore, be surprised when we see how Ptolemy and the greatest of ancient geographers have erred, owing to the impossibility of fixing with even tolerable accuracy the longitudes of different places. It is likely that their practice of constantly landing might have in some degree supplied their deficiency in this particular; but we have now no record of any astronomical observations which were made at sea, by even the most skilful of ancient navigators. A sort of dead-reckoning—an observation of the position of the sun during the day, or of certain stars during night—was the haphazard mode by which their positions at sea were chiefly ascertained. If they had been accustomed to steer a direct course instead of following the coast line, or if they had been acquainted with the properties of the compass, or of any instrument by which the bearings of the different headlands could have been determined, they might, having found their latitude, have depended, as mariners in modern times have been often obliged to depend, with some confidence upon their dead-reckoning. The wonder is that they should ever have ceased to hug the land, and that they really ventured on the long voyages they unquestionably accomplished.

Mariner's compass.

Some writers have attempted to show that the Arabians and the Chinese were acquainted with the mariner's compass even in those remote ages; but for this idea there does not seem to be any warrant whatever. Certain it is that Marco Polo, who made voyages on the Chinese seas in native boats, nowhere alludes to it; while Niccola de' Conti, who navigated the Indian waters in an Indian vessel, in 1420, after the properties of the magnet were known in Italy, expressly states that the mariners had no compass, but were guided by the stars of the Southern Pole, the elevation of which they knew how to measure. Nor is there any reason to believe that the Chinese had any greater knowledge, though there may be in some Chinese books a notice of the physical fact that, by constant hammering, an iron rod becomes magnetized—in other words, has imparted to it the property of pointing to the north and to the south.

Such a discovery, so important for purposes of

navigation, would at once have been recognised, and could not have been kept secret for ten centuries. Moreover, there is really abundant evidence to show that the compass had been long in use among the nations of the West before it was adopted by the Chinese; Dr. Robertson having justly remarked that in Arabic, Turkish, and Persian, there is not only no original word for it, but that the name they give it is the Italian *bossolo:* nay, further, that the Arabians have nowhere recorded any observation by them of the variation of the needle.[1] We may add that Dr. Robertson's view is completely confirmed by Sir John Chardin, one of the most learned of Eastern travellers, who made special inquiries on this subject. "I have sailed," says he, "from the Indies to Persia in Indian ships when no European has been on board but myself. The pilots were all Indians, and they used the forestaff and quadrant for their observations. These instruments they have from us, and made by our artists, and they do not in the least vary from ours, except that the characters are Arabic."[2]

Speed of ancient ships.

A few notices remain to us of the time occupied in the performance of different voyages by ancient vessels, from which we may deduce the general fact, that though owing to their construction—being generally from three to four times as long as they were broad, with shallow keels, and rarely other than square sails—they could not have made much way

[1] Hist. of India; Notes and Observations, p. 333—and below, p. 233.

[2] Chardin's Travels, p. 441 *et seq.*

on a wind, they were capable of considerable speed when the wind was right aft. Thus Pliny states that a merchant-ship passed from Messina to Alexandria in six days; another from the Pillars of Hercules to Ostia in seven; another from the nearest port of Spain in four; another from Narbonne in three, and another from Africa in two.[1] So, too, Arrian relates that the ship in which he sailed on the Euxine accomplished five hundred stadia (or, as is more probable, three hundred stadia) before mid-day;[2] and St. Luke tells us that he ran from Rhegium to Puteoli (one hundred and eighty-two miles) by the second day after he had started:[3] but, in all these cases, we may be quite sure that the sailors had (as St. Luke distinctly states was his case) a good stiff breeze abaft.

[1] Nat. Hist. xix. 3, 4. [2] Peripl. Mar. Eux. c. 7.
[3] Acts xxviii. 13.

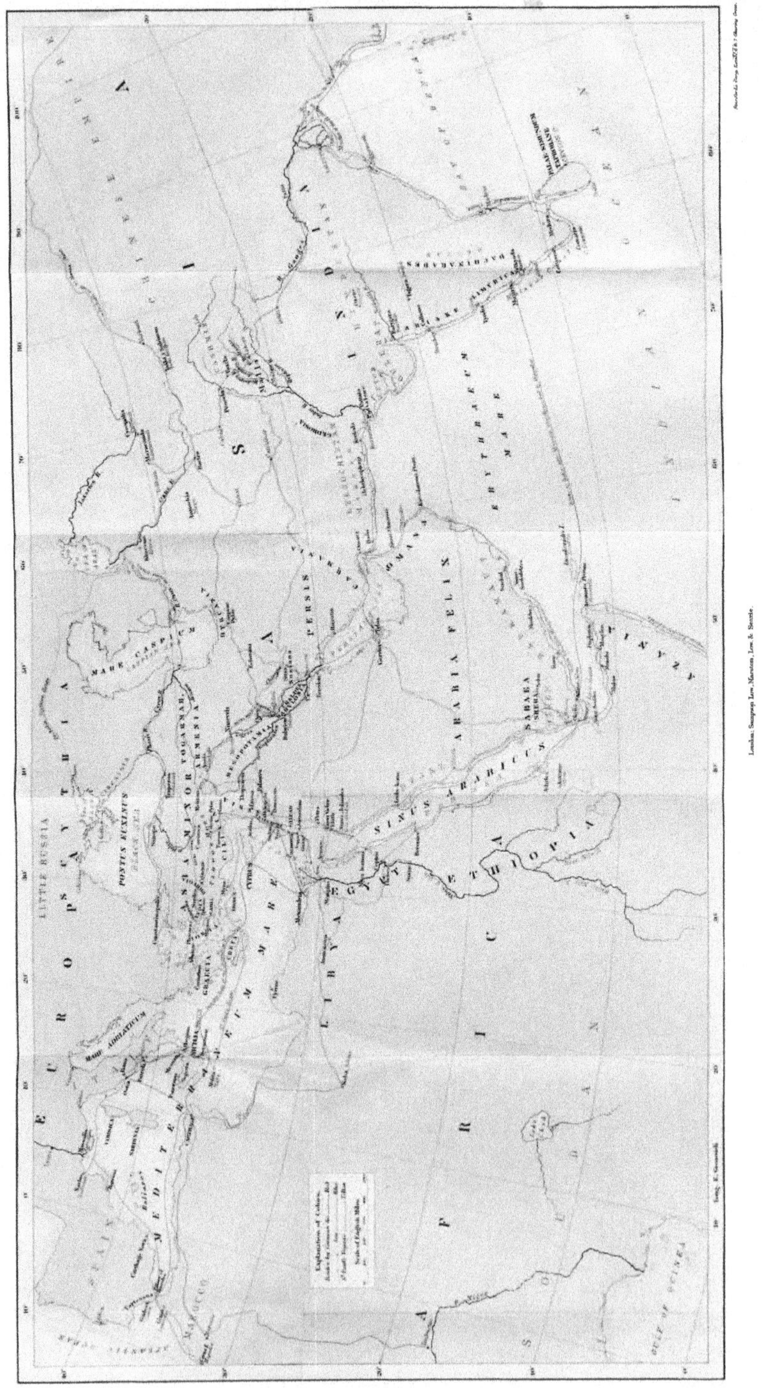

The material originally positioned here is too large for reproduction in this reissue. A PDF can be downloaded from the web address given on page iv of this book, by clicking on 'Resources Available'.

MERCHANT SHIPPING.

CHAPTER I.

Maritime commerce of Antiquity—Coasting—Tyre—Argonautic Expedition—Queen Semiramis—The Phœnicians—Early notices of them—The prophecy of Ezekiel—Trade in tin—Origin of the name "Cassiterides Insulæ."—Amber—Mainland trade of Phœnicia—Cause of prosperity—Carthage—Utica—Commercial policy—Trade with Spain—Trade in Africa—The commercial policy of Carthage—Limits of trade.

Maritime commerce of Antiquity.

WHEN different tribes were desirous of exchanging with each other the commodities their countries respectively produced, their first consideration would naturally be the means of transport; and though we may not be able to fix the period when it commenced, the interchange of goods by barter must have been nearly coexistent with the existence of man himself. In the most ancient times the chief commercial routes were undoubtedly overland; but it may safely be assumed that at a scarcely less early period trading vessels had begun to creep along the shores of the Red Sea, Persian Gulf, and Mediterranean, and to pass from island to island amid the land-locked waters of the Levant.

There can, indeed, be no doubt that, till a period comparatively recent, the characteristic of all early navigation was that of a coasting trade, the mariners seldom quitting the land except when constrained to do so by some unavoidable necessity, such as the violence of a gale or the force of currents, or when a great saving of distance could be effected by crossing the mouths of deep bays where the headlands were at a moderate distance from each other.

Coasting. But a coasting navigation is really subject to greater difficulties and dangers than any other, and hence has in all times had the property of forming the most expert seamen. Thus it was that the seamen of Tyre found their way to Carthage, and ultimately through the pillars of Hercules to Gades and the tin-bearing islands of the West: and thus, too, the States of Tyre and of her great colony, Carthage, for centuries maintained their power and lofty position in the midst of nations in other respects greatly their superiors. By the prosecution, too, of coasting voyages the Portuguese, in later ages, passed the Cape of Good Hope, and reached the East Indies. Indeed nothing was more likely to advance discovery than voyages of such a character, for which the position of the three continents of the ancient world afforded considerable natural facilities, especially when taken in connection with the two long narrow seas known as the Red Sea and the Persian Gulf. Again, the Mediterranean, with its subordinate portions, comprising the Adriatic and the Levant, with the Black Sea and the Sea of Azov, was peculiarly adapted for the commencement of an over-sea trade with a shipping still rude and with sailors little skilled; while its position in the centre, as it were, of these three continents, surrounded by the most fruitful and civilized regions of the then known world, prepared it, naturally, to be the principal scene of such an intercourse.

It should also be remembered that the Mediterranean possesses the singular advantages of a very considerable number of excellent harbours and roadsteads, with numerous islands, projecting promontories, and deep bays, affording excellent shelter for small undecked craft; and, more than this, that the two nations who were, in remote ages, the most eminent among its merchant navigators, the Tyrians and Carthaginians, were, as a rule, peaceful traders, and slow to take up arms except in self-defence. The Indian Ocean, within prescribed limits, and the Persian and Arabian Gulfs, afforded somewhat similar facilities, from the moderate distance between the opposite shores, and from the periodical winds, which change their direction twice in the year—a fact which could hardly fail to have been early recognised, though the reason of this change may have remained long unsuspected. Bearing, therefore, these physical facts and conditions in mind, it is not unreasonable to believe that long and distant voyages were accomplished with no greater nautical science than has been generally conceded to the most ancient mariners.

We find, too, as might be supposed, that the nations who held in their hands the means of conducting the largest amount of maritime commerce were the most prosperous as well as the most powerful. The small state of Phœnicia, of which, Tyre.
in its most prosperous days, Tyre was the capital, though insignificant in territory and population,

as compared with either Syria or Egypt, possessed in some respects far greater power than either. Holding, during many centuries, the command of the sea, she was able, in great measure, to control them as she pleased, and to prohibit their intercourse with any nations that could not be reached by their caravans. Phœnicia, therefore, as the leading maritime state at the earliest period to which any reliable records ascend, is entitled to the first consideration in any work having for its object an historical account of Merchant Shipping. To trace the course of the extensive maritime trade of the Phœnicians is to elucidate the progress of navigation in ancient times.

Argonautic Expedition.

Before, however, we speak of the Phœnicians we must briefly notice two maritime adventures, which, though fabulous in most of their details, were highly estimated by the ancients, and had, doubtless, some foundation in fact. The first of these, the Argonautic Expedition, as it was called, was evidently a commercial enterprise, promoted by reports of abundant deposits of gold along the eastern shores of the Black Sea. It is remarkable that the name of the ship from which the expedition itself derived its appellation is almost certainly taken from the Semitic word *arek*, "long,"[1] suggesting that it was perhaps the first "long" ship, and indicating a direct connection with the Phœnicians, who spoke the dialect to which this name belongs.

Queen Semiramis.

The second is the celebrated legend ot Queen Semiramis, and of the fleet she employed the Phœnicians in building, which is given at great

[1] Gesen. Hebr. Lex. p. lxxix.

length by Diodorus.[1] That such a fleet was ever built, or that Semiramis invaded India by its means, may well be questioned; but, since the interpretation by Sir Henry Rawlinson of the Assyrian inscriptions, we know that Semiramis is not a mythical personage, but a real queen within historical times. In the Assyrian Hall at the British Museum stand two statues of the god Nebo, each bearing a cuneiform inscription, with the statement that they were made for Queen Semiramis by a sculptor of Nineveh. Semiramis was, in fact, the wife of the Assyrian king who is mentioned in the Bible under the name of Pul.[2]

The Phœnicians.

To recur to the Phœnicians. There has been much discussion as to whence they came; and many able writers a few years since, as Bochart and Heeren, held the view that they were the same as the Canaanites. Modern research, however, fully confirms the judgment of Herodotus,[3] that they were really immigrants from the shores of the Persian Gulf; thereby, in themselves, affording an illustration of that great law of migration westwards, of which that of Abraham and of his family, and that of Chedorlaomer from Elam to the valley of the Jordan, are the earliest recorded instances. There seems, indeed, to have been a marked distinction between the Phœnicians and the Canaanites; the former having been a peaceable mercantile population, generally on terms of good will with the Jews, while the Canaanites were a fierce and warlike race. The names, too, of many of the Phœnician cities in Syria are believed to be of Hamite, and not of

[1] Diod. ii. 16–19. [2] 2 Kings xv. 19. [3] Her. i. 1.

Semitic origin, as, for instance, those of Askalon, Arka, Aradus, Gaza, and, most probably, those also of Sidon and Tyre.

It is remarkable that a district, whose people became so famous in the early history of the world, should have been confined within so limited an area; for the average breadth of Phœnicia never exceeded twelve miles, while sometimes it is considerably less. In length it was about two hundred and twenty-five miles, from Aradus in the north to Joppa in the south.

But if its territory was small, its position was admirably fitted for the grandest development of over-sea trade; and Tyre itself occupied pre-eminently the situation best fitted for carrying on the commerce of the then known world. We shall, therefore, briefly trace the course of that commerce, with a sketch of the chief places to which the Tyrians traded, and with some notice of the colonies they founded in the prosecution of this object; for to the activity of this remarkable people we owe the first link connecting the civilization of the East with Europe and Western Africa.[1]

Early notices of them.

The inhabitants of Phœnicia are first mentioned as Sidonians of the coast (though the name Phœnician also occurs), whose trinkets, like those of Autolycus, captivated the maidens of the Grecian islands,[2] and the produce of the Sidonian looms is said in the Iliad[3] to have been used for the most costly offerings to the gods. A little later we are able to trace them to Cyprus, Carthage, Malta, Sicily, the Balearic Islands, and, through the Pillars of Hercules, to

[1] Herod. i. 1; Mela, i. 12. [2] Odys. xv. 414, &c.· xiv. 29.
[3] Il. vi. 290.

Cadiz on the shores of the Atlantic. At first, probably, kidnapping went hand-in-hand with more legitimate trade; but, even in remote times, the presence of the Phœnicians must have been deemed beneficial, or Pindar would not have compared his own relations with his patron Hiero to those of a Phœnician merchant.[1] Indeed there is no recognised value in the dealings of the civilized with the uncivilized when they first meet; hence those Phœnicians need not be deemed unjust who exchanged the pottery of Athens against the ivory of Africa.[2]

Phœnician commerce was probably at its highest when Nebuchadnezzar, with the view, it is likely, of obtaining a powerful navy, made his famous attack upon Tyre. Hence the description of Tyre, and of her dealings with the nations around her, in the celebrated prophecy of Ezekiel, ch. xxvii., has great value as showing what her state was (about B.C. 588) when ruin was immediately impending over her; and it becomes worth while to give an attentive consideration to the statements of the prophet, who was evidently well acquainted with the history of Tyre. Thus, after stating that Tyre was "a merchant of the people for many isles,"[3] Ezekiel tells us that her "ship boards" were made "of fir-trees of Senir," her masts of "cedars from Lebanon," her oars "of the oaks of Bashan," and the benches of her galleys "of ivory, brought out of the isles of Chittim."[4] It is true that doubts have been expressed as to the fitness of some of these materials for the purposes mentioned; but it is, perhaps, best

The prophecy of Ezekiel.

[1] Pyth. ii. 125.
[2] Scyl. c. iii.
[3] Ezek. xxvii. ver. 3.
[4] Ver. 5, 6.

not to strain to the uttermost a description obviously poetical. The "ivory" here noticed is most likely box-wood,[1] the abundant produce of Corsica, Italy, and Spain, of the "Isles of Chittim," or Western Europe.

"The inhabitants of Zidon and Arvad" (Aradus, now Ruad,) "were thy mariners;"[2] but Tyre kept the command of her ships in her own hands, for "thy wise men, O Tyrus, that were in thee, were thy pilots."[3] "The ancients of Gebal," Ezekiel continues, "and the wise men thereof were in thee thy calkers. All the ships of the sea with their mariners were in thee to occupy their merchandise;"[4] that is, besides their own shipping, they largely employed those of surrounding and seafaring peoples, as those of Cyprus, and probably of Rhodes and Crete. "Fine linen with broidered work from Egypt was that which thou spreadest forth to be thy sail; blue and purple from the isles of Elishah was that which covered thee."[5] The isles of Elishah are generally supposed to be the Greek Archipelago, and Pausanias states that the purple of the coast of Laconia, which was but little inferior to that of Tyre itself, was used for the decoration of awnings.[6] "Javan" (the Ionian Greeks) "Tubal, and Meshech" (probably the people of the southern coasts of the Black Sea) "they were thy merchants; they traded the persons of men and vessels of brass in thy market;"[7] a trade in slaves which has survived to the present day from the neighbouring district of Circassia; as, also, many of

[1] Cf. Plin. xvi. 16; Diod. v. 14; Virg. x. 135.
[2] Ezek. xxvii. ver. 8. [3] Ver. 8. [4] Ver. 9.
[5] Ver. 7. [6] Paus. iii. 21 [7] Ver. 13.

the brazen vessels procurable at Mosul and other Turkish entrepôts derive their copper from the mountain districts of the Taurus.

Again, "They of the house of Togarmah traded in thy fairs with horses and horsemen and mules,"[1] a species of merchandise equally existent now in Armenia (or Togarmah),[2] that country being still as famous for its horses and mules as it was then. The constant denunciations of the prophets show how the baneful trade in slaves prevailed of old.[3] The Mossynoeci and Chalybes were famous for their mineral wealth;[4] and the prophet adds, "Tarshish was thy merchant by reason of the multitude of all kind of riches; with silver, iron, tin, and lead, they traded in thy fairs."[5] "The ships of Tarshish did sing of thee in thy market."[6] Tarshish has been identified by some with Tartessus in Spain, by others with other places; but the probability is that the phrase "ships of Tarshish" was an accepted term for any vessels with large and rich cargoes, like our name "Indiamen." Ancient history abounds with notices of the mineral wealth of the Spanish Peninsula. Aristotle tells us that silver was once so abundant there, that the Phœnicians not only freighted their ships with it, but even made their anchors of that precious metal;[7] and iron, lead, salt, corn, and wine, were among its most common productions.[8]

Trade in tin.

Tin, which has been often attributed, as by the

[1] Ver. 14. [2] Cf. Strab. xi. 553. [3] Joel iii. 6; Amos i. 6, 9.
[4] Plin. xxxiv. 2; Fest. in Virg. Æn. xii. 6.
[5] Ezek. xxvii. ver. 12. [6] Ver. 25.
[7] De Mirab. Ausc. 147; cf. Diod. v. 35.
[8] Lucret. v. 1256; Strab. iii. 147 and 159; Polyb. x. 10; Plin. xxxiv. 15; Martial, iv. 35.

prophet, to Spain, probably came thence only in small quantities;[1] though some is, indeed, still found in Porto, Beira, and Bragança, and was exhibited in the Exhibition of 1862. The great bulk, however, of this metal was brought from the *Cassiterides Insulæ*, unquestionably the Scilly Islands, and from Cornwall; partly, as may be readily believed, by Phœnician vessels which sailed thither from Gades, and partly from St. Michael's Mount, whence it was conveyed, through France, on the backs of horses, as Diodorus has pointed out, to the great Roman colonies of Marseilles and Narbonne.[2]

In the Museum at Truro is still preserved a pig of tin, supposed by some to be one of the original Phœnician blocks. It is impossible to assign even a probable period for the commencement of the tin trade; but this is certain, that some of the earliest objects in metal which have come down to us, are formed of an alloy of copper with tin, generally in nearly the same proportions, *viz.* ten to twelve per cent. of tin. Such monuments are the nails which fastened on the plates of the so-called Treasury of Atreus at Mycenæ, the instruments found in the earliest Egyptian tombs, the bowls and lion-weights from Nineveh, and the so-called "celts" from European graves. All these facts tend to show that the ancient world must have been acquainted with tin at a very remote period.

Origin of the name "Insulæ Cassiterides."

There has been much discussion as to the meaning of the word *cassiteros*, which has no equivalent in either the Semitic or the Greek families of languages; on the other hand, the Sanscrit name for tin, *kastira*,

[1] Plin. iv. 34; xxxiv. 47; Strab. iii. 147.

[2] Diod. v. 38, 5.

is almost the same. It seems, therefore, not improbable that the Phœnicians, while still in their old homes on the Persian Gulf, may have found their way in pre-historic ages to India, and may there have met with it, as it is abundant at Banka in the Straits of Sumatra; then, when in later days they found it again in even greater abundance in England, that they gave it the name they had previously adopted from the far East.[1] The trade in tin was so valuable that the Phœnicians did their best to keep secret the locality whence they obtained it; and Strabo tells a curious tale of a merchant captain, whose ship was pursued by the Romans, and who preferred stranding his vessel to allowing her to fall into their hands, whereby the secret would have been discovered; and moreover, that on his return home, he recovered from his government the value of the ship he had thus sacrificed for the public weal of his country.[2]

Amber.

Another very important trade may be noticed here, though it is not strictly of Phœnician origin, that in *amber*. This semi-mineral substance, as is well known, is procured chiefly from the shores of the Baltic, though it is not unknown elsewhere. There is a curious record of what was supposed to be its discovery, in Pliny's account[3] of an exploratory voyage by Pytheas, of Marseilles, who named the island whence he obtained it Abulus. Xenophon of Lampsacus, however, calls the island Baltia—whence obviously our Baltic. The amber trade is strangely

[1] *Vide* Lassen ap. Ritter's Erdkunde, v. p. 549; and cf. Hom. Il. xxiii. 503, who was clearly aware of the practice of tinning.

[2] Strabo, iii. 5. For further details of the tin trade, *vide* Herod. iii. 115; Arist. de Mundo, viii. 3; Polyb. iii. 37; Strab. v. 10; Phillips' Mineralogy, p. 249.

[3] Plin. iii. 26.

mixed up with one of the most poetical of ancient legends, that of the daughters of Phaethon, who are said to have been changed into poplars, and to have wept amber by the banks of a river called Eridanus, generally identified with the great river of Italy, the Po. But there was also an Eridanus on the Baltic shores, which has left traces of its name in that of a small river still flowing near the modern town of Dantzig. Tacitus, referring to amber as an article of commerce—the native name of which he states to be *glesum* (*glass?*)—refers to the Suionæ, who dwelt along those shores, and had vessels differing from the Roman type in that they were equally high at prow and stern. This is even now characteristic of what are called Norway yawls.[1]

Mainland trade of Phœnicia.

It is not so easy to trace the course of Phœnician commerce with the countries on the mainland to the north, east, and south, as it is in the case of the islands of the west. But here, too, the statements of the Prophet come to our aid, and enable us to fill up an outline which would have been otherwise very incomplete. Thus we find Ezekiel saying, "The men of Dedan were thy merchants . . . they brought thee for a present horns of ivory and ebony,"[2] and "precious cloths for chariots."[3] So Syria,[4] Dan and Javan,[5] and "the merchants of Sheba and Raamah,"[6] dealt with Tyre in precious stones, fine linen, broidered work, and gold. From "Judah and the land of Israel," from "Minnith and Pannag," she obtained "wheat and honey, and oil and balm;"[7] from Damascus, "the wine of Helbon and white

[1] Tac. Germ. 44, 45. [2] Ezek. xxvii. ver. 15. [3] Ver. 20. [4] Ver. 16. [5] Ver. 19. [6] Ver. 22. [7] Ver. 17.

wool;"[1] and from "Arabia and all the princes of Kedar," lambs and rams and goats.[2] Lastly, to those "of Persia, and of Lud, and of Phut," she was indebted for her mercenaries, for they "were in thine army, thy men of war: they hanged the shield and helmet in thee; they set forth thy comeliness. The men of Arvad with thine army were upon thy walls round about, and the Gammadims were in thy towers: they hanged their shields upon thy walls round about; they have made thy beauty perfect."[3]

The probability is that most of the Tyrian commerce with the East was carried on by the aid of caravans passing through Arabia Felix to Petra, and thence to the western seaports of Gaza, Askalon, and Ashdod.[4] Many of the more precious articles were obtainable direct from Arabia;[5] spices, of which cinnamon and cassia (the produce of the same plant, *Laurus cassia*), were of great importance, were best procured thence up to the discovery of Ceylon;[6] while some, like the "bright iron" and the calamus (*Calamus aromaticus*) point to India itself for their origin. The "bright iron," for which Diodorus states that the Arabians exchanged equal weights of gold,[7] is perhaps the famous *Wootz* steel.[8] Asshur and Chilmad, who were "thy merchants in all sorts of things, in blue clothes, and broidered work, and in chests of rich apparel, bound with cords, and made of cedar,"[9] point to articles of commerce for which, from a very early period, Babylon and Nineveh were

[1] Ezek. ver. 18. [2] Ver. 21. [3] Vers. 10 and 11.

[4] The Azotus of Herod. iii. 5.

[5] Cf. Strab. xvi. 777; Diod. ii. 50, for gold in "nuggets."

[6] Cf. Vincent. ii. 702. Ezek. v. 19. [7] Diod. iii. 45.

[8] Cf. Ritter, Erdk. v. 521; Michael. Spicel. ii. 173. [9] Ver. 24.

famous.[1] We may also gather that it must have been for the extension of Babylonian commerce, from the Persian Gulf to Damascus on the north, that Nebuchadnezzar built Teredon, near the present Bussorah.[2] The mode of packing rich garments, like those described in Ezekiel, is one still in use among the natives of Upper India.

We may add that civilization owes to the Phœnicians the invention of the alphabet; and, probably, that of the well-known weight of ancient Greece, the *mna*, or *mina*, which is found on certain lion-weights from Nineveh, bearing bilingual legends in Assyrian and Phœnician, their value being expressed in the latter tongue:[3] they also discovered the Cynosure (called after them, Phœnice), the last star in the Little Bear, which, as nearly identical with the Pole Star, gave superior fixity to their observations;[4] while they are said to have noticed at Gades the connection between the moon and the oceanic tides.[5]

Cause of prosperity.

It is not difficult to discern the principal causes of the success and prosperity of these Phœnician traders, which we may be sure did not rest, as some writers[6] have supposed, on an extensive system of piracy. This, and other evils of a similar character, may have existed among them, as elsewhere, for a certain period; but they would not have ruled the maritime

[1] Cf. Nahum iii. 16; 2 Kings iii. 4; Plin. H. N. viii. 48; and the "goodly garments of Shinar," for the secreting of which Achan was punished, Josh. vii. 21.

[2] Euseb. Præp. Evang. ix. 41.

[3] Norris, ap. Trans. As. Soc. xvi. 221.

[4] Manil. Astron. i. 304; Hygin. Astron. ii. 2; Callimach. Fragm. 94.

[5] Strab. i. 173.

[6] Heeren. As. Nat. i. pp. 30, 285.

commerce of the world, had not their power rested on foundations far more firm than those of robbery and plunder. No nation has ever become great merely by lawless acts. We believe their success was chiefly due to the practice of dealing with any one who was willing to deal with them, and to the encouragement they invariably gave to perfect freedom of intercourse. Nor must it be forgotten that they largely imported the raw materials of other countries, assorting their various products to suit the demand, and transporting them when thus assorted, together with their own manufactures, to all parts of the world.

Their practice, indeed, was as perfect as their policy was wise. The merchants of Tyre were the first to establish the system of factories or agencies, where they were able not only to dispose of their several cargoes to the best advantage, but to collect the produce of other lands so as to be ready for shipment on the arrival of their fleets. Every nation was, in fact, their merchant; just as every nation is, at the present moment, manufacturing or producing something for England.

Again, to the Tyrians belongs the credit of the establishment of the first regular colonies; some of which, as Carthage, probably far surpassed in wealth and power those of the mother city—nay, what is more, they succeeded in planting their colonies on terms so liberal as to retain through all time an affectionate remembrance from their children; for we know that, as Tyre refused the aid of her fleet to Cambyses when he wished to attack Carthage,[1] so Carthage offered

[1] Herod. iii. 17, 19.

a refuge to the inhabitants of Tyre when besieged by Alexander.[1] Thus, without the aid of conquering armies, this remarkable people spread over the remotest parts of the then known world, establishing the arts of peace among nations previously buried in darkness and barbarism, and making the "solitary places of the earth to rejoice." No commercial nation of either ancient or modern times presents a history, so far as we can trace it, more worthy of imitation than that of Phœnicia. Liberal, by comparison, in its policy, and enlightened in its intercourse with other peoples, it offered, in the plenitude of its power, an example to the ancient world of what industry and a sound policy could effect—a course worthy of imitation, even now. All nations "were merchants of Tyre;" that is, all nations found it to their advantage to be on good terms with such a people; and it would be well if some of the nations of our own times could be persuaded to act on Tyrian principles, and if, instead of checking free intercourse by the imposition of high protective duties, they would do as Tyre did 2600 years ago, invite all nations to be their merchants.[2]

Carthage. Of all her colonies, Carthage was the one of which Tyre had the best reason to be proud. Situated on a peninsula, in Lat. 36° 55′ N., 10° 20′ E., with a long

[1] Diod. ii. 190.

[2] Xenophon, in his "Œconomics," c. 18, gives some interesting details of a large Phœnician merchant ship which he went over, when at anchor in the Piræeus. He appears to have entered into conversation with the "prow's-man" (who probably acted as supercargo), and to have been greatly surprised at the care with which everything was arranged, so that it could be got at at once. From the phraseology Xenophon uses it would seem that such a vessel came, in his day, annually to Athens. Heliodorus (v. 18) speaks, too, of the "beauty and magnitude of Phœnician ships."

narrow neck of land westward, forming a double harbour for ships of war and commerce, it is believed to have been founded between B.C. 878 and B.C. 826, the Roman writers, as a rule, assuming Carthage to have been only a collection of huts till Dido[1] came. On the other hand, Utica[2] is distinctly stated from *Phœnician records* to have been in existence two hundred and eighty years before Carthage. As, too, it was earlier in date, so did it long survive the greater city, being, according to Strabo, in his time, the metropolis of Northern Africa. Utica appears also as an independent power in the treaties between Carthage and the Romans. Utica.

The headland first occupied by the Tyrians, near the harbour now called the Goletta, is exactly the kind of place Thucydides[3] says the Phœnicians always selected; a promontory easy of defence and commanding an adjoining port. Modern travellers have recognized in the "Hill of St. Louis,"[4] the site of the ancient Byrsa (itself a genuine Phœnician word, meaning *fortress*).

Commercial policy.

Unfortunately, no ancient historian has given us any reliable information as to the means whereby Carthage raised herself so far above the other Phœnician colonies. But these may be in part traced to the natural fertility of her soil, the excellent situation of the city for carrying on a large inland as well as maritime commerce, and, above all, to the firmness with which she adhered to the enlightened policy of

[1] Virgil. Æn. i. 421.

[2] Arist. de Mirab. Ausc. c. 146. Strabo, xvii. p. 832. Polyb. iii. 24.

[3] Thucyd. vi. 2.

[4] Barth. "Wanderungen," p. 94. Sir Grenville Temple's "Excursions," ii. 37. Admiral W. H. Smyth's "Mediterranean," p. 92.

her founders. The Carthaginians closely followed the example of the Tyrians, in establishing colonies of their own, whenever they could do so advantageously, their first object being maritime commerce, a preference being, therefore, naturally given by them to islands such as Sicily, Sardinia, Corsica, the Baleares, and Melita (Malta). "Carthage," says Aristotle,[1] "continually sent out colonies composed of her citizens into the districts around her, and by these means gave them wealth. It is a proof," he adds, "of a mild and intelligent government, that it assists the poor by accustoming them to labour." Thus the Carthaginians, while they enriched themselves, increased the prosperity of surrounding states and tribes; and, by promoting colonization, prevented the too great increase of their home population. Many of their colonies embraced the rich provinces to the west of Carthage, and the territory under the immediate control of the republic was little less than two hundred geographical miles in length. As the native population of these provinces comprised many of the nomad tribes, the Carthaginians were enabled to direct their attention to the inland trade of Africa, by caravans which crossed the Libyan Desert, and penetrated as far as the Niger and Æthiopia on the one hand, and to Upper Egypt and the Nile on the other.

There is no justice in the assertion that Carthage ever exhibited a lust of conquest. Throughout her whole career she seems to have acted in the spirit of her Tyrian ancestors; as long as her merchants were free to trade, her neighbours were not dis-

[1] Arist. Polit. ii. 11, vi. 5, and Heeren i. p. 40.

turbed, her naval reputation in later days having been mainly caused by the necessity of protecting her commerce and her colonies from the piratical attacks of other nations. With Spain, for instance, she maintained for centuries extensive and peaceful commercial relations: nor was it till the Greeks and Romans had become the most daring marauders in the Mediterranean, that Carthage, in self-defence, fitted out a navy, and thus became a great naval power. That these peaceful employments were crowned with success, we learn from the universal testimony of antiquity, it being generally admitted that, in the manufactures she had transplanted from Tyre and Sidon, she greatly surpassed in excellence whatever reputation the parent state had acquired. Moreover, we have still extant a series of coins of extraordinary beauty, struck for her no doubt, in many instances, by Greek artists of Sicily and Magna Græcia, yet which could hardly have been intended, as some numismatists have thought, for only her colonial cities of Panormus, Segesta, &c.[1]

Acknowledged by Polybius[2] to have possessed hereditary pre-eminence in nautical matters, with the undisputed dominion of the sea for a long period, it may be fairly assumed that her ships were then unrivalled. Indeed Aristotle states that the Carthaginians were the first to increase the size of their galleys from three to four banks of oars.

Trade with Spain.

As the Carthaginians followed in the wake of the Phœnicians, it is impossible to ascertain the exact

[1] The question of the reality of Carthaginian coins has been fully examined by Müller, "Études Numismatiques," and by Vaux, "Numism. Chron." vol. xxi.

[2] Polyb. i. 7, 16.

period of their colonization of Spain; but it is well known that Gades (Cadiz) was one of their earliest and most important commercial entrepôts, and that thence they sent expeditions to the south and to the north, along the western shores of Africa and Europe, securing for themselves the most favourable positions as marts for their merchandise.

Their first expedition to the western shores of Africa was that of Hanno, it is said, with sixty ships, of fifty oars each, and an incredible number of emigrants. Though all traces of their settlements have long since been obliterated, there is no reason to question the fact that such a voyage was really made, that Hanno did reach the small island of Cerne (probably the modern Arguin in N. Lat. 20.5), that he laid the foundations of six towns, or trading stations, and that he proceeded farther along a coast, inhabited by negro races, for a period of twenty-six days, in all probability passing Cape Verde, even if he did not visit the islands of that name.[1]

About the same time Himilco[2] was sent to explore the north-western coasts of Europe, founding, as he proceeded, if we may believe the very curious poem of Festus Avienus, settlements even in Britain and Ireland. The whole of this story (which has been carefully translated by Heeren, "Asiatic Nations," i., p. 502, and appendix) is well worthy perusal; and is almost certainly based on reliable traditions or records. Among other things, the navigator speaks of men who dwelt in lands rich in tin and

[1] Plin. ii. 169. Hanno's "Periplus," ap. Geogr. Græc. Minor. Hanno's voyage was really rather one of discovery.

[2] Plin. ibid.

lead; who used boats made of skins and leather; of the Œstrymnades, or Scilly Islands; of the ancient trade between them and Tartessus; and of a sea where weeds abounded so much that navigation was impeded (probably part of the Sargasso). Nor ought it to be forgotten that many antiquaries, more perhaps formerly than now, have been of the opinion that metallic objects of unquestionably Phœnician workmanship have been found in Irish bogs.

Trade in Africa.

On the western coast of Africa, the island of Cerne was the chief Carthaginian depôt; the goods from the merchant vessels being here unladen, and placed under tents, to be conveyed thence in smaller vessels to the continent. This trade itself was conducted wholly by barter. The method is well described by Herodotus. "The Carthaginians," says he,[1] "are wont to sail to a nation beyond the Pillars of Hercules, on the Libyan coast. When they come there, they transport their wares on shore and leave them, and, after kindling a fire, go back to their ships. Upon this signal the natives come down to the sea, and placing gold against the wares, again return. The Carthaginians then again approach, and see whether what they have left be sufficient. If it be, they take it and depart; should it, however, not be enough for their wares, they again go back to their ships and wait; and the other party bring more gold, until the strangers are satisfied. But neither party deals unfairly by the other, for the one touches not the gold till the value of the wares be brought, nor the other the wares until the gold be taken away."

A similar system of silent barter has been noticed

[1] Herod. iv. cap. 196; cf. Scylac. "Periplus," c. 112.

by many travellers. Thus Captain Lyon states that "In Soudan, beyond the desert, in the countries abounding in gold, there dwells an invisible nation who are said to trade only by night. Those who come to traffic for their gold, lay their merchandise in heaps, and retire. In the morning they find a certain quantity of gold dust placed against every heap, which, if they think sufficient, they leave the goods, if not, they let them both remain until more of the precious ore is added."[1] Hoest says the same thing in the case of very large caravans, from Marocco to Timbuctoo. "The Moors enter not into the Negro country, but only go to a certain place on the frontiers, where one of each party exhibits and exchanges the goods, without scarcely opening their lips."[2]

The commercial policy of Carthage.

The commercial treaties between Carthage and Rome, to which fuller reference will hereafter be made, show that if the duties levied were in some cases heavy, they were not differential or protective, but chiefly with the object of securing a sufficient revenue. That, like all commercial nations, the Carthaginians were jealous of competitors need not be doubted, but while other nations were content with profits derived from intercourse among their own people, Tyre and Carthage sought the trade of all nations and erected entrepôts where required for this commerce.

At the same time, it must be borne in mind that free trade, pure and simple, as now understood, could, in ancient times, have been possible only with a very considerable modification; especially where, as was the case with Carthage and Tyre, a large portion of the dealings with barbarous nations was

[1] Lyon's Narrative, p. 149. [2] Hoest, p. 279.

by barter; for competition, while tending seriously to reduce the profits, could not then have increased the demand to an extent equivalent to the reduction in price. As long as the savage is kept in ignorance, he is ready to exchange goods of great value for mere trifles, and rivalry would only serve to enlighten him as to their actual value. Moreover with uncivilized nations whose wants are limited, it is impossible to create a demand adequate to the loss accruing from open competition. Hence Carthage watched these branches of her trade with peculiar jealousy, and, while throwing wide open the harbours of the capital, closed as far as possible her colonial ports to the shipping of rival nations.

It seems, therefore, unreasonable for Heeren to call the commercial policy of Carthage "paltry and selfish:"[1] for if she did guard the colonial trade which her genius and industry had created, her policy generally, as compared with that of contemporaneous nations, was as liberal as that of Great Britain now is in comparison with that of the United States of America. Carthage acted on principles of reciprocity, while her neighbours were rigid protectionists. She was ready to grant, as her treaties show, reciprocal privileges to all nations ready to deal with her on similar conditions; and on such terms, she dealt largely with Greece and with Egypt during the reign of the Ptolemies, and even with Rome.

Limits of trade.

The trade of Carthage, as might be anticipated from her position, was almost entirely with the west, her chief rivals being Sicily, Italy, and Massalia (Marseilles), who prevented her from obtaining any-

[1] Heeren's "Ancient Nations of Africa," vol. i. p. 159.

thing like an exclusive monopoly. Yet the abundant details given by Herodotus, Diodorus, Aristotle, Strabo, Terence, and Plautus, show clearly that, even with these places, her commercial relations attained considerable dimensions. The wines and oils of Sicily and Italy found their best market in Carthage, the return being black slaves from Central Africa. Malta, Corsica, Elba, produced fine cloths, wax and honey, and iron, respectively; while the mines of Spain, with her great port Cadiz, the entrepôt for tin from Britain, before the Massalians brought it overland through France, produced the largest and most enduring portion of her revenue.

To her commerce with the interior of Africa by means of caravans mention has already been made; and it is scarcely necessary to add that the details which Herodotus and other ancient writers give of this trade, read much like a page out of Livingstone, or Baker, or Du Chaillu. Then, as now, the wants of the respective populations were much the same; if the interior could send abundance of ivory or gold-dust, salt, a need of their daily life, could be procured only from the Mediterranean shores. Lastly, it is certain that Carthage, like the United States of America in modern times, was mainly indebted for her navy to her merchant service, inasmuch as in times of peace she set apart scarcely any shipping for merely warlike purposes.

CHAPTER II.

Earliest caravan trade—Ophir—Port of Ezion-geber—The voyages of the Jewish ships—The inland commerce of Solomon—Babylon—Gerrha and Tylos—Babylonian commerce—Assyrian boats—Lydia—Ionia—Caria—Phrygia—Scythians—Their caravan routes to India, *viâ* the Caspian.

Earliest caravan trade.

REFERENCE has already incidentally been made to a few of the caravan routes of very ancient times: these and other more important routes will now and hereafter be considered somewhat more in detail, as, antecedently to the invention of boats, there must have existed some interchange of commodities between different nations and tribes on land, by the agencies of different kinds of beasts of burthen; and, here, the records of Holy Writ are, as in so many other cases, the first available; the earliest caravan noticed in history being that mentioned in the 37th chapter of the book of Genesis, v. 25: "behold, a company of Ishmaelites came from Gilead with their camels bearing spicery and balm and myrrh, going to carry it down to Egypt;" and again, v. 28: "Then there passed by Midianites merchantmen; and they drew and lifted up Joseph out of the pit, and sold Joseph to the Ishmaelites for twenty pieces of silver."

Here there is a clearly defined trade at a very

remote period of authentic history, and one which there is no reason to suppose was even then new or unusual.

Moreover, a somewhat subsequent statement, "all countries came into Egypt to Joseph for to buy corn" (Gen. xli. 57), proves that Egypt was already what it remained for many centuries, the granary of adjacent, and even of distant nations; while some of the goods she received from Palestine in exchange were in great demand for the embalmment of the Egyptian dead.

This the first regular trade appears to have been conducted wholly by camels, the "ships of the desert:" an animal marvellously adapted by Providence for the toil it has to undergo in traversing for many continuous days almost waterless deserts.

It is worthy of note, too, that in the earliest notice we have of any trade at all, we find slave-dealing in full operation; and, supposing for a moment the Biblical date B.C. 1862 to be correct, it is an interesting though accidental coincidence, that in the year 1862 *after* Christ, the same inhuman commerce was finally put a stop to in the United States by the direct action of its government.

But the brief words of Genesis imply more than is at first obvious—they imply a trade with Arabia—possibly even with the yet more remote India; for balsam and myrrh are products of the Arabian province, Hadramaut, and the spices may have come either thence or from India. In like manner there is reasonable probability for believing that in the remotest ages there was a trade between Egypt and the borders of the Persian Gulf and Indian Oceans;

indeed, recent researches strongly lead to the belief that the Egyptians, like the Phœnicians, were immigrants from the same neighbourhood, and connected, therefore, with the chief cities of Chaldæa, such as "Ur of the Chaldees," the primitive Babel, and other sites, the great mounds of which have been partially explored by Loftus and Taylor, though it is not as yet possible in all cases to assign to them their true ancient names. Babylon, the great city of Nebuchadnezzar, did not then exist, nor could Nineveh have been of importance, at least commercially. All the evidence available, and especially that obtainable through the latest interpretation of the Cuneiform Inscriptions, tends to show that the greatest people in the earliest period were the Chaldæans—a race probably older than the Egyptians, and like them of Hamite origin—the true inventors of alphabetic writing, astronomy, agriculture, navigation, and of other sciences, which the Semites, in after days, claimed as their own exclusive discoveries.

It was in connexion with this trade that the ports at the head of the Ælanitic gulf came first into existence. As the caravans of Edom or Idumæa passed to and fro between Egypt and the borders of Arabia, the foundation of Elath and Ezion-geber would be but the satisfying of a necessary want; becoming, when seized by King David, places of much greater importance than they could have been in the hands of Hadad, or of any other petty Idumæan prince.

David would seem to have been the first, in connection with caravans from Petra and from the west, to open up, by means of a line of ships, that trade with "Ophir" which his son Solomon afterwards made so

Ophir.

famous. Where and what "Ophir" was, has been the subject of innumerable essays by men of learning, but to enter into a discussion of this uncertain though interesting inquiry, would be out of our province. Let it suffice that the first notice in the Bible[1] clearly means by "Ophir" some place in Arabia, where great wealth was found, and was no doubt applicable afterwards to all other similar places. Those writers who, relying on the native Indian names of some of the products said to have come thence, assert Ophir to be the name of a people near the mouths of the Indus, advance opinions more ingenious than convincing. If Ophir were an Arabian entrepôt for the trade of India, the occurrence of Indian names for certain Indian products would be as natural as the use in English of the Persian word *shâl*, which we pronounce as they do, "shawl." Then David's "gold of Ophir" may have been simply descriptive of quality, as we used to speak of "guinea-gold."[2]

Be this, however, as it may, it is certain that to David the Jews owe their first practical knowledge of the result of successful commerce, though a careful consideration of the story of his life suggests that his coffers were filled, not so much by any legitimate trade, however extended, as by the conquest and plunder of his neighbours. Though probably not averse to royal monopolies, the fashion of his day, David was a great warrior, and it is likely, indeed it is so stated on more than one occasion, that it was by the capture of Philistine (Phœnician) towns,

[1] Gen. x. 29.

[2] Taking all things into consideration, it looks very much as if the Saphara of Ptolemy (vi. 7, 41), described as a metropolis of Arabia, was the original Ophir.

the overthrow of Moab, the plunder of Hadadezer, the garrisoning of Syria and of its chief city, Damascus, and the extortion of heavy tribute as the condition of peace, that David accumulated the enormous wealth which he proposed devoting to the building and decoration of the future Temple at Jerusalem:[1] but God said, "Thou shalt not build an house unto my name, because thou hast shed much blood upon the earth in my sight."[2]

To Solomon more strictly belongs the great commercial results of a long and peaceful reign, materially aided as this was by the king's personal superintendence, by his visits to Elath and Ezion-geber, by his treaty of amity, mutual forbearance, and important commercial arrangements with Hiram, King of Tyre, and last, not least, by the extraordinary fame he thus obtained, leading, to the memorable visit to him by the Queen of Sheba, and to the display of his wisdom and wealth, till she felt, on beholding them, that "there was no more spirit in her."[3]

Port of Ezion-geber.

Dean Stanley, in his "Lectures on the History of the Jewish Church," has eloquently described the position of Solomon's chief port, where, he says,[4] "Ezion-geber, the 'Giant's backbone,' so called, probably, from the huge range of mountains on each side of it, became an emporium teeming with life and activity; the same, on the eastern branch, that Suez has, in our own time, become on the western branch of the Red Sea. Beneath that line of palm trees which now shelters the wretched village of Akaba, was then

[1] 1 Sam. xviii.; xix. 8; xxvii. 8; 2 Chron. viii. 17, &c.
[2] 1 Chron. xxii. 8.
[3] 2 Chron. ix. 4.
[4] Stanley Lectures, xxvi. p. 182.

heard the stir of ship-builders and sailors. Thence went forth the fleet of Solomon, manned by Tyrian sailors, to Ophir, in the far East, on the coast of India or Arabia. From Arabia also, near or distant, came a constant traffic of spices, both from private individuals and from the chiefs. So great was Solomon's interest in these, that he actually travelled himself to the gulf of Akaba to see the port."

It appears that the fleets though manned by Tyrian sailors, were under charge of Jewish supercargoes, who were responsible for the stores and merchandise, and conducted all the trading operations. This happy alliance materially extended the commerce of both countries; for shut out from the Mediterranean by the inefficiency of the ports of Palestine, and with no communication with the Indian Ocean, except by caravans traversing the Arabian desert, the Jewish people could in no other way have derived material advantages from the valuable and much coveted trade of the East. For the first time, too, the trade of Europe was opened to the Jews through their connexion with the Tyrians; while, on the other hand, the merchants of Tyre found in Israel a large and lucrative field for the full development of their commerce.

The voyages of the Jewish ships.

So far as can now be ascertained, the joint fleets of Hiram and Solomon sailed periodically from the Ælanitic or Akaba gulf, for the East, somewhere between November and March, when the winds are favourable for a voyage down the Red Sea. Thence, probably, a portion of the ships shaped their course for the south-east shores of Africa, from the straits of Bab-el-Mandeb, to Zanzibar and Sofala; while a second portion coasted to the northward till they reached the shores of Beloochistan, Baroach (Barygaza), and even the western coasts of Hindostan. Over-sea voyages from Arabia to India were doubtless of considerably later date, when the character and use of the monsoons had been more or less ascertained. "Every three years once came the ships of Tarshish, bringing gold, and silver, ivory, and apes, and peacocks;"[1] a length of time which, at first sight, seems scarcely credible, yet is accounted for by the habits of those early mariners. The merchants of those days had no factors as consignees of their produce or home manufactures, with orders to have ready a cargo in return. They were therefore obliged to keep their ships as a floating warehouse until the exported cargo had been sold, and the produce of the country they were to take in exchange was ready for shipment. Indeed Herodotus states, what seems to have been a common custom, that when their stock of corn was exhausted, the mariners landed at some convenient spot, sowed corn, and reaped the harvest, before proceeding with their voyage.[2]

The inland commerce of Solomon.

There is some difficulty, looking at the present desolate and barren state of Palestine and of the districts around it, in realizing the possibility of such vast productiveness as the story of Solomon evidently implies; and the face of the country must have greatly changed in the last two thousand eight hundred years, for, now at least, the land of the Edomites, and a great portion of Arabia from the Persian Gulf to the Euphrates on the one side, and to the Red Sea on the other, is perfectly barren. Yet,

[1] 2 Chron. ix. 21. [2] Herod. iv. 42. Voyage of Pharaoh Necho.

that Babylonia was once of extraordinary fertility we know from the statements of Herodotus, and it is possible that much of Palestine, now withering under the bane of Turkish despotism, might revive with better and wiser treatment.

Mr. Rich[1] states that Babylonia "is not cultivated to above half the degree of which it is susceptible;" and General Chesney[2] says "that those portions of Mesopotamia which are still cultivated, as the country about Hillah, show that the region has all the fertility ascribed to it by Herodotus."[3]

But though the Jewish trade under Solomon had reached proportions so unusually large, these soon fell away and dwindled almost to nothing under his successors. With his death came wars and divisions; Jehoshaphat lost his ships at Ezion-geber, the Edomites revolted, the Syrians under Rezin seized the port, till at length it fell into the more powerful grasp of Tiglath Pileser, who thus finally destroyed the only maritime career in which the Jewish people had ever taken an active or successful part.

Babylon. There is reason to believe that it was not many years before the time of David that the great cities of Mesopotamia, strictly so called, Babylon, and Nineveh, made themselves known as commercial entrepôts, for the storing of goods on their way from the East to the West; and that at first, and for a considerable period, Babylon was of the two the most

[1] Rich, "First Memoir," p. 12.

[2] Chesney, Euphrat Exped. ii. 602-3.

[3] Cf. also Ammianus ("March of Julian," xxiv. 3) and Zosimus (iii.) with Layard ("Nineveh" ii. 6), and Ker Porter (ii. p. 355), for the luxuriance of the date-bearing districts, and the general sylvan character of many of these plains.

important. Placed advantageously so as to make available both the Euphrates and Tigris, Babylon secured easy communication with the interior of Asia, and was able, therefore, to supply all the surrounding populations with the produce of the far East. She soon became what the prophet calls her, "a land of traffic—a city of merchants," partly, no doubt, because the navigation of the Persian Gulf presented fewer difficulties and dangers than that of the Red Sea, while her traders were largely aided by the Phœnician settlement of Tylos among the Bahrein Islands and by Gerrha, a port on the western shores of the Persian Gulf.[1]

In Babylon itself there were manufactories of cotton and linen, which, with the maritime imports not required for the use of the great city, were carried by water as far as Thapsacus and thence distributed by caravans all over Asia.

Gerrha and Tylos.

Gerrha was a place of large trade, and its merchants and ship-owners are probably as old as any recorded in history, for they were not merely the factors for the precious commodities of Asia and Europe, but, in conjunction with the Midianites and Edomites, conducted the first caravans on record. From the remotest times they carried on an extensive trade with the Phœnicians in spices and aromatics, and with Babylon in mineral salt and cotton, which the island of Tylos produced in great abundance. In-

[1] It has been supposed that the Babylonian vessels passed along the Persian Gulf, from Bussorah to Crokala near Kurachi, and that they there met the vessels of Gerrha and Tylos, and proceeded onwards along the western coast of Hindustan to Ceylon; but there seems little probability that any ships strictly Babylonian found their way to India. Probably between Ceylon and Babylon there was more than one transhipment of Indian and other produce.

deed, the words of Herodotus in his first chapter clearly indicate the existence of such an ancient trade conducted by aid of the Phœnicians.

Babylonian commerce.

Though frequently interrupted by the great internal revolutions of Asia, in which Babylon was constantly compelled to take part, and though the trading routes between Babylon and Tyre lay through wild and inhospitable deserts, the intercourse between them continued for many centuries, nor ceased, so far as we know from history, till the final overthrow of Babylon by Cyrus and the Medes and Persians.

Of the objects of this commerce a tolerably certain account has been preserved; and among these are found corn (which has been supposed to be indigenous in Babylonia), dogs of an extraordinary breed, carpets, cotton and woollen fabrics, woven and embroidered with figures of mythic animals and famous alike for their texture and workmanship and for the richness and variety of their colours. These native products were exchanged for spices, ivory, ebony, cinnamon and precious stones. The *sindones*, or flowing garments, of Babylon had a great reputation from remote times, for it was "a goodly Babylonian garment," which tempted Achan to his destruction (Josh. vii. v. 21); and, centuries after Babylon had almost ceased to be counted among the nations, an Edict of Diocletian, A.D. 284, the purpose of which was to regulate the maximum prices of articles in the empire, speaks of several products of Babylonian manufacture.[1]

[1] This Edict is a great curiosity. It was first copied by Sherard in 1709 at Eski-Hissar (Stratonicæa), and this copy is preserved in the Harleian MSS. at the British Museum, No. 7509. Leake, "Asia Minor," pp. 229–239. It has been recently (1866) re-edited by Mr. W. H. Waddington with great care.

Herodotus[1] has given a curious description of the boats seen by him when he was at Babylon—made of willows from Armenia, sewn round with hides, so that they must have as much resembled the Welsh coracles still in use, as they do some of the boats on the Assyrian monuments.

Assyrian boats.

If, indeed, we may assume that there was little difference between Assyrian and Babylonian boats, the recently disentombed monuments of Nineveh will afford excellent evidence of their character, whether for purposes of war or pleasure, and confirm remarkably the accuracy of the "Father of History." Mr. Layard remarks, that vessels (or rather rafts) of an exactly similar construction were used by him for the conveyance of the sculptures he discovered, from Nimrúd to Bussorah. They were generally built of twigs and boughs, and covered with skins smeared with bitumen, to render them water-proof. Other boats represented on the sculptures would seem to have been constructed of planks of poplar, fastened together by wooden pins or trenails, and in some instances by iron nails. But, though using boats and rafts of a rude type for the conveyance of merchandise, there is no reason to suppose that either the Assyrians or the Babylonians had any naval tastes. Like the Egyptians and the Jews, when they wanted vessels of large dimension or strength, they had recourse to their Phœnician neighbours. Thus, Phœnician shipwrights built the vessels for Sennacherib's invasion of Chaldæa; as they were said to have done for Semiramis.[2]

[1] Herod. i. 194. Compare, also, description of boats at Rhapta (Arrian's Peripl. c. 16); and the name derived from the way the boats were made by being sewn together.

[2] See Journ. of Roy. Asiat. Soc. xix. 154.

D 2

Again, Shalmaneser, when about to besiege Tyre, manned his ships with Phœnician sailors.[1]

It is probable that the vessels on the Assyrian sculptures range in date from Tiglath Pileser I., B.C. 1110, to nearly the fall of the empire, B.C. 625. The earliest are those of wicker work, covered with skins.

(LAYARD, II. Series, Pl. 28.)

On other sculptures we see:—

(1.) Vessels—carrying two chariots, and apparently constructed of planks, with a double arrangement of oars, one set for steering, the other for rowing (Layard, I. Series, Pl. 15, 16).

(2.) —— conveying planks, large stones, &c. Layard, II. Series, Pl. 10, 12, 13, &c.).

(3.) —— carrying horses (Layard's Nin. and Bab. p. 232).

In one instance, where a huge carved block of stone is being moved (one of the great bulls weighing 10 tons), the boat is evidently a flat-bottomed barge or raft.

[1] Menander ap. Joseph. Ant. Jud. ix. 14.

After the Cypriote expedition, the Assyrian boats show signs of improvement, hence a lighter and more ornamental class of vessel; one of the best has the prow in the form of a horse's head.

Others have a broad top to their masts, not unlike the crow's nest, visible in some of the medieval boats, represented on the Corporate seals of different English port towns.

Lastly, we find vessels wherein the oarsmen are obviously placed so as to row to the best advantage. The ships are generally *biremes*, with perhaps thirty rowers, and are decked.

On the deck of the second of these last illustrations two figures may be noticed with white head-dresses or veils; these are, no doubt, the wives who are accompanying their husbands in the expedition. The circular objects attached to the sides of the ships are probably the shields of the warriors. The rowers are evidently placed on a lower as well as on an upper deck.

(LAYARD, I. Series, Pl. 71.)

(LAYARD, I. Series, Pl. 71.)

No representations of naval engagements have as yet been met with on the Assyrian bas-reliefs, but they may be found hereafter.

The sculptures further show, contrary to what was long the received opinion, that the ancients possessed mechanical contrivances for diminishing manual labour, not unlike those now made use of. Indeed, the genius that planned and carried out the sculptures at Nineveh, might have been deemed equal to the knowledge of the pulley, or of the wheel and axle; and such we find to have been the case. In the museum at Leyden there exists a well made pulley, brought from Egypt; and on a bas-relief from Nineveh we clearly discern that the old mechanical contrivances differed inappreciably from those of modern days. Similar appliances would certainly have been adopted on shipboard, and ancient vessels must have been furnished with pulleys, or such other simple mechanical contrivances as were required for raising the anchor, hoisting heavy sails, or otherwise assisting manual labour.

In fact, the sculptures exhibit most of the common implements in actual use, as the saw, the pickaxe, the adze, and the handspike (or lever of the first class) Moreover, there are still preserved in the British Museum specimens of the metallic parts of all the above-named instruments.

Having called attention to the more important nations, the Tyrians, the Carthaginians, the Babylonians and the Assyrians, some other peoples who, in the ancient history of the world, played an important part, as maritime or naval states, require to be noticed, but more briefly.

Among these are the following: Lydia, Ionia, Caria, Phrygia, Sinope, Cilicia, and Scythia.

To take first Lydia. There can be no doubt that **Lydia.**

the Persians deemed the conquest of Lydia one of the most important of their achievements, in the erroneous belief that the Lydians were a great naval power. The Lydians had a navy, and may have built it themselves (though Heeren thinks not); but their real wealth lay in the great power of their capital, Sardes,[1] and in the fertility of the plains above and below it. The city has well nigh perished, but the meadows, once her joy, still retain their marvellous luxuriance. Moreover, that Lydia was very early a state unusually rich, may be inferred from the gold coins still occasionally found there. These, it is now believed, are the oldest specimens of coined money, a fact affording a striking proof of the accuracy of Herodotus,[2] who, as a Greek, would naturally have given the first origin of coinage to Argos, or to some other Greek state.

Ionia. Next in order, as memorable for their sea-faring and trading abilities, are the inhabitants of Phocæa, Ephesus, and Smyrna, who long contested with the Phœnicians the supremacy of the Archipelago; cities too, which, in a humbler degree, would seem to have worked out an inter-commercial system, much resembling the Hanseatic League of later days.

Caria. Miletus, again, as the capital of Caria, achieved no small maritime renown, and was the parent of colonies maintaining their sway for centuries along the inhospitable shores of the northern side of the Black Sea. "Her extensive commerce," says Heeren, "was not confined to the Mediterranean, but sought to monopolize the navigation of the Euxine and of the Sea of

[1] Dion. lxxiv. Herod. i 80. Fellows' "Asia Minor," p. 281.
[2] Herod. i. 91.

Azov."[1] Again, Phrygia, one of the earliest commercial populations of Asia Minor, was famous for its capital, Celænæ, a great internal entrepôt, and, in a less degree, for the possession of Sinope, itself a colony of Miletus, and a port which until now has attracted to itself a very considerable trade with the populations on the shores of the Black Sea. Phrygia.

The Scythians, with boundaries perfectly undefinable, but who may be roughly described as the inhabitants of the great Steppe country, now known as Little Russia, and of the districts north of Circassia, for centuries played an important part in the commerce of the ancient world. Though chiefly nomads, they were also, to a great extent, carriers by land, while no inconsiderable section of their population devoted itself to agriculture. Strangely, however, they cultivated, not that they might themselves enjoy the produce, but that they might sell it to other nations. From the same districts, embracing Odessa, and from the ports of the Sea of Azov, vast quantities of corn are still annually imported into England.[2] Scythians.

Nor was this all: like the modern inhabitants of the eastern shores of the Black Sea, the Scythians were also notorious for their extensive traffic in slaves, the countries situated to the north and east of this inland lake affording then, as now, inexhaustible magazines for this lucrative branch of commerce: they at the same time extended thence their trading operations far into the interior of Asia. "As far as the Argyppæi" (the

[1] Heeren's "Asiatic Nations," vol. i. p. 70.

[2] The fisheries of the Black Sea were also particularly famous in ancient times, the brackish waters of the Sea of Azov providing excellent breeding grounds. Plin. ix. 15. Ælian. De Animal. xv. 5. Athen. vii. p. 303. Polyb. iv. c. 5.

modern Calmucks), says Herodotus,[1] "the country is well known; and also that of the other nations which we have mentioned before. For it is often visited either by the Scythians, of whom inquiry may easily be made, or by the Greeks of the commercial towns on the Borysthenes [Dnieper] and Pontus. The Scythians who go into these districts usually carry on their affairs in seven different languages, by the assistance of the same number of interpreters."

Their caravan routes.

The Scythian caravans probably crossed the southern end of the Ural mountains, and passed on, round the Caspian Sea, to Great Mongolia and the Sea of Aral. Travelling with immense herds and numerous beasts of burden, they were able to conduct with advantage the overland trade through Asia Minor; following, during part of their journeys, a road which Herodotus carefully describes and to which reference will hereafter be made.

Herodotus states that their principal trade was in furs, and that it had been carried on from time immemorial. They also probably dealt largely in horses,[2] and other beasts of burden, and exchanged the manufactures of the West for such animals, and for furs and metals of various kinds, including gold, which was apparently to be procured in considerable quantities.

To India, *via* the Caspian.

These routes, as well as those through Bactra (Balkh) and Maracanda (Samarcand), the two principal marts for Indian merchandise, were all in connection with the Caspian Sea, across which, Herodotus informs us, there existed an organised system of

[1] Herod. iv. 24.

[2] Some of the names of the tribes near the Caspian, as the Arimaspi, bear names which are compounded of the Sanscrit word for "horse."

navigation.[1] On this point Heeren remarks:[2] "In the Macedonian period, the productions of India and Bactra were carried down the Oxus to the Caspian Sea; then over this sea to the mouths of the Araxes and Cyrus; after that by land to the Phasis, where they were once again conveyed by water to the different cities on the coast of the Euxine Sea."[3]

By means such as these, the chief trade between the western shores of the Mediterranean, the Black Sea, and the East was carried on during the earliest periods of history. Babylon, Susa, and Nineveh, on the one hand, with David and Solomon on the other, having been the chief causes alike of its early success and of its vast extension.

[1] Herod. i. 203.

[2] Heeren's "Asiatic Nations," vol. ii. p. 32.

[3] There seems reason to doubt whether the Oxus ever flowed into the Caspian Sea—it now flows into the Aral. (See Alex. Burnes's "Journey to Bokhara," ii. p. 188.) On the other hand, Conolly believed he crossed the bed of the river which did formerly flow by one branch into the Caspian. ("Travels," i. p. 50.) Dr. Vincent goes so far as to express his belief that communication between the west and east, by one of the routes specified above, was even more ancient than that by the Red Sea. ("Commerce of the Euxine," p. 113.)

CHAPTER III.

Egypt—Commerce—Sesostris—Naucratis—The Nile—Sailors of Egypt —Their boats—How navigated—Mode of building them—Cargo barges—Their rig—Steering—Passage and cargo boats—Boat for the conveyance of the dead—Variety of boats, and their superiority—Prosperity of Egypt under the Ptolemies, B.C. 283—Canal over the Isthmus—Ptolemy's great ship—Analysis of her dimensions —The Thalamegus, her size and splendour—Great size of other Egyptian monuments—Probability of such vessels having been constructed—Hiero's great ship—Not unlike a modern inland American steamer—Details of her construction, accommodation, outfit, and decorations — Greek ships—Habits of piracy—Corinth—Athens—The size of her ships as described by Herodotus—Discrepancy between the different accounts.

Egypt. THE ancient history of Egypt is to be found almost exclusively in the works of Herodotus and Diodorus Siculus; but it has been materially supplemented, and in many respects confirmed by the researches of modern scholars. Moreover, from the time when Young[1] discovered the key to the hieroglyphical

[1] Dr. Young, not Champollion, was the first to discover the true method of deciphering the hieroglyphics by determining that "certain characters in the Proper Names, whatever may have been their original import, were employed to represent sounds." This he published, in 1819, in the "Supplement to the Encyclopædia Britannica." Two years later, in 1821, M. Champollion published at Grenoble a work in which he still asserted "that hieroglyphics are not phonetic," and "that hieroglyphical symbols are the signs of things, and not the signs of sounds."

writings, a flood of light has been thrown upon it by the labours of Champollion, Lepsius, Bunsen, Birch, De Rougé, Chabas, Goodwin and Wilkinson; the works of the last-named writer being especially full of information with reference to its ships and commerce.

Of the period of the commencement of civilization in Egypt there is no reliable information, nor are modern scholars at all agreed as to the evidence deducible from Herodotus, as compared with the monuments. There is no certainty about the age of Menes, or about the reign in which the Exodus took place; even the date of the invasion of Judæa by Shishak is not undisputed; and it would require more materials than are yet at our disposal to harmonize all the Biblical with the Monumental records. There can be no doubt, however, that the country was richly cultivated and fully peopled many centuries before the classical nations, or even the Phœnicians, were known as merchants or warriors. As already noticed, there is further reason for believing that the populations depicted on the sculptures were not originally natives of the Valley of the Nile, but immigrants thither from Chaldæa and its neighbourhood.

The skulls of Egyptians from the mummy-pits are Caucasian, and have no affinity with those of Africa, and the grammar of their language is not Semitic. Again, the name "Egypt" is not found on any of the early monuments: the country is simply called "*Cheme*," the "black-land"; the "land of Ham," the "Caphtorim" (Genesis x. 14). Moreover, the complexion and features of the people prove that the immigrants did not appreciably mingle with the primitive population, the lineaments of many of even the existing inhabitants still showing these marks of Asiatic origin.

Commerce. Egypt under the Pharaohs was almost entirely an agricultural country; commerce and manufactures (excepting in the case of cloths of various descriptions) were neglected. With a soil of unexampled richness, annually renewed by the Nile floods, the Egyptians acted wisely in devoting their attention chiefly to the development of their own vast natural resources.

The paintings on the walls of their tombs, and other monuments, suffice to show the attention the early population paid to agricultural pursuits; for there was obviously no higher tribute to the memory of a deceased landowner than to represent him overlooking his labourers in the field, cultivating the soil, or reaping, and carrying, in nets and baskets, the produce to the thrashing floor. In fact, apart from the records of Herodotus, valuable as they undoubtedly are, the monuments furnish a great amount of information, with regard to the state and progress of the arts and sciences among this ancient people. To measure and to calculate the fitting seasons for their various religious ceremonies, they observed, with much accuracy, the courses of the heavenly bodies, especially those of the sun and stars; at the same time keeping a careful registry of their movements, little, if at all, inferior to that of the Chaldæans. But while a practical acquaintance with geometry was a necessity to the men who constructed the Pyramids and the great dams and dykes required for the complete utilizing of the periodical inundations of the Nile, the study of this exact science was still more stimulated by the mechanism necessary to enable them to transport from the quarries the enormous blocks of stone of which the Pyramids and temples were constructed, some of these having to be brought for more than five hundred miles. Such works could not have failed to demand considerable mechanical invention.

Nor indeed is this all. Remains still existing show that the Egyptians were well skilled in the use of metals, and in their application to delicate as well as rough work. The paintings in the tombs, and abundant drawings preserved on the Egyptian *papyri*, demonstrate also their knowledge of at least the elementary branches of the Fine Arts; while their colossal statues exhibit great power in the working of sculptures in a very hard and untractable material.

Sesostris.

During the earliest periods there is no record of any large vessels having been in use, for those employed for the conveyance of the huge blocks of stone from the quarries were doubtless rather rafts or barges than boats. In the reign, however, of Rameses II. (the Sesostris of the Greeks) we hear of vessels of large dimensions; these, however, it is most likely were all of Phœnician origin, and simply hired for use during his foreign expeditions. Prodigious sculptured memorials of this king exist all over Egypt, and there is still a curious relief of him at the Nahr el Kelb near Beyrût, which was seen by Herodotus.[1] Tacitus[2] further tells us that others were shown to Germanicus when in Egypt. It is not necessary here to discuss the vexed question of the conquests of Sesostris; it is enough to suggest that, in whatever extensive expeditions by sea he

[1] Herod. ii. 109. [2] Tacit. Ann. ii. 60.

may have been engaged, he was indebted to the Phœnicians for his fleet—and that, by their agency if at all, he was able to destroy "the Khairetans of the sea and the Tokhari" (probably the Cretans and Carians), nautical races, who, from the mythical till the commencement of the historical period, were highly esteemed by the Greeks for their skill as sailors. A figure discovered by the Rev. G. C. Renouard, and engraved in Texier's "Asie Mineure"[1] is almost certainly the Sesostris of Herodotus. It is on the highway from Sardes to Smyrna, but the inscriptions on it are no longer legible.

There seems no reason to suppose that the native population of Egypt was at any time of its history accustomed to nautical pursuits. As the Phœnicians supplied the navy of Sesostris, so other foreign shipping were engaged in the later times of Egyptian history. Hence it was that the famous port of Naucratis was founded on the Canopic mouth of the Nile, foreign merchants and sailors being restricted to this and to one or two other places: a practice recalling the custom of the Chinese up to a very recent period. Herodotus says that the abodes of these foreign settlers were generally called "Camps;"[2] and gives some details which show how jealously the Egyptians provided against the advent of strangers to any but the one port of Naucratis. "There was," he says, "no other in Egypt for them" (the merchants). "If a merchant or a ship-owner entered any other branch of the Nile than that of the Canopic mouth,

Naucratis.

[1] Texier, "Asie Mineure," ii. p. 304. Cf. Herod. i. 106.

[2] Herod. i. 112, 154. Compare also Strabo, xvii. 1147. Joseph. Ant. Jud. xiv. 8.

he was compelled to swear he had come there against his will through stress of weather; and he was required to sail in his own ship to the Canopic mouth, or to have his cargo transported in barges, should the winds prove adverse, round the Delta, to the factory at the port of Naucratis, which had an exclusive privilege."[1]

In the reign of Amasis (B.C. 556) special privileges were granted to the Greeks by that king, with protection to those who made Naucratis their place of abode; while for those who did not care to reside there permanently, but were simply sea-faring traders, he appropriated sites for temples and altars to their gods, and sanctuaries where their lives and properties would at all times be secure. But these privileges seem to have been restricted to the Greeks; for when another nation claimed a similar protection, Herodotus[2] simply remarks that "they claim what does not belong to them."

Thus the Greeks became the sole agents and ship brokers through whom business could be transacted at Naucratis, and, though at first reluctantly admitted within its sacred soil, they, in the end, largely aided in promoting the wealth and prosperity of Egypt. The merchandise imported by them gave rise to new fashions and new wants, and by degrees, the introduction of Greek manners and customs produced an influence over nearly the whole of Egypt, and prevailed in spite of numerous revolutions throughout the rule of the Persians till the time of Alexander the Great.

But the Nile itself was, after all, the chief source or cause of the wealth of Egypt. Although the only The Nile.

[1] Herod. ii. 179.

[2] Herod. ii. 178.

river in the world which has during so long a course so few tributaries of any magnitude, it has, or rather had, several mouths, and these, with various canals, were the principal high roads for Egyptian traffic. The external character of the greatest of these canals (the Bahr-Jusuf, or "River of Joseph"), which runs parallel with the Nile on its western side from a little below Cairo for three hundred and fifty miles, though now no longer navigable, rendered it, up to the opening of the Suez Canal in 1869, the most important work of the kind in Egypt. Nor were there wanting canals which received the surplus of the inundations of the great river.

Sailors of Egypt.

The sailors of Egypt—a numerous class—were chiefly boatmen employed on the Nile and the canals—bargemen rather than seamen. So vast, however, was the trade on this river that, according to Herodotus, no fewer than seven hundred thousand sailors (persons, we must presume) assembled on board different vessels on the occasion of one of the principal festivals;[1] while, then as now, during the periodical inundations, a large portion of the population were compelled to live in boats and barges, where fairs and markets were also held, giving fresh impulse to trade and navigation.

Their boats.

Herodotus has furnished an interesting description of how the Egyptian boats and barges were built. From the acantha[2] tree the Egyptians cut planks

[1] Herod. ii. 60.

[2] The Acantha is a species of Mimosa, or Acacia, still common in Egypt, and the origin of our "gum Arabic," perhaps the same as the Shittim wood of Exodus. The present boats are built of it. The Egyptians exported "fine linen" for sail-cloths to Phœnicia (Ezek. xxvii. 7). Hempen (Herod. vii. 25) and palm ropes (not papyrus) were used for the tackle. The process of making them may be seen on

about two cubits in length, arranging them like bricks. "They attach them,"[1] he adds, "to a number of long poles till the hull is complete, when they lay the cross planks on the top from side to side. They make no use of ribs, but caulk the seams with the papyrus; they make only one rudder, and that is driven through the keel. They use a mast of acantha and sails of papyrus. These vessels are unable to sail up the stream unless they have a brisk breeze, but are towed from the shore. They are thus carried down the stream. There is to each a raft made of tamarisk, wattled with a band of reeds, and a stone, bored through the middle, of about two talents[2] in weight; the raft is fastened to the vessel by a cable, and allowed to float down in front, while the stone is held by another cable at the stern; by this means the raft, by the stream bearing hard upon it, moves quickly, and draws along the 'baris' (for this is the name given to these vessels); but the stone being dragged at the stern, and sunk to the bottom, keeps the

How navigated.

---

the tombs at Beni-Hassan and Thebes, and specimens of them have been often found. The modern boatmen place a stone aft to keep the boat's head to the stream. Col. Chesney (ii., p. 640) found the Arabs using a bundle of hurdles and a stone for the *kufahs* on the Euphrates, exactly as described by Herodotus. *Baris* occurs in Æschylus, technically, as an Egyptian boat (Suppl. 815 and 858); see also Plutarch, Isis, c. 18; Iamblichus De Myst. 5, 6. All their larger, and even their market boats, had cabins. Wilkinson adds that there is as much difference now as of old in the size of the boats; and that there are some (which can only navigate the Nile during the inundation) which are rated as high as twenty-four thousand bushels of corn. The war vessels of the eighteenth and nineteenth Dynasties had a single row of twenty to fifty oars, like the Greek *penteconters*.

[1] Herodotus, book ii. c. 96.

[2] A talent is about sixty-five pounds weight.

vessel straight. They have very many of these vessels, and some of them carry many thousand talents."

Mode of building them.

The following drawing, taken from Champollion's "Description de l'Egypte," furnishes monumental proof of the accuracy of Herodotus, in his description of their construction.[1]

Men may be seen building a boat, much resembling a modern barge, with a high poop, and a long bow, apparently binding bands of papyrus round the boards, while others are bringing, on their backs, baskets filled with reeds, to be twisted into similar bands. But the larger vessels must have been fastened together (though Herodotus does not mention this) by either metal bolts, or trenails.

Herodotus, therefore, probably refers to the smaller craft employed upon the Nile.

Cargo barges.

Many interesting drawings of these river boats are to be found in Wilkinson's "Manners and Customs" of that ancient people. Most of them have been copied from ancient monuments, and have evidently had their imperfections corrected, as far as practicable, by a reference to the boats and

[1] See also Rawlinson's "Herodotus," vol. ii. p. 132.

barges of modern times, similarly employed. For instance, the following sketch, taken originally from one of the paintings on a tomb at Kom-el-Ahmars,[1] near Minieh, represents, in many respects, one of the large Nile barges still in use. From having twenty-two oars on each side, her length could hardly have been less than from eighty to one hundred feet, and her form shows considerable capacity for cargo.

Like the other boats of the Nile, this vessel has only one sail, but the mast appears to have been Their rig.

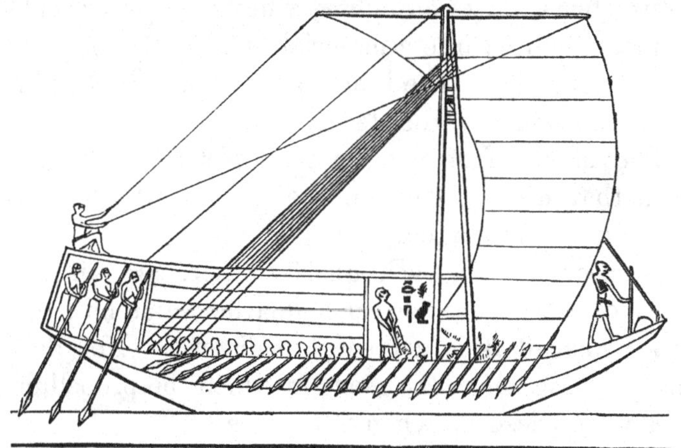

composed of two spars of similar size, secured by backstays to her after-part. It is not easy to understand why two spars should have been used; but it is possible that by these means a large and heavy sail might in stormy weather be lowered on either side, according to the direction of the wind; this, however, would require some mechanical contrivance not indicated. If the yard was a fixture aloft, moving

[1] Rawlinson's "Herodotus," vol. ii. p. 156.

on a pivot, the sail may have been triced up and furled to it: the cross bars, at the top of the masts, serving to enable the sailors more easily to furl the sail, tend to confirm this supposition. Although such a mode of furling the sail would be inconvenient and full of risk, if the ship were exposed to heavy seas, it would answer very well for barges on the Nile, as the yard and sail, when furled, would be entirely clear of the cargo while loading or unloading. It has been supposed that the sail, in this vessel, was made of papyrus, as noticed by Herodotus; but it may be doubted whether papyrus could be manufactured into a material sufficiently tough to form a large sail. The braces are apparently worked by a man seated in the stern.

Steering. The mode of steering here depicted is different from that usually seen on the monuments, for, instead of a single oar, passing through the stern frames, or one on each quarter, there are, in this instance, three on the same quarter; and how this was managed it is not easy to discern. Nor does the drawing show the mode in which the propelling oars were triced up when not in use.

Tacitus[1] speaks of Germanic tribes who used a rudder at each end; but the practice was not general, and none of the Egyptian boats or barges were thus fitted, or had more than one sail, in these respects resembling the earliest of the Greek vessels. Sometimes a single rudder, instead of working in a rowlock, or in a porthole through the stern, was applied outside, merely over the stern-rail, and held in its place by a stout thong. This imperfect mode of steering was,

[1] Tacit. Annal. ii. 6, and De Morib. German. c. xliv.

however, confined to the rudest river craft, and of these we have a model in the museum at Berlin, as well as a painting at Thebes. The Berlin model shows also the position of the rowers, the arrangements of the mast, yard, and rigging, the place of the pegs and mallet, for fastening the vessel to the shore, and the landing planks, which were always kept in readiness at the bow, in charge of the man stationed there, to fathom and report the depth of the water. This boat is decked, the cabins occupying only a portion of the middle, like the pleasure vessels of the Nile, or the passage-boats at Diarbekr. But in most of the larger boats the cabin resembled our "round house," extending from one side to the other, and was often sufficiently spacious to contain cattle, horses, and general stores.

Passage and cargo boats.

In another drawing, Wilkinson exhibits another description of Nile boat. Here there is a single rudder or paddle, passing through the counter, and evidently worked by some kind of machine attached to the post against which its handle rests. Or it may be worked on the one side, as the drawing is not very distinct, somewhat after the style in use in large boats or river barges of the present day. Its general character suggests that it is a passage-boat, as it has a round house, with windows at each end and a semblance of decoration for the upper yard. This yard is fitted with lines, for the purpose of drawing it down with the sail when furled to the lower yard.

One of the illustrations subjoined, taken from a bas-relief at Thebes, represents a double cattle-boat;[1]

[1] See also Rawlinson's "Herodotus," vol. ii. p. 137.

in other words, two canal boats lashed together when descending the Nile, much like the "monkey-boats," or "wussers," employed on the Thames or Severn. In the cabin a man is represented, inflicting the bastinado on a boatman; an occurrence probably not unusual, as we find it on the ordinary cattle-barge of the period. In the same boat a cow eats hay out of a net, precisely resembling the *sherif* now used in Egypt. These boats are without masts. The "house" appears to be of a light and a temporary character, and as the sailors on the top are

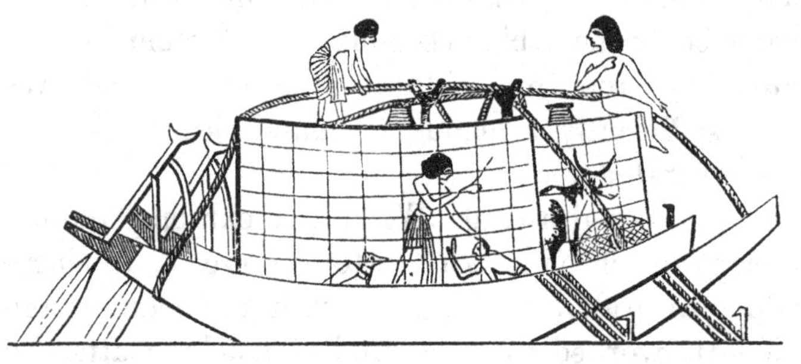

evidently making a rope fast to bind it together, it may be inferred that such houses were chiefly used when these vessels were employed in the conveyance of cattle, and that they could be removed at pleasure.

Boat for the conveyance of the dead.

In Champollion's great work, we find a sketch of another boat, in this instance carrying a bier. It is taken from a bas-relief on the tomb of Beni-Hassan. Here two rudders, one on each quarter, are clearly represented. Their upper extremities are, by some mode not easily understood, attached to separate upright posts, and the helmsmen appear to hold lanyards or bow-lines for the regulation of the rudders, proving that mechanical appliances of one sort or another were then in use as tillers to assist the steerage.

Although a tolerably accurate impression may be formed from the monuments of the various kinds of vessels employed on the great river and the canals, there is, beyond these, no evidence of the form and dimensions of their other vessels. We may, however, presume that, till the times of the Ptolemies, the Egyptians did not build any large sea-going ships; one reason of this probably being, that Egypt, within her own territory, had no forest timber adapted for such a purpose. Hence, indeed, as is well known, arose the sanguinary wars so long and so fiercely waged between the Ptolemies and the Seleucidæ—the inheritors from the Tyrians of the forests of Lebanon, who, mindful of the elder times, as well as of the value of this property, were little inclined to give the Egyptians the means of becoming a powerful maritime people.

Variety of boats, and their superiority.

But though, from the scarcity of suitable timber,[1] and the repugnance of its people to sea-faring pursuits, Egypt was never destined to occupy a position of any influence as a maritime nation, it surpassed all others of the old world in the number, variety, and excellence of its boats for inland navigation. Beyond those already described there were others of the most fanciful description, in form and rig. The mode of keeping the sail flat introduced only a few years ago by the famous yacht *America*, whose sails were lashed to spars to prevent them from bellying, was, after all, only the double yard used by the Egyptians four thousand years ago. The painted eye upon the

[1] Egypt produced no forest timber nor any lofty trees, except the date-palm and sycamore, of which the mummy cases are made.

bow, still so common in the Mediterranean, was a favourite mode of decorating the boats of ancient Egypt. Modern ship-owners of all nations have adopted their plan of deck-houses; and the decoration of the stems and sterns of their ships are in some respects not unlike those of the Nile during the reign of the Pharaohs. But the ancient Egyptians carried the decorations of their vessels sometimes to a ludicrous extent. They were frequently wont to paint even the masts, sails, and yards in the most variegated and gaudy colours. A lotus leaf usually adorned the blade of the rudder, and some other design that of the oars, the prevailing colours being, red, yellow, or green.[1]

Prosperity of Egypt under the Ptolemies, B.C. 283.

The conquest of Egypt by Alexander put an end to the internal convulsions which had so long disturbed that country, and gave new life to its trade, and Alexandria became the entrepôt of the trade of India and the West. Favoured after his death by wise counsellors and enterprising monarchs, Egypt flourished under the rule of the Ptolemies, and devoted more attention to maritime commerce than she had hitherto done. Ptolemy, son of Lagos, by a judicious exercise of sovereign authority, and by encouraging by all means in his power sea-faring pursuits and free intercourse with other nations, collected a considerable body of traders at the new city; and perceiving what had been the intentions and policy of Alexander, steadily endeavoured to follow in his footsteps.

It was during this long and prosperous reign that the celebrated Pharos at Alexandria was erected

[1] See an elaborate drawing of a ship in Rawlinson's "Herodotus," vol. ii. p. 157.

by Sostratus of Cnidus,[1] at the cost, it is said, of eight hundred talents; and though Pliny doubts the value of such buildings, and seems to think of them rather as snares to the navigator,[2] Cæsar fully approved of the Alexandrian one.[3] The upper storeys had windows, looking seaward; and fires therein at night lighted ships into the harbour. A few similar structures are mentioned in ancient history as those at Ostia, Ravenna, Brundusium, Capreæ, and Gessoriacum (Boulogne). In England, it is believed that we have remains of two similar structures—the Pharos in Dover Castle, and at Moel Van in Flintshire.

Upon the front of the Alexandrian Pharos there was written the appropriate inscription: "King Ptolemy to the God the Saviour, for the benefit of sailors."

Canal over the Isthmus.

More than one of the followers of Ptolemy I. pursued the same course, and encouraged their subjects in the promotion of commerce. Thus Philadelphus, his son, made a fresh attempt to cut a canal a hundred cubits in breadth, between Arsinoe (on the Red Sea, not far from Suez) to the Pelusiac or eastern branch of the Nile. But though he failed to carry out his plan, as Necho had done two centuries before,[4] he built on the south-western shores of the Red Sea the port of Berenice, so that goods from Alexandria could be carried on camels' backs for shipment, either from Myos Hormus, or from this new port; while stations were erected on the road, so as to facilitate the commercial intercourse between the Mediterranean and

[1] Plin. xxxvi. 12. [2] Plin. xxxvi. 86. [3] Cæsar, Bell. Civil. iii. 93.

[4] Herod. iv. 42. The canal was really commenced by Rameses II., and, probably, only re-opened by Necho and Darius.

the Red Sea. Thus Egypt, mainly through his instrumentality, enjoyed a line of commerce to India uninterruptedly until the period of Augustus Cæsar, when Egypt became a province of the Roman Empire.

Although, as we have seen, the Egyptians were not naturally fond of maritime occupations, it is certain that, during the sway of the Ptolemies, an Egyptian fleet was maintained in the Mediterranean of sufficient size to command that sea, and to afford effectual protection to their merchants and ship-owners. Appian, in his preface, enumerating the naval and military forces of Ptolemy, the son of Lagos, says that he had five hundred galleys, two thousand smaller vessels, and eight hundred *thalamegi*, or pleasure boats; and Lucian[1] states that he saw in Egypt a vessel of the country, one hundred and twenty cubits long, thirty broad, and twenty-nine deep.

Again, another Ptolemy (Philopator) appears to have been no common enthusiast in ship-building, for he constructed vessels of a size far in excess of any before his day, either in his own or in any other country—ships, indeed, as much larger than any then known, as the Great Eastern is larger than any vessel built in modern times.

Ptolemy's great ship. One of these extraordinary vessels is described at length in Athenæus,[2] from an Alexandrian historian named Callixenus. The following are some of her chief peculiarities: she is said to have been two hundred and eighty cubits long, thirty-eight broad, and fifty-three from the highest part of the stern to the water; she had four rudders, each thirty cubits long; and the oars of the *thranitæ* were thirty-

[1] Lucian. Navig. 5. [2] Athen. v. 37.

eight cubits long, with handles necessarily weighted with lead. She had two heads, two sterns, and no fewer than seven beaks, one of them much larger than the rest. She carried on board four thousand rowers, and about three thousand mariners, besides a large body of men under her decks, and a vast quantity of stores and provisions. She was launched by means of a contrivance invented by a Phœnician, one, indeed, which might probably have been adopted with success for the launching of the Great Eastern, and, assuredly, at less cost.

Various imaginary drawings have been made of Ptolemy's great vessel; but as none of them appear to answer the only description of her which has been preserved, or to fulfil the requirements of a structure meant to float in safety, an endeavour has been made, in the drawing annexed, to illustrate this remarkable ship, which was "well proportioned in an extraordinary degree."[1] If the cubit be taken at eighteen inches, Ptolemy's ship was four hundred and twenty feet in length, fifty-seven feet beam, and had seventy-two feet depth of hold: proportions which, as far as regards the length and breadth, accord very well with those of the large steam-ships of our own time; but the depth is so great and so much out of proportion to the length and breadth, that there is no doubt a mistake in the figures. The depth was much more likely to have been twenty-eight cubits, for which forty-eight has, through some misapprehension, been substituted. There is no doubt, also, a mistake in the height of the stern above the water, for though the ships of the

Analysis of her dimensions.

[1] See a further examination of her by Leroy, Mémoires de l'Acad. d'Inscriptions, t. xxxvii.

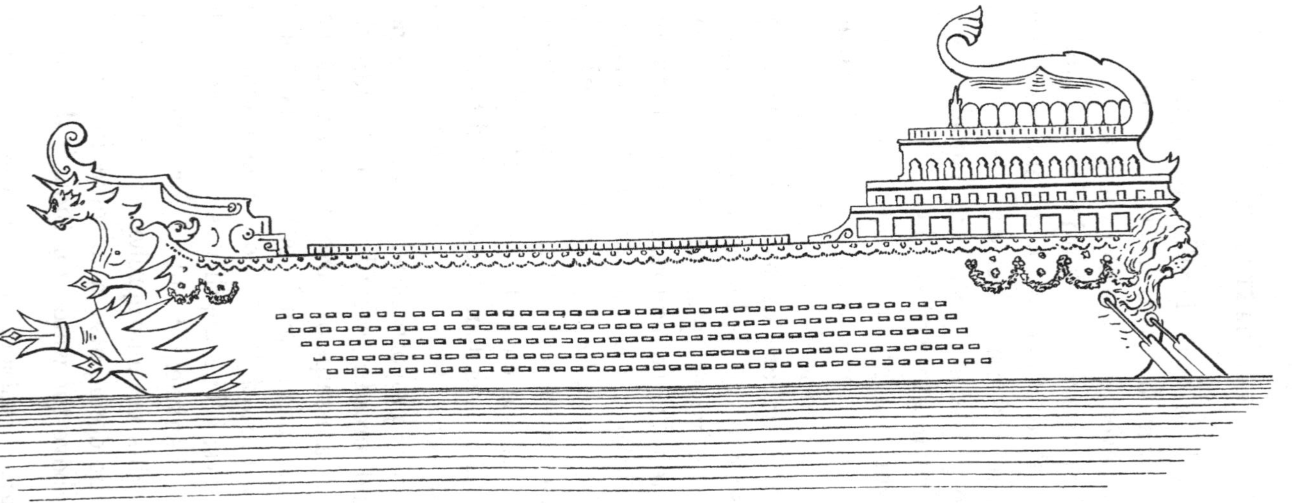

GREAT SHIP OF PTOLEMY PHILOPATOR.

ancients had frequently very high poops or enormous castles erected aft, a practice which prevailed up to the seventeenth century, it is hardly possible to conceive that the highest portion of the poop of Ptolemy's ship was fifty-three cubits, or about eighty feet above the water. The object of having so many as seven beaks is not easily understood; two of them may, however, have been placed at the bluff, or rounds of the bows, so as to protect, in some measure, the oars from being destroyed by the ship of an enemy sheering alongside. "Some of them," we are informed, "were fixed to the ears of the ship."

Nor is it easy to understand what is meant by the "ears," unless they represent that portion of the head or bow where the cat-heads are now placed. A beak in that place would protect the upper bank of oars, while another below it, a little above the water-line, would guard the lower banks. Though inferior in length, breadth, and capacity to our modern wonder, the Great Eastern, Ptolemy's huge vessel could hardly have been meant for sea-going purposes, if the dimensions given of her depth, and the height of her poop, are accurate; nor could seven or eight thousand men, besides a "large number under deck," have been accommodated in her 'tween decks; but, though the nautical knowledge of the present day renders it difficult to accept all the recorded details of this extraordinary vessel, it is not necessary to agree with the writers who altogether deny her existence. The four thousand rowers could perfectly well have been placed at their stations, though it is most likely that she was never used except for display, or as an object of ornament or luxury.

Other writers insist that the oars, by reason of their length, would be unmanageable; but in approaching the question of rowing such ponderous vessels, which more properly belongs to and shall be treated of in a subsequent portion of this work, it will be found that the oars described by Callixenus are not longer than those which have been used in galleys, of which authentic accounts exist. It may be denied that four thousand men could have been made available as oarsmen in any vessel; but if it be possible to work the upper bank of oars, which shall hereafter be shown to be practicable, it will be found on examining the drawing and number of oar-ports, that with ten men to each oar, two thousand rowers could be placed at their stations on each side of the vessel, or, in all, "four thousand rowers," as described by Callixenus.

The Thalamegus, her size and splendour.

Nor was this the only vessel of huge dimensions constructed during the reign of the Ptolemies. Callixenus describes another, the Thalamegus, or the "carrier of the bed-chamber" which was half a stadium (three hundred feet) in length, thirty cubits wide, and forty cubits high. From his elaborate description we learn that she was fitted with every conceivable luxury, and in a style of magnificence much superior to that of any other ship or floating structure of the period; with "colonnades," "marble stairs," and "gardens," whence it may safely be concluded that this vessel was never meant for sea-going purposes. But there is no reason to question her existence. Such a vessel might have remained moored on the Nile, or on one of the great lakes or canals, as a pleasant place of resort during the hottest months of an Egyptian summer.

When, indeed, the colossal character of all Egyptian monuments (more especially those of the Pyramids, now known to have been in some cases tombs, as that of Mycerinus,) and that, too, of their temples, statues, and canals, is borne in mind, the presumption is strong that this love of the colossal extended to other Egyptian works, and further, that in a country where so much mechanical genius was displayed, the construction of one or two great ships would not form an exception, even though a seafaring life may have been repugnant to the habits and tastes of a majority of the people. Plutarch, in speaking of the great war-ships built by Demetrius, observes, that while these could really be used, the still larger ship of Philopator "was a mere matter of curiosity, for she differed very little from an immovable building, and was calculated more for show, as she could not be put in motion without great difficulty and danger."

Great size of other Egyptian monuments.

During the last three thousand years the steady tendency of commercial enterprise has been towards the West, and may, in its circuit from New York to California, even cross the Pacific and restore commercial life to Assyria, Phœnicia, and Egypt. Three thousand years hence London may have become a city of ruins, which an Egyptian antiquary may, in the interests of science, consider worthy of a visit. By the year 4873 all references to Ptolemy's ship, constructed five thousand years before, may have been destroyed, but some account of the Great Eastern, built on the banks of the Thames in the nineteenth century of the Christian era, may have endured. The supposed Egyptian traveller may seek diligently for some proof that such a vessel was really built and

Probability of such vessels having been constructed.

launched, yet all he may ascertain, by a careful measurement of the ruined docks, will be that not one of them was large enough to receive her: he will, therefore, conclude that what he has read about her was but the vainglorious romance of the historian of the day.

Hiero s great ship.

The Egyptian monarchs were, however, not alone in their desire of building ships of gigantic proportions; but found a worthy rival in Hiero, king of Syracuse; nay, more, while the Syracusan ruler constructed a vessel scarcely if at all inferior to that of Ptolemy, this ship surpassed the Egyptian one in accomplishing at least one successful voyage. No details have been preserved of the dimensions of Hiero's ship; but from the description of the cargo she carried, of the number of her decks, and of the structures of various kinds above her hold, she must have been of even greater cubic contents than Ptolemy's ship.[1]

Not unlike a modern inland American steamer.

The probability is that Hiero's vessel was simply an enormous barge, and that, on this barge or hulk there were erected, much after the fashion of the steam-vessels on the rivers and inland waters of America, one or more decks or tiers of houses, suited to carry wool or other kinds of light cargo, or capable of being fitted up for passengers, as occasion might require. It is, however, more likely from the description we have of her, that the decks immediately above the hold were reserved entirely for cargo, and that the houses upon deck were appropriated to the passengers and the crew.

It is stated that, for the construction of this mag-

[1] A long account is given of her by Athenæus (v. 40–44), who makes use of three distinct words for the trenails, the ribs, and the upright supports of the side planks.

nificent vessel, Hiero cut down on Mount Etna trees enough to have built sixty triremes; procuring stores of trenails, &c., from Italy and Sicily, ropes from Spain, and hemp and pitch from the banks of the Rhone; and watching himself over the progress of the works. To launch her effectively, Archimedes invented a screw of great power; and the building was pushed on with such rapidity, that, in six months from the time she was commenced, great progress had been made, every part as it was finished (referring no doubt to the sheathing of the bottom and to the interstices on the upper decks or houses) being covered with sheets of lead. She is further said to have had twenty banks of oars, and three entrances, the lowest leading to the hold, the next to the eating-rooms, while the third was appropriated to the armed men. On both sides of the middle entrance thirty rooms, each containing four couches, were assigned to the soldiers; the sailors' supper-room held fifteen, and there were, besides, three cabins, each containing three couches. The floors of these rooms were composed of stone mosaic work, bearing on it a pictorial representation of the whole story of the Iliad. There was also a temple to Venus of cypress inlaid with ivory, furnished with rich and valuable goblets and vases. This great ship was fitted with four wooden and eight iron anchors; and the mainmast, of a single tree, was procured after much search from the mountains of the Bruttii.

Details of her construction; accommodation, outfit, and decorations.

But the most remarkable part of the story is that relating to her freight, as it is stated that one or two of the launches belonging to this ship, built, it may be presumed to attend upon her, were able themselves to carry three thousand talents (about eighty tons); and these tenders are said to have put on board of the *Alexandrian* "sixty thousand measures of corn, ten thousand jars of Sicilian salt fish, twenty thousand talents' weight of wool, and of other cargo twenty thousand talents, all of which was in addition to the provisions required for the crew." It is further stated that she was sent to Alexandria, partly because Hiero discovered he had no harbours in Sicily that could contain her, and partly because he had heard that at that time there was a dearth of corn in Egypt. She bore upon her the following curious inscription: "Hiero, the son of Hierocles the Dorian, who wields the sceptre of Sicily (sends this ship), bearing in her the fruits of the earth—a rich gift to all Greece and her islands. Do thou, O Neptune! preserve in safety this ship over the blue waves."

There is no more reason for doubting the existence of this ship than there is for questioning the vessel constructed by the Egyptian king; though, in each case, there may be some exaggeration in the description preserved. Vessels not differing much from her in form may be seen on the Mississippi and traverse the stormy lakes of America; they even trade along her shores, exposed to the boisterous waves of the Atlantic; and hence it may be reasonably inferred that, though not well adapted for sea-going purposes, Hiero's ship may have made, in perfect safety, voyages to both Greece and Alexandria.

Greek ships.

Although the Greeks were for many centuries well known alike for their intellectual abilities and for their zeal as merchants and traders, Herodotus speaks with some contempt of their geographical knowledge in the time of Xerxes, and says they were so ignorant of the position and distance of places, that they could with difficulty be prevailed upon to advance as far as Delos,[1] and that all the countries beyond that island and in the vicinity of Ionia were avoided by them. "They believed," he adds, "that it was as far from Ægina to Samos as from Ægina to Gibraltar."

Habits of piracy.

On the other hand, history clearly demonstrates that each Greek power, as it became famous, turned its attention to the sea as a source of wealth and greatness; and that, during the struggles between the Lacedæmonians and Athenians, Philip of Macedon, with a powerful fleet under his command, swept the seas of the pirates and marauders, enriching himself by the spoils. The Greeks, moreover, paid a marked attention to the mode of conducting their local commerce, forbidding their vessels to sail with more than a specified number of men on board. Plutarch, quoting from a more ancient author,[2] names a limit of five persons only to each vessel; while others, referring to later periods, speak of a general law applicable to all Greece, which fixed the maximum crew of its merchant ships at one hundred men. These restrictive navigation laws were passed professedly for the suppression of piracy; but in those days, the strong were generally held to be right and the weak to be wrong, for even Philip resorted to the practice he had denounced, to recruit his finances at

[1] This is surely an exaggeration, as the passage through the islands to Asia Minor *must* have been familiar to them. Even the Spartans were used to the voyage (Herod. i. 70, 152; iii. 47, 57). The reason was rather, as Mr. Grote suggests, "fear of an enemy's country, where they could not calculate the risk beforehand" (vol. v. p. 198).

[2] Plutarch in Thes. c. 19, where "trireme" is used in the sense of any vessel.

the siege of Byzantium. Nor, indeed, are such principles wholly forgotten at the present day; for, even now, while Great Britain captures and destroys at sea the private property of the people with whom she may happen to be at war (which is simply the right of the strong confirmed by ancient usage and unhappily still sanctioned by international maritime law), she does not allow depredations similar in their character to be perpetrated by nations that sell their prisoners as captives of war. We, like Philip of Macedon, denounce in others what we ourselves practise, because it is sanctioned by usage and by law. Who will say that the destruction at sea of the goods of private individuals is not as barbarous as the practice which still prevails among illiterate African chiefs? England, in this matter, simply overlooks the beam in her own eye, though sacrificing much to extract the mote in that of other and less civilized nations.

Corinth. Corinth, once so celebrated, was among the first of the Greek states to avail herself of the many advantages nature had given her. Built a little to the west of the isthmus connecting the Peloponnesus with northern Greece, she was destined by her position to be the entrepôt of both. Nor did her people fail to appreciate this, for, contrary to what Herodotus states generally of the Greeks, the Corinthians are known to have been expert sailors, and to have made navigation and ship-building their study, being, as Thucydides remarks (i. 13), the inventors of the trireme.[1]

[1] Cicero, de leg. Agrar. ii. 32; Eurip. Troad. 1097; and Hor. Od. i. 7, 2, exactly describe the geographical position of Corinth. The Phœnicians must have been there early, as a mountain at Corinth bore the name of the "Phœnician" (Ephor. ap. Steph. Byz.), and the

In maritime pursuits, and by an extensive commercial intercourse with the neighbouring states, they amassed great wealth. Corinth also affords a striking instance that the cultivation of commerce can be successfully combined with a taste for the most refined arts, for the Corinthian column continues to this day the finest type of architectural beauty; while Corinth was famous in antiquity for her celebrated artists, and their works.[1]

The writers, however, of ancient Greece have left but few particulars either of the merchant vessels or of the trade in which they were engaged. Of the character and habits of its seamen, or of the remuneration they received, the accounts are brief and fragmentary, though we know that after the time of Demosthenes their wages were provided for by a tax B.C. 326.
upon property. In cases of emergency, it would seem that men of substance in Greece, besides paying the whole of this special tax, fitted out at their own expense numerous vessels for the service of the state, and that a patriotic and generous rivalry prevailed among them, inducing them to do their utmost for the good of their country. From this laudable public spirit arose, in a great measure, that enlarged and enlightened system of commerce with foreign nations, for which the Greeks have been in all times conspicuous, and which still largely prevails among the leading Greek merchants resident in England.

"Phœnician Athene" was also worshipped there (Tzetz. ap Lycophr. (658. The Corinthians, too, were the founders of Syracuse and Corcyra (Corfu) and of many ports along the coast of Greece. The principal port of Corinth (represented on a coin of Antoninus Pius) was called Cenchreæ, and is noticed in Acts xviii. 18, and Romans xvi. 1.

[1] Plin. xxxiv. 7; xxxvii. 49; xxxv. 15, 151; xxxvi. 178; xxxv. 152, &c.

Athens.

Athens, too, though in a less degree than Corinth, was also a place of commercial importance; for though at some distance from the sea, it possessed three harbours—the Piræeus, Munychia, and Phalerum, themselves forming a city as large as, if not larger than, Athens herself. From the harbour of the Piræeus a large foreign trade, chiefly in corn, was carried on with the countries bordering on the Black Sea and the Crimea, as well as with Palestine and Egypt. The Piræeus contained extensive warehouses for the reception of various descriptions of produce, as well as a large portico or arcade, where, after the fashion of eastern bazaars, manufactures of every description were exposed for sale.

This portico (technically called the Deigma, or Show-Place) was in fact the Royal Exchange of Athens, where her merchants transacted business with those of Syria and of Asia Minor, who resorted thither in great numbers; and though Athenian commerce, even at its best times, was small when compared with that of Tyre, Carthage, or Miletus, Athenian merchants held a high position in ancient times.[1]

But, if commercially inferior to some other states, Athens maintained the highest rank among the naval cities of the ancient world, though it is difficult from such records as still exist to determine either the size or the number of the vessels belonging to her or to other Greek states.[2]

[1] The actual boundary stone of the mercantile port of the Piræeus, of the date of the Peloponnesian war, was found *in situ* in 1842 (Ulrich's Athen. 1843). Themistocles planned, and Pericles carried out the building of this port-town (Paus. i. 1; Schol. Arist. Equit. 974; ibid. 547).

[2] The few following facts are, perhaps, worth recording. Thus, an

The superiority of Athens was, however, due to political rather than commercial causes; and her people were chiefly famed for their daring and prowess as warriors at sea. To the Athenians, Greece was mainly indebted for her freedom from the Persian yoke. It was the Athenian fleet that resisted successfully the gigantic navy of Xerxes; and the description of this fleet, by Herodotus, is almost the only information we possess with regard to the size of Greek ships, and of the relative maritime power of the different Greek states. Describing the naval force which defeated the Persian fleet off the promontory of Artemisium, Herodotus states:[1]—"The Greeks engaged in the sea-service were these. The Athenians furnished one hundred and twenty-seven vessels to the fleet; but the Platæans, from a spirit of valour and zeal, though inexperienced in the sea-service, assisted the Athenians in manning the ships. The Corinthians furnished forty ships, the Megarians twenty; the Chalcideans manned twenty, the Athenians having furnished them with ships; the Æginetans eighteen; the Sicyonians

The size of her ships as described by Herodotus.

oar cost 5 drachmæ (Andoc. p. 81); and Lucian, Dial. de Mort. 4, charges the anchor for Charon's boat at 3 dr. The *tropoter* cost 2 obols; a needle for sewing the sail, 3 obols; and the pitch, wax, nails, &c, 2 drachmæ more. Again, Demosthenes speaks of a *bottomry* bond of 3000 drachmæ; and Polyænus states, generally, that a ship cost a talent. Usually the State found the hull, and the trierarch the fittings. In the naval service the pay and the provisions were generally joined together: 20 minæ was good pay for a month, and the complement of a trireme about 200 men; the proportion of sailors, rowers, and fighting men varying considerably at different times. The *thranitœ* got the best pay (Arnold's note, Thucyd. vi. 43). The whole equipment of shipping (for war) was under the control of *trierarchs* (Böckh, Publ. Economy of Athens, bk. iv. c. 11).

[1] Herodotus, book viii. ch. 1 and 2.

twelve; the Lacedæmonians ten; the Epidaurians eight; the Eretrians seven; the Trœzenians five; the Styreans two; and the Cêans two ships, and two penteconters; the Opuntian Locrians also came to their assistance with seven penteconters." Of the individual size of these vessels no mention is however made; but speaking, in another portion of his history, of the preparations made to resist the invasion of Xerxes, Herodotus[1] says: "Now the Grecians from Thrace, and the islands contiguous to Thrace, furnished one hundred and twenty ships; with crews in number amounting to twenty-four thousand men," equivalent to two hundred fighting men a ship. The same author further remarks,[2] that "Clinias,[3] son of Alcibiades, at his own expense, joined the fleet with two hundred men and a ship of his own:" on the other hand, Xenophon states that the Athenians in this celebrated war put on board a fleet of a hundred sail only one thousand marines, and four hundred archers, which is only fourteen men to each vessel, besides the rowers.

B.C. 481. The fleet of Xerxes, Herodotus adds,[4] amounted to twelve hundred and seven triremes, carrying two hundred and forty-one thousand four hundred men, or two hundred men to each vessel, exclusive of Persians, Medes, and Sacæ, who served as marines, thirty to each ship, in addition to the crew. The vessels must, therefore, have been larger than those of the Athenians, described by Herodotus and Xeno-

[1] Herodotus, book vii. ch. 185.

[2] Ibid. book viii. ch. 17.

[3] This Clinias, who was killed at the battle of Coronæa, in B.C. 447, was the father of the famous Alcibiades. Plut. Alcib.

[4] Herod. vii. 184.

phon. But besides the twelve hundred and seven triremes, Xerxes is said to have brought with him three thousand transports and penteconters, with many light boats, and long horse-transports, so that his whole naval force must have consisted of four thousand two hundred and seven vessels of one sort and another: a number almost as inconceivable as the reputed catalogue of his combined land and sea force, even though he brought, as was said of him, "all Asia in his train."

This vast fleet had the misfortune to encounter a great storm on the coast of Magnesia, in which four hundred vessels, besides store ships, were totally wrecked; and so great were the spoils from the derelict ships that, according to the testimony of Herodotus,[1] one Ameinocles, who owned the land on the coast, became immensely rich from the quantity of gold and silver Persian cups which were afterwards found. Having described the coast of Magnesia, Herodotus says:[2] "The ships of the first row were moored to the land, while the others behind rode at anchor; and as the beach extended but a little way, they had to anchor off the shore in eight rows. Thus they passed the night, but at daybreak, after serene and tranquil weather, the sea began to swell, and a heavy storm, with a violent gale from the east, which those who inhabit these parts call Hellespontias, burst upon them. As many of them, then, as perceived the gale increasing and were able from their position to do so, avoided the storm by *hauling their ships upon the beach*, and both they and their ships escaped. But such of the ships as the

[1] Herod. vii. 190. [2] Ibid. vii. 188.

storm caught at sea were driven ashore; some near the place called Ipni, "the Ovens," at the foot of Pelion, others on the beach; some were dashed on Cape Sepias itself; some were wrecked near the cities of Meliboea and of Casthanæa. The storm was indeed irresistible."

Hauling the ships on shore seems to have been customary in those days; for, in another place, (when referring to the ship-canal Xerxes[1] had ordered to be cut to the north of the headland of Athos,) Herodotus[2] remarks that "it was possible, without any great labour, to have drawn his ships over the isthmus."

Discrepancy between the different accounts.

It is not easy to account for the discrepancy in the statements about the number of men each of the vessels carried, or to comprehend the facility with which they were drawn up on a beach in the face of an approaching storm, or how they could, as Herodotus suggests, have been transported across the isthmus. Possibly Herodotus was misinformed as to the number of men in each of the vessels. Curiously enough, the descriptions preserved of the fleets and

[1] Some ancient, as well as many modern writers, have questioned the story of this canal (Cf. Juvenal, x. 173, 174); but later researches have shown that there are undoubted remains of this great work. Captain Spratt, R.N., has surveyed it thoroughly, and has published an account and map thereof in the "Journ. Roy. Geogr. Soc." v. 17. The canal now forms a line of ponds, from 2 to 8 feet deep, and from 60 to 90 broad, extending from sea to sea. It is cut through tertiary sands, which would naturally fall in, as Herodotus states (vii. 23). Previously to Spratt, the genuineness of this work had been maintained by Choiseul-Gouffier, Voy. Pittor. ii. i. 148; Colonel Leake, "Northern Greece," ii. 145; and Sir George Bowen, "Athos," p. 57. Moreover, we can hardly fancy that Herodotus could be in error about a work of such magnitude, and executed only thirty-six years before he publicly read his history at the Olympic Games, B.C. 445.

[2] Herod. vii. ch. 24.

maritime exploits of Cyrus, and of other great conquerors, partake of the same character as these recorded of Xerxes, and are equally inconsistent, when we look to the capacity of the vessels as compared with the apparent ease with which they could be moved about on dry land. Although the ancients had capstans, of which Herodotus speaks, and were conversant with pulleys, and with the best mode of transporting, by means of manual labour, aided by blocks and rollers, heavy weights across land, it is difficult to understand how any vessels competent to convey between two and three hundred men each, could, just as a storm was coming on, have been hauled high and dry upon a beach with sufficient speed.[1]

A vessel of size sufficient to take that number of men even for a short distance and across a smooth sea, must have been, according to the present mode of measurement, of at least seventy tons register. But no vessel of that tonnage, or of three-fourths that size, could be drawn up on a beach, much less across an isthmus, with the facility the narrative of Herodotus presumes, unless the ancients had methods for transporting their vessels on shore of which no accounts have been preserved. A vessel of fifty-five tons register might hold between two and three hundred men, and transport them, in a calm, across the smooth and narrow waters of the Hellespont; but to attempt to make a voyage of no greater

[1] There is no doubt that the ancients did adopt this plan of hauling vessels over land to a great extent; a portion of the Isthmus of Corinth was called *Diolcus*—as the spot where the ships were so drawn across. Hesych. ad voc. Cf. Thucyd. iii. 81; iv. 8. Horat. Od. i. 4, 2.

distance than from Constantinople to Athens, in the craft of those days, measuring fifty-five tons, with so many men on board, would be attended with very considerable risk, and, this too, without taking into consideration the convenience of the troops, or the space required for their stores and accoutrements.

CHAPTER IV.

Route *viâ* the Cape to India, discovered by the Phœnicians, B.C. 610–594—Voyage of the first Eudoxus—Story of the second Eudoxus (of Cyzicus)—Opinion of Dr. Vincent on the circumnavigation of Africa—Remarks upon his opinion—Routes to India and to the East by land—Origin of the caravans—Resting places—Their management—The more important routes—Eastern—Southern—Northern—The character, size, and discipline of the caravans—The route from Sardes to Susa, described by Herodotus—Between Tyre and Gerrha—Length of journey—Importance of Petra—Intercourse between Syria and Babylon—Value of the trade of Babylon—Caravan routes from that city—to Candahar—Cashmir—Ecbatana, and Peucela—on the Indus—Earliest land and sea combined routes—Commercial efforts of Alexander in the East, and the impetus he gave to the development of the trade with India by the erection of Alexandria, B.C. 331—Time of the departure of the fleets—Residence of the merchants and course of trade from Alexandria to the East—Value of the trade with India—The ports through which it was conducted—Course of the voyage to India—Outwards—Homewards—The vessels engaged in the trade with India—The nature of their cargoes—Immense demand at Rome for the luxuries of the East, and the enormous prices paid for them—Imports and exports to and from Pattala—Barygaza or Baroach—Musiris—Cape Comorin—Ceylon—Time of departure of the fleets for Africa and the coasts of Arabia—Rhapta, or Quiloa—Sofala—Articles of commerce — Moosa—Yemen, or Arabia Felix — Its great wealth, and the importance attached to its trade—Kane—Sachal—Moskha—Maskat—Omana.

Route *viâ* the Cape to India, discovered

It has been often questioned whether the ancients had really any geographical knowledge south of the farthest point reached by Hanno, or, speaking geneby the Phœnicians, B.C. 610-594.

rally, far south of the Cape Verde Islands; but some of the statements preserved in their writings are too definite to have been the mere creation of imagination. We shall, therefore, briefly examine these assertions. To take first the account in Herodotus,[1] of the famous voyage undertaken by the orders of Pharaoh Necho. His words are: "As for Libya, we know it to be washed on all sides by the sea, except where it is attached to Asia. This discovery was first made by Necho, the Egyptian king, who, on desisting from the canal he had begun between the Nile and the Arabian Gulf, sent to sea a number of ships manned by Phœnicians, with orders to make for the Pillars of Hercules, and return to Egypt through them, and by the Northern sea (the Mediterranean). The Phœnicians took their departure from Egypt by the way of the Erythræan sea, and so sailed into the Southern ocean. When autumn came they went ashore wherever they might happen to be, and, having sown a tract of land with corn, waited until the grain was fit to cut. Having reaped it, they set sail again; and thus it came to pass that two whole years went by, and it was not till the third year that they doubled the Pillars of Hercules, and made good their voyage home. On their return, they declared—I for my part do not believe them, but perhaps others may—that in sailing round Libya, they had the sun on their right hand."

But what Herodotus disbelieved, from ignorance of the principles of spherical geography, affords the strongest confirmation of the report of the Phœnician mariners; for, in sailing westwards, south of the line,

[1] Herod. iv. c. 42.

the sun would at noon appear on the right hand of the observer, and not on his left, as in sailing westwards in the Mediterranean. Herodotus relates a second story,[1] how one Sataspes was sent, during the reign of Xerxes, by way of punishment, on a voyage through the Pillars of Hercules, with orders to sail round Africa; and states that this man, after having occupied many months in traversing unknown seas and sailing along strange coasts, doubled a cape called Soloeis (Cape Spartel), and thence returned to Egypt. Sataspes gave a minute account of his journey, and of the strange, dwarfish men (probably Bosjesmans) he had met with; but Xerxes, either not crediting his tale, or angry because of his cowardice in turning back, ordered him to be impaled.[2]

Voyage of the first Eudoxus.

A third expedition is reported by Pliny,[3] who states, on the authority of Cornelius Nepos, that a certain Eudoxus, his contemporary, in an attempt to escape the pursuit of Ptolemy Lathyrus, passing down the Arabian Gulf, came at length to Gades; and further, on the same authority, that Cœlius Antipater had seen a man who had made a commercial voyage from Spain to Æthiopia. Lastly, we have the memorable narrative in Strabo,[4] of Eudoxus of Cyzicus. This Eudoxus, he tells us, was sent with sacrifices and oblations to the sacred games of Proserpine, and travelled through Egypt in the reign of Ptolemy VII. (Physcon). It befell that during his stay there, a certain Indian was brought

Story of the second Eudoxus (of Cyzicus.)

[1] Herod. iv. c. 33.

[2] It is probable that Sataspes got as far as the Gulf of Guinea, and was then stopped by the south-east trade-winds. It is to avoid these that our ships, bound to India *viâ* the Cape of Good Hope, stand across to South America.

[3] Plin. ii. 169.

[4] Strab. ii. 81.

to the king, by his officers employed along the Arabian Gulf, with the report that he had been found in a ship, alone and half dead, and that they knew not who he was or whence he came, as he spoke a language unintelligible to them.

Strabo further states that this Indian, when, after a certain time, he had acquired a sufficient knowledge of the Greek language, related how, after leaving the coast of India, he had lost his course, and reached Egypt alone, all his companions having perished of hunger, adding that he would point out to any persons sent with him by the king the best and quickest route by sea to that part of India whence he had started. Eudoxus, who had previously prevailed on the king to attempt the exploration of the Nile, was able to carry out the wishes of the Indian, by sailing to India in a vessel under his own charge and with the Indian as his pilot. It appears, further, that the voyage was successful, and that Eudoxus brought back in due time to Egypt, in exchange for the presents he had taken with him, aromatics and precious stones, some of which, he said, were collected among the pebbles of the rivers, while others were dug out of the earth.

On the king's widow, Cleopatra, succeeding him on the throne, Eudoxus was despatched on a second voyage, with a still richer cargo, for purposes of exchange; but his previous good fortune did not, on this occasion, attend him; for, on his return, he was driven by adverse winds on the south coast of Æthiopia, where he is said to have conciliated the inhabitants by presents of grain, wine, and cakes of pressed figs, articles the natives did not possess, receiving in exchange a supply of water and pilots for his voyage. Before, however, taking his departure, he had made himself acquainted with a few words of their language, and having ascertained that the portion of a prow he had seen on the beach, representing the head of a horse, belonged to a vessel which the natives said had come from the west, he took it with him to Egypt, where he exhibited it in the market-place. Some of the Egyptian pilots, it is further stated, on examining this figure head, recognized it as that of a vessel which had sailed from Gades (Cadiz), beyond the river Lixus,[1] and had not returned. She was one, they said, of a class of vessels styled "horses" (from the figure of that animal borne upon the prow), which were employed in fishing around Maurusia as far south as Lixus.[2]

Eudoxus, from the account of the pilots, inferred the possibility of circumnavigating Africa, and resolved to attempt it, first visiting various parts of Europe to procure the necessary funds. Having succeeded in doing so, he equipped one large ship, and two swift boats of considerable size, embarking merchandise of various kinds, as also physicians and singing boys, no doubt to cure and delight the natives of the places he proposed visiting. No particulars are given of this voyage except that he unfortunately lost his ship, and returned to Egypt. It must be added, that Strabo doubts the story of Eudoxus, and sneers at the

[1] Larachi or Al Arish, on the coast of Marocco.

[2] Humboldt, in confirmation of this statement, quotes the case of a counterpart for the horse's head belonging to the Gades-ship, referred to by Eudoxus, as having occurred in the remains of a ship of the Red Sea, which was brought to Crete by westerly currents, according to the account of the trustworthy Arabian historian Masudi.—Humboldt's "Cosmos," vol. ii. p. 389.

discovery of the head of the Spanish ship, thus casting ridicule on a statement which has at least the merit of being circumstantial, and which tends to confirm the general correctness of the narrative as well as the authenticity of the voyage round the Cape in the days of Pharaoh Necho, related by Herodotus.

But Strabo, to whom posterity is indebted for a vast amount of ancient geographical knowledge, was in this case merely the exponent of the ignorant prejudices of his age. Of the fact there is little doubt. Few persons who have studied the observations of Rennell, Humboldt, and Heeren, on this subject, without reference to the questionable extent of the voyages of the Carthaginians under Hanno, will doubt the accounts preserved by Herodotus and Strabo; though both these distinguished authors treat as romance the circumstances they have recorded.

Opinion of Dr. Vincent on the circumnavigation of Africa.

These voyages have, however, been seriously questioned by a modern writer of no mean authority, Dr. Vincent,[1] who denies altogether any circumnavigation of Africa previously to the expedition of the Portuguese. "Nothing is more easy," he says, "than to affirm the accomplishment of these great attempts, where an author clogs himself with neither circumstances nor particulars; but whenever we obtain these, as we do in the journal of Nearchus, or the Periplus, we find, indeed, that the ancients performed great things with slender means; but we see also plainly what they could not do. We see with such vessels as they had, they could neither have got

[1] Periplus of the Erythræan Sea, vol. ii. p. 189 *et seq.*

round the Cape of Good Hope, by adhering to the coast, where the violence of the ocean must have been insupportable, nor could they have avoided this by standing out to sea, as they had neither the means nor the knowledge to regain the shore, if they had lost sight of it for a single week." He further asserts, that no voyages were accomplished except by coasting; and that no vessels were accustomed to cross the stormy waves of the ocean except, perhaps, the ships of the Veneti, in Brittany, noticed by Cæsar.

And yet there is abundant ground for believing that the Phœnicians as well as the Carthaginians carried on a regular trade with Cadiz, and could hardly have failed to visit the British Isles; moreover, they must have often done so at seasons when they would have been liable to encounter heavy gales in the Bay of Biscay. Again, near the commencement of the Christian era, the vessels of Crete engaged in the commerce between Rome and Alexandria were evidently ships of considerable dimensions; and though, from their style of build and rig, they may not have been well adapted for long over-sea voyages, there seems no valid reason why they should not have made a coasting voyage round Africa. Besides, as the southern portions of that vast continent were doubtless as thickly peopled as the north, why should the traders on the east coast have limited their voyages and explorations to Sofala, and those on the west coast to Cape Corrientes? Even if so distant a trade did not prove sufficiently remunerative to encourage constant voyages, this is no reason why such a voyage should never have been made, or why the stories in Herodotus and Strabo should be deemed to have no foundation in fact. The admitted coasting character of all the early voyages in antiquity, is really one of the best arguments in favour of the longest of these expeditions; so that what Dr. Vincent states in support of his views, tells against the objection he raises, and tends to confirm the probability of the stories as we have them.

Remarks upon his opinion.

He further admits that the very "inferior vessels" of ancient times *did* cross the Indian Ocean from Africa, and from Arabia to India, when the nature of the monsoon winds was first fully understood, fifteen hundred years before Vasco de Gama made his celebrated voyage; and that long before even that early period Solomon's ships found their way to Sofala.

Nor does he doubt that the Carthaginians under Hanno had explored the western shores of Africa, at least as far as the Equator. Now, if so much be admitted, it is not easy to understand why the rest should not be conceded also. It is true that no account has been preserved of the size of the ships built at Ezion-geber; but, considering the length of the voyages it is agreed they accomplished, there is no reason why they should not, on an occasional voyage, have safely doubled even the stormy promontory of the Cape, and also, perhaps as occasionally, have found their way to the East Indies.

Routes to India and to the East by land.

Previously, however, to the time of Solomon, communication with the East was, as has been incidentally noticed, chiefly carried on by caravans, themselves in many instances vast undertakings. The camels, or "ships of the desert," put it in the power of many of the ancient nomad tribes to become carriers through sandy and otherwise impenetrable deserts;

and, as Moses was forbidden to molest the sons of Edom during the Jewish passage through the Wilderness,[1] it is reasonable to infer that there was, even in his time, a considerable commerce carried on through the country of Edom, or Idumea, by means of caravans. Again, Gideon, when he conquered Midian, a few years afterwards, found among the Midianites, an Idumean tribe, abundant gold and camels and many other proofs of a large traffic, by which they had evidently long flourished. He "demanded for his reward the ear-rings of the men, and the chains that were about the camels' necks;"[2] decorations alike attesting the value of the animals, and the extent and wealth of the commerce in which these people had been engaged.

B.C. 1453.

Indeed, when we consider the extent of the Asiatic continent, its sterile deserts, and its geographical features, together with the lawless hordes that roamed over them, it would seem to have been impossible for any but a numerous company to conduct a trade across it in safety and with success. Hence it became necessary to collect companies of travellers or merchants in sufficient numbers, either to defend themselves, or to pay for the protection of a body of guards. Moreover, as it frequently happened that the merchants of any one district were too few to cope with the marauders they were likely to encounter on their journey, some central depôt or rendezvous was named where the smaller caravans might meet. These were not a matter of choice, but of established custom.

Origin of the caravans.

Happily, in the deserts they had to cross, Nature had allotted to the traveller occasional spots,

[1] Numbers xx. 14.
[2] Judges viii. 24–26.

Resting places. though few and far between, where he could obtain rest for himself and his beasts of burden under the shade of a cluster of palm trees, with the additional refreshment of invigorating springs of cool, fresh water. These places of repose naturally became entrepôts of commerce, where merchants from all parts exchanged their commodities; and, hence, some of them, as Palmyra and Petra, became wealthy and magnificent cities, and the sites of temples and sanctuaries, to which the pilgrim and the merchant alike resorted. From these and other great centres, the leading caravans took their departure on their distant and dangerous journeys by routes as untraceable to the eye as the track of a ship on the ocean.

Their management. The entire management or safe conduct of the great Asiatic and Arabian caravans was confided to the nomad tribes,[1] who provided the means of transport and directed their movements. In their hands was necessarily placed the important duty of breeding and rearing the camels,[2] and, in the transport of the goods of the merchants across the desert, they acted much as ship-owners now do in the conveyance of goods across the ocean; such duties, then as now, forming a separate and distinct branch of commercial enterprise. These undertakings vast in themselves—for it would require about four thousand camels to transport the amount of produce and manufactures constituting the cargo of a single modern Indiaman—formed an important trust. Articles of great value, in proportion to their bulk, such as silks, perfumes, balsams, and rich manufactures of various sorts, besides gold and silver, were entrusted

[1] Macpherson, i. pp. 7, 8. [2] Heeren, Gen. Introd. p. xxv.

to the care of those who had charge of the caravan, and who had dangers even greater to encounter than the perils of the sea. Nor was their responsibility limited to merchandise. All classes, as well as merchants, availed themselves of these caravans, so that arrangements had to be made on a large scale, and often for months before the caravan started, for the means of conveyance and for the requisite supply of water and provisions.

The more important routes.

Besides Petra and Palmyra, the cities of Sardes, Babylon, Gerrha, Damascus, and Susa were all peculiarly well situated for carrying on a large inland commerce; and these places, with Thebes and Memphis, were as famous in their day as great commercial entrepôts, as London, Liverpool, Glasgow, New York, Marseilles, or Hamburg are in our own time. At the period to which we now refer, Arabia, including Asia Minor, and the northern portion of Africa, may be said to have been divided into four great caravan routes, with numerous tributaries. The first embraced the traffic between Egypt and Palestine; the second extended from the coast of Syria, including the trade of Phœnicia with Babylon and Assyria, through the plains of Mesopotamia to the north, and along the shores of the Red Sea to the south; the third traversed Asia Minor to the north; and the fourth route lay through Africa, with Thebes as its centre, and the Nile and ports of the Red Sea as its outlets.

Eastern.

But Arabia, of all countries, was the most frequented by caravans. From Petra, where vast numbers of travellers met, an important and lucrative trade was carried on with Yemen and the fertile districts of the south, especially with that portion of the great peninsula which lies between the Persian and Arabian Gulfs, where it is washed by the Indian Ocean. In a commercial point of view, Yemen was one of the most important countries through which the caravans passed; not merely on account of its own productions, but from being at a very early period a depôt of Indian as well as of Ethiopian merchandise, and the principal mart in those days for spices, perfumes, and especially frankincense.

Southern. That branch of the caravan trade between Palestine and Egypt, mentioned in the Mosaic records, is also noticed by Herodotus, who states that the transport of Egyptian and Assyrian wares was the first business carried on by the Phœnicians.[1] Tyre also sent large quantities of wine into Egypt, receiving in exchange the "fine cotton and embroidered work" of which Ezekiel speaks.[2]

In somewhat later times, Babylon became one of the principal places to which the Phœnicians directed their attention, and traces are still to be seen of the cities which marked alike the course and the extent of this inland traffic.

Northern. In considering the account in Ezekiel, we have already noticed the trade between Tyre and the nations on the Black Sea such as "Tubal and Meshech": where a portion of the trade was probably by caravans, especially that from "Togarmah" (Armenia), whence the Tyrians obtained "horses of noble and common breeds, and mules for their wares." The same is probably true of the vessels of copper imported thence into Tyre, the same range of mountains (the Taurus) affording at present similar productions.

[1] Herod. i. 1.

[2] Ezek. xxvii. v. 7.

The character, size, and discipline of the caravans.

Though conducted wholly by nomad tribes, these caravans were, nevertheless, as complete in their organization and control, as the modern India-men which now occupy their place. Frequently consisting of between one and two thousand persons, with numerous horses and many thousand camels, they had a captain (pasha) of their own choice, to whom all owed and gave implicit obedience. Separate officers were likewise appointed to regulate the march, to perform the duties of treasurers and pay-masters, to superintend the servants and the cattle, to take charge of the baggage and merchandise, and to make the necessary arrangements for encampment. Thus the caravans had each their captain, their pilot, their purser, and mates, who had their respective duties to perform like those of the officers of the merchant-man of the present day. It was a point of honour that each traveller should assist the other; and if the humblest fell into difficulties, he had only to claim the assistance of his companions. If a camel broke down, or even if its load was thrown to the ground, the whole line halted until the accident was repaired.

On the main routes, special seasons, well known to the merchants and travellers, were appointed for the arrival and departure of the caravans. Their departure was an animated sight. For several days, persons destined for the journey were hourly arriving at the rendezvous with their camels, horses, and merchandise. Provisions had to be provided, and plans arranged for the comfort and safety of all who were about to undertake so long and hazardous a journey. The risk of falling short of food, or of being lost in the deserts, and the danger of attack from the predatory tribes infesting them, required a careful arrangement and strict discipline; but, though generally well armed, the merchants often adopted the safer plan of paying a fixed sum to the Bedouins, to secure a safe transit for themselves and their goods.

Some of the routes, were provided with numerous resting-places and caravanserais, so that travelling along these lines was comparatively safe and easy. Herodotus[1] furnishes a description of one constructed by Cyrus, king of Persia, which was originally, it is true, for military purposes, but which proved also to be of great importance to the merchants trading between the leading cities of Persia, Asia Minor, Babylonia, and India.

The route from Sardes to Susa, described by Herodotus.

Starting from Sardes, not from Smyrna and Ephesus, there appears to have been one continuous road to Susa (a city second in importance only to Babylon itself). "Royal stations and magnificent caravanserais," says Herodotus, "continually succeed each other in all parts of it, and it passes through an inhabited and safe region all the way. First (from Sardes) there are twenty stations through Lydia and Phrygia, or ninety-four parasangs and a half (about two hundred and eighty-three miles). Leaving Phrygia we come to the river Halys, near which there is a guarded passage, necessary to be passed on our way over the river. On the other side of the river we come to Cappadocia, and through this country to the Cilician mountains, comprehending twenty-eight stations, or a hundred and four parasangs. We penetrate into these mountains through two sets of

[1] Herod. v. 52.

gates, at each of which there is a guard posted, and then traverse Cilicia, a space of three stations, or fifteen parasangs and a half. The river Euphrates, which can only be passed by a ferry, separates Cilicia from Armenia, in which there are fifteen stations, or fifty-six parasangs and a half. There is one place where a guard is posted, and four rivers which are crossed in boats. The first is the Tigris, the second and third bear the same appellation,[1] without being either the same river or flowing from the same country, as the first of them comes out of Armenia, and the other out of the land of the Matienians; the fourth is the Gyndes, which Cyrus dispersed by digging for it three hundred and sixty branches.[2] From Armenia into the land of the Matienians there are four stations; and eleven stations, or forty two parasangs and a half, from this country into that of the Cissians (Khuzistan), as far as the river Choaspes, which must likewise be passed in boats; and on the banks of this river stands the city of Susa. Thus, in the journey from Susa to Sardes, there are one hundred and eleven stations with the same number of caravanserais."

Here, then, is a record, four hundred and fifty years before our era, of a well made road of more than one thousand miles in length; and this road is still in existence.[3]

[1] These are the greater and lesser Záb.

[2] Referring, probably, to the numerous canals this great conqueror cut, for purposes of irrigation as well as navigation, between the Euphrates and Tigris.

[3] "Royal stations" were the abodes of the king's couriers. Cf. Herod. viii. 98. These couriers were very rapid, like the Indian *hurkâreh* of the present day. Strabo (xv. p. 725) states that Alexander's order for the execution of Parmenio, given near Herât, was conveyed eight hundred

Between Tyre and Gerrha.

The trading routes between Babylon and Tyre, and more especially between Tyre and Gerrha[1] lay, in both cases, through long and uninterrupted deserts; a course, some have thought, chosen as better enabling merchants to preserve the secrecy of their business, and the real character of the wares in which they were trading. Baalath and "Tadmor in the desert"[2] (Baalbek and Palmyra) were, it is supposed, founded by Solomon with the intention of obtaining for himself a share of the commerce which the Phœnicians were at that time carrying on with Babylon and other inland cities.

Length of journey.

Here many caravans assembled, and thence diverged to their different destinations. Those destined for the East proceeded by way of Palmyra,[3] and to this day, the commercial road from Damascus to the Euphrates runs close to the ruins of that city. Seven days were occupied in the journey from Baalbek to Palmyra, four of them in passing through the desert which lay between that city and Emesa (Hems), another celebrated city of Syria. From Palmyra, other four days were required to reach Thapsacus,[4] where the caravan had the choice either of following the

---

and fifty miles in eleven days, to Ecbatana. The present route from Smyrna to Baghdad, is nearly the same as that described by Herodotus, from Sardes to Susa; it turns a little to the N., to avoid the arid deserts about the Upper Euphrates and the Upper Tigris, and passes Sart (Sardes), Allah Shehr (Philadelphia), Kaisariyeh, Malatiyeh, Diarbekr, Mosul, Arbil (Arbela), and Kerkuk (Circesium). If Herodotus went to Babylon, he would have gone by this route as far as the river Gyndes (Diyala), where the route from Babylon to Ecbatana crossed it, as is clear from the account of the march of Cyrus. (Herod. i. 189.)

[1] Strabo, xvi. 766.

[2] 1 Kings ix. 18.

[3] Plin. v. 87. Procop. Bell. Pers. ii. 5. Gibbon, c. xi.

[4] Xenoph. Anab. i. 4, 11.

course of the Euphrates, or of passing through the plains of Mesopotamia. The southern, or rather the southern and eastern routes, passed through Palestine (where Joseph was sold to the caravan of Midianitish merchants) into Egypt, terminating at Memphis on the Nile. The eastern route diverged from it to Petra,[1] a place perhaps more celebrated than any other in the inland trade of ancient times. From Petra, there were two great routes to the East, both terminating in Gerrha on the Persian Gulf. Opposite to this place, and about fifty miles distant, lay the island of Tylos,[2] a settlement of the Phœnicians, as already stated. One of the routes lay along the line of the eastern shore of the Arabian Gulf, but at some distance from it, except where it touched Leuke Kome, and, most probably, Mecca also, till it reached Saba or Saphar, perhaps, as already suggested, the Ophir of Solomon, a distance of twelve hundred and sixty geographical miles from Petra, or a caravan journey of seventy days; thence the route lay through a great desert to Gerrha. The other route was almost a straight line through a more northern desert, from Gerrha to Petra, and was probably that by which Europe was first supplied with the produce of India.

Importance of Petra.

While Gerrha was the chief commercial city of Arabia to the east, Petra,[3] the capital of the Nabathæans, may be considered as occupying a similar position in the north-west of that country. A city equal in opulence to Gerrha, it constituted the chief western mart of the Arabian spices and frankincense, of which immense quantities were consumed in Egypt. Here important fairs were periodically held for the

[1] Plin. vi. 144. [2] Plin. vi. 28. [3] Strab. xvi. 779. Diod. Sic. xix. 98.

exchange of different commodities; and here the traders from the south met the merchants of Syria, and bartered the luxuries of the East for the manufactures of Tyre, and of the other cities of Phœnicia and Syria.

According to the testimony of Ezekiel, the whole of this trade was carried on by barter, being an exchange of merchandise for merchandise, in which even the precious metals were included.

Inter-course between Syria and Babylon.

Many of the caravans of the northern route unloaded their merchandise on the banks of the Euphrates, whence it was shipped for Babylon and Susa, or conveyed through the canals, some of which were of considerable magnitude.[1]

Value of the trade of Babylon.

Situated between the Indus and the Mediterranean, with a productive soil, and commanding, by means of the Euphrates and Tigris, every communication with the interior, and, by the Persian Gulf, with India and the eastern shores of Arabia, the Babylonians, until they were brought under the yoke of Persia, carried on a commercial intercourse with surrounding nations which for many ages was second only to that of the Phœnicians. Babylon stood in its relations with the East somewhat as Tyre in its dealings with the West. Hence the traffic between these two great centres of ancient commerce was necessarily of an important character. Nor indeed was it ever seriously interrupted, except when the ambition of Nebuchadnezzar vainly prompted him to attempt the capture,[2] if not the destruction, of Tyre. Each

[1] See note on principal canals of Babylonia, by Sir H. C. Rawlinson, in Rawlinson's Herodotus, i. p. 571.

[2] It is not distinctly stated anywhere that Tyre was actually taken;

had its own spheres of commerce and its own means of usefulness, and those of Tyre must have been materially impaired, if not annihilated, by the siege of thirteen years, whether the Babylonian monarch did or did not succeed. While Tyre increased in strength and wealth, spreading her colonies over the west, Babylon continued her dealings with her and with the nations dwelling on the Euxine and the Caspian Seas. By means of her caravans, canals, and rivers, Babylon became also the chief entrepôt for Western Asia, where the merchants of many countries assembled to exchange their merchandise; and such it remained for ages. Neither the heavy yoke of Asiatic despotism, nor the devastating sword of conquering nations, could destroy, though they might for a time overshadow, its splendour. It was only when the Persians, feeling no interest in sea-borne commerce, and dreading the incursions of the maritime powers, blocked up the Tigris, that its commercial greatness began to decline.

Although Babylon did not reach the zenith of B.C. 604.
its power till Nebuchadnezzar made it his capital, everything leads to the supposition that, for many ages, it had been the seat of science and civilization, and had carried on an extensive intercourse with distant as well as with neighbouring nations. Highly skilled in astrology and in astronomical observations, to which the clearness of the sky and the brightness of the stars offered every encouragement, the Babylonians were, however, not familiar with either the science or practice of navigation; but that

but the inference from Ezek. c. xxvi. is that it was—or the prophecy has remained unfulfilled.

they, in connexion with the Chaldeans, possessed an over-sea maritime commerce when their power was at its height, may be inferred from the writings of Isaiah:[1] "Thus saith the Lord, your deliverer; For your sakes have I sent to Babel, and thrown to the ground all obstacles, and the Chaldeans, whose cry is in their ships." While however they carried on a large inland trade in vessels of their own, their oversea commerce was most probably conducted by the Phœnician ships of Tylos, or by the Arabians. Indeed, Heeren,[2] quoting Agatharchides, shows that the merchants of Gerrha sent to Babylon in *their own ships* the produce of India, as well as frankincense and other perfumes from Arabia Felix. Of these the consumption must have been enormous, for Herodotus states that no fewer than a thousand talents were annually consumed by the Chaldeans in the temple of Belus alone.[3] Besides, there was a large overplus, which was conveyed up the Euphrates to Thapsacus, and then distributed by caravans over the whole of Western Asia.

Caravan routes from that city,

While Babylon constituted the emporium on the river Euphrates, the city of Opis,[4] on the Tigris, a few miles above Baghdad, formed another centre of commerce, to which the merchants of Gerrha had, with much success, directed their navigation from very early times, until interrupted by the Persians. From Opis, an important caravan route lay across Mesopotamia to Aradus, near Tyre; while from Susa, taking first a northerly direction, there diverged another route almost due east to Candahar, and thence

to Candahar,

[1] Isaiah xliii. 14. [2] Heeren, i. p. 438. [3] Herod. i. 183. [4] Arrian, vii. 7.

by one of the branches of the Indus into Cashmir,[1] running almost in a continuous line with the road through Asia Minor mentioned by Herodotus. This great eastern route has been fully described by both Strabo and Pliny, who derived their knowledge chiefly from the writings of the companions of Alexander. Cashmir,

According to these accounts, it appears to have gone directly east in about 36° N. latitude to Ecbatana, the capital of Media, and thence to the Caspian gates, through which everything coming from the west necessarily passed. On the north lay the Hyrcanian mountains; on the south an impenetrable desert; and on one portion of the route there was the narrow defile, about eight Roman miles in length, which Pliny describes as having been cut through the rocks.[2] From the Caspian Pass, the road led with various considerable turns till it reached Peucela on the Indus. From Alexandria in Ariis (Herát), and Ortospanum (Kâbul), other routes turned off into Bactriana, and thence proceeded into Great Tatary and Central Asia.[3] As there was considerable commercial intercourse between the neighbouring inhabitants of the city of Bactra (Balkh) and of Upper India, another route ran due north to Marakanda (Samarcand); and Heeren is of opinion that caravans traversed the desert from Badakhshan to Serica (China), and from that country to the Ganges. Ecbatana, and. Peucela, on the Indus.

Herodotus relates that from the Greek establishments on the Black Sea there were commercial routes through Central Asia, over the Ural Mountains to the country of the Calmucks of Great Earliest land and sea combined routes.

[1] Arrian, iii. 16. [2] Pliny, vi. 17. [3] Strabo, p. 782.

Tatary.[1] These different highways will be found laid down on a map, which has been prepared for reference (see Frontispiece), wherein will also be found the courses adopted by the vessels of ancient times in the navigation of the Asiatic seas, which, as far as can now be ascertained, was chiefly confined to the Arabian and Persian Gulfs, and the Indian Ocean. The periodical winds in these gulfs when once ascertained, rendered navigation comparatively easy, but, in navigating the Indian Ocean at the time of Alexander's expedition, the monsoons were either not generally known to extend across the Indian Ocean, or were not made available to any great extent. Voyages, in the days of Herodotus, and for three centuries afterwards, were almost wholly of a coasting character.

Commercial efforts of Alexander in the East, and the impetus he gave to the development of the trade with India, by the erection of Alexandria, B.C. 331.

Although Alexander endeavoured, when he took possession of Babylonia, to remove the obstructions by which the Persians had blockaded the river Tigris, and, by this and other means, hoped to restore the maritime commerce they had destroyed, he was only partially successful; hence, subsequently, the great bulk of the sea-borne trade between the Western and Eastern world reverted to the Arabian Gulf, and, with a few unimportant deviations, continued in that route until the Portuguese successfully doubled the Cape of Good Hope. For some time, however, after his death this new trade was materially retarded by the anarchy which occurred on that event; nor did it thoroughly revive until Ptolemy Philadelphus established an embassy on the coast of Hindustan, and, at the same time, built the port of Berenice, on the Red Sea, at

[1] Herod. iii. chap. 24.

the eastern end of the great commercial road from Coptos on the Nile.

Ptolemy, son of Lagos and father of Philadelphus, as soon as he had taken possession of Egypt, established the seat of his government in Alexandria, entering readily into the schemes which had led Alexander, a few years before, to lay the foundations of that city. With a rapidity truly astonishing, merchants from all parts flocked to the new city, so that in a space of time incredibly short the commerce of the East came to be carried on in the channel which the sagacity of Alexander had anticipated for it.

By a prudent exercise of authority, by many acts of liberality, and, above all, by the fame of a mild and judicious administration, Ptolemy drew so many inhabitants to this place that it soon became one of the most populous and wealthy cities in Egypt. Ptolemy had possessed, as he well deserved, the confidence of the great conqueror more perfectly than any of his other officers; hence he knew better than any of them that Alexander's chief object in founding Alexandria was to secure the advantages arising from the trade with India. His long and prosperous reign enabled him to carry out this purpose with great success; while his general attention to the requirements of a wide maritime commerce is exemplified by his construction of the celebrated Pharos, at the mouth of the harbour of Alexandria, of which mention has already been made.

From Alexandria the course of trade with the East seems to have at first passed to Arsinoe, the present Suez, but the difficulties and dangers of the navigation of the northern extremity of the Red Sea, led to the formation by Ptolemy Philadelphus, on its western shores, of the harbour of Myos Hormus, as well as the more important roadstead of Berenice, whereby direct communication with the outer ocean was greatly facilitated, and due advantage could be taken of the prevailing winds within the Straits. Goods were conveyed by the Nile to Coptos, and were thence transported over land by caravans to Myos Hormus, or Berenice. To render these routes more easy and endurable during many days' march through torrid deserts, Philadelphus sought out the needful springs, and established caravanserais at these necessary halting places. Pliny[1] and the Itinerary of Antonine[2] give a list of them; and it is worthy of record, that Belzoni recognized traces of many of these routes when he visited that country.[3]

Time of the departure of the fleets.

From both Myos Hormus and Berenice the fleets appear to have sailed in the month of September for Arabia, as well as for various ports on the coast of Africa; and in July for India. These periods, from the course of the prevailing winds, were the best adapted for proceeding upon such voyages. In the first instance, clearing, as we may presume they would do, the Straits in the month of November, they would probably fall in with a wind during that month which would carry them down the coast of Africa, and enable them to return with equal facility in the course of the following months of May and June. By sailing in July from Berenice, or Myos Hormus, they would reach Bab-el-Mandeb before the 1st of September, and would thus have a fair wind for nearly three

[1] Plin. vi. 102.

[2] Itin. Antonin. p. 172.

[3] Belzoni, "Travels," ii. p. 36.

months. Thence they could easily reach the shores of Malabar, even by adhering to an almost strictly coasting route, in the forty days, in which, as we learn from Pliny, that portion of the voyage was usually performed.[1]

Residence of the merchants, and course of trade from Alexandria to the East.

The merchants who carried on these important trades, both under the Ptolemies and the Romans, resided chiefly, if not altogether, at Alexandria; and though the Ptolemies, for their own interest, were willing to extend, as far as possible, mercantile privileges, the law of Egypt still required (as in the case of Naucratis) the employment of an Alexandrian factor for the transaction of the merchant's business: a custom which in a great measure accounts for the immense wealth of Alexandria.

It is clear that the prevailing winds must now have been studied with care, and the intercourse between West and East so arranged as to admit of the utmost possible advantage being derived from them. Towards the latter end of July the annual, or Etesian (north), wind commences its influence and extends from the Euxine Sea to Syene in Upper Egypt.[2] As a northerly wind, prevailing at the time of the year when the Nile is at its greatest height, it affords an excellent opportunity of advancing against the stream. Hence the voyage from Alexandria to Coptos, a distance of three hundred and eight Roman miles, was usually performed in twelve days.[3]

The Canopic branch of the Nile (the nearest to Alexandria) was then the chief navigable approach to Egypt from the sea. From its entrance a canal

[1] Plin. vi. 104.
[2] Herod. ii. 20, compared with vi. 140; vii. 168. Plin. vi. 102.
[3] Pliny, ibid.

had been formed connecting it with Alexandria, so that traders from Coptos could pass through it without landing their cargoes at Alexandria, and without paying the custom-dues exacted from other vessels.

It is worthy of remark, that though Berenice was built by Philadelphus, the real value of its position was not at first recognised; nor was it fully appreciated till the discovery of the regular uniformity of the winds at certain seasons of the year gave a special impetus to the trade with the far East.

It is needless to inquire when the monsoons were first noticed: it is enough to know, that even if the principle of them was ascertained at a remote period, little or no use was made of this knowledge by the Alexandrian merchants till about the reign of Claudius, and of the successful voyage of Hippalus. The Romans perceiving the great advantage Hippalus had made known by his adventurous voyage justly named the monsoon wind after him.

These winds, now so familiar, extend with a variety of modifications over all the seas of India, from Japan to Madagascar. Their general course is north-east and south-west, with some fluctuations, and they commence blowing from the north-east in October, though it is not till November that they blow steadily from that quarter, and continue to do so for four months. They begin again to fluctuate about the month of March, and do not blow steadily from the south-west till April or May, when they often increase to a strong gale. Previously to the discovery of the monsoons, commercial adventure with the more

[1] Hippalus is believed to have lived in the reign of the Emperor Claudius.—Vincent, i. pp. 47–49.

remote regions of the East had been generally carried on in comparatively small vessels, that crept cautiously along the windings of the coast. As soon however as Hippalus had shown the uniformity of these periodical winds, vessels of a larger and of an improved description were constructed; and so great was the impulse thus given to the trade between Europe and India, that it soon became a subject of apprehension at Rome, lest the empire should be drained of its specie to maintain the commerce with India. According to Pliny,[1] silver, to the value of nearly a million and a half sterling was annually required to pay for the spices, gems, pearls, and silks then imported through Egypt.

Value of the trade with India.

From the earliest historic period, the productions of India have, indeed, been in almost incessant demand by the nations of the West, and from even the mysterious reign of Semiramis, the queen of Assyria, to our own time, the possession of India has been in turn the envy of them all. To Great Britain, India has perhaps been of less special value since the differential duties were abolished and its ports thrown open to the shipping and commerce of the world; but still that empire is a prize she would not readily relinquish. To her merchants it has been a source of immense wealth, and among her people its produce, either as articles of necessity or luxury, is now as eagerly sought after as it was in the palmy days of Tyre, of Rome, or of the Italian republics. Vast quantities of silver are still gathered from all parts of the Western world, for export to the East, in exchange for the products of India; and complaints have been

[1] Plin. vi. 101.

frequently made, even in our own times, of the quantity of the precious metals sent from Europe to pay for these commodities. Yet, so far from this being a just grievance, nothing can be more certain than the prosperity of a people, who have thus at their disposal, from one source or another, vast superabundant stores for exportation and exchange for the raw material or even the luxuries of the East.

The ports through which it was conducted.

When Rome came into possession of Egypt, its commercial intercourse was conducted chiefly through the port of Berenice, while the port of Myos Hormus was in a great measure abandoned. Yet some trade was still carried on from this port as also from Leuke Kome, on the north-western coast of the Red Sea, near the entrance to the Gulf of Akabah. The whole of these ports being in possession of Rome, there were custom-houses established at each, with Roman officers to collect the duty of twenty-five per cent. imposed on *all* articles of import and export, as well as Roman garrisons to enforce its payment, where necessary. Caravans from Petra and from the shores of the Mediterranean, brought to Leuke Kome the manufactures and other produce of the North, destined for shipment to the East, while Berenice became the chief port for the manufactures of Rome and of the West, which were conveyed up the Nile, by the route described, to Coptos, and thence forwarded by caravan. Caravans also, from Thebes and other places in Upper Egypt, were the agents of an extensive trade through Berenice and Myos Hormus.

Course of the voyage to India.

Pliny, as has been stated, when compared with Arrian, gives a clear account of the length of time required to make the voyage from Berenice to the straits of Bab-el-Mandeb, a distance between of five and six hundred miles; and the whole of this question has been fully examined by Dr. Vincent.

It would seem that the chief anxiety of the fleets of those days arose from the intricacy and consequent danger of the navigation, even with a favourable wind, within the Straits, and hence that vessels invariably anchored during the night when an opportunity offered. But after passing Bab-el-Mandeb, the steady influence of a favourable monsoon enabled the pilots to make a continuous and comparatively rapid passage. Those ships destined for the more distant voyage to Malabar remained at Okelis (the modern Ghella or Cella), near Aden, for a longer time than those whose destination was only Guzerat. The pilots had observed from the commencement of this new route to India, that the interval between the change of the monsoons was invariable, not merely fluctuating, but that in June and July the weather sometimes proved so tempestuous as to render the navigation of the Indian Ocean perilous, if not almost impracticable; that in August and September the winds become more settled, and that by the month of October fine weather, with steady breezes, could be depended upon. Accordingly, one portion of the fleet, which left Berenice about the 10th of July, arriving at the mouth of the Arabian Gulf within a month, remained at Okelis for a week, ten days, or a fortnight, and by this arrangement the vessels bound for the coast of Malabar reached their destination at the best season of the year.[1]

Outwards.

[1] Dr. Vincent's "Periplus," p. 288.

Homewards.

The homeward voyage was regulated by the same experience. Remaining on the coast of India from the end of September, or beginning of October, to the early part of December, two months of the finest weather were thus obtained for the discharge of the vessels and the disposal of their cargoes, as also for taking on board the return lading in exchange. The 13th of January was fixed as the latest date for leaving the coast; and it is here worthy of remark, that the original order for the fleets of Portugal, fifteen centuries afterwards, was subject to a similar regulation. Quitting the coast of India on or about the 10th of January, they would easily reach Aden in twenty or thirty days, where they would most probably remain until they could derive the benefit of the Gunseen winds, which, from about the middle of March, blow steadily from the south for fifty or sixty days, and thus have a fair wind to carry them to Berenice. Thus the winds prevailing in the Gulf at different seasons of the year were as valuable to the ancient ships as the true monsoons in the Indian Ocean.

The vessels engaged in the trade with India.

It is much to be regretted that no descriptions exist of the character of these fleets, of the men by whom they were navigated, or of their merchant owners. It seems, however, a reasonable conjecture that they were in many respects similar to the vessels the Romans employed in the grain trade between Alexandria and Egypt, of which St. Paul's ship may be considered as a type. In all likelihood they were chiefly owned by the merchants of Rome and of Alexandria, and commanded by men from the Grecian and other maritime states of the Roman empire; the crew, on the other hand, were probably

Arabians, as the natives of Arabia are known to have been from remote times settled on the western shores of India. Indeed, we learn the same fact from the historian of Vasco de Gama's celebrated voyage, who speaks of the vast number of Arabians whom the Portuguese found settled at Calicut, and engaged in commercial and maritime occupations.

The nature of their cargoes.

The products of India were at no period sought after with greater avidity than when Rome became mistress of the world. Tyre, in the plenitude of her power, or Babylon in her greatest magnificence, were, compared with Rome, moderate in their expenditure upon luxuries. It was this extravagance which led Pliny to make the complaint to which we have just referred, of the drain of precious metals to the East; in itself just, because they were sent to purchase articles of luxury as expensive as they were superfluous, instead of necessaries and raw materials capable of conversion for the wants of the people, or of re-exportation to other countries. Enriched by the spoil and tribute of nearly every portion of the then known world, the inhabitants of Rome had acquired a taste for every kind of luxury, and had resolved to obtain it, regardless of the cost. Whatever was rare commanded fabulous prices. To supply their demands, new and extraordinary efforts became necessary to obtain from the East the articles they required. Silks, precious stones, and pearls, were eagerly sought after, but spices and aromatics were even greater objects of solicitude. Fortunes expended upon frankincense had, they thought, the combined effect of raising them in the estimation of their neighbours, and of securing the favour and

Immense demand at Rome for the luxuries of the East, and the enormous prices paid for them.

friendship of the gods. The greatest extravagance was displayed on the funeral pile, which, as well as the body about to be consumed by the flames, was frequently covered with the most costly spices. Nero is reported to have burnt at the funeral of his wife Poppæa, a quantity of cinnamon and cassia greater than the countries from which it was imported were capable of producing in one year;[1] and two hundred and ten burdens of spices are said to have been strewed upon the pile which consumed to ashes the body of Sylla.

Among the precious jewels brought from the East, pearls were most in demand, and for the finest and rarest of these the most extraordinary prices were given. Julius Cæsar is said to have presented the mother of Brutus with one for which he had paid 48,457*l.*; and if we may credit the statement of Pliny, the famous pearl earrings of Cleopatra were valued at 161,458*l.* sterling.[2] That silk was an article greatly prized is not a matter for wonder, when we consider the variety of elegant fabrics into which it may be fashioned, and how much it must have added to the splendour of dress so eagerly sought after by the luxurious inhabitants of Rome. Its price was so exorbitant that women of eminent rank and opulence alone could afford to use it; but this did not render the demand for it less eager. Contrary to what usually happens in the ordinary operations of trade, an increased demand for it had not the effect of increasing the quantity imported to a sufficient extent to materially reduce the price, for in the reign of Aurelian, more than two hundred and fifty years

[1] Plin. xii. 83.

[2] Plin. ix. 119-121. Gibbon, ch. 3.

from the time of its being first introduced into Rome, silk continued to be valued at its weight in gold. No doubt this arose in a great measure from the fact that the merchants of Alexandria, by whom the silk was imported, had no direct intercourse with China, the only country in which the silkworm was then reared, while the place of production was too remote, and the means of increasing the supply then too limited, to meet the greatly increasing demand.

Imports and exports to and from Pattala.

Arrian has left the fullest information now obtainable with reference to the commodities in his time, which constituted the chief articles of commercial intercourse between Europe and India. Pattala, on the river Indus, was then the first mart for the vessels arriving from Egypt, and from Leuke Kome. He states that the outward cargoes consisted of woollen cloth of a light fabric, linen in chequer work, glass vessels, wine, and aromatics of a sort unknown in India, besides some precious stones, wrought silver, coral, borax, and specie. For these were received cotton cloths, silk thread, and silk stuffs of different sorts, black pepper, sapphires, and other gems, as well as various kinds of spices.

Barygaza or Baroach.

Barygaza, on the same coast, soon, however, became a more important mart than Pattala; and, by the minute description Arrian has given of its position, that port would seem to correspond with Baroach, on the great river Nerbudda, by means of which it had navigable communication for many hundred miles into the rich interior of India. The articles of import and export were much more various and

[1] Arrian, the merchant, must not be confounded with the famous Arrian of Nicomedia; nothing is, however, known about him.

abundant at Barygaza than at Pattala. Besides those already mentioned, Arrian enumerates among the former, Italian, Greek, and Arabian wines, brass, tin, lead, girdles or sashes of curious textures, white glass, red arsenic, black lead, and gold and silver coin. Among the exports were the onyx and other gems, ivory, myrrh, various fabrics of cotton, both plain and ornamented with flowers, and pepper. At Musiris, the port Hippalus reached when he first took advantage of the monsoons, the articles imported were much the same as at Barygaza; but, as it lay nearer to the eastern parts of India, the commodities exported from it were more numerous and more valuable. Pearls are specified as being there obtainable in great abundance and of extraordinary beauty, besides a variety of silk stuffs, rich perfumes, tortoise-shell, different kinds of transparent gems, especially diamonds, and pepper of the best quality.

Musiris.

Cape Comorin.

Although Arrian, from the accurate description he has given of it, would seem to have sailed along the coast as far as Cape Comorin, the southernmost point of the Indian peninsula, the ships from Berenice do not appear to have traded with any place on the coast south of Musiris, where, however, various Egyptian commodities were to be found. Probably these articles were received in exchange for the produce of the East, brought by native vessels from the countries near the Ganges, or from Malacca and China to Ceylon. Many native vessels were, however, evidently confined, in their trading operations, exclusively to that coast. Although the island of Ceylon was the great mart or depôt, where the manufactures and produce of the West were exchanged for those

Ceylon.

of the then far distant and almost unknown East, it is probable that the ships from Egypt did not, at least during the early portion of their operations, proceed as far as that island, but that their cargoes were transported thither in the native coasters, and there bartered for silk and for other commodities produced in Ceylon, or in the countries to the eastward of it. In all likelihood the merchants of Alexandria were deterred from sending their ships as far as Ceylon, through fear of the dangers of which Pliny has preserved a report. "The sea," he remarks, "that lies between the island and the mainland, is full of shallows, not more than six paces in depth; but in certain channels no anchor has ever found a bottom. For these reasons," he adds, "the vessels are constructed with prows at each end, so that there may be no necessity for tacking in channels which are extremely narrow."[1]

Time of departure of the fleets for Africa and the coasts of Arabia.

While the fleets for India sailed in July, the vessels destined for the various ports on the coast of Africa or Arabia took their departure with equal regularity in the month of September. By clearing the gulf before November, they made certain of a favourable wind down the eastern coasts of Africa, and had ample time to transact their business, and to return with the change of wind by the following May. Abdooli, contiguous to Orine, was the first port of call for the African traders. Here large quantities of ivory and horn were shipped, brought from Axume, an inland town eight days' journey from the coast, and an important mart for their collection and sale, as it lay in the central part of the district, where

[1] Pliny, vi. 82.

both the elephant and the rhinoceros were killed in great numbers. From Abdooli, the fleets, after passing through the straits of Bab-el-Mandeb, reached Malao, Moondus, Mossulon, and Daphnon, four harbours, or rather roadsteads, of some commercial importance, which lay not far from each other on the line of coast extending to the eastward. At all of these places boats or rafts had to be used for the transport of goods and produce between the ships and the shore, as no attempt had been made to construct wharves. After rounding Cape Aromata, the extreme eastern point of the African continent, they shaped their course to the south, steering about S.S.W., along the coast of Azania, calling at various places, including Melinda, until they reached Rhapta or Quiloa, in about nine degrees south latitude. The merchants of this place had many ships of their own employed in the trade, on board of which they had Arabian commanders and factors, employing such only as had experience of the country, or as, having contracted marriages with the natives, understood the language, and were familiar with the navigation.[1]

Rhapta, or Quiloa.

Arrian gives a picture of these people, and of their habits, resembling much that presented to the Portuguese, fifteen centuries afterwards, when they first cast anchor off Quiloa. Here, too, as well as from the more northern port of Melinda, a trade seems, though we have no positive knowledge of the fact, to have been carried on with India in ages before Hippalus. Corn, rice, butter or ghee, oil of cinnamon, cotton in the web, and in the flock for stuffing, sashes, and

[1] Dr. Vincent's "Periplus," vol. ii. p. 170.

"honey from the cane called sugar," had, long before Arrian, been articles of commerce imported thence. "Many vessels," he says, "are employed in this commerce, expressly for the importation of these articles; and others, which have a further destination, dispose of part of their cargoes on this coast, and take in such commodities as they find here in return." The cargoes specified are just such as could be now imported from India.

From Quiloa the Egyptian fleets appear to have traded as far south as Sofala, obtaining thence the produce of Æthiopia as well as of Abyssinia, and rhinoceros horns, tortoise-shell, myrrh, and odoriferous gums, frankincense, cinnamon of a common description, and slaves of a superior order, principally for the Egyptian market. In exchange, Alexandria sent cloths of various kinds, and linen, glass, porcelain, white copper for ornaments and for coin; brass for the manufacture of culinary vessels, bracelets and ornaments for the legs, such as are still worn in Abyssinia; iron for weapons of all sorts, as well as hatchets, adzes, knives, and daggers, manufactured and ready for use. The invoices also mention drinking vessels of brass, large and round; denarii or Roman specie, for the use of the merchants resident on the coast; Laodicean (or Syrian) and Italian wines; gold and silver plate, according to the fashion of the country, as presents for the native kings; jackets, watch-coats, coverlids, Indian cotton, besides cotton in its raw state; sashes of variegated colours, and cloths with the nap on, of various sorts, suited for the barbarian coasts. Tin, the produce of the British mines, formed likewise an article of export from Berenice

Sofala.

Articles of commerce.

and Leuke Kome, to the coast of Africa, although only in small quantities. Plated silver, and flint glass, or crystal, were shipped to a considerable extent; while corn from Egypt constituted one of the most bulky articles of export to the more populous of the places we have named.

Moosa. The merchants of Alexandria, likewise, carried on an extensive and valuable commerce with various ports in Arabia, especially with Moosa, at the entrance to the Red Sea, a place believed to have had a very ancient trade with India. Moosa also imported large quantities of coffee from Africa, and, mixing it with the coffee of Arabia, sold the adulterated article as the produce of the latter country. Its imports from Egypt consisted, among other manufactures, of various descriptions of cloths, and of clothes made up after the Arabian fashion, with sleeves plain and embroidered. Its merchants gave in exchange the produce of their own country, and that of India, imported in their own vessels from Baroach.

Yemen, or Arabia Felix. There are few lands more extolled in ancient history for their natural richness, both as regards its mines and the productiveness of its soil, than Yemen, or Arabia Felix, the country of the Queen of Sheba, of which Moosa was the chief port. Though separated from India by an open sea, it was yet intimately connected with it by nature; a sky of great serenity enabling its mariners to make full use of the stars as their guides, and thus sparing them the labour and anxiety of slowly creeping along the coast, as was elsewhere necessary. Arabia was above all others the native country of frankincense, of myrrh, and of other aromcati perfumes, productions then held in such

Its great wealth,

repute, that scarcely one of the then most civilized nations of the world would have dared to offer a gift to their gods without them.

Greek and Hebrew writers alike speak of the country of the Queen of Sheba as one of the richest of the ancient world. The Hebrew poets cite the names of its various cities and harbours, and their writings overflow with descriptions of its many treasures. No sooner had the Greeks obtained a knowledge of these regions than they extolled to the utmost the boundless riches concealed in Arabia Felix. "Its inhabitants, the Sabæans," remarks Diodorus[1] quoting from Agatharchides, "not only surpass the neighbouring barbarians in wealth and magnificence, but all other nations whatever. In buying and selling their wares they maintain among all nations the highest prices for the smallest quantities. As their distant situation protects them from foreign plunderers, immense stores of precious metals have accumulated among them, especially in the capital. Curiously wrought gold and silver drinking vessels in great variety, couches, tripods with silver feet, and an incredible profusion of costly furniture in general, abound there."

and the importance attached to its trade.

The whole of this vast wealth would seem, by the remarks of Diodorus, to have been derived, not from war and plunder, but by the prosecution throughout many ages of peaceful commerce and unwearied industry. "Before merchants," observes Arrian, "sailed from India to Egypt, and from Egypt to India, Arabia Felix was the staple both for Egyptian and Indian goods, much as Alexandria is now for

[1] Diodorus, iii. 46.

the commodities of Egypt and foreign merchandise;" a testimony fully borne out by abundant statements in Holy Scripture. Isaiah, Jeremiah, and Ezekiel all speak in glowing terms of the great wealth of Arabia Felix. Nowhere, too, were the civilizing effects of commerce more noticeable than in Arabia Felix. Although Dr. Vincent remarks that "the importance of this commerce, as it appears in the "Periplus," is manifestly far inferior to the representation of it in Agatharchides," he adds, "still it is evident that the manners of the people in this quarter of Arabia were civilized, that the government was consistent, and that the merchant was protected. This character, as we learn from Niebuhr, Yemen still maintains, in preference to the Hijar and the whole interior of the peninsula. The same security is marked as strongly by the "Periplus" in Hadramaut; and the whole coast on the ocean being commercial, *the interests of commerce have subdued the natural ferocity of the inhabitants*."[1]

It would appear that, before the settlements at Moosa and Okelis, the ships from Persia, Caramania, and the Indus came no farther than the coast just outside the straits, near the modern Aden, and that here the fleets of Egypt met them and exchanged their articles of commerce. Many writers, too, on this subject, have maintained that the fleet of Solomon, though fitted out with the view of going as far as Sofala, did not proceed beyond the Straits of Bab-el-Mandeb, and that they there exchanged the produce of the West for that of India, Yemen, and Africa. We, however, adhere to the opinion already expressed,

[1] "Periplus," vol. ii. p. 317.

that at least a portion of Solomon's fleet visited both the Indus and the eastern coast of Africa. It is not, in itself, likely that seamen so enterprising and adventurous as the Phœnicians, would have failed in accomplishing any voyage wherein the ships of other nations had been successful; nor, viewing the profits the Arabians derived from their intercourse with the East, can it be supposed that the merchants and shipowners of Phœnicia would have cut short their voyages at the Straits of Bab-el-Mandeb, knowing too, as they could not fail to have known, many commercial reports about a vast country to the east abounding in riches, which the Arabians had reached by sea. It seems also more than probable that they had, at the same time, learnt something of the character of the winds which favoured such voyages, and their reasoning must have been, "What the inhabitants of the sea coasts of Arabia and Africa can perform by vessels in every way inferior to those of Phœnicia, we can accomplish so much the more successfully by means of our well appointed fleets."

The Arabians had also a considerable intercourse with the East from Kane,[1] a port on the south-western shores of Arabia, in Hadramaut, a place enjoying a direct intercourse with Sana, and thence by the great caravan route with Saba. The merchants of Kane traded, on the one hand, with Baroach, Sindh, Ormus, and Persia, and on the other, with Egypt, whence they imported wine, corn, cloths suited for the Arabian market, salt, brass, tin, resin, specie, wrought plate, carved images, and horses, and exported various commodities common to the country, Kane.

[1] Pliny, vi. 104, identified by Welsted with Hisn Ghorab, ii. p. 421.

and especially frankincense and aloes. From Kane the Arabian vessels, and afterwards some of the Egyptian traders in the time of Arrian, proceeded along the coast to the north-east until they reached Sachal, on the shores of Hadramaut, their chief trade being incense, which, according to Arrian, was there "collected by the king's slaves, or by malefactors condemned to this service as a punishment." Most of the incense, however, was sent through Thomæra, the capital of the Gebanites, to Gaza, on the coast of Palestine, by way of Petra, by the important caravan route already noticed, and continued in a great measure to find its way to Egypt by this inland route even after the merchants of Alexandria had established a regular maritime commerce with the East.

Sachal.

Moshka.

From Sachal the traders on the coast proceeded to Moskha, where vessels from Baroach and Larike, on the Gulf of Cambay, if too late for the favourable monsoons, usually endeavoured to exchange their Indian muslins for the frankincense of the place. From this place, also, native vessels made a coasting voyage till they reached Maskat and Kalaiso. Near these ports they were able to cross the gulf at its narrowest parts, and steered nearly due north, or about N.N.E. for the port of Omana, which evidently takes its name from Oman in Arabia, and was, doubtless, a colony of Arabs, established on the coast opposite to their own, for the purpose of approaching nearer to Western India. From Omana they steered almost due east along the coast of Beloochistan until they reached their destination at the mouth of the Indus or in the Gulf of Cambay.

Maskat.

Omana.

Although Omana was the centre of commerce between Arabia and India, and afterwards became a place of great commercial importance, no produce of the latter country appears to have been shipped from it at the time of Arrian. Dates in large quantities were then, as they were long afterwards, its chief articles of export; as also, coarse cloths, wine, slaves, some gold, and many pearls. Here were built for the Arabians the vessels they employed in the Persian Gulf, and along the whole line of the coast, their hulls consisting of planks sewed together, without nails. To this day similar vessels, known as *frankees* and *dhows*, may be seen in great numbers, engaged in much the same trade their ancestors followed two or three thousand years ago.

We have now given a brief outline of the routes by land and by sea, by which commerce was conducted with the East, before the commencement of the Christian era, and the map we have prepared (see frontispiece) may assist our readers in tracing the different routes. Of the maritime commerce of India itself, and of the trade and shipping of the East during the earliest periods of history, we shall attempt to furnish an outline in the following chapter.

CHAPTER V.

Ancient India—Expedition of Sesostris—Doubts of Dr. Robertson with regard to it—Hindustan, its early commerce, and the probability, from its great value, of its having attracted Sesostris—The conquests of Darius, and of Alexander—Trade with China—Its maritime intercourse—A comparison of the Chinese boats with those of the ancient Britons—The conquests of Alexander in India, B.C. 327-5—The gain to commerce by his conquests—The spread of knowledge—His march into India—Preparations for the voyage down the Indus—Departure of his fleet from Nicæa, B.C. 326—Description of the vessels employed—Progress of the fleet—Establishment of new cities on the banks of the Indus—Character of the vessels engaged on the voyage from the Indus to Susa—Time occupied—Future voyages—Death of Alexander, B.C. 323—Eastern India—Ceylon—Internal commerce of India—Manufactures of India—State of the trade of India from the sixth to the ninth century—Change in the course of trade—Persian trade with India—The Muhammedans, A.D. 622—The extent of their commerce with the East—The trade between Constantinople and India and China.

Ancient India.

It is impossible to say at how early a period the commerce of India assumed a civilized form, and from the rude barter of the savage became a regular system of exchange and account. The opinion of ancient as well as of modern writers, is almost unanimous in considering the Hindus as one of the oldest civilized nations in the world; but their most ancient records are so blended with fables, that it would be a waste of time to attempt to separate fact from fiction. Nor shall we do more than allude to the supposed conquests of Sesostris and Semiramis, as these are now generally held to have no historical foundation. That the civilization of India may reach back two or three thousand years before the Christian era is, however, not improbable, as the oldest of the Indian sacred writings, the Vêdas, are believed by the best Sanscrit scholars to have been handed down by tradition from about B.C. 1500.[1]

The historian who attempts to trace the operations of men in their commercial pursuits during very remote ages, and to mark the various steps of their progress, will soon have the mortification of finding that the period of authentic history is limited to the time assigned to it in Holy Writ; and that all the speculations about the high civilization of the Hindus before the period usually assigned to the Deluge are mere dreams of antiquarian enthusiasm. There is no reason to doubt that the narrative usually attributed to Moses is the most ancient we can now obtain, whatever modern philosophers may say to the contrary; and it is on the whole, unquestionably, the most in conformity with the facts now deducible from antiquarian or linguistic research. Many centuries must have intervened before the first heathen historian, Herodotus, wrote; and it is simply idle to attempt to write a consecutive record of commercial enterprise for any period preceding written history, as even the sculptured monuments of Egypt and Nineveh add scarcely anything to the pages of the

[1] The earliest dated MS. (a Syriac one, now in the British Museum) is dated in the first decade of the fifth century of our era. The Alexandrian codex may be a few years earlier. The oldest Egyptian inscriptions may ascend to B.C. 2000: that on the Moabite stone, perhaps, to B.C. 890.

Bible. Dr. Robertson, who wrote before anything was known of the meaning of the hieroglyphic writing of Egypt, expresses grave doubts about the Indian expedition of Sesostris, resting as this story does on the unsupported testimony of Diodorus Siculus; but, though portions of it may be fabulous, others may be true.

Expedition of Sesostris.

Doubts of Dr. Robertson with regard to it.

"Credulity and scepticism," he says,[1] "are two opposite extremes into which men are apt to run, in examining the events which are said to have happened in the early ages of antiquity. Without incurring any suspicion of a propensity to the latter of these, I may be allowed to entertain doubts concerning the expedition of Sesostris into India, and his conquest of that country. Few facts in ancient history seem to be better established than that of the early aversion of the Egyptians to a seafaring life. Even the power of despotism cannot at once change the ideas and manners of a nation, especially when they have been confirmed by long habit, and rendered sacred by the sanction of religion. That Sesostris, in the course of a few years, should have so entirely overcome the prejudices of a superstitious people, as to be able to fit out four hundred ships of war in the Arabian Gulf, besides another fleet which he had in the Mediterranean, appears to be extremely improbable. Armaments of such magnitude would require the utmost efforts of a great and long established maritime power."[2]

[1] Robertson's "Hist. Disquis. on India," note i. p. 179 (ed. 1791).

[2] It may be added, that while Herodotus alludes to other portions of the history of Sesostris, he omits the tale of his Indian conquests; that Strabo rejects it altogether (xv. p. 85); while Arrian equally doubts it.

On the other hand, we may remark that, though the extent of his fleet, especially of vessels large enough to undertake so distant a voyage as that to India, is, under any circumstances, very questionable, the aversion of the Egyptians to a sea-faring life, would not in itself be an insuperable objection against the probability of great and distant expeditions, since, as we have already shown, the Phœnicians must have had considerable fleets at an early period; and Sesostris (or whoever he may be supposed to represent), is said to have employed Phœnician ships and sailors. Nor does Herodotus's omission of the expedition attributed to the Egyptian monarch, prove that no such undertaking could have been carried into effect. We must, in fact, be wary of rejecting the possibility of some conquest or of some expedition, while we reject unhesitatingly what is on the face of it fabulous, as the story of the seventeen hundred associates of Sesostris, who were born on the same day as the king, and were still alive: moreover, with regard to Strabo, it should be remembered, that he, like Herodotus, has doubted more than one story, which there is, nevertheless, sound reason for believing. The first duty of an historian is to separate, to the best of his judgment, fact from fiction, and especially, not to reject what may have taken place, because the account of it is mixed up with questionable or exaggerated anecdotes.

Hindustan, its early commerce, and the probability, from its great

There are many reasons for supposing that Hindustan, to this day famous for its riches, was at a very early period the seat of a lucrative commerce and of much accumulated wealth. As such it would be the envy of other nations, and more especially of

value, of its having attracted Sesostris.

ambitious monarchs. The narrative of Arrian shows that this commerce was then regulated by sounder principles, and carried on in a more civilized manner, than it was fifteen centuries afterwards when Vasco de Gama first visited the shores of India. As numerous elements of wealth and luxury, usually found scattered over various regions of the earth, were the natural products of Hindustan, it might be expected that a country so highly favoured should, through the mists which over-hang the dawn of history, have loomed forth imposingly in very ancient times as the special abode of luxury and refinement.

But while not admitting the extravagant descriptions in the Hindu poets and historians of the glory and wealth of their country, any more than the whole of the Egyptian story of Sesostris, there is no reason to doubt that the civilization of India dates from a period as early as that of Egypt, and that the fame of its riches may have led to more than one attempt to achieve its conquest. The Râmâyana, one of the most ancient Hindu books, where it informs us, in the glowing language of its poetry, that Ayodhya[1] (Oude), one of the leading commercial cities of India, was "filled with merchants and artificers of all kinds"; that "gold, precious stones, and jewels were there found in great abundance"; that "every one wore costly garments, bracelets, and necklaces"; that "the town always resounded with the noise and bustle of men and women, like the shouts of contending armies"; that "the great men were ever going to and fro upon chariots, elephants, and prancing steeds"; and that "the

[1] Heeren, vol. ii. p. 227, in his "Asiatic Researches," believes this city to have been founded from 2,000 to 1,500 years before the Christian era.

gardens of pleasure were always crowded with eager inquirers after their friends and lovers," may have furnished an exaggerated description of its wealth, but far from a fabulous one, as the fame of that great city seems to rest on satisfactory evidence.

The conquests of Darius,

Of the actual commercial resources of India we have, however, no reliable accounts previous to the conquests of Darius and to the successful navigation of the Indus by his fleets. In his time, the country through which he passed was represented to be very populous and highly cultivated; and though his conquests did not extend beyond the district watered by the Indus, below Peucela, we cannot but form a high opinion of its opulence in ancient times, as well as of the number of its inhabitants, when we learn from Herodotus that the tribute Darius levied upon it was nearly one-third of the whole revenue of the Persian monarchy.[1] But it was only when Alexander, two hundred years later, undertook his celebrated expedition, that sufficient knowledge of India was obtained to enable us fully to realize the real amount of its wealth, and some of the actual conditions of its civilization and commerce. Up to that period the more valuable commerce between Europe and India was conducted mainly by caravans passing through Bactra[2] (Balkh), "the mother of cities," as it has been called from its great antiquity. From this important seat of inland Asiatic trade, the Oxus on the N.W., the Indus on the E. and S., and the Ganges to the S.E., stretched long branching arms, and thus afforded ready means for the distribu-

and of Alexander.

[1] Herod. iv. 42-44; iii. 84.

[2] Pliny, who calls this city Bactrum, points out the peculiarity of its double-humped camel, yet seen on the Bactrian coins (vii. 87)

tion of the contents of the caravans to the most populous districts. Founded, as is believed, before the dawn of history, Bactra was for many centuries the most flourishing mart of Eastern commerce; the western and the northern roads into India passed through it; and the ruins still surrounding it for miles attest its former size and splendour.

It was the obvious policy of the Bactrian people, holding as they did in their own hands the advantage of a great trade, to give as little information as they could of the actual sources whence came the wealth or the luxuries in such demand with the merchants of the West. Hence the dismal tales of the sandy deserts to be traversed, of the many dangers to be surmounted, and of the terrible "griffins," which, according to Herodotus and Ctesias, were the guardians of the gold-bearing districts.[1] Even Arrian, the shrewd Alexandrian merchant, speaks of the land whence the glistening hanks of silk were obtained—the land of *Thina* (China), as a country practically inaccessible. "It is not easy to get there," he says, "and of those who attempt the journey, few are ever seen again. Once a year there come to the borders of Thina, a set of ill-formed, broad-faced, and flat-nosed savages, who bring with them their wives and children, and carry great burdens in mats. They stop short at a certain place between their own territory and that of Thina, where, seated on their mats, they celebrate a kind of festival, and then, having disposed of their goods, of which their silk is the chief, to the people of Thina,

Trade with China.

[1] Herod. iii. 116; iv. 27. Ctesias, ap. Ælian Nat. Animal. iv. 27 Mela, II. c. 11.

they depart to whence they came. The country situated beyond Thina is unexplored, either in consequence of cold and severe frosts, which render travelling thither very difficult, or because the immortals have so willed it."[1]

The early navigation of China, like its commerce and everything else connected with the history of that remarkable country, is involved in the utmost obscurity, but there is no reason for accepting the extravagant antiquity to which the Chinese themselves pretend. Modern researches bring down the period of early Chinese civilization to a date comparatively recent; and, though it is likely that, from an early period, some of their vessels may have reached Hindustan or Ceylon, it is equally clear that their chief commercial operations with the nations of the West, previous to the time when the merchants of Alexandria established a regular trade with the coasts of Malabar, were conducted by means of the caravans already described, and, at the same time, with as much secrecy and mystery as possible.

Its maritime intercourse.

Our knowledge of the early maritime routes to the far East is almost exclusively confined to what has been already stated with reference to those between Europe and Arabia and the western shores of Hindustan. Beyond those shores, all that is certain is, that vessels from China, from Bengal, and from other parts of the East, traded with Ceylon, and that some of the products of China found their way by circuitous routes, probably after passing through many hands, to the great central mart of Alexandria; nor, indeed, is there any greater certainty or know-

[1] Arrian, "Periplus," c. 64, 65.

ledge about the character of the early Indian vessels, for, like the Egyptians, the Indians were not, and are not, as a nation, a seafaring people. Those Indians who followed seafaring pursuits, were then, as now, of the lowest caste; hence the inference is natural that their shipping would exhibit a corresponding inferiority in construction.

Pliny[1] says that their boats consisted chiefly of a large description of cane or bamboo, split down the middle, and capable of carrying three persons; and Arrian remarks that, in his time, the vessels employed on the Malabar coast were very inferior to those of most other nations. He says the small vessels, called *madara*, have their planks sewn together with coir—the inner fibre of the cocoa-nut—like some of the native vessels of Arabia. Others, he adds, were long vessels, *trappaga* and *cotymba* (in the native dialect),[2] used by fishermen and pilots of the port of Barygaza. But besides these, there were double canoes, which were lashed together, and were by his description not unlike, though much inferior to, those of the South Sea Islands, of which, from Captain Cook's description, the following is an illustration (Page 131).

The Chinese junk of the present day probably affords a tolerably accurate representation of the Chinese merchant vessel of two or perhaps three thousand years ago; for all that is known of China,

[1] Plin. xiv. 162. Cuvier (ap. Rawlinson's Herod. iii. 98) speaks of a bamboo (*Bambus arundinacea*) which grows to the height of sixty feet. Colonel Yule states that the largest bamboos are in the Malay Islands and Cambodia. He has seen them from eighty to one hundred feet high. "Early Travels to India," 1867, p. 93.

[2] Arrian, "Periplus," c. 44.

and of the habits of its population, tends to show that they have adhered to established types with even more than Oriental tenacity.[1] In the "Asiatic Researches" (vol. vi. p. 204) is a representation of one of the oldest Chinese merchant vessels which have been preserved: it exhibits a model almost as perfect as any of their vessels of our own time.

Moreover, the ordinary junk now in use for the coasting and inland navigation of that country, will

be noticed as forming an exact counterpart of many of the Egyptian vessels engaged on the trade of the Nile, and, more especially, that called *paro*, another description of trading craft very common in China: while the account given by Sir George Staunton of some of the small vessels of China exhibits a

[1] Sir John Herschel has called attention to the fact that the Chinese have preserved registers of comets and other celestial phenomena for more than a thousand years before the Christian Era. "Familiar Lectures," p. 94, 1868.

A comparison of the Chinese boats with those of the ancient Britons.

remarkable similitude between these and the ancient boats of Britain. "The boats," he says, "commonly in use among them, consist of five planks only, joined together without ribs or timber of any kind. These planks are bent to the proper shape by being exposed some time to a flame of fire. They are brought to a line at each end, and the edges are joined together with wooden pins, and stitched[1] with bamboo split into flexible threads, and the seams

SMALL JUNK. PARO.

afterwards smeared with a paste made with quick-lime from sea-shells and water. Others are made of wicker-work, smeared all over, and rendered water-tight, by the same composition as is used for the former. The owners affect to paint eyes upon the heads of all these boats, as if to denote the vigilance requisite in the conduct of them. They are remarkable for standing the sudden shock of violent waves, as well as for being stiff upon the water, and sailing expeditiously. The boat belonging to the chief of

[1] Friar Oderic (ap. Colonel Yule, p. 57) speaks of vessels, like the ancient boats at Rhapta, stitched with twine, without any iron, employed along the coast approaching the modern site of Bombay.

the district was built upon the same plan, but on a larger scale, had a carved and gilt head, bearing some resemblance to that of a tiger, and a stern ornamented with sculpture, and painted with a variety of designs in lively colours. In these boats the principal sitters are generally at the stem, instead of being near the stern, as is the custom of Europe."

Considering themselves to be the most ancient and the most learned of people, the Chinese were too vain to learn from others; they thought they knew more than anybody else, and they think so still; for, having daily before them some of the most magnificent European ships of modern times, they still retain the ancient form of the junk. To a people so fond of money, and so industrious, one would have thought that the fact of such vessels conducting the most valuable trade on the Chinese coast, would have induced them to make some endeavour, by means of shipping better found and better fitted than are any they possess, to retain a trade for centuries originally and exclusively their own.

Nowhere are their failings in this respect better exemplified than in the report of the embassy under Lord Macartney, sent from Great Britain to Pekin in 1792. "It is not uncommon," remarks the writer of this report, "on board Chinese vessels to have maps or sketches of their intended route, with the neighbouring headlands cut out or engraved upon the back of empty gourds, the round form of which corresponds in some sort to the figure of the earth. Such a similitude may have sometimes contributed to render these sketches somewhat less erroneous, but the advantage is accidental, for neither the astronomers nor navigators of China have varied much from the first rude notions entertained among mankind, that the whole earth was one flat surface, in the middle of which the Chinese took for granted that their own empire was situated, thence emphatically styled by them, the 'empire of the middle;' all other countries surrounding it being, in their estimation, comparatively small, and lying towards the edge, or margin of the earth, beyond which all must be a precipitate and dreadful void."

The conquests of Alexander in India, B.C. 327–5.

With the conquests of Alexander commence our first really historical knowledge of India. For, if Alexander left behind him, at his premature death, the fame of a mighty conqueror, he no less deserves that of a great civilizer, by the wisdom he displayed in opening up new channels of commercial intercourse.[1] In the foundation of Alexandria (B.C. 332) he showed how keenly he was alive to the value of the commerce between Europe and the East, while he was, at the same time, the first to lay down the principle that the command of the sea secures the possession of the land; and to carry that principle into practice, by raising his fleets from insignificance until they held dominion over all waters accessible to them. Alexander saw that the extension of the commercial intercourse of his people would do more to consolidate his power than military conquest; hence he had the wisdom to establish in the path of his conquests, ports, cities, and institutions, with which his name has been, and will be, imperishably associated. Although there will always be some

[1] See an excellent life of Alexander by Archdeacon Williams. "Family Library," No. iii. 1829.

persons who can see nothing but desolation and ruin in the paths of a great conqueror, who deem great soldiers the necessary enemies of mankind, and who cannot recognise either the foresight or the motives of men such as Alexander the Great, yet even they must admit that the world ultimately reaped a rich harvest through the creation of Alexandria, and that his triumphs in Asia gain additional renown from his efforts to increase geographical knowledge, and to bring India, by means of a more rapid communication by sea, nearer to Europe than it had ever been before his time.

Nor were the designs of this great conqueror confined to an increase of facilities for conducting with greater rapidity and safety the commercial intercourse of the nations of the West, requiring, as these did for their daily wants, commodities India could alone supply. Alexander created new channels of trade, and fresh wants, and fresh hopes for each country he successively overcame. Instead of devastation and misery marking his progress through Syria and Asia Minor, these countries were greatly enriched by his sovereignty, while their inhabitants secured more freedom and prosperity than they had ever enjoyed under their native princes. Egypt, under the dynasty of the Ptolemies, the first founder of which, Ptolemy the son of Lagos, was one of Alexander's most trusted generals, obtained a commercial preeminence it had not enjoyed during any previous period of its history. Again, when Alexander advanced into the district now known as the Panjâb, he conferred many advantages on the natives, and imparted to them much practical and valuable know-

The gain of commerce by his conquests.

ledge. Almost everywhere he founded Greek cities or colonies (Plutarch gives their number as seventy), diffusing the manners and customs of his own people over the vast tracts of land from the temple of Ammon in the Lybian oasis to the banks of the Indus. Thus he brought into contact with his own refined and civilized Greeks, not merely Oriental nations that were highly gifted in their own way, but also the semi-barbarous tribes of many lands, teaching them the advantages of commercial intercourse, and extending by its influence the comforts which habits of industry can alone bestow, together with the many blessings civilization confers. His conquests, like the discoveries of Columbus, made known the existence of rich regions before unsuspected, and countries where millions of the human race could find remunerative occupation.

Articles of commerce, of which the Western World had had no previous experience, were thus brought to light. Rice produced from irrigated fields; a cotton tree of a superior growth, which, from its fine tissues, furnished the materials for the manufacture of paper; various descriptions of spices and opium; wine made from rice, and from the juice of palms;[1] wool from the great bombax tree;[2] shawls made of the fine hair of the Thibetan goats; silken tissues of various kinds; oil from the white sesamum; and perfumes of the richest description. These and other products, for the most part new to the Western World, soon became articles of universal commerce, while some of them were transported to Arabia, and thence to the shores of the Mediterranean.

[1] Arrian, Ind. vii.

[2] Strabo, book xv. p. 694.

But, beyond numerous commercial advantages, the Macedonian campaigns opened a large and beautiful portion of the earth to the influence of a highly-gifted race, who courted the society of the most learned men of the countries they conquered. Hence the geographical knowledge of the Greeks was more than doubled in the course of a very few years by the extraordinary and enlightened conquests of their chief.

The spread of knowledge.

While the comparison of notes between the geometricians, naturalists, and astronomers of two of the most learned nations of ancient times proved of immense benefit to mankind, we cannot doubt that the scientific knowledge of the Greeks, when brought to bear upon the practical experience of the Hindus with regard to the prevailing winds, mainly induced Nearchus to start without fear on his celebrated voyage, and, at the same time, encouraged the merchants of Europe to seek out new means of communication with a country producing in such abundance the articles they prized so highly.

The expedition through the northern portions of India, and the voyage from the Indus to the Euphrates, if not the greatest of the exploits of Alexander, were certainly, in many ways, the most important up to that time in the history of commerce and navigation.

His march into India.

Arrian, whom we have had so often the pleasure of quoting, has preserved copious extracts from the journal of Nearchus, and the information thus obtained has been thoroughly investigated by Dr. Robertson, in his "Disquisition on the Knowledge the Ancients had of India"; by Heeren in his "Asiatic Nations"; and most fully of all by Dr. Vincent in his "Commerce and Navigation of the Ancients in the Indian Ocean."

With a view to secure the commerce Tyre had so long and so successfully carried on with India, Alexander, early in his career, as has been shown, established the great Egyptian port which still bears his name; and other events soon gave him the opportunity of obtaining the sovereignty of those regions that supplied the rest of the world with so many precious commodities. After his victory over the Persians, the pursuit of Darius led him across Asia, from the Caspian Sea to Maracanda (Samarcand), and during this adventurous march he naturally learnt many things, not only of the tribes through whom he passed, but also of India itself, with which those tribes had much commercial intercourse. Decisive and prompt in his resolutions, he accordingly set out from Bactra (Balkh), crossed the great chain of mountains that constitutes the north-western boundary of India, and, passing the Indus, marched on towards the Ganges and the rich provinces of the south-east, now comprehended under the general name of Hindustan.

Nor would he have hesitated in pushing onwards to the then capital of India, Palimbothra (now Patna), had he not been compelled by the remonstrances of his native troops to retrace his steps homewards. Being, however, unable to persuade his troops to cross the Hyphasis (now Setlege), and to pass on to the conquest of India, Alexander fell back upon the Hydaspes (now Jelum), where he found that the officers to whom he had entrusted the construction and collection of as many vessels as could be got ready, had so well executed his orders, that they

Preparations for the voyage down the Indus.

had assembled a numerous fleet, consisting of two thousand vessels, according to Strabo, or, according to Arrian,[1] of about eight hundred boats, thirty-one of which were ships of war, and the rest such as were usually employed in the navigation of the river. But, whichever number be right—and with the dense population of the Panjâb, the larger one, comprehending anything and everything that could float, is doubtless possible—it is certain, if we except that of Xerxes, that this flotilla was one of the largest which had as yet, at least within historical times, been got together.

It is very likely that, by his eight hundred, Arrian may have meant only those employed for transports and fighting vessels, not deeming it worth while to reckon up every small craft Alexander may have pressed into his service. Moreover, Strabo[2] has remarked that in the neighbourhood of Nicæa, whence the army embarked, there was an abundant supply of fir, pine, cedar, and of other timber, fit for the construction of boats and barges; while Arrian further records the fact that Alexander, before he himself had reached the Indus, had already caused a number of vessels to be built in the country of the Assacani (the Afghâns), and to be sent down the Kophen (or river of Kâbul) to Taxila (Manykyala). It was, probably, during the preparation of this great fleet that Alexander obtained his most valuable information about the state of inner or further India, both with regard to the commerce of the country, and to the different places with which the natives traded. Many of the natives, too, embarked with him, either for the purpose of conducting the fleet, or with a view to

[1] Arrian, Exped. Alex. v. 3.

[2] Lib. xvi. p. 752.

their own advantage; and, besides the natives who rendered their services in the collection, fitting out and navigating the fleet, it is further stated that an ample supply of mariners was obtained from a number of Phœnicians, Egyptians, Cypriotes, Ionians, and others from the shores of the Hellespont, and from the Ægean islands, who had accompanied the army, in various capacities, as camp followers.[1]

Departure of his fleet from Nicæa, B.C. 326.

Thus prepared, the expedition started from Nicæa on the 1st October, B.C. 326. The voyage down the river is described rather as a triumphal procession than a military progress. The size of many of the transport vessels, and of the barges for the conveyance of horses, the splendour of the equipments, the clang of arms, and the sound of musical instruments, attracted the natives in vast numbers to the banks of the river, as wondering spectators to the pomp. Nor, probably, were they less surprised at the measured chant of the rowers, and the dashing of the oars in the still waters: subjects on which all the historians of this remarkable expedition have dwelt in detail, doubtless thereby conveying an accurate account of this remarkable exploit. But though there can be no doubt of the general truth of the story as handed down to us by Arrian, the descriptions of the vessels which composed it are, in some respects, inconsistent with each other. The transports were probably short flat vessels, to which the ordinary small barge of the present day bears, perhaps, a greater resemblance than any other craft.

Description of the vessels employed.

[1] Vincent, vol. i. p. 122. It is worthy of remark that not a single native of Southern Greece—even of Athens—is mentioned among the leading followers of Alexander. Nearchus was a Macedonian of Amphipolis; three other naval chiefs were from Cos, Teos, and Cyprus.

The galleys are said to have been long and sharp, some of them having two banks of oars; others were "half-decked vessels;"[1] while some of them had keels so deep, that they could not be beached without risk of their destruction. "As the tide fell," remarks Dr. Vincent,[2] "the vessels were left on ground; but upon the return of the flood those only that had settled upright in the mud or ooze, escaped unhurt, while all that lay inclined upon the harder ground, were exposed to the most imminent danger, and several were lost." As any vessel, however, that is of sufficient stability to float upright, would, when the tide returned, rise to it, it is very probable that the cause of these occasional accidents was leakage, through straining or from carelessness in beaching them on uneven ground. The greater part, however, of the craft consisted, no doubt, of open boats and barges, and especially that portion of it which had been built on the upper branches of the Indus, and then transported overland to the Hydaspes.

Progress of the fleet.

The expedition having been disposed of in various divisions, had orders to observe a due distance from each other in their movements, so that no confusion might arise, its speed being at the same time regulated so as to accommodate itself to the motions of the army on the shore. Three vast armies, moving in separate divisions, encumbered with baggage as well as with munitions of war, with no roads prepared for them, and, for the most part, following the sinuosities of the river, must have had numerous difficulties to surmount. It is, therefore, unlikely that they were

[1] Vincent's "Commerce in India," vol. i. p. 169.

[2] Ibid. vol. i. p. 171.

able to maintain their combined movement with anything like order, or to average in their progress as much as the fifteen miles a day Dr. Vincent considers a fair estimate for them. Still less is it possible that they could have accomplished the six hundred stadia, or seventy miles, in the time Pliny has recorded. The estimate of Curtius of forty stadia, or four miles and three quarters a day, is unquestionably nearer the truth, as we know that the fleet was nine months floating down a distance of little more than one thousand miles. Moreover, there were constant delays and interruptions, arising from the arrangements Alexander considered it necessary to make with the different tribes and provinces through whose territory he had to advance.

Establishment of new cities on the banks of the Indus.

At the junction of the Acesines with the Indus, Alexander established his first city on the banks of that river. The site was judiciously chosen, as a city placed in such a position would necessarily partake of all the commerce that passed up the Indus, to be distributed by means of its various tributaries, from Candahar and Kâbul on the west, to Upper India and Thibet on the north and north-east: moreover, being the centre where all the streams united, it must, consequently, derive equal emoluments from the commerce that passed downwards to the coast.[1] From the establishment of this and of other cities on the banks of the Indus, all of which he fortified, it is evident that the Macedonian conqueror destined that river to be the eastern frontier of his empire, and saw that, by holding the command of it,

[1] Vincent, i. p. 136. No modern site has as yet been recognised for this city; nor is Wilson sure. Ariana. Antiq. p. 207.

he would combine, by means of a river navigation to the eastern portion of his dominions, a maritime commerce with the richest portions of the interior of India.

On the arrival of the expedition at Pattala, in after days a place of great commercial importance for the maritime trade with the West, Alexander made arrangements for despatching Nearchus, with the largest and best portion of his fleet, to the Euphrates, he himself proceeding with the bulk of his army, by land, to Susa and Babylon. The importance of Nearchus' expedition cannot be too highly estimated, as on its success greatly depended the carrying out, with thorough efficiency, that widely extended system of commerce by sea, between India and Europe, Alexander obviously had in view, and of which the fleet, under the command of Nearchus, was to serve as the pioneer. The opening of the Indus, on the one hand, and the establishment of Alexandria in Egypt on the other, are evidences of a comprehensive scheme of commercial intercourse between all the leading points of the then known world. Alexander could scarcely have failed to perceive that the junction of the great ports of the East and of the West, with well selected stations, at proper intervals between them, would secure the stability of his vast empire; indeed, no other device could have provided for it so well, or could, at the same time, have enabled him to hold in his own hands by far the largest and most valuable trade known to the merchants of ancient times.

Although Nearchus in his journal enters into the most minute details of his voyage from the Indus to Susa on the Choaspes, it is remarkable that he has

Character of the vessels engaged on the voyage from the Indus to Susa.

given no account whatever of the size or number of vessels under his command. An attentive perusal of his story shows however, clearly enough, that they were of the smallest description of craft then in use for sea-going purposes. During the whole voyage they closely hugged the land, invariably anchoring during the night; and though occasionally, when the wind was fair and strong, the journal records a run of sixty, and once of even eighty miles, the average distance did not exceed twenty-five, add to which, the joy of the crew when they reached Karamania, and formed a naval camp on shore, indicates but too plainly that, on board, they had been uncomfortably crammed from want of space.[1]

Time occupied.

The voyage itself is recorded with great care by Nearchus; and Heeren, in his "Asiatic Nations,"[3] gives a condensed account of it, which is alike interesting and clear, especially in that portion of it referring to the leading outlines of the coast. It is interesting to read in the records of Nearchus that he speaks of the marauding habits of a people who, having reached a high state of civilization, and even refinement, seem to have degenerated from what they were two thousand years ago, and to observe that, by even this circumstance, the navigator by sea and the traveller by land, of our own time, can recognize the accuracy of his description.[3]

[1] Vincent, "Commerce in India," vol. i. p. 326.

[2] Ibid. vol. i. chap. ii. p. 431.

[3] In 1838, the author, then a young man in command of the *Olive Branch*, a barque of four hundred tons, sailed along the whole of this coast, frequently following the route which Nearchus had taken, and sometimes obliged to anchor on account of the intricacy of the navigation, as Nearchus had done, overnight. He can, therefore, confirm the accuracy of Heeren's condensed description of the voyage in its

The whole time occupied on the voyage from the mouth of the Indus to Susa, appears to have been 146 days—five lunar months and six days, and not seven months, as stated by Pliny.[1] In calling attention to this fact, Dr. Vincent remarks that a modern vessel can perform in three weeks the passage which Nearchus was five months in accomplishing. "Within the memory of man," he adds,[2] "a voyage to India required eight or nine months; but Dr. Robertson mentions that, in 1788, the *Boddam* East Indiaman reached Madras in 108 days, and it has since been performed in 96." To this we may add that the voyage to India (Bombay), by way of Marseilles, Egypt, and the Red Sea, is now performed in 28 days; that auxiliary screw steam-ships from Liverpool and London perform the voyage, by way of Gibraltar and the Suez Canal, to Bombay and Ceylon, heavily laden with cargoes each way, and back to England in 80 days; and that by means of the electric telegraph we can now communicate with any portion of that vast empire in a day, practically in a few minutes if there are no obstacles in the way.[3]

But conquests in Asia and Western India were not

difficulties and dangers; and can testify to the abundance of the dates, which formed a portion of the author's return cargo to Bombay; and also, he may add, to the "robbers" by whom he was attacked when conveying, from an inland town in the vicinity of Bushire, some treasure which was destined for his ship.

[1] Lib. vi. p. 136. [2] Vincent, vol. i. p. 695.

[3] *The Telegraph.* Telegraphic communication with India is now so far perfect, that electricity outstrips the speed of the earth, as it frequently happens that messages transmitted from Calcutta at noon to London are delivered by the Indo-European Telegraph Company at 10.30 A.M. Communication between London and Teherán (the terminus of the Indian Government lines) is actually instantaneous.—*Times*, 5 April, 1870.

sufficient to satisfy the ambition of Alexander, which knew no limits short of the then known world. Future voyages. Whether he really contemplated the circumnavigation of Africa, and also its subjugation, is a matter of doubt, but it is a well established fact that he had in view the conquest of the whole of Arabia. With that object, he commissioned Nearchus, with the ships he had brought from the Indus, supplemented by forty-seven vessels from Phœnicia, which had been built in pieces and conveyed overland to Thapsacus, and by others constructed on the spot, of cypress, the only wood Babylon afforded, to form a fleet, and take command of this second great maritime expedition. Two of the vessels brought from Phœnicia are described as of five banks, three of four, twelve of three, while thirty were rowed with fifteen oars on a side.[1] The object of Alexander was evidently not so much conquest as colonization. To prepare the way for Nearchus, three single vessels were despatched at different times down the Arabian side of the Persian Gulf, to learn the nature of the coast, the character of the soil, and the best sites for stations or towns. One of these vessels had instructions to circumnavigate Arabia, and to proceed up the Red Sea as far as Suez,[2] though it does not appear whether she ever reached her destination.

Nearchus would, no doubt, have accomplished the task allotted to him by Alexander, but when the expedition was ready to start, the Macedonian conqueror lay on his death-bed. Death of Alexander, B.C. 323. In the midst of the fever of which he died, he, according to the diary of one of his officers, "transacted business with his officers, and

[1] Vincent, vol. i. p. 509.

[2] Pliny, xii. c. 11.

gave directions about the fleet."[1] On the following day, though "the fever now ran very high, and oppressed him much, he nevertheless ordered the principal officers to attend, and repeated his orders in regard to the fleet"; and on the day of his death, when unable to speak, it would appear by the diary preserved in the extracts made from it by Arrian, that his last thoughts were directed to the conquest and colonization of Arabia. His untimely death, however, not only put an end to this project, but also to all his other splendid schemes.

As is well known, the body of Alexander was hardly cold, ere the great empire he had founded fell to pieces, and was parcelled out among those who had been his ablest lieutenants; but, though for a while suffering from the rude conflict of rival selfishness, it is a remarkable fact that the commercial relations between the different provinces he had overrun had been so well established by the sagacity of the conqueror, that on the final restoration of tranquillity, the Macedonian dominion, and with it Greek principles of trade and mutual intercourse, prevailed throughout Asia, no province succeeding for many years in shaking off the yoke. Even in the distant East, though those portions of it subdued by Alexander for a while joined a native chief Sandracottus (Chandra-gupta), the ruler of a powerful nation on the banks of the Ganges, whose plan was to attack those parts of the Macedonian dominions bordering on his territories, order was soon restored; while Alexander's immediate successor in the government of the East, Seleucus, who had

[1] Arrian, "Exp. Alex." vii. 25.

carefully studied the principles of his great master, conceived so clear an idea of the importance of a commercial intercourse with India, that he marched into that country, and, entering into relations with Ptolemy the son of Lagos, established on a firm basis the trade between the Red Sea and Hindustan, as described in the previous chapter.

Eastern India.

Of the more eastern portions of India little was then known. Indeed, so late as the geographer Ptolemy, so erroneous are his ideas of the size and position of even the great island of Ceylon, and of the peninsula of Hindustan, that it is certain he obtained the information he has recorded from the reports of persons of no scientific acquirements. His description of the character of the coasts and of the chief ports are, on the other hand, more accurate than might have been expected, considering that his only source of information was from the lips of unscientific sailors or merchants who had merely visited the places he notices. Thus, in his account of Ceylon, we find a fair description, not only of the sea coast of the island, but of the trade then carried on, and, especially of the nature of the intercourse conducted by the different nations who frequented its excellent harbours. Ptolemy, also, notices the productions for which Ceylon was then celebrated, as rice, honey, ginger, aromatic drugs, pearls, and precious stones, and especially the beryl and the hyacinth. He likewise mentions gold and silver, with a special reference to its elephants and tigers. Indeed, his description of the island resembles in all material points that given by Cosmas Indicopleustes, four centuries later. Both agree in stating that the shores were occupied by foreigners, who held the harbours and the chief seats of commerce, leaving the interior to the aboriginal inhabitants.

Ptolemy speaks also of many small islands west of Ceylon—doubtless the Maldives—and of those to the eastward, now called the Sunda Islands, more especially of Jabadia (now Java), which he describes as the richest of them all. Many other islands are also noticed by him which cannot now be identified; it seems also probable that he knew something of the Straits of Sunda, between Java and Sumatra. Indeed, he mentions boats peculiar to the Java sea, as observed also by Pliny, constructed of planks fastened together by trenails instead of iron. Moreover, his account of India beyond the Ganges, and of the various ports and cities of the peninsulas of Malacca and Serica (China), proves at least this, that long before his time these countries were accessible to navigators, and that Ceylon was the common mart for the trade of all the vessels bound thence to the westward.

From the "Periplus" of Arrian still more accurate information is obtainable, and especially with regard to the Malabar coast he himself visited: from his report we learn that Cochin and Travancore then carried on a flourishing trade, and that Palæsimundum, the capital of Ceylon, was considered by him to contain upwards of two hundred thousand inhabitants, an estimate more likely to be true of the whole island than of the capital alone. Palæsimundum was on the northern side of the island, probably on or near the bay of Trincomalee, one of the finest harbours in India, although then, as now, the port and harbour of Galle on the south appears to have been

Ceylon.

the chief rendezvous for merchant vessels. A glance at the map will show that for this purpose Galle is eminently well placed.

Nor can the commercial reputation of Ceylon be said to have ever waned; for of this island alone it may be said that, during all the changes in the course of commerce, since the Phœnicians of Gerrha first, as we believe, explored the western shores of the Indian peninsula, Ceylon has maintained her natural position as the great maritime entrepôt between the East and the West. Here, doubtless, the voyagers from each distant land met, as it were, on neutral ground, none of them, perhaps, for many ages, extending their own commercial relations beyond it. We have also Pliny's statement that the Singhalese ambassadors to Rome, in the reign of Claudius,[1] asserted that their countrymen had reached China by an overland route through India and across the Himalaya, before ships had attempted the voyage thither; while it is further certain that Ceylon also reaped the full share of the advantages maritime adventure derived from the discovery of the monsoons, and that, during the period when Rome carried on, by way of the Red Sea, an extensive commercial intercourse with the East, this island was, as it had been for so long, the chief emporium of the far East.

Passing on to the time when the transfer of the seat of empire was made from Rome to Constantinople, and when the Persians vied with the merchants of Egypt and the ship-owners of Arabia to divert the course of the Oriental trade from the Red Sea and Alexandria to the Euphrates and the Persian Gulf, Ceylon con-

[1] Pliny, vi. 88.

tinued to be the great rendezvous alike for the traders of the West and the East.[1] Nor has it lost in any way its ancient fame as a place of call. At the harbour of Galle the steamships from Europe, by way of the Red Sea, destined for Calcutta and the ports of China, now exchange their passengers and specie with the lines of steamships which trade to the ports of Australia; while traders from Bombay to Bengal, and other ports of the East, still make it the centre to which, and from which, their respective routes converge or diverge. Again, India within itself has, from the earliest period of authentic history, carried on a large internal commerce both by land and sea. Rice and other necessaries of life must have been transported from the countries along the Ganges, where they grow abundantly, to the sandy shores of the peninsula; and cotton, though manufactured with the same activity on the coasts as in the interior, differed so much in each district, in its texture and mode of preparation, that a large interchange of its various kinds must naturally have occurred. Again, the mode of life, especially in such cities as Ayodhya (Oude) implies the existence of a multitude of wants, natural and artificial, which could only be supplied by a corresponding system of active commerce between the different parts of India.

Internal commerce of India.

It is clear, from Ptolemy, that along the shores of the Indian peninsula there were a number of ports known to the traders of his time by the name of "Emporia," or places of rendezvous; but, as Dr. Robertson has pointed out, we have no means now of

[1] Ammianus speaks of ambassadors from Ceylon to the Emperor Julian, xx. 4.

determining whether these, or most of these, were simply ports for native vessels, or for the larger ships that conveyed the merchandise of Alexandria and of the West. It seems, however, probable from his strange ignorance of the real size of Ceylon (in which ignorance he nearly equals Arrian), that even then direct communication with that island was not very common; add to which, that, beyond the Golden Chersonesus, Ptolemy has noticed but one emporium, a fact clearly showing that few, if any, reports had reached him of the trade beyond the present site of Singapore.

Manufactures of India.

But, however little we may know of the outline of the coasts of India, or of its harbours to the eastward of Cape Comorin, previous to the Christian era, there can be no doubt of the comparatively high state of civilization then prevalent among the Hindus generally, and of their skill in manufactures.

So great was the variety of cloths manufactured by it even in the days of Arrian, who gives them in detail, that we can hardly suppose the number to have afterwards much increased. In the "Periplus"[1] we read of the finest Bengal muslins; of coarse, middle, and fine cloths; of coarse and fine calicoes; of coloured shawls and sashes; of coarse and fine purple goods, as well as of pieces of embroidery; of spun silk and of furs from Serica: and it is further recorded that the Greeks who visited India in the train of Alexander the Great, were struck with the whiteness and fineness of the texture of the cotton garments of the Hindus. Moreover, it is quite possible that the "coloured cloths and rich apparel," noticed by Ezekiel as brought to Tyre and Babylon, were partly,

[1] Arrian, "Periplus," 13 to 36.

at least, the production of India. Again, frequent mention is made of these coloured cloths and fine garments by the poet of the Râmâyana, and of "the rich woollen stuffs," perhaps the shawls of Cashmir, still among the richest portions of female attire in Eastern countries. Herodotus, also, speaks of the bark of trees being used in India from very remote times, for the purpose of manufacturing a species of cloth, extensively worn by pious hermits and penitents. All these facts establish beyond any question the great antiquity of Indian civilization.

India, like Asia Minor and Arabia, had its caravans. In those of the south, elephants were chiefly employed; for the whole of the peninsula being traversed by rocky mountains, could scarcely, if at all, admit of the employment of camels. The Ganges and its tributary streams, however, afforded great facilities for the commercial intercourse of Northern India, though Arrian adds also, and truly, that many of the rivers of the south were equally available for trade, and that along the eastern and western coasts extensive use was made of country-built boats. Indeed, when we consider the high antiquity of the pearl fisheries of Ceylon, we cannot doubt that such a coasting trade was carried on for many hundred years before his time.

At particular periods of the year caravans proceeded to Benares and Juggernaut, sanctuaries to which hundreds of thousands of pilgrims resorted for purposes of commerce and devotion long before the Christian era; and, as markets and fairs were established, and depôts for goods erected, partly in the interior, but particularly on the coast, to meet the wants of the vast concourse of pilgrims and traders, there must, at such times, have been considerable employment for the native vessels, beyond what was required in the pearl fisheries and in the ordinary course of traffic.

Though from the age of Ptolemy the trade between Western Europe and India was carried on by the way of Egypt, Rome and Constantinople being alike supplied by the agency of the merchants of Alexandria, we have not, till the reign of Justinian, any further
A.D. 527-65 information concerning the progress of the over-sea trade, or of any discoveries with reference to the more remote regions of the East. In the course, however, of his reign, Cosmas (commonly called, from the
A.D. 535. voyages he made, Indicopleustes, an Egyptian merchant), went on more than one occasion to India; and when, in after days, he renounced the pursuits of commerce, and became a monk, he composed in the solitude and leisure of his cell, several works, one of which (his "Christian Topography") has been preserved.[1] It is not, indeed, a work of any special merit, consisting, as it does, chiefly of fanciful views about the shape of the globe. With a condemnation of the notions of Ptolemy, and of other "speculative" geographers, it contains, however, much curious and reliable information with reference to the countries he had himself visited, and especially, to the western coast of the Indian peninsula. Indeed, from the
A.D. 150. time of the merchant Arrian to that of Marco Polo, Cosmas, who traded on the coast of Malabar about
A.D. 1271-95. the middle of the sixth century, is the only writer of note who gives any account of the maritime and commercial affairs of India, during a period of twelve centuries.

[1] This treatise of Cosmas exists in Montfaucon: Bibl. Nov. Patrum. ii. p. 336.

State of the trade of India, from the sixth to the ninth century.

From Cosmas we learn that, in his day, great numbers of vessels from all parts of India, Persia, and Æthiopia, were in the habit of trading with Ceylon; and that the island itself had "numerous fleets of ships belonging to its own merchants." He reckons the tonnage of these vessels "as generally of about three thousand amphoræ";[1] adding that "their mariners do not make astronomical observations, but carry birds to sea, and letting them go, from time to time, follow the course they take for the land." Cosmas further remarks, that "they devote only four months in the year to the pursuits of navigation, and are particularly careful not to trust themselves on the sea during the next hundred days after the summer solstice, for within those seas it is, at that time, the middle of winter." But the "numerous fleets of ships" he refers to were, probably, the property of Arabian merchants settled in the island, navigated by their own countrymen, and not by the natives of Ceylon. The Singhalese, indeed, in ancient and modern times alike, have shown an apathy in all matters connected with navigation, the more remarkable as, by its position and the character of its coasts, Ceylon is singularly well adapted to be the nursery of an able race of seamen. The boats now found there are all copies from models supplied by other nations; even their strange canoes, with out-riggers and a balance log, are but repetitions of the boats of the islanders of the Eastern Archipelago; while their *ballams*, canoes of a larger and more substantial description, are borrowed from the vessels of Malabar. It is curious that, to this day, the gunwales of their dhows are frequently topped by wicker-work, smeared with

[1] One thousand amphoræ are equal to about thirty-three tons.

clay to protect the deck from the wash of the sea, much after the fashion of the bulwarks of the mythical craft of Ulysses.

It is remarkable also that in the enumeration of the exports of the island of Ceylon given by Arrian, no mention whatever is made of cinnamon. Nor does Cosmas refer to it. "I have searched," says Sir Emerson Tennent, in his work on Ceylon, "among the records of the Greeks and Romans from the earliest time, until the period when the commerce of the East had reached its climax in the hands of the Persians and Arabians: the survey extends over fifteen centuries, during which Ceylon and its productions were familiarly known to the traders of all countries, and yet in the pages of no author, European or Asiatic, from the earliest ages to the close of the thirteenth century, is there the remotest allusion to cinnamon as an indigenous production, or even as an article of commerce, in Ceylon. I may add, that I have been equally unsuccessful in finding any allusions to it in any Chinese work of ancient date."[1] This is, in fact, but another, though a striking instance, of the secrecy with which the ancients conducted the more valuable portions of their trade, and fully confirms the notice of the cinnamon trade of Herodotus, who could only have obtained his information about it from the merchants[2] or mariners who traded along the shores of Malabar or of Æthiopia to the south of Zanzibar. He speaks of it as so mysterious in its growth, and so difficult to obtain, that the most exorbitant prices were given for it in the markets of Europe; adding that, though in great demand in Tyre, Carthage, Miletus, and Alexandria, the merchants

[1] Tennent's "Ceylon," vol i. p. 575.

[2] Herod. iii. 111.

kept the secret of its *provenance* as the Carthaginians kept that of British tin.

The trade which the Romans "opened" with India by the way of the Red Sea, was conducted by them with success for more than five centuries; but we learn from Cosmas that, but a short time before his travels, they had met with a new and powerful rival in the Sassanian rulers of Persia, who, having overthrown the Parthians, and restored the ancient faith and monarchy of Persia, made early and vigorous efforts to acquire a share in the lucrative commerce of India. Following in the course of the early Phœnicians, the Persians with their ships commenced anew this eastern trade with India, and, in return for the productions of their own country, received the precious commodities of Hindustan, conveying them up the Persian Gulf, and, by means of the rivers Euphrates and Tigris, distributing them through every province of their empire. Rome being then in its decline, a powerful rival, such as Persia, could hardly fail to injure, if not to entirely destroy, the commerce the merchants of Alexandria had for ages nurtured with so much care. Moreover, the voyage from Persia to India, being much shorter, and attended with fewer dangers, led to an increase of the intercourse between the two countries, which the Greek merchants of Alexandria vainly attempted to resist. Even then, if Cosmas be trustworthy, few Europeans visited the eastern part of India, but were content to receive thence its silk, spices, and other valuable productions, either by caravans or the agency of native vessels.

Change in the course of trade.

Persian trade with India.

About this period, China carried on the most prosperous trade of any of the nations of the East, both by land and sea. Her caravans passed through Asia and Tatary, and her merchants conducted an extensive business with the provinces bordering on the Caspian, and in some cases with the more distant nations to the west and the north. Four hundred Chinese vessels are said to have been seen in the port of Ormuz, at the entrance of the Persian Gulf, and China is stated to have then received ambassadors from all the countries of Asia, as well as from Constantinople, and the Khalif of Baghdad, thus holding a direct intercourse with the whole civilized world. The vessels of China, however, had ceased to repair to the Persian Gulf long before the Portuguese made their appearance in Calicut; but from the time of Cosmas to that of Marco Polo they appear to have shared with the Arabians and Persians the carrying trade of the East, and to have even extended their voyages to the remote island of Madagascar.

The Muhammedans, A.D. 622.

Within a hundred years after the death of Justinian, an event happened, which occasioned a revolution still more considerable in the intercourse of Europe with the East. A prophet and a conqueror arose in Arabia; and within forty years of his death a great part of Asia, and Africa, with no inconsiderable portion of Europe, had been subdued, and the dominion of the followers of Muhammed extended from the shores of the Atlantic to the frontier of China, with a rapidity of success to which there is nothing similar in the history of mankind. "Egypt," remarks Dr. Robertson, "was one of their earliest conquests; and, as they settled in that inviting country, and kept possession of it, the Greeks were excluded from all intercourse with Alexandria, to which they had long resorted as the chief mart of Indian goods. Nor was this the only effect which the progress of the Muhammedan arms had upon the commerce of Europe with India. Prior to the invasion of Egypt, the Arabians had subdued the great kingdom of Persia, and added it to the empire of the Khalifs."[1]

Finding their new subjects engaged in the trade with India, and sensible of the vast advantages to be derived from it, the Muhammedan rulers turned their attention to it with even greater vigour than ever the Persians had done; and pursuing the same course they had followed, their enterprising merchants soon advanced far beyond the boundaries of ancient navigation as known to the nations of the West, bringing many of the most precious commodities of the East directly from the countries in which they were produced. Having founded the city of Bussorah on the western banks of the great stream formed by the junction of the Euphrates and Tigris, they thus secured the command of these two rivers, so that this entrepôt soon became the seat of a maritime commerce second only to Alexandria in its greatest prosperity. Although their knowledge of navigation scarcely exceeded that which the Phœnicians possessed when they launched their expeditions from Gerrha some two thousand years before, the followers of Muhammed had extended, as early as the ninth century, their voyages beyond the Gulf of Siam, carrying on with Sumatra, and other islands of the Indian Archipelago, a regular commerce, and extending their trading operations even to the city of Canton. At many of the intervening ports numerous Arabian merchants and ship-owners settled with their families, so that the Arabian language was understood, and

The extent of their commerce with the East.

[1] History of India, s. iii. p. 99.

spoken at most places of any importance between the mouths of the Euphrates and Tigris, and Canton.[1]

The Muhammedans were, however, not without rivals in this lucrative trade, as the Chinese themselves, who, seemingly, were much more enterprising then as navigators than they are now, no longer limited their communications with the traders of the West to the Island of Ceylon; but, rounding Cape Comorin, traded directly with the ports of Malabar and of the Persian Gulf, sometimes proceeding as far as the Euphrates, but more frequently terminating their voyage at Siraf, near to the mouth of that gulf. While these Eastern nations were thus extending their operations, the people of Europe found themselves excluded almost entirely from any intercourse with either India or China. The great port of Alexandria was under the control of the Muhammedans, and they, and the Christian subjects of the Khalifs, had, in their own extensive dominions, sufficient demand for all the Indian commodities they could import. Consequently the trading towns of the Mediterranean were obliged to seek fresh, or rather to re-open old, routes to the East, to obtain their supplies. Nor was this a task easy of accomplishment; and the difficulties surmounted in accomplishing it furnish a proof that the luxuries of the East were then in as great demand as they had ever been in ancient times.

The trade between Constantinople, and India and China.

Indeed the fabulous prices obtained for silk and various other articles of Indian produce enabled the trader to overcome any difficulty. Starting from the banks of the Indus, he found his way by one of

[1] The Malay and many local dialects are still chiefly written in Arabic characters.

the early routes, already described, to the river Oxus, or directly to the Caspian, and thence to Constantinople, which became, even more than it had hitherto been, the great centre of European commerce. The intercourse between Constantinople and China was much more difficult and dangerous; as in this case the trader had to proceed to the western provinces of the Chinese empire, and, having purchased his silk, to convey it by caravans, for an average of ninety days, to the banks of the Oxus, and along that stream to the Caspian; thence he followed the course of the river Cyrus, as far it was navigable, and, after a five days' march overland, found his way to the Euxine, by the river Phasis.[1]

Such were the different means of conducting the commercial intercourse between Europe and the East in ancient times, and such they practically continued, amid various minor changes and through many wars and vicissitudes, up to the period when Vasco de Gama discovered the new and better way to India by doubling the Cape of Good Hope. We shall hereafter glance at the maritime commerce of India from the ninth century up to the time when the Portuguese landed on its shores, with some notices of the celebrated travels of Marco Polo, of the expulsion of the Arabians from its trade, and of the decline of the vast influence so long exercised by the Moors; but in the meantime we must endeavour to trace the maritime commerce of Rome, and especially of the Italian Republics, which afterwards exercised more influence in commercial affairs than the "mistress of the world" had done during her most prosperous days.

[1] Robertson's "History of India," p. 106.

CHAPTER VI.

Rome—The repugnance of the Romans to seafaring pursuits—Single-banked galleys of the Liburni—The fleets of Rome—Their creation and slow progress—The form and construction of their galleys—War with the pirates of Cilicia—First treaty with Carthage, B.C. 509—Its purport—College of merchants, established B.C. 494—No senator allowed to own ships, B.C. 226—Cicero's opinion of merchants—Contempt for mariners—Reduction of Egypt, B.C. 30, and trade with India—Customs' duties—The excise—Bounties on the importation of corn, A.D. 14—System of collecting the taxes—Value of the trade with Alexandria—Its extent—Vessels of Spain—Pharos or light-house at Gessoriacum—The shipping described by Tacitus—Rhodians—Their maritime laws—System of accounts in use at Rome—The corn trade of the city—Port of Ostia.

Rome.

IN a previous chapter an outline has been given of the commerce and navigation of the Carthaginians in succession to that of the Phœnicians. A rapid glance will now be taken of the shipping and progress of the maritime commerce of the great nation that destroyed Carthage, and, by the valour of its arms and the vigour of its political system, rather than by its genius and industry, extended its dominions over the whole of Italy, Syria, Egypt, and Western Asia, ultimately reducing to the condition of provinces all the habitable portions of Europe.

Great as soldiers, the citizens of Rome had, however, a repugnance to maritime affairs. "Their ambition," remarks Gibbon,[1] in his history of their

[1] Gibbon, c. 1. Horat. Od. i. 3. Tacit. Germ. c. 34.

decline and fall, "was confined to the land; nor was that warlike people ever actuated by the enterprising spirit which had prompted the navigators of Tyre, of Carthage, and even of Marseilles, to enlarge the bounds of the world, and to explore the most remote coasts of the ocean. To the Romans the ocean remained an object of terror rather than of curiosity."

The repugnance of the Romans to sea-faring pursuits.

Unlike the Phœnicians and Carthaginians, the Romans had no inclination to expeditions of mere discovery, and never cared to become acquainted with any country whose remote situation appeared to defy their arms. Vain of their own power and of the extent of their dominions, they did not hesitate, in almost every instance, to bestow the name of barbarians on the civilized inhabitants of India as well as on those of other parts of the world, whose manners or customs were indistinctly known to them. Despising commercial pursuits, they looked to Greece and other nations to regulate their over-sea trade and to supply their wants; and when their fleets obtained the dominion of the sea, their object was less to protect their rapidly extending maritime commerce than to consolidate and preserve their power and dominion upon the land. In the reign of Augustus the plan of fixed naval stations was, for the first time, adopted; two being appointed, one at Ravenna to command the eastern, the other at Misenum to command the western division of the Mediterranean. By this time the Romans had learned from experience that galleys of more than three banks of oars were unsuited for real service, and consequently their more important fleets, from the reign of Augustus, consisted almost exclusively of the light and swift vessels

Single-banked galleys of the Liburni.

known as Liburnians, from the people who were the first to build them.

Single-banked galleys of the Liburni.

Occupying a district a little north of the present Dalmatia, and devoting their attention almost exclusively to sea-faring pursuits, the Liburnians[1] had obtained a great reputation for their knowledge of the art of navigation. Provided with excellent harbours, and holding in their grasp many of the small islands of the Adriatic, which afforded them shelter from storms and a convenient rendezvous for their swift craft, they unfortunately made but little distinction between the duties of the honest trader and the predatory habits of the buccaneer: but to them Octavianus was mainly indebted for his victory over Antony at Actium, and Rome itself for the introduction of a better and swifter type of war-vessel.[2]

The fleets of Rome.

Although Ravenna and Misenum were the principal stations of their navy, the Romans had fleets at various other places. Forty ships and three thousand soldiers then guarded the waters of the Euxine; a very considerable force was stationed at Frejus (Forum-Julii); numbers of Roman vessels cruised in the English Channel to preserve the communication between Gaul and Britain; while, throughout the whole period of her supremacy, a strong force was maintained on the Danube and Rhine to protect the empire from the inroads of the Northern barbarians. But these fleets were the slow growth of centuries; and the navies of Rome were for a long time of comparatively little note, and obtained celebrity only when the first Punic war roused her citizens to ex-

[1] Livy, x. 2; xliii. 48. Cæs. Bell. Gall. iii. 5. Horat. Epod. i. 1.

[2] Plut. Vit. Anton. c. 66.

traordinary exertions to deprive Carthage of its maritime supremacy.[1] Roman fleets were then constructed and spread over the Mediterranean with such rapidity that the Carthaginians would not credit the reports of their number and equipment. In their construction they displayed the energy they had ever shown when they had once determined on their plan. Skilled artisans, from friendly or subjected states, were ready to execute their orders, and the banks of the Tiber resounded with the noise of the axe, the adze, the hammer, and the mallet. Nor is there any reason to suppose that the first fleet Rome sent forth to oppose the powerful squadrons of the Carthaginians was so much inferior to the galleys of Augustus as has been supposed by some writers.[2] But the real character of the Roman vessels cannot now be ascertained; as no Roman historian has thought it worth his while, probably from ignorance on such matters, to give details from which they could, even in imagination, be constructed.

Their creation and slow progress.

The form and construction of their galleys.

It is, however, reasonable to suppose that they

[1] The first Roman ships were probably little better than the boats used on the Tiber, called from their thick coarse planks *Naves Caudicariæ*—whence Appius Claudius, A.U.C. 489, B.C. 264, who first induced his people to fit out a fleet, obtained the name of Caudex (Senec. de Brev. Vit. 13. Varro de Vit. Rom. 11). According to Polybius a stranded Carthaginian ship was their first good model (i. 20, 21), though this is hard to reconcile with Livy, ix. 30, 38. Possibly their first ship of war was copied from one of Antium (Livy, viii. 14). The treaties with Carthage long before the Punic wars prove that the Romans had a fleet even then—though, probably, of a very inferior kind.

[2] Instances occur in which fleets were fitted out with great rapidity—green wood being necessarily used. Thus Scipio fitted out a large fleet within forty-five days after the timber had been felled (Liv. xxxiii. 45), and Julius Cæsar in thirty days, at Arles, against the people of Marseilles (Cæs. B. Civ. i. 34).

were much the same as the ships of the Greeks and Carthaginians, or of the merchant vessel, already described, in which St. Paul made his celebrated voyage, and that their form and dimensions were regulated by the services they were expected to perform. In a note we subjoin a list of the number of fleets the Romans are known to have had in the brief space of twenty years, as they will give a better idea than anything else of the vigour of their administration, and of the energy wherewith, in the best days of the republic, they surmounted disasters which would have crushed to the ground a less self-reliant people.[1]

But so far as commerce is concerned, it was only when they had brought the third Punic war to an end, and had destroyed the great trading cities of Carthage and Corinth,[2] that the Romans really began to devote their abilities to commercial pursuits, and recognize in the site of one of them (Corinth), a great centre of trade for Asia, Western Greece,

[1] 1. At the commencement of the first Punic war a fleet was hastily built and, under the command of C. Duilius, destroyed that of the Carthaginians, B.C. 260.

2. A second fleet was prepared, and a great victory was won over the Carthaginians near Agrigentum, B.C. 256.

3. A third fleet was fitted out in B.C. 250, and nearly destroyed off Drepana, in the next year.

4. About the same time a fourth fleet, conveying stores to the army besieging Lilybæum, was entirely destroyed, together with the store ships, by a hurricane off Camarina.

5. A fifth fleet was built, B.C. 241, to relieve Lilybæum, which had now been besieged for eight years.

This fleet, under C. Lutatius Catulus, defeated the Carthaginians, and put an end to the first Punic war in B.C. 241.

During the second and third Punic wars no fleets were employed, except as transports.

[2] Carthage fell in B.C. 146, Corinth in B.C. 141.

and Italy. Hence it was that, when the Corinthian people joined the Achæan League, for the preservation of the independence of Greece, the Romans found an excuse for the capture, though not for the plunder and destruction of Corinth.

War with the pirates of Cilicia.

By the burning of these two great towns, instigated as these acts doubtless were, in no small degree, by a lust for plunder, the Romans not merely lost, for a time, the advantages they might have derived from a continuation of the trade hitherto successfully conducted by the Carthaginian and Corinthian merchants and shipowners, but drove those of the latter class, who had saved their property, and who had no other means of subsistence, to join Mithradates, and to convert their ships, as circumstances allowed or encouraged, into ships of war, privateers, or pirates. Persons of rank and capital then embarked to an extent previously unknown in marauding expeditions, with the object either of personal gain, or of the destruction of the maritime commerce of Rome. The organization of this confederacy was of the most formidable character. They erected forts, watch-towers, arsenals, and magazines; and from Cilicia, their citadel in chief, their squadrons swept the seas. Hence their historical name of the Cilician pirates. Every merchant ship that ventured forth became either their prize or their prey. Commerce was seriously interrupted; and the citizens of Rome lost their usual supplies of corn. The piratical ships increased in numbers and in daring; they infested the coasts of Italy, plundered the temples, and even ascended the Tiber in search of spoil. At length Pompey put an end to their power, by a brilliant victory at

B.C. 67. Coracesium, and in a campaign of only forty days' duration.[1]

Having cleared the seas of the ships of this confederacy, the merchants of Rome were free to carry on with more prospect of success the leading branches of a commerce which had for centuries yielded large profits to the merchants of Corinth and of Carthage. Hitherto commerce had been held an ignoble occupation for Roman citizens, nor were there apparently any facilities for its encouragement, or any advantages sought in their commercial intercourse with strangers. Indeed, in their first treaty with the Carthaginians, the earliest record of any commercial treaty, the Romans were satisfied with conditions which restricted any extension of such maritime trade as they then possessed. "Let there be friendship," says the treaty, "between us and the Romans, together with their allies, on the following terms and conditions. Let not the Romans nor their allies navigate beyond the Fair Promontory. If they be driven by storm or chased by enemies beyond it—*i.e.*, westward of it—let them not buy or receive anything but what is necessary for repairing their vessels, and for sacrifice; and let them take their departure within five days of the time of their landing. Whatever merchant or ship-owner may arrive on the business of merchandise let him pay no duty, except the fee of the broker and the clerk. Let the public faith be security for the seller, for whatever is sold in the presence of these officers—that is to say, whatever is sold in Africa or Sardinia. If any Romans arrive at that part of Sicily which is subject to Carthage,

First treaty with Carthage, B. C. 509.

[1] Details of Pompey's triumph for this cause are given in Pliny (vii. 98.)

let them have impartial justice. Let not the Carthaginians do any injury to the people of Ardea, Antium, Laurentium, Cercii, Tarracina, nor to any of the Latins who shall be subject to Rome. Let them not attack the free towns of the Latins. If they shall take any of them, let them deliver it up to the Romans free of any damage. Let them build no fort in the land of the Latins. If they make a hostile landing in the country, let them not remain all night in it."[1]

Its purport.

This convention gives a higher idea of the relative power of Rome at that early period, than is to be gathered from the annalists. It is clear that even then she must have had a naval force of some importance, while the Latins are distinctly called the "subjects" of Rome. It further shows very clearly how trade was then conducted. The prohibition of sailing beyond the Fair Promontory was no doubt inserted, lest, by directing their attention to maritime commerce, the Romans should deprive the Carthaginians of a portion of their valuable trade with Spain. Probably with the same view an interdiction was also placed against the Romans trading with the fertile coasts of Africa, in the vicinity of the Lesser Syrtis, showing that an occasional merchant vessel must, even at that early period, have ventured as far. But the Carthaginians were obviously at that time strong enough to dictate, to a considerable extent, their own terms, and the Romans too weak to resent this dictation.

College of merchants established, B.C. 494.

It seems likely that this treaty induced the Romans to pay more attention to commercial pursuits than they had previously done, for Livy[2] states that within

[1] Polybius, iii. 22. [2] Livy, ii. 27.

a few years of its execution, a college of merchants, the precise nature of which is not known, was established at Rome; centuries, however, elapsed before the State afforded any real encouragement to commercial intercourse with other countries. Indeed, as far as can now be ascertained, the supply of corn for the capital formed the chief and for ages almost the only article of commerce worthy of senatorial notice, as any scarcity in the supply of that necessary article invariably produced tumults among the people.[1] But it was only when their increasing wants obliged them to direct attention to foreign trade, that the law so far encouraged ship-building, as to exempt from municipal taxation those vessels employed in the importation of corn. Every other trade with foreign countries was restricted to a certain class of the citizens, who, with constitutional jealousy, restrained the senators from embarking in what was likely to prove highly remunerative. Quintus Claudius, a tribune of the people, proposed a law, and carried it against the Senate, Caius Flaminius alone assisting him, that no senator or the father of a senator should be proprietor of a sea-going ship of a greater capacity than three hundred amphoræ.[2] A vessel of this very limited size might be large enough to carry the produce of their own lands to market; but, in the opinion of the citizens no Roman senator ought to take part in general mercantile operations which might lead him, perhaps, to neglect his duties to the State.

No senator allowed to own ships, B.C. 226.

[1] "As long as the corn-fleets arrived duly from Sicily and Africa, the populace cared little whether the victory was gained by Octavian or his generals."—Liddell's "Hist. of Rome," p. 628.

[2] Livy, xxi. 63.

Nor were any relaxations made in these laws during the most flourishing periods of the empire. On the contrary, as was the case during many previous centuries, noblemen, persons filling exalted offices, and great capitalists, were forbidden the exercise of any trade whatever, lest they should by such means become suddenly rich, and thus draw down upon them the envy of the people.

The emperors Honorius and Theodosius, in consolidating these laws, state that "as trade might be carried on with greater ease among men of base extraction, the respect due to persons of quality renders it necessary to deprive them of the full liberty of trading." And Cicero observes, that "Trade is mean if it has only a small profit for its object: but it is otherwise if it has large dealings, bringing many sorts of merchandise from foreign parts, and distributing them to the public without deceit; and if, after a reasonable profit, such merchants are contented with the riches they have acquired, and purchasing land with them retire into the country and apply themselves to agriculture, I cannot," says the great orator, in quite a vein of aristocratical condescension, "perceive wherein is the dishonour of that function."[1]

Cicero's opinion of merchants.

From the whole tenor of this legislation it is easy to understand why persons engaged in seafaring pursuits were so long despised; and that the strongest measures were necessary to secure for them even ordinary justice. Naturally, however, when, on the destruction of Corinth and Carthage, a more extended trade arose, the prejudice against mariners somewhat abated, though among the nobility and great land-

Contempt for mariners.

[1] Cicer. De Offic. i. c. 151.

owners of Rome, a lasting aversion prevailed against seafaring men. In the time of Cicero, the advantages of foreign commerce were only beginning to be felt at Rome, for previously her traders had been simply retailers of corn and provisions. But when the empire of the seas fell indisputably into the hands of the Romans, there arose merchants and large owners of sea-going ships, who in their operations with distant countries realised colossal fortunes, and were thus deemed by Cicero and his class worthy of being distinguished from the mere retailers; and thus, too, in Rome, as has befallen elsewhere, wealth at length supplied the place of birth and genius, Roman merchants entering at last into friendly relations with even its proudest landowners and citizens, and Rome itself becoming the depôt for numberless articles produced abroad. "The most remote countries of the ancient world," remarks Gibbon, "were ransacked, to supply the pomp and delicacy of Rome. The forests of Scythia afforded some valuable furs. Amber was brought overland from the shores of the Baltic to the Danube, and the barbarians were astonished at the price which they received in exchange for so useless a commodity. There was a considerable demand for Babylonian carpets, and other manufactures of the East; but the most important and unpopular branch of trade was carried on with Arabia and India."[1]

Reduction of Egypt, B.C. 30, and trade with India.

No event, however, proved more advantageous to her merchants than the reduction of Egypt to a Roman province, which was finally effected by Octavianus after the battle of Actium. The Romans thus not merely recovered the regular supply

[1] Gibbon, c. 2.

of corn they always so much needed, but obtained a monopoly of nearly all the trade between India and Europe. Though affording a vast source of wealth to those engaged in it, the trade with India was unpopular with the bulk of the Roman people, who saw a few individuals enriched by its incredible profits, while the country was drained of specie to pay for every conceivable article of luxury. The raw materials which alone could afford remunerative employment to the Roman manufacturers were too costly in their transit to constitute, as they do now, the chief articles of import; and the natives of India and of Arabia were so well satisfied with the productions and manufactures of their own territories, that silver was almost the only article they would receive in exchange from the Romans. Pliny computed the annual loss arising from these exchanges at eight hundred thousand pounds sterling;[1] and Gibbon has noticed that a pound of silk was at one period esteemed of the same value as a pound of gold.[2]

But though it is a mistake to suppose that in the ordinary course of commerce, the export of the precious metals entails a loss when exchanged for produce and manufactures, Pliny had some reason to dread the results, while the industrious citizens had ample cause for complaint when they saw the whole wealth of the empire exchanged for pearls, precious stones, or costly aromatics required only for the funeral pageants of a few wealthy citizens. Nor is it hard to understand the accumulation of great riches about this period at Rome, when we reflect on the number of valuable provinces over which its rulers

[1] Pliny, H. N. xii. 84.

[2] Gibbon, c. 2.

had the power of almost unlimited taxation. Gibbon estimates the income of these provinces during the reign of Augustus at from fifteen to twenty millions of our money.[1] Customs, too, were introduced during this period, and were followed by a regulated scheme of excise, whereby both the real and the personal property of the Roman citizens were made subject to a system of taxation from which they had been exempt for more than a century and a half.

Customs' duties.

But in great empires, such as Rome, the natural balance of money soon establishes itself. The wealth at first attracted to the capital, as the chief place of abode for the aristocracy, by degrees finds its way to the industrial people in the provinces, to be employed in the development of arts and manufactures, and is thus spread throughout the whole kingdom, to find its way back to the capital, through the medium of those who, having by commerce or otherwise accumulated a superabundance, resort thither to spend it. In the reign of Augustus and of his successors, the duties also imposed on every kind of merchandise found their way through numerous channels to Rome, the great centre of opulence and luxury, so that, in whatever manner the law was expressed, the Roman purchaser, rather than the provincial merchant, paid the tax. A higher duty was imposed on articles of luxury than on those of necessity, varying from an eighth to the fortieth part of the value of the commodity; and the productions raised or manufactured by the labour of the people were wisely treated with more indulgence than was shown to the luxurious products of India and Arabia.[2] "There is

[1] Gibbon, vol. i. c. 6.

[2] Pliny, vi. 101; xii. 84.

still extant," remarks Gibbon,[1] "a long but imperfect catalogue of Eastern commodities which, about the time of Alexander Severus, were subject to the payment of duties: cinnamon, myrrh, pepper, ginger, and the whole tribe of aromatics, a great variety of precious stones, among which the diamond was the most remarkable for its price, and the emerald for its beauty; Parthian and Babylonian leather, ebony, ivory, and eunuchs; and we may observe," adds this great historian, "that the value of these effeminate slaves gradually rose with the decline of the empire." A.D. 222.

The excise.

Although the excise seldom exceeded one per cent. *ad valorem*, it embraced whatever was sold by private contract, or in the markets by public auction, from the largest purchase of lands and houses, to those minute objects which have a value only from their infinite number and daily consumption. Against taxes of this description there were, as there have ever been in all countries, loud complaints on the part of the people; but when the emperor endeavoured to substitute for these obnoxious and vexatious imposts a new tax of five per cent. on all legacies and inheritances, the nobles of Rome, who were more tenacious of their property than of their freedom, were, in spite of their indignant murmurs, compelled to acquiesce in the imposition of a land tax.[2]

The annual tributes, customs, and direct taxation of the provinces, tended still further to produce the balance of values. The farmers were paid with their own money. The Romans laid not only heavy duties upon the natural products of every country subject to their sway, but also an export duty on produce

[1] Gibbon, c. 6.

[2] Dion, lv. and lvi.

sent away, as well as an import duty on any article brought in for the consumption of the provinces. A transit duty was even levied on goods and produce of British origin during their passage through the Roman province of Gaul. At the other extremity of the empire, on the coasts of the Arabian Gulf, the same system of fixed taxation was enforced; but the high prices we have named as prevailing at Rome for foreign goods of all kinds, especially those of India, Arabia, and Babylonia, rendered this taxation comparatively light. The *Portorium*[1] or tax on produce or manufactures brought by sea, resembled greatly the custom duties levied at the ports of Great Britain during the present century; they were exacted by officers of the public revenue, at harbours, rivers, and sometimes also at the passages of bridges. On the other hand, besides the relief from municipal taxation, an adequate and regular supply of corn was deemed so essential that shipowners were offered liberal bounties to bring it from abroad. In the reign of Tiberius, it is stated by Tacitus,[2] that, as the people murmured at the oppressive price of grain, the emperor settled its price to the buyer, and undertook to pay two sesterces a measure to the corn-dealers and importers. More than this, the Emperor Claudius, unlike the rulers of some of the nations of our own time, whose systems are too often prohibitory of the importation of the staple article of food for the people, urged the ship-

Bounties on the importation of corn, A.D. 14.

A.D. 41.

[1] *Portoria* existed from early times; were abolished by Metellus Nepos, A.U.C. 694, and were restored by Augustus. The senate under Nero declared that such taxes were absolutely necessary.—Tacit. Ann. xiii. 50. Cicero, in Pison. c. 36.

[2] Tacitus, b. ii. c. 87.

owners to make voyages during the winter, when they usually laid up their vessels, and besides confirming to them the allowances sanctioned by Tiberius, with relief from municipal taxation, took on himself all losses, at the same time securing the importers a certain rate of profit.

Of the several impositions introduced by Augustus the five per cent. on legacies and inheritances was the most fruitful as well as the most comprehensive. Farmed like nearly all other taxes (for in every age the best and wisest of the Roman governors adhered to this pernicious method of collecting the principal customs), the burden was increased by the insolence and cupidity of the collectors; hence, when two centuries afterwards Caracalla doubled the already heavy impost, this act of oppression nearly cost him his throne and his life.[1] Yet, in spite of the extravagant luxury of the wealthier classes, the enormous value of the imperial commerce, together with the extent and wealth of the provinces, enabled the government to maintain for a long time an expenditure which, under other circumstances, could not have been endured; and much, indeed, of this wealth was really due to the possession of Egypt, apart altogether from the large commercial profits derived from Alexandria. Besides corn, Egypt supplied the imperial city with flax and linen of various qualities, cotton goods, costly ointments, marble, alabaster, fine alum, salt, gums, and the papyrus, from which paper was manufactured at Rome. Three hundred thousand

System of collecting the taxes.

A.D. 211.

Value of the trade with Alexandria.

[1] Gibbon, c. vi., has relied on a passage in Dion., lxxvii., which the best commentators doubt. The edict seems to have been made by M. Antoninus, and was perhaps fathered on Caracalla from his general unpopularity.

of the million inhabitants of Alexandria consisted of Roman citizens, but its merchants and ship-owners were chiefly emigrants from Greece or of Grecian origin.

Although the value of the trade with Egypt, which comprised the chief portion of that with India and Arabia, was in itself greater than any other, it fell far short of supplying the numerous wants of Rome. Caravans traversed, as they had done centuries before that city became mistress of the world, the whole latitude of Asia in two hundred and forty-three days,[1] from the Chinese ocean to the sea coast of Syria, to supply her with the silk her rich citizens were always eager to obtain. Nor could Egypt alone supply her demands even for corn and cattle. That fertile country, which stretches from the southern foot of the Alps to the shores of the Mediterranean, grew large quantities of corn for Rome, and reared numerous cattle for her market, while from Northern Italy she drew her supplies of salt provisions for the use of her troops and mariners. The Sabine country also furnished wheat, rice, and barley; and thence large quantities of wine were imported, as well as from Corsica, Sardinia, and Sicily. Timber, suitable for ship-building purposes, was extensively imported from Etruria. Genoa exported largely, for the use of the Romans, wood for furniture, coarse wool for the clothing of their slaves, hides, and honey.

Its extent.

There was likewise a very considerable trade between Malta and the Tiber in white cloths of wool

[1] Gibbon, c. xl. Procop. Persic. i. 20. Cf. Isidore of Charax in Stathm. Parth., who gives the stations in the Persian empire, and Amm. Marcell. lib. xxiii., who enumerates the provinces.

and linen. Greece, and the Greek islands, Samos, Cos, and Thrace, furnished green marble, dyes, cambrics, and earthenwares; and from the Euxine were imported wax, hemp, and pitch, and wool of the finest quality; while the ancient trade with Persia, through Trebizond, remained unbroken during the Roman supremacy, greatly increasing when Constantinople became the eastern capital of the empire. Phrygia produced alabaster; Miletus woollen goods, and Tyrian purple; and Sidon and Tyre, glass manufactures and rich work in embroidery. From Africa proper the Romans imported very considerable quantities of corn, drugs, and horses, together with the wild elephants and lions required for their gladiatorial exhibitions.[1]

Next to Egypt, Spain was the largest seat of their foreign trade. Its products of lead, iron, copper, silver, and gold, were sources of vast wealth; and the corn, wool, wine, oil, honey, wax, pitch, dyes, and salted provisions of a superior quality afforded a large and lucrative commerce to the merchants, ship-owners, and manufacturers of Rome. Indeed, so extensive were the commercial transactions carried on in the Spanish Peninsula, that nearly as many ships were employed in its trade as in that with the whole of Africa. Nor need we doubt that the vessels so occupied were as large as those engaged in the Egyptian trade already noticed. New Carthage (Cartagena), Saguntum, Tarragona, and Bilbilis (Bilboa), even then famous for its steel, had a large commercial intercourse with Rome, in provisions, cordage, and linens of

Trade with Spain.

[1] The Roman laws went further than the game laws of England, as an African was not permitted to kill a lion, even in his own defence.

remarkable whiteness and texture. The province of Gaul formed a rich appendix to the Roman empire, though the only ports directly connected with the Tiber were Massalia (Marseilles), Arelate (Arles), and Narbo[1] (Narbonne), at that period the most frequented and most populous city in Gaul. Narbonne has since suffered the same fate as Ostia, the silting up of its port having entirely destroyed its value.

The chief exports of Gaul appear to have been gold, silver, and iron from its own mines; linens from every part of the country; corn and cheese of superior quality; with excellent salt pork, and tartan cloths. Burdigala (Bordeaux,) on the Garonne, was its chief port on the west, and on the north the Portus Itius (by some supposed to be Wissant, near Cape Grisnez, but more probably Boulogne). At this port, called afterwards Gessoriacum,[2] and whence Cæsar sailed for Britain, was the lighthouse constructed by Caligula, some remains of which are said to have existed in the early part of the seventeenth century. This tower, or Pharos, the first lighthouse on record for any part of the coasts of the North Sea or English Channel, stood upon the promontory or cliff which commanded the port. Of an octagonal, form (if Bucherius is right in supposing the building he has drawn to be the remains of Caligula's structure), it was twenty-five feet in breadth, and the circumference of the whole at the base two hundred feet. It had twelve storeys or spaces for galleries, rising above each other. Each storey diminished in diameter as you ascended, and on the top of the tower

Pharos, or lighthouse at Gessoriacum.

[1] Pliny, iii. 31.

[2] Sueton. Calig. c. xlv. Mela. iii. 2. Sueton. Claud. c. xvii. Eginhardt says that Charlemagne repaired this tower (Vit. Car. Magn.).

a fire was kindled every evening at sunset, and served as the beacon light for the guidance of mariners.

Tacitus[1] has preserved a description of the expedition of Germanicus, but his "Annals" throw little light upon the state of that portion of the Roman navy which assisted in the conquest of Germany, and frequented the northern seas about the period when the first lighthouse was erected in the English Channel. Indeed his description very imperfectly represents either the vessels or seamen of those maritime nations, who, becoming subject to Rome, largely aided her alike in her naval and in her commercial victories. Of these none have left a more lasting record of their existence as a maritime people than the Rhodians. Alike celebrated for their skill as navigators, and their honesty and shrewdness as merchants, they excelled all others as jurists. Their laws relating to navigation were introduced into the Roman code, and formed the groundwork of maritime jurisprudence throughout the civilized world. Colonized, no doubt, by some of the more civilized nations of Western Asia, and probably by the Phœnicians, the Rhodians from their position, in a small island and on the great highway of commerce, as well as from their skill in astronomy and in navigation, soon took a prominent part among nations more populous and powerful than themselves. Accessible to all the surrounding naval powers, and deriving their chief commercial wealth from their trade with Egypt, the Rhodians from the first made it their business

The shipping described by Tacitus.

Rhodians.

[1] Tacit. Annal. ii. 6. They were mostly broad flat-bottomed boats, with rudders at each end.

to keep the police of the surrounding seas; and having punished the pirates who then infested the Mediterranean with exemplary severity, pursued their trade as merchant navigators with equal security and success.

During the great struggle between Ptolemy and Antigonus, the Rhodians naturally sided with the former; and hence were compelled to undergo one of the most celebrated sieges of antiquity, by Demetrius Poliorcetes the son of Antigonus: their resistance, however, was so remarkable that, on raising the siege, B.C. 304, Demetrius, out of respect for their prowess, is said to have presented them with the engines he had employed against them during the siege. The value of these engines was so great as to enable the islanders to erect the colossal statue of Apollo[1] (the work of Chares of Lindus, who was engaged on it for twelve years), which is known in history as one of the Seven Wonders of the world. Placed, according to the usual (though probably fabulous) story, with extended legs on the two moles forming the entrance of the smaller harbour, and in height seventy cubits, all vessels entering and leaving passed under it. But this memorable statue was overthrown, only fifty-six years after its erection, by an earthquake (224 B.C.), which destroyed the naval arsenals and a great portion of the once famous city; and, though liberal promises were made towards its restoration, there is no satisfactory evidence that it ever was replaced.[2]

[1] The head of Apollo, on the fine tetradrachms of Rhodes, is believed to be a copy of the head of the Colossus.

[2] Strab. xiv. p. 654. In the time of Strabo and Pliny it was lying as it had fallen. Plin. xxxiv. 41.

But the Rhodians, in their laws, have transmitted to posterity a monument of their maritime wisdom, more enduring than the brass of which the Colossus was composed. These laws were for ages the sovereign judges of controversies relating to navigation. Even the Romans in such questions almost invariably appealed to their judgment. Indeed the Rhodian laws were held in such respect, that, on an appeal being made to Marcus Aurelius by one Eudæmon of Nicomedia, whose goods had been plundered on the wreck of his ship, that emperor replied: "I am the sovereign of the world; but the Rhodian law is sovereign wheresoever it does not run contrary to our statute law."[1]

Their maritime laws.

It would further appear, that the Rhodians were the first to establish rules, subsequently accepted universally, with regard to co-partnership, and the remuneration of the commanders, officers, and seamen, by shares in the profits of the ship, much in the same manner as is still done among whaling vessels. Again, they framed laws to be observed by freighters and by passengers while on board ship; they affixed penalties on the commander or seamen for injuries done to goods on board of their vessels, from want of sufficient tarpaulins or proper attention to the pumps, and for carelessness or absence from their duties. They also imposed penalties for barratry, for robbery of other ships, or for careless collisions, awarding a special and severe punishment to any one who ran away with a ship which had been placed under his

[1] Justin. Digest. xiv. 2, and the comment thereon by Sir Patrick de Colquhoun ("Summary of the Roman Civil Law," vol. iii. pp. 137-142.

charge. Punishments were likewise enforced for plundering wrecks, and a compensation allotted to the heirs of seamen who lost their lives in the service of the ship. The Rhodians were also the first to make regulations affecting charterparties and bills of lading, as well as contracts of partnership or joint adventures. They laid down rules for bottomry, for average and salvage, specifying a scale of rates for recovering goods from the bottom, in one and a half, twelve, and twenty-two feet and a half water; and also for the payment of demurrage.[1] The whole of these rules were copied by the Roman legislators and incorporated with the Roman laws; and having been thus handed down to the States of Europe, they constituted the main features of the laws known as the "Rôles d'Oleron," and the "Hanse Town Ordinances of 1614 and 1681," besides forming the basis of that English system of maritime law, which was brought to almost human perfection by the wisdom of Lord Mansfield.

System of accounts in use at Rome.

While the Romans were indebted to the Rhodians for their maritime laws, it seems likely that they gained their knowledge of accounts and book-keeping from the Greeks of Crete, who had themselves acquired the elements of this knowledge from the Phœnicians. It is, however, more than questionable whether the Romans improved upon the art. The private arrangements of the Roman merchants and ship-owners respecting the systematic practice of book-keeping were exemplary. Accounts were not actually enforced, as in

[1] One Rhodian Law quoted in the Digests decreed that *silk*, if saved, when shipwrecked, from wetting, should pay a salvage of ten per cent. as *being equal in value to gold.* Cf. Vopisc. in Aurel. c. xlv.

some modern nations, by positive enactment, but as it was deemed base to charge what was not justly due, so it was held to be nefarious to omit entering what was due to others. The Roman merchants were evidently well acquainted with book-keeping by single entry, as they kept their accounts, *Rationes*,[1] in a book or ledger called *codex*, with headings in columns *accepti* or *expensi* (the received and the paid away); they had also a book containing each debtor's or creditor's name, and they posted in the ledger, at least once a month, the various items of debit and credit, which it was incumbent on every trader to state fairly and punctually. They had likewise a sort of waste-book (*adversaria*); and it was deemed a suspicious circumstance if entries in this rough book were neglected, and not duly entered on the *codex*[2] in the regular course of business. But though the system of single entry adopted by the Roman merchants and ship-owners much resembles that of modern times, their books were entirely different from those now in use among the traders of Europe and of the United States of America. They were rather rolls[3] of papyrus, each roll or page being divided into columns. The *codex* or ledger contained the separate accounts, in accordance with the still prevailing practice, headed with the proper name and titles of the respective parties, every transaction being duly transferred or posted into it for permanent observation and record. The ledger

[1] Orelli. Inscript., Nos. 1494, 2973, &c. Cf. Horat. Ars. Poet. v. 329.

[2] Cicer. pro Rosc. 2, 3, and 9, where the whole argument turns on the point that Roscius's creditor, Fannius, claimed simply on the assertion of a note in his "adversaria." This, Cicero argues, is no valid claim at all.

[3] "Volumina," whence our "volumes."

was then, as it is now, legal evidence, producible in courts of justice in cases of dispute. It contained in its debit and credit divisions the full account of each transaction. When the *adversaria*, containing the temporary memorandum of the transactions, on which necessary alterations were made before the particulars were transferred to the ledger at the end of each month, if not more frequently, was full, it was thrown aside or destroyed, the ledger being the only record preserved of the transactions which had been completed.

Although the Romans were slow in becoming a great naval power, it is clear that very soon after the battle of Actium they became as powerful at sea as on land; all the leading seafaring states having by this time become subject to the engrossing power of the empire, and there being no longer any naval power to contest with them the supremacy of the Mediterranean Sea: hence, for many years, there was no employment for their fleets, except to protect their commerce and to keep open the communication with the distant colonies of the empire. But long after Rome had swept the sea of her greater opponents, marauders of different races continued to prey upon commerce, so that her merchant traders, engaged on distant voyages, invariably took on board a number of Roman archers to guard their ships from pirates. These men were engaged either to protect the ship when an emergency arose,[1] or to man the oars, and, like the marines of our own time, acted

[1] In our own time, merchant ships have carried fire-arms for their protection, and up to within the last few years there was an armoury on board of all merchant vessels.

as soldiers, or performed those portions of the sailor's duties to which they had been trained.

The corn trade of the city.

Although, unfortunately, no clearly defined records of the maritime commerce of Rome at any period of her history have been preserved, its extent may be conjectured by the number and wealth of her citizens. One million and a quarter of people,[1] including nearly all the wealthy inhabitants of the empire—for these flocked to the capital in great numbers—would at any time require a large fleet of merchant ships to supply their varied wants. Even during the time of the Roman commonwealth, the vessels engaged in the corn trade alone of the city were so numerous, that medals were struck in commemoration of the traffic, bearing upon them the representation of the prow of a ship, and the inscription, "By decree of the Senate, for the purchase of corn." That trade, as well as all others, increasing with the spread of the metropolis, must, in the reign of the Cæsars, have required an amount of shipping to supply its wants far in excess of that of any other city of either ancient or modern times. If one steamship now performs the work of at least three sailing vessels, each of equal capacity to the steamer, then, considering the dilatory movements of ancient vessels, it will not be an exaggerated estimate to allow six thousand tons of shipping as necessary to conduct the same amount of transport as one steamship of a thousand tons would now perform. Allowing, therefore, that Rome

[1] Gibbon, c. xxxi. under A.D. 408, estimates the probable population of Rome at 1,200,000 souls; and his reasoning seems satisfactory. Its present population probably does not exceed one-sixth of this amount. David Hume has an interesting essay, "Of the Populousness of Ancient Nations," in which he examines this and other similar questions.

was not one half the size of London, and presuming that it required one half the amount of supplies from abroad, the shipping employed in its over-sea trade would be more than twice as great as that now necessary to supply the wants of the inhabitants of the metropolis of Great Britain.

A.D. 41. Previous to the reign of Claudius[1] the chief over-sea intercourse with the city was carried on by way of Puteoli, now Pozzuoli, near the Bay of Naples, about seventy miles from Rome. Here the larger description of vessels, employed in the trade of Alexandria and of Spain, discharged their cargoes; but the inconvenience and expense of land carriage became so enormous, especially upon low priced and bulky articles, such as corn, as to fully justify the cost of erecting the new port of Ostia, and the embanking and deepening of the Tiber. Half a century afterwards, the Emperor Trajan, remarkable not merely for the splendid edifices erected during his reign, in almost every part of the empire, but for the interest he took in maritime affairs, constructed, to meet the increasing wants of the provinces, the present Civita Vecchia, as well as the town and port of Ancona on the Adriatic, where may still be read an inscription on the monument of marble he raised at the extremity of the Mole, dedicating the harbour to the use of the mariners who frequented those seas.

Port of Ostia.

But the port of Ostia was the most useful monument of Roman greatness in connection with shipping established by the empire, and has been described as one of the boldest and most stupendous works of

[1] Claudius began, and Nero and Trajan completed, this great work.

Roman magnificence.[1] The accidents to which the precarious subsistence of the city was continually exposed in a winter navigation (a matter more worthy of serious consideration than the costs of transit) and in an open roadstead, had suggested to the genius of the first Cæsar this useful design, which was executed under the reign of Claudius, and finally completed under Nero. Within the artificial moles which formed its narrow entrance, and advanced far into the sea, "the largest vessels then engaged in the trade of Rome securely rode at anchor;" and in its deep and capacious basins, which were situated on the north bank of the Tiber, every facility was afforded for the discharge of their cargoes. This great work was represented on numerous coins and medals of the period, of which the following, struck by the Emperor Nero, furnishes a fair example.

But Ostia must have borne more resemblance to a wet dock of the present day than to a harbour or "port." At the entrance was a tall tower, which served as a beacon by day, and a lighthouse by night for the guidance of vessels coming into the harbour.[2]

[1] Gibbon, c. xxxi. See also Admiral W. H. Smyth's "Mediterranean."

[2] Pliny, xxxvi. 83.

CHAPTER VII.

Roman empire—The cause of its decline—First invasion of Goths, A.D. 217—Their habits—Defeat the Emperor Decius, A.D. 257—Rebellion of Egypt, A.D. 273—Franks and Allemanni—The Veneti on the coast of Gaul—Constantinople founded, A.D. 323—Its commercial advantages and harbour—The extent of its ancient trade—Black Sea and Sea of Azov—The trading vessels on—Oppressive taxation—The laws affecting shipping—Constans and Julian—Produce of certain lands applied to the sea service—Neglect and decline of commerce, and sufferings of the people—Siege of Rome by Alaric and the Goths, A.D. 408—Genseric—His capture of Rome—Rise of Constantinople—Customs' duties—Silk trade—Naval expedition of Justinian against the Vandals, A.D. 533, and conquest of Carthage—Rise of the Muhammedan power, A.D. 622—Rapid conquests; of Jerusalem, A.D. 636; of Alexandria, A.D. 638; and of Africa, A.D. 647—Sieges of Constantinople, A.D. 668-675.

Roman empire.

FROM the close of the last Punic war to the middle of the third century after Christ, the Romans were the greatest if not the only enemies of Rome. The extravagance and heedless folly of her citizens were in themselves enough to ruin a less powerful nation. Without competitors, she maintained a position for centuries which, under other circumstances, the lavish expenditure of her people would have destroyed in as many years. The mistress of the world could do as she pleased; and the industry of the country districts was heavily burdened to support, in indolence and luxury, its rulers at Rome. Under such circumstances as these a fall must have come sooner or later; and so we find that even under the excellent government of the Antonines the decay of the imperial system had fully commenced. On their removal, and on the accession of such princes as Commodus, Caracalla and Elagabalus, the decay was much more rapid, till at length commerce, the true index of the real state of a nation, failed to recover its former position, even with the willing and active support of Alexander Severus. Nor was it possible that the corruption of Rome throughout its whole administration could be long kept a secret. On her distant and outlying provinces she had jealous enemies, burning to avenge past injuries and insults, and eagerly awaiting the opportunity of finding or making an entrance through her armour.

The cause of its decline.

A.D. 212–235.

Already in the reign of Caracalla, the Goths had begun to move southwards from their earliest known haunts in south Prussia and Poland,[1] but their advance was for a time checked by that emperor. This was their first attempt at marching in the direction of Rome. A little later, in the reign of Philippus, they seized a great part of the Roman province of Dacia (Hungary), and from this time their attacks,

First invasion of Goths, A.D. 217.

[1] Much confusion has been made by various writers on the subject of the Goths and Vandals, and, perhaps, by the majority of them, these tribes have been somewhat carelessly classed together. The real fact is, they were two distinct branches of the one great nation of the Suevi. The distinction of Ostro (or Eastern) and Visi (or Western) Goths was made in the third century, when they broke into Dacia. Those from Mecklenburg and Pomerania were called Visi-Goths; those from south Prussia and north-west Poland took the name of Ostro-Goths.

A.D. 249. though from time to time repelled, became more frequent and more destructive. Under their two great divisions of Ostro-Goth and Visi-Goth they waged a continual predatory war against Rome, becoming able eventually to wrest from the Romans the whole of Italy, and to capture the haughty city itself.

Their habits. The character of the Goths has probably been sketched with sufficient accuracy by Tacitus in his famous essay "De Germanis," as that of a wild, illiterate, brave nation, preserving in their habits and ordinary mode of life their original savage character. They possessed nothing that could be called a city; but dwelt in rude and temporary huts wherever game and water were abundant. "The characteristic," says he, "of all these nations is the round shield, the short sword, and obedience to their kings."[1]

Such were the people who, more than any others, caused the disruption of the Roman empire. Devastating the country on all sides, as they advanced through the Ukraine into Thrace, and having captured the city of Philippopolis, and defeated and slain the Emperor Decius, they were for a while checked by an ignominious peace, and by the payment of a considerable sum in money by his successor, Gallus, which only showed the weakness of the empire, and stimulated them to fresh attacks. The province of Dacia, ceded to them by Aurelian, was one of the first steps in advance they secured; for, though often repulsed with great loss, their perseverance was indomitable, while they showed an aptitude for war

Defeat the Emperor Decius, A.D. 257.

[1] Tacit. De Germanis, c. 43.

remarkable among men in other respects so ignorant; their recovery from crushing defeats being often scarcely less glorious than their victories. Thus, when joined with the Vandals in the expedition that ended in the possession of Dacia, they soon made themselves masters of the Black Sea. An enormous army needs an ample fleet; but it would seem that the fearless courage of the Goths made up for want of skill in the construction of their transport vessels. The natives of the coasts of that sea had for centuries made use of very frail boats for its navigation;[1] and there is no reason for supposing that the Goths had better ships than Tacitus describes as on the Euxine in his day. Speaking of a sudden invasion of Pontus, A.D. 69, that historian says: "The barbarians even insolently scoured the sea, in hastily constructed vessels of their own, called 'cameræ,' built with narrow sides and broad bottoms, and joined together without fastenings of brass and iron. Whenever the water is rough, they raise the bulwarks with additional planks, according to the

[1] The Ukraine and Black Sea boats of the middle ages resembled in most respects, but with little or no improvement, those of more ancient times. They usually had ten or fifteen oars of a side, and rowed faster than the Turkish galleys. They had one mast, which carried an ill-shaped sail, used only in fine weather, as their crews preferred to row when it blew hard, and when, to prevent the waves from washing on board, they formed temporary bulwarks of reeds, which were more conveniently carried than planks. If about to undertake a hostile expedition by sea, it was not uncommon to employ at once from five to six thousand Cossacks skilled in seafaring matters, to construct the necessary number of boats, and as sixty hands could complete one in a fortnight, they could finish at least two hundred of them in a month, well-armed and ready for action. In these frail craft, the hardy mariners of the north frequently crossed the whole extent of the Black Sea, sometimes performing the voyage from the Borysthenes to Anatolia in from thirty-six to forty hours.

increasing height of the waves, till the vessel is covered in like a house. Thus they roll about amid the billows, and as they have a prow at both extremities alike, and a convertible arrangement of oars, they may be paddled in one direction or another, indifferently and without risk."[1]

It was in such frail craft as these that the Goths committed themselves to a sea with which they were wholly unacquainted, yet, under the guidance of local and impressed mariners, they succeeded in surprising the city of Trebizond, wherein immense treasures had been collected for safety, its capture, with many of its merchants, being the reward of their daring.

Seven years after obtaining possession of Dacia they were, however, again driven from it by Probus; but the skill and courage of these barbarous tribes were always conspicuous at sea; and in no instance more so than in the case of a party of Franks, who had been settled near the sea coast, and who, being suddenly seized with the desire of returning to their homes, surprised a small fleet then on the Euxine, and were thus enabled to carry out their plan. Unskilled in the art of navigation, and unacquainted with any other except the Baltic and the Black Seas, these adventurers made their way through the Dardanelles into the Mediterranean, and, after sacking Syracuse and other towns, boldly steered through the Straits of Gibraltar, entered the Atlantic with a degree of

[1] Tacit. Hist. iii. 47. Strabo, xi. c. 12, notices the same native boats, to which, like Tacitus, he gives the name of "cameræ," or "house-boats." They carried, on an average, twenty-five men each.

hardihood almost unparalleled, and made a triumphant passage to the Batavian or Frisian coasts.[1]

Though repeatedly defeated, their successes, together with the steady advance of other barbarian hordes from the north, were sufficient to destroy the *prestige* which had for centuries made Rome invincible. A general spirit of revolt was now awakened in all the provinces. Even Egypt, so long the most docile of the slaves of Rome, was aroused into active rebellion by Firmus, a wealthy merchant of Alexandria, who, after plundering that city at the head of a furious mob, maintained, though for only sixty days, the imperial purple, published edicts, and raised an army, supported, as he boasted vaingloriously, from the profits of his paper trade.[2]

Rebellion of Egypt, A.D. 273.

The dangerous secret of the wealth and weakness of the empire once clearly discerned, new swarms of barbarians, encouraged by the successes of those who had gone before them, sprang into existence, overran the northern districts, flooded Gaul and Spain, and carried desolation and terror almost to the very walls of Rome. Of these the most formidable were the Franks, or Freemen, who now occupied the Rhenish frontier, and the Allemanni, a name now generally held to imply a confederacy of many tribes of German origin. As in the case of the Goths, their first successes were of short duration, and, after three bloody battles, Aurelian was able to drive them out of Italy, securing, at the same time, by the overthrow of Zenobia and the destruction of Firmus, a short breathing time for the distracted empire. But the

Franks and Allemanni.

[1] Gibbon, ch. xii. Zosimus, i. p. 66. Panegyr. Vet. v. 18.

[2] Ibid. ch. x. Vopiscus, ap. Hist. Aug. Script. pp. 220–242.

policy now, though not for the first time, adopted by the Roman generals, was not one likely to succeed against the hosts now arrayed against the empire. The principle of building walls of great size and length, which had failed in England and in Scotland, failed even more conspicuously when adopted by Probus,[1] who, at the head of his legions, still maintained vigorously the prowess and the name of ancient Rome. His wall, two hundred miles in length, from the Danube to the Rhine, could be of little real value against an active and experienced enemy; indeed, Gibbon stated the truth when he said, "The experience of the world has exposed the vain attempt of fortifying an extensive tract of country." Nor did Probus's second scheme of enlisting in the Roman armies large levies taken from tribes but partially conquered, prove, as might have been anticipated, a more effective source of security and strength. It must, indeed, have been clear to any persons of observation, that no permanent stability could be secured for a government which wasted its means by acts of wanton and revolting extravagance, such as those which Gibbon has so eloquently described in his "Decline and Fall" of the great empire.

The barbarians, ever on the alert, now discovered that there were traitors within the Roman camps who gave fresh assistance to their inroads. Such a traitor was Carausius, not, as Stukeley imagined, a descendant of the blood royal of Britain, but a Dutch soldier of fortune, of the tribe of the Menapii. Tampering with the fleet he commanded in the name

[1] Gibbon, ch. xii.

of Maximian, he crossed with it from Gessoriacum (Boulogne), and, seizing on Britain, proclaimed himself Augustus and struck money with his effigy. For seven years he maintained his ill-gotten power, A.D. 287. but, though at length murdered by his lieutenant, Allectus, Carausius deserves some historical remembrance as the first creator of a British-manned navy.

In the reign of Diocletian events somewhat similar occurred. The Britons again revolted; Egypt was again the scene of fresh discord and confusion, and though the various attempts to throw off the Roman yoke still proved abortive, the general decline of intellectual power among the Roman people became so apparent that fresh enemies arose against her in almost every quarter. The Veneti, who, four centuries before, had given Julius Cæsar[1] no little trouble ere he reduced them to subjection, perceiving the weakness of Rome and the impunity with which her territory had been ravaged by the Northern hordes, rose in arms against her, and exercising an arbitrary dominion over the seas that washed their coasts, exacted tribute from all strangers, and for a while successfully bade defiance to Rome, whose mariners dreaded the navigation of the Bay of Biscay.

The Veneti on the coast of Gaul.

The reign, too, of Diocletian, who seems to have had an especial dislike for Rome and the senate, saw the commencement of a new system of imperial government, which, afterwards more fully developed by Constantine, led to the removal of the chief seat of government to Constantinople, a change which exerted a vast influence on commerce, and essentially

Constantinople founded, A.D. 323.

[1] Cæsar, Bell. Gall. iii. 8.

Its commercial advantages,

altered the course of navigation. The splendid position of Constantinople, especially for all purposes of sea-borne trade, has been fully noticed by every author who has treated of this subject; and it seems probable that, when brought into communication with the whole of Europe, by means of the railways now fast approaching completion, it will rival in greatness any commercial city of the continent. The new route to India by way of the Suez canal, of which advantage will, no doubt, be taken by the establishment of a line of steamers to Port Said, cannot fail to afford it such facilities for becoming a great depôt for the produce of the East Indies, that it will be the fault of its government and of its merchants if it does not again assume and surpass the rank it held soon after its re-construction by Constantine the Great. Gibbon's description of its position is as applicable now as ever.[1] "The imperial city," he remarks, "may be represented under that of an unequal triangle. The obtuse point, which advances towards the east and the shores of Asia, meets and repels the waves of the Thracian Bosphorus. The northern side of the city is bounded by the harbour; and the southern is washed by the Propontis, or Sea of Marmora: the basis of the triangle is opposed to the west, and terminates the continent of Europe."

and harbour.

"The epithet of 'golden' in 'Golden Horn,'" he adds, "was expressive of the riches which every wind wafted from the most distant countries into the secure and capacious port of Constantinople. The river Lycus, formed by the conflux of two little

[1] Gibbon, ch. xvii.

streams, pours into the harbour a perpetual supply of fresh water, which serves to cleanse the bottom, and to invite the periodical shoals of fish to seek their retreat in that convenient recess. As the vicissitudes of the tides are scarcely felt in those seas, the constant depth of the harbour allows goods to be landed on the quays without the assistance of boats; and it has been observed that, in many places, the largest vessels may rest their prows against the houses, while the sterns are floating on the water. From the mouth of the Lycus to that of the harbour this arm of the Bosphorus is more than seven miles in length. The entrance is about five hundred yards broad, and a chain could be occasionally drawn across it to guard the port and city from the attack of a hostile navy."

The Hellespont, in its winding course, is about sixty miles in length, with an average breadth of three miles; its lower end, where Xerxes is believed to have built his bridge of boats, is celebrated as the spot where Leander, in ancient times, is said to have swum across, and which has, in modern days, been certainly so crossed by Byron,[1] Ekenhead, Colquhoun, and others. Altogether Constantinople would seem to have been formed by nature as an important entrepôt for commerce; and this was peculiarly the case in ancient times, as caravan routes placed it in communication, not merely with the cities of Mesopotamia, but also with those on the Indus and the Ganges, thus securing for it the trade with the Euxine

The extent of its ancient trade.

[1] "He could, perhaps, have pass'd the Hellespont,
As once (a feat on which ourselves we prided)
Leander, Mr. Ekenhead, and I did."
BYRON, "Don Juan," cant. ii. 105.

and the Caspian, and even the silk trade of China. With the Bosphorus and the Hellespont for its gates, whoever secures possession of these important passages can always shut them against a naval enemy, and open them to the peaceable fleets of commerce.

Black Sea and Sea of Azov.

Although the trade of the Black Sea was considerable, even in remote times, it greatly increased after the foundation of Constantinople. Across this sea a large portion of the goods of Asia found their way; while gold from Colchis; and from the surrounding coasts, corn, leather, flax, honey, wax, flocks of sheep and goats, furs, medicinal herbs, and timber suitable for ship-building, found a ready mart in the markets of the new city. The fisheries of the Euxine and the Bosphorus still maintained their ancient reputation. Sturgeon and tunny-fish, abundant in the Black Sea,[1] had, of old, fetched excessive prices in Greece and Italy, and, under the Greek emperors, contributed largely to the revenues of the state. The city of Byzantium, also, raised large sums annually from dues levied on shipping passing through the Straits.

The *Palus Mœotis*, or Sea of Azov, and the Tauric Chersonesus, now the Crimea, became, after the time of Constantine, places of importance; while Theodosia (now Kaffa) and Tanais (the present city of Azov) grew to be of great commercial value when occupied by the Genoese. Of these, Azov, Panticapæum (Kertch), and Odessa (probably at or near the ancient Olbia), have retained an extensive trade in corn, wool, and tallow, to the present time, the

[1] Plin. ix. 15. Horat. ii. Sat. v. 44. Ovid, in Halieut. v. 98.

latter being now the most enterprising commercial port on the shores of the Black Sea.

The trading vessels on.

The rude vessels the Goths used in crossing the Black Sea were probably fair specimens of the ordinary craft in which the early maritime commerce along its shores was conducted. The largest of the corn ships employed within the Euxine and Azov seldom exceeded in capacity from two hundred and fifty to three hundred and fifty quarters of wheat, or from fifty to seventy tons. Some of those which passed on to the Mediterranean may have been larger, for then, as now, there was considerable difference (though not nearly so great as in our own day) in the size of merchant vessels. It was not, however, until Constantinople was founded, and revived the trade with Egypt, that ships of great dimensions were constructed there, specially for the purposes of commerce. Gibbon[1] has described as "canoes," consisting of a single tree hollowed out, the vessels used on the Black Sea by the Goths in their descent on Trebizond; but no one will believe that, with all their rash bravery, they actually trusted themselves to boats so small as this view suggests; nor, indeed, does the passage in Strabo to which Gibbon has referred, imply all that he has deduced from it. Many vessels, vastly superior in build to the simple monoxyle, must have existed; though their construction may easily have been so inartistic that they were scarcely safer than canoes.

To increase as rapidly as possible the size and magnificence of the new capital, the opulent senators

[1] Gibbon, ch. xxvi.

of Rome and the great landowners or merchants of the eastern provinces were, at first, induced to make it their place of residence by the assignment to them, on the part of Constantine, of many of the palaces and of the costly mansions he had erected. In time, however, such encouragements became unnecessary and were gradually abolished. The court, and the fact that Constantinople had become the chief seat of government, attracted to it the wealthiest inhabitants of the provinces; while others were induced to dwell there through motives of interest, business, or pleasure, so that, in less than a century from the time of its foundation, Constantinople rivalled, if it did not equal, Rome herself, in population and in wealth. Nor does it seem to have been much less extravagant or less luxurious than the Western capital in life and morals, for the magnificence of the first Cæsars was largely imitated by its founder. The natural results followed in the form of an oppressive system of taxation, which fell heavily upon the trading portion of the community. Tributes of corn were exacted from Egypt, and the poorest traders, the industrious manufacturers, and the most obscure retail dealer, were, with the rich merchants, alike obliged to admit the officers of the revenue into a partnership of their gains.

Oppressive taxation.

This general tax on industry, which was collected every fourth year, appears to have caused such lamentation, that the approach of the period for collecting it "was announced by the tears and terrors of the citizens, who were often compelled, by the impending scourge, to embrace the most abhorred and unnatural methods of procuring the sum at which their property had been assessed."[1] From the nature of this tax, it may be inferred that it was arbitrary in its distribution, while, from the rigorous mode of its collection, it could hardly fail to be both unequal and oppressive in its operation. The income tax of our own time has been frequently denounced for its inquisitorial character and the irregularity of the burden imposed on different sections of the people; and if it be difficult now to ascertain, in various branches of trade, the actual amount of a trader's gains, it must have been far more so in ancient days, when the precarious profits of art or labour were capable of only a discretionary valuation.

It is certain, however, that laws pressing heavily on the merchant were now greatly modified in favour of those who followed maritime pursuits—a remarkable fact, as contrasted with the former legislation of Rome and the contempt in which seafaring persons had been previously held. The emperors Valentinian, Theodosius, and Arcadius exempted the ship-owners and the sailors who navigated their vessels, from the payment of taxes, on the ground that the merchant was enriched by foreign trade, while the mariners had all the trouble and risk. The fifth title of the thirteenth book of the Theodosian code referred exclusively to their interests; while the ninth law under that head, enacted by the emperors Constans and Julian, further shelters them from personal injuries and protects them "from all costs of violent proceedings, as well as extortions, ordinary and extraordinary." Nearly two hundred years afterwards the Emperor Justinian considered it politic to

The laws affecting shipping.

Constans and Julian.

A.D. 527.

[1] Gibbon, ch. xvii.

incorporate this law into his celebrated code;[1] the same exemptions being granted by that emperor, in his fourth and fifth law under the same table as
A.D. 364 and 375. the Theodosian code. The laws of the emperors Valentinian, Valens, and Gratian, embodied in the Code of Justinian, likewise forbid, on pain of death,
A.D. 379–395. that any one should insult the persons of mariners, while the special enactments of Arcadius, Honorius, and Theodosius treated them with the like respect. The same code furnishes another law of Gratian, Valentinian, and Theodosius, wherein these privileges are confirmed and ordered to be continued for ever.

Such extraordinary privileges conferred on the seafaring population of the empire—privileges unknown in any other country or in any other age—were probably enacted in order to revive the nautical spirit which had been so long practically treated with contempt. No doubt, special bounties were needed to ensure the import of corn and the construction of vessels adapted to this purpose. Indeed, the necessity of a constant and steady supply of food sufficient to meet the wants of the people, and to prevent the tumults which too frequently arose whenever there was a prospect of a scarcity of corn, sufficiently accounts for the encouragement afforded to this particular trade. But in the later days it was found necessary to create laws to raise further in the social scale the seafaring classes. Indeed this seems the only reason why the emperors Valentinian, Theo-

[1] Cod. Justinian, bk. ii. tit. i. sec. 3. By this code six per cent. was pronounced to be the ordinary and legal standard of interest; eight was allowed for the convenience of manufacturers and merchants, while twelve was granted to nautical insurance.

dosius, and Arcadius should have issued ordinances to prevent persons adopting the sea as a profession who had previously exercised any mean and disgraceful employment;[1] endeavouring thus, so far as laws could do so, to counteract the deep-rooted prejudice against seafaring pursuits. By the decrees of Constantine and Julian, sailors were even raised to the dignity of knighthood; while Valentinian, Valens, and Gratian enjoined that persons filling the functions of mariners should be admitted into the society of men of the most honourable and aristocratic parentage, and even into the senate.

Produce of certain lands applied to the sea service.

But while the Roman laws enacted at the new capital conceded so many privileges to persons who adopted the sea as a profession, the state also required the possessors of certain lands (making this, indeed, the condition of the grant) to perform the functions of public mariners; but this arrangement was so contrived that actual personal service was not enforced, although the expense of substitutes was charged on the lands. The nature of this scheme is fully explained in the Theodosian Code,[2] where the rights of the state and of the parties are defined. When these lands were sold, the law enforced the same obligations upon the purchasers; and the emperors Valentinian and Valens enacted, that if they passed into the hands of strangers, they should revert to "mariners," on conditions regulated by the experience and practice of the previous fifty years. On the other hand, those persons who were employed in the service of the state

[1] Theodosian Code, bk. xiii. tit. v. secs. 14, 16, and 18.
[2] Book xiii. tit. vi. secs. 5–10.

were not permitted, in such voyages, to carry any private merchandise; moreover, the owners of vessels engaged in certain trades were required to hold them at the disposal of the state. In spite, however, of all these laws, the encouragement proposed or provided by them came too late.

Neglect and decline of commerce,

But while a new life was being gradually infused into the empire by the creation of Constantinople, overgrown wealth and luxury, with the evils following in their train, indolence, waste, and extravagance, were only too surely working out the downfall of old Rome. Capital, which ought to have been used as a provision for fresh channels of employment for an increasing population, was devoted to pleasure and folly; while no middle class arose to create fresh capital by its industry and to supply the place of the annual waste. In no age or country have the extremes of wealth and poverty been so great; even the provincial merchants came not to the capital to increase its wealth, but rather to waste their own substance. They sought to rival, in display, the ancient noblesse; they rented their palaces to enjoy their society, and were ready to spend fortunes derived from commerce to win a ready entrance into their salons.

So early as the Augustan age, Livy and Pliny have alluded to the then enormous accumulation of wealth in Rome; the former describing the mass of treasure accumulated there as something fabulous;[1] the latter stating that there were side-boards in his time groaning under more solid silver than

[1] Livy, xxx. 45. Plin. xxxiii. 50. Gibbon, ch. xxxi., quoting from Ammianus Marcellinus.

had been transported by Scipio from vanquished Carthage. Besides all this removable wealth in the shape of plate, there was, no doubt, a still greater supply in jewels and precious stones, in gold ornaments and in the current metallic coin of the empire. Unlike their poor and invincible ancestors, who were not distinguished from the meanest of the soldiers by the delicacy of their food or the splendour of their apparel, the nobles of Rome, in its latter days, were not merely fond of the most ostentatious display, but magnified the rent rolls of their estates, too frequently living in accordance with their imaginary rather than with their actual incomes. The "Satires" of Juvenal portray but too distinctly the corruption of manners which had in his time (the reign of Domitian) extended to the female portion of the population.[1]

History, it has been truly said, repeats itself; and the reading of the lengthened description Ammianus has given of the extravagance of Rome reminds us of too many of the gay assemblies so frequently met with in our own time. Nor is his description of the manners of the Roman nobility wholly unlike what may too frequently be now seen in the conduct of those persons who measure their importance by their wealth and gay equipages, or who, by their rapid acquisition of large fortunes, and their method of dealing with them, used to be known in England as "Nabobs," but who now bear a less flattering name.

While such was the state of the upper, the middle classes, who derived their subsistence from their skill and industry, and who, in all communities, **and sufferings of the people.**

[1] Juvenal, Sat. iii., and *passim*.

constitute the mainstay of a nation, had become comparatively insignificant, the still lower orders being reduced, in most instances, to abject poverty. Large allowances of bread were daily served out at the public expense; and, in one year, three millions six hundred and twenty-eight thousand pounds of bacon are said to have been distributed to the needy masses, as well as oil, indispensable alike for the lamp and the bath, to the extent of three hundred thousand English gallons; but the poor citizens had become almost as indolent and depraved as their rulers. In the baths, constructed in every part of the city with imperial magnificence for the indiscriminate use of the senators and the people, the meanest Romans idled away their time. For a small copper coin[1] they could there purchase the daily enjoyment of a scene of pomp and luxury which might well have excited the envy of princes. Baths, the extent of which we can now scarcely comprehend, surrounded with granite pillars from the quarries of Egypt and adorned with the precious green marble of Numidia, with streams of ever-running hot water from mouths of bright and massive silver, were the hourly resort of dirty and ragged plebeians without shoes or mantles.

Siege of Rome by Alaric and the Goths, A.D. 408.

Such was the state of the western capital of the once proud and powerful Roman empire, when the Gothic army first appeared before it. The barbarian Goths had greatly improved in discipline since they made their first invasion of Italy; they were well organised, and under the absolute control of Alaric,

[1] About half of a farthing. Horat. i. Sat. iii. 136. Juvenal, Sat. vi. 146.

a commander in whom they had a confidence approaching to devotion. Their first action against the city itself was rather in the nature of a blockade, for they cut off all communication with it by land, while they held the mouths of the Tiber; hence, in spite of their rage and humiliation, the Romans saw at once that they had no alternative but submission, and it is to the credit of the victorious leader of the Goths that the terms he imposed were neither severe nor extravagant.

From Rome Alaric continued his march into Tuscany, where vast numbers of enslaved barbarians flocked to his standard; so that with the reinforcement of a large body of Goths and Huns, who had fought their way from the banks of the Danube, he had now, under his command, an army sufficient to overawe the whole of Italy. By this time the *prestige* of Rome had gone for ever; she was now destined to become the frequent prey of the barbarians of the north, till the tribes of Germany and Scythia, who had so long coveted her wealth, at length accomplished her destruction.

The first half of the century which saw Rome blockaded was full of events, all tending towards her final overthrow. Spain, separated from the enemies of Rome by her insular position and the Pyrenean mountains, had been almost undisturbed for four
hundred years by foreign invaders or civil wars. It A.D. 409.
was her turn now. Ten months after Alaric's attack on the capital, the Vandals and other barbarous tribes found their way thither, and plundered her rich and
prosperous cities, her valuable mines, and her fruitful A.D. 413.
plains. Soon afterwards Africa revolted; the consul,

Heraclian, assumed the title of emperor, and prepared a vast fleet for the invasion of Italy; but though
A.D. 427–439. he failed in his designs, Carthage and the whole of Africa were prepared, by this outbreak, for subjugation by the Vandals under Genseric, their able and energetic leader. Revolutions arose in Gaul. Its most opulent provinces became the prey of the barbarians, and its fairest and most fertile lands fell into the hands of rapacious strangers, and were assigned for the use of their families, their slaves, and their
A.D. 409–426. cattle. About the same time the regular forces were withdrawn from Britain, and the defenceless islanders abandoned to the Welsh and Scotch semi-savages and to the Saxon invaders. We cannot, therefore, be surprised that, reduced as she was by constant wars and invasions, distracted by the folly and weakness of her own people, and despoiled of her best provinces, the Imperial City itself fell an easy prey to the Vandal hosts of Genseric.

Genseric. Having made himself master of Carthage, and having confiscated all the estates belonging to the Roman nobles and senators, Genseric at once resolved to build a fleet for the blockade of the Tiber, and to treat the Imperial City as she had treated Carthage. His bold resolve was executed with steady and active perseverance. The woods on Mount Atlas afforded an inexhaustible supply of timber suitable for his purpose, while the Moors and Africans, alike skilled in the arts of shipbuilding and navigation, were ready to execute commands which held out the hope of unlimited plunder. Nor, indeed, was Genseric without other and certain inducements to act at once on the plan he had proposed to himself. In the first place, he could hardly have failed to know that since the invasion of Alaric, the nobles and senators of Rome had sunk into their former state of apathy and indolence; that they were giving no heed to the dangers besetting their capital, while they had taken no warning from the losses they had sustained by the frequent invasions of the barbarians. "Sufficient for the day is the evil thereof" had become their maxim and that of the Emperor Maximus, who, however incapable of administering an empire, might at least have ascertained the extent and the object of the naval preparations on the opposite shore of Africa. Yet, like his nobles, he was content to await in luxurious ease the approach of the enemy, careless alike of any means of defence, of negotiation, or of retreat.[1]

His capture of Rome.

Within three days of a popular tumult which closed in ignominy the life of another feeble emperor, Genseric advanced from the port of Ostia to the gates of the defenceless city. An unarmed procession, headed by the bishop and clergy, met him and implored his mercy. But, though the barbarian conqueror promised to spare the unresisting multitude, to protect the buildings from fire, and to exempt the captives from torture, Rome and its inhabitants were given over to the licentious mercies of his army—a tardy but terrible revenge for the Roman sack of Carthage. During fourteen days and nights there was one almost uninterrupted scene of plunder and sacrilege, and all that remained of public or private wealth, of sacred or profane treasure, was

[1] Gibbon, ch. xxvi.

transported to the vessels of the Vandal king. The "gold table" and "the golden candlestick with seven branches," which, three and a half centuries before, Titus had carried away from Jerusalem, were now transferred, by a barbarian conqueror, from Rome to Africa. The gorgeous decorations of the Christian churches, and of the Pagan temples, constituted a rich prize to the host of Genseric. Having time to collect and ships to transport any removable article of value in the capital, the conqueror spared neither church nor temple, dwelling-house, nor palace. The magnificent furniture and massive plate with which the palace of the emperor was furnished, were gathered up with disorderly rapine; even brass and copper were not beneath the notice of the Vandals, and were, whenever found, as carefully removed as articles of gold and silver. The Empress Eudoxia herself, at whose instigation, it is said, Genseric had been led to undertake his expedition, was compelled, with her daughters, to follow as a captive in the train of the conqueror, and to expiate, during a seven years' exile in Africa, a treason of which her subjects alone had any ground of complaint.[1]

Rise of Constantinople.

When Rome fell, the sovereign of the eastern empire claimed, and long maintained, the fictitious title of Emperor of the Romans, adopting the hereditary names of Cæsar and Augustus, and declaring himself the legitimate successor of the imperial rulers of Rome; and, indeed, if mere splendour was enough to support such a claim, the emperors of Constantinople were well justified in all their assertions. The palaces of Constantinople rivalled, if

[1] Gibbon, ch. xxxii.

they did not surpass, the gorgeousness of Rome in her proudest days; while in barbaric "pomp and circumstance," and in their Oriental and tawdry magnificence, they unquestionably stood alone. Moreover, the emperor at Constantinople was inaccessible alike to the complaints of his own people and to the menaces of his enemies, the peninsular position of the city rendering it during many centuries impregnable against the attack of foes from without, so that the barbarian armies which had swept Europe and Africa from end to end, turned aside from a fortress no military knowledge or skill then available could have reduced.

For some time it would seem that Genseric remained undisturbed, for Leo, the eastern emperor, was little disposed to avenge his brother of the west. At length, however, he was obliged, or persuaded, to join Egypt and Italy in an attempt to deliver the Mediterranean from the sway of the Vandals, Genseric having become as oppressive on land as he was formidable at sea. By extraordinary exertions a vast fleet was collected, chiefly, as the historians inform us, at the cost of the emperor himself; but it was feebly commanded, and its destruction inevitable as soon as it should come into collision with so veteran a general as Genseric. Though it would seem that, at the first landing near Carthage, the attack on the Vandals was successful, their wily leader, obtaining from the commander of the Greeks a hollow truce, and watching the opportunity of a favourable change of the wind, suddenly launched his fire-ships on his unsuspecting foes. More than half their fleet was destroyed, and Genseric was again ready to complete the final destruction of Rome.[1] "Leave the determination to the winds," was the favourite reply of the Vandal king when asked whither he meant to steer; "they will transport us to the guilty coast whose inhabitants have provoked Divine justice."

During the fifty years that intervened between the fall of the Roman empire of the West, and the memorable reign of Justinian, Italy revived and flourished under the good and wise government of a Gothic king, who, with abilities equal to those of Genseric, had few of his vices and none of his predatory habits. During that period, also, the vast changes which had taken place in the ancient provinces of Rome had become consolidated, and out of these had arisen various independent nations destined to occupy a conspicuous position in the maritime commerce of the world. The rude tribes of the North had, to some extent at least, been blended with the more civilized and refined inhabitants of the South ; and an admixture of races had taken place, which, though adverse for a while to the cause of learning, was of solid advantage to the people, tending, on the one hand, to save from entire annihilation the little refinement still preserved, and, on the other, softening and materially improving the hardier and ruder tribes. Constantinople, undisturbed by foreign invaders, reaped the advantages of a prosperous commerce, and when Justinian ascended the throne, was one of the most important commercial cities in the world.

Fortunate in the choice of his generals, and sup-

[1] Procop. Bell. Vandal, 1.

ported by eminent lawyers, the thirty-eight years' A.D. 537.
reign of Justinian was equally distinguished by his conquests and by his laws, to the maritime portion of which we have already referred. In his reign, the empire of the Vandals in Africa was overthrown, and the kingdom of the Ostro-Goths, in Italy, destroyed by Belisarius and Narses; while Rome was restored to the Romans, and the chief power placed in the A.D. 547.
hands of the descendants of its original population. A.D. 553.
In their hands it remained, generally, in a state of peace till, nearly two hundred years afterwards, it A.D. 728.
became independent under the rule of the Popes. But the expenses of the many public buildings Justinian erected—among which must be mentioned the great church (now the Mosque) of Sta. Sophia—together with those incurred in his many wars, obliged him to impose several new and vexatious imposts on his people. Beyond a supply of corn, free of cost, for the use of the army and capital, he levied heavy customs' dues on all vessels and merchandise passing the Bosphorus and Hellespont, which had hitherto been open to the freedom of trade. Customs' duties.

Happily for the people, the empire of the East possessed vast natural advantages, which, in some measure, counteracted the injurious effects of heavy taxation. Blessed by nature with superior soil, situation, and climate, her people could bear burdens which would have ruined the inhabitants of countries less favourably situated. Embracing the nations Rome had conquered, from the Adriatic to the frontiers of Æthiopia and Persia, the capital of the East had the means within herself, in spite of tariffs, apparently ruinous, of creating and maintaining an extensive and lucrative inland and maritime commerce. Egypt still largely supplied her with corn, and afforded many other advantages; commerce gradually extended itself along the coast of the Mediterranean; and as her own wants in food and dress were many, these combined, afforded a large and varied field for employment. The Asiatic love of dress was duly—if not unduly—exhibited by the ladies of Constantinople; and if Aurelian complained that a pound of silk at Rome cost twelve ounces of gold, we may well believe that Justinian saw with concern the Persians intercepting and obtaining a monopoly of this important trade, and the wealth of his subjects continually drained by a nation of fire-worshippers.

Silk trade. An unexpected event, however, afforded Justinian the means of cultivating in his own dominions that much prized article. Christian missionaries were then, as they have often been since, the harbingers of commerce, as well as of peace and good-will towards all men. Some of them who had settled at Ceylon, or, perhaps, more probably on the coast of Malabar, were induced, with a view of proselytising the Pagans, to follow the footsteps of trade to the extremities of Asia. Two of their number remained in China, and, in the course of their missionary occupations, observed that the common dress of the Chinese consisted of silk, at the same time noticing the myriads of silkworms, whence the raw material was produced. Having carefully collected a large number of the eggs in a hollow cane, they conveyed them to Constantinople, and, imparting their discovery to Justinian, were liberally rewarded, and encouraged to pursue the propagation of the valuable insect. Under their direction the eggs were hatched at the proper season by the artificial heat of dung; and the worms thus produced living and labouring in a foreign climate, Europe ceased to be dependent for her supply of this now necessary article on the chances of war or of Asiatic caprice.[1]

Naval expedition of Justinian against the Vandals, A.D. 533,

But the mind of Justinian was more occupied by foreign conquests than by commerce. Among his earliest maritime expeditions may be ranked the invasion of Africa and the overthrow of the Vandals, the preparations for which were not unworthy of the last contest between Rome and Carthage. Five hundred transports, navigated by twenty thousand mariners of Egypt, Cilicia, and Ionia, were collected in the harbour of Constantinople. If the smallest of these are computed at thirty, and the largest at five hundred tons, the average will supply an allowance liberal, if not profuse, of about one hundred thousand tons, for the reception of thirty-five thousand soldiers and sailors, and five thousand horses, with military stores and provisions sufficient for a three months' voyage. When the fleet lay moored ready for sea before the gardens of the palace, the Patriarch, amid great pomp and solemnity, pronounced his benediction for its safety and success; and when the emperor had signified his last commands, the expedition, at the sound of a trumpet, got under way. It was attended with the most complete success. Carthage became subject to Justinian; and the Romans were again masters of the sea—a position they maintained until a more formidable power arose

and conquest of Carthage.

[1] Gibbon, c. 40. Procop. Gothic. iv. c. 17. Anced. c. 25: Theoph. Byzant. ap. Photium.

in the East, which declared war against the empire both by land and by sea.

Rise of the Muhammedan power, A.D. 622. It is not our province to trace the progress of that power, nor indeed of that of any nation, except as may be necessary to furnish an idea of the extent of its maritime commerce, so far as this can be ascertained from the limited sources of information now extant. Muhammed had not only introduced a new religion, but his warlike successors propagated their newly accepted faith by the sword with a success unparalleled in the history of the world. Nor were their exploits confined to the land. The Arabians, distinguished by the name of Saracens (that is, specifically "the *Easterns*"),[1] who, from the earliest period of history, were skilled as navigators, and daring as seamen, had by this time become not merely an important
A.D. 633. but a powerful maritime people. Masters of Persia and of the whole of the Arabian Gulf, the "true believers," soon extended their conquests into Syria, nominally to abolish "infidelity," but with a clear eye to the advantages of commerce.

Hatred of the Christians, love of spoil, and contempt for danger were the ruling passions of the Saracens; nor could the prospect of instant death shake their religious confidence, nor stay a course of conquest, on all occasions made in "the name of the most merciful God." Bozrah and Damascus soon
Rapid conquests; fell into their hands, as well as Abyla, thirty miles distant, where the produce and manufactures of the country were then collected at a great annual fair.
of Jerusalem, A.D. 636; Three years afterwards Jerusalem was besieged and taken, and the Syrian seaports captured. The

[1] *Al Sherki.*

possession of Tyre, not yet wholly obliterated, and of the province of Cilicia, secured them the command of the whole of the eastern Mediterranean. Extending their conquests to the shores of the Euxine, they threatened—indeed, for a short time, besieged—Constantinople, though in this, and in subsequent attempts, they failed with heavy loss.[1] These facts show how early in their history they were able to extend their conquering and marauding expeditions both by land and by sea. Egypt was an easy and rich prey to them. But Alexandria, still a great and flourishing city, offered the most strenuous resistance to the invaders. Abundantly supplied, and easily replenished with the means of subsistence and defence, her numerous inhabitants fought for the dearest of human rights, religion and property; and if the Emperor Heraclius had been awake to the public distress, fresh armies might have been poured into the harbour before the fleet of the Saracens had taken up their position before it. But the power of the Infidels prevailed, and after a siege of fourteen months, and the loss of twenty-three thousand of their men, the standard of Muhammed was planted on the walls of the capital of Egypt. In ten years more Africa, from the Nile to the Atlantic Ocean, fell into their hands. Shortly afterwards Cyprus, Rhodes, and Sicily were taken; Spain overrun, except the Asturias and Biscay; and Capua and Genoa became their possession by conquest.

of Alexandria, A.D. 638; and of Africa, A.D. 647.

Although it cost the Saracens a siege of fourteen months, and a heavy loss of men, before they were able to take Alexandria, Constantinople from its

Sieges of Constantinople, A.D. 668–675.

[1] Gibbon, vol. ix. ch. 51, p. 425.

stronger position offered a still more determined resistance. In the first siege thirty thousand Moslems are said to have been slain; but the destruction which awaited them on the occasion of the second was by far the heaviest reverse their arms had as yet sustained. Commanded by their ablest general, at the head of one hundred and twenty thousand men, they had deemed success certain, and little anticipated the serious resistance the city really made. The Greeks were, however, resolved at all costs to force back these terrible invaders, who had plundered almost with impunity so many lands. All persons not provided with the means of subsistence for a year's siege were ordered to leave the city, the public granaries and arsenals were abundantly replenished, the walls restored and strengthened, and engines for casting stones, or darts of fire, were stationed along the ramparts or in vessels of war, of which an additional number were hastily constructed. The Greeks, on perceiving that the Saracen fleet had been largely reinforced from Egypt and Syria, were at first induced to offer the large ransom of a piece of gold for each person in the city; but, on the contemptuous rejection of this proposal, the Muhammedan chief imagining he had the game in his own hands, they determined on a most daring expedient to get rid of the fleet that threatened their destruction. As it slowly approached, with a fair wind and over a smooth sea, overshadowing the Straits like a moving forest, the Greeks suddenly launched fire-ships[1] into the

[1] The Greek fire was prepared chiefly from *naphtha*, with which there was mixed sulphur and pitch, extracted from evergreen firs. The admixture, when ignited, produced a fierce and obstinate flame, which burned with equal vehemence in every direction, and, instead of

midst of the dense mass, and involved in one general and terrible conflagration their own and every vessel of the invading squadrons. The destruction of the Saracenic Armada was complete.

The fate of the Saracen army, though not quite so disastrous, was one of heavy loss and great suffering, materially increased by a severe frost which covered the ground with snow for more than one hundred days. In the spring the survivors, aided with new levies of troops from Africa, made a fresh attempt to storm the city; but, on this proving as futile as their former efforts had been, they at length withdrew, and for seven hundred years more Constantinople was spared the desecration of the Infidel flag.

---

being extinguished, was nourished and quickened on the application of water. Sand, urine, or vinegar, were the only known applications which could damp its fury; the Greeks styled it appropriately the *liquid* or *maritime* fire. For the annoyance of the enemy, it was employed either by sea or by land, and with equal effect in battles or in sieges. Sometimes it was poured from the ramparts of a besieged city from large boilers, or launched in red-hot balls of stone or iron, or darted in arrows and javelins, twisted round with flax or tow which had been soaked in this inflammable oil. On other occasions it was deposited in fire-ships, and thence often, by some unexplained contrivance, blown through long tubes of copper, which were planted on the bow of a galley, and fancifully shaped into the mouths of savage monsters, that seemed to vomit a stream of liquid and consuming fire. Its composition was jealously concealed, and the Greeks terrified their enemies, not merely by the fire itself, but by the reports currently believed that its knowledge had been revealed, by an angel, to the first and greatest of the Constantines for the special use of the people of the eastern portion of the Roman empire. The secret was kept by them for more than four hundred years.

CHAPTER VIII.

Constantinople, A.D. 718–1453: its increased prosperity—Manufactures of Greece—System of taxation, and of expenditure—Fleets, and mode of warfare—Struggle for maritime supremacy—Scandinavians—Muscovites, their trade and ships—Russians; their early commerce, and attempts to capture Constantinople—Their ships—The Normans, and their expeditions—Establish themselves in Italy, A.D. 1016—Amalfi—Futile attempts of the Normans to take Constantinople, A.D. 1081–1084—Rise of Venice—The cause of its prosperity—Spread of the Scythians, Huns, or Turks, A.D. 997–1028—The Crusades, A.D. 1095–1099—Siege of Acre, A.D. 1189—Armistice, A.D. 1192—Fourth Crusade, A.D. 1202—The effect of the Crusades on the commerce of Constantinople, and on its fall—Power of Venice, A.D. 1202; her ships join in the Crusade, which was afterwards altered from its original design—They besiege and take Constantinople, A.D. 1204—Commerce declines under the Latins, but revives on the restoration of the Empire, A.D. 1261—Genoa—Genoese settlement at Galata and Pera—Arrogance of the Genoese, who at last rebel, A.D. 1348, and declare war, A.D. 1349—The progress of the Turks, A.D. 1341–47—Their fleet—First use of gunpowder and of large cannon—The Turks finally become masters of the Eastern capital, A.D. 1453.

Constantinople, A.D. 718–1453: its increased prosperity.

ALTHOUGH the Greeks had suffered considerable hardship during the thirteen months they were besieged by the Saracens, the siege was no sooner raised than they returned to their usual occupations with increased energy. The losses they had sustained, by an interruption to their maritime commerce, and the curtailment of their home manufactures, required to be met with renewed vigour. Fresh commercial projects were formed and carried into effect with remarkable energy; circumstances favoured their efforts; trade rapidly increased, manufactures flourished; and, as the cities of the West had fallen with the decline of the ancient empire, Constantinople secured a large portion of their commerce, and became a centre of commercial intercourse, equalled only in wealth and influence by Baghdad, the capital city of the Arabian Khalifs.

Nor was her prosperity transient in its nature. During nearly three centuries Constantinople continued to be the principal seat of commercial exchange, increasing in power and influence as the Christians of Syria, Egypt, and Africa respectively shook off the yoke of the Khalifs, and returned to their allegiance to the emperor of the East. Those who had gone to settle in the capital took with them whatever portion of their movable wealth had eluded the search of their oppressors, and Constantinople thus acquired the fugitive trade of Alexandria and Tyre. The chiefs of Armenia and Scythia, flying from hostile or religious persecution, were alike hospitably entertained, and their followers encouraged to build new cities, and to cultivate waste lands within the limits and under the protection of the empire. Increased facilities were afforded to persons engaged in trade and manufactures, and some symptoms of a liberal policy may be traced in a law exempting from personal taxes the mariners of the Peloponnesus, the workmen in parchment and purple, and the manufacturers of linen, wool, and silk. These arts not merely afforded employment to many persons in Constantinople, but to a still greater number in Corinth, Thebes, and Argos. Moreover, from the reign of Justinian to the twelfth century, Greece was the only country in Christendom possessing silkworms, or workmen familiar with the art of preparing their produce.

Manufactures of Greece.

Gibbon describes the manufactures of Greece, during the period of Constantinople's greatest prosperity, as unequalled in elegance and fineness by any similar manufactures of either ancient or modern times. "The gifts," he states, "which a rich and generous matron of Peloponnesus presented to the Emperor Basil, her adopted son, were doubtless fabricated in the Grecian looms. Danielis bestowed a carpet of fine wool, of a pattern which imitated the spots of a peacock's tail, of a magnitude to overspread the floor of a new church, erected in the triple names of Christ, of Michael the Archangel, and of the prophet Elijah. She gave six hundred pieces of silk and linen of various use and denomination; the silk was *painted* with the Tyrian die, and adorned by the labours of the needle; and the linen was so exquisitely fine, that an entire piece might be rolled in the hollow of a cane."[1] The value of these manufactures was estimated according to the weight and quality of the article, the closeness of the texture, and the beauty of the colours; some, too, of the embroidery is said to have been of the most exquisite description.

System of taxation,

But though the mariners and some of the manufacturers were relieved from personal taxation, we have the authority of Benjamin of Tudela, who visited

[1] Gibbon, ch. liii. Constantine, Vit. Basil. ch. lxxiv–lxxvi.

Constantinople in the twelfth century, for the statement that the taxes fell very heavily on the ordinary shopkeepers, and on the merchants of foreign countries who frequented the capital.[1] Nor, indeed, could this have been otherwise, where a system of pomp and luxury was promoted by the imperial rulers, scarcely less than that which had mainly caused the ruin of Rome.

But, besides this, vast sums of money were required to maintain the army and navy, as the command of the Mediterranean, from the mouth of the Tanais (Don) to the Columns of Hercules, was always claimed and often possessed by the successors of Constantine. To secure an adequate fleet, the capital was filled with naval stores and skilled artificers; the native Greeks, from long practice among their own bays and islands, formed excellent sailors; while the trade of Venice and Amalfi also supplied an excellent nursery of seamen for the imperial squadrons.

and of expenditure.

Fleets, and mode of warfare.

"Some estimate," remarks Gibbon,[2] "may be formed of the power of the Greek emperors by the curious and minute detail of the armament which was prepared for the reduction of Crete. A fleet of one hundred and twelve galleys, and seventy-five vessels of the Pamphylian style, was equipped in the capital, the islands of the Ægean Sea, and the seaports of Asia, Macedonia, and Greece. It carried thirty-four thousand mariners, seven thousand three hundred and forty soldiers, seven hundred Russians, and five thousand and eighty-seven Mardaites, whose fathers had been transplanted from the mountains of Libanus. Their pay, most probably of a month, was computed

A.D. 960.

[1] Voyage of Benjamin of Tudela, book i. ch. v. p. 44–52.

[2] Gibbon, c. liii.

at thirty-four centenaries of gold, about one hundred and thirty-six thousand pounds sterling. Our fancy is bewildered by the endless recapitulation of arms and engines, of clothes and linen, of bread for the men and forage for the horses, and of stores and utensils of every description, inadequate to the conquest of a petty island, but amply sufficient for the establishment of a flourishing colony."

Struggle for maritime supremacy.

For several centuries of that period, often termed, though with some injustice, "The Dark Ages," the contests for the maritime supremacy of the Black Sea and Mediterranean were incessant. One barbarous nation succeeded another just as their lust for plunder was stimulated by the wealth of peaceful and unwarlike communities. The Goths and Vandals were followed by the Franks, the Bulgarians, and the Hungarians. Then arose the Russians and Normans, each contending for the chief rule at sea, or for the plunder such superiority enabled them to secure. After these came the Turks, the onward wave of the Tatars and of the Mongols of Central Asia, who, under various names and dynasties, overran the eastern empire, at the period of the Crusades to the Holy Land. Neither the Bulgarians nor the Hungarians were, however, a maritime people. The former took possession of a district of country south of the Danube; and the latter directed their attention to the conquest of the territory, a portion of which they still occupy. Both tribes, with the Turks, were descendants from the same races; and all of them originally, while following pastoral pursuits, had been trained to a military life. With tents made from the skins of their cattle, and dressed in furs, the produce of the hunt, they were easily housed and clothed. Possessing within themselves every want, and trained from their infancy to the use of arms and horses, they were most formidable opponents; the immense hordes with which they advanced generally enabling them to carry all before them.

Previous to the tenth century all the nations, or rather tribes, east of Germany were heterogeneously classed as Scythians. Being almost entirely nomadic, they as a rule disdained commerce, and held peaceful arts, the certain signs of civilization, in contempt. Those of them who were accustomed to the sea made piracy their chief occupation, and gloried in their marauding expeditions. Of these the Scandinavians were among the most daring. Scandinavians; Impatient of a bleak climate, and narrow limits, they were ever ready to make the most distant and hazardous voyages, exploring every coast that promised either spoil or settlement. Though the Baltic was the first scene of their naval achievements, they extended their operations far beyond those seas, and were frequently found in the Euxine, where, with others of the northern tribes, they committed considerable havoc, and, from their superiority in arms and discipline, were greatly feared. About the tenth century there, however, arose among these barbarous hordes of the north the Slavonians, a tribe then occupying Lithuania, but soon better known as the Mus- Muscovites covites, who directed their attention to commercial pursuits. Occupying the chief ports of the Baltic, these people traded in leather, wool, flax, hemp, lead, and amber, receiving in exchange wine, manufactured iron, with dry goods, and a limited supply of silk in the web. But, however intrepid and disposed to persevere in commercial pursuits, their vessels were of the rudest description, and their knowledge of maritime affairs, or of the science and art of navigation, was far behind that of the most ignorant of the nations of the South. Nevertheless the Muscovites extended their trading operations farther to the south and east than any of the northern nations had hitherto done; and, not satisfied with the limited markets on the shores of the Baltic, they visited as traders the North or Arctic Ocean, and the Black and Caspian Seas. The internal navigation of the rivers Dwina, Don, and Volga, extending almost from Archangel to Astrakhan, afforded an almost inexhaustible field for inland and maritime commerce. Every year increased the demand from the western countries of Europe for their furs, salt, dried fish, train oil, honey, flax, and caviare; till at length they also started a trade with Persia by the Black Sea, and with India by the Caspian, being thus the first of modern nations to avail themselves of the ancient overland routes to the far East. St. Petersburgh and Moscow still carry on a considerable commercial intercourse with China by the same means.

their trade and ships.

Although it was not until the ninth century that the Russians are mentioned by name, their monarchy, within one century afterwards, obtained an important place in the map of Constantine, Novgorod and Kief being then considerable entrepôts of commerce. "Between the sea and Novgorod," remarks Gibbon,[1] "an easy intercourse was discovered; in the summer through a gulf, a lake, and a navigable river; in the

Russians: their early commerce,

[1] Gibbon, c. lv.

winter season, over the hard and level surface of boundless snows. From the neighbourhood of that city, the Russians descended the streams that fall into the Borysthenes; their canoes, of a single tree, were laden with slaves of every age, furs of every species, the spoil of their bee-hives, and the hides of their cattle; and the whole produce of the north was collected and discharged in the magazines of Kiow." Thence, after many perils, they ultimately reached Constantinople, and exchanged their cargoes for the produce and manufactures of Greece, and often for the spices of India. A few of their countrymen settled in the capital and the provinces, under full protection of their persons and effects; but they soon abused the hospitality of the Greeks, by inciting those whom they had left behind to make no less than four attacks on the capital city during the first two hundred years of their settlement. They had seen, tasted, and envied the wealth of Constantinople; and then, as in more recent times, they hoped to revel in luxuries they were too barbarous to obtain by honest trade.

and attempts to capture Constantinople.

Their ships.

The vessels used in their first onslaught were in the form of canoes, scraped out of the long stem of a beech or willow tree. "This slight and narrow foundation," says Gibbon, "was raised and continued on either side with planks, till it attained the length of sixty, and the height of about twelve feet. These boats were built without a deck, but with two rudders and a mast, to move with sails and oars, and to contain from forty to seventy men, with their arms and provisions of fresh water and salt fish."[1] In their

[1] Gibbon, c. lv.

A.D. 865. first enterprise, and with an insignificant fleet of two hundred vessels, the Russians, under the princes of Kief, passed the Straits without opposition, and occupied for a short time the port of Constantinople,
A.D. 904. from which, however, they soon retreated. In the
A.D. 941. second, they do not appear to have met with any better success; and the third, though chosen when the Greeks were greatly harassed, and when the naval powers of the empire were employed against the Saracens, proved most disastrous to the Russians. "Fifteen broken and decayed galleys were boldly launched against the enemy; but instead of the single tube of Greek fire, usually planted on the prow, the sides and stern of each vessel were abundantly supplied with that liquid combustible. The engineers were dexterous; the weather was propitious; many thousand Russians, who chose rather to be drowned than burnt, leaped into the sea; and those who escaped to the Thracian shore were inhumanly slaughtered by the peasants and soldiers."[1]

These attempts at naval invasion continued at long intervals, and with varied success; but the fourth and last, ending in the destruction of twenty-four of the Greek galleys, was brought to a close by treaty. The Greeks found that, though victorious, every advantage lay on the side of the Russians; their savage enemy gave no quarter; their poverty promised no spoil; while their impenetrable retreats deprived the conqueror of the hopes of revenge. The Greeks were, therefore, not unwilling to grant liberal terms to their invaders, the terror these attacks caused being increased by a supposed prophecy. "By the vulgar

[1] Gibbon, c. lv.

of every rank," remarks Gibbon, "it was asserted and believed that an equestrian statue in the square of Taurus was secretly inscribed with a prophecy, how the Russians, in the last days, should become masters of Constantinople,"[1]—a belief which, as we know, was still largely shared in, even so recently as the Crimean war of 1854–6.

The Normans and their expeditions.

Towards the decline of the Saracen empires, the Greeks had to contend with the Normans or Northmen, a race as daring and adventurous as the Russians, and much more skilled in sea-faring pursuits. This remarkable people had recently left their frozen homes in Norway and adventured upon unknown and distant oceans, penetrating as far as the Mediterranean with numerous fleets, and rendering themselves more dreaded by their maritime genius than the Russians or Saracens had ever been. Ravaging Flanders, France, Spain, and Italy, after an infinite series of piratical exploits, they compelled Charles the Simple to cede and assign to them A.D. 918. the large territory now known as Normandy; and, following up this success by various adventures in the south of Europe, obtained for themselves a great name and influence. Thus the Norman kingdoms of Naples and Sicily, during the eleventh century, played an important part in the drama of the history of Italy and of the eastern empire.

Establish themselves in Italy, A.D. 1016.

It is not our intention in this work to follow the Normans in their conquests or defeats, except in so far as these bear on their maritime exploits, and on their connection, limited though this may be, with commerce. At first, a large number of them appear

[1] Gibbon, c. lv.

to have earned their daily subsistence by the sword, having constantly mixed themselves up in the domestic quarrels then incessantly raging between the rulers and people of the southern states of Italy; till at length, chiefly through the aid of the Duke of Naples, whose cause they had espoused, they secured their first settlement in Italy. Within eight miles of his residence, he built and fortified for their use the town of Aversa, granting to them, also, a considerable tract of the fertile country in the vicinity, over which they were vested with complete control. Year by year numerous pilgrims from all parts of Europe, but especially from the north, found shelter under the independent standard of Aversa, and were quickly assimilated with the manners and language of the Gallic colony. But the Norman power soon extended far beyond the infant and limited colony of Aversa, and embraced the whole of the territory, which for centuries, and, indeed, until the last few years, was known as the kingdom of Naples. Within that territory, thirty miles from Naples, stood the commercially celebrated republic of Amalfi.

Amalfi.

Although the port of Amalfi, from which the republic derived its name, is now an obscure place, no western harbour then contained a more enterprising maritime population. Its position, not unlike that of Tyre, afforded great facilities for carrying on an extensive sea-borne commerce. Hence it was that Amalfi, in its day, had a very extensive intercourse with all parts of the then known world, and was among the earliest of the Italian republics to hold in its hands the trade of the Mediterranean. Long before the Venetians and Genoese had become famous, this small but indefatigable republic assumed the office of supplying the western world with the manufactures and productions of the East, and that trade proved then, as has been the case in all ages, a source of immense profit. Though the city contained only fifty thousand inhabitants, its wealth was enormous, and its merchants, who had correspondence with all parts of the coasts of the Mediterranean, dealt largely in the commodities of both Arabia and India. Their settlements in Constantinople, Antioch, Jerusalem, and Alexandria, acquired the privileges of independent colonies. No city or seaport of those days contained more mariners who excelled in the theory or practice of navigation and astronomy than Amalfi; indeed, it was long supposed, that to the skill of one of the seamen of this city, the world owed the discovery of the mariner's compass.[1]

But, after three hundred years of great prosperity, arising entirely from the energetic, and, at the same time, honest pursuit of commerce, Amalfi, oppressed by the arms of the Normans, was at last brought under their rule. Shorn of its independence, and depressed in spirit, the city was soon after attacked by the jealousy of Pisa, one of its commercial rivals; A.D. 1137.

[1] There seems much doubt about the story of the invention of the mariner's compass by Flavio Gioga, an Amalfite, in A.D. 1307. The city had ceased to have any commercial importance since its sack by the Pisans in A.D. 1137 (Sismondi, i. p. 303); while, on the other hand, Hallam shows that the compass was known as early as A.D. 1100 (Mid. Ages, iii. 394); and Wachsmuth proves that it was used in Sweden in A.D. 1250 (Ersch und Grüber's Encycl. iii. 302). The Italian *bussola*, from the French *boussole*, comes again from the Flemish *Boxel* (box);—hence, probably, our term of "boxing" the compass. It was most likely a northern discovery.

but the ruined palaces of its merchants, and the remains of an arsenal and cathedral, still attest its former splendour and importance.[1]

Not satisfied with the possessions they had already secured in Italy and with their conquest of Sicily, the Normans next resolved on the conquest of Constantinople itself.

Futile attempts of the Normans to take Constantinople, A.D. 1081-1084.

Their first attempt was made from the port of Otranto, where, after a preparation of two years, they had collected a fleet of one hundred and fifty vessels, and thirty thousand men, including one thousand five hundred Norman knights. But this expedition proved a calamitous failure. The Normans were no longer the experienced or adventurous mariners, who had explored unknown oceans, from Greenland to Africa; hence, in a great storm they encountered at the mouth of the Adriatic, many of their ships were shattered, while others were dashed on shore and became hopeless wrecks. Besides, a new, and a naval, enemy had arisen in the Venetians, who, at the solicitations and promises of the Byzantine court, were ready enough to aid in the overthrow of the hated Normans, and, with a view of tempting commercial advantages for themselves, to assist in defending the capital of the East. And so it befell, that what the storm had spared of the Norman fleet, the Venetians and Greek fire destroyed; add to which, the Greek populations,

[1] Hallam remarks that "it was the singular fate of this city to have filled up the interval between two periods of civilization, in neither of which she was destined to be distinguished. Scarcely known before the end of the sixth century, Amalfi ran a brilliant career as a free and trading republic, which was checked by the arms of a conqueror in the middle of the twelfth."—Mid. Ages, iii. 300.

sallying from their towns along the southern shores of Italy, carried slaughter and dismay to the tents of the chiefs of the Norman invaders.

But three years afterwards, their indefatigable duke (Robert Guiscard) resumed the design of his eastern conquests; preferring, on this occasion, as the season was far advanced, the harbour of Brundusium to the open road of Otranto for the assembling of his fleet of one hundred and twenty vessels. However, in the interval Alexius, the emperor, had assiduously laboured to restore the naval forces of the empire, obtaining at the same time, at an exorbitant price, the aid from the republic of Venice of thirty-six transports, fourteen galleys, and nine galiots, or ships of unusual strength and magnitude. The goods and merchandise of the rivals of the Venetians at Amalfi were taxed to raise the required sum; and by granting special privileges, such as the licence or monopoly of trade in the port of Constantinople, with the gift of many shops and houses, Alexius propitiated the good will of the Venetian merchants. But this expedition was so far successful, that the Normans captured and destroyed many of the vessels of the combined fleets; it failed, however, to take Constantinople, against which the Normans relinquished any attempts worthy of notice after the death in the following year of their prince, Guiscard.

Rise of Venice.

While the power and name of the Romans was passing away under the imbecile rule of the Greek emperors, and commerce and navigation shared in the general decay, a new maritime power, the State of Venice, destined to become the greatest of the Italian republics, was imperceptibly increasing in strength and renown. From the time when the A.D. 452. inhabitants of that portion of Italy, now known as Venetian Lombardy, were driven by Alaric, the barbarian conqueror, to seek refuge in the small islands of the Adriatic, near the mouth of the Brenta, their progress had been one of almost uninterrupted prosperity. Devoting their attention exclusively to the pursuits of commerce, and avoiding, by every means in their power, interference with the affairs of their neighbours, the Venetians drew towards their infant colony all whose habits and tempers induced them to seek industrial pursuits. Among these, many families of Aquileia, Padua, and other towns, fleeing from the sword of the Huns and similar barbarous tribes, found a safe but obscure refuge. A modern writer[1] has eloquently described Venice as "immoveable on the bosom of the waters from which her palaces emerge, contemplating the tides of continental convulsions and invasions, the rise and fall of empires, and the change of dynasties;" and certainly no description could be more true of the splendour and position of Venice, and of the policy of its rulers, when at the height of its prosperity.

The cause of its prosperity. But many centuries elapsed from the time when the infant colony was planted, before "the water fowl, who had fixed their nests on the bosom of the waves,"[2] obtained a prominent and independent position as a great maritime nation. Although in the early career of the Venetians their independence was more especially due to their determination to attend to their own affairs, and not to trouble themselves with

[1] Sismondi, Republ. Ital. du Moyen Age, i. p. 203.
[2] Cassiodor. Var. l. 12. Epist. 24.

those of their neighbours, at a later period the western[1] and eastern empires, in turn, claimed authority over them, and thus they were invaded and at last conquered by Pepin, father of Charlemagne, though ultimately restored to the Greek empire in the tenth century. The Venetians therefore can hardly be considered as a really independent republic till they had acquired the maritime cities of Dalmatia A.D. 997.
and Istria, including the people of Ragusa, the posterity of the mariners who, in classical times, owned and manned the fast sailing Liburnians. The population of these coasts still retained the piratical habits of their ancestors; and having in some respects identical interests to defend, were not unwilling to place themselves under the strong government of the Venetians. From that period the Venetians carried on, for between four and five centuries, a most important commercial intercourse with other nations, and exercised, as a trading people, more influence than any other country had done before them. The long duration of this enterprising republic, with its maritime greatness and vast commerce, will, with the story of the sister republics of Genoa and Pisa, form a subject to which we shall frequently have occasion hereafter to refer. It is enough now to remark that these cities, all favourably situated for conducting an extensive maritime

[1] The power of Venice at this early period (A.D. 774) is well shown by the aid it gave to Charlemagne, at his request, during his siege of Pavia, of twenty-four galleons said to have carried six thousand horse and foot. This fact has been recently illustrated by Mr. W. De Gray Birch, of the MS. Room of the British Museum, who has published a contemporary leaden tablet, in which it is recorded. (Archæol. xliv. pp. 123–136. 1872.)

commerce, were among the first to revive the genuine spirit of trade in the south of Europe after it had been almost annihilated by the repeated inundations of the barbarians.

Spread of the Scythians, Huns, or Turks, A.D 997–1028. A.D. 1074–1084.

The nomad Tatar, or so-called Scythian populations, have been already slightly noticed; the rapidity with which they spread their arms over Asia having been a matter of surprise to every historian who has written on the subject. About the time of Mahmud of Ghazna, after having overrun the West of India, an important section of them settled in great force in Asia Minor. Opposed to the Greeks and their religion, they became the most powerful enemies the eastern Roman empire had yet encountered; and their occupation of the Holy Land, with their conquest of Jerusalem, led to conflicts with the Greeks only less terrible than had been the earlier wars between the Saracens and the nations of the West. Their ignorance of navigation alone deferred for a time the fall of the eastern empire, though internally weak and decrepid, chiefly owing to the blow it received during the Crusades, and from which it had never recovered.[1]

A.D. 1076–1096.

The Crusades, A.D. 1095–1099.

The first Crusade, made about twenty years after the conquest of Jerusalem, had for its object the recovery of the Holy City from the infidel. To replace the Cross in Palestine, where the Crescent had been impiously raised, was a duty the whole of Christendom considered itself bound to accomplish. But the Christians in their enthusiasm undertook a task as wild as it was disastrous, and one, too, so miserably planned, that three hundred thousand of the

[1] Speaking of Timúr, Gibbon observes, "the lord of so many myriads of horse was not master of a single galley," c. lxv.

first Crusaders lost their lives, either by fatigue and hunger or by disease and the weapons of the Saracens, before they rescued a single city from their grasp.

The second Crusade called into action the whole of the West, from Rome to Britain. At its head were displayed the banners of the dukes of Burgundy, Bavaria, and Aquitaine; and the kings of Poland and Bohemia obeyed the summons of the leader of an army estimated at more than four hundred thousand men. But the numbers appear to have been still greater in the third Crusade, which was made both by sea and land, and included the siege of Acre, graphically described by Gibbon[1] in his "Decline and Fall of the Roman Empire." After the surrender of Acre, and the departure of Philip, Richard of England, whose name was long an object of terror among the Saracens, led the Crusaders to the recovery of the sea-coast; and the cities of Cæsarea and Jaffa, afterwards added to the fragments of the kingdom of Guy de Lusignan, fell into his hands, as Jerusalem would also have done, had he not been deceived by the envy or the treachery of his companions. But Plantagenet and Saládin became, in time, alike weary of a war so tedious and disastrous in its results, especially as both had suffered in health. An agreement between them was, after much delay, brought about, and was, naturally, disapproved by the zealots of both parties alike—the Roman pontiff and the Khalif of Baghdad. Its leading features were, that Jerusalem and the Holy Sepulchre should be open, without hindrance or tribute, to the pilgrimages of the Latin Christians; and that during three years

A.D. 1147.

Siege of Acre, A.D. 1189.

Armistice, A.D. 1192.

[1] Gibbon, c. lix.

and three months all hostilities should cease. In the following year Saládin died; and, immediately after the conclusion of the treaty, Richard returned to Europe "to seek a long captivity and a premature grave."

But the spirit of religious warfare did not rest. Will it ever do so? A fourth Crusade soon followed. In this case, however, the Crusade was directed from Syria to Constantinople; and as there was an armistice between the Crescent and the Cross, the self-constituted avengers of the latter quarrelled among themselves—the restoration of the western empire by Charlemagne having created differences between the Greek and Latin Churches, which had in course of time become serious feuds, to be settled only by bloodshed. The aversion existing between the Greeks and Latins had been manifested in the three first expeditions. Though alike opposed to the creed of the Muhammedans, the pride of the emperor of the East was wounded by the intrusion of foreign armies, who claimed the right of traversing his dominions, and of passing under the walls of the capital. He urged, not without reason, that his subjects were insulted and plundered by the rude strangers of the West; perhaps, too, he secretly envied the bold enterprises of the Franks.

Fourth Crusade, A.D. 1202.

While, however, the passage of vast armies in their pilgrimage to the Holy Land roused feelings of animosity between the two great sections of professing Christians, they very materially increased their commercial intercourse, and enlarged their knowledge without abating their religious prejudices. Constantinople proved, commercially, of great importance to the

The effect of the Crusades on the commerce of Constantinople,

West, as the then chief entrepôt of exchange with the distant nations of the East, and as requiring for the wants of her own wealthy and luxurious people the productions of every climate. From her situation she invited the commerce of the world, and the art and labour of her numerous inhabitants, while it balanced the imports, afforded profitable employment to the number of foreign merchants resident at Constantinople, and to their ships in which her over-sea trade was chiefly conducted. After the decline of Amalfi, the Venetians, Pisans, and Genoese, had introduced their factories and settlements into the capital of the empire, had acquired possession of land and houses, and had greatly increased in numbers, intermingling by marriage, and in all the social relations of life, with the natives. Constantinople was therefore largely indebted for her prosperity and wealth to the foreign merchants resident in, or frequenting her port; and, hence when these demanded the right of worshipping in accordance with the Latin forms of Christianity, the emperor, who had tolerated a Muhammedan mosque,[1] was unable to refuse the demand of the Christians of the West. A.D. 1148.

But his good intentions, and those of his successor, Alexius, were stopped by a popular tumult, which ended in a terrible massacre of all the Latins whom the vengeance of a mob, headed and applauded by the Greek priesthood, could reach. Many, however, of the foreign merchants had escaped on the first alarm to their vessels, and in these they proceeded to the western ports to seek protection and redress for the wrongs inflicted upon themselves and their countrymen. and on its fall.

Joined in their appeal by the son[2] of the dethroned

[1] Gibbon, c. lix.

[2] Gibbon, c. lx.

monarch, Alexius Angelus, who had escaped in the disguise of a common sailor on board an Italian vessel, their case was at once promised consideration, and was soon after brought under the notice of the leading pilgrims of the West, Baldwin, Count of Flanders, and the Marquis of Montferrat, then assembled at Venice, to negotiate with that republic for shipping to convey them on the Fourth Crusade.[1] For many centuries the inhabitants of Venice had been considered as a portion of the subjects of the Greek empire; but when their power and influence had greatly increased, notably by the acquisition of the cities on the coasts of Istria and Dalmatia, the extent of their maritime commerce entitled them to assume an independent position. "The sea was their patrimony;" and with the chief command of the western shores of the Mediterranean, the Venetian galleys had now secured the still more lucrative commerce of Greece and Egypt.

Power of Venice, A.D. 1202.

Nor were they simply traders: Venetian glass and silk manufactures had an early reputation; while their system of banking and of foreign exchange, which they worked on a much more extensive scale than any other

[1] It seems worth while to append here a note concerning the results of the principal Crusades.

First Crusade.—Preached by Peter the Hermit, and led by Robert Guiscard and Godfrey de Bouillon, chiefly against the Seljuk Turks, A.D. 1096. Jerusalem taken, A.D. 1099.

Second Crusade.—Preached by St. Bernard, and led by Louis VII. and Conrad III., A.D. 1146. Stopped by the Seljuk Turks, by their victory at Iconium (Konieh), A.D. 1147.

Third Crusade.—To avenge the capture in A.D. 1187 of Jerusalem by Saladin; and led by Frederick Barbarossa, Richard Cœur-de-Lion, and Philip of France, A.D. 1188. Results: Acre, Joppa, and Askalon taken from Saladin, A.D. 1192.

Fourth Crusade.—Led by Baldwin, Count of Flanders, with aid from Venice, A.D. 1202. Results: taking of Zara and of Constantinople, A.D. 1204.

The remaining Crusades were, comparatively, unimportant.

nation, gave them a great commercial preponderance in the south of Europe. To assert these rights and to protect the freedom of their subjects, they are said to have been able to equip at very short notice one hundred galleys; but their usual policy was essentially that of merchants, and was almost wholly regulated by their trading interests. In their religious dogmas the Venetians avoided the schism of the Greeks without yielding a servile obedience to the Roman pontiff; while an unrestrained intercourse with the Muhammedans, as well as with other nations, encouraged in her people a spirit of toleration unknown to the Crusaders.

Her ships join in the Crusade, which was afterwards altered from its original design.

Venice was, therefore, in no haste to launch into a holy war, and the appeal of the pilgrim ambassadors, "sent by the greatest and most powerful barons of France, to implore the aid of the masters of the sea for the deliverance of Jerusalem," though ultimately successful, was granted only with reservation and mainly on selfish conditions. The Crusaders, after considering these (they had, indeed, little option), determined to assemble at Venice, so as to start on their expedition on the feast of St. John of the ensuing year; the Venetians, at the same time, engaging to provide flat-bottomed vessels enough for the conveyance of four thousand five hundred knights and twenty thousand foot, with the necessary provisions for nine months, together with a squadron of fifty galleys. The pilgrims, on the other hand, promised to pay the Venetians, before their departure, eighty-four thousand marks of silver; any conquests by sea and land to be equally divided between the confederates. These exorbitant demands were acceded to, the enthusiasm of the people enabling fifty-two thousand marks to be collected and paid within a short time.

But the expedition was diverted from its original design. Thirty-two thousand of the promised marks being still wanted to complete the stipulated sum, the Doge, Henry Dandolo, offered to waive this claim, provided the combined forces were first employed in the reduction of Zara, a strong city on the opposite shores of the Adriatic, which had recently thrown off its allegiance to Venice. After much discussion and many differences of opinion this proposal was accepted, and proved fully successful; but the sack of Zara scattered wide the seeds of discord and scandal; and many were shocked that the arms of professing Crusaders should have been first stained with the blood, not of the Infidel, but of the Christian.

The presence of this great force revived the hopes of the young Alexius, while the tale of the massacre of the Latins at Constantinople seemed to demand a punishment adequate to its atrocity. The separate interests of many and various parties supported his appeal; the Doge hoped to increase the commercial power of Venice by humbling that of the eastern capital; Alexius was warmly backed by Philip of Germany and the Marquis of Montferrat; while the promises of the young man himself were liberal enough to suggest more than a suspicion of his honesty. In the end it was determined to make a further diversion of the hosts originally consecrated to the deliverance of Jerusalem, and to employ them on what to the miscellaneous multitude must have been the far more congenial office of ravaging and plundering the Greek empire. It can, indeed, hardly be supposed that many of the Crusaders could have believed themselves bound to aid in the restoration of an exiled prince as a step in any way necessary for the recovery of Jerusalem; while the savage treatment the unfortunate Jews met with at their hands in every city they passed through, shows how little their enthusiasm for the Cross was tempered by anything resembling Christianity. The large majority were, doubtless, mainly swayed by the hope or the certainty of public plunder or private gain.

They besiege and take Constantinople, A.D. 1204.

Although the boldest hearts were appalled by the report of the naval power and impregnable strength of Constantinople, the Venetians vigorously urged on the scheme, seeing clearly that for them it was now or never, and that, with the aid of the formidable forces at their disposal, they would be able to avenge themselves for many insults and injuries they had received from the Byzantine court. No such armament had, indeed, for ages, if ever, assembled on the waters of the Adriatic. Consisting of no less than one hundred and twenty flat-bottomed vessels for the horses; of two hundred and forty transports filled with men and arms; of seventy store ships laden with provisions; and of fifty stout galleys prepared to encounter any enemy, the expedition presented a most imposing appearance.

Favoured with fine weather and a fair wind the fleet made rapid progress, and, without interruption or loss, anchored, after an unusually quick passage, at Abydos, on the Asiatic side of the Hellespont. But here a strong gale sprung up, and swept them to the eastward, and so close were they brought to the city, that some volleys of stones and darts were exchanged between them and the ramparts. Most of the invaders then beheld, for the first time, the capital of the East; and few cities can boast of so imposing an appearance; nor could it fail to create a deep impression on the minds of the invaders. Vain, indeed, would have been the attempt of the Crusaders to conquer such a city had its people been united, or its ruler a man of ability and honesty. The sixteen hundred fishing boats of Constantinople could in themselves have manned a fleet, which, with their fire-ships, would have been sufficient to have annihilated the forces of the Crusaders; but the negligence of the prince, and the venality of his ministers rendered the great city under their charge an easy prey. There was of course a show of resistance, but it was so feeble that the tower of Galata, in the suburb of Pera, was quickly stormed, and easily captured by the French; while the Venetians forced the boom or chain that was stretched from the tower to the Byzantine shores, captured or destroyed twenty Grecian ships of war, and made themselves masters of the port of Constantinople.

During the sixty years that the Latins held in their hands the empire of the East, the Greek emperors kept their court and maintained a feeble dignity at Nicæa (Nice), the most important city in Bithynia. Yet, though at that city a certain show of pomp and power was maintained, the removal of the empire from Constantinople, and the sway there of the Latin princes, produced the most disastrous effects on the trade of the capital: a race alien in religion and language, and anarchy withal, were not, indeed, likely to be favourable to peaceful arts or commerce. When, however, the Greek empire was afterwards restored in the person of Manuel, that wise monarch paid little heed to the factions of the Venetians and of other republicans from Italy, but encouraged their industry by many privileges, and allowed them

Commerce declines under the Latins,

but revives on the restoration of the empire, A.D. 1261.

full use of their own customs. Thus the merchants resident at Constantinople preserved their respective quarters in the city, trading thence whither and how they pleased.

Genoa.

The early history of Genoa was not unlike that of Venice; in so far at least, that, like it, Genoa had been for some centuries under the control, if not the vassal, of the eastern empire: at the period, however, to which we are now referring, the Genoese had a large colony at the seaport town of Heraclea, in Thrace. From this place the gratitude of the Greek emperor, Michael, recalled them, at the same time giving them the exclusive privilege of the suburb of Galata—a settlement whereby, more than by anything else, the commerce of the Byzantine empire was revived.[1]

Genoese settlement at Galata and Pera.

Though indulged in the use of their own laws and magistrates, the Genoese were required to submit to the duties of subjects, and undertook, in case of a defensive war, to supply the Greek emperor with fifty empty galleys and fifty more completely armed and equipped. In consideration of these services, and to afford them protection from the Venetian fleets, the Genoese were allowed the dangerous privilege of surrounding Galata with a strong wall and wet ditch, with lofty towers and engines of war on their ramparts. No wonder that, having secured so much, they should seek to acquire more, and that, within a short space of time, they had covered the adjacent hills with their villas and castles, each fort being connected with the next, and protected by new fortifications. Nor, as was natural, did they stop here; they

[1] Gibbon, ch. lxiii.

soon sought to possess themselves of the whole trade of the Black Sea, long the especial patrimony of the emperors of Constantinople, and a prerogative which, in the reign of Michael, had been acknowledged by even Bibars, the Mamluk Sultan of Egypt.

Nor, having resolved on the end, were they long in hesitating about the means to it; first, in seemingly friendly alliance with the Greeks, they secured for their colonies at Galata and Pera the bulk of the corn trade; while, at the same time, their fishermen supplied the wants of the city, the salt fish largely required by the Catholic nations, and caviare for the Russians. Next, they secured for themselves the produce of the inland caravan trade with the remote East, which still, as formerly, found its way by the waters of the Oxus and the Caspian to the eastern shores of the Euxine. In almost every case, their course of business was a strict monopoly, the Venetians and all other rivals being carefully excluded from any participation in their trade. So powerful, indeed, did they become, that, while they awed the Greeks into a reluctant submission, they resisted effectually, at their chief settlement, Caffa,[1] the inroad of the Tatar hosts. The demands of the Genoese merchants were in proportion to their rapacity, and at last they actually usurped the customs and even the tolls of the Bosphorus, securing for themselves alone a revenue of two hundred thousand pieces of gold, of which they reluctantly doled out to the emperor thirty thousand.

Arrogance of the Genoese,

[1] So late as Chardin, four hundred sail of vessels were occupied at Caffa during forty days in the corn and fish trade. ("Voy. en Pérse," i. pp. 46–48.) Clarke found it wholly demolished by the Russians ("Travels," i. p. 144)—and so it is now.

The usurpations of the Genoese, which extended over nearly a century, every year increasing in their arrogance, ended, as might have been anticipated, with a demand for the empire itself. Having been refused some commanding heights at Pera, on which to erect additional fortifications, they embraced the opportunity of the emperor's temporary absence from his capital to rise in open rebellion. "A Byzantine vessel," remarks Gibbon,[1] "which had presumed to fish at the mouth of the harbour, was sunk by these audacious strangers; the fishermen were murdered. Instead of suing for pardon, the Genoese demanded satisfaction; required in a haughty strain that the Greeks should renounce the exercise of navigation; and encountered with regular arms the first sallies of the popular indignation. They instantly occupied the debatable land; and by the labour of a whole people, of either sex and of every age, the wall was raised, and the ditch was sunk with incredible speed. At the same time, they attacked and burnt two Byzantine galleys; while the three others, the remainder of the imperial navy, escaped from their hands; the habitations without the gates or along the shore were pillaged and destroyed; and the care of the regent, of the empress Irene, was confined to the preservation of the city. The return of Cantacuzene dispelled the public consternation; the emperor inclined to peaceful counsels, but he yielded to the obstinacy of his enemies, who rejected all reasonable terms, and to the ardour of his subjects, who threatened, in the style of Scripture, 'to break them in pieces like a potter's vessel.' . . . . The merchants of the colony, who had

who at last rebel, A.D. 1348,

[1] Gibbon, ch. lxiii.

believed that a few days would terminate the war, already murmured at their losses; the succours from their mother-country were delayed by the factions of Genoa; and the most cautious embraced the opportunity of a Rhodian vessel to remove their families and effects from the scene of hostility."

and declare war, A.D. 1349. The peaceful counsels of the emperor having proved of no avail, the Byzantine fleet in the spring of the following year attacked Pera by sea, while the Greek troops assaulted its walls and ramparts. The attack, however, wholly failed; the Genoese carried all before them, and, crowning their galleys with flowers, they added to this insult the throwing, by means of their engines, of large stones into the very heart of the imperial city. To insults such as these even Cantacuzene could not submit; but, discerning clearly his own weakness, it occurred to him that other and known enemies of Genoa might do for him what he had not strength to do for himself: hence his appeal to Venice, as the great naval rival of Genoa, and a yet more fatal coquetry with the Turkish hosts, who by this time were in full possession of the wide plains of Asia Minor.

Nor were the Venetians slow to accept an offer likely to lead to the humbling of enemies so inveterate. The war assumed proportions nowise foreseen, and fluctuated for more than a century with alternate success, but with ultimate ruin to the Genoese, whose audacity had provoked it. During the whole of this struggle the eastern empire practically counted as nothing, and would, but for the intervention of the Venetians, have sunk into a province of Genoa. The connection, however, with the Turkish tribes led to more deplorable disasters, in that, owing to the weakness of the emperor, an opportunity was now, for the first time, afforded to them of obtaining a footing on the sacred land of Europe itself. The progress of the Turks, A.D. 1341–1347.

The time had indeed come when a Greek emperor, more fearful of his own life than of the honour of his people, could seek the advice, if not the direct aid, of the enemies of his faith and country. The Turks, seeing the chance of great ultimate advantages, were not unwilling to grant his requests. Under the pretence of protecting one of their race, who had taken up his residence at the Greek court, they assembled at Smyrna a fleet of three hundred vessels and twenty-nine thousand men, in the depth of winter, and casting anchor at the mouth of the Hebrus, under the further pretext of guarding their fleet, landed nine thousand five hundred of their men; thus for the first time establishing themselves on the continent of Europe. A position, however small, thus obtained, the further spread of the Turkish arms was but a question of time. In a few years they were settled in their new homes; a little later, the whole province of Roumania and of Thrace fell into their hands; and, in less than forty years from their first arrival, all the country round Constantinople, including Adrianople, which they had made their western capital, became subject to them. From this time the fate of Constantinople was sealed, and the overthrow of the Cross by the Crescent but a question of a few years. Their fleet. A.D. 1353. A.D. 1360–1389.

Various reasons, however, prevented the immediate capture of Constantinople; nor was it till sixty years after the Turks had secured Adrianople, that Muhammed II., who had unceasingly sighed for its possession, resolved, by an attack of sufficient magnitude, and at any cost, to make it the centre of the Muhammedan arms and religion, and to haul down the Christian banner, which for more than a thousand years had waved over its battlements. Nor was he unsupported by many favouring accidents, of which the most valuable was the discovery of gunpowder, as this engine of destruction rendered the Greek fire of comparatively little advantage, and left success to those who had best studied the qualities of the new explosive compound.[1] Muhammed at once devoted himself to its serious study, the result being that the cannon he cast for the siege of Constantinople are generally admitted to have been greatly superior to any weapons of the class hitherto invented.

First use of gunpowder, and of large cannon.

While Muhammed threatened the capital of the East, the Greek emperor implored in vain the assistance of the Christian powers of the West, who were either too weak or too much engaged with their own contentions, even where favourably disposed, to render him assistance. Even the princes of the Morea and of the Greek islands affected a cold neutrality, while the Sultan indulged the Genoese in the delusive hope that they would still be allowed to retain the advantages they had possessed under the empire as regarded their trade with the city and on the Euxine.

The Turks finally become masters of the Eastern capital, A.D. 1453.

But Constantinople did not fall without a desperate and bloody struggle; and had the zeal and ability of its inhabitants equalled the heroism of the last Constantine, the banner of the Cross might have floated even until now over the great city of the Eastern Empire.

[1] The precise era of the invention and application of gunpowder is involved in doubt, and has formed the subject of many learned disquisitions, not the least interesting of which will be found in the 1st and 2nd vols. of Bishop Watson's "Chemical Essays."

CHAPTER IX.

Ancient galleys—Different descriptions—Their outfit—Beaks—Stern—Masts and sails—Oars—Mode of rowing—Single-banked galleys—French galley—General Melvill's theory—Charnock's theory—Vossius's views—Mr. Howell's plan—Plan of Revd. J. O. W. Haweis (Appendix No. 1)—Our own views—Biremes—Triremes—Quadriremes—Quinqueremes—Hexiremes and larger galleys—Suggested plan of placing the rowers—Summary.

Ancient galleys.

FREQUENT reference has been made in the course of this work to the row-galleys of the ancients, and no subject connected with shipping has called forth more conflicting opinions: nor is this surprising. Most ancient writers who refer to it are less or more at variance with each other; while the representations on coins and monumental sculptures are generally on so small a scale as to afford little assistance in its elucidation. Within the last two centuries numerous authors have endeavoured to solve the problem how these galleys were classed and rowed, and to establish a system of propulsion which, while applicable to every class, would harmonize with the accounts preserved of the size of these vessels and of the number of rowers employed on board of them.

Different descriptions.

Galleys appear to have been rated by their bank of oars, that is, uniremes had one, biremes two, triremes three, quadriremes four, quinqueremes five, and so forth, up to the enormous ship of Ptolemy Philopator, which we have already noticed. But the chief point of controversy has been what constituted a bank.

According to Homer,[1] the Greek fleet at the siege of Troy consisted entirely of uniremes. They were then undecked, with the exception of a platform at each end on which the archers or principal fighting men stood, and were guided by oars or sweeps at both extremities so as to ensure rapid evolution. Pliny[2] states that the Erythræans were the first who built biremes. Various ancient writers give the Corinthians the credit for having been the first to construct triremes. "And now Greece," remarks Thucydides,[3] "began to construct navies and to apply herself more assiduously to nautical affairs. The first who introduced a change in the structure of vessels, so as to form them very nearly in the present mode, are said to have been the Corinthians; and *triremes* are thought to have been built first for Greece at Corinth. It appears, too, that Ameinocles, a Corinthian ship-builder, also constructed four such vessels for the Samians."

B.C. 430. Although triremes, in the time of Thucydides, and for some centuries afterwards, were more approved for purposes of war than any other description of vessel, the authority of Pliny, Athenæus,[4] Polybius,[5] and others is sufficient proof that vessels of four, five, six, and ten banks of oars were built;—that Alexander increased the number of banks to twelve;

[1] Hom. Il. ii. 510. Od. xii. 409, &c.

[2] Plin. vii. 207, cf. Cic. ad Attic. xvi. 4. The *biremis* was often a little boat managed by two oars. Horat. iii. 29, 62. Lucan, viii. 562.

[3] Thucyd. i. c. 13. [4] Athen. v. 37. [5] Polyb. in Excerpt.

—that Philip, father of Perseus, had a galley of sixteen banks;[1] and—that vessels of four and five banks were frequently engaged in war. The triremes, however, were much more numerous than any other class of galleys except those which had only one bank of oars. Themistocles built three hundred triremes for the purpose of carrying on the war against Ægina; and obtained a decree authorizing the construction of a further, but limited number of these vessels from the produce of the mines of Laureium.[2] By his influence twenty triremes were annually built by the Athenians so as to maintain in efficient order a permanent fleet of from three to four hundred vessels of this description.[3] Triremes consisted of two classes, fighting ships and transports. The former were propelled at great speed, frequently reaching seven to eight miles an hour; the number of rowers employed on each varying from fifty to two hundred. The transports were bulkier and stronger vessels, and, though armed, were not brought into action except in cases of urgent necessity.

No mention is made of any vessel with more than B.C. 431-403.
three banks of oars having been employed in the
Peloponnesian war, but quadriremes and quinque- B.C. 400.
remes were known in the reign of Dionysius I., of B.C. 255.
Syracuse, and were employed by the Carthaginians in the first Punic war, who had also in their service some vessels of the hexireme and septireme class. From the ease, however, with which the Romans captured these large vessels (even allowing for their superior energy and vigorous mode of close action), they were evidently much less efficient in proportion

[1] Liv. xlv. 34. [2] Plutarch, Themist. c. 4. [3] Plut. ibid.

to their size than triremes. Nevertheless, according to the testimony of Plutarch, very large galleys were in high favour with Demetrius Poliorcetes,[1] whom he represents as a prince possessing superior knowledge of the arts, and of a highly inventive turn of mind. This prince, he states, caused several of fifteen and sixteen banks to be built, he himself superintending their construction; and so formidable are these vessels said to have appeared, that Lysimachus, when he had ocular confirmation of the reports he had heard of their strength and capacity, raised the siege of Rhodes rather than encounter them in action. Plutarch also states that Antony[2] possessed a fleet of no less than five hundred armed vessels, magnificently adorned, having eight and ten banks of oars, and that he selected the best and largest of them for the celebrated battle of Actium. However exaggerated some of the accounts preserved of these very large galleys may be, and however imperfect and inconsistent the descriptions of them by ancient authors, their existence has been established beyond all doubt.

Their outfit.

With reference to their outfit, it is sufficient to state that, in nearly every instance, they were highly ornamented with figures carved on the bow and stern. Below the bow, and between it and the fore-foot or keel, there was generally a projecting piece of very strong timber, to which was attached either a ram's head, sharp metal bolts, cleavers, or some other instrument of destruction. These beaks were at first constructed so as to be visible above the water, but

Beaks.

[1] Plut. Vit. Demet. c. 10.

[2] Plut. Vit. Anton. c. 4. Hor. iv. ii. 4. Virg. Æn. viii. 691. Dio. L. 33.

afterwards they were immersed, like the beaks of the iron-clad rams of our own time, themselves evidently copies from the original Grecian and Roman designs. The most trustworthy illustrations of these have been taken from the Trajan column and a few

coins of the period, of which the accompanying drawings are fair representations. Nearly the whole of the ancient war-galleys had their bows and

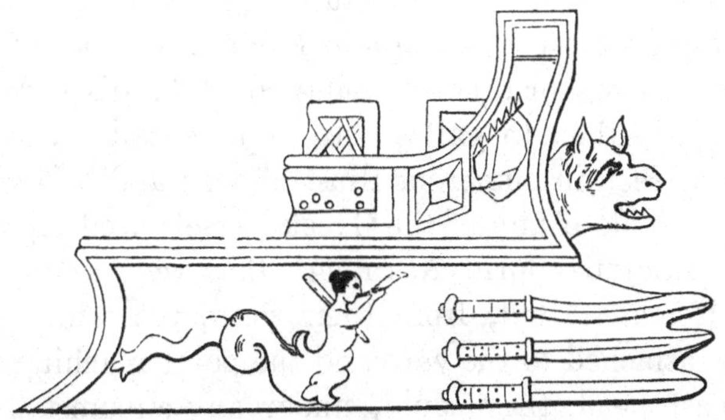

sterns considerably elevated above the level of the deck. From the former, or the "*coursier*"—centre platform—an officer regulated the duties of the rowers; whilst the pilot directed, from the quarter-deck, the course of the ship. In many cases, this officer sat under a highly ornamented canopy, from Stern.

which he issued his commands, and behind it there was usually carved the image of the tutelar deity of the galley. From the flag-staff floated her ensign or private signal; and, sometimes, a large vane on the taffrail pointed to the direction of the wind. On the column of Trajan a lantern is shown suspended close to the stern in one of the galleys. Each trireme carried two wooden ladders and three "spreads," poles of different lengths. Although the oars were the chief means of propulsion, almost every vessel

Masts and sails.

above the size of a trireme had either one or two masts, but one of them, from raking forward and being comparatively small, resembled in many respects a bowsprit, so that, practically, there was only one mast except in very large vessels, which, with the yard and square sail attached, usually completed their rig. The portion of the mast immediately above the yard formed a "top," or structure similar to a basin, serving for the purpose of a look-out or as a place from which arrows or other missiles could be discharged. All the Athenian galleys had square sails only, as may be seen in numerous illustrations; and it is very questionable if any of the Greek vessels used topsails of a triangular form, Δ, though they were known to the Romans;[1] but, from their form, the wide part being attached to the yard and the point reaching the topmast head, they could, under any circumstances, have been of very little service, and none whatever when the wind was abeam or before the beam.

Oars.

The oars varied in size according to the bank on which they were used, of course increasing in length

[1] As noticed in the Introduction to this work, these sails were called Suppara. Lucan, v. 429. Stat. Sylv. ii. 2, 27. Senec. Epist. c. 77.

as they ascended. Their length in a trireme is stated at from 9 to 9¼ cubits, but no mention is made ot the part of the vessel to which they belonged. An oar, however, of only fourteen feet in length could have been of no service unless used on the lowest rank and almost on a level with the water. Those employed in the smallest wherries of the Thames are from twelve to fourteen feet long. Thucydides,[1] in describing the attack of the Peloponnesian commanders on the Piræeus, the harbour of Athens, remarks, "The plan was that each sailor should take with him his oar, his cushion and his thong, and go by land from Corinth to the sea over against Athens, and, proceeding with all speed to Megara, should put off with forty triremes which happened to be at Nisæa, their naval station, and sail immediately for Piræeus." From these remarks it may be inferred that none of the oars belonging to a trireme were of greater weight than one man could carry for a distance of four or five miles; and that only one man was stationed at an oar, unless "his oar" might be construed as meaning the oar under his charge. But though no mention is made of different-sized oars having been used on board of a trireme, there can be no doubt that the oars of the ancients differed far more in size than those of the river barge or man-of-war sweeps as compared with the sculls of the Thames wherry of modern times.

This is clear from the fact that while various ancient writers mention oars of 9½ cubits in length, Athenæus distinctly states that the oars belonging to Ptolemy Philopator's large ship were thirty-eight cubits long.[2]

[1] Thucyd. ii. c. 93.

[2] Athen. v. c. 37.

Here we have a specific account of oars varying from fourteen to fifty-seven feet in length, the latter requiring to have lead embedded in their handles as a counterpoise to the weight outside the rowlock.[1] Besides, it is clear that the oars must have increased in size according to the banks on which they were employed. In the case of the oar fifty-seven feet in length, if worked from a great height a large portion of it would require to be inboard—say nineteen feet against thirty-eight; and even the one-third would not, at a line of nine feet above the water, be sufficient as a counterpoise, unless the shoulder of the oar were of unwieldy thickness or heavily weighted by lead. In all single-banked vessels the oar worked on the gunwale, and was kept in its place by means of a leather thong. In larger galleys it passed through an oar-port. Various ancient writers assert that there was only one man to each oar, and add, that he sat, when rowing, on a single bench or small stool attached to the ribs of the vessel, and within a very short distance from the *scalmus* of his oar.

Mode of rowing.

But these assertions, though they increase the difficulty of solving the intricate problem of how galleys, with more than one bank of oars, were propelled, can have no weight when opposed to practical experience. It is clear, without any testimony beyond our knowledge of the physical power of man, that no one man, however herculean, unless he had the aid of machinery, of which there is no proof, could work an oar in the manner described. Indeed, we know that in ancient galleys of every description, above the smallest uniremes, more men than

[1] Athen. v. c. 37.

one *were* frequently employed upon the same oar. Such was the case in the celebrated Liburnian[1] galleys, already described.

Here the question arises how many men could, with convenience, sit on each bench? Presuming that, in the case of an oar fifty-seven feet in length, one-third, or nineteen feet, remained within board, there would, allowing fifteen inches for each rower, be space for fifteen men to work at the one oar; and if the men who sat within six feet of the row-port were of no service, there is still ample space left to place ten effective rowers.

If in comparatively modern times, when rowers were by no means crowded, eighteen inches for each man abreast was considered more than sufficient, we may infer that five men to an oar was far from an unfrequent practice in manning the state galleys of the Italian Republics. But while there is no difficulty in understanding how five or even ten men could be rendered serviceable in working the oars of single-banked galleys, a great difficulty arises when we inquire how that number of men could effectively handle the upper bank oars of the quadriremes and quinqueremes. On these and on many other matters the accounts of the ancients are conflicting: nor do the imperfect illustrations on ancient monuments and on coins materially assist in their elucidation. Assured of the fact that there were many vessels of much larger dimensions than even quinqueremes propelled by oars, we have to consider *how this was done*. Now the only mode of arriving at correct

[1] Dio. xxix. 32. Horat. Epod. i. 1. Veget. iv. 33. Sueton. Vit. Calig. c. 37.

conclusions on this, the most conflicting and intricate of all the problems connected with shipping which ancient authors have left for solution, is to trace the progress of the galleys themselves, from the single-banked craft or unireme upwards.

Single-banked galleys.

With the exception of the extraordinary Liburnian galleys, every account extant leads to the conviction that the single-banked galleys of the Venetians and Genoese resembled in many respects those of the Romans and ancient Greeks. Drawings of Venetian galleys, to which references will hereafter be made, have been preserved, but, as no detailed account of them exists, we are obliged to seek for information from a writer of a comparatively modern date.[1]

French galley.

In its leading features, a French galley, constructed somewhere about the close of the seventeenth century, would appear to have resembled those of Venice and of Rome of a similar class. She is described as having been one hundred and fifty feet long and *fifty feet broad*; but there is evidently a mistake in the description of her width, as there is no record of any war galley, either ancient or modern, where the length was only three times the breadth of beam. They were invariably from five to ten times longer than they were wide. All writers on the ships of the ancients or of the middle ages are agreed upon this point; nor is there any account of a vessel propelled by oars of our own times, which

[1] In the "Monthly Magazine," vol. xviii., London, 1758, p. 445, there is a review of a work, entitled "The Memoirs of a Protestant condemned to the Galleys of France," written by himself, which contains, in minute detail, a description of a French galley in which, in the year 1701, he was condemned to labour. The account was originally published at the Hague, and was afterwards translated into English, 2 vols. 12mo.

is not at least six times longer than she is wide; therefore, it is safe to assume that the French galley of one hundred and fifty feet in length did not much exceed thirty feet in width. In other respects, with the exception of the length of oars, the description of this single-banked galley is evidently quite reliable.

The author says, that she "consists but of one deck, which covers the hold; this hold is in the middle nine feet, but at the sides of the galley only six feet high. By this we may see that the deck rises about a foot in the middle, and slopes towards the edges to let the water more easily run off; for when a galley is loaded, it seems to swim under water, at least the sea constantly washes the deck. The sea would then necessarily enter the hold by the apertures where the masts are placed, were it not prevented by what is called the *coursier*. This is a long case of boards fixed on the middle or highest part of the deck, and running from one end of the galley to the other. There is also a hatchway into the hold as high as the *coursier*. From this superficial description, perhaps, it may be imagined that the slaves and the rest of the crew have their feet always in the water; but the case is otherwise; to each bench there is a board raised a foot from the deck, which serves as a footstool to the rowers, under which the water passes. For the soldiers and marines there is, running on each side along the gunwale of the vessel, what is called a *bande*, which is a bench about the same height with the *coursier*, and two feet broad. They never lie here, but each leans on his own particular bundle of clothes in a very incommodious posture. The officers themselves are not better accommodated, for the chambers in the hold are designed only to hold the provisions and naval stores of the galley."

The author then proceeds to state that the French galley had a chamber in the poop or raised deck, only large enough to hold the captain's bed; that, contiguous to it, were compartments for the more valuable stores; and, after remarking on various details, he adds, that she had twenty-five benches for the rowers on each side of the vessel. These fifty benches, which were four feet apart, and ten feet long, are described as having been "covered with sackcloth, stuffed with flocks, and over this is thrown a cow-hide, which, reaching down to the *banquet* or footstool, gives them the resemblance of large trunks. To these the slaves are chained, six to a bench, along the *bande* runs a large rim of timber, about a foot thick which forms the gunwale of the galley. On this, which is called the apostic, the oars are worked. These *are fifty feet long*, and are poised in equilibrio upon the afore-mentioned piece of timber, so that the thirteen feet of oar which come inboard are equal in weight to the thirty-seven feet outboard; and as it would be impossible to hold them in the hand, because of their thickness, they have handles by which they are managed by the slaves."

If the oars of this vessel, which in their leading features no doubt resembled those of the large single-banked galleys of the ancients and of the middle ages, were fifty feet in length, then a beam of thirty feet would not suffice for oars of that enormous length. But if the beam was only one-fifth of her length, we may assume that the oars were not more than thirty-nine feet long, especially as that length would be amply sufficient for propelling a single-banked vessel. In that case the oar would be "thirteen" feet inboard as described, affording abundance of space for six slaves to be stationed at it, although the two nearest the side would be of comparatively less service in rowing. To enable the rowers, and especially those who were stationed nearest the centre of the galley, to work with effect, their benches must have been placed in a slightly oblique position.

From this description, there is no difficulty in understanding the character of the uniremes; it is only when we come to inquire what was meant by biremes, triremes, and so forth, and how they were propelled, that the most conflicting statements are met with. Although Scheffer,[1] General Melvill, and others, have bestowed an immense deal of learning in their endeavours to prove that each oar was rowed by one man only, and that the banks were placed directly one over the other, the bulk of the testimony of ancient writers, confirmed by experience, is opposed to any such views. Besides, the most casual inquiry will show that it would be impracticable to row any galley with more than two banks of oars on the plan suggested. Every additional rank adds to the difficulty in a greatly increased ratio; and if hexiremes were efficient ships, which, on the authority of Polybius they were,[2] it would have been altogether impracticable to propel them by oars on the plan suggested.

[1] The curious treatise by Scheffer, entitled "I. Schefferi de varietate Navium," is preserved in Gronovius's "Thesaurus Antiq. Græc." vol. viii fol. In the same vast collection are treatises by Bayfius, Doletus, and Laurentius, on similar subjects, which are worthy of examination.

[2] Polyb. i. c. 23.

It might be unnecessary to offer any further remarks on this branch of the subject, had not Mr. Mitford, the celebrated historian of Greece, expressed so strong an opinion in favour of it. "The most satisfactory conjectures," he remarks, "that I have met with by far, are those of General Melvill."[1] It may, however, be here explained that General Melvill, in common with other writers, had previously entertained the opinion that the number of banks were measured by the number of men at an oar. That is to say, a unireme, he considered, had only one man placed at an oar, a bireme two, a trireme three, and so forth, up to the great ship of Ptolemy Philopator, which had, according to this theory, forty men to each of its fifty-seven feet oars. As the General on examination found such a theory to be untenable, he conceived the idea that in no case was there more than one man to an oar. "He," then,[2] "set himself to investigate the subject for confirmation of this opinion on fact, as he should find that fact to turn out in the descriptions of sea-fights and other naval transactions, as given by the ancient authors, particularly Polybius, Cæsar, Livy, and Florus." Impressed with his new idea, it occurred to him, that "the indispensable requisites were, that in the arrangement of the rowers within, each side ought to have been such as to admit of the greatest number possible, that they should be so placed as not to impede each other; that they should be enabled to row to the best advantage;

General Melvill's theory.

[1] Mitford's Hist. of Greece, vol. ii. p. 194.

[2] Pownall's "Treatise on the Study of Antiquities," Appendix, no. iii., pp. 236–40.

and that the highest tiers, both in respect to length and weight, should be sufficiently manageable: from these grounds the discovery immediately resulted to him, which was, that by a combination of two obliquities between the galley and a rower's gallery running along its waist part, projecting outwards from a small distance above the water's edge, with an angle of 45°, and rows of horizontal seats of about two feet in length, fixed obliquely upwards from the bottom of this gallery against this obliquely projecting part of the side, with no more space betwixt them in all directions than should be found necessary for the free movement of men when rowing together, a quincunx or chequer order would be formed, with all the above-mentioned requisites, to the highest degree of advantage which could co-exist consistent with each other."

It is not easy to understand the General's scheme by this description of it. He lays down, practically enough, some essential points which require to be considered; but while the oar adapted for the lowest banks might be "sufficiently manageable," the oars of the upper banks, even if well balanced, could not be effectively worked by one man. Nor is it easy to understand what is meant by "rows of horizontal seats, of about two feet in length, fixed obliquely upwards from the bottom of this gallery." However, the General caused a model of a quinquereme to be erected against a high wall belonging to his house in London, which was of the same proportions as would have been required for a "fifth part of a real galley." The model is said to "have held, in a very small space, but with sufficient ease, the rowers of five tiers, of six men in each, lengthways, making one-fifth the rowers on each side of a quinquereme, according to Polybius, who mentions three hundred as the whole number of rowers in it, besides one hundred and twenty fighting men." But this further explanation does not assist in the elucidation of his theory of "one man to each oar." On the contrary, it rather tends to confuse, unless the General means that there were one hundred and fifty row-ports on each side of the quinquereme mentioned by Polybius, which would be absurd.

But the impracticability of the whole plan is shown when an examination is made of the space that would be required to place, single file, three hundred rowers at the oars of a quinquereme.

The sweep of an oar is measured by its length, and would require a certain defined space for its movement, irrespective of the number of men at work upon it. The single-banked French galley already described was one hundred and fifty feet long, having twenty five benches on each side, requiring a length of one hundred feet. All other accounts, as well as experience, show that the benches were, and required to be, three feet apart: and, allowing one foot for the breadth of the bench, each oar would require a space of four feet in a horizontal line. According to the General's theory there would be thirty oar-ports on each bank, which, allowing for their obliquity, would require the gallery attached to the side of his galley to be somewhere about two hundred feet in length for the accommodation of the rowers. No doubt such a vessel could be built, but it is very questionable if any such vessel *ever was built.* Ptolemy Philopator's ship would have required two thousand oar-ports on each side, to afford employment to her rowers. There is, however, another equally valid objection to the General's scheme: a bank of oars means something whereby one class of galleys could be clearly distinguished from another class. Ships of war, up to a comparatively recent period, were rated as mounting so many guns, just as ancient galleys were rated by their banks of oars; the one measured the fighting, the other the propelling power. But if, according to the General's plan, triremes or quinqueremes were known by the number of banks, what was the measure of vessels of the larger size? for he does not profess to work any galley on his plan with more than five tiers; nor does he maintain that the size of his galley was measured by the number of her oars, which would depend upon her length. In whatever way this scheme is examined it will be found to be altogether untenable.

Charnock's theory.

Charnock, in his "History of Marine Architecture,"[1] has evidently devoted more space than thought to the elucidation of this intricate subject. While he, with all other writers on the subject, accurately describes "uniremes" as "those galleys or vessels which had only one row of oars extending between their masts, or perhaps the entire length of the vessel," he breaks down at the first step beyond a unireme, when he says that "the biremes had one tier of oars between their masts, and another abaft the main or principal mast." Indeed, all theories must necessarily fail which cannot be made applicable to vessels of every

[1] Vol. i. p. 47.

description; and it is no solution of the difficulty to deny, as Mr. Charnock and others have done, the existence of vessels beyond a certain size, when it is found that a theory practicable within certain limits would be altogether impracticable if carried beyond them.

That this would be the case in Mr. Charnock's plan he himself admits. He says that a trireme was a galley more formidable than the bireme, "having one tier of oars extending between the masts, a second abaft the mainmast, and a third forward, near the prow or stem before the foremast." The quadriremes he describes as having had "their oars ranged like the triremes, with the difference of having two tiers of oars one above the other, abaft the mainmast." "The quinqueremes," he adds, "were also of the same description, with the addition of the second tier of oars forward." He then goes on to state that "the octoremes had two tiers of oars in the midships, and *three* at the stem and stern, making in all eight." This is no doubt an easy method of solving the difficulty, so far as regards biremes, triremes, quadriremes and octoremes, but our author fails to explain how his principle can be applied to vessels of a larger description, or even how the number of rowers each of these classes are said to have contained was placed at the oars. The latter he does not attempt, and as summarily dismisses the former by questioning the existence altogether of any vessels with more than three tiers of oars placed either directly or obliquely above each other, in the face of the most ample evidence to the contrary. However, the theory Mr. Charnock considers unanswerable would not be the most perfect in practice, even in vessels of an inferior class to the octoreme. The oars would be more effective in midships than at any other part of the vessel, yet our author places the greatest number of these aft and forward, near "the prow or stem and near the stern." If there is any merit in his scheme, it would consist in placing the three banks in midships, and one aft in the case of a quadrireme; one aft and one forward in the case of a quinquereme; and two instead of three near the "stem and stern."

Vossius's views.

The whole of the question of rowing ancient galleys has been exceedingly well put by Vossius, in his "Dissertation on the Construction of Ancient Ships."[1] Speaking of the largest of all these ships, of which any record remains, he says: "If we compare the oars that must necessarily have been used on board of this (Ptolemy's) ship with those by which the modern galley is worked, and allow for their different proportions in respect to length, we must also keep in view a similar comparison in regard to their size and thickness, and we shall then have a correct idea of their relative dimensions, as well as their strength." He then goes on to remark, "Let us now consider in what manner the four thousand rowers, which are said to have been employed on board this vessel, were employed or stationed at the forty banks of oars. It is not my intention," he continues, "to combat or examine what many learned men have

[1] Vossius' Treatise, entitled "I. Vossii de Triremium et Liburnicarum constructione dissertatio," is printed in Graevii Thes. Antiq. Roman, vol. xii. fol. See also "Charnock's History," vol. i. p. 52., etc.

already written on this subject, both in France and in other countries. Their opinion is certainly correct in respect to the tiers of oars being placed obliquely over each other. Existing remnants of antiquity convince us clearly of the fact; but there still remains a much heavier difficulty to be got over: it is, in what manner the oars of the upper tier could be worked and managed by one person only; for it is denied that more than one was stationed to each oar, and the perplexity of the enigma is not a little increased by the assertion that a very small part of the oar reached within board. It is well known that there are no weights whatever which, by the proper assistance and combination of mechanical power, may not be moved even by a single person; but we are at the same time certain, that the greater the weights are, so much the slower can they be moved. Oars, it must be remembered, become almost useless unless they are impelled with quickness and spirit, as well as brought back to their original station, for a renewal of the stroke with equal celerity. The mechanical powers are of no use in this instance, as the law remains fixed and immutable, that any operation which, in the ordinary course of things, requires ten men to perform it, and one only is employed, may indeed be executed by that one, but will require a period ten times as long to perform it in; for nature will not suffer herself to be deceived, or her laws perverted by any such vainly-hoped-for advantage."

While Vossius was of opinion that no vessel had ever more than seven tiers of oars,—though he does not show how that number could have been worked, —he, for the reasons just quoted, arrived at the conclusion "that in the lower tier one man only was stationed to an oar, which being short, and but trivially elevated above the surface of the water, he might be able to work without much difficulty." He then explains that, in his opinion, as to which there can be no question, "the oars in all superior tiers, as they increased in height from the water, increased also in length, within board as well as without, leaving room for a greater number of rowers to work, each in progressive proportion to their length;" but he draws a false conclusion from right premises when he remarks that the difficulty consists "not in so many tiers, but in the number of seats of rowers comprised in one oblique tier."[1]

Such are the views of a few of the leading writers on this intricate question. While agreeing with Vossius in the opinion that the oar-ports were placed obliquely in the sides of the vessel, and that the number of men to an oar was regulated by its length and position, there are many objections to his theory that the galleys of the ancients were classed, either by the number of men or by the number of their seats; and any seaman who takes the trouble to put the theory into practice will find that even the principle of obliquity will not admit of the effective working of more than five tiers of oars.

Each theory, however, contains less or more

[1] In the course of our examination of this subject we have received from the Revd. J. O. W. Haweis, of Colwood, Crawley, in the county of Sussex, a paper so ingenious and original, that, though we doubt its practicability, we have much pleasure in printing it in the Appendix to this volume.—See Appendix No. 1, pp. 625–8.

truth; and by a careful examination of the whole, the problem which has occupied the attention of so many writers may be successfully solved, if there be less attempt to harmonize statements made by ancient authors, who were not practically conversant with the subject, or whose writings have been misquoted or imperfectly interpreted. All writers agree in the opinion that the uniremes had only one bank or tier of oars, and there is no difference of opinion with regard to the mode of propelling these vessels. Although "seated" (and this expression has led to much controversy), the rowers, in the case of large vessels, doubtless, rose simultaneously to their oars at the word of command, stretching out the handles as far as the allotted space would permit, and then throwing themselves back uniformly upon their seats, and, with their whole weight, propelling the galley forwards. This mode of rowing may be seen in the Mediterranean and elsewhere at the present day.

Writers differ with regard to the number of men placed at an oar; but herein there is, practically also, no difference of opinion, for the number of men at an oar must depend on the size of the vessel. A jolly-boat has never more than one man at an oar, but a launch has two, and, in the phraseology of our own time, launches thus rowed are called "double-banked," although this expression was not applicable to the galleys of the ancients. Nor is there much difference of opinion with reference to what was meant by a bireme. Apart, therefore, from direct testimony, there can be no doubt that a bireme (as a rule) meant a vessel, not with two rowers to an oar, but with two banks or tiers of oars. Some writers, as already explained, have maintained that the oar-ports were placed directly one above the other; but this could only be possible in vessels such as the bireme. On the other hand, a careful examination of Trajan's column, and of other remains of ancient sculpture, proves that the oars were placed *obliquely* over each other: thus, on coins of the Emperor Gordian, two tiers of oars so placed are very conspicuous. If, however, any doubts still exist on this point, they are entirely set at rest by the recent discoveries of Layard and others.

The illustration on the next page, a copy of an alabaster slab found at Kouyunjik, the site of ancient Nineveh, clearly shows the oar-ports arranged obliquely on the broad side of the galley. The only further question is, to what extent this principle could be applied, so as to place at work the vast number of rowers some galleys are said to have carried, and also to afford accommodation for the troops and stores.

Mr. Howell's plan.

Mr. Howell, a comparatively modern writer,[1] adopts many of the views of Vossius, but differs from him in that he maintains that it would be impossible to work with effect more than five banks of oars. As his views are more in accordance with our own than those of any other writer, we shall refer to them at greater length, although differing also from him in some of his most important conclusions. And here it ought to be stated, that all modern writers, Mr. Howell included, appear to have given

[1] "An Essay (pamphlet) on the War-Galleys of the Ancients." By John Howell. W. Blackwood: Edinburgh, 1826.

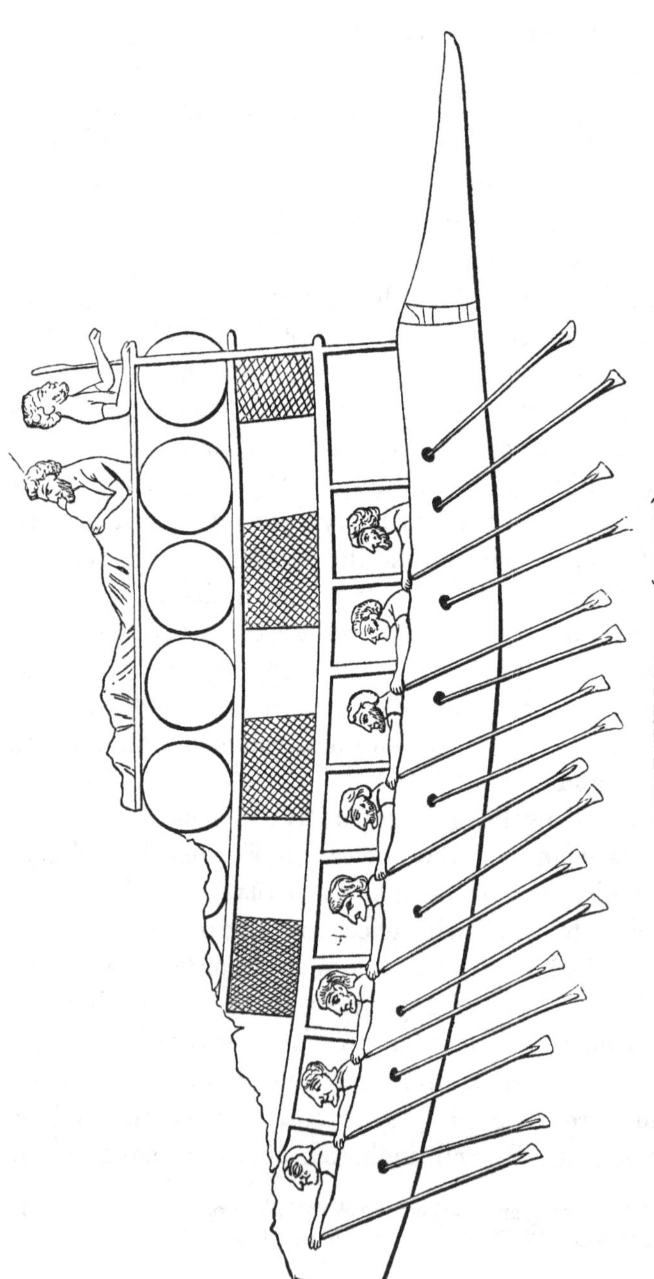

GALLEY FROM KOUYUNJIK (NINEVEH).

too little consideration to the facts, that ancient galleys varied quite as much in size as the vessels of modern times, that their power or dimensions were not, in all cases, measured by the number of their banks of oars, and that in proportion to the number of rowers the capacity of the hold would require to be increased. A war-galley would be comparatively useless if she had not ample capacity for fighting men, and for their munitions of every kind, besides stores, including water. All these points must, however, have been fully considered by the ancients, who evidently saw, when they wished to have more than thirty oars on each side of a galley, that an increase could not be obtained on the single-bank principle without constructing her of an unwieldy length in proportion to her depth and breadth, and thus sacrificing an unnecessarily large amount of space. Consequently, they invented the bireme, whereby they could, in little more than the length required for fifteen oars, place double that number without any corresponding sacrifice of space; while in the trireme, they would in nearly the same length obtain space for three times the number of oars, and secure for the use of the soldiers and stores ample accommodation and any extra length they might desire.

Mr. Howell, in discussing this principle as applicable to quinqueremes, shows that, by adopting the oblique ascent, the rowers of the first and highest bank can be placed so as not to interfere with the rowers on the second, their oars having space to play free of the benches before them. "That a bank or bench of oars," he adds, "never contained more than five oars, I think, can be proved, whatever the size of the galley was, whether a bireme or trireme, up to the galley of Philopator, which had forty banks, nine feet being the highest point from the water for the *scalmi*, from which they could pull with effect."[1]

Mr. Howell, in confirmation, as he conceives, of this opinion, quotes Athenæus;[2] but, though there is nothing in the description of the great ship to lead to the conclusion that the *scalmi* of her highest bank of oars were only nine feet above the level of the water, we agree with Mr. Howell that an oar could not be worked effectively at a greater height, and that the seats of the rowers were arranged by the system of obliquity, so as not to interfere with each other. We, however, differ from him in other respects. "A Greek trireme," he remarks, "at the time of the invasion of Xerxes, had from one hundred and fifty to one hundred and sixty rowers and forty armed foot, while the average-sized Persian triremes carried two hundred rowers and thirty soldiers." Presuming these to be established facts, Mr. Howell endeavours to make his theory harmonize with them. "I have shown," he says, referring to the French vessel, of which we have furnished particulars, "that a modern galley pulling fifty oars has six rowers on a bench. If I am correct," he continues, "a trireme pulled thirty oars, that is, three banks, five oars in each, thus:—

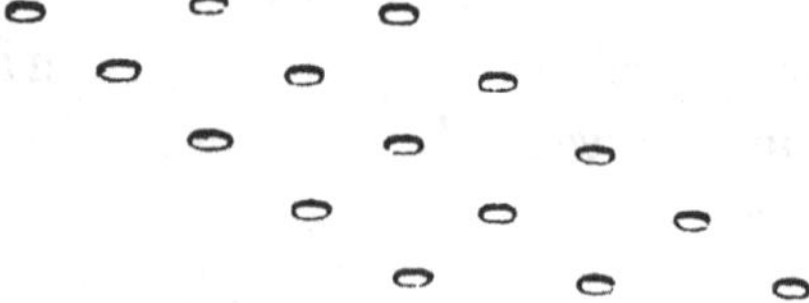

[1] Howell's Pamphlet, p. 48. [2] Athen. v. c. 37.

Now, to a vessel of her bulk, with elevated poop and stern," he goes on to state, "less than five men cannot be allowed to each seat. Thus there are twenty-five rowers in each bank, and six times twenty-five make one hundred and fifty." But though this mode of calculation (which, by the way, does not allow for any "watch-and-watch" or reliefs[1]) makes the Grecian galley agree with his scheme of manning her so far as regards the number of rowers, it is based upon the presumption that every oar had the same number of men. But this could not have been the case; for even if five men could be placed to advantage on each of the upper tiers of oars, two of them, at least, would be useless on the lower tiers of a vessel of this size, as they would not have space to work at it. The same fallacy runs throughout his arguments in other places. Thus he accounts for the Persian trireme with her two hundred men, by saying that she "must have had six men to an oar, which is not improbable, the Asiatics being not so athletic as the Greeks. Six times thirty," he adds, "is one hundred and eighty, leaving twenty men for casualties, etc., etc."

This is an exceedingly easy mode of attempting to solve an intricate question; but Mr. Howell, instead

[1] Although Homer (Odys. xiii. v. 81–95) states that Ulysses was rowed from Corcyra (Corfu) to Ithaca, a distance of eighty nautical miles, without apparently any resting of the oarsmen, there is no proof that ancient galleys were propelled *continuously* by their oars, or for a longer period on a stretch than the one set of rowers could endure. To this day the Malay pirates sometimes row more than ten hours without change, and are fed at their oars. Nor is there anything to show how many spare men were carried for reliefs, in case of accident.

of overcoming the difficulty, only increases it when he says that there must have been six men to an oar, for six men would be less easily placed at each of the lower tiers of oars than five. Nor does he aid in the solution of this vexed problem when he comes to deal with vessels of five banks. Practically his arguments are the same, and show the mistakes which learned men are liable to make when dealing with questions requiring experience as well as learning. "Polybius," remarks Mr. Howell, "informs us the crew of a quinquereme was three hundred rowers, and one hundred and twenty fighting men. Now a quinquereme," he reasons, "having five banks, thus—

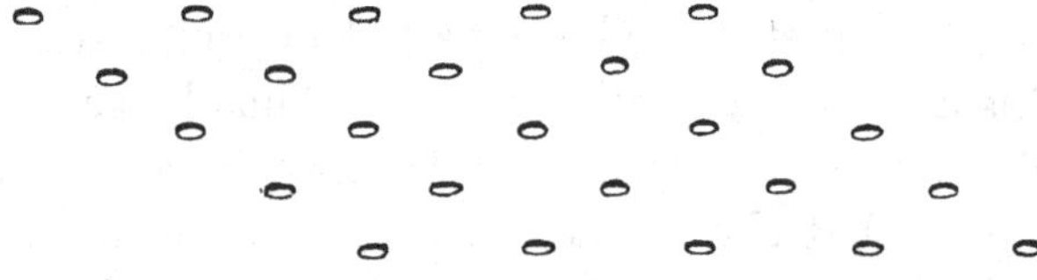

pulled fifty oars, or twenty-five aside, the same number as the modern galley. As by this arrangement, adding to the banks of the galley," he continues, "did not add to her height, and not in any great degree to her length, seven feet being sufficient for a bank, I think the addition of one man to an oar was all she could require. Six times five is thirty, and ten times thirty, three hundred. Both of these," he concludes, by saying with evident self-satisfaction, "are remarkable coincidences, and tally better with the description of ancient authors than any solution that has yet been given."

"I shall now," he continues, "show how remarkably it agrees with Athenæus; thus taking in the whole range and applying to all, a thing it could never do were it not near the truth. The tesseracontoros having," he adds, "forty banks, five oars to a bench, makes her have two hundred oars of a side, or four hundred in all. Considering her size, she could not have less than ten men to an oar." The Liburnia of Caligula, according to the testimony of Suetonius, had, he states, that number of men to an oar, forgetting that she was a single-banked galley, and consequently he concludes that that number was attached to each of the four hundred oars in Philopator's ship, which "gives four thousand, the number mentioned by Athenæus." Here again he overlooks the impracticability of placing ten men at each of the lower tier of oars.

Our own views.

Now, while there can be no doubt that all vessels had their ports placed obliquely in cases where there were more than one tier of oars; that there were vessels of five tiers of oars thus placed and no more, and that the Grecian trireme had one hundred and fifty rowers, and the Persian two hundred, it is clear from the descriptions of ancient authors that there were many triremes of much smaller dimensions, especially from the facility with which they were hauled upon the beach: while there were others carrying even more men than the galleys he refers to.[1] But presuming Mr. Howell to be correct in his supposition, that a trireme derived her name from "having three rows of five tiers and no more," as he illustrates, then a bireme would derive her

[1] Thucyd. i. c. xciv., etc., etc.

name because she had only two rows of five tiers, thus :—

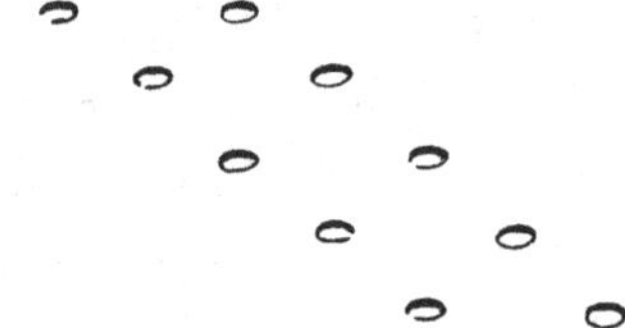

Biremes. No practical man, however, could entertain the idea that ten oars, arranged as he suggests, would be as efficient as a similar number in single lines or even in double tiers; nor would a galley of this size be nearly so efficient as she would be with her ports in a horizontal line, for she would be much too high in proportion to her length. Similar remarks apply with nearly equal force in the case of triremes.

The perusal of ancient authors, as well as experience, leads to the conviction that galleys, from the unireme to the quinquereme inclusive, had their oars arranged not merely in oblique vertical rows, but also in horizontal rows according to circumstances. Besides, the plan illustrated on the sculpture from Nineveh is much more practicable than the one Triremes. suggested by the theory of Mr. Howell. A galley with only ten oars on a side would be more efficient if they were placed as follows :—

than if arranged in the manner suggested by Mr. Howell. Nor would they occupy more space, the saving of which evidently induced the ancients to increase the number of tiers.

As the galleys of the ancients must have varied very much in their capacity and dimensions, it would be more reasonable to suppose that, from the unireme to the quinquereme inclusive, they derived their names from the number of oars placed horizontally over each other, rather than from the number of oblique rows as suggested by Mr. Howell. That is to say, though a trireme bore that name because she had three tiers of oars placed thus :—

she was, nevertheless, still a trireme, if she had four, five, ten, or even twenty oblique rows of oar-ports, only she would be a trireme of a larger size, just as we have or had frigates—single-decked vessels, which have varied in size from 600 to 6,000 tons. A trireme might therefore be a much more powerful vessel than a quadrireme or quinquereme. On a similar principle, a quadrireme would have four horizontal tiers of oars, as follows :—

Quadriremes.

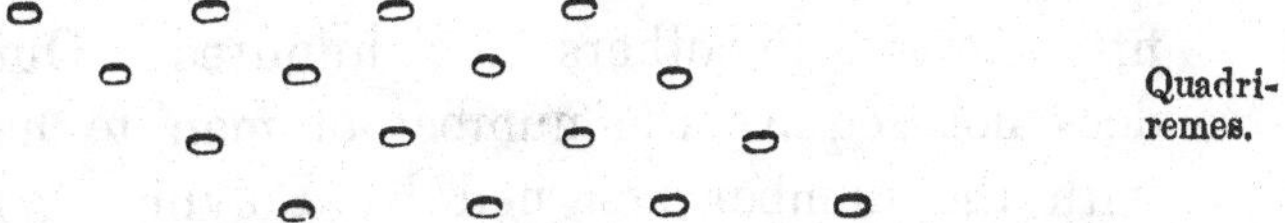

but, as in the case of the trireme, she would still be a quadrireme, only of a larger size, if she had more than four oblique rows. There is, however, a limit beyond which oars could not be worked when placed over each other in any fashion. That limit would be reached at the fifth horizontal row, and, for the reasons already named, a sixth row, however obliquely placed—for obliquity has also its limits—would be useless. Therefore, while a quinquereme had five horizontal rows, and the same number of oblique rows, forming a *quincunx* thus—

Quinqueremes

a galley must have acquired another name when she had *more than five of these oblique rows.* For instance, vessels with six oblique rows were, in our opinion, called hexiremes; with seven rows, septiremes; with eight rows, octoremes, and so forth; up to Ptolemy Philopator's tesseracontoros. That the number of men placed on board the ships of the ancients was regulated, as at present, by the work they had to perform, and by the size of the ship, there can be no doubt; but the number of men had nothing in itself to do with the class or grade of the galley. In some triremes there may have been only fifty rowers, in others five hundred. Our theory does not require the number of men to harmonize with the number assigned by Polybius, Athenæus, and other authors, to differently-rated galleys. Thus, in the trireme, with the thirty oars and one hundred and fifty rowers, it would not be necessary to place five men at *each* oar, as Mr. Howell has proposed.

Hexiremes and larger galleys.

Six men to each of the oars of the highest bank,

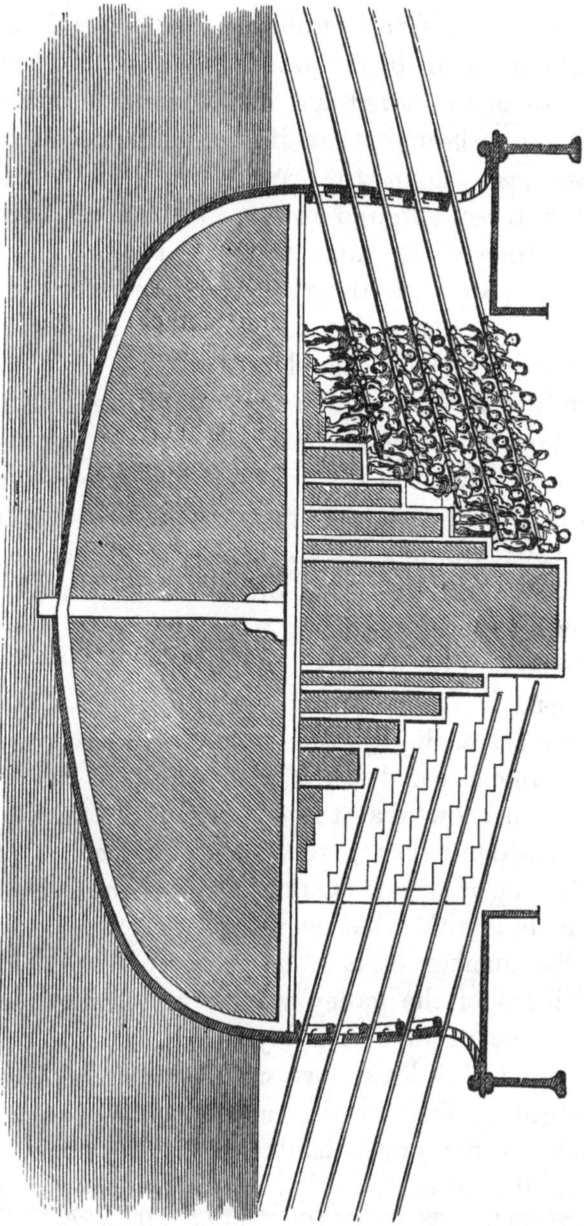

TRANSVERSE MIDSHIP-SECTION OF A QUINQUEREME.

Suggested plan of placing the rowers.

five to each oar of the second, and four men to each oar of the third bank, would give the requisite number of one hundred and fifty rowers, who would be far more effective than if placed in the manner he describes. So in the case of the quinquereme, with her three hundred rowers, instead of placing six men (presuming there were no reliefs) to each of her fifty oars, our theory, while it equally solves the difficulty created by the statement of Polybius (a difficulty which could only arise in quinqueremes with so large a crew as three hundred rowers), is one which could be carried out with much more practical effect; for, by placing on the 1st bank 8 men $\times$ 5 = 40; 2nd, 7 $\times$ 5 = 35; 3rd, 6 $\times$ 5=30; 4th, 5 $\times$ 5=25; 5th, 4 $\times$ 5=20; there would be 150 on each side, or 300 rowers in all, as represented on the preceding page, in the transverse midship-section of what a quinquereme really must have been.

Before proceeding to examine in detail how rowers thus arranged could work with effect, it will be desirable to show that the outline of the vessel, of which a section is here given, corresponds not merely with the imperfect information obtained from ancient authors, but with what would be practicable. To work the number of men here shown, the breadth of the beam of the galley would, presuming every rower on board to be employed at the same time, require to be, at least, forty-two feet, which would allow eighteen feet for the range inside of each of the oars on the upper bank, and six feet for the width of the raised midship-deck, where the hatches were placed. That width would allow for oars fifty-four feet in length, which would be ample where the highest row-port was nine feet above the level of the water; and as thirty men would be able to work on each oblique row, a hexireme, of no greater width, could carry three hundred and sixty rowers, a septireme four hundred and twenty, an octoreme four hundred and eighty, and so forth. In the case of a tesseracontoros, with no greater beam, two thousand four hundred rowers could find employment; but as vessels of that enormous size—if, indeed, more than this one was ever built—were very considerably wider,[1] it would be an improvement on the plan proposed by Mr. Howell, of ten men to each of the four hundred oars, to place fourteen rowers upon each of the oars of the upper bank, twelve on the second, ten on the third, eight on the fourth, and six on the fifth or lowest bank, which would give the required number of four thousand, though, in either case, many of the men would be more ornamental than serviceable. There is, however, no doubt that about three thousand men could be placed so as to row in each individual case with effect if they were apportioned to their oars in somewhat the scale of ten, nine, seven, six, and five, or say, thirty-seven men to each of the forty banks or oblique rows of oars, which would leave one thousand and forty for reliefs.

If the men were arranged in the manner suggested, and as represented in the following front view of their positions when placed at their stations before they commenced work on board of a trireme, the various objections which have been raised to the plan of working oars placed one over the other are removed.

[1] Ptolemy's ship had a beam of 57 feet.

A practised eye will at once perceive that rowers thus arranged could work with great effect and simultaneously, without in any way interfering with

the movements of each other. Nor would there be any difficulty in placing to the best advantage, as may be seen in our illustration (see p. 285) of the tranverse midship-section of the quinquereme, the large number of three hundred rowers required for vessels of that class.

If this theory be correct, then the problem of how the various classes of galleys were rowed is solved; for, if this was the principle of their classification, the difficulty does not increase with their dimensions, as is the case in all other theories ; the extreme height of the highest bank of rowers, either in the case of the quinquereme, or in that of any of the larger vessels, being not necessarily more than nine feet above the water.

At the word of command from the officer, who

walked upon the elevated portion of the deck, and guided by the leading men, who were stationed at the inner end of the oars, the rowers, when seated, stretched the handles of their oars as far aft as their arms would permit, as shown in the following representation:—

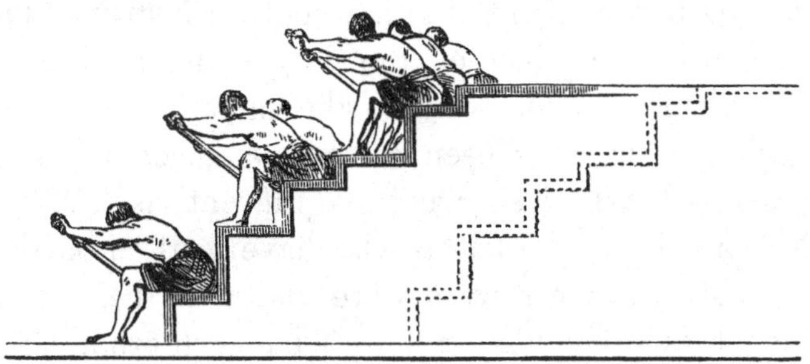

The action of the rowers would, however, in some measure be regulated by the size of the galley and the space at their disposal. Placed alternately, those who worked at the lower tiers would, in all galleys, have full swing for their oars, as the footstools of the rowers who sat above them would not interfere with the free action of their bodies, though such might appear to be the case by the side representation, which in itself, and without reference to the front view, necessarily fails to show their exact position. But while the men in small galleys, no doubt, rowed from their seats, there is every reason to suppose that in the larger vessels, where great numbers of rowers were employed, they rose, if seated, and after moving forward, according to the space at their disposal, threw themselves backward into their seats with an impetus as simultaneous and harmonious as it would be possible to attain without the aid of a machine to regulate their joint action. Indeed, the ancients practised this art with the greatest care, and the rowers were frequently exercised on benches erected on the shore, and their harmonious movements were sometimes made an object of display in their theatres. In nearly every case they plied their oars to the sound of either vocal or instrumental music, so that a fleet of the larger description of galleys, when under way on the smooth waters of the Levant, must have been, as various ancient authors describe, a heart-stirring and magnificent display.

Vossius, Le Roy, and all who have written on the subject of how the rowers were placed at their oars, though they differ less or more from each other, and fail, as we conceive, to propound a theory applicable to vessels of every class, agree in the opinion that the rowers were divided into classes, and that the *thranitæ*, who pulled the longest and highest oars and had the greatest amount of labour, "were exposed to the darts of the enemy." For these reasons they received, as we learn from Thucydides, the highest pay; and from the same authority we ascertain that even the largest description of galleys "were *not* decked *throughout*." [1]

These statements are important, as they show a thoroughly organized system among the rowers, without which it would have been impossible to make available, in a limited space, large numbers of men, and in so far as they answer objections, frequently raised, to the employing so many men close together in the hold of a ship. In our illustration (p. 293) it will be seen that by our theory the galleys

[1] Thucyd. i. c. xiv.

were only decked somewhat less than halfway across, a large space remaining open for ventilation, while the rowers of the upper tier were above the level of the deck, and were consequently exposed to the darts of the enemy.

As far as we can now judge from the writings of the ancients, first-class galleys were divided into compartments, not unlike the steamers of our own day, verifying the adage that there is "nothing new under the sun;" and certainly this holds true on comparing the bows of the war galleys of the ancients with the iron-clad rams of modern times. Our theory, therefore, after the most careful inquiry, is that *the paddle-wheel steamer of to-day resembles in her structure* (though materially improved, and possessing the vast advantage of mechanical power) *the row galley of the ancients.* Her machinery and coal bunkers are distinct and separate from the hold, cabins, or any other portions of the ship; while the engines and the paddle-wheels take the position and act the part of the rowers and their oars. Here modern genius and skill, as in a thousand other instances, substitutes mechanical for manual labour. The modern paddle, in its revolutions, performs exactly the same duty as the oars of the ancients in their simultaneous movements, and the well-trained crews of the Grecian and Roman galleys in their action at the oars were, so far as is traceable, almost as regular as the beat of the paddle-wheel.

Nor was it necessary to appropriate for the use of the rowers, even when three hundred men were engaged, a larger space in the ship than would now be required for a steam engine of one hundred and fifty horse-power, and her fuel for twenty days. A glance at the illustration will show that, by the plan suggested, the whole of the fore and after holds, with the midship portion of the galley, besides a large space below the platform of the rowers, could be appropriated to cargo and stores, the fore and after main-decks to troops, while the rowers themselves could be berthed in that portion of the vessel where they performed their daily toil, and where there would be space, however uncomfortable, for their beds and scanty apparel.

By reference to the accompanying deck plan, and by comparing it with the midship-section previously given, it will be seen that though the portion of the galley occupied by the rowers was open, it could be covered with an awning in warm, and by a tarpaulin in wet, weather. To have enclosed this space would have been fatal to the men, who, especially during the summer months, when the galleys were chiefly employed, could not have existed, much less have laboured in a confined hold.

In confirmation of this opinion, Thucydides, in describing the galleys of the Bœotians and of Philoctetes, of whom Homer also writes, says, "Nor had they, as yet, *covered* ships;"[1] and we find in the "Iliad" such expressions as, "He marched upon the *hatches* with long strides;"[2] and in the "Odyssey," where Ulysses is preparing to encounter Scylla, "upon the *hatches* of the prow of the ship he went."[3] Mr. Howell, in opposition to the views of most translators, remarks that the hatches should be construed

[1] Thucyd. c. x. [2] Hom. Il. xiv. [3] Hom. Odys. xii.

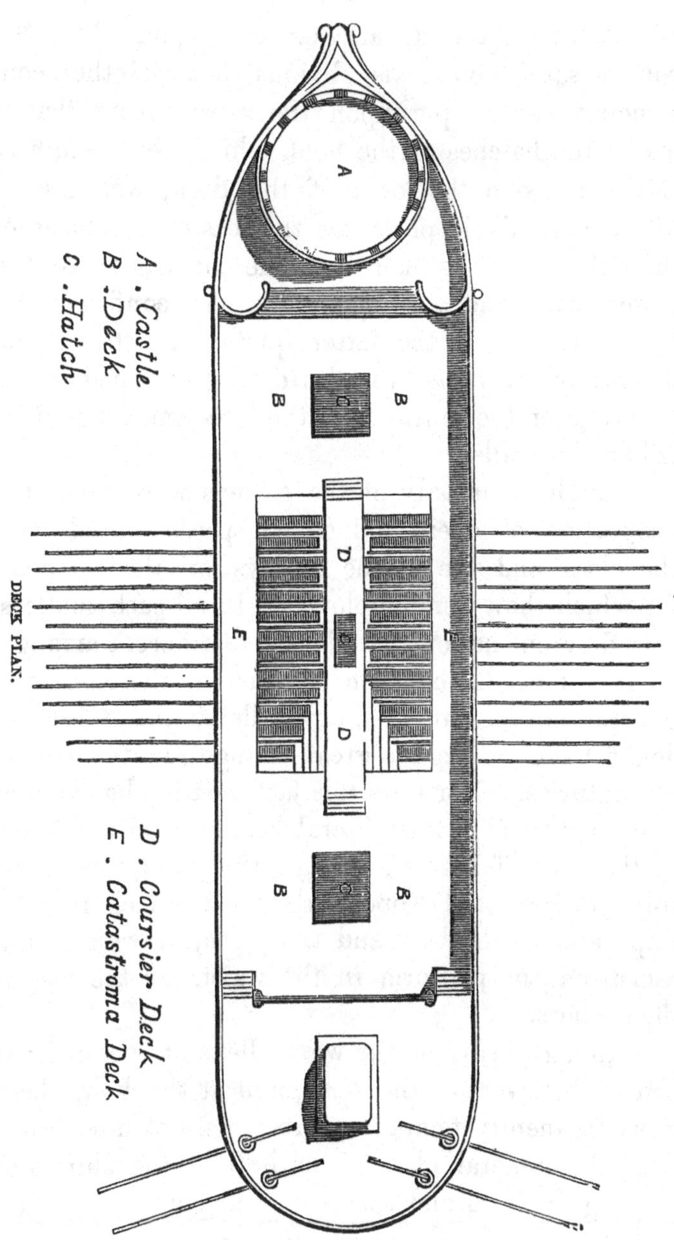

DECK PLAN.

as meaning "the thwarts or seats upon which the rowers sat:"[1] but it is obvious that no other construction can be put upon the word except that it meant the hatches of the hold, which, being slightly elevated above the level of the deck, would be a much more likely place for the master or officer of the galley to walk than upon the thwarts where the rowers sat; and this opinion is also confirmed by the expression in the latter quotation, where "the hatches *of the prow*" are distinctly mentioned as the covering of the entrance to the fore-compartment or hold of the galley.

Though parts only of the galleys were open, the proportion of open and closed spaces varied with the class and size of the galleys or the purposes for which they were employed. In all such matters, also, different nations had doubtless different arrangements, if not in the form, at least in the outfit and general equipment of their galleys, and these no doubt have undergone great changes in the course of centuries. Nor does this fact modify the opinion that "hatches" in their literal sense are meant; for, in the time of Homer, though the galleys were all single-banked and "open," they had a deck in midships and at the bow and the stern, as well as the catastroma or platform in the waist, for the use of the soldiers.

Although many of the war-galleys of the ancients had high towers at the stern, and at the bow, these were frequently temporary erections, not interfering with the general plan of the hull of the ship, and varying in form and size; the oar-ports, too, could

[1] Howell's Pamphlet, p. 7.

not have been of the form generally drawn. They are more likely to have been ▭ oblong, fashioned so as to allow the oar—which in galleys of many banks could only have been unshipped by being passed outwards—to be brought pretty close alongside of the vessel when the rowers ceased work. In regard to the seats, stools, or benches of the rowers, so frequently mentioned, and which have created a good deal of controversy, the plan here suggested satisfies all these requirements, for to each rower a separate seat or stool attached to the oblique benches or steps is appropriated. The height of each of the oar-ports above the level of the water in that of the quinquereme, and in all vessels of greater dimensions, would be as follows:—

	ft.	in.
From the first or lowest *port* to water-line	2	0
Distance between 1st and 2nd port . . .	1	9
" " 2nd " 3rd " . . .	1	9
" " 3rd " 4th " . . .	1	9
" " 4th " 5th " . . .	1	9
	9	0

So that the height of the sill of the port on the fifth or highest bank would be nine feet above the water-line.

The space between the rowers, seated on their respective benches or platforms, doubtless varied according to the size of the galley. While from four to six feet between each rower seated on the same level would be ample in the case of uniremes, biremes, or triremes, galleys of the larger class, in many cases, most likely had an intervening space of from six to even ten feet, so as to afford room for the sweep of the handles of the oars, and to enable the rowers to walk one or two steps forward, and then throw themselves backwards with greater impetus into their seats, as already described.

Summary. The conclusions at which we have arrived may be condensed as follows :—

1. Ancient galleys were classed or rated according to their number of banks, rows or tiers of oars.

2. All galleys above the unireme had their oar-ports placed obliquely above each other in horizontal rows.

3. No galley had more than five horizontal rows.

4. Every galley, from the unireme to the quinquereme inclusive, derived its name or class from the number of *horizontal* rows.

5. All galleys, above a quinquereme, were likewise classed according to the number of rows. In their case, however, the *oblique* rows were counted; but, in all cases, from the smallest to the largest, including Ptolemy's tesseracontoros, *each row, whether oblique or horizontal, was a distinct bank of oars,* which, like the number of guns, wherever they were placed, in wooden men-of-war, *constituted the only basis for their classification.*

6. The portion of the galley appropriated to the rowers and their oars was as separate from the other portions of the vessel as is the machinery of a paddle-wheel steamer. The rowers, also, like modern engineers and stokers, were entirely distinct from the seamen and marines; and among them were leaders and crack rowers, who were as indispensable to get the galley under way and keep the rest of the rowers in time as are the engineers of our own day, who

start and keep the machinery in proper working order.

In a word, the row-galley constituted the steamship of the ancients, as distinguished from their sailing vessels. She had sails to aid her progress when the winds were fair, as a steamer now has, but the one depended on her oars as much as the other now does upon her machinery; and, however vast the improvements, there is really no difference in principle between the galley of the ancients and the steamship of to-day. In practice they are the same, except that steam is substituted for manual labour. An oar is a paddle, and the blades of the oars fastened together, like the spokes round the axle of a wheel, and projecting into the water, constitute the paddle-wheel of modern times.

CHAPTER X.

Britain: its maritime position, and limited extent of over-sea trade—The vessels of the Ancient Britons, and the larger kind used by the Veneti—Encouragement by law to construct superior vessels—Britain and its inhabitants little known—Cæsar's reasons for invading Britain—First invasion, B.C. 55—Size of his transports—Second invasion, B.C. 54—Cæsar's preference for small vessels—Violent storm, and great loss of ships—Final action on the banks of the Thames—Cæsar makes terms with the Britons, and re-embarks his legions—Advantages derived by the Britons from their intercourse with the Romans—Conquest of Britain, A.D. 43: its state of civilization—Speech of Caractacus—The course of commerce with Rome—Inland water traffic—Transit duties—Articles of commerce, and knowledge of manufactures and of the arts—Colchester and its mint—London—Agricola, A.D. 78–85—His fleet sails round Britain—The influence of the rule of Agricola on the Britons—Hadrian, A.D. 120—State of commerce in and after his reign—The Caledonian incursions—Piratical invasions of the Germans—Carausius seizes the fleet of Maximian, and declares himself Emperor of Britain—Welsh and Scots, A.D. 360—Saxons, A.D. 364—Their ships—State of the Britons when abandoned by the Romans.

Britain: THE successful career which has distinguished the Royal Navy of Great Britain in her contests for many centuries on the ocean, and the vast proportions to which her merchant shipping has extended during the present generation, render the details of her incipient attempts at navigation one of the most interesting portions of her domestic history. Nor is the task to obtain these a difficult one. The early annals of the ancient Britons, though very limited with regard to their shipping and maritime commerce, have been so often thoroughly investigated that little remains to be done beyond collecting the leading facts which antiquarian industry has preserved, and endeavouring to re-produce them in a manner as pleasing and instructive as possible.

Its maritime position,

Separated from the rest of Europe by a sea, which in winter is very boisterous, and in summer often disturbed by currents and uncertain winds; surrounded by a coast full of danger, and with the channels to its principal havens interspersed with treacherous sand-banks, the ancient Britons must have been an adventurous race to launch their frail barks, for even a limited voyage, on waters so often disturbed by storm and tempest. Their trade, moreover, during the early periods of their history, was very inconsiderable, notwithstanding the convenient situation of their island for carrying on an extensive commerce; and the greater number of their vessels were of the rudest description. Cæsar speaks of them as being, even in his time, of the slightest construction, with the keels and ribs framed of some light wood and covered with leather; and Lucan[1] says "they were constructed of osiers, twisted and interwoven with each other, and then covered with strong hides." In such vessels as these the Britons worked their way along their iron-bound and tempest-tossed shores, and frequently made the passage to Ireland and the coasts of Gaul. From the fact, however, that they carried on a trade, though limited,

and limited extent of over-sea trade.

The vessels of the ancient Britons,

[1] Lucan, Phars. iv. cf. Fest. Avienus, "Ora Maritima," v. 80–130, and Plin. iv. c. 16.

in their own vessels with the Veneti on the coasts of Brittany, sometimes extending their voyages to the river Garonne, it is a fair inference that they possessed other vessels of a larger and stronger description, and that they had learnt something of ship-building from the Veneti, and, possibly, from the Phœnicians. But if it were true, as has been asserted by more than one author, that when the Britons undertook a voyage they abstained from food till it was completed, these voyages must have been very short, indeed, not longer than to Gaul or Ireland.

As has been already noticed, some almost circular boats, made of wicker-work, are still in use in Wales, and may fairly be supposed to represent a similar class of boats of much earlier times. On the other hand, we know pretty well, from Cæsar's description, the character of the larger and stronger vessels of the Veneti.[1] Thus from him we learn that they were built flatter than the Roman merchant ships, for convenience in navigating shallow waters, and that having erect stems and full bows, they were well adapted to resist the violence of the waves in a storm; while he further admits that, as they were constructed entirely of oak, they were not easily damaged by the sharp iron beaks of the Roman galleys. Such vessels could hardly have failed to attract the attention of the Britons, with whom the Veneti long maintained friendly and commercial intercourse, while it is very probable that, from them, the Britons learnt the art of constructing ships of war. But though it is likely that their intercourse with the Veneti may have had some advantages, it is, at the same time, probable

and the larger kind used by the Veneti.

[1] Cæsar describes the ships of the Veneti, B. G. iii. 13.

that there was no marked improvement in the form and construction of the greater number of British merchant vessels till the Emperor Claudius bestowed by law various privileges upon those persons who built vessels of a superior class for trading purposes.[1] As these privileges, however, only applied to ships capable of carrying ten thousand Roman modii, or about three hundred and twelve quarters of wheat, it is further evident that the framer of the law was desirous of encouraging the building of a larger and better class of vessels than then existed. But though a vessel capable of carrying only about sixty tons weight is much less than the average size of the coasters of the present century, little or no increase had apparently been made in their dimensions even three hundred years afterwards; for the trade in corn alone between Britain and the ports of Gaul required for its conduct, in the reign of Julian, eight hundred vessels.

Encouragement by law to construct superior vessels.

Although Britain had been for so many centuries more or less known to the Phœnicians, the Carthaginians, and the neighbouring continental tribes, it continued up to the time of the invasion of Julius Cæsar, B.C., to be a *terra incognita* to the rest of the ancient world; the preservation of such ignorance having been no doubt a matter of state policy with those who had some acquaintance with it, in order that the monopoly of their trade might not be interfered with by any interlopers. Hence, too, the stories sedulously spread of the barbarous character of its inhabitants, of the naked bodies painted with colours in imitation of beasts of prey, though Cæsar himself only says that "they stained

Britain and its inhabitants little known.

[1] Sueton. Claud. c. 18. Cod. Theodos. v. 13, 5.

themselves blue with woad, and wore their hair long, with moustachios."

On the other hand, there is good reason for believing that the Britons of the south and south-eastern parts of England were by no means the barbarians some writers have asserted. It is certain that they were of the same race, and nearly connected with the Belgæ of the opposite continents, for Cæsar tells us that many names of cities in the two countries were the same; that their manners greatly resembled those of the Gauls;[1] that Divitiacus, a king of one of the Belgian tribes, was also the ruler of a wide district in England,[2] much as in later times our Edwards and Henries held large provinces of France; that Cingetorix, though ruler of the Treviri on the Moselle, was also a king in Kent;[3] and that the buildings of South Britain and Gaul bore a great similarity one to the other.[4] More than this, we know that the languages of the two countries, divided as they were from one another only by the narrowest part of the English Channel, must have been, as Tacitus[5] states, very similar—a fact partially supported by Cæsar's mission to England of Comius, the chief of the Atrebates (Artois), that he might advocate the cause of the Romans in the British language.[6]

We know further that the southern portions of England were then thickly peopled, and that the Britons were in some respects so far in advance of their neighbours that the Gauls used to send their sons to England for the purpose of learning the sacred rites of the Druids, an order of priests, be it

[1] Cæs. Bell. Gall. v. 12, 14. [2] Ibid. ii. 4. [3] Ibid. v. 22.
[4] Ibid. v. 12. [5] Tacit. Agric. c. ii. [6] Cæs. Bell. Gall. iv. 19.

remembered, who made use of Greek letters for both their public and private transactions.[1] It is further clear, from Cæsar's narrative, that there must have been no inconsiderable extent of land under cultivation, and therefore cleared, at least partially, of forests, probably for the most part among the Cantii, or men of Kent, whom he calls the "most polished;"[2] moreover, if Cassivelaunus had only one-tenth of the "four thousand war chariots" mentioned by Cæsar,[3] he must have required roads, and well-made roads, too, along which to manœuvre them; not forgetting also the fact, that the construction of such chariots implies considerable mechanical skill. Cæsar adds, that the Britons made use of iron which they obtained from their maritime districts, a statement confirmed by the existence, till within a recent period, of numerous furnaces in the Weald of Sussex, for the extraction of iron from the iron sand of that district.[4] The extremely barbarous Britons, to whom the popular stories refer, were no doubt those of the more northern and central districts—Celts, who had been driven back by the advancing tide of the Belgæ of Northern France.

Cæsar's reasons for invading Britain.

The invasion by Cæsar was the result of various and mixed circumstances, among which we may well believe one inducement to have been the desire on his part of making his rule in Gaul pre-eminently famous by the subjugation, under Roman rule, of

[1] Cæs. Bell. Gall. vi. 13, 14. [2] Ibid. v. 10. [3] Ibid. v. 15.

[4] Sussex was the chief seat of the iron manufacture of England till coal became abundant. In the reign of Queen Elizabeth seventy-three furnaces are said to have been at work, and the last, at Ashburnham, was only blown out in 1827. The railings round St. Paul's Cathedral (temp. Queen Anne) are made of Sussex iron.

an island about which so many stories were current among his countrymen. Britain, described in Virgil[1] as "beyond the limits of the known world," was supposed to be rich in gold and silver, with an ocean fertile in pearls;[2] indeed, Suetonius speaks of it as a popular belief, that it was in quest of pearls that Cæsar crossed the Channel. But a more probable reason for his proposed attempt is that alleged by Napoleon III., viz., his having found the natives of Britain invariably aiding his enemies in his Gallic wars, and especially in his conflict with the Veneti, during the summer of the year of his first invasion, B.C. 55.[3] Moreover, intestine divisions[4] had about that time broken out in England, and hence there was then a better chance of Roman success than there would have been had the islanders stood firmly together to resist the invader.

Having resolved then to make the attempt, Cæsar looked about him to procure information about the unknown island: but here he was completely foiled; for the Gauls stood too well by their friends and relations in Britain to volunteer the information they might easily have given the Roman commander. The Veneti, as might have been expected, did what they could to thwart him, while the Morini, dwelling around and to the east of Boulogne, are specially mentioned as friendly to the Britons.[5] Moreover, Cæsar himself remarks that no one but merchants ever visited Britain, [6]unless, indeed, they fled thither for their lives; Britain having been then, as now, the

[1] Virgil, Eclog. i. 67. [2] Tacit. Agric. Sueton. Cæs. c. 46, 47.
[3] Cæs. Bell. Gall. iv. 18. [4] Ibid. v. 16. [5] Dio. xxxix. 51.
[6] Cæs. Bell. Gall. iv. 18.

refuge for continental exiles of all classes. In spite, however, of these adverse circumstances, increased in some degree by the lateness of the season, Cæsar judged it best to make the attempt, hoping, probably, to strike an effective blow before the petty states in Britain had had time to weld themselves into a compact body, although, too, he had an almost certain prospect of an uprising in his rear of the only half-subdued Gauls as soon as his legions were fully employed in Britain. He therefore, as a last chance of procuring news about the island, despatched one of his lieutenants, C. Volusenus, in a "long ship" (*i.e.*, light war-galley),[1] giving him orders, as soon as he had made the necessary inquiries, to return to him with all possible speed; a step which showed clearly what his intentions were, and led to an embassy from the Britons, offering terms of submission he, perhaps, disbelieved, at all events declined accepting.

First invasion, B.C. 55.

Cæsar soon after collected about eighty vessels of burden, placed in them two legions, and, having made his final arrangements, started for England from Boulogne at midnight on August 26, B.C. 55, having on board a force of about eight thousand men. Eighteen other transports conveyed about eight hundred horses for the cavalry.[2] Beyond the number of the vessels, Cæsar has left us no information

[1] Cæs. Bell. Gall. iv. c. 21.

[2] It would be out of place here to discuss the vexed question of the places, respectively, whence Cæsar started from France, and where he landed in England. We can only say that, having read the several memoirs on this subject, by Halley, d'Anville, Dr. Guest, Master of Caius Coll., Cambr., the Astronomer Royal, and Mr. Lewin, we are inclined to think that the essay by the last-named writer (London, 1859) is the most consistent with the language of Cæsar himself. In the following pages, therefore, his views have been generally adopted.

in regard to them, and no indication of their capacity beyond the incidental statement that two of the galleys, which on his return got adrift, carried altogether three hundred men.

The number of men constituting a legion varied very much during the different periods of Roman history, and, in Cæsar's time, amounted to about five thousand two hundred and eighty men, all told; but as Cæsar obviously took with him as few troops as possible, intending his first descent upon England to be rather a visit of observation than a conquest, it is likely that the whole number of his force did not exceed what we have stated, making for each of the eighty galleys a complement of somewhere about one hundred men.

Size of his transports.

At present about three hundred passengers can be accommodated in a sailing vessel of one thousand tons register on a distant voyage; but, in coasting vessels, the number is very much greater.[1] It may therefore be assumed that the average size of the vessels in which Cæsar embarked his legions on this occasion was not more than one hundred tons register. The horse transports[2] may have been somewhat larger, as more than thirty-three horses, with their

[1] By the Passengers Act, which applies to all British possessions, except India and Hong Kong, the space allowed in passenger ships to each statute adult is not to be less than 15 clear superficial feet in the poop or in the upper passenger-deck, nor less than 18 clear superficial feet on the lower passenger-deck; and the height between decks is not to be less than 6 feet for the upper passenger-deck, nor less than 7 feet for the lower passenger-deck. Each person of twelve years and upwards, and two children between one and twelve years, count as an adult.

By the 16 and 17 Vict. cap. 84, however, the governors of colonies may, by proclamation, reduce this space to 12 superficial feet in the case of passengers, *being natives of Asia and Africa*, sailing from their governments.

[2] Cæs. B. G. iv. 32, 33.

provender, water, and attendants, could not well be conveyed in a vessel of less register than one hundred tons, even on so short a voyage as from Boulogne to Romney[1] or Lymne, performed, as this voyage was, with a fair wind, in fifteen hours, or at the rate of about two miles an hour. The ships of burden or transports were all flat-bottomed, that they might float in shallow water, and be more expeditiously freighted.

Although the facts preserved with regard to the ships which Cæsar employed on his first invasion are of the most meagre description, they are sufficient to show that they drew comparatively little water, or the men could not have "jumped" out of them, and made good their footing on the beach with their standard and arms against the whole British force: most likely, they were rather good stout-decked or half-decked barges than the ordinary sea-going coasting vessel, which, if one hundred tons burden, would draw, when laden, from seven to eight feet of water. There is no record of the ports where these vessels were constructed; but some of them, Cæsar tells us, had been employed by him, earlier in the same year, in his war with the Veneti.

Second invasion, B.C. 54.

The vessels employed in Cæsar's second invasion were somewhat similar in form to those in the first; but his army on this occasion consisted of five legions, with two thousand cavalry, for the transport of which he had about six hundred boats; there were also twenty-eight war-galleys.[2] If we appropriate

[1] It seems a reasonable conjecture that in the name of Romney (*i.e.*, Roman marsh or island) we have a relic of Cæsar's invasion.

[2] Cæs. B. G. v. 2.

one hundred vessels for the transport of the two thousand horses, and from seventy to one hundred for the transport of stores and munitions of war, and, if the number conveyed was about twenty-seven thousand men, the rate would be forty-five men to each vessel, so that the vessels on the second and more important expedition were, on an average, only about one-half the size of those which had been engaged on the first, and, like those, consisted, probably, in great measure of undecked and flat-bottomed boats or barges.

Cæsar's preference for small vessels.

One of the reasons Cæsar assigns for the preference he gave in his second expedition to small vessels was, that he had learned by his experience of the frequent changes of the tide in the Channel that the waves were not so violent as he had expected, and, therefore,[1] that smaller boats were sufficient for his purpose; but this does not seem to be a very satisfactory view. It is true that when wind and tide are together the violence of the waves is modified materially; but when they are opposed, their violence is greatly increased. We should rather suppose that, in preferring open row boats to sailing vessels for his second expedition, Cæsar had more especially in his mind the facility with which they could be beached. One effect of Cæsar's selection of this large flotilla became, however, at once manifest in the terror it caused to the Britons, who, instead of resisting his landing, fled precipitately in all directions at the sight of so numerous a squadron, and retired into the interior. The debarkation of the troops on the second invasion was therefore effected without

[1] Cæs. B. G. v. 1.

obstruction; and the vessels, after having discharged their freights, were anchored in Dungeness Bay. Finding that the British forces had retreated in the direction of Canterbury, then, as now, the capital of Kent, Cæsar determined on a rapid advance, most probably crossing the river Stour at Wye, about twelve miles from Lymne, near to which, as before, he had disembarked. Challock Wood, a considerable military post in the wars between the kings of Kent and Sussex, is, with reasonable probability, believed to have been the scene of the first encounter between the British and Roman forces. In this battle, though on the whole successful, it is clear that Cæsar had not much to plume himself upon; moreover, it was followed by a great disaster, in a gale which wrecked forty, and more or less disabled the whole of the vessels in which he had crossed the Channel. But the Roman general was not dismayed; having collected those least injured, he hauled them up on the shore, threw a rampart around them to preserve them from the attacks of the Britons, and leaving Labienus to collect fresh ships in Gaul, at once placed himself at the head of his legions.[1]

Violent storm and great loss of ships.

The British force having, however, gathered strength in the interval, now assumed a more threatening aspect; as Cassivelaunus, king of Hertfordshire and Middlesex, having triumphed in the wars in which he had been engaged at the time of Cæsar's first invasion, now claimed dominion over the whole of the south-east of England, and was, therefore, able to oppose the new assault on Britain

[1] The "Invasion of Britain by Julius Cæsar," by Thomas Lewin, Esq., M.A., 1859.

with a vast army, aided, it is said, with no less than four thousand chariots.[1]

Final action on the banks of the Thames.

But though some of the encounters were at first of doubtful success, the steady discipline of the Romans forced back the hosts of Cassivelaunus, and Cæsar apparently followed his retreating forces, first, in a north-westerly, and then in a direction due north, till they arrived at the banks of the Thames, a little to the west of Walton bridge. Here Cassivelaunus resolved to resist the further progress of Cæsar,[2] but was

[1] Cæs. B. G. v. 19; and Roach Smith's "Antiquities of Richborough, Reculver, and Lymne. Lond. 1850."

[2] It is generally supposed that Cassivelaunus, in execution of a well concerted plan, retired, followed by Cæsar, from the banks of the Stour along the southern side of the chalk hills running from Wye to Dorking, and then down the right bank of the Mole to the nearest point of the Thames at "Coway stakes," situated between Walton and Shepperton. In the year 1855, the author of this work purchased the principal property in the latter parish, and a few years afterwards that of Halliford, so named from the ford at Coway, where the Romans are supposed to have crossed the Thames. Since then he has resided almost constantly in the Manor-house of Shepperton, which, on the authority of Stukeley and of other antiquaries, occupies the site where Cæsar pitched his camp after the final defeat of the ancient Britons. The paddock, about fourteen acres in extent, attached to his house, is said to have derived its name from the fact that there the battle between the Romans and Britons raged in its greatest fury, and that there it ended, with great carnage, in the overthrow of Cassivelaunus. In the recent Ordnance maps, as well as in some maps of an ancient date, this paddock is described as "War-close field, from which there has been dug spears, swords, and great quantities of human bones."

Cæsar in his Commentaries remarks (book v. c. xvii): 'Cæsar, perceiving their design, marched the army to the river Thames, towards the territory of Cassivelaunus; that river was fordable only at one place, and there with difficulty. When he arrived, he saw that the enemy was drawn up in great force at the opposite bank of the river; but the bank was fortified with stakes fixed in front; stakes also of the same kind were driven into the bed of the river, concealed from view by the stream. Cæsar, learning this from the prisoners and deserters, having sent the cavalry before, ordered the legions to follow closely. This the soldiers did with such celerity and vigour, their

defeated in a well contested action, which rendered any further struggle against the Romans in that part, at least, of England, hopeless.

The legions of Cæsar had suffered so severely in this campaign, that he was equally glad with the native princes to enter into negotiations for peace; and, on the conclusion of these, he withdrew his army to Gaul, in little more than two months after his disembarkation at Lymne. As his homeward journey across the Channel lasted but eight hours, he must have had the wind in his favour.

Cæsar makes terms with the Britons, and re-embarks his legions.

When the magnitude of the preparations which Cæsar made for his second expedition are considered, it can hardly be doubted that his intentions were to subjugate the whole of Britain. Tacitus, however, in his life of Agricola, confesses that Cæsar, in his two campaigns, only made the discovery of Britain; that, though victorious, he was unable to maintain his position;[2] that, on leaving the island, not a single Roman was left behind him; and that, for

heads only seen above water, that the enemy could not sustain the shock of the legions and cavalry, but abandoned the banks and betook themselves to flight.

Besides the traces of a great Roman camp, still distinctly visible on the brow of St. George's hill, about two miles from Coway stakes, the footprints of the legions are to be seen in many places round Shepperton, and have been noted by Bede, Roy, Camden, Salmon, Gale, Stukeley, and other antiquarian writers. To these the author may add his own testimony, having found, in different parts of the property (especially when cleaning out a ditch which runs through War-close), various Roman coins and spikes, resembling spear-heads. Other relics of the Romans, such as urns, have frequently been dug from the gravel-pits opened during his time in different fields in the parish.

[1] Tacit. Agric. c. 13; and Strabo confirms this view (iv. c. 4.).

[2] Ibid. c. 15.

Advantages derived by the Britons from their intercourse with the Romans.

nearly a hundred years afterwards, the Britons were as free as ever, and paid no tribute to the imperial city.[1] Yet the Romans and ancient Britons were alike gainers by their mutual intercourse; for, from this period, their commercial intercourse rapidly increased. The corn and cattle of the Britons rose to a value hitherto unknown, while iron, and pearls of an inferior description, were eagerly sought after by the Romans. A new and vast field was opened up for their tin, lead, wool, and skins. Their slaves,[2] and dogs, of a remarkable breed, were in great demand; and were readily exchanged for the cut ivory, bridles, gold chains, cups of amber, drinking glasses, and trinkets of various kinds which the Romans exported. A considerable trade also arose between the two countries in lime, marl, and chalk, and in the manufacture of baskets, graceful in design, and curious in workmanship, for which the Britons were famous.

Conquest of Britain, A.D. 43.

Its state of civilization.

Beyond these facts, however, nothing is known of what passed in Britain between the time when Julius Cæsar left it, and the period when it first became a Roman province under Claudius. When, however, the armies of Claudius landed upon its soil, the Britons had advanced far beyond the painted savages who first exchanged their tin for the trinkets of Phœnicia; and although, in the remote portions of the island, there were still to be found many barbarous tribes, the inhabitants of the coast and of the commercial cities were then scarcely less civilized

[1] Tacit. Ann. xii. 34.

[2] Strabo speaks, from personal observation, of the large stature of the Britons whom he saw at Rome.

than they were a thousand years afterwards at the period of the Norman Conquest. London, or Londinium, is described by Tacitus as a place then of considerable trade, though not dignified with the name of a colony, and as the chief residence of the merchants. Clausentum[1] (old Southampton), and Rutupi (Richborough) were commercial ports of some importance, and were occupied by traders who dealt largely with those of Gaul, and extended their business even to Rome itself.

Traders from the neighbouring coasts, but more especially from that section of the Germans known by the name of Belgæ,[2] who centuries before had settled on the opposite coast between the Rhine and the Seine, were, in many cases, the intermediate dealers between the Britons and the continental tribes. The whole country was then, as had no doubt been the case for some time previous to the invasion, divided into several small states presided over by chiefs, who are dignified by historians with the title of king. Ptolemy, in his geography,[3] mentions various towns in different parts of Britain of sufficient importance in his time to be recorded, all tending to show that a state of civilization then prevailed throughout the island, and that barbarism and savage life were the exception rather than the rule.

Amongst the towns noticed by Ptolemy may be mentioned Isca Damnoniorum (Exeter); Durnium (Dorchester); Venta Belgarum (Winchester), which

[1] Generally considered to be represented by the village of Bittern, about one and a half miles up the Itchen, above the present Southampton.

[2] Cæs. B. G. vi. 13 and 14. Ibid. v. 14.

[3] Ptol. Geogr. ii. c. 3.

was a place of great fame in his time; Aquæ-solis (Bath), so called from its hot waters; Ischalis, now Ilchester, and Guildford in Surrey (Noviomagus). Numerous towns and seaports are also noticed by him, as, for instance, in Kent, Rochester, Dover, and Lymne; and in the west and north-west of England, Gleva (Gloucester); Deva (Chester); and near it Uriconium (Wroxeter), the curious remains of which have been quite recently explored;[1] Carlisle and Mona (Anglesey), the great seat of the Druidical worship. In the interior of the country we may record, as among the most famous of the Roman stations or colonies, Eboracum (York); Lindum (Lincoln); Camalodunum (Colchester); Corinium, (Cirencester); and Dorovernia (Canterbury); at or near all of which places extensive Roman remains may still be seen.

The principality of Wales, formerly comprehending the whole country beyond the Severn, was supposed by Tacitus[2] to have been originally peopled by emigrants from Spain, and here too may be still traced the vestiges of several Roman camps, as at Usk and Caerleon. At Stonehenge and Abury, in Wiltshire, are still more ancient remains, monuments of great interest, both for the size and the elegant disposition of the stones of which they are formed; and which, at the same time, denote considerable progress in the mechanical arts at a period antecedent, perhaps, by centuries to the invasion of Cæsar.[3] Wherever we go, we find that the Britons

[1] "Uriconium, or Wroxeter," by T. Wright, F.S.A. Lond. 1872.
[2] Tacit. Ann. xii. c. 31.
[3] "Abury Illustrated," by W. Long, M.A. Devizes, 1858.

at the commencement of the Christian era occupied a position, which, if far short of the high state of civilization the Romans had reached, was greatly superior to that of most of the northern nations of Europe, or to that of the Goths and Vandals, when, three centuries afterwards, they overran the empire and became masters of the imperial city.[1]

Speech of Caractacus.

Indeed, the famous speech of Caractacus, when taken captive to Rome, shows a nobility of character, nay, we may add, an amount of civilization that would not have been anticipated. "If I had made," said the noble Briton, "that prudent use of prosperity which my rank and fortune enabled me to do, I might have come hither as your friend rather than as your prisoner; nor would you have disdained the alliance of a king descended from illustrious ancestors, and

[1] Nor can we omit noticing here a matter which has in former times been much disputed, whether or no there are any coins, clearly British, antecedent to the invasion of Cæsar. On the evidence of all the best MSS. of Cæsar's Commentaries, especially of a very fine one of the tenth century in the British Museum, we find Cæsar distinctly stating that the Britons "use either brass money or gold money, or instead of money, iron rings, adjusted to a certain weight." (Cæs. Bell. Gall. v. 10. E. Hawkins' "Silver Coins of England" (1841), pp. 9–14. Evans' "Coins of the Ancient Britons," pp. 18 and 285. Lond. 1864.) It was only about the seventeenth century that the editors of Cæsar, Scaliger leading the way, corrupted this passage and made him assert that only substitutes for money were used by the natives. All the facts are in favour of the MSS., for coins of gold, sometimes of silver, but very rarely of copper, are found in different parts of England, and as is evident to any eye, are in form, fabric, and type, constructed on a model differing essentially from any thing of Roman origin. Indeed, as is well known to numismatists, the original British coins were constructed on Greek models, and, however rude, may be traced back, step by step, to the gold money (staters) of Philip, the father of Alexander the Great. Plenty of coins exist of the time of Cæsar's second invasion and of Cunobeline, who was alive in the reign of Claudius; the first, in a purely British (*i.e.*, Greek) type, the second, with an obvious imitation of those of the Romans—and perhaps executed, as some have thought, by Roman artists.—Tacit. Annals, xii. 31–36.

ruling over many nations. My present condition, degrading as it is to me, reflects glory on you. I once had horses, men, arms, and money; what wonder is it if I was reluctant to part with them! Your object is to obtain universal empire, and we must all be slaves! If I had submitted to you without a blow, neither my own fortune nor your glory would have been conspicuous, and all remembrances of me would have vanished when I had received my punishment; but spare me my life, and I shall be a lasting monument of your clemency."

The course of commerce with Rome.

When the course of events is considered, it is not surprising that the ancient Britons should have made less opposition to Claudius than they had done ninety-seven years before to Julius Cæsar. They had learned in the interval the advantages to be derived by intercourse with a much more wealthy and more polished people than themselves. They saw that not only the enlightenment of the mind accompanies civilization in its progress, but that, as civilization increases, it creates wants which require to be supplied, and luxuries which crave to be satisfied.

The routes taken by merchants and travellers continued for many centuries much as they had been in the earliest times. Claudius, however, when he left Rome for the seat of war in Britain, set sail from the port of Ostia at the mouth of the Tiber, went by sea to Massalia (Marseilles), and afterwards journeying, partly by land and partly by the rivers till he reached the coast of Gaul on the English Channel,[1] crossed over to Britain, and there joined "the forces which awaited him near the Thames." "There

[1] Dion. Cass. lx. c. 21.

were then four ports," remarks Strabo,[1] "at which voyagers generally crossed from the mainland to the island, at the mouths respectively of the river Rhône, the Seine, the Loire, and the Garonne; but the travellers who crossed from the country about the Rhine did not set sail from the mouth of that river, preferring to pass through the Morini and to embark at its port of Boulogne."

The ordinary traffic of those times was conveyed either on the backs of mules or horses, across Gaul, as was the case with tin, or by the rivers of that country: indeed, for a long period the merchant vessels of Britain were not of a construction to brave the heavy gales and stormy seas of the rude Atlantic, while Gaul was a country peculiarly favoured in the conveniences it afforded for such an inland water transit. Everywhere intersected by navigable rivers running in very opposite directions, goods could be carried between the Mediterranean and the English Channel, or the shores of the Atlantic, with little assistance of land carriage. From Narbo, an ancient commercial port of first-class importance already noticed, goods were carried a few miles overland and re-shipped on the Garonne, which carried them to Burdigala (Bordeaux). In the same way the Loire, the Seine, and the Rhine afforded navigable facilities into the very heart of the country, while all of them were easily connected with the Rhône or its great navigable branches, thus completing the inland water-carriage between the Mediterranean and the western and northern shores of Gaul.

Inland water traffic.

British goods destined for Rome, or for any port of

[1] Strabo, iv. 2.

the Mediterranean, were chiefly conveyed by either of these inland routes, or across country by the few highways or beaten tracks then in use.[1] In the centre of this inland conveyance, at the junction of the Rhône with the Saône (Arar), and within an easy distance of the other navigable rivers flowing in the opposite direction, stood the great inland emporium of Lyons (Lugdunum), a city then of much commercial importance and second only to Narbo. This inland navigation, while of material advantage to the inhabitants of the districts traversed, was, even before the Roman conquest, a source of considerable emolument to the proprietors of the lands adjacent to the rivers, as they were thus able to levy a toll or transit duty on the boats passing through their territories. These duties, we may presume from Strabo, were transferred to the Roman coffers soon after Gaul became a Roman province, as he distinctly asserts that (in his day at least) the duties on the imports and exports of Britain constituted the only species of revenue derived from Gaul by the Romans.[2] It is, moreover, not likely that the government of Rome would permit its subjects to levy dues for their own individual benefit.

Transit duties.

Articles of commerce,

"The commercial and friendly intercourse," remarks Macpherson in his Annals of Commerce,[3] "between the Britons and Gauls, which had subsisted before the invasion of Julius Cæsar, still continued, and was probably increased in consequence of the greater assortment of goods now in the hands of the Romanized Gallic merchants." Tin, which was still

[1] Strabo, iii. p. 119; ii. p. 190; iv. pp. 279, 318. Diod. Sic. v. s. 22.
[2] Ibid. ii. p. 176; and iv. p. 306. [3] Ibid. i. p. 132.

the chief article of British commerce, after being cast into cubic masses, remained, and long continued, the general staple of the British trade. "But besides it," continues the same author, "there was then exported to Gaul, either for sale in that country, or for further transit, lead, corn, cattle, hides, under the description of which, perhaps, wool is included; gold, silver, iron, ornaments for bridles, and various toys made of a substance which the Romans called ivory, but more probably the bone of some large fish; ornamental chains, vessels made of amber and of glass, with some other trifling articles; also precious stones and pearls; slaves, who were captives taken in the wars carried on by the tribes against each other; dogs of various species, all excellent in their kinds, which were highly valued by the Roman connoisseurs in hunting, and by the Gauls, who used them not only against wild animals in the chase, but also against their enemies in the field of battle; and bears for the sanguinary sport of the Roman circus, though probably not so early as the age of Augustus."

and knowledge of manufactures and of the arts.

Brass, brazen vessels, salt, and earthenware, were then, with the lighter articles and trinkets previously named, the chief articles of import from Gaul into Britain. Though chiefly occupied in pastoral and agricultural pursuits, the ancient Britons, from the character of their exports, evidently understood, not merely the arts of extracting tin and lead and even gold silver and iron from their mines, but were skilled in the manufacture of objects in glass and amber, and also in some works purely ornamental, as well as in the conversion of iron to many useful purposes. Skins were no doubt still used as articles of dress by many of the less civilized inhabitants who resided in the remote parts of the island; but those Britons who occupied the frequented parts of the coast, or the chief towns, were, from the observations of Cæsar, clothed in better and more comfortable garments, very likely in woollen cloths. As manufactures in wool were among the earliest arts which first brought England into notice as a great commercial nation many centuries afterwards, it is reasonable to suppose that woollen fabrics may, even in early times, have been part of the staple of the country.

Colchester, and its mint.

Colchester, the principal city of eastern Britain, was made by Claudius,[1] at the commencement of the Christian era, as appears from his coins, a Roman colony. Here Cunobeline, king of the countries lying between the Thames and the Nen, established a mint, of which as many as sixty varieties have been engraved by Mr. Evans.[2] No descriptive account of this ancient town has been preserved, but it is reasonable to suppose that, as the capital in which the king resided, it was better built than the "fenced collection of huts" Cæsar describes.

London.

Some doubts have been expressed as to the very early antiquity of London; and, on the whole, it is most likely that it was not till Claudius had appointed Plautius to the supreme command of the island, that the Romans directed their attention to London,[3] and established it as the chief commercial

[1] Dion. lx. 21.

[2] J. Evans, "Coins of the Ancient Britons," p. 284, &c. Lond. 1864.

[3] Details of early London in Ptol. i. 15; vi. 8. Tacit. Ann. xiv. 33. It is first mentioned by Tacitus.

centre for the arts and manufactures of Kent and of the valley of the Thames, over which river, if the testimony of Dio can be relied on, the Britons had already constructed a bridge somewhere near the site of the lowest of the existing structures. Ten years afterwards, in the reign of Nero, we hear of the now famous city, the greatest and wealthiest the world has ever seen, having become the residence of a great number of such dealers as the Romans dignified with the title of merchants, and between whom and the small traders of Rome, Cicero drew, as we have already noticed, so marked and so supercilious a distinction. A.D. 61.

It is not the province of this work to follow in detail the course of Roman conquest. It is sufficient to state that the Romans only gained their footing in Britain by slow degrees, and that the legions which had conquered other countries almost as soon as they marched into them, had to encounter many a sturdy foe, and to achieve many a hard-earned victory, ere they obtained full control over a people, who, though fully alive to the advantages of a commercial intercourse with Rome, cherished a love of independence unsurpassed by any other nation of antiquity. Indeed, it was not until the governorship of Agricola that Britain could in any sense be called a Roman province; and that Agricola succeeded where other generals, such as Plautius and Ostorius Scapula, had failed, is mainly attributable to the care and gentleness of his administration, and to his obvious desire to make the chains he had forged for the British as agreeable as possible to them. Agricola was the first Roman general who had penetrated into

Agricola, A.D. 78–85

His fleet sails round Britain.

Scotland; he was also the first to sail round the whole country, an undertaking then of no ordinary danger, especially at the advanced season of the year when it was performed. It is a striking remark of Tacitus that the harbours of Ireland, which one or two centuries before had been visited by the Gauls, and perhaps at a still earlier period by the Carthaginians, were then better known to continental merchants by means of their commerce than to those of Britain.

The influence of the rule of Agricola on the Britons.

Altogether the rule of Agricola proved as remarkable as it was certainly at variance with the usual habits and practices of Roman proconsuls. When once he had laid down the sword, he encouraged a taste among the Britons for the pleasures of civilized life; first exhorting, then assisting them to build temples and places of public resort, and commending and rewarding those who were assiduous and forward in such pursuits: in this way he hoped to subdue their restless spirit, and to give scope to their excitement in other pursuits than those of war. He also took care to have the sons of their chiefs instructed in the liberal sciences, inducing many of them to study the Roman language, which they had previously despised, to copy the manners and customs of Rome, and even to adopt the costume of its citizens. Nor were his efforts confined to the improvement and amelioration of their social position. He had learned, from the conduct of those who had preceded him in the government of Britain, how little arms avail to settle a province, if victory is followed by grievances and oppressions; he therefore displayed his superior wisdom by removing every just cause for complaint. Beginning with himself, and with those around him, he regulated his own household, so that in its conduct it might be an example for others to follow; his domestics, according to Tacitus,[1] were not allowed to transact any business concerning the public; and, in promoting or rewarding the soldiers, he was induced to do so by no personal interest or partiality, nor by the recommendations of centurions, but by his own opinion and knowledge of them. By such means as these Agricola, by degrees, reconciled the Britons to the government of Rome; and, though their love of independence was never actually subdued, they were content to live, if unopposed, in peace, and in friendly intercourse with the invaders of their soil. Caledonia alone kept up an angry hostility to the yoke of Rome, and seized, on the departure of Agricola, the castles and forts he had raised in various parts of Scotland.

Hadrian, A.D. 120.

During the thirty-five years which elapsed after the recall of Agricola, until the reign of the Emperor Hadrian, the Roman historians, from whom alone we derive our information, hardly deign to notice the island; while, as is well known, no native records, or even what might perhaps have been a copy of a native record, have come down to us: indeed, it may be seriously doubted whether letters were at all generally known beyond the schools of the Druids. There is, however, every reason to suppose that the Britons pursued with persevering industry those commercial occupations we have already named; that the advice and example of Agricola had not been given in vain, or neglected on his departure; and, that, long ere that time, trade and commerce must

State of commerce in and after his reign.

[1] Tacit. Vit. Agric. c. 19.

have taken deep root in the island, as the city of London had even then given tokens of its aptitude to become the mercantile capital of the world.[1] The pearl fisheries, abandoned afterwards from the inherent defects of British pearls, were developed to an extent hitherto unknown; and a trade was opened out in oysters, which were actually conveyed, probably by one of the overland routes, to Rome, to satisfy the cravings of the epicures of the imperial city. Indeed, they were in such demand as to form a subject for the poet's satire.

> "Could at one bite the oyster's taste decide,
> And say if at Circæan rocks, or in
> The Lucrine lake, or on the coasts of Richborough,
> In Britain, they were bred."[2]

Another extensive trade, the manufacture of baskets, is casually mentioned, in the same strain of wit, by another Roman poet in the following lines:—

> "Work of barbaric art, a basket, *I*
> From painted Britain came, but the Roman city
> Now call the painted Britons' art their own."[3]

The Caledonian incursions.

We also learn, incidentally,[4] that the people of the northern part of Scotland, although the shores swarmed with fish, did not eat them, but subsisted entirely by hunting and on the fruits of the earth.

Not satisfied with the possession of the forts Agricola had erected for the protection of the Britons against the Caledonians, the Emperor Hadrian, who visited the island in person, finding that they had extended their warlike and predatory excursions to the south of the Tyne, was compelled to drive them

[1] Tacit. Ann. xiv. 33.
[2] Juvenal, Sat. iv. 140.
[3] Martial, xiv. 99.
[4] Dion. lxvi. 12.

back to their mountain fastnesses by the superior force of fresh legions. Alarmed, however, by their daring and intrepidity, or not considering it worth while to follow them north of that river, he caused the wall to be built which still bears his name, from the Eden in Cumberland to the Tyne in Northumberland, to restrain them from again making incursions into the Roman province. Hadrian's rampart, however, was soon breached, for seventy miles of wall required more soldiers to protect it than the Romans could spare, and though subsequent walls were built at different times, all of these proved equally ineffective in repressing the advances of the Picts: till, at length, Severus was compelled to purchase a peace by money which his arms had failed to secure.[1]

Piratical invasions of the Germans.

But Rome had innumerable difficulties to contend against in the government of Britain beyond the inroads of the Caledonians, who had ever spurned and resisted her rule. The Franks and other German nations had for some time invaded the coasts adjacent to them with piratical incursions, and had reaped a rich harvest from the plunder of the sea-coast towns and of the vessels of the traders employed between Britain and Gaul. In order to repress these sea-robbers, the Emperor Maximian built a fleet of ships, the command of which he gave to Carausius, an officer of great experience in naval and military affairs, to whose history we have already alluded. Though a traitor to the government he professed to serve, and possessing himself no claims to the allegiance of the Britons, there is no doubt that the island

Carausius seizes the fleet of Maximian, and declares himself Emperor of Britain.

[1] For further details, see Rev. J. C. Bruce, "The Roman Wall from Tyne to Solway." 4to., 1867.

prospered under his brief rule, and for the first time was able to claim the proud title of mistress of the northern seas, a title, however, she soon lost, and only regained after tremendous struggles, twelve centuries afterwards. Britain, during the seven years' reign of Carausius, seems to have possessed more wealth and prosperity than during any similar period of Roman rule, while the flourishing state of the arts at that period of her history is shown by the number and elegance of his coins, three hundred varieties of which, in gold, silver, or copper, are now preserved in different numismatic collections.

But though Britain may have flourished in material prosperity under Carausius, no Roman emperor could have allowed his rebellious acts to remain unchastised, and hence, after a long preparation, Constantius was sent to England with a powerful force, and in a short space of time restored the imperial sway; not the less easily, perhaps, that Carausius had in the meanwhile been murdered by his lieutenant Allectus. No mention is made of the number of ships or troops constituting the expedition of Constantius, but it must have been on an extensive scale, as it captured in its first attempt the port of Boulogne, with part of the British fleet.[1]

Welsh and Scots, A.D. 360.

Nor do historians afford much information with regard to the affairs of Britain from the death of Constantius, father of Constantine the Great, until more than fifty years afterwards, when its Roman subjects were seriously harassed by the Welsh on the west,

[1] An attempt has been made by one or two writers to connect the name of Carausius with the "War of Caros" in the so-called "Poems of Ossian." For this there will be some pretence, whenever it shall be shown that Ossian exists, except in the brain of Macpherson.

and the Caledonians on the north, who ravaged the frontiers and spread terror throughout the now civilized provinces of Britannia Romana. Nor was this all: while harassed by the descendants of the Celts, the Germanic Saxons invaded England on the east and south, startling the Romans and their subjects by the daring intrepidity with which they skimmed over the roughest seas in "boats of leather," and, without respect of persons or property, plundered and carried off everything worthy of removal. Besides these frail craft the Saxons, however, possessed more than one description of vessel altogether superior to their leather-covered boats, called by the old historians in Latin, *Kiulæ*; in Saxon, *Ceol*, or *Ciol*; and in English, *Keels*.[1] Some writers also maintain that they had strong open boats adapted to warfare at sea.

Saxons, A.D. 364.

Their ships.

That these German rovers possessed larger vessels than even their war-galleys is ascertained by the fact that, within seventy or eighty years after they first gained a secure footing in Britain, they received a reinforcement of "five thousand men, in seventeen ships,"[2] or at the rate of about three hundred men to a ship, besides provisions, stores, and munitions of war. But of their form, size, or equipment no accounts have been preserved, and it can, therefore, tend to no useful purpose to

[1] Camden describes Kiulæ as a general name for all Saxon vessels. Other writers say that Kiula meant "long ships," *i. e.*, men of war, or galleys, whatever might be their precise shape. *Keel* now represents a description of barge which has long been in use in the north of England, and especially on the Tyne, built to hold twenty-one tons four hundred-weight, or a keel of coals.

[2] Macpherson's "Annals of Commerce," i. p. 217.

attempt, as Mr. Strutt has done, the reproduction of the supposed types of the vessels of Canute, as all such drawings are only the creations of fancy.

It may be reasonable, however, to infer that the better class of Saxon vessels were copies of the Roman or British galleys, used by Carausius or Constantius, possibly with some addition, such as higher bulwarks, fitting them the better to resist the stormy and pitching sea of the German Ocean. However slow the progress of improvement may have been among a body of merchants and ship-owners, whose property was perpetually exposed to depredation and destruction, there can be no doubt that the princes of those days in Britain and through-out northern Europe availed themselves of all the resources of the time to display their maritime consequence and power to the best advantage. It can, indeed, be hardly questioned that the long and comparatively peaceful intercourse between the seamen of the north and the south must have familiarized the Vikings with such improvements in the construction of shipping as had been worked out by the nations bordering on the Mediterranean; and though, for short and hasty expeditions, the Northmen or the Saxons may have been willing to trust themselves to small or ill-constructed open boats, there is no reason to suppose this would be the case, either when they had heavy and bulky merchandise, or their best and bravest warriors, to convey in safety on long and perilous voyages.

On the invasion of the Celts and of the Teutonic tribes, the inhabitants of Britain were unable to make an adequate defence. Unlike their hardy forefathers, who had needed no aid but their own good right hands, they had become accustomed to look for protection to their Roman masters, and to delegate to others what they ought to have achieved themselves. Nor were the northern tribes their only foes. Besides their new invaders, they had to contend with gangs of Roman soldiers, who, cheated of their pay by their officers, infested the highways as robbers, and extorted provisions from the natives.[1]

State of the Britons when abandoned by the Romans.

It might have been supposed that the Britons, improved in learning, in agriculture, in manufactures, and in the arts and sciences by four centuries of Roman instruction, would have become a great and flourishing people. They had, indeed, natural advantages superior to all their rivals, in the possession of some of the finest harbours in the world, of minerals, and of a soil as fruitful, if not more so than that of any of the countries around them. But while Rome had raised the Britons in the social scale, and imparted to them knowledge of the highest value for the development of their vast natural resources, she had, especially towards the close of her career, greatly weakened them, by the heavy drafts of their best sons for employment in local wars, or to be posted far away as garrisons in distant provinces. It is, therefore, probable that Rome left our forefathers comparatively poorer and, assuredly, in a weaker condition than they were when she usurped the government of their island.

[1] Bede places the final withdrawal of the Roman forces from England, and the consequent misfortunes which befell the native Britons, at just before the siege of Rome by Attila, A.D. 409. Eccles. Hist. i. c. 2. See also "Uriconium," by T. Wright. 8vo., 1872.

Of the origin of the Saxons, whose aid the Britons are said to have sought after the departure of the Romans, nothing is distinctly known, except that they had, for some time previously, made themselves masters of the territory lying between the Elbe and the Rhine, pushing forwards their conquests or occupation of the country as far as the coasts of Zealand, part of the present kingdom of Holland. Their occupation of England was probably exceedingly gradual, the south and east having been early peopled with these strangers, so that the so-called Saxon conquest was really, therefore, rather the slow result of their increasing numbers than of such a development of military or naval genius as is seen in the later inroads of the Danes or of William the Norman.

CHAPTER XI.

The early Scandinavian Vikings settle on the coast of Scotland and elsewhere—Great skill as seamen—Discovery of ancient ship, and of other early relics—Incursions of the Saxons and Angles into Britain; and its state soon afterwards—London—Accession of Offa, A.D. 755—Restrictions on trade and commerce—Salutary regulations—Charlemagne's first treaty of commerce with England, A.D. 796—Extension of French commerce, A.D. 813—Commerce of England harassed by the Danes—Their ships, and the habits of their owners—Increase of the Northern marauders—Language of the Northmen still spoken by mariners in the North—Accession of Alfred the Great, A.D. 871: his efforts to improve navigation, and to extend the knowledge of geography—Foundation of a royal and commercial navy—His voyages of discovery and missions to the East—Reign of Edward the Elder, A.D. 901–25, and of his son Athelstan, A.D. 925–41—Edgar's fleet, and his arrangements for suppressing piracy—The wisdom of his policy—Ethelred II., A.D. 979–1016—Sufferings of the people—Charges on vessels trading to London—Olaf, king of Norway, his ships, and those of Swein—Love of display—Mode of navigating—Canute, A.D. 1016—Reduction of the English fleet—Prosperity of commerce—Norman invasion, A.D. 1066—Number of vessels engaged, and their form—State of trade and commerce—Exports—Manufactures—Wealth—Imports—Taxation—London specially favoured—Chester specially burdened—State of the people at the time of the Conquest.

The early Scandinavian Vikings

AMONG the numerous tribes which overran Europe during the third, fourth, and fifth centuries, it would not be easy to give to any one a position of superiority over the others in the theory and practice of maritime commerce. Requiring wider

settle on the coast of Scotland, and elsewhere.

fields for their energy, and a soil more suited for a superabundant population than could be found amidst the barren mountains of Scandinavia or in the northern portions of Germany, the first object of most of them, as was the case with the Goths and Vandals, was, doubtless, to obtain greater means of subsistence. But desolate hills, and a string of small islands along a deeply indented coast, with deep and narrow water between them and the mainland, afforded a natural home for the Vikings' tribe; while the mainland itself became available as a great sea-fortress for countless fleets.

By the physical structure of the country, there run out from a solid centre of mountain-land a multitude of rocks, like great prongs, with deep gulfs between them filled from the sea. These are the celebrated Fiords, which send branches or inlets through the mountains on either side, some of them longer than the longest sea lochs of the West Highlands of Scotland. Except in the few places where large rivers make deltas of silt, the rocks run sheer down into deep water, so that vessels can lie close to the land in the smallest crevices or bays. The entrances to wide stretches of fiord are sometimes so narrow, and consequently so easily defended, that the people speak of the stones rolling from the tops of the high rocky banks, and bounding across the water, so as to strike the opposite shore. It was of little consequence to the Vikings that the soil around them was hard and barren, for the value to them of that soil was in protection, not in produce. The only articles they required for home industry were the timber, iron, and pitch, for the building of their vessels, and the fish which abounded in their narrow seas. All their other wants were provided by plunder from the industrious and affluent communities of other lands.

In the Hebrides and the sea-lochs of the Highlands they found harbours of retreat the same in character, though not in greatness, as those they left behind them; and we may fairly suppose that it was for these, not necessarily for any temptation in the prospect of plunder, that those districts were frequented by them. Hence it was that the Orkney and other Northern Isles, and even a great part of the north of Scotland, came in hand more naturally to the monarch ruling in Norway than to the king of the Scots.

When we find these sea-rovers in the north-west of Scotland and in Ireland, it becomes obvious, and is confirmed by facts, that they took the north-east coast of Scotland and the northern islands in their way. As the Shetland Islands are not more than two hundred miles distant from the mouths of two of their greatest fiords—the Hardanger and the Sogne, it may be inferred that these islands, or Caithness, was their first landfall, where they could swarm off to the Faroes or Iceland, on the one side, or to Scotland, England, and Ireland, on the other.

Great skill as seamen.

As the Vikings must have been thorough seamen, with a great capacity in the handling of their vessels, it is to be regretted, for the sake of arts and inventions, that we have not a fuller knowledge of the details of their craft, and of their method of working them. With, perhaps, the exception of the Phœnicians and Carthaginians, their achievements in navigation were on a scale unknown in the world of ancient history. Whether or not they were the first discoverers of Vinland (or North America), they quickly found their way to the Mediterranean, and were known on every European coast from Iceland to Constântinople. Their rapid movements directly across wide, stormy oceans show a start in seamanship passing at once beyond the capacity of the earlier navigators who crept along the shore. Their ordinary galleys were adapted to the Mediterranean, where they were used down to the seventeenth century. They had small square sails merely to get help from a stern wind, their chief mode of propulsion being oars; but it may be reasonably supposed that the Vikings, when they performed, as they so often did, the feat of sailing from their place of retreat straight across a stormy ocean, and of pouncing unexpectedly on the opposite shore, had made considerable advance in the rigging and handling of sailing vessels.

From incidental allusions in the Sagas, it is believed that a fleet fitted out for fighting and plunder was accompanied by lumber ships to carry slaves for the drudgery work, provisions, munitions, and perhaps the heavier portion of the plunder. As to the size of their light narrow war ships, it has been calculated by an ardent and skilful student of the habits of the Norsemen, that one favourite vessel, "the Long Serpent," must have been above a hundred feet in length.[1] The monk of the Irish house of St. Gall, who tells the story of Charlemagne weeping when he saw a pirate fleet in the Mediterranean, also tells how

[1] Laing's Transl. of the Heimskringla, p. 135.

the emperor's acute eye at once detected, from the build and swiftness of the vessels, that their purpose was not trade but mischief.[1]

Some remarkable discoveries in Denmark have revealed recently the remains of a plank-built boat sufficiently complete to admit of the entire reconstruction of the vessel as it floated. If we compare this vessel (see page 336) with the accounts of the hide-covered coracles which carried the Scots from Ireland, or with the lumbering canoe cut out of the solid wood, such as may still be seen on the lakes of Bavaria, we obtain at a glance the measure of the high capacity of those who built the vessels for the Vikings. The Northern antiquaries have fixed her date as "the early iron age," probably about the fifth century. Close examination has led to the conclusion that she was entirely a row-boat, with no arrangement for help from canvas; "yet it is seventy-seven feet long, measured from stem to stern, and proportionally rather broad in the middle."[2]

Discovery of ancient ship and of other early relics.

It immediately recalls the light handy boats of smaller size still used on the Norwegian coast, and in the Shetlands; and its structure is so thoroughly adapted to a union of lightness, speed, and strength, that it has been compared with the class of vessels now called clippers.

[1] Monach. Sangall. De rebus Caroli Magni ap. Muratori. Antiq. v. 1.

[2] Full details of this, and of two other less perfect vessels discovered about the same time, at Thorsbjerg and Nydam, in S. Jutland, are given in the very interesting work by Mr. C. Engelhardt, entitled "Denmark in the early Iron Age," Lond. 4to. 1866. From the frontispiece of this work the accompanying plate has been taken. Special attention has been called to it by Mr. J. H. Burton, to whose "History of Scotland" we are indebted for some of the notices of the Scandinavians.

ANCIENT DANISH VESSEL.

There are peculiarities in its structure, testifying to the abundance both of material and skilled labour. The timber or heavy planks, for instance, instead of being sawn into boards of equal thickness—or thinness—throughout, are cut thin where thinness was desirable, but thick at points of juncture, that they may be mortised into the cross-beams and gunwale, instead of being merely nailed. The vessel has two bows, or rather is alike at bow and stern, with thirty rowlocks, and it is noticed that these, along with the helm, are reversible, so as to permit the vessel to be rowed with either end forward.[1] The gunwale rises with the keel, at each extremity, into a high beak or prow, a notable feature of the Norwegian boats of the present day. The build is of the kind technically called "clinker," each plank overlapping that immediately below, from the gunwale to the keel: in the peat-moss containing these remains many other testimonies to wealth and industrial civilization, especially to boat-building, were found.

It is alike interesting and instructive to trace the progress of these northern tribes, and the mechanical means at their disposal which enabled them to construct vessels which could in safety navigate distant

[1] We have also a record of the discovery in England of two very ancient oak boats of considerable size. The first was found in 1822, in a deserted bed of the River Rother, near Matham, in Kent, and has been fully described in the Archæol. vol. xx. p. 553. This boat, which was sixty-three feet long by fifteen feet broad, appears to have been half-decked, and to have had at least one mast. It had been caulked with moss. The second was found in 1833, at North Stoke, near Arundel, in what was formerly a creek running into the River Arun. This boat, which was made of the half of a single oak-tree, hollowed out like a canoe, was thirty-five feet four inches long, and four feet six inches broad. It is now preserved in the British Museum, having been presented to that institution by the Earl of Egremont.—*Vide* Archæol. vol. xxvi.

seas, for there can be no doubt that these wild adventurers, barbarous as they undoubtedly were, became, in the hands of Providence, useful instruments for saving from extinction a large portion of the human race, who, under the Roman rule in the later days of its folly, had become unable to maintain their position either as independent nations, or as provinces of the imperial city. Surely it was good for mankind that the Goths and Vandals became masters of Rome, when Rome in her last decay could no longer govern herself.

Incursions of the Saxons and Angles into Britain;

Nor was the change of people to the disadvantage of Britain. Though not to the same extent, the Romanized Britons had imbibed the vices of their rulers, and were too effeminate to defend the lands the Romans had, in their extremity, abandoned. The coming of a new race, the Saxons and Angles of Schleswig, was needed to revive the energies of a population who had not been able to drive back the far more barbarous Picts, though, for a long time, under the Anglo-Saxon rule, also, commercial enterprise in Britain remained at a low ebb. For a while, indeed, even the faint light of learning, which remained when the Romans left, appears to have been almost extinguished by the long-continued and bloody wars which, during this gloomy period, depopulated the country and desolated the cities of Britain.

and its state soon afterwards.

Almost everything that is known of the state of Britain, and of its commerce and manufactures, from the time of its evacuation by Rome till the commencement of the eighth century, is derived from the ancient biographies of the Saints, then the chief, if not the sole, histories of the Western world; and faint indeed is the glimmering of light which these writers throw upon the state of navigation during those periods.[1] From these writers we get the story of the first Saxon expedition, together with the traditional tales of Hengist and Horsa, and of the fifteen hundred men, and the three long vessels or "ships" they came in. No reliance can, however, be placed, as Mr. Kemble has shown, on this statement; nor is it likely that the vessels of the northern pirates were superior to those Saxon craft already noticed, in which, on their second expedition, the Saxons are said to have landed seventeen thousand men on the shores of Britain.

Indeed, the accounts of the internal state of Britain and Ireland during that portion of the dark ages to which we now refer, so far as regards its trade and manufactures, are of the most meagre description; and the little we do find is rather in the form of incidental notices in books devoted to other objects than commerce or science. For instance, it is merely to an incidental remark of the venerable Bede[2] that we are indebted for the earliest notes of London after the abdication of the Romans. Speaking of the East-Saxons, at the commencement of the seventh century he says that "their metropolis is the city of London, which is situated on the bank of the aforesaid river (Thames), and is the mart of many nations resorting to it by sea and land;" adding

London.

[1] St. Patrick flourished from A.D. 432, the year of his mission to England, to 493; St. Brigit, about 500; and St. Columba, from 522–97. The venerable and more trustworthy Bede, who mentions Horsa by name (Eccles. Hist. i. c. 15), lived at a much later period, A.D. 750.

[2] Bede, ii. 3.

that "King Ethelbert built the church of St. Paul, in the city of London, where he and his successors should have their episcopal see."

That the Britons then possessed no naval force fitted to compete with the Saxons is clear, from the fact that their contests with them were invariably carried on by land, and that no effectual resistance by sea was offered to the vast numbers of Saxons and Angles who poured into the island. It is, indeed, not improbable that the Romans, when they assumed the government of Britain, discouraged the inhabitants from the creation of a fleet, which might endanger their possession of the island, a fact which would naturally account for the inferiority of the Britons when matched against invaders, who, from the nature of their previous lives, were more at home on the sea than on land.

Accession of Offa, A.D. 755.

One only of the kings of the Heptarchy, Offa of Mercia,[1] exerted himself to resuscitate the declining trade and commerce of Britain. Offa, having in view the raising of a naval force to defend his dominions, encouraged his subjects to fit out ships, and to carry goods in their own bottoms instead of trusting for transport to so large an extent as they had hitherto done, to the vessels of foreign nations. But his praiseworthy efforts were only transient in their character. Some of the English traders who resorted to the continent (including Rome and Venice), in order to evade payment of the customs exacted from them in their transit through France, pretended to be pilgrims on their journey to the

[1] The kingdom of Mercia comprised the midland and western counties.

imperial city, whose baggage was exempted from duties. This attempt to evade the duties was discovered, and reported to Charlemagne by his collectors of customs; the payment of the duties was enforced, and the goods of the English merchants, consisting chiefly of works in gold and silver, for which English workmen were then famous, and which were in great demand in Italy,[1] were seized and confiscated until the pleasure of the emperor was known. The merchants appealed to Offa for redress, who, by way of retaliation, laid an embargo upon the French shipping frequenting his ports. Thus differences arose between Charlemagne and Offa which continued for some years, and thus the improvement in commerce which, since the time of the Roman dominion in Britain, had been well-nigh extinguished, was nipped almost in its bud. These differences, combined with the incessant wars then waged between the Anglo-Saxons and their remote ancestors, the Danes and Norwegians or Northmen, for the supremacy of the Northern Ocean, prevented for the time all hope of any permanent improvement in the maritime commerce of Britain.

Restrictions on trade and commerce.

Nor, indeed, did the laws of the Saxon kings afford much encouragement to the development of trade. Those of Kent, which were considered as patterns for the other kingdoms, enacted that if any Kentish Saxon should buy anything in London, and bring it into Kent, he should have two or three honest men, or the Portreeve (the chief magistrate of the city), present at the bargain.[2] By the same laws, no man

[1] Muratori, Antiq. v. 12.

[2] Laws of Hlothar and Eadric, ap. Schmid's Anglo-Sax. Laws, c. 1–5, p. 11. Leipsig, 1858.

was allowed to buy anything above the value of twenty pence, except in a town, and in the presence of a magistrate or some other trustworthy and responsible witness. Similar, and even greater restraints were imposed on bartering one commodity for another. In fact, during a considerable period of time, no bargain could be contracted without the personal presence of some principal person or chief magistrate as a witness; a restrictive system, which may have been necessary when few, if any, of the traders could write, and disputes were frequent and inevitable, but which, like some laws of much more recent times, seriously retarded the progress of commerce. It is curious to note that the origin of every protective or restrictive law, even from the infancy of commerce, has proposed for its object the securing individual profits or the supposed safety of the revenue. At this period of English history the king claimed a portion of the price of all goods imported or sold within his dominions above the value of twenty pence; a practice which we learn, from an entry in Domesday, prevailed till after the Norman invasion. It is there stated that a certain per centage of everything bought or sold in the borough of Lewes was to be paid to the Portreeve (royal tax collector), and especially the sum of fourpence for every man sold as a slave within its boundaries.[1]

Salutary regulations.

The limited trade of the Saxons was, however, regulated by some salutary provisions, such as that preventing the execution of bargains and sales on Sundays, on which day the people were, without exception, expected to assemble for the performance

[1] Scriptores Brit. Gale, p. 762.

of their religious duties. The contests, on these grounds, between the clergy and people were as violent then as now, but with this difference, that modern legislation strikes at the humble retailer, whereas in those days the great merchant was equally compelled to obey the law. Not that we are to suppose that no trade was done clandestinely under the guise of these Religious Assemblies—the origin, no doubt, at least partially, of the Statute Fairs of later ages—but this is certain, that bargains, though planned and discussed, could not be completed till the next "lawful" day.

But though the maritime commerce of England made little progress till the reign of Alfred the Great, there can be no doubt that it derived various advantages from the impulse given to that of the neighbouring country of France by the exertions of Charlemagne, as that wise and able monarch is justly deemed to have laid the foundations of French trade with distant countries. Nowhere do we find a more striking instance of his *tact* than is displayed in his letter to Offa, with the object of renewing the commercial relations between France and England:[1]

Charlemagne's first treaty of commerce with England, A.D. 796.

"Charles by the grace of God, king of the Franks and Lombards, and patrician of the Romans, to our venerable and most dear brother Offa, king of the Mercians, greeting. First, we give thanks to Almighty God for the sincere Catholic faith, which we see so laudably expressed in your letters. Concerning the strangers, who, for the love of God and the salvation of their souls, wish to repair to the thresholds of the Blessed Apostles, let them travel in

[1] William of Malmesbury, s. 17, and M. Paris Vit. Offæ.

peace without any trouble. Nevertheless, if any are found among them not in the service of religion but in pursuit of gain, let them pay the established duties at the proper places. We also will, that merchants shall have lawful protection in our kingdom according to our command; and if they are in any place unjustly aggrieved, let them apply to us or our judges, and we shall take care that ample justice be done to them."

Extension of French commerce, A.D. 813.

It is, further, no small evidence of the effect produced by the energetic rule of Charlemagne that, only a few years later, the merchants of Lyons, Marseilles, and Avignon, confiding in his power and fame, and in the friendship between him and Harún-al-Rashíd, whose ships were then supreme in the Mediterranean, made a joint plan for sending vessels twice a year to Alexandria, whither no Christian vessels had adventured since it came into the possession of the Muhammedans. The spices of India and the perfumes of Arabia were then for the first time brought direct to their own port of Marseilles by the merchants of France, and one of the most ancient trades was thus re-opened.[1] From Marseilles these goods were conveyed by one of the inland continental routes we have already described, up the Rhône and the Saône, then re-embarked on the Moselle for the Rhine, and, by means of this latter river, distributed through Germany and the northern countries.

Nor can we doubt that England would have followed where France had so cleverly led the way,

[1] Macpherson, i. p. 251; and compare Monach. Sangall, i. c. 13, ap. Muratori, Antiq. v. 1.

but for the ruin caused by the ceaseless incursions of the Danes, who, having effected their first landing on the island of Thanet,[1] soon made good other settlements in the northern and eastern portions of Britain whence they were never wholly expelled till the Norman conquest. As a maritime people the Danes equalled, if they did not surpass, all the nations or tribes of the north of Europe, and possessed, even at this early period of their history, vessels superior and more varied than any of their northern competitors, and rivalling all others for many centuries afterwards. These vessels were chiefly distinguished by the name of Drakers and Holkers; the former of which has been supposed to have derived its name from the figure of a dragon on its bows. These and other vessels are said to have carried the ancient Danish flag of the raven at the top of their masts.

Commerce of England harassed by the Danes.

Their ships,

The *Holker* was originally a small boat, hollowed out of the trunk of a tree, but in process of time the word "hulk" was used evidently for vessels of larger dimensions, adapted for the conveyance of troops, and even for landing them with facility on a beach; hence it is probable that it bore much resemblance to the ordinary barge. But this name was first applied to light vessels used for exploring purposes, or for "scouts," and other swift craft engaged in carrying despatches. The Danes and most of the other Scandinavian nations had also another kind of vessel they called Snekkar (serpent), apparently shorter in proportion to her breadth, and therefore not unlike

[1] This first Danish invasion is said to have taken place A.D. 753. Macpherson, i. p. 247; and Chronic. Augustin, ap. Twysden.

the ordinary Dutch merchant galliot of the sixteenth and seventeenth centuries.[1]

Nature furnished abundance of materials to the mariners of the north for the building of their vessels; indeed, to this day, the primeval forests of Norway and Sweden supply vast quantities of timber, for ship-building and other purposes, to the European markets. The outfit of these vessels seems to have been singularly inexpensive—even provisions were supplied to them but scantily—their commanders being constantly in the habit of landing in the course of their passage to replenish their limited stock of meat, wine, and beer. Indeed this practice became a constant tax upon the people of the countries they visited, and whom they but too frequently pillaged of their whole stock of provisions. Nor was this all: it was customary in Sweden and Norway to compel the people of the maritime districts to hold in readiness a stated number of ships for the use of the king and, nominally, for purposes of defence: these vessels were, however, not unfrequently used for warlike and predatory expeditions, a custom which doubtless led to many of the unwarrantable attacks, whereby England and other parts of Europe were in succession, and for many ages, laid waste. From this marauding and unconquerable race, the daring and hardy sailors of England had their descent; and the adventures of this progeny of the Scandinavians, in more recent times, show that they have retained for many ages the adventurous, and too often lawless, spirit of their ancestors.

and the habits of their owners.

[1] Sir H. Nicolas (" Hist. Roy. Navy," i. p. 10) states that the Snekkar, or Serpent, was manned by twenty rowers. See also Depping, " Hist. des Exped. Maritimes des Normands." i. 71–73.

The piratical expeditions of the Northmen were more easily suppressed in France than in England, where, among the numerous islands contiguous to her coasts, their vessels could take refuge. Thus Wales suffered severely from their marauding attacks; the island of Anglesey was more than once pillaged by them; while, in Ireland, they long held the ports of Dublin, Waterford, Limerick, and Cork. A Danish king resided in Dublin and in Waterford; and the invaders preserved their warlike spirit and predatory habits long after the remaining portions of the kingdom had acquired peaceful habits.[1] The Scandinavian language survived the independence of the Northern pirates; and, centuries after these had ceased to dominate the seas, a Norse dialect was still spoken. Even to this day remnants of this original language remain in the Orkneys and Shetland Islands, and is often used among the seafaring population, especially for the ordinary nautical expressions employed on board of their ships.

Increase of the northern marauders.

Language of the Northmen still spoken by mariners in the North.

When Alfred ascended the throne, he found England overrun by the Danes, so that for a short time he was obliged to dissemble and to conceal himself, with the few faithful subjects who had not deserted him. In his retreat, however, he was the better able to arrange future plans, as he at once perceived that without an effective maritime force his island must be ever at the mercy of every piratical

Accession of Alfred the Great, A.D. 871:

[1] Macpherson, in his "Annals of Commerce," vol. i. p. 254, says that "the Norwegians and Danes, under the names of Ostmen (*i.e.* eastern men), Gauls, Gentiles, Pagans, &c., were the chief, or rather the only commercial, people in Ireland, and continued for several centuries to carry on trade with the mother countries, and other places on the west coast of Europe, from their Irish settlements."

adventurer. He accordingly determined to meet the enemies of England on the sea, and having studied the best models of the Danes, and added many improvements of his own, his efforts were in the end completely successful. His galleys are said to have been twice as long as those of the enemy, and to have carried sixty oars. They were also loftier and better built, and proved of much greater speed.[1]

his efforts to improve naviga- tion,

and to extend the know- ledge of geography.

Alfred, who, by the attention he devoted to maritime pursuits, has justly earned the title of the "Father of the British Navy," was also the first native of Britain who made an attempt to extend the science of geography. Having obtained information from Ohthere, a Norwegian,[2] and from other sources, of the Baltic Sea and adjacent countries stretching to the extreme northern regions of Europe, he corrected many of the prevailing errors of geographers. Ohthere, who had coasted along the country of the Fins, now known as Lapland, and had passed the North Cape and penetrated into the bay where Archangel now stands, speaks of the vast abundance of whales and seals along that northern coast, and gives a description of the mode of life of the natives, which is not unlike that of the ancient Scythians. They brewed no ale; mead was the ordinary drink of the poorer classes; while the rich drank a species of liquor prepared from the milk of goats.

But though Alfred was successful in raising, after four years' labour, six small vessels, with which he put to sea and overcame seven of the Danish ships,

[1] See Saxon Chronicle A.D. 897, Florence of Worcester; Simeon of Durham, the Chronicle of Melros; and Pauli, "Life of Alfred," p. 212.

[2] Pauli, "Life," &c., p. 178.

capturing one and driving back the rest, intestine troubles compelled him for a considerable time to neglect maritime affairs: after some years, however, having induced those of the Danes whom he had brought under subjection to embrace Christianity, he assigned them lands in the kingdom of the East Angles, and made it their interest to defend that portion of Britain with which, from their own repeated descents upon it, they were most familiar. These newly settled people possessed many vessels, were skilled in ship-building, and excellent mariners, and thus aided him effectually in fitting out a powerful fleet with which he encountered, with varied success, the Danish ships who still claimed the dominion of the northern seas. Many of his subjects were likewise persuaded to acquire the art of navigation, to study for themselves the best mode of conducting naval warfare, and to devote their attention to commercial and maritime pursuits, which, while they increased the number of merchant vessels, laid at the same time the surest foundation for the creation and maintenance of a royal navy.

Foundation of a royal and commercial navy.

The exertions of his people were so energetically supported by their king, that at length a fleet was raised sufficiently powerful to guard the sea coast, and protect the foreign trade of the country. Nor were the defences of the sea-port towns, and especially those of London, where the chief commercial wealth of the country had been collected and stored, forgotten.[1] In addition to these judicious measures, he introduced new manufactures, and

[1] If Asser is correct in his statements, London had been almost destroyed by the Danes just before the accession of Alfred.—Asser, "Vit. Alfred," p. 51.

discovered new articles of growth which, if exported, would prove a considerable source of profit to those merchants who undertook their shipment to other countries. It was by such means, by liberal and wise laws, and by well conceived arrangements for the best development of the natural resources of England, that he greatly increased the wealth of his people, and laid the foundation of that powerful royal and commercial navy, which, through many vicissitudes, has continued, though often neglected, to be the pride and boast of the English people.

His voyages of discovery and missions to the East.

Nor, indeed, was this all. Alfred, also, sent out ships on voyages of discovery to the south as well as to the north; and, having opened communications with the patriarch of Jerusalem, obtained from him much information on various important subjects, which ultimately proved of great value to his people: moreover, if William of Malmesbury can be relied on, he sent Sighelm, bishop of Sherbourne, with many gifts to the Nestorian Christians of St. Thomas, at Maliapur, on the Coromandel coast, and received from them in return various products of Indian growth and manufacture.[1]

[1] William of Malmesbury, Gest. Reg. Angl. 24, a. Some of the jewels of curious manufacture which Bishop Sighelm brought home were to be seen among the treasures of the church at Sherbourne; and Asser says that King Alfred one morning gave him a silk robe, and as much frankincense (incense) as a man could carry; from which it may be inferred that, after the visit of Sighelm, a trade was opened out between England and India, or with other countries of the East, where frankincense was produced or stored. For the Christians in Malabar, see a curious story in the "Legenda Aurea;' in Buchanan's "Christian Researches;" in the Journal of Bishop Heber; and in Thomas's "Prinsep's Indian Essays," vol. ii. p. 214. Sighelm, who had previously been sent to Rome by King Alfred, is thought by Pauli to have been a layman, as his name is not found in the episcopal registers of Sherbourne.—Life of Alfred, p. 146.

To Alfred the Great, England also owes the first attempt to secure a more speedy and equal distribution of justice by the division of the kingdom into hundreds and tithings, combined with a careful survey of the whole country, known as the "Book of Winchester," the model probably of the later and still more famous Domesday Book. The laws of the Anglo-Saxons were also revised, and a code was formed with selections from the best of those of other nations. The wisdom and the justice of Alfred first raised England out of the darkness of one of the darkest ages, and secured for her a position at sea she had never previously held; and, though a thousand years have since passed away, we cannot but think that those statesmen who are now devoting their attention to the commercial and maritime interests of their country would do well to study the policy of Alfred at a period of bigotry, superstition, and ignorance, when piracy at sea, and plunder on land, afforded a large source of remunerative employment to the people.

Reign of Edward the Elder, A.D. 901–925, and of his son Athelstan, A.D. 925–941.

His son Edward followed his example in the care he bestowed on his fleet; and, though much of his time was occupied in constructing castles to keep back the ever encroaching Danes, he was able to equip and to maintain during his reign one hundred ships to protect trade and guard the coasts. But his son, Athelstan, displayed even greater anxiety to increase the power of his fleet, being at the same time the first English monarch who, by his laws, made trade a road to honour. One of these laws enacted, that if any merchant or mariner successfully accomplished three voyages on the high seas with a ship and cargo of his own, he should thenceforth be advanced to the dignity of a Thane and entitled to all the privileges attaching to his rank; and he, at the same time, established mints in such towns as enjoyed any considerable amount of foreign trade, with the necessary provisions to ensure the purity and just weight of the coins issued.[1] These salutary laws and other prudent regulations had the effect of considerably improving trade during his reign.

William of Malmesbury has preserved the record of a gift by Harold, king of Norway, to Athelstan, about the year 931, of a ship adorned with a golden prow, having a purple sail, and armed with a complete bulwark of shields. A similar arrangement of shields may be seen on many of the ships delineated on the Bayeux tapestry.[2]

Edgar's fleet, and his arrangements for suppressing piracy.

From the death of Athelstan to the accession of Edgar, there are no incidents in connection with shipping or commerce worthy of record. Edgar, however, greatly increased the royal navy; nay, the monkish writers of the period assert that he had three or four thousand vessels, an exaggeration not requiring refutation.[3] Edgar, besides living in considerable splendour, spent large sums of money on

[1] Thorpe, "Ancient Laws of England," p. 31; and Macpherson, vol. i. pp 266–268. There is another order of Ethelred, "that the ships of war should be ready every year at Easter."—Ancient Laws, p. 137.

[2] William of Malmesbury, i. p. 215.

[3] The Saxon Chronicle gives to his predecessor, Edward the Elder, a fleet of some hundreds of ships, but this number is evidently too indefinite for any historical purpose. (Sax. Chron. A.D. 911.) If the charter granted to Worcester by this king in A.D. 964 be genuine, which Kemble doubts (Cod. Diplom. Ævi Saxon. ii. 404), he would seem to have been the first English monarch who claimed the "sovereignty of the sea."

monastic foundations; hence the only historians of his day took care to sound his praises with their highest notes. The more effectually to repress the ravages of the Danes, he is said to have divided his fleet into three divisions, and to have sent each squadron to separate stations, thus, for the first time, stationing his ships in a systematic manner along the English coasts, so as to guard against surprise, and protect the merchantmen trading with his seaports. Nor was he satisfied with the mere organization of his plans. Every summer he himself visited the fleets, making excursions from station to station, and by his vigilance kept the sea from being disturbed by marauders, thereby greatly contributing to the strength of his kingdom.

The wisdom of his policy.

But though he has been credited with numerous victories, nay even with the complete subjugation of Ireland, it is clear that his policy was really one of peace and progress, and that he was anxious to maintain peace as the best safeguard for progress by the maintenance of a force sufficient for that purpose, rather than by increasing it to such dimensions as might have overawed his neighbours and rendered it an aggressive one. To be prepared for war is undoubtedly a guarantee for peace; but a naval force exceeding what is necessary for the protection of its shores and commerce is dangerous to the nation which has created it, as other nations then naturally increase their forces, and a rivalry in arms arises, with war for its probable result. Edgar evidently knew where to draw the line, and having secured the safety of his dominions from foreign aggression, he devoted his attention to the improvement of his internal affairs.

Thus, to facilitate commerce, all money coined in the kingdom was decreed to be of one kind in its relative value,[1] so far as regards receipts and payments; and the Winchester measures were fixed as the standard of all measures throughout the country. Many restrictions were enforced as to the method of transacting business; and no one was permitted to buy or sell except in the presence of two or more witnesses. Every member of a tithing was required, if he went to a distant market, to inform the borstholder, not merely what he intended to purchase or dispose of, but on his return to declare into what transactions he had entered. Restrictions, however, which would be ruinous to modern commerce may have been necessary in its infancy.

Ethelred II., A.D. 979–1016. Sufferings of the people.

The annals of the long and disastrous reign of Ethelred II. afford but one continued picture of rapine and plunder. "The Danish and Norwegian robbers," remarks Macpherson, in his Annals of Commerce,[2] "now united, and led by Swein, king of Denmark, and Olaf Trygvason, who afterwards became king of Norway, spread the horrors of slaughter, captivity, and desolation over all the country. After wasting the lands, and utterly extinguishing cultivation and industry, they compelled the miserable people to bring in provisions for their subsistence; and they moreover extorted in the name of tribute, as the price of peace, but in reality the premium for invasion, the enormous sums of ten thousand pounds of silver in the year 991, sixteen thousand pounds in

[1] Bp. Wilkins, "Leg. Saxon." p. 78. Nearly eighty mints of Edgar's money are known. Hawkins's "Silver Coins of England," p. 57.

[2] Vol. i. p. 275. A list of all these Danish invasions may be consulted in Sir H. Nicolas's "Hist. Royal Navy," vol. i. pp. 10–28.

1007, and forty-eight thousand pounds in 1012. After which the greatest part of the country sunk under the power of the Danes."[1] Nor was this all. London itself was burnt; extraordinary inundations prevailed in different parts of the country, followed by contagious disorders destructive of both man and beast.

Yet amid all the desolations of this unhappy reign, some attention was paid to maritime and internal commerce, and a law was passed commanding every proprietor of 310 hides[2] of land to furnish a ship for the protection of the State; the result being a larger naval force than had ever been collected before.[3] Fresh regulations were also made with reference to the coasting trade. Boats arriving at Billingsgate were required to pay a toll of a halfpenny, a penny, or four pennies, according to their size and build. Each vessel with wood left one piece as toll or tribute; boats with fish coming to London bridge (first mentioned, according to Spelman, in the reign of Ethelred)[4] paid either one halfpenny, or one penny, according to their size. Foreign merchants from Rouen, Flanders, and Liege, frequenting the Port of

Charges upon vessels trading to London.

[1] This was the well-known tax called "Dane geld," imposed, apparently for the first time, about A.D. 991; see also Saxon Chron., A.D. 994, 1002, 1007. Stow, p. 114, ed. 1600.

[2] Mr. Kemble, in an elaborate chapter on the "Hide," has determined that it was probably a little less than 100 statute acres of arable land. ("Anglo-Saxons," vol. i. c. 4, p. 88–121.) It is clear, however, that the word was often used for a much smaller, though indefinite extent of land. In Bosworth's Anglo-Saxon Dictionary (*in voc.* Hyde) many examples are quoted, showing that it was popularly held to be as much land as "could be tilled in a year by one plough."

[3] Saxon Chron., A.D. 1009.

[4] London Bridge is noticed in the Saxon Chronicle under A.D. 1016. The first stone bridge is said to have been commenced, A.D. 1176, and finished, A.D. 1209.—Stow's Survey, pp. 50, 52, 682.

London with their ships and manufactures, were in some respects privileged, but were still required to pay the duties, and forbidden to "forestall the market to the prejudice of the citizens." At Easter and Christmas the German merchants,[1] resident in the city, were further required to pay for the privilege of trading two pieces of grey cloth and one piece of brown cloth, ten pounds of pepper, five pairs of gloves, and two casks of wine. The larger description of vessels engaged at this period in the foreign trade, appear to have discharged their cargoes on the Middlesex shore at wharves or jetties, between the Tower and London bridge, while the smaller craft lay above bridge, chiefly in the Fleet river near the port of Ludgate, where many of the merchants then resided. Within the limits of the Fleet to the west, and of Billingsgate to the east, were to be found the warehouses and dwellings of all the traders, and the chief portion of London was then, and, indeed, for two or three centuries after the Conquest, embraced within those limits.

Olaf, king of Norway, his ships,

Olaf, who had given so much trouble to Ethelred, having by his piratical excursions gained considerable knowledge of the wants of various countries, endeavoured on his accession to the crown of Norway to encourage commerce in his own country. With this object he founded Nidaros, now known as Drontheim, and made it an emporium for trade. He also built various ships of war, larger than had ever been seen in the Northern seas. One of these,

[1] Then called "Emperor's men," the forerunners, probably, of the "Merchants of the Steel-yard." See also Brompton, p. 897, quoted by Macpherson, p. 277, and "Ancient Laws," p. 127; Prynne, "Annales," p. 105.

the Dreki, or "Dragon," is described as having a hull one hundred and eleven feet in length, with thirty-four benches or thwarts for rowers. Her head and stern were finely adorned with carved work, elaborately gilt, and from the description of her which has been preserved, she must have resembled in many respects the state galleys of the Italian republics during the fourteenth and fifteenth centuries, thus showing very considerable advancement in the science of ship-building among the nations of the north.[1]

Some record has also been preserved of the ships with which Swein, the father of Canute, made a descent in A.D. 1004 on the coasts of Norfolk. Each vessel had a high deck, and their prows were ornamented with figures of lions, bulls, dolphins, or men, made of copper gilt; at their mast-heads were vanes in the shape of birds with expanded wings to show the quarter whence the wind blew. Swein's own ship, also called "the Great Dragon," is said to have been built in the form of the animal whose name it bore; its head forming the prow, and its tail the stern. It bore also a standard of white silk, having in the centre a raven with extended wings and open beak, which had been embroidered by three of that monarch's sisters.[2]

and those of Swein.

Nor need we suppose that there was much exaggeration in the chronicles describing these and other ships of that time. It was evidently a period when gorgeous displays were not uncommon. Only a few years later, Earl Godwin, to appease the wrath of

[1] Snorro, "Hist. Olaf. Trygv." cc. 124–8.

[2] "Heimskringla," vol ii. p. 125. Cf. Reginæ Emmæ Encomium, ap. Script. Rer. Normann. pp. 166, 170.

Love of display.

Hardicanute, presented him with a ship, the prow of which was richly decorated with gold;[1] and Macpherson has recorded how the step-father of Olaf, though usually a plain man and good farmer, would, on state occasions, dress himself in "breeches or trousers of Cordovan leather, and clothes made of silk, with a scarlet cloak over them. His sword," remarks the same writer,[2] "was richly adorned with carving in gold, and his helmet and spurs were gilded. His horse had a saddle embellished with golden ornaments, and a bridle shining with gold and gems."[3]

It is probable that such decorations were not unfrequently the prizes of piracy rather than of fair trade: for, though some of the people of the southern portions of Norway are said to have been considerable traders to England, Ireland, Saxony, Flanders, and Denmark, yet their attachment to trade in no way interfered with occasional amusements of a very different kind, or with quartering themselves during the winters on the countries of the Christians. Nor were they particular in their objects of plunder. In the periodical fairs of Germany, which were established about this period, a large portion of the merchandise brought to them for sale consisted of slaves of both sexes; ordinary slaves of either sex realizing about a mark, or eight ounces of silver,

[1] "Florence of Worcester," p. 623, who calls the vessel a "trierem."

[2] "Annals of Commerce," vol. i. p. 279.

[3] It may not be generally known that a considerable number of the charters and deeds preserved in the collections of the British Museum, and of the libraries of the Bodleian and of Magdalen College at Oxford, bear seals impressed with ancient Roman, and occasionally with Greek, gems, all, or nearly all, of which are now lost.

while three times that sum was frequently given, at these northern fairs, for female slaves who were "fair in form and beautiful in countenance." Helmold relates that he saw seven thousand Danish slaves at one time exposed for sale in the market at Mecklenburg.[1]

Long before the compass was known, the seamen of Norway, like the ancient mariners of the Island of Ceylon, regulated their track through the ocean by the flight of birds set free from on board their vessels; a proof that, in regions of the world far removed from each other, the same primitive practices prevailed. It is related of Flok,[2] a famous Norwegian navigator, that when about to set out from Shetland[3] to Iceland, he took with him some crows on board of his ship. Under the impression that he had made considerable progress in his voyage, he liberated one of these birds, which, seeing land astern, flew for it; whereby Flok, considering that he was nearer Shetland or Faroe "than any other land, kept on his course for some time, and then sent out another crow, which, seeing no land at all," returned to the vessel. At last, as he conceived, having accomplished the greatest part of his voyage, a third crow was set at liberty, which seeing land ahead immediately flew for it, and Flok, following his guide, fell in with the east end of the island of Iceland.

Mode of navigating.

Happily, the accession of Canute to the throne of

[1] Thorkelin's "Essay on the Slave Trade," pp. 4–9.

[2] Arngrim Jonas. For the story of the Singhalese sailors, see Plin. H. N. vi. 83.

[3] The Shetland as well as the Orkney Islands were then in the possession of the Norwegians, and Sutherland, the most northern portion of Great Britain, obtained this title as the land to the south of the Orkneys.

Canute, A.D. 1016. Reduction of the English fleet.

England had put a stop to the cruel wars so long waged between the Danes and English, and commerce once more began to flourish; the influence and dread of this prince being so great, that he found it unnecessary to maintain more than forty[1] ships at sea to protect his coasts and his maritime commerce, a number which was afterwards reduced to sixteen.[2] Indeed, so far from entertaining any apprehensions of an inclination to revolt among the English, he frequently made voyages to the Continent, once proceeding even as far as Rome, where he met the Emperor Conrad II. and other princes, from whom he obtained, for all his subjects, whether merchants or pilgrims, a complete exemption from the heavy tolls usually exacted on their visits to that city.[3] Canute, indeed, by his conquest of Norway, represented in his own person both the English whom he had subjugated, and the Danes, who had been their constant and persevering rivals, thus uniting under one sovereignty all the maritime nations of the north.

A.D. 1031.

Prosperity of commerce.

Under such favourable circumstances as these, the trade and shipping of England could hardly fail to prosper, although there are no records left whereby we can measure their extent or character. But as Canute materially increased the number of mints[4] throughout the kingdom, and as the merchants of

[1] Saxon Chron. A.D. 1018.

[2] This fact is mentioned, incidentally, in the Saxon Chronicle under the reign of Hardicanute, A.D. 1039.

[3] William of Malmesbury gives a letter from Canute to the English nobility stating his success in this matter, ii. c. 11.

[4] See Ruding, "Annals of the Coinage of England," and Hawkins, "Silver Coins of England." No other English king had so many mints, at least 350 of the names of his moneyers having been preserved.

London had become sufficiently powerful to be the chief instruments in placing his son Harold upon the throne at his death,[1] it may be inferred that the mercantile community, while requiring a greater amount of currency for the conduct of their business, had likewise become an important element in the State. It is further recorded, that the merchants of London, with the *seamen* of that city, many of whom had probably become Thanes, mingled with the nobility and performed a leading and conspicuous part at the coronation of Harold at Oxford, who soon afterwards increased the wages of the sailors of his fleet, giving to each of them eight mancusses[2] (2*l.* 16*s.* 8*d.*) annually; but when Hardicanute increased his navy to seventy-two ships,[3] a further advance was required to be made in the wages of the seamen, who were discontented with the remuneration they received.

During the short period of the restoration of the Saxon monarchy the Danes resumed their marauding expeditions; but, after ravaging the coasts of Wales and Sussex, they were repulsed with great slaughter by the English under Harold II., who was however less successful in resisting the Norman invasion under William the Conqueror, whose accession constitutes a new era in the commercial and maritime, as well as in the political and general, history of Britain.

Norman invasion, A.D. 1066.

[1] Saxon Chron., A.D. 1036.

[2] Saxon Chron., A.D. 1039–40. A mancus was worth about seven shillings and a penny, sterling. Spelman (p. 387) has pointed out that accounts differ as to whether we are to read here mancusses or marks, and that these two denominations of money were sometimes interchanged.

[3] Saxon Chron., A.D. 1039.

The stories as to the number of vessels under the orders of the Conqueror on this memorable expedition are very conflicting. Some writers have asserted that the total number amounted to no less than three thousand, of which six or seven hundred were of a superior order, the remainder consisting chiefly of boats temporarily built, and of the most fragile description. Others place the whole fleet at not more than eight hundred vessels of every sort, and this number is likely to be the nearest to the truth. There are now no means of ascertaining their size; but their form may be conjectured from the representations of these vessels on the famous roll of tapestry still preserved at Bayeux, from which the following has been copied.[1]

Number of vessels engaged,

and their form.

It is related that when William meditated his descent upon England, he ordered for that purpose

[1] It will be observed that in this, as in other boats, in the tapestry, the steersman holds the sheet in his left hand. The man at the mast-head may indicate the sailor whom Wace (who heard the story from his father) says William sent aloft to look out.—Will. Poict., p. 199.

"large ships" to be constructed at his seaports, collecting, wherever they could be found, smaller vessels or boats to accompany them. But even the largest must have been of little value, as the whole fleet were by his orders burned and destroyed as soon as he landed with his army, so as to cut off all retreat and to save the expense of their maintenance.[1]

Those of our readers who have visited the north of Scotland, during the herring-fishery season, will readily notice the resemblance to the traditional form of the war vessels of the Saxons in the eleventh century exhibited by the larger boats owned by the present Wick or Lerwick fishermen. But as we have more than once had occasion to observe, though we are greatly indebted to antiquaries for their researches, the few drawings of ancient vessels preserved are scarcely objects of instruction. Even the vessels on the Bayeux tapestry give us little that is definite, and we can hardly infer from them more than that we see in them an ideal but imperfect representation of the boats which were hastily constructed for William the Norman; while we may at the same time feel sure that the Saxon and Danish ships in ordinary use must have been stronger and

[1] Mr. Freeman, who has recently and most fully examined every record relating to the Norman invasion, states that he finds the largest number of ships recorded to have amounted to 3000, the smallest to 693. Most of the ships were gifts from the great barons or prelates. Thus, W. Fitz-Osborn gave 60; the Count de Mortain, 120; the Bishop of Bayeux, 100; while the finest of all, that in which William himself came over, was presented to him by his Duchess Matilda, and was called the "Mora." (E. A. Freeman, "Norman Conquest," vol. iii. c. 15, pp 376–1381. 1869.) Sir H. Nicolas has examined at considerable length the evidence of the Bayeux Tapestry, pp. 63–66.

better adapted to encounter stormy weather and rough seas than the vessels of a similar size and class in the Mediterranean. All details respecting them must, however, be conjectural; and a drawing of one class, even if accurate, may give as faint an impression of ships of another class, as the collier of to-day would afford of a modern Indiaman or Ocean-Steamer.

Nor, indeed, is it likely that the Conqueror's fleet included many ships of a superior class or size, as we know that the great bulk, if not the whole of them, were built or collected, and fitted between the first of January and the latter end of August. Norman writers of the period state that their merchant vessels or transports were in length about three times their breadth, sometimes propelled by oars, but generally by sails: their galleys appear to have been of two sorts, the larger, occasionally called galleons, carrying in some instances sixty men, well armed with iron armour, besides the rowers. The smaller galleys, which are not specially described, doubtless resembled ships' launches in size, but of a form enabling them to be propelled at considerable speed. Besides these, the Normans would appear to have also used, for purposes of war, small light boats covered with leather resembling those already described.[1]

It is almost as difficult to arrive at any sound conclusion with regard to the actual state of trade and

[1] Judging from the records of the chronicles of the period, it seems that William the Conqueror had not at any time a fleet capable of competing with those of the Northmen, who appear to have made descents on the coasts much as they had done in earlier years. Cf. Saxon Chronicle for the years 1069, 1070, 1083; and Selden, "Mare Clausum," c. xxv.

commerce in England at the time of the Conquest as it is with regard to the shipping. Agriculture, which had been in so flourishing a state under the Roman government, that large shipments of corn were frequently made to the Continent, had been much neglected during the long wars between the Britons, Saxons, and Danes; and there is no instance on record of any export of grain of any sort during the whole period of the Anglo-Saxon rule. On the other hand, in unfavourable seasons, the Britons did not grow enough for themselves, though the country must have been thinly peopled, and, consequently, but too frequently suffered severely from famine. In the account of the sales of church property and of other estates, many records of which are still extant,[1] we find that land even of the best quality seldom realized a higher price than five pounds[2] of silver for a hide of land, showing that while the people must have been widely scattered few persons were in opulent circumstances.

State of trade and commerce.

Wool was however produced to a considerable extent, the rich pastures of England having furnished from the earliest ages ample food for large flocks of sheep. By the eighth law of King Edgar, the highest price which could be taken for wool was somewhat less than three-fourths of a penny for a pound; and though there is no positive information on the subject, the Flemings, who were then and for some centuries afterwards the chief manufacturers of fine woollen goods for the whole of Europe, must have bought wool

Exports.

[1] See the histories of Ramsey and Ely, and others.

[2] No data exist from which we can calculate with any certainty the value of a pound of silver in the Conqueror's reign.

largely in the markets of England, and carried it away to be spun and woven in their own country. Lead was frequently used for the roofs of churches and other buildings; and from the records in Domesday Book it is clear that, during the reign of Edward the Confessor, there were iron works in the neighbourhood of Gloucester, of a date perhaps as early as the Roman colonization.[1] Although there is no account of the exportation of any metals in the age now under consideration, it is reasonable to suppose that the demand at home and abroad for lead, tin, and iron, could never have wholly ceased, and that they must have formed a considerable part of the few exports during the Anglo-Saxon period.[2]

Horses, it may be presumed, were sometimes exported, as King Athelstan made a law against carrying any out of the kingdom except as presents.[3] The natives of Britain, too, were not unfrequently exported to the Continent and even to Rome, the handsome figures of these female slaves naturally attracting much attention. The merchants of Bristol and of Northumberland appear to have been the chief dealers in this inhuman traffic, the former finding in Ireland the readiest and the largest market for their slaves.[4]

Concerning the ordinary description of manu-

[1] Pliny states that lead was found so abundantly on the surface in Britain, that a law was passed to limit the supply. H. N. xxxiv. 49; cf. also Wright's "Uriconium," pp. 6, 7, 8.

[2] Matthew Paris, Hist. p. 570. Camden, Britan. p. 134.

[3] Wilkins, "Leges Anglo-Saxon." p. 52.

[4] William of Malmesbury, i. c. 3. Wharton, "Angl. Sacr." ii. p. 258. According also to Bede, it appears that the sight of English slaves in the market-place at Rome first led Gregory to think of evangelizing the country.—Hist. Eccles. ii. c. 1.

factures, the meagre chronicles of the period furnish little information. We find, however, that Northumberland was then comparatively famous, as it has been ever since, for the manufacture of glass, while the English jewellers and workers in gold surpassed those of most other nations. Nor were the women of England less famous for their taste and skill in the embroidering of silk of various colours interspersed with threads of gold and silver. So famous, indeed, were they in this description of work, that when William the Conqueror sent to his patron, Pope Alexander II., the banner of Harold wrought for him by them, it was remarked that "it might be greatly admired even in Constantinople,"[1] then the wealthiest and most refined city of the world; and similar presents made by him to the church of Caen in Normandy are said to have been "such as strangers of the highest rank, who had seen the treasures of many noble churches, might look upon them with delight; and even the natives of Greece and Arabia, if they were to travel thither, would be equally charmed with them."[2]

Manufactures.

Wealth.

At this early period there must have been a considerable amount of accumulated wealth in England, to have enabled Canute to have expended the vast sums he is said to have done on his pilgrimage to Rome, or to have allowed Edward the Confessor to build the Abbey of St. Peter's at Westminster, and many other churches, at an enormous expense. Nor do the resources of his treasury appear to have been drained by all this expenditure; for the

[1] William of Poictiers, p. 216.

[2] Ibid. Muratori, Antiq. v. coll. 404, 405.

quantity of money the Conqueror took from Harold enabled him to be, in the words of his biographer, "incredibly liberal" to the Church of Rome:[1] moreover, that some of the nobles had great wealth, may be inferred from the present of Earl Godwin to Hardicanute already alluded to, together with the other rich gifts which he bestowed upon the Church.[2]

Imports. But the governing class and the great ecclesiastics must have had in those days the bulk of the wealth of the country in their hands; indeed, the limited extent of trade, and the character of the imports of the period, demonstrate plainly that such was the case. Silk, and similar expensive articles of dress, precious stones, perfumes, and other oriental luxuries, purchased in the ports of Italy or at Marseilles, are, with one or two extraordinary exceptions, the only items the historians of the period record as having been brought from foreign countries: these exceptions, strange to relate, consisted of portions of legs, arms, fingers, and toes, supposed to have belonged to canonized saints. It is almost impossible now to conceive that such articles constituted, at any period of English history, important items of her imports. There is, however, no doubt of the fact; and so high in estimation were such remains held, that Egelnoth, archbishop of Canterbury, is said[3] to have purchased at Paris, on his return from Rome, an arm of St. Augustine for one hundred talents of silver and one talent of gold;

[1] William of Poictiers, chaplain to William the Conqueror, speaks of his rich gifts to Rome, p. 206.

[2] William of Malmesb. p. 43.

[3] Ibid. p. 42.

while Elfsig, abbot of Peterborough, gave no less than five thousand pounds of silver for a headless body, which some knavish dealer had pronounced to be that of a distinguished saint.[1]

By the records of Domesday, nearly all the cities and boroughs of England appear to have been, in the reign of Edward the Confessor, the property of the king, or of some noble to whom the inhabitants looked for protection and paid a rent or borough-mail. London, Winchester, York, and Exeter alone enjoyed exemptions from taxes imposed on other cities of the kingdom. London was afterwards especially favoured by the Conqueror, who, recognizing the great importance of that city, endeavoured to conciliate the goodwill of the inhabitants by a charter, which not merely confirmed all the privileges they had previously possessed, but enjoined that "every child should be his father's heir after his death." To William the City owes the jurisdiction of the Thames,[2] the conservancy of which is even now to some extent in its hands, the Lord Mayor being still *ex-officio* chairman of the present board for that purpose. The inhabitants, or burgesses of London, also enjoyed the highly-prized privilege of hunting in the extensive chases of Chiltern, Middlesex, and Surrey, which, with the conservancy over the Thames, was confirmed by subsequent charters, and especially by that of Henry I.

Taxation.

London specially favoured.

It is clear that the taxes imposed on the seaport as

[1] Saxon Chron. The list of relics preserved (till quite recently) in the Escurial in Spain, would satisfy the wildest curiosity of any owner of a "rag and bone shop." Cf. also W. of Malmesb. De Pontif. 5. Bede, Hist. Abbat. Weremouth.

[2] Thom. Chron. ap. Twysden, ed. 1793.

well as inland towns, were not arranged by any systematic law. Thus, for no especial reason that can now be discerned, Chester was taxed far more heavily than any other city in the reigns of both William I. and his predecessor, Edward. Dover again paid 18*l.* annually, but the burgesses, who were required to provide twenty ships, carrying twenty-one men each, for fifteen days in the year, were exempted from all tolls throughout the country. Sandwich was placed on a similar footing, but only paid 15*l.* per annum. In Southwark, the king claimed a duty on all vessels entering the "dock," and levied a toll on those that used the strand for the delivering or loading of their cargoes. Colchester paid two marks of silver, and also, as a composition for the rent of six pennies on every house, 15*l.* 5*s.* 4*d.*, of which 4*l.* was paid by the coiners. Yarmouth, which had seventy burgesses, was taxed to the extent of 27*l.* by toll to the king and earl. In Ipswich there were eight hundred and eight burgesses paying custom to the king, but the amount is not stated.

Chester specially burdened.

No determinate principle can now be discerned why such dues were exacted, small towns being in many cases required to pay more than others of double their size. In some places the taxes were paid in produce or merchandise—as, for instance, at Gloucester, where, besides 36*l.* levied in toll, the inhabitants had to contribute twelve gallons of honey, and one hundred iron rods to the king's ships, together with a few other petty customs. Again, Leicester had also to provide honey, and twelve burgesses to supply the king's army, and four horses to carry arms and stores to London when any maritime expedition was about to sail from the Thames. In Shrewsbury the king levied a tax of ten shillings on the marriage of every maid, and twenty shillings on that of every widow, besides numerous taxes upon the people in the shape of services or customs; and in Hereford, the king had one hundred and three tenants, including six blacksmiths, who performed certain services in lieu of rents, while the burgesses had, among other burdens, to provide "a bear, and six dogs for the bear." At Sandwich, forty thousand herrings were demanded for the use of the monks of the neighbourhood.[1]

State of the people at the time of the Conquest.

In many places, the records of Domesday show that considerable portions of the inhabitants were too poor to pay any taxes. Thus, in Norwich, while six hundred and sixty-five are rated among the burgesses, there are no less than four hundred and eighty heads of families who had no means of contributing. Notices are also preserved of the number of houses at that time in a state of decay or disuse: thus, at Winchester, whole streets and many churches were in a state of ruin; in Thetford, there were one hundred and twenty houses empty; in Ipswich, more than three hundred and twenty-eight falling to decay. In Chester, once so flourishing and so heavily taxed, there were, soon after the Conquest, two hundred and five houses lying waste; while, in York, four hundred houses were so much decayed, as to pay only one penny each, or even less; five hundred and forty were waste, and paid

[1] For these and other references to Domesday, see Macpherson, i. pp. 293–7, and i. pp. 303–7.

nothing; and one hundred and forty-five were occupied by Frenchmen, who were relieved from the tax.

But while poverty and oppressive taxation ground down the masses of the people, the nobles abandoned themselves to the excesses of gluttony, drunkenness, and promiscuous concubinage, frequently not scrupling to consign the objects of their lust, and even their own offspring, to the miseries of slavery, for paltry sums of money to be squandered in wretched folly. Learning was almost at as low an ebb as it had been at the commencement of the reign of Alfred; while the middle classes, with some, though few, exceptions, were, in many respects, no better than the nobles, and trade and commerce languished and declined. Such was the state of things in England when the Norman conqueror landed on its shores.[1]

[1] The above particulars are derived from the records of Domesday, which were, however, never completed for several of the northern counties, possibly owing to the great northern up-rising against William the Conqueror. It is also remarkable that there are no notices of London and Winchester in the Conqueror's Domesday. (See Spelman's Gloss. s. v. Domesday, and Ayloffe's Calendar, p. xviii.) For Winchester, there was a separate register known as the "Winchester Book." A portion of the *original* survey, with the title of "Inquisitio Eliensis" (from which that in Domesday has been *reduced*) has been recently discovered in the British Museum, and will shortly be published, under the direction of the Royal Society of Literature, by Mr. N. E. S. A. Hamilton, Librarian to the Society, and late of the Dep. of MSS., British Museum.

CHAPTER XII.

Increase of the English fleet, A.D. 1066—Its participation in the Crusades to the Holy Land—Departure of the English expedition—Arrival at Messina—Number of ships—Their order of sailing—Arrival at, and capture of, Acre, 10th June, 1191—Richard returns to England—Maritime laws founded on the "Rôles d'Oleron"—Power to pledge ship and tackle—The sailors consulted—Laws relating to hiring—Drunkenness—Sickness—Damage to ship and cargo—Quarrels—Mooring of ships—Partnership in freight—Food—Obligation to carry the ship to her destination—Rules as to sailors—Demurrage—Bottomry—A bad pilot forfeited his head—Punishments—Shares in fishing vessels—Wreckers—Jetsam and flotsam—Royal fish—Timber of wrecks—Remarks on these laws—Code of Wisby—Magna Charta, A.D. 1215—Henry III., A.D. 1216—Naval actions—Cinque Ports—Increase of piracy—Measures for its suppression—Treaty of commerce with Norway, A.D. 1217, and facilities afforded to foreign merchants—English merchants first open trading establishments abroad—Origin of the Hanseatic League, A.D. 1241—Corporate seals—Sandwich—Poole—Dover—Faversham—Stanhope, vice-admiral of Suffolk—Duties of the Cinque Ports—Increased privileges to foreign merchants—Letters of marque first issued—Law for the recovery of debts, and adjustment of average—Shipping of Scotland, A.D. 1249—Extremely liberal Navigation Act—Chief ports of England, and extent of its shipping and commerce—Edward II., A.D. 1307-1327—Edward III., A.D. 1326-7-1377—Extension of English commerce—The discovery of coal—First complete roll of the English fleet, A.D. 1347—Quota of different ports—Pay of soldiers, sailors, &c.—War renewed, A.D. 1354—Death of Edward III., A.D. 1377—State of the merchant navy during his reign—Loss sustained by war, and encouragement afforded thereby to foreign nations—Rapid increase of the trade of Flanders—Trade between Italy and Flanders—Commercial importance of Bruges and Antwerp—Wealth of Flanders, and extent of its manufactures and commerce—Special privileges to her merchants—Progress of the Hanseatic League, and its system of business: its power too frequently abused.

Increase of the English fleet, A.D. 1066.

THE accession of William the Conqueror to the throne of England produced important changes in the maritime affairs of that country, and gave to its over-sea commerce greatly increased security and stability. In their anxiety to recover the throne of Canute, the Danes had prepared a fleet for the purpose of invasion, which obliged the Conqueror to summon to his aid the whole of the naval resources of the island. Dover, Sandwich, and Romney were each called upon to provide, at their own expense, twenty vessels, equipped for sea, with crews of twenty-one men and provisions for fifteen days.[1] Rye and Winchelsea rendered similar assistance, and in return had conferred on them privileges similar to those which had been granted to the former places by Edward the Confessor. These ports were then for the first time styled the Cinque Ports, by which distinctive title they have ever since been known. Other ports had also to provide their quota. The fleet thus provided by the Conqueror was so fully maintained by Rufus, his second son and successor, that the learned Selden dates England's maritime supremacy from that very early period. Still, for more than a century after the Conquest, her ships seldom ventured beyond the Bay of Biscay on the one hand, or the entrance to the Baltic on the other; and there is no record of any long voyages by English ships until the time of the Crusades, which, whatever they may have done for the cause of the Cross, undoubtedly gave the first great impetus to the shipping of England. The number of rich and powerful princes and nobles, who embarked their fortunes in these

[1] Domesday Book.

extraordinary expeditions, offered the chance of lucrative employment to any nation which could supply the requisite amount of tonnage; and English shipowners made great exertions to reap a share of the gains.

Its participation in the Crusades to the Holy Land.

The Earl of Essex appears to have been the first English nobleman who fitted out an expedition for the Holy Land, while, twelve years afterwards, Richard Cœur de Lion, on ascending the throne, made vast levies on the people for the same object; and, with the aid of Philip II. of France and of other princes, resolved to attempt to save the Cross from the grasp of the Infidels. Extraordinary exertions were made throughout both countries to provide the requisite armaments; and, towards the close of 1189, two fleets had been collected, one at Dover, to convey Richard and his followers (among whom were the Archbishop of Canterbury, the Bishop of Salisbury, and the Chief Justice of England) across the Channel; and a second and still larger one at Dartmouth, consisting of numerous vessels from Normandy, Poitou, Brittany, and Aquitaine, for the conveyance of the great bulk of the Crusaders, to join Richard at Marseilles.

Departure of the English expedition.

This expedition from Dartmouth set sail, under the command of Robert de Sabloil and Richard de Camville, towards the end of April 1190, and, after a disastrous voyage, showing clearly the incompetence alike of both officers and ships, succeeded in reaching Lisbon, where they committed such a series of disgraceful outrages upon the inhabitants, that seven hundred of them were for a time imprisoned: thence, they passed on, and at length, on the 22nd of August, reached Marseilles, from which, after a brief delay for necessary repairs, they followed the kings to the Straits of Messina, where they were all assembled on the 14th of September.[1]

Arrival at Messina.

Vinisauf[2] has described in glowing language the appearance of the fleet as it entered Messina. "As soon as the people heard of its arrival," he says, "they rushed in crowds to the shore to behold the glorious king of England, and at a distance saw the sea covered with innumerable galleys, and the sounds of trumpets from afar, with the sharper and shriller blasts of clarions, sounded in the rear, and they beheld the galleys rowing in order nearer to the land, adorned and furnished with all manner of arms, countless pennons floating in the wind, ensigns at the ends of the lances, the beaks of the galleys distinguished by various paintings, and glittering shields suspended to the prows. The sea appeared to boil with the multitude of the rowers. The clangour of their trumpets was deafening; the greatest joy was testified at the arrival of the various multitudes, when thus our magnificent king, attended by crowds of those who navigated the galleys, as if to see what was unknown to him, or to be beheld by those to whom he was unknown, stood on a prow more ornamented and higher than the others, and, landing, displayed himself elegantly adorned to all who pressed to the shore to see him."

Number of ships.

It was not, however, till the following year

[1] Peter Langtoft says that Richard's own ship was called the "Trenche-le-mer," a good name for a swift sailing vessel; and the name of Trenchemer occurs frequently in subsequent records, even as late as Henry V., as that of commanders of ships.

[2] Geoffry de Vinisauf, ap. Gale, Script. Hist. Anglic., vol. ii.

(April 10) that the fleet actually got under weigh for the Holy Land, numbering one hundred ships[1] (that is, of a larger kind), and fourteen busses. Each of the large ships carried, it is said, besides her crew of fifteen sailors, forty soldiers and forty horses, and provisions for one twelvemonth. The commander was also aided by fourteen other picked men, whom the chronicler calls "slaves." But these, and other accounts of the capacity of ancient vessels are, like too many of the tales about shipping, not now reconcilable. We can only account for the numerous discrepancies as to the size of the vessels and the number of men and horses embarked, by some misapprehension on the part of the writers, or by some confusion in their application of the nautical expressions used by ancient writers, few of whom had any practical knowledge of the subject.

Their order of sailing.

Vinisauf describes the fleet as proceeding in the following order. Three large ships, filled with soldiers and stores, formed the van. The second line consisted of thirteen vessels, described as "dromons and busses;"[2] the third of fourteen vessels; the fourth of twenty; the fifth of thirty; the sixth of forty, and the seventh of sixty; the king himself, with all his galleys, forming the eighth line, and thus

[1] These numbers are given from Richard of Devizes (p. 17), who appears to be the only writer who gives details of the fleet at Messina. The number given subsequently, during the passage of Richard to the Holy Land, by Vinisauf and others, is considerably larger, and probably comprehends vessels of all descriptions.—Sir H. Nicolas's "Hist. Roy. Navy," vol. i. p. 77, &c.

[2] Buss, Bussa, Buscia, or Burcia, and Dromon, or Dromond, seem to have been used indifferently for large vessels. As the specific name given to the large ship belonging to Saladin which Richard I. captured, it has been supposed that the word Dromond is of Arabic origin.—Spelman in voc. Dromunda.

bringing up the rear for the better protection, as was considered, of the whole convoy. The lines were sufficiently near for a trumpet to be heard from one to the other; and each ship also was near enough to her consort to communicate by hailing. But though such an order of sailing might have succeeded during fine weather, the fleet was soon after dispersed during a gale off Ætna, the crews being "sea-sick and frightened;" while three ships were wholly lost on the island of Cyprus and their crews drowned, together with the Vice-Chancellor of England, whose body was washed on shore, with the Great Seal tied round his neck.

Arrival at, and capture of, Acre, June 10, 1191.

After the successful capture of Acre, and a truce, as its consequence, with Saládin, Richard set out for England, where, however, he did not arrive till 13th March, 1194. On landing at Sandwich, he was received "amidst the joyful acclamations of his subjects," or, as we may presume, of those chiefly who dwelt in the seaport towns; for these could hardly have failed to greet joyfully a monarch who had opened out the means of affording ample and lucrative employment to their shipping and seafaring population. Nor, indeed, were the merchants less handsomely remunerated; for to them, the progress of the Crusades procured the opportunity of developing many new and valuable markets for commercial enterprise.

Richard returns to England.

Prevented by the jealousy and the restrictive policy of the Italian cities, English traders had hitherto not ventured on voyages so distant as the Levant, the general policy of the republics of the south throwing various difficulties in the way of foreign shipping. By the Crusades, however, the eyes of English merchants and mariners were alike opened to the successful undertakings of the Mediterranean traders; to them also is largely due the constitution of England's first shipping code, based, as this was, on more ancient laws, with many improvements derived from the increased knowledge due to the recent experience of her mariners.[1]

Maritime laws founded on the "Rôles d'Oleron."

By the first article in these laws a master had power to pledge, with the advice of his mariners, the tackle of the ship for the necessary provisions; but could not sell the hull without special authority from the owners. Previously, it had not been thought safe

Power to pledge ship and tackle.

[1] The whole of these and of the more ancient maritime laws have been recently edited (A.D. 1828–1847) by a learned French lawyer, M. Pardessus. According to his researches, it appears most probable that these documents belong to the ancient French code, called the "Rôles ou Jugemens d'Oleron." It is impossible to determine now who first compiled them, hence they have been claimed for different nations and tribes; Selden, Coke, Prynne, Godolphin, and others, deemed them of English origin, and due to Richard I., but there is no evidence that he ever went to Oleron. M. Pardessus has shown from the authority of MSS. at Oxford and in the British Museum, and from their coincidence with a very early translation into Spanish, that the first twenty six articles are the most genuine. The others he considers to be later additions, as, indeed, their intrinsic evidence tends to show. The place of the departure of the ships being generally Bordeaux suggests that they were originally embodied for the coasting trade of the west of France.—Pardessus' "Collection de lois Maritimes," Paris, 4to, 1828–47. Sir Harris Nicolas, quoting from Brompton, Hoveden, and others, states that Richard drew up at Chinon, on his way to Marseilles, what he calls "the earliest articles of war." ("Hist. Roy. Navy," pp. 89–91.) Still more recently (1871) Sir Travers Twiss, in his edition of "The Black Book of the Admiralty," has examined very fully the real or supposed claims of Richard to be the author or the editor of the "Rôles d'Oleron." In doing so he quotes a memorandum of 12 Edw. III. (A.D. 1284), stating that these laws (*i.e.*, the ten last articles of the Rôles) "were by the Lord Richard, formerly king of England, on his return from the Holy Land, corrected, interpreted, and declared, and were published in the island of Oleron, and were named in the French tongue (Gallica lingua) 'La Ley Olyroun.'"—Introd. pp. lvii.–lviii.

to entrust any one with the command of a ship unless he was a part owner or a freeman; but, by the laws of Richard I., these restrictions were abolished, and the qualifications and duties of the captain for the first time defined by statute. Everything on board being placed under the master's care, he was required to understand thoroughly the art of piloting and navigation, that he might control the pilot. In a merchantman, the first officer was then practically the master, the second, the pilot;[1] the third, the mate; the fourth, the factor or supercargo; then followed his assistant, and after him came the accountants, surgeon, steward, four corporals, cook, gunner, and coxswain, the two latter having their quarters before the mast with the ship's crew, but receiving higher wages.

The sailors consulted.

By the second article if a vessel lay in port, waiting for weather and a wind, the master was instructed, when the time for departure arrived, to call together his ship's company and inquire what they thought of the wind and weather. A difference of opinion arising, he was bound to be guided by the majority, and was legally responsible, if any accident happened, to make good damages caused by his unsupported act. It was, in fact, a standing rule for the master to act with the advice of the greater part of his ship's company and of the merchants, if any were on board.

The third clause provided, that if the ship's crew should not, unless under compulsion, do everything in their power to save the vessel and cargo from shipwreck, they should forfeit their wages. If they

[1] We need not point out that the order of precedency differs nowadays. The supercargoes in after years claimed priority in everything except in that which related to the navigation of the vessel.

saved a part of the cargo they were sent home, by raising money on the goods so saved.

The fourth article, relating to salvage, was very similar to that enacted by the Rhodian law, the allowance of the half, third, or tenth of the articles saved being regulated according to the depth of the water out of which they were raised. Any promises extorted by danger were either void or not too strictly interpreted.

The fifth article provided, that no sailors in port should leave the vessel without the master's consent. The practice of the time required that the sailors should carefully look after everything that related to the preservation of the ship and goods; and if any damage accrued by their absence without licence, they were punished by a year's imprisonment and kept on bread and water. If any accident happened so as to cause death, resulting from their absence, they were flogged. Special punishments were by law, as well as practice, inflicted for damaging the cargo; and very detailed instructions were given how certain goods were to be stowed and delivered. The laws in all cases against desertion were very severe. In some places the sailors were marked in the face with a red-hot iron, so that they might be recognised as long as they lived.

Provision was, however, made for such seamen as ran away by reason of ill-usage;[1] while in the case of a double engagement, the master first hiring a sailor was entitled to claim him, and any master

Laws relating to hiring.

[1] Some of the following rules are noted in the "Ordinances made by King Richard to be observed among sea-faring men." See Appendix No. 2, 628.

knowingly engaging a hired sailor, was amerced in double the amount of wages. The sailor became entitled to his discharge on four grounds: in the event of his being made master or mate of another ship; if he married, in which case, however, he was obliged to refund what he had received; if he made any proviso in his articles for quitting the ship; and if the voyage was concluded, and the ship disarmed and unloaded, with her sails, tackle, and furniture taken away and secured. Provision was also made for compensation to the sailor, in the case of a master giving him his discharge at his pleasure only and without lawful cause. A master, however, could dismiss a mariner for incompetency, especially a pilot, and in such cases no wages were payable. Unqualified persons were in many cases punished for having accepted situations on board for which they were incompetent; and a sailor proved by two witnesses to have any infectious distemper, could be put on shore. The law quaintly laid down that a master might turn away any quarrelsome or thievish, factious fellow, but as to the latter, "he should have a little patience to see if he can be brought to reason."

Drunkenness.

By article sixth, drunkenness, quarrelling, and fighting, were severally punishable, and mutinous mariners were compelled to refund their wages. Mariners wounded in the service of the ship were provided for. The seventh regulation stipulated that in the case of sickness seizing any of the crew while in the service of the ship, they were to be sent on shore with a ship's boy to attend upon them. The eighth prescribed the formalities to be observed in throwing goods overboard to lighten the ship, which

Sickness

were much in the same way as had been laid down in the Rhodian laws. Similarly the proportional average, pound for pound, payable by each party so damnified, was framed upon the French law, *livre à livre*. The ninth article applied to the destruction of the masts and sails, in order to save the ship and cargo; and the rules to be followed were nearly the same for collecting the averages as those which are now adopted. The tenth article relates to damage arising from imperfect dunage, for which the master and mariners were liable to the merchant in the event of any injury, through neglect in this respect, to his merchandise.

Damage to ship and cargo.

Article eleventh refers to damage of goods, or loss of wines or other liquids, by the breaking in of the head of the cask, and generally to all damage arising from improper stowage. It would appear that persons, like the present Stevedores, who look to the stowage of the cargo, existed at a remote period, with the title of *arrimeurs*, or stowers. They were then paid by the merchant, and their business was "to dispose the cargo properly, stowing it closely, and arranging the several casks, bales, boxes, bundles, in such a manner as to balance both sides, fill up the vacant spaces, and manage everything to the best advantage." There was also a class called Sacquiers, who were very ancient officers. Their business was to load and unload vessels with cargoes of salt, corn, and fish, to prevent the ship's crew defrauding the merchant by false tale, or otherwise cheating him of his merchandise.

Quarrels.

The twelfth article throws great light upon the existing manners of the sailors of those days. The master having hired his crew was invested with the duty of keeping peace. He was, in fact, their judge. If any of them gave the lie to another at a table, where there was wine and bread, he was fined four *deniers*; but the master himself offending in that way had to pay a double fine. If any sailor impudently contradicted the master, he was fined eight deniers; and if the master struck him, whether with the fist or the open hand, he was required to bear the stroke; but if he struck more than one blow the sailor might defend himself; whereas, if the sailor committed the first assault, he had to pay one hundred *sous*, or lose his hand. It would appear that the master might call the sailor opprobrious names, and in such case he was advised to submit, and hide himself in the forecastle out of his superior's sight; but if the master followed, the sailor might stand upon his defence, for the master "ought not to pass into the forecastle after him."

The thirteenth article[1] enacted, that, if a difference arose between the master and the seaman, the former ought to deny him his mess thrice[2] before he turned him out of the ship. If the latter offered satisfaction and was refused and turned out of the ship, he could follow the ship to her port of discharge and claim full wages. The master not taking any seaman in his stead, in such cases, rendered himself liable for any damage accruing. The Hanseatic laws required

[1] This is the fourteenth article in Pardessus, p. 333. His article thirteen relates to charter-parties to different places between Bourdeaux and Yarmouth.

[2] The old Gascony phrase was *Oster la touaille*, which signifies denying him the table-cloths or victuals for three meals, by which was understood one day and a half.

the master not to give the seamen any cause to mutiny; nor to provoke them by calling them names, nor wrong them, nor "keep anything from them that is theirs, but to use them well, and pay them honestly what is their due."

Mooring of ships.

The fourteenth and fifteenth articles relate to the regulations of mooring ships, and to injuries sustained through "striking against each other." The law of damage is laid down at great length, and buoys, made of empty barrels, pieces of any description of light wood, baskets, or any articles which float buoyantly on the top of the water, are required to be used to prevent accidents and show where the anchors lie, when in port.

Partnership in freight.

The sixteenth clause required the master to ask the crew, when a ship was ready to load, "Will you freight your share yourselves, or be allowed for it in proportion with the ship's general freight?" and the sailors were there and then bound to answer, and make their election.[1] If they elected to take their risk, a curious practice resulted. In the event of taking on board a cask of water instead of a cask of wine, they might deal with their own stowage as of right; and, in the event of throwing cargo overboard, to lighten the ship, they had the privilege of refusing to throw over a cask of water in preference to a cask of wine. If the water, however, was thrown overboard, the mariner came in upon the general average; although, by the common law of England, a tun of water was never rated, pound by pound in value, with a tun of wine.

[1] The fishermen of Blankeness, on the Elbe, and the sailors of the Levant, and in various other places, still navigate in shares for wages.

Food.

By the seventeenth clause the sailors of Brittany were restricted to one meal a day from the kitchen, while those of Normandy had two meals; and when the ship arrived in a wine country, the master had to provide them with wine.[1] The practice of serving out a certain allowance of food is very ancient, and to prevent jealousies, complaints, and quarrels on this account, the law prescribed a specified quantity to be supplied to each man exactly alike. When wine was provided, the mariner had one meal per day, but when water alone was served out, he had two meals.

Obligation to carry the ship to her destination.

The eighteenth article provided, that when a ship was unladen, the sailors could demand their freight; but from those of them having neither bed, chest, nor trunk on board, the master could retain a portion of their wages, till the vessel was brought back to her final port of destination. It was ruled that the wages were not due till the work had been entirely done, unless a special agreement subsisted to the contrary, for "freight was the mother of wages."[2]

Rules as to sailors.

The rights of sailors hired per day, or week, or month, where freight was not procurable, were secured by the nineteenth article, which stipulated that if an engagement was broken off by war, pirates, or the command of his sovereign, the seaman was entitled to have a quarter part of his wages for the full term of his engagement.

The twentieth clause provided that, when in a foreign port, only two sailors from the ship might go

[1] This article affords some evidence that these laws were drawn up in France for French sailors.

[2] Pardessus refers to an unedited Rhodian Law, as having suggested this article, p. 337.

on shore at a time, and take with them one meal of victuals, "as much as they can eat at once," but no drink. They were bound to return to the ship in season, so as not to lose a tide, and they were held responsible for any damage resulting from their default.

Demurrage.

The twenty-first clause related to detentions, and provided for the payment of demurrage. If a merchant, having freighted a ship, did not load her by the time appointed, he was bound to make compensation for such delay, and the sailors were entitled to a fourth part of the amount; the remainder being allotted to the master, he finding the crew in provisions. Formerly, eight days were allowed the merchant to unload, which afterwards was extended to fifteen. But that did not affect the payment of freight, which was required to be paid in eight days, whether the ship was discharged or not. The master could not detain the goods on board for freight, but when in a boat or lighter, he was entitled to stop them until he was satisfied.

Bottomry.

The twenty-second clause relates to selling goods on board, to provide for the ship, in which the laws of bottomry were enforced.[1]

A bad pilot forfeited his head.

The twenty-third clause was a frightful instance, copied from the so-called Rhodian laws,[2] of barbarous legislation. It enacted that if a pilot, or "lockman,"[3]

[1] It was further ordained, that the wines on board the ship should be sold at the price customary at the place to which she had come.

[2] It has been shown by Pardessus and others that these so-called "Rhodian Laws" are a compilation of the eleventh and twelfth centuries, and distinct from the one famous Rhodian Law whose title, "De Jactu," has been preserved.

[3] Pardessus retains this form of the word, but the MSS. read "lodman" (*i.e.* leading-man, pilot), which is probably the true form. —See Brit. Mus. Add. MSS. 7965, fol. 89, &c.

for such was the term applied to harbour pilots, undertook to carry a vessel into port, and the vessel miscarried through his ignorance, and he had no means to make good the damage, or otherwise render full satisfaction, he was condemned to lose his head.[1] While the twenty-fourth clause actually gave the master, or any of the mariners, or merchants on board, power to cut off the head of the offender without being bound in law to answer for it; they were only required to be very certain that the unlucky lockman who was hired at every river to guide the ship, in order to avoid rocks, shelves, shoals, and sand-banks, had not wherewith to make pecuniary satisfaction.

Punishments.

The twenty-fifth clause aimed at altering "the unreasonable and accursed custom" of lords of the coast, where a vessel was wrecked, claiming and seizing the third or fourth part of the ship, leaving only the remainder to the master, the merchant, and the mariners. "Therefore, all pilots who, in connivance with the lords on the coast," or to ingratiate themselves with such nobles, ran the ship on shore, were doomed to a most rigorous and unmerciful death on "high gibbets near the place where these accursed pilots brought the ship to ruin, which said gibbets are to abide and remain to succeeding ages on that place, as a visible caution to other vessels that sail thereby." The lords or others, who took away any of the goods, were also declared to be "accursed," and were frequently punished as "robbers and thieves." Indeed the twenty-sixth clause

[1] A French law, so late as Aug. 22, 1790, sent a pilot to the galleys for three years who accidentally lost his vessel; and sentenced him to death if he did so wilfully.—Pardessus, p. 341.

declared that, "If the lord of the place be so barbarous as not only to permit such inhuman people, but also to maintain and assist them in such villanies, so that he may have a share in such wrecks, the said lord shall be apprehended, and all his goods confiscated and sold, in order to make restitution to the parties, and himself be fastened to a post or stake in the midst of his own mansion-house, which being fired at the four corners, all shall be burned together; the walls thereof shall be demolished, the stones pulled down, and the place converted into a market-place for the sale of hogs and swine only, to all posterity."[1]

The frightful severity of this punishment was adopted to stop even greater barbarities inflicted upon wrecked mariners, in addition to the plundering of the ship and cargo. Neither the Gauls nor Britons hesitated to sacrifice strangers cast on their shores; and, unfortunately, the piracies of the Scandinavians and the Normans had the effect of perpetuating this sanguinary custom. Foreigners cast on shore were too frequently immediately despatched, and the right of plundering a wrecked ship extended alike to friend and foe. The execution of pirates, and such as were condemned for crimes committed on the high seas, and their being left to hang in chains by the water side, has survived in practice even to the present century.

Clause twenty-seven relates to the adjustment of losses by any accident resulting from an inferior outfit, and stipulates that when a vessel arrived at

[1] These and the following Articles, which, doubtless, faithfully represent the manners of the times, are found in early editions of Garcia and Cleirac, but not in the MSS.—Pardessus, p. 346, note 3.

her port of discharge, she was to be hauled up on dry ground, the sails taken down, and everything properly stowed away; and that then the master ought to consider an increase of wages, "kenning by kenning."[1]

Shares in fishing vessels.

The twenty-eighth, twenty-ninth, and thirtieth clauses adjust the respective shares of fishing vessels, when several were working in partnership, and provide that in the case of the loss of one vessel, the representatives of the parties who had perished could claim their quota of the fish caught as well as of the fishing instruments. They further relate to the salvage of shipwrecked vessels, in which the right of all shipwrecked persons to their goods is fully maintained; and refer to derelict ships and goods whose owners have been drowned, stipulating that such goods be kept a year, and if not claimed in that time be vested in the Church under certain conditions.

Wreckers.

The thirty-first clause provides that any wreckers who plundered a ship, or who, "more barbarous, cruel, and inhuman than mad dogs, did sometimes, to gain their apparel, monies or goods, murder and destroy poor distressed seamen; in this case, the lord of the country ought to execute justice on such wretches, to punish corporally as well as pecuniarily, to plunge them in the sea till they be half dead, and then to have them drawn from the sea and stoned to death."

[1] "Kenning" is a very ancient word in sea language. It means view, or course, "course by course," and was employed when navigation was performed by views and by observation from one land to another, prior to the use of the compass. Admiral W. H. Smyth, in his "Sailor's Word Book," states that "it was a mode of increasing wages formerly, according to whaling law, by seeing how a man performed his duty."

The thirty-second to the thirty-sixth articles inclusive refer to the laws of jetsam and flotsam, and provide that goods thrown overboard to preserve the ship and cargo do not change their proprietorship. Whilst the thirty-seventh clause relates to strays of the sea, such as whales[1] and other oil-fish, stipulating that if a man on horseback could reach the stray with his lance it was deemed a royalty belonging to the lord. But if the fish was found farther off the shore, the lord had no right to it, though afterwards brought or driven on shore. **Jetsam and flotsam.**

The five clauses which followed regulated the prevailing customs relating to sturgeon, salmon, turbot, the sea dragon, the sea barbel, and in general all fish fit for a king's table; besides oil-fish such as whales, and porpoises, or of any fish of which oil could be made, and in which the lord had a title to a share. All other fish were declared to be the property of those who caught them in the sea, whether in deep or shallow waters; whilst the forty-third and forty-fourth clauses adjusted the title to goods which had become derelict. The forty-fifth provided that a vessel cutting her cables and putting to sea through stress of weather was entitled to recover their value. Buoys were directed to be placed over the anchors, and any person detaining them from the lawful owners was to be reputed as "a thief and a robber." **Royal fish.**

The forty-sixth and forty-seventh articles applied to the timber of wrecks, when the crew were lost and had perished. The pieces of the ship were declared to belong to the owners, notwithstanding any custom **Timber of wrecks.**

[1]. For notice of whales caught so far south as Biarritz, see "Syllabus of Rymer's Fœdera," Appendix No. 8, p. 648, s. a. 1338.

to the contrary. "And any participators of the said wreck, whether bishops, prelates, or clerks, shall be deposed and deprived of their benefices respectively." If they were laymen, they incurred the penalties previously recited.

Remarks on these laws.

Whatever opinion may be entertained of the barbarous character of the punishments enforced by these laws, it is undeniable that they are framed in a spirit of wisdom and justice towards the ship-owner. The lawless spirit of piracy, prevailing along the coasts in the time of Richard I., rendered it absolutely necessary, if a merchant navy was desirable, to protect the ships and the mariners, as well as the goods in them, by the stern authority of the civil law. The experience that Richard had acquired in sea affairs during his voyage to the Holy Land, made him sensible of the necessity of introducing into England the most salutary maritime regulations in force abroad. Accordingly the above code, of which we have furnished only a brief abstract, was established by him, or shortly after his death, to afford protection to those persons and interests, on which he saw clearly the commercial prosperity of England in great measure depended.

Code of Wisby.

At a later period, the merchants of Wisby[1] framed their laws on the Rôles d'Oleron, which became, in fact, during the succeeding century and subsequently, the authoritative rule for deciding all maritime controversies not only in the Hanse Towns,

[1] In the island of Gothland, Baltic. These laws are believed to have been reduced to three, their present form, by Magnus, who became king of Sweden in A.D. 1320. (Pardessus, p. 426.) They are almost identical with those in the Rôles d'Oleron, North German names of places of departure, &c. being substituted for Bordeaux, &c.

but among all nations on the Baltic Sea. Further, it was declared by the forty-first article of Magna Charta, A.D. 1215, "that all merchants shall have safe conduct to go out of or come into England, and to stay there. To pass either by land or by water, and to buy and sell by the ancient and allowed customs without any civil tolls (an excessive tax on sales), except in time of war, or when there shall happen to be any nation at war with us."

Magna Charta, A.D. 1215.

Lord Justice Coke, in his comments on this famous charter,[1] is of opinion that the merchants here mentioned were strangers, as few Englishmen at that time traded directly with foreign countries; some years elapsing before an English association began conducting, on its own account, a foreign trade with English wool, tin, lead, and leather. But during the reign of King John, the merchant navy found abundance of profitable employment, for the wars he engaged in required a large amount of tonnage. Moreover, the ship-owners and seamen are known to have supported him in his contentions with the nobles;[2] and William of Malmesbury speaks of the fame of London for its extensive commerce, and of the crowd of foreign merchants, especially Germans, who flocked there, and filled the Thames with their ships. Bristol, also, appears from the same authority to have been then a flourishing port for ships from Ireland, Norway, or other foreign parts. But the people, and especially the monks and nobles,

[1] Cap. 30.

[2] King John, in his edict of Hastings, A.D. 1200, ordered his captains to seize and to confiscate the cargoes of every ship that did not strike their topsails to them. (Selden, "Mare Clausum," ii. c. 26.) He is also said to have destroyed the whole naval force of France. Trivet, "Ann. ad ann. 1214," quoted by Spelman, in his Glossary.

complained loudly of the taxes levied for the hire of the merchant shipping, although a large portion of the great wealth amassed by the ecclesiastics of the period was undoubtedly derived from trade, and most likely from their private and personal investments in maritime pursuits.

Henry III., A.D. 1216.

When Henry III. ascended the throne, and the barons arrayed themselves in opposition to Louis of France, their former ally, so many actions by sea ensued that the maintenance of the navy became a necessity. An English fleet of forty galleys and other vessels attacked and defeated a French squadron of more than double its size; the English, on the authority of Matthew Paris,[1] attacking their opponents by "a dreadful discharge of arrows from the crossbow-men and archers," rushing against them with their iron beaks, "and availing themselves of their position to windward by throwing pulverised quicklime into the French, whereby the men were blinded." In this celebrated action, which some have called the commencement of England's dominion of the sea, the vessels contributed by the Cinque Ports[2] greatly distinguished themselves, and obtained thereby further privileges. Thus they were commissioned "to annoy the subjects of France,"—in other words, to plunder, as they pleased, not merely the merchant vessels of that country, but "all they met of whatever nation, not sparing even their own

Naval actions.

Cinque Ports.

[1] M. Paris, p. 298. Ann. of Waverl. p. 183. Gale, ap. Robert of Gloucester, p. 515.

[2] See Appendix No. 4, pp. 629–632, for charter of Edward I. (1272–1307) to the Cinque Ports. This appears to be the earliest charter that has been preserved, but it is only confirmatory of the charters given by previous kings.

acquaintances and relations,"[1]—a system of piracy which other Channel ports were not slow in adopting. Indeed, between the privateer and the pirate there was then so little distinction that, when Henry attempted to suppress these lawless acts, he found it necessary to hang indiscriminately about thirty of the most guilty.

Increase of piracy.

But piracy, under the plea of retaliation, rapidly spread among the ships of other nations. The Normans, Scotch, Irish, and Welsh fitted out their marauders, pillaging not merely every vessel they could successfully cope with at sea, but also various towns along the coast. The whole Channel swarmed with pirates, and the spoils of rapine were too often preferred to the slower acquisitions of honest industry by those who thought themselves powerful enough to be robbers; a state of things naturally much increased during the long contest between Henry III. and his nobles. During this period, indeed, foreign commerce was almost annihilated. Wines, which used to sell for forty shillings, realized ten marks; wax rose from forty shillings to eight marks, and pepper from six pennies to three shillings a pound; while the scarcity of ordinary merchandise, especially of salt, iron, steel, and cloth, together with the stagnation in all exportable articles, owing to the interruption to navigation, was so great, that the industrial classes and many of the merchants were reduced to want and beggary. Still more stringent measures were therefore found necessary to sweep the seas of these pirates; for the English nation had become seriously alarmed. A great increase was consequently made

Measures for its suppression.

[1] M. Paris, p. 589.

in the fleet. A lord high admiral, and guardian of the sea and maritime ports, by the name of Topham, was for the first time appointed; and to him all ships of war were rendered responsible for their conduct.

But though so much trouble had arisen from pirates and other marauders, many changes of great importance in the development of the maritime commerce of England were inaugurated during the long, though generally feeble, reign of Henry III.

Treaty of commerce with Norway, A.D. 1217, and facilities afforded to foreign merchants.

Thus a treaty of friendship between England and Norway[1] formed one of his earliest acts, whereby the merchants and subjects of both kingdoms obtained full liberty of personal intercourse. The merchants of Cologne[2] were then also allowed to establish a hall or factory (known as their Guildhall), which soon became the general rendezvous in London of all German merchants, and the place of business where they disposed of their merchandise, and found safe and comfortable abodes; while, not long afterwards, they were allowed to trade at all the fairs throughout England.[3] French ships, laden with corn, wine, or provisions, then received permission to come into, or go out of, English ports unfettered by former restrictions. A quay was formed at Queenhithe, where vessels belonging to the Cinque Ports could discharge their cargoes; and here, also, the first fish market was established.

[1] There is constant notice of intercourse between England and Norway during this period of English history. See Appendix No. 3, p. 629.

[2] This was about A.D. 1220. This "Guild-hall" ("Gildalla Teutonicorum") was distinct from the guildhall of the merchants of the Steel-yard. (Madox, Hist. Excheq. ii. 2.) The former obtained a charter from Henry III. in A.D. 1259. Rymer, Fœd. v. 2.

[3] Hakluyt's "Voyages," vol. i. p. 130.

Liverpool then first became known as a place of maritime trade, although it continued to be ranked as a "village," attached to the parish of Walton, till as late as 1699.[1] Brunswick was invited to have commercial dealings with England, and protection was afforded to its citizens. In Henry's reign, too, there were built at Yarmouth, Winchelsea, and other ports, many vessels of a superior description to any that England had hitherto produced.[2] During the same period an association of English merchants obtained privileges from the Earl of Flanders (A.D. 1248), and established in the Netherlands depôts of English wool, lead, and tin. These adventurers were long known as the merchants of the staples of England. Previous to the reign of Henry III. all foreign merchants had been compelled to sell their goods on board their vessels; but in consideration of a payment of 100*l.* (cash) towards a supply of fresh water for the city of London, and of fifty marks to the lord mayor (annually), the merchants of Amiens, Nele, and Corbie, and of Normandy, were then allowed to land and store their cargoes.[3]

English merchants first open trading establishments abroad.

Origin of the Hanseatic League, A.D. 1241.

The formation of the Hanseatic Association was, however, the most important commercial event of Henry's reign. Though its origin, like that of many other great communities, cannot be precisely ascertained, it seems probable that it arose out of an agreement, entered into in the year 1241 between the merchants of Hamburg and Lubeck, to establish a guard for the mutual protection of their merchandise

[1] Atkins's "Manchester," p. 332. Liverpool appears to have had burgesses as early as A.D. 1207. Rot. Patent. 9 Johan.

[2] M. Paris, p. 889.

[3] Stow's "Survey of London," p. 130. Rymer, Fœd. vol. v. p. 105.

against robbers; a precaution the more necessary, as men of the first rank were then but too ready to profess openly the trade of robbery on land, and of piracy on the seas.[1] As this powerful corporation, the most important in the commercial history of the middle ages, in time exercised great influence over the commerce of England, and of the whole of the north of Europe, we shall have frequent occasion to refer to its commercial operations.

It is to be regretted that no reliable information as to the number, size, or form of the English merchant vessels of this period has been preserved. We have, consequently, been obliged to seek information on this subject from the Corporate Seals of different towns which have fortunately been preserved, and are represented in the following drawings.

Corporate Seals.

Sandwich.

1. Is a corporate seal of the cinque port Sandwich, of about the date A.D. 1238. This curious seal shows that English ships were then provided with sails, which were furled aloft as at the present time, and, further, that they carried their long-boat on deck amid-ships, as do most merchant vessels now.

Poole.

2. A seal of the town of Poole, A.D. 1325, exhibits a sheer of remarkable height, with the representation of the castle aft and forwards, the name of which is preserved in the present word "forecastle," for the portion of the vessel towards the bow. The anchor may also be noticed, hanging clear over the bows and ready for use.

Dover.

3. Is an exceedingly well preserved seal of Dover, of A.D. 1284, exhibiting similar elevated portions at

[1] Lambecii, Orig. Hamburg, ii. p. 26.

SANDWICH.

POOLE.

the stern and bow for the use of the fighting men, with a curious representation, also, of a sailor ascending the shrouds, across which, no doubt, ratline lines were placed, though these can hardly be detected in the drawing. This seal has some other special details, as on the forecastle two men blowing trumpets in different directions; on the after deck, a man steering with a long oar over the side; and on the main deck, two sailors apparently coiling the cable.

DOVER.

Faver-sham.

4. Is the seal of about the same period of the town of Faversham. It is remarkable for the amount of detail preserved on it. On this, as on the seal of Sandwich, two sailors may be noticed seated aloft on

the yard in the act of furling the sail. On the deck is an officer giving the word of command, and in the castle over the poop a man holding a standard. On the fore deck are five soldiers variously armed with spears and axes, and, near the top of the mast, is the castellated object often observed on similar seals, indicating the crow's nest.

FAVERSHAM.

Stanhope, vice-admiral of Suffolk.

5. A seal of Michael Stanhope, vice-admiral of Suffolk, of a somewhat later date, is remarkable in that it represents a ship with *four* masts and a bowsprit. Each mast has a single yard, with the lug sail furled on the three smaller ones, and set on the fourth and largest. The bow is ornamented with a crocodile's head, his back appearing to form the roof of the forecastle. Over the bow is the anchor triced up to the side of the vessel.[1]

[1] The following are the legends, on the five seals, respectively:—
1. SANDWICH—SIGILL. CONSILII. BARONVM. DE. SANDWICO.

Duties of the Cinque Ports.

By the charter granted in the twenty-second year of the reign of Edward I., the Cinque Ports[1] were bound to provide, at any time the king passed over the sea, not less than fifty-seven ships fully equipped, each to have twenty armed soldiers maintained at the cost of the ship-owner for fifteen days. Soon afterwards,

MICHAEL STANHOPE, VICE-ADMIRAL OF SUFFOLK.

the constable of Dover Castle set forth, in a proclamation, the proportion of ships which these and other ports, admitted to certain privileges, were bound to furnish. The total number thus collected amounted

2. POOLE—SIGILLVM. COMMVNE. DE. LA. POLE.
3. DOVER—SIGILLVM. COMMVNE. BARONVM. DE. DOVORIA.
4. FAVERSHAM—SIGILLVM. BARONVM. DE. FAVERSHAM.
5. SUFFOLK—SIGILLVM. MICHAELIS. STANHOPE. ARMIGERI. VICE· ADMIRALLI. COMITATVS. SVFFOLCIE.

[1] See Appendix No. 4.

to seventy-eight vessels, of which Hastings had to supply eighteen; Bekesbourne, in Kent, seven; Rye, five; Winchelsea, ten; Dover, nineteen; Folkestone, seven; Faversham, a similar number; and Sandwich with Deal and other minor places, five: the whole to be ready and properly "armed and arrayed," each to carry twenty men besides the master and mariners, who were to serve five days at the expense of the ports and afterwards at that of the king's.

The nucleus of a national navy was thus established. In cases of emergency, other vessels were obtainable from London or built for the occasion by the government; and to make certain of a still further supply, the whole merchant service were required to be ready within forty days from the time of the summons. The "Cinque Ports," for their five days' service, paid the masters sixpence, and the sailors threepence per day.[1]

Increased privileges to foreign merchants.

Although the reign of Edward, like that of his predecessor, was unfortunately marked by many contentions at home and abroad, the interests of commerce were not neglected, and foreigners obtained privileges far beyond any they had previously enjoyed.[2] Those, for instance, who repaired to England were not merely granted full quiet and security, but they were exempted from all differential duties and special restrictions, and from the payment of either "murage, pontage, or pavage," although in cities they were only allowed to sell their goods by wholesale, except

[1] Hakluyt's "Voyages," vol. i. p. 17.

[2] A charter granting these privileges will be found at length in Hakluyt, vol. i. p. 135. It was confirmed by Henry IV. and Henry V.

in the case of spices or mercery wares. Goods of any kind might be exported or imported, with the exception of wine, which could not be re-exported without a special licence. Foreign merchants were also allowed to take up their abode at any town or borough in the kingdom, subject only to the civil and municipal laws of the country. The crown promised not to seize their goods without making full satisfaction. Bargains were to be enforced after the "earnest penny" had passed between the buyer and seller; and all bailiffs and officers of fairs were commanded to do justice without delay, from day to day, "according to the law of merchants." Before goods were weighed, it was stipulated that both buyer and seller were to see that the scales were empty and of equal balance, and all weights were to be of one standard. When the scales were balanced, "the weigher" was expressly required to remove his hands. Moreover, in all trials by jury, in which strangers were interested, the jury was to consist of half Englishmen and half foreigners.

Letters of marque first issued.

It was also in the reign of Edward I. that letters of marque appear to have been for the first time issued. A merchant of Bayonne,[1] at that time a port of the English dominions in Gascony, had shipped a cargo of fruit from Malaga, which, on its passage along the coast of Portugal, was seized and carried into Lisbon by an armed cruiser belonging to that country then at peace with England. The king of Portugal, who had received one-tenth part of the property, declined to restore the ship and cargo, or make good the loss; whereupon King

[1] Rymer, "Fœdera," v. p. 691.

Edward's lieutenant in Gascony granted the owner of the ship and his heirs licence, to be in force for five years, to seize the property of the Portuguese, and especially of the inhabitants of Lisbon, to the extent of the loss he had sustained and of the expenses of recovery.

Law for the recovery of debts,

It was likewise during the reign of Edward (10th Oct., 1283) that parliament passed the famous "statute of merchants," which gave a remedy for the due recovery of debts, "as for want of such a law many merchants were impoverished, and many foreign merchants desisted from trading with England." It is remarkable that, in the required process, the debtor was supposed incapable of writing, and was, therefore, required to put his seal to a bill drawn by the mayor's clerk, who thereupon affixed the royal seal prepared for that purpose. If, on judgment against him, the debtor was proved to have no property, he was imprisoned and fed on bread and water until the just demands of the creditors were satisfied.

and adjustment of average.

Nor were Edward's commercial enactments confined to those we have thus briefly noticed; for, understanding that certain citizens of London,[1] together with other merchants of England, Ireland, Gascony, and Wales, were in the habit of compelling the barons of the Cinque Ports and others to pay an average on articles which ought to have been exempted, as in the case of goods thrown overboard in storms, he ordained that the vessel with her apparel, provisions, and cooking utensils, "the master's ring, necklace, sash, and silver cup," as well as the freight for the goods brought into port, should be free of all such

[1] Ibid. v. p. 298.

payments: on the other hand, that all other things in the vessel, not excepting even the seamen's bedding, should bear a proportion of the loss incurred, and that the master should not be permitted to claim freight for goods so thrown overboard.[1]

Shipping of Scotland, A.D. 1249.

In Scotland, as might have been expected, commerce was of even slower growth than in England, nor was it till the reign of Alexander III. that there was any real maritime force; and although the vassals of Scotland, as, for instance, the king of Man, were required to contribute ships for the use of the state in proportion to their lands, the king does not appear to have considered that such merchant vessels as these were of much value, as he passed a law whereby his merchants were prohibited for a limited period from exporting any goods in their own vessels, "because some of them had been captured by pirates, and others lost by shipwreck and by arrestments in foreign ports." Of course, the inevitable result followed that, for a time, the merchant vessels of Scotland were totally extinguished. The enactment, however, for some unaccountable reason, seems to have given satisfaction, as the historians of the period remark that—"in consequence of these laws the kingdom abounded in a few years with corn, money, cattle, sheep, and all kinds of merchandise, and the arts flourished."[2] It is, indeed, possible that Scotland may have imbibed the spirit of extreme liberality in its maritime policy which then prevailed throughout England, where it was evidently supposed that foreign merchants brought wealth which England could not otherwise have obtained. It is,

Extremely liberal Navigation Act.

[1] Act. ii. Edward I.

[2] Ayloffe's Calendar, p. 335.

perhaps, remarkable that we have no notice of any trading port of Scotland except that of Dunbar, which, at that time, was subject to the English crown.

Chief ports of England,

Fortunately, however, a document has been preserved which furnishes the names of the chief ports of England during the reign of Edward I.[1] It is interesting and instructive. They were then as follows: Dover, Sandwich, Romney, Winchester, Rye, Hythe, Faversham, Hastings, Shoreham, Seaford, Portsmouth, Southampton, Dartmouth, Lymington, Weymouth, Poole, Humble, Lymne, Sidmouth, Chichester, Teignmouth, Frome, Fowey, Looe, Bodmin, Wareham, Falmouth, Bristol, Haverford-West, Caernarvon, Caermarthen, Landpadanour, Conway, Chester, Bridgewater, Cardiff, Oystermouth, Rochester, Gravesend, Northfleet, London, Harwich, Ipswich, Dunwich, Orford, Yarmouth, Blackney, Lynn, Boston, Wainfleet, Saltfleet, Grimsby, Hull, Ravensburg, Scarborough, Tynemouth, Newcastle-on-Tyne, Berwick-upon-Tweed, and Dunbar. Such were the principal ports of England at the commencement of the fourteenth century. Some of these places are now hardly known for their trade, while the very names of others among them have long since disappeared. How changed since then are the seats and centres of England's maritime commerce!

and extent of its shipping and commerce.

But we know nothing of the amount of shipping belonging to these ports for more than half a century afterwards; nor, till a comparatively recent period, of the extent of business carried on in England. Had

[1] The Act of Edward I. prohibiting the exportation of bullion, and relating to his new coinage, was ordered to be sent to all the chief ports in the kingdom. For the wages of the sailors in the fleets of Edward I., see Appendix No. 5, pp. 632–4.

such records been preserved, we should probably have seen that in the port of Liverpool alone, then scarcely recognisable, a larger amount of tonnage now arrives and departs during a week or even a day, than entered and left all these ports in the course of a year. The only document in the shape of statistics referring to shipping of the thirteenth century that can be discovered, is a return which states that, in the year ending 20th November, 1299, there arrived in the port of London, and in all the other ports of the kingdom, except the Cinque Ports, seventy-three vessels with cargoes of wine, of which the smallest had not less than nineteen tuns on board, from each of which the king, by ancient law, had the right to take, at a fixed price, two tuns for the use of his household.

But even this return conveys but a very vague and imperfect idea of the number of vessels then belonging to England, or of the extent of its maritime commerce; moreover, the importation of wine was then much larger in proportion to that of other articles of commerce than it is now. The Cinque Ports, from their wealth and exclusive privileges, were, doubtless, large consumers of wine and had great facilities for its storage.[1] London had long been, as it is now, pre-eminently the port for wine. To Edward I. is due the selection of the Vintry (a name still remaining) on the banks of the Thames, where vessels delivered their cargoes

[1] To this day the visitor to the quaint old town of Winchelsea may observe under houses, now cottages, extensive cellars—some with roofs of Gothic arches. The Ward-robe books of the 25th, 29th, and 32nd years of Edward I. (now in the British Museum) give ample details on all these subjects.

alongside the wharf. Thence they often proceeded up the river Fleet, as far as Holborn Bridge, to take in their return cargoes, the smaller ones occasionally ascending even as far as Battle Bridge, near the present station of the Great Northern Railway at King's Cross.

Edward II., A.D. 1307–27.

The twenty years' reign of Edward II. is not marked by any events worthy of note relating to maritime commerce. Retrogression rather than progress was the result of his policy and of his constant troubles and contentions with neighbouring nations. When, however, he had been deposed, indeed almost immediately after the accession of Edward III., a considerable step in advance was made by the grant of fresh patents and charters to secure for the merchants of England further staples on the Continent. Nearly the whole of the wool trade had been previously carried on by foreigners, but the English now aimed at having "staples" in Brabant and Artois as well as in Flanders, whither they could freely send their own wool and dispose of it themselves from their own entrepôts. And in this they at length succeeded; for with their own capital they bought their wool, and exporting it in their own bottoms to a staple in Holland, Flanders, or France, disposed of it in those countries without the intervention of any second party or foreign merchant. This privilege was considered at the time a great step in advance; but now it is not easy to understand how the laws of any country could have withheld from its merchants the right to trade wherever or whenever other nations did not object.

Edward III., A.D. 1326–7—1377.

Extension of English commerce.

Such changes in the mode of transacting business

tended materially to enlarge the knowledge of the English merchants, acquiring as they did from year to year, by their intercourse with the more refined and intelligent merchants of Holland and France, much information on subjects they might have learnt at an earlier period of their history had their rulers not embroiled them in constant wars with the very nations with whom they were now in direct communication. Again, though it is certain that, at least on the western side of England, the Romans had worked coal on or near the surface,[1] the opening of the great coal-fields near Newcastle first took place in the reign of this wise monarch—though, curiously enough, its value was sooner appreciated by foreigners than by the people of the country in which this vast source of wealth was found. For a considerable period after its discovery, the consumption of coal was supposed to be so unhealthy that a royal edict prohibited its use in the city of London while the queen resided there, in case it might prove "pernicious to her health."[2] On the other hand, while England was thus prohibiting the use of the article which has made her by far the most famous commercial nation of either ancient or modern times, France sent her ships laden with corn to Newcastle, receiving coal as their return cargoes,

The discovery of coal.

[1] Mr. Wright, in his excavations at Uriconium (Wroxeter), found abundant evidences of the use of coal. Roman candles have also been met with in some of the neighbouring mines. As early as A.D. 1253 there was a lane behind Newgate, in London, called Sea-coal Lane. Ayloffe's Calend., p. 11. It appears also that coal was used in A.D. 1337 in the manufacture of iron anchors. See "Syllabus of Rymer's Fœdera," Appendix No. 8, p. 648, s. a. 1337.

[2] Stow's "Survey of London," p. 925.

and her merchants were the first to carry this now great article of commerce to foreign countries.

For the first time we obtain also at this period something like reliable information with regard to the extent of trade of England and the number and size of her merchant vessels. Hitherto everything with regard to them, and indeed to the vessels of almost all other countries, has been, in a great measure, a matter of conjecture, the accounts preserved being so conflicting that scarcely more than the vaguest idea of their form or size can be ascertained. Nor, indeed, so far as we know, were there any returns of the actual strength of the navy of England or of the number of vessels which each port could send to sea on an emergency, until Edward III. ordered a roll to be prepared of the fleet he employed in the blockade and siege of Calais.[1]

First complete roll of the English fleet, A.D. 1347.

From the details given in this roll we have the means of forming a tolerably correct impression of the merchant shipping of the time; and it is remarkable how small was the proportion of ships and men which the king himself supplied. Many of the ports, it will be seen, supplied a larger number of both than the king himself, these being, obviously, the merchant shipping at other times employed in the foreign trade of the country. This interesting document clearly shows that from the earliest period up to the siege of Calais, as was also the case for a long period subsequently, the

[1] See Appendix No. 6, pp. 634–6, where the original documents preserved in the Cotton and Harleian Collections are given in parallel columns, to show their variations. At the end of this roll are also notices of some of the more remarkable items in the repairs of Edward III.'s galleys from another contemporary MS. Appendix No. 7, pp. 636—641.

English fleets were composed almost exclusively of merchant ships, contributed by the chief ports in the kingdom or in the dependent provinces.

Quota of different ports.

That Yarmouth, in Norfolk, should have supplied the largest number of vessels, is probably due to its herring fisheries, and to the great quantities of wool which were then shipped from that port to Brabant and the ports of Flanders and Holland.[1] Again, Fowey, in Cornwall, furnished more seamen than London, in all likelihood on account of the tin trade; while the now extinct port of Winchelsea, in Sussex, occupied the first position amongst the Cinque Ports, perhaps from its neighbourhood to the then chief ironworks in the country. Those places directly interested in foreign trade contributed rateably, in accordance with its extent, and not with reference to the number of their inhabitants. For instance, the city of York furnished only one small vessel with nine men on board; whilst the town of Newcastle, now becoming important as the port of shipment of sea-borne coals, furnished no fewer than seventeen ships.

Pay of soldiers, sailors, &c.

We also learn from this record that the Prince of Wales, who distinguished himself greatly in the expedition, had as his wage 20*s.* per diem; the Bishop of Durham, 6*s.* 8*d.*; thirteen earls 6*s.* 8*d.* each; forty-four barons and bannerets, 4*s.*; one thousand knights, 2*s.* Esquires, constables, captains and leaders, of whom there were four thousand and twenty-two, received 1*s.* each. Masons, carpenters, smiths, en-

[1] It appears also from the warrants contained in a MS. of the Harleian Collection, No. 433, that besides the trade with Iceland from Bristol, many vessels went thither from the ports of Norfolk and Suffolk. See Appendix No. 12, p. 654.

gineers, tent-makers, miners, armed gunners, from 10*d.* to 3*d.* per day; mariners, 4*d.*; whilst the Welshmen on foot had 4*d.* and 2*d.* But this roll is also valuable for what it omits to tell us. Thus if it be the record of the fleet before Calais, we cannot doubt that England then had many other vessels of naval and commercial importance, for, even at this period of English history, we find organized piracy was not extinct: thus, in November 1347, a Spanish fleet piratically seized and sunk (for the two nations were then at peace) ten English ships, on which a fleet of fifty ships was immediately sent to sea to make reprisals. In this fleet the King himself, with the Prince of Wales, and many of the nobility, embarked, and attacked off Winchelsea forty large Spanish carracks, fully manned and armed, and richly laden with cloth and other valuable commodities, capturing no less than one-half, and sinking or disabling most of the others.

War renewed, A.D. 1354.

Unfortunately, in 1354, France again became the scene of war, which ended in the celebrated battle of Poictiers under Edward the Black Prince. In the campaign which followed the expiration of the truce, consequent upon the capture of the French king and the most of his army on the field of Poictiers, Edward collected a fleet of no less than eleven hundred vessels, in which were embarked one hundred thousand men, by whom Paris was successfully invaded; but at the siege of La Rochelle his good fortune deserted him, and his whole fleet, then under the command of the Earl of Pembroke, became the prize of the combined squadrons of France and of Castile. Although, on pressing demands for succour. Edward was enabled to fit out a fresh fleet of four hundred ships, of which he personally assumed the command, fortune and the winds proved adverse; and, after having been nine weeks at sea, he was unable to effect a landing on the French coast. Greater reverses followed, and the vast territories which the English possessed in France, and which they had maintained at so great a cost, soon sank into comparatively insignificant proportions. The death of the Black Prince, in 1376, preyed so heavily upon the king that he only survived him for twelve months; and in June, 1377, he died, after a reign of more than half a century, broken-hearted at the loss of his brave and distinguished son.

Death of Edward III., A.D. 1377.

State of the merchant navy during his reign.

Although Edward, throughout the whole of his long reign, had encouraged a liberal commercial policy, and had devoted, in an especial manner, his attention to naval affairs, it was impossible for maritime commerce to flourish in the midst of turmoil and war. England, though she lost the greater portion of her unnatural territory in France, may have preserved, as against the fleets of that country, her superiority at sea, and her wars with France on the one hand, and with Scotland on the other, may have developed the natural bull-dog courage of her seamen; but war, while it lasted, transferred the bulk of her over-sea carrying trade to the ships of Spain, Flanders, Holland, and of the Mediterranean nations, the whole energy of her people, which might have been better employed in the development of her natural resources and manufactures, having been devoted to war and to the creation of its instruments of destruction. Commissioners were even summoned to London to hold a sort of naval parliament during these struggles with France, and to render an account of the number of vessels which each port could supply to the naval force of the country. The press warrants authorized the appointed officers to seize not merely all vessels lying in the several ports, but every vessel which came from sea during the continuance of the commission; and these vessels were frequently compelled immediately to discharge the whole of their cargoes, although their last port of destination had not been reached, till Edward, during the greater part of his reign, had actually more than one-half of the merchant vessels of the kingdom in his service.[1] Operations such as these could not fail to seriously injure the maritime commerce of England, and, at the same time, afford encouragement to foreigners to absorb her over-sea carrying trade.

Loss sustained by war, and encouragement afforded thereby to foreign nations.

But although the ships of Spain and of the Mediterranean were at first the chief gainers by this state of things, those of the more northern nations of Europe soon became, from the same causes, the most formidable commercial rivals of England. While the English were engaged in unprofitable conflicts, they were steadily increasing in wealth and commercial greatness. Flemish ship-owners, taking advantage of the constant disputes of England with France and Scotland, acquired a considerable portion of the trade which would otherwise have fallen to England, and materially increased their business relations with the Mediterranean, with Egypt, and the East. Nor were they alone in their efforts. The advantages to be derived from distant commerce had

[1] Rymer's "Fœdera."

now become known to all the nations of the North; while they were rapidly gaining an insight into the most profitable mode of conducting it, and ascertaining the class of goods best adapted for the markets of the East, and the description of vessels most suitable for carrying on the trade.

Rapid increase of the trade of Flanders.

The people occupying the Netherlands, observing on the one hand how English genius and energy were being wasted in war, and, on the other, perceiving the vast progress of the Italian republics, and the wealth which their inhabitants had accumulated by their intercourse with the East, endeavoured, and with success, to imitate their example. Besides being carriers by sea they became themselves large manufacturers, opening up an extensive trade with Persia through the medium of Constantinople, and enjoying during the reign of Baldwin, Count of Flanders, an amount of prosperity second only to that of Venice, then the chief of the Italian republics. Protected by the franchises which their energy had wrung from their lords paramount, the inhabitants of Flanders were thus induced to apply themselves with vigour to commercial and manufacturing pursuits. Almost every town emulated its neighbour in works of usefulness or taste, exhibiting alike their habits of industry and their inventive genius. Their population increased to an astonishing extent, their wealth in a yet greater ratio; and the modern traveller may note in buildings still extant the superabundant pecuniary resources of that period, and the joint results of freedom from war and of unwearied industry.

Somewhere towards the close of the thirteenth century the merchant vessels of the Italian republics first began to frequent the markets of the Netherlands, and in 1318 Venetian ships brought to Antwerp spices, drugs, and silk-stuffs. The Hanseatic League, which had now become a commercial association of considerable importance, readily entered into relations with the Italian traders, so that the markets of Flanders became the best supplied of any in the north of Europe with the products and manufactures of the Mediterranean, Arabia and India, furnishing in exchange from their factories a variety of fine cloths in assortments adapted to the wants of the Eastern people. Thus, while England was distracted and impoverished by war, foreign merchants found safety and protection, and became greatly enriched, under the government of the Count of Flanders. The Flemings were satisfied with moderate duties. Whilst clearing their coasts of pirates and of hostile corsairs to the utmost extent in their power, they in all cases respected the property of shipwrecked vessels, which had too often been considered the prize of any promiscuous wrecker, and encouraged traders from all nations to frequent or settle on the banks of the Scheldt and the Meuse, many of whom realized large profits out of England's folly or misfortunes.

Trade between Italy and Flanders.

During the period of the commercial splendour of the Netherlands, Bruges and Antwerp were the chief entrepôts of the north of Europe for foreign goods. The former of these, in the course of the fourteenth century, had successfully negotiated favourable commercial treaties with the German empire, as also with Spain, Portugal, England, Scotland, and Ireland, which, in the following century, were extended with

Commercial importance of Bruges and Antwerp.

great advantage to Venice, Genoa, and Aragon; but, towards the close of the fifteenth and the beginning of the sixteenth century Bruges was surpassed by Antwerp, where, after the discovery of the passage to India by the Cape, Flemish vessels trading with the East landed their cargoes. Antwerp had, indeed, previously to that period enjoyed a large and profitable maritime commerce. Apart from the many advantages which the port possessed, the liberal policy established by the Duke of Brabant and the privileges he conferred on foreigners had induced English, German, Genoese, and Florentine merchants to make it a rendezvous for their ships, and a depôt for storing their goods, whence they were distributed throughout the continent and the whole of the north of Europe.

Wealth of Flanders, and extent of its manufactures and commerce.

Some idea may be formed of the importance of Flanders and the Low Countries, and how they then surpassed all the other nations of northern Europe in wealth and commercial enterprise, from the fact that Ghent had no less than forty thousand looms constantly at work in the manufacture of cotton and woollen cloths. She likewise supplied in great abundance, and of superior quality, serges, fustians, and tapestries. Courtray possessed, in the sixteenth century, six thousand weavers' looms; Ypres, four thousand, which produced very fine cloths, especially those of the scarlet colour so frequently specified in the tariffs of the countries of the South and East; while the Cloth Hall of that place was considered one of the most beautiful edifices of all Flanders. Oudenarde supplied tapestries which rivalled those of Arras: Tournay was famed for a peculiar description of serges. Louvain, though somewhat injured by the growth of other places, had employed in the fourteenth century four thousand looms; Mechlin, three thousand four hundred; and Brussels was, even at that early period, renowned for its woollen fabrics.[1]

Middleburgh, in Zealand, had then attracted to its market the merchants of Italy, Spain, and Portugal, who trafficked in its manufactures as well as in the productions generally of the country. Haarlem wove in its looms an extraordinary quantity of fine cloth and velvets much in request by the wealthy and prosperous Italian republics. The Low Countries received in return from Venice, spices, drugs, perfumes, cotton-prints, and silk stuffs. Genoa, Florence, Ancona, and Bologna, despatched also to Holland their silks, cloths of gold and silver, corselets, pearls, cotton, silk twist, alum, oils, and other articles of manufacture and produce. France sent to her ports the fine cloths of Paris and of Rouen, the common velvets of Tours, and the linen yarns of Lyons, besides wines in great abundance.

Special privileges to her merchants.

About this period the merchants of Brabant, Flanders, Zealand, and Holland, obtained from the king of France the privilege of establishing agencies in her chief commercial cities. Spain was likewise then largely engaged in over-sea commerce, and competed with the merchants of France and Italy in importing to the North sugar, cotton, dye-woods, and other articles of foreign growth; but it appears

[1] The great wealth of Flanders at this time is well shown by the fact that, in A.D. 1339, the Duke of Brabant paid Edward 50,000*l.* as the dowry for his daughter on her espousal to Prince Edward.—Rymer, Fœd. v. pp. 113, 118.

that they were so much molested by pirates, especially by the English, that in 1340 the cities of Ghent, Ypres, and Bruges, were obliged to seek and obtain from Edward III. a safe conduct[1] for the merchant shipping of Catalonia, Castille, and Majorca. In spite, however, of the king's protection, so daring and regardless of all law were these marauders, that a few years afterwards two vessels laden with valuable cargoes, and sent by the merchants of Barcelona and Valencia for Flanders, were captured by pirates from Bayonne, and carried into an English port.[2]

Progress of the Hanseatic League,

The Hanseatic League having now become by far the most important commercial association in Europe, its merchants entered with zeal into the rich and prosperous trade which made Flanders and the Low Countries so conspicuous in the annals of the commercial history of the period. More than seventy cities and towns were associated with the League. Its chief agencies, firmly established at Bruges in Flanders, at Bergen in Norway, and at Novgorod in Russia, entirely monopolized for many years the trade of these countries. Its agents and factors, all of whom were mercantile men, were guided by rules and instructions emanating from head-quarters at Lubeck, and from these they had no power to deviate unless under extraordinary circumstances. They were not permitted to have any common interest with strangers, or to trust their goods no board any other merchant ships than those belonging to the places with which the association was in league. Wholly

and its system of business.

[1] See a specimen of the "Safe Conduct" usually given on these occasions from a MS. in the Harleian Collection. Appendix No. 6.

[2] Rymer's Fœd. v. pp. 179–203.

occupied in extending their own privileges and in securing for themselves the business of any place where they had established themselves, they soon became obnoxious to their rivals, and their counting-houses were frequently exposed to popular fury. When unable to obtain redress for the outrages thus committed against it, the League closed its warehouses, and its members withdrew from the place. They could inflict no more severe punishment for the wrongs they had sustained; indeed, the withdrawal of their trade was often considered so great a calamity to the inhabitants, that large concessions were made and new privileges granted to induce their return. More than once the League transferred their quarters from Bruges to Dordrecht in Holland, and, on each occasion, obtained fresh grants before they agreed to resume business in the former city.

Its power too frequently abused.

But the League was unable to obtain at Bruges the power and influence it too frequently exercised at other places; for it had there to contend with men of business habits and of considerable wealth, whose firms had long conducted business with distant countries, and who held large stocks of the same description of merchandise from which the League itself derived its chief profits. Moreover, the Flemings of Bruges imported in their own ships, or in those of the nations with whom they were in direct correspondence, the products of the East, the manufactures of Italy, and the wines of the South. At other places, however, and especially in the North, where the League had comparatively few competitors and none whom it could not crush when necessary, it exercised, at times, an overbearing dominion. Arrogant and despotic, it even claimed the right of having submitted for its sanction the question of the succession of the Danish princes to the throne. At Bergen it persecuted with inveterate rancour any foreigner who attempted to oppose it in trade; and, at Novgorod, it behaved in such a manner as more than once to arouse the severe displeasure of the Russian government. Nor did it hesitate, when it suited its purpose, to carry on maritime wars, frequently exercising the power of an European sovereign; and more than one potentate of the North experienced the terrible ravages caused by the fleets of this powerful and haughty commercial association.[1]

[1] The following are the most important dates in connection with the history of this celebrated confederacy.

Great German Hansa established A.D. 1241, with the view of clearing the Baltic and adjacent coasts of pirates. Their first cities were Lubeck and Hamburg, then Bremen, ultimately Bergen and Brunswick; they were supported, generally, by the emperors as a commercial counterpoise to the feudal nobility—Lubeck was chosen as queen of the Hansa.

In 1281 the citizens of the Hanseatic League were placed on the same footing as those of London.

From A.D. 1303 to 1475 they possessed many houses in London, with a jury, half English, half foreign, to try their causes, and two English aldermen to act as their chiefs. This was the period of their greatest power. The power of the League began to decline in 1547, after the death in this year of Henry VIII. Though Edward VI. renewed their privileges, the English "Merchant Adventurers" proved too strong for them.

In 1666 their buildings of the Steel-yard were burnt in the great fire of London, but were reconstructed in 1680.

In 1852 the premises of the Hanseatic League were finally alienated, and are now built over by the Cannon Street railway station.

CHAPTER XIII.

Treaties with Spain and the merchants of Portugal—Early claim of the right of search—Restrictive laws against the English, and in favour of foreign traders—Accession of Richard II., A.D. 1377—Character of the imports from Italy—Sudden change of policy—First Navigation Act, A.D. 1381—A rage for legislation—Relaxation of the Navigation Act, A.D. 1382-8—Free issue of letters of marque; and of commissions for privateering—Special tax for the support of the Navy, A.D. 1377—Superiority of English seamen—Their intrepidity and skill—Chaucer's description of the seamen of his time—Henry IV., A.D. 1399-1413—Disputes between the Hanse and the English merchants—Agreement for guarding the English coasts—Henry V., A.D 1413: his liberal policy, and ambition—The extent of his fleet—Size and splendour of the royal ships—Prologue of the "Dominion of the Sea"—England first formally claims dominion of the sea, about A.D. 1416—Prerogatives conferred thereby—First accounts of revenue and expenditure, A.D. 1421—Law for the admeasurement of ships and coal barges—Henry VI. crowned, A.D. 1422—Marauding expedition of the Earl of Warwick—Distress among shipowners not royal favourites, A.D. 1461—Fresh legislative enactments—First "sliding scale" applied to the importation of corn—Relaxation of the laws by means of treaties, A.D. 1467—Treaties of reciprocity—Extension of distant maritime commerce, A.D. 1485—First English consul in the Mediterranean, A.D. 1490—The advantages derived from reciprocal intercourse.

Treaties with Spain and the merchants of Portugal.

ALTHOUGH Edward's thoughts had been directed almost exclusively to the wars with France and Scotland, he found time to extend English enterprise beyond its then comparatively narrow limits by an advantageous treaty with Spain[1] in A.D. 1351, consisting mainly of an offensive and defensive alliance, so that neither nation were to afford any assistance to their enemies, nor injure each other, the merchants and seamen of both countries having, at the same time, full liberty to proceed by land or sea wherever they pleased with their merchandise. Spanish property found in any vessel taken by the English was to be restored to the owners, and English property similarly situated to be respected by Spanish captors; moreover, Spanish fishermen were permitted to fish on the coasts of England and Brittany, and were allowed to enter any English ports on the payment of the same duties and customs to which English vessels were subjected. A nearly similar treaty was concluded with Portugal in the name of the merchants, mariners, and communities of Lisbon and Oporto, in which, however, curiously enough, no mention is made of the king of Portugal.[2]

Early claim of the right of search.

With the Flemings, treaties were made of a more restrictive character; thus, they were not to carry goods belonging to either the French or Spaniards; nor were the ship-owners of these countries allowed to become burgesses, so as to sail with Flemish papers. The papers of the Flemish ships were required to state the contents of their cargoes and their port of discharge, and to be attested by the magistrates of the port of departure, and also by the Count of Flanders. These treaties[3] contain the first suggestion of the simulation of a ship's papers, so

[1] Rymer's Fœd. v. p. 719; Macpherson i. pp. 544–5.

[2] In A.D. 1353; Rymer's Fœd. v. p. 763.

[3] Rymer's Fœd. vi. p. 659. The date of this famous treaty appears to be Aug. 4, 1370. Macpherson i. p. 577.

as to secure the ship and cargo from capture by making their owners denizens of a neutral power. Then arose, for the first time, those claims to the "Right of search" which England so long insisted upon, and maintained against the world in arms; claims not yet relinquished, though now rarely enforced. It must not, however, be supposed from these so far salutary regulations that Edward or his council had any knowledge of sound commercial legislation; for, in 1303, every English merchant was commanded to restrict his business to one commodity only, and to select at once the article he would trade in.[1] Five years afterwards they were by law prohibited from importing wine from Gascony, though, at that time, an English dependency;[2] while, with singular inconsistency, the Parliament of England, by an Act of 1378,[3] perceiving "the advantages derived from the resort of merchant strangers," gave foreign merchants permission to remain in the kingdom as long as they had occasion, and to buy or to sell, wholesale or retail, provisions, spices, fruits, furs, silk, gold and silver wire or thread, and numerous other small wares. The merchant strangers could likewise dispose of various descriptions of cloths, linen, canvas, and other bulky articles of manufacture, in any city, fair, or market, though in quantities of not less than a piece, it being the privilege of freemen only to dispose of them by retail as well as wholesale, with the exclusive right also of retailing wines, foreigners being restricted to their sale in the casks in which they were imported.

Restrictive laws against the English, and in favour of foreign traders.

Accession of Richard II., A.D. 1377.

[1] Stat. 37, Edw. III. cc. 5, 6.
[2] Stat. 42, Edw. III. c. 8.
[3] Stat. 1, 2, Rich. II. cc. 1, 2.

In consequence of these changes in the laws, the merchants of Genoa, Venice, Catalonia, Aragon, and of other western countries, brought their carracks, galleys, and vessels of various descriptions to the ports of England, where, disposing freely of their merchandise, they received in exchange, wool, tin, lead, and other articles the produce of that country: Southampton proved so convenient and favourite a port of resort, that a Genoese merchant of great opulence offered to raise it to a pre-eminence above any other port of Western Europe, as the depôt for the Oriental goods the Genoese had hitherto conveyed to Flanders, Normandy, and Bretagne, provided the king would allow him to store his goods in the castle of Southampton. We cannot doubt that had this offer been accepted, this port would have become, to the great advantage of England, the entrepôt for the supply of the northern markets of Europe. The foul murder of this enterprising stranger, in the streets of London, put an end to his wisely-imagined scheme, English merchants ignorantly supposing that their own trade would prosper the more by the prevention of his plan.[1]

Character of the imports from Italy.

From the accident of a Catalan ship, bound from Genoa to Sluys, the port of Bruges in Flanders, having been wrecked at Dunster in Somersetshire, an insight is obtained into the nature of the cargoes shipped at that period from Italy to Flanders. The merchants, in claiming the restoration of her cargo, enumerate its contents, viz., sulphur, wood, ginger, green and cured with lemon juice; raisins, writing paper, flax, white sugar, prunes, cinnamon, pepper,

Feb. 10th, 1380.

[1] Walsingham, pp. 227–553.

and a few other articles of minor importance;[1] thereby showing that this ship was freighted with the produce of India as well as of the Mediterranean. For all of these England might then have become the depôt, but her merchants could not, as yet, discern the advantages of a free intercourse with foreign nations; they still believed that a ruinous competition and the loss of their bullion would be the probable results; and in this spirit persuaded Parliament[2] to prohibit, unless under special circumstances, the exportation of bullion, either in the shape of coin or otherwise. They pretended, further, that under the existing regulations all their carrying trade passed into the hands of foreigners, who, in point of wealth, commercial experience, and command of shipping were far superior to themselves.

Sudden change of policy.

Doubtless, there was some justice in these complaints. Foreigners, by law, were able to undersell the English in their own markets, as they could bring goods from foreign ports at rates of freight which would have been unremunerative to the shipowners of England. The first Navigation Act[3] was consequently passed, but, as one extreme frequently begets another, this law proved to be one of the most restrictive kind against foreign vessels. What effect it produced upon English shipping we have been unable to ascertain, as there are no statistical returns nor accounts, however crude, now extant, of the shipping and commerce of this period; but, unless it enhanced the rates of freight to the

First Navigation Act, A.D. 1381.

[1] Rymer's Fœd., vol. vii. p. 233, and Macpherson i. p. 590. In A.D. 1383, a large Genoese ship bound to Flanders was driven by stress of weather into Sandwich. Walsingham, p. 296.

[2] Stat. 1–5, Rich. II. c. 2.

[3] Ibid. c. 3.

injury of the consumer, it could not have benefited those in whose interests it had been passed; while, on the other hand, any increase in the rates of freight would assuredly have tended to diminish the number of ships employed. The law of Edward I., in so far as it granted special privileges to foreign traders and their shipping, though it may have been necessary at the period, was certainly unjust towards the merchants and ship-owners of England; and it is not, therefore, surprising that they embraced the first opportunity to resort to extreme retaliatory measures against their wealthy and powerful foreign competitors.

Nevertheless, there was less wisdom in Richard's law, "to freight none but English ships," than there was in Edward's answer to a petition to expel foreign shipping from his ports, "I am convinced that merchant strangers are useful and beneficial to the greatness of the kingdom, and therefore I shall not expel them:" but, while Edward's policy encouraged the establishment of foreign trading associations in England, a clear advantage to the people generally, his ship-owners unquestionably suffered, as they had to struggle against laws the especial object of which had been the encouragement of foreign maritime enterprise. Edward would have displayed greater wisdom and sounder policy had he simply placed "merchant strangers" on an equal footing with his own people, and his country would have been spared the conflicts of navigation laws, which have raged with greater or less bitterness almost to the present day.

As was natural, a protective system once inaugurated, other classes besides the ship-owners claimed its presumed advantages.[1] Thus, immediately afterwards, Richard issued a general proclamation, prohibiting the exportation of corn or malt to any foreign country, except to the king's territories in Gascony, Bayonne, Calais, Brest, Cherburg, Berwick-upon-Tweed, and other forts held for his majesty.[2] Nor was this all; frivolous pretensions led to frivolous laws: thus, the fishmongers of London were prohibited from buying any fresh fish to sell again, except eels or pikes.[3] No cloths could be exposed to sale except of a manufacture sanctioned by law;[4] dealers in provisions of all kinds were placed under the control of the mayor and aldermen of London;[5] no one was permitted to carry corn and malt, or food, or refreshments of any kind to Scotland;[6] while laws were passed with the idle object of maintaining the relative positions of the different classes of society, as though their rulers were hopeless of talent, industry, or honesty reaping their natural reward. Parliament actually enacted that no servant should remove from one hundred to another, unless travelling upon his master's business; the wages for agricultural labour were fixed by law; children employed in husbandry up to twelve years of age were to be confined to that description of employment for life; farm servants were prohibited from carrying

A rage for legislation.

[1] Among other persons, the Pope succeeded in carrying from the town of Bristol, in 1382, a prodigious quantity of goods (the list is given in full in Rymer's Fœd. v. pp. 356–7, 577–90) *without paying any duty.*

[2] Rymer's Fœd., vol. vii. p. 369.

[3] Stat. 1–6, Rich. II. c. 11.

[4] 7 Rich. II. c. 9.

[5] 7 Rich. II. c. 11.

[6] Ibid. c. 14.

weapons, except bows and arrows for practice on Sundays and holidays; while enactments scarcely less absurd kept down the mechanics and labourers of the cities and boroughs.[1]

Relaxation of the Navigation Act, A.D. 1382–8.

But these evils found their natural remedy: the evasion of such restrictive laws was so general, that those affecting shipping were relaxed almost as soon as they had come into operation. In October, 1382, permission was given to English merchants in foreign ports, if they did not find in them sufficient native tonnage for their purpose, to ship their goods for England in foreign vessels;[2] aliens were allowed[3] to bring fish and provisions into any town or city, preparing them for sale in any manner they pleased; lastly, in 1388, it was enacted, in direct opposition to the recently adopted restrictive policy, that foreign merchants might sell their goods by retail or wholesale in London or elsewhere, any claims or privileges of corporations or individuals notwithstanding, while the late impositions on their merchandise were, at the same time, declared illegal and of no effect.[4]

It is alike curious and instructive to examine the many and inconsistent laws passed about this period to regulate maritime commerce, and to compel Englishmen as well as foreigners to conduct their business otherwise than they would have preferred for their own interests. Thus, in 1390,[5] foreign merchants bringing goods to England were required to give security to the officers of customs at the port of

[1] Stat. 12, Rich. II. cc. 3–9, A.D. 1388. These rigid rules seem to have arisen from a reaction against the concessions extorted from the feeble king by the insurrections of 1380 (Wat Tyler) and 1381.

[2] Stat. 1, Rich. II. c. 10.

[3] Stat. 1–6, Rich. II. c. 10.

[4] Stat. 2, Rich. II. cc. 7, 9.

[5] 14 Rich. II. c. 1.

landing, that they would invest half of the proceeds in wool, hides, cloths, lead, tin, or other English commodities; while another law passed in the same year[1] provided that a merchant, drawing a bill of exchange on Rome or elsewhere, should lay out the whole money received for it within three months on articles of English growth or manufacture. But perhaps the most curious and unmeaning Act of this year was one[2] which, in order "to keep up the price of wool," forbade any Englishman to buy that article from any one but the owners of sheep or of the tithes, unless in the staple, or to purchase wool, except on his own account for sale at the staple, or for manufacture into cloth: he was also forbidden to export either wools, hides, or wool-fells; although, by the same Act, full permission to do so when and how they pleased was granted to foreigners. By another Act, the merchants of England were obliged to export their merchandise in English vessels only; and the ship-owners were desired to carry them for "reasonable freights"!

Free issue of letters of marque,

Few reigns, in proportion to its extent, were likewise more prolific for the issue of letters of marque than that of Richard II. They were freely granted, for the purpose of revenging or compensating hostile aggressions on individuals, and also to enable the English creditor to recover debts, not only from foreign countries, but likewise from natives of his own country, whose property he could thus conveniently confiscate. Among the most conspicuous of these were the letters granted in 1399 to John de Waghen, of Beverley, against the subjects of the

and of commissions for privateering.

[1] 14 Rich. II. c. 2.

[2] 14 Rich. II. cc. 4, 5.

Count of Holland, because that prince had not compelled two of them to pay some money due to Waghen; while orders were actually issued to detain all vessels and property in England, belonging to Holland and Zealand, till the Count should determine this affair "according to justice."[1] The people of Dartmouth took the lead in these semi-piratical acts, as they held from the king a general privateering commission, whereby they brought away (1385) various rich vessels from the mouth of the Seine, one of which, according to the testimony of Walsingham,[2] bore the name of "Clisson's Barge"[3] (Clisson being at that time Constable of France), and "had not its equal in England or France;" while one of their merchants, with a fleet of his own, captured no less than thirty-three vessels, with fifteen hundred tuns of Rochelle wine.[4]

There can be no doubt that, at the period of Richard's accession, the English navy was in a very neglected state, and wholly unfit to protect even the comparatively small number of English merchant vessels then engaged in foreign commerce. France, with fifty ships under the command of Admiral Sir John de Vienne, had made a descent on Rye, and, after plundering that town and neighbourhood, had levied a contribution of one thousand marks upon the inhabitants of the Isle of Wight; on the same

[1] Fœdera, vol. viii. p. 96. It would seem that Waghen did not, on this occasion, gain his object, as his letters of marque were renewed in 1412 and 1414. Fœdera, v. p. 733.

[2] Fœdera, vol viii. p. 318.

[3] It is, perhaps, worth remarking that, through the whole of this period, the name of every vessel employed is carefully recorded on the MSS., these names being almost as various as those at present existing.

[4] Knyghton col. 27–35.

occasion pillaging and burning Hastings, Plymouth, and Dartmouth; while the Scots, under Mercer, one of their most daring adventurers, plundered every English vessel that fell in his way, and thereby realised enormous booty.[1] The English government became, at length, seriously alarmed, and were induced, in October 1377, to pass the first law on record, whereby dues were levied on all merchant vessels frequenting English ports, for the purpose of restoring and maintaining an efficient royal navy.[2] The only exceptions made were those in favour of ships bringing merchandise from Flanders to London, and of the traders from London to Calais with wool and hides; every other vessel leaving the Thames was required to pay sixpence per ton; while a similar tax, payable weekly, was levied on boats engaged in the herring-fisheries, and one-third that amount on all other fishing-boats. A monthly duty of 6*d.* per ton had likewise to be paid by colliers, as well as by all merchant vessels sailing from any port in England to Russia, Norway, or Sweden.[3] In the belief that the Navy thus created would be applied as proposed, this tax was readily voted and as willingly paid by the shipowners; but, in the end, it was appropriated to entirely different purposes. There seems, in those days, to have been a restless desire, scarcely now wholly forgotten, to interfere with the affairs of other

Special tax for the support of the Navy, A.D. 1377.

[1] Sir H. Nicolas, from the various chronicles, &c., of the time, has well traced the course of this French plundering expedition. (Hist. Roy. Navy, ii. p. 260–264.) Mercer was ultimately crushed, not by the "Royal Navy," but by the courage and power of a London citizen, John Philpott, who was created twice Lord Mayor in 1377 and 1378. Walsingham, p. 213.

[2] Fœd., vol. vii. p. 220.

[3] Rot. Parl. iii. 63.

countries. Thus the "grand fleet," when equipped, sailed under the command of the Duke of Lancaster and besieged St. Malo ineffectually, the natural result being that French cruisers ravaged the coasts of Cornwall, while a combined fleet of French and Spanish galleys sailed up the Thames to Gravesend, plundering and destroying the towns and villages along the Kentish shores.[1]

Here again the merchant service came to the timely aid of the state.[2] The hostile galleys, on their way down the Channel with the view of ravaging every defenceless place on the coast, were met by a fleet of west-country merchantmen,[3] who had united for their mutual defence, and thus, for the present, checked their further course. Though their vessels were generally much smaller than those of the Spaniards and often more than over-matched by their superior equipment, the English far surpassed the seamen of the south in daring skill and hardihood. By the boldness of their attack, especially during inclement weather, they often, as in the present instance, achieved victories over their better found and more scientific adversaries. They had, however, a long career of thankless, though of noble and patriotic, struggles. Heavily taxed for the maintenance of a fleet, too often used for purposes of no concern to the nation, they were still obliged to create one of their own to protect their commerce and to defend their homes, at a time, too, when legislative enactments threw nearly the whole of

Superiority of English seamen.

[1] Rot. Parl. ii. 42, iii. 46, quoted by Nicolas, ii. pp. 274–5.

[2] Here, again, the munificence of John Philpott is especially noticed. Walsingham, p. 248.

[3] In July 1380. Walsingham, p. 249.

their carrying trade into the hands of aliens and strangers.[1]

Their intrepidity and skill.

But while narrow prejudices and mistaken legislation depressed the maritime commerce of the country, English sailors continued to maintain, in spite of every national blunder and vicissitude, their superiority in activity and skill. During the whole period from the Conquest to the end of the fourteenth century, they showed the highest genius and daring in navigating their ships, and more and more courage in their contests with the French, as the sphere of their efforts became extended. The testimony of contemporary historians, foreign as well as English, attest this opinion; and the imperishable glory and renown of their exploits, under circumstances of the most adverse character and in the face of apparently insurmountable difficulties, contributed in a great measure to the extension of the maritime power of England over that of most other nations. The splendid victory of England off the Swyn, in 1340, had been mainly owing to the superiority in naval tactics of her seamen, a race, it must be remembered, not trained to fight in the disciplined manner of modern times, but, as has so often been the case on subsequent occasions, chiefly distinguished for their bravery, hearty exertions, and extraordinary, but natural skill.[2]

[1] The records of Parliament, at this period, are each year full of these natural complaints, to which Richard and his ministers appear to have paid little attention. See, especially, Rot. Parl. iii. p. 102. s a. 1382.

[2] Rymer, Fœd. v. pp. 195–97. Knyghton col. 2577. Stowe, p. 369. This is believed to have been the first naval victory gained by the king in person since the days of Alfred. Sir H. Nicolas suggests that the gold nobles struck by Edward III. in 1344, on which the king is

Chaucer's description of the seamen of his time.

Among the most graphic descriptions of the character of the English seamen of the fourteenth century, is that of the renowned Chaucer[1] in his "Prologue to the Canterbury Tales." Although it is the picture of a hardened, reckless "felawe," who made no scruple to drown the prisoners whom he captured—"by water he sent them home to every land"—it affords an excellent insight into the manners and customs, as well as the dress, of the seamen of his time. Indeed, the poet's description gives a good idea of the free-and-easy character of seamen at all periods of English history; a class of men scarcely less distinct and peculiar in their habits now than then; and while equally expert and ready in tempestuous weather, no less fond, when at ease on shore, of "their draught of wyn," or of their glass of grog.

"A schipman was ther, wonyng fer by Weste:
For ought I woot, he was of Dertemouthe
He rood upon a rouncy, as he couthe,
In a gown of faldying to the kne.
A dagger hangyng on a laas hadde he
Aboute his nekke under his arm adoun.
The hoote somer had maad his hew al broun;

---

represented standing in a large ship, were struck in allusion to, if not in commemoration of, this action. (Hist. Roy. Navy, ii. p. 223.) Selden quotes the lines:

"For foure things our noble sheweth to me,
King, shippe and sword, and power of the sea."
Mare Clausum ii. c. 25.

The same writer also gives this line:

"Thus made he *Nobles* coyned of record,"

in honour, apparently, of the capture of Calais A.D. 1347.

[1] Chaucer is generally believed to have been born in 1328, and to have died in 1400: it is certain that he flourished in the time of Edward III. and of Richard II. The orthography of this extract is from Bell's ed. of Chaucer, 1855.

And certeinly he was a good felawe.
Ful many a draught of wyn had he drawe
From Burdeux-ward, whil that the chapman sleep.
Of nyce conscience took he no keep.
If that he foughte, and hadde the heigher hand,
By water he sente hem hoom to every land.
But of his craft to rikne wel the tydes,
His stremes and his dangers him bisides,
His herbergh and his mone, his lodemenage,
Ther was non such from Hulle to Cartage.
Hardy he was, and wys to undertake;
With many a tempest hadde his berd ben schake.
He knew wel alle the havenes, as thei were,
From Scotlond to the Cape of Fynestere,
And every cryk in Bretayne and in Spayne;
His barge y-clepud was the Magdelayne."

It was, however, impossible, even with the aid of such daring and skilful mariners, for England to maintain her position at sea, or her commerce, in the face of the laws we have attempted briefly to describe, and the lawless acts of too many of those of her people engaged in maritime pursuits.

Henry IV. A.D. 1399–1413.

The reign of Henry IV., opening with conspiracies at home and troubles abroad, afforded at first little hope of improvement in the laws affecting English maritime commerce; that monarch, however, was able to make arrangements with Prussia so as to restore the long interrupted commercial intercourse between the two countries;[1] while two years later he concluded a treaty with the Hanse Towns. By this treaty were also settled many claims of those merchants and ship-owners against English cruisers, who, however, in turn, alleged that their property had been captured and destroyed by the Prussians, and

[1] Voluminous papers on this subject are given in Hakluyt, vol. i. p. 157, *et seq.*; with the letter of Henry IV. to the master-general of Prussia, together with the treaty itself, and the Hanse-Towns agreement.

their countrymen taken from their ships and thrown into prison. The merchants of Lynn, especially, "complained pitifully[1] that four of their ships, with cargoes on board, consisting chiefly of cloth and wine, were captured on their way to Prussia, some of their people being slain, while some were grievously injured, and others put to extreme ransoms."

Disputes between the Hanse and the English merchants.

On the other hand, the complaints of the Hanse Towns merchants were not confined to losses sustained by the piratical acts of the cruisers, who, after due inquiry, really appear to have been the greatest delinquents; they alleged also not a few infringements by English traders of their chartered privileges. They urged that many new charges and duties had been exacted from their goods and shipping; that, besides the ancient duty of 3*s.* 4*d.* upon every sack of wool, a charge of 1*s.* 7*d.* was imposed by the town of Calais; that the officers of the Customs over-rated the value of their goods, exacting duties for various kinds of cloths formerly exempted by the charter of merchants; that, in order to remove their goods from one port of England to another, they had to pay duties twice over; and that needless delays were created, whereby they often lost the market for their goods, which were, further, sometimes damaged by lying three or four weeks on the wharves. This, they asserted, was mainly due to the neglect of the officers of the Customs. The English commissioners retorted that the Hanse merchants had combined to destroy the commerce and manufactures of England by

[1] Rymer's Fœdera, vol. viii. pp. 601-603. Hakluyt, vi. pp. 154–157. There seems some doubt as to the date of this transaction. See Macpherson, i. p. 625.

refusing to hold intercourse with their merchants in the Hanse Towns, or to buy English cloth from Englishmen, and that they had even imposed fines on those who had English cloth in their possession. They accused them also of passing the goods of merchants not belonging to the Hanse under their name, to avoid paying the proper duties.[1]

These differences, which had their origin mainly in absurd laws framed to protect one nation from competition with another, though, in reality, by endeavouring to put a stop to all intercourse between nations, affording encouragement to violent dissensions, private warfare and piracy, were at last settled by the payment of modified sums to each of the claimants; but while England had to pay 32,326 nobles, there was found to be due to her people only 766! a pretty convincing proof that she had been by far the greater delinquent in fitting out these piratical expeditions.

Agreement for guarding the English coasts.

Although Henry made extraordinary exertions to provide England with a royal navy, the entire guardianship of the sea from May 1406 to Michaelmas of the following year was entrusted to her merchant vessels,[2] the law requiring their owners "to maintain certain ships on the seas." They were further empowered to select out of their body two fit persons, to whom the king granted commissions to act as his admirals. As a recompense for their services, the owners of the vessels thus employed were allowed

[1] Macpherson has collected from various sources all the details of the disputes between the Hanse and English merchants, of which the above is a condensed notice, vol. i. pp. 620–623, s.a. 1408–9.

[2] Rymer's Fœd., vol. viii. p. 437.

three shillings per tun on all wines imported during that period, and twelve pence per pound on the value of all other merchandise exported or imported, with the fourth part of the then existing subsidy on wool and leather. Although the king complained shortly after these privileges were granted that "they had not sufficiently guarded the seas according to contract," the system of entrusting, if not wholly, at least in a great measure, the protection of its shores and maritime commerce to its merchant ship-owners, prevailed for many years: indeed, as already shown, it was upon them that England mainly depended in her maritime wars. In those early days they had also their own wrongs to redress as well as those of the nation.

Henry V., A.D. 1413: his liberal policy,

When Henry V. ascended the throne, he, according to Rymer, confirmed the privileges which had been granted by some of his predecessors to foreign merchants and shipping frequenting his kingdom.[1] From the same authority[2] we learn that the king, who held the sole right of drawing bills of exchange for the use of persons visiting the papal court, Venice, and other places abroad, leased this right for three years at the annual rental of 133*l.* 16*s.* 8*d.*, afterwards increased to 208*l.*, the contractor being bound not to export any gold or silver on account of the bills he drew. Merchants, however, trading with these places were allowed to draw bills for their merchandise, but for no other purpose. In his reign also the exemption from the obligation of carrying the staple goods to Paris, granted to the

[1] Rymer's Fœdera, v. ix. p. 26–72. [2] Ibid. v. ix. p. 13, ap.

commercial states of Italy and Spain by the act of the second year of Richard II., was renewed.

The short and, as it has been called, "brilliant reign of Henry V." was disastrous to the commercial interests of England, in that it was devoted more to foreign conquests than to the internal affairs of his people. He had, indeed, hardly ascended the throne (March and April 1413), when he resolved to assert his claim to the crown of France by force of arms. Every vessel in England, of twenty tons and upwards, was pressed into the service and ordered to assemble at London, Southampton, Sandwich, Winchelsea, and Bristol, ready for immediate action. Nor could the ports of England supply his wants. Commissioners were despatched to engage on hire whatever vessels could be obtained in Holland and Zealand; his whole force, when collected ready for the invasion of France, consisting of fifteen hundred vessels, English and foreign, manned to a large extent by crews collected through the instrumentality of the press-gang.[1]

and ambition.

Perhaps no finer fleet had before been despatched from the shores of England, but it was created at an enormous cost. In vain the Parliament remonstrated against the outlay, and "humbly" represented that the conquest of France would be the ruin of England, while the merchants and ship-owners, exhausted by former unprofitable wars, were equally opposed to what they considered a vain-glorious expedition. But Henry paid no attention to either their remonstrances or prayers. He had fixed his mind upon the expedition. The expense was to him a matter

The extent of his fleet.

[1] Fœdera, ix. pp. 215, 216–218, 238. Walsingham, p. 390.

of little or no consideration. Observing that the vessels brought to the assistance of the French by the Castilians and Genoese were larger and better than any he possessed, he ordered to be built at Southampton[1] the "Trinity," "Holy Ghost," and the "Grâce de Dieu," vessels said, from their size, rig, and power, to have been "such as were never seen in the world before."[2] But his two flag-ships, styled the king's chamber and his hall, in one of which he embarked, were, from the descriptions preserved of them, the most magnificent of his fleet. Adorned with purple sails, whereon the arms of England and France were embroidered, they represented this proud monarch's court and palace upon the sea.

Size and splendour of the royal ships.

Although Henry doubtless achieved his object by restoring Normandy to the dominion of England, the success of his expedition, however barren in its ultimate results, was mainly due to his command of the Channel.

A document in metrical verse, illustrative of the war, and written about this period, gives so graphic an account of the then existing state of maritime commerce, and so well points out the wisdom of England in maintaining her supremacy at sea, that a few extracts from it cannot fail to be interesting and instructive to our readers. It pro-

[1] The same names of ships, and the place of their construction (then called Hampton), are given in the "Dominion of the Sea," as preserved in Hakluyt, vol. i. See also the Chronicle of the Church of the Holy Trinity at Winchester, in which, too, is a notice of the action off Harfleur A.D. 1416. Sir H. Nicolas, quoting from the "Issue Roll" of Henry V., states that 496*l.* was paid at Southampton for the "Holy Ghost," and 500*l.* for the "Grâce Dieu;" but this could have been only a portion of the real cost of these ships. (Hist. Roy. Navy, ii. 406.)

[2] Hakluyt, vol. i. pp. 187–203.

bably contains the views of the most enlightened men in England on the impolicy of the course of continental conquest on which Henry had embarked. This curious production, which occupies twenty-one or twenty-two folios of closely printed black letter in Hakluyt, and has been frequently referred to and quoted by writers upon English shipping, is entitled—

"Here beginneth the Prologue of the Processe of the *Libel of English policie, exhorting all England to keepe the sea, and namely the narrowe sea*; and shewing what profite commeth thereof, and also what worship and saluation to *England* and to all Englishmen."

Prologue of the "Dominion of the Sea."

However much the people of England may at the time have been flattered by Henry's heroic deeds of arms, it is evident from this poem that a large class were thoroughly convinced of the impolicy of the aggressions of their monarch. But the all-important point the author has in view is the necessity of maintaining the command of the Channel as the only true safeguard of the shores of England; and almost every statesman since then has endeavoured to carry into effect what the author in his quaint old language so strongly recommends:

"The true Processe of English policie
Of otterward to keepe this regne in
Of our *England*, that no man may deny.
Ner say of *sooth* but it is one of the best,
Is this, that who seeth South, North, East and West,
Cherish marchandise, keepe the admiraltie;
That we bee Masters of the narrowe sea.

"For *Sigismond*[1] the great Emperour
Wich yet reigneth, when he was in this land

[1] The Emperor Sigismund came to London May 7, 1416, to try to make peace between England and France.

With King *Henry* the Fift, Prince of Honour
Here much glory, as him thought, he found,
A mightie land which had take in hand
To werre in *France*, and make mortalitie,
And euer well kept round about the sea.

"And to the king thus hee sayd: My Brother,
(When hee perceiued two Townes *Caleis* and *Douer*)
Of all your Townes to chuse of one and other,
To keepe the sea and soone to come ouer
To werre outwards and your regne to recouer:
Keepe these two Townes sure, and your Maiestee
As your tweyne eyne: so keepe the narrowe sea.

"For if this sea be kept in time of werre,
Who can heere passe without danger and woe?
Who may escape, who may mischiefe differre?
What Marchandie may forby bee agoe?
For needs hem must take trewes every foe:
Flanders and *Spain* and othere, trust to mee,
Or ellis hindred all for this Narrow sea.

"Therefore I cast mee by a little writing
To shewe at eye this conclusion,
For conscience and for mine acquiting
Against God and ageyne abusion,
And cowardise, and to our enemies confusion.
For FOURE things our Noble sheweth to me,
KING, SHIP, and SWERD, and POWER of the SEA."

In the first chapter of his poem the author gives a very lucid account of the course of the commerce then carried on between England, Spain, and Flanders. No mention is made of France, as England was then engaged in hostilities with that country; but from Spain English merchants imported figs, raisins, wine, dates, licorice, oil, grains, white pastile soap,[1] wax, iron, wool, wadmolle, goat fell, saffron, and quicksilver; and, from Flanders, fine cloth of Ypres and of Courtray were carried in Spanish ships homewards, with fustians and also linen cloth. These cargoes requiring necessarily to pass between Calais and Dover going and coming, Spain and

[1] Query, Castile soap.

Flanders being then mutually dependent, while the raw material of the Flemish manufactures came from England, it followed that the interest of both these powers lay in keeping peace with that country, or the Flemish factories would be starved. In the second chapter the trade with Portugal is described. It represents that Portugal is England's friend, her shipping resorting thither to trade in wines, wax, grain, figs, raisins, dates, honey, Cordovan leather, hides, &c., all of which merchandize were carried in great quantities to Flanders, justly described as the largest "staple" or market at that time in all Christendom. But Portugal is accused of being changeable; "she is in our power while we are masters of the narrow seas."

In the third chapter, it is stated that the people of Bretagne were great rovers on the sea, and had often done much havoc on the coasts of England, landing, killing, and burning to her great disgrace, but that they durst not be her open foes so long as she had possession of the narrow seas. The vigour of Edward III. is extolled in granting letters of reprisals to the seamen of Dartmouth, Plymouth, and Fowey, by which the pirates from Brittany, especially those from St. Malo, were extirpated. The trade of Scotland is reported to have consisted of wool, wool-fells, and hides; but her wool was sent to Flanders to be dressed, as it was not equal in quality to the English wool, with which it was often mixed before being manufactured. Scotland, we are also informed, brought from Flanders mercery and haberdashery in great quantities: moreover, one-half of these Scottish ships were then generally laden home from Flanders with cart-wheels and wheel-barrows. The writer remarks that the Scotch ships must pass by the English coast on their way to Flanders, and might therefore be easily intercepted,

> "——If they would not our friends bee
> We might lightly stoppe hem in the sea."

The trade of the Easterlings,[1] Prussia, and Germany, consisted of copper, beer, bacon, bow staves, steel, wax, pottery, pitch and tar, fir, oak planks, Cologne thread, wool cards, fustian, canvas, and buckram, exported to Flanders; whence were carried back silver plate and wedges, and silver (which came to Flanders in great plenty from Bohemia and Hungary); also woollen cloths of all colours. "And they aventure full greatly unto the Bay For salt that is needefull;"

> "They should not passe our streems withouten leve
> It would not be, but if we should hem greue."

There then follows a description of the commerce of Genoa, whose merchants resorted to England in great caracks "arrayed withouten lacke," with cloth of gold, silk, black pepper, woad, wool, oil, cotton, rock-alum, taking as a return cargo, wool, and woollen cloth made with home-spun wool, proceeding frequently from England to Flanders, then the chief market of north-eastern Europe.

> "If they would be our full enemies,
> They should not passe our streems with marchandise."

[1] The ancient word Easterlings or Osterlings (whence Sterling) signifies from the east, and embraces the inhabitants of all the seventy-two Hanse Towns.

The trade with Venice is next detailed in original and explicit terms, and extends to great length.

> "The great Galees of *Venice* and *Florence*
> Be well laden with things of complacence
> All spicery and of grossers ware:
> With sweete wines all maner of chaffare,
> Apes and Japes and marmusets tayled,
> Nifles and trifles that little have avayled:"

and so forth.

The author then alludes to the frauds committed by the Italian bankers and factors, all which he strongly and with the deep feelings of patriotic prejudice animadverts upon and condemns. He shows the disadvantages English merchants laboured under in point of trade with foreign markets. He claims at least reciprocal advantages, and after showing how valuable the trade is likely to become, he concludes—

> "Keep then the sea, shippes should not bring ne fetch,
> And then the carreys wold not thidre stretch:
> And so those marts wold full evil thee,
> If we manly kept about the sea."

In his eighth chapter the author describes the trade of Brabant, Zealand, and Hainault, both by sea and land, and expatiates upon the value of English merchandise, adding that the English are the best customers at all the foreign fairs;

> "As all the goods that come in shippes thider,
> Which Englishmen bye most and bring it hither."

He laments with deep regret the neglect of English shipping for the guard of the sea.

> "A prince riding with his swerd ydraw
> In the other side sitting, soth it is in saw
> Betokening good rule and punishing

In very deed of *England*, by the king.
And it is so, God blessed mought he bee.
So in likewise I would were on the sea,
By the *Noble*, that swerde should haue power,
And the ships on the sea about us here."

Throughout the whole document the dominion of the sea is urgently enforced, and the insolence of certain ships of the Hanse Towns loudly complained of. The folly of English merchants colouring the goods of foreigners is also condemned. The ninth chapter relates to the trade with Ireland, of which it furnishes a copious account. The author mentions gold and silver ore as being produced there in large quantities, and urges the importance of quelling the wild Irish, and keeping the country in strict obedience, all which, he states, cannot be done without good ships, and being masters of the seas. The trade of Iceland is also mentioned, and its important fisheries; and here follows a distinct mention of the mariner's compass, as having been recently introduced by merchant mariners.

There can be no doubt that the mariner's compass was at this period in general use as the "shipman's card" on board of English vessels; and further, that English seamen were extensively employed in the trade with Spain and Brittany.

"Of *Island* to write is litle nede
Saue of stock-fish: yet forsooth indeed
Out of Bristowe (Bristol), and costes many one,
Men haue practised *by nedle and by stone*[1]

---

[1] It used to be thought that "lodemenage" had some connection with the mariner's compass, but this is not the case. The word is a hybrid, part English, part French, and means "pilotage." It is used several times in that sense in 3 George i. c. 13. Compare with it,

Thiderwardes, within litle a while,
Within twelue yeer, and without perill
Gon and come, as men were wont of old
Of *Scarborough* unto the costes cold.
And nowe so fele shippes this yeere there ware
That moch losse for unfreyght they beare."

This chapter concludes with some remarks upon the importance of Calais, criticising several incidents in the reigns of Edgar, Edward III., and Henry V., and concluding with a most energetic exhortation to all English statesmen to consider the deep national importance of his arguments concerning English commerce, navigation, and the dominion of the sea, upon which he re-asserts that the peace, prosperity, and security of their island essentially depend.

"The ende of battaile is peace sikerly,
And power causeth peace finally.
Keepe then the sea, about in special
Which of *England* is the town-wall.
As though *England* were likened to a citie,
And the wall enuiron were the sea.
Kepe then the sea, that is the wall of *England*:
And then is *England* kept by Goddes hande;
That as for any thing that is without,
England were at ease, withouten doubt."

That the author of these curious metrical rhymes represented the feelings of the age is, in some measure, confirmed by the fact that, towards the close of the reign of Henry V., the Parliament of England, for the first time, asserted their right to the dominion of the sea in all their more important formal documents, or rather to its sovereignty. "The Commons do pray," ran these documents, "that seeing our

England first formally claims dominion of the sea, about A.D. 1416.

"Loadsman" (the priest), "Loadstar," and "Loads-stone," all agreeing in their composition with "load," *i.e.* some leading or guiding influence.

sovereign lord the king and his noble progenitors have ever been lords of the sea," &c., &c. Nor were these claims, then, whatever they may have been in former ages, nominal titles. Without citing the opinions of Hugo Grotius, and other jurisconsults, on the necessity of a prince proclaiming by an overt act that he is lord of the sea, there can be no doubt that the English, from the earliest periods, did at least assert, if unable at all times to maintain, the dominion of the English Channel and a large portion of the North Sea. In the year 1674[1] the extent of the dominions of the British sovereign in the eastern and southern sea was ascertained and admitted to reach from the middle point of the land of Vans Staten, in Norway, to Cape Finisterre in Spain; a large extent of sea which England then asserted, and has since the reign of Charles II. maintained by many hard-fought naval engagements. Indeed, so far back as the reign of King John, we have already noticed, in the records of his marine laws, one to the effect that if a lieutenant of a king's ship encounter any vessel or vessels, laden or unladen, that will not strike and veil their bonnets[2] at the command of the lieutenant of the king, they were to be taken and condemned.

[1] See Treaty of Charles II. with the States-General.

[2] "The bonnet is belonging to another saile, and is commonly used with none but the missen, maine, and fore-sailes, and the sprit-sailes. I have seene, but it is very rare, a *top-saile bonnet*, and hold it very useful in an easie gale, quarter-winde, or before a wind. This is commonly one-third as deepe as the saile it belongs to; there is no certaine proportion, for some will make the maine-sail so deep, that with a showele bonnet, they will latch all the mast without a drabbler." Manwayring, Sir H., "Seamen's Dictionary presented to the late Duke of Buckingham," Lond. 4to, 1644. See also "The Sailor's Word-Book," by Admiral W. H. Smyth, Lond., 1867.

That this right was not then a barren title may be assumed from the fact, that it involved mercantile interests of the most important character, within the limits named, which were guarded with the utmost jealousy for centuries. The prerogative claimed by the crown included, 1st, the royalty of granting the liberty of fishing for pearl, coral, amber, and all other precious commodities. 2nd. The power of granting licences to fish for whales, sturgeon, pilchard, salmon, herring, and all other fish whatsoever, as then exercised in Spain and elsewhere. 3rd. The power of imposing tribute and custom on all merchant ships, and fishermen, trading and fishing within the limits of the sea, subjected to private dominion, in the same manner as if enjoying the state's protection in its dominion on land. 4th. The regular execution of justice, by protecting the innocent, and punishing delinquents for all crimes committed within the limits described, protection being due to all who paid homage and tribute. 5th. The power of granting free passage through such sea to any number of ships of war belonging to any foreign prince, or of denying the same according to circumstances, in like manner as foreign potentates may grant or deny free passage of foreign troops through their territories by land. This right being exercised in peace as well as during war, all foreign vessels whatsoever, whether ships of war or others, navigating within those seas, and there meeting any of the ships of war or others bearing the colours of the sovereign of such seas, "are required to salute the said ships of war by striking the flag, or lowering," as we have just mentioned, "one of her sails, by which

Prerogatives conferred thereby.

sort of submission the saluters are put in remembrance that they have entered a territory in which there is sovereign power and jurisdiction to be acknowledged, and protection to be expected."[1]

Although from the earliest periods of history successive nations have periodically claimed the sovereignty of certain seas, England appears to have been the only one of either ancient or modern times which not merely asserted and maintained that power in the English Channel and neighbouring waters, but was fully acknowledged to possess it by other nations, who admitted "the striking or veiling the bonnets" to be a ceremonious homage in recognition of her absolute sovereignty.

First accounts of revenue and expenditure, A.D. 1421.

Towards the close of the reign of Henry V. an account is, for the first time, published of the revenue of the kingdom. It appears to have amounted, in 1421, to the sum of 55,743*l.*, obtained chiefly, if not altogether, by duties upon commerce; the customs and subsidy upon wool alone amounting to more than one-half, or 30,000*l.*; while the small customs, and a duty of twelve pence in the pound in value on other goods, realized 10,675*l.* Out of that year's revenue there was expended no less than 38,619*l.*[2] in the custody and defence of Calais, Scotland, and Roxburgh, and their "marches;" while the custody

[1] Ordinance of Hastings. Sir Harris Nicolas has thrown some doubt on this ordinance of King John, because we have no record that he was ever at Hastings; on the other hand, Sir Travers Twiss—who is supported in his view by Sir Duffus Hardy—shows that he may easily have been there, and issued it in the second year of his reign, A.D. 1201. (Black-Book, p. L.)

[2] This heavy expense doubtless applies to a time of war; but the return speaks also of previous debts of Henry IV. on Calais which had not been paid off.

and defence of England and Ireland were maintained for the comparatively moderate sum of 6,990*l.* The officers of customs at London and the outposts received 821*l.* for their services, but the salaries of "dukes, earls, knights, esquires, and the abbess of Shene," amounted to 7,751*l.* A sum of 4,370*l.* was likewise charged on the customs for "annuities," but no mention is made of how they were appropriated. A lump sum of 3,507*l.* appears to have been paid, without distinguishing the items, "to the king's and queen's household and wardrobe; the king's works; the new tower at Portsmouth; the clerk of the king's ships; the king's lions, and the constable of the tower; artillery; the king's prisoners, ambassadors, messengers, parchment, and the Duchess of Holland;"[1]—a curious enough medley, but perhaps not more promiscuous than some of the estimates of our own time, frequently smuggled in one sum through Parliament, from the difficulty and delicacy of defending many of them if produced in detail.

Law for the admeasurement of ships and coal barges.

Immediately before the close of the reign of Henry V., an Act[2] was passed requiring all ships to be measured according to prescribed forms, so as to ascertain their tonnage or capacity, and preclude the possibility of one ship deriving advantage over another. By a clause in this Act, the barges, or "keels," then employed in the conveyance of coals from the colliery wharves to the ships in the Tyne were also required to be measured and marked by the Crown. From that day, until now, every keel contains 21 tons 4 cwt. of coals, and in the north of

[1] Fœdera, vol. v. p. 113.
[2] Act 9 Henry V. Stat. 1, ch. 10.

England the capacity of a ship is still better undertood by the number of keels she can carry than by her registered tonnage.

Henry VI. crowned, A.D. 1422. It is not our province to notice the long and terrible wars between the Houses of York and Lancaster which followed the accession of the infant Henry VI. to the throne of England.[1] War, in all cases, would seem to have encouraged hordes of marauders to fit out armed vessels, too frequently under the pretence of the national defence, but practically for their own gain and aggrandisement. But the war which now raged for supremacy between the rival claimants to the crown of England was, perhaps, the one of all others which offered the greatest encouragement to these disgraceful expeditions. Forms of licence were hardly necessary, as the flags of Lancaster or of York were sufficient covers to many crimes. Thus, under plea of aiding the cause of the House of York, the Earl of Warwick, "the king-maker," fitted out a fleet on his own account, with which he attacked, in the Straits of Dover, a fleet of *Genoese merchantmen* bound for Lubeck, with a cargo of Spanish merchandise, of which he captured six, rendered worthless twenty-six, slaughtered one thousand of their crews, and plundered merchandise to the value of 10,000*l.* sterling, with the loss, it is said, of only fifty of his own men. In the face of such an act as this, perpetrated by one of the most exalted of the English nobility, who filled the highly responsible office of

Marauding expedition of the Earl of Warwick.

[1] To what extent England had been depopulated by the wars with France, may be seen from the fact noticed in the Act 9 Henry V. Stat. 1-5, that the sheriffs were to remain in office, instead of being changed annually, because a sufficient number of persons duly qualified for the office could not be found.

governor of Calais, the reader of English history need not feel surprised at the acts of piracy which too frequently disgrace its pages. On the dethronement of Henry VI., after an inglorious reign of nearly forty years, the Earl of March, who had shortly before become Duke of York by his father's death on the field of Wakefield, was proclaimed king of England as Edward IV.

Distress among ship-owners, not royal favourites. A.D. 1461.

These intestine commotions and civil wars, combined with the impolicy of the crown, had reduced the merchant shipping of England to a state of great distress. A few merchants, however, during the long but unfortunate reign of Henry VI. had been, by special favour, enabled to realize large fortunes. John Taverner, a ship-owner of Kingston-upon-Hull, having built in 1449 one of the largest merchant vessels of the period, received a licence to take on board wool, tin, lambs'-skins, hides, or any other merchandise, the property of English or foreign merchants, and carry them to Italy, on "paying alien's duty."[1] William Canynge, an eminent merchant of Bristol, who sent his factors to foreign parts, was likewise favoured by letters from the king to the grand master of Prussia and the magistrates of Danzig, recommending to their good offices the representatives of "his beloved and honourable merchant."[2] Although prohibited by Act of Parliament, Canynge, when mayor of Bristol, on account of services said to have been rendered to the king, had a special licence to employ two ships, of whatever burden he pleased, during two years, in the trade between England and Iceland and Finmark, and

[1] Fœdera, xi. p. 258. [2] Ibid. xi. pp. 226–27.

to export any species of goods not restricted by the staple of Calais.[1] Canynge appears to have been one of the most important ship-owners of England of the period. He is said to have possessed ships of four, five, and even nine hundred tons burden, which were far above the average size of the merchant vessels of the period. On one occasion he supplied Edward IV. with two thousand six hundred and seventy tons of shipping, a fact recorded on his famous monument in the church of St. Mary Redcliffe, Bristol, itself one of the most beautiful structures of the fifteenth century.[2]

Fresh legislative enactments.

As the commercial legislation of England, previously to the reign of Edward IV., had been full of irregularities and inconsistencies, exhibiting itself as at one time liberal in the extreme to foreigners against its own subjects, at another retaliatory to its own prejudice and unwise in its prohibitions; this monarch, on his accession to the throne, introduced various legislative measures professing to regulate upon something like fixed principles the maritime commerce of the country. Thus Parliament, in the third year of his reign, granted the king, for life, a subsidy of 3*s.* upon every tun of wine imported, and a poundage of twelve pennies in perpetuity on the prime cost of all goods exported or imported for the defence of the realm and especially for the guard of the sea. Another Act

[1] Fœdera, xi. p. 277.

[2] See interesting details of William Canynge (the ancestor of George Canning), in "Illustrations of the History of Bristol," p. 280, 1853, by S. Lucas, M.A., the first editor of "Once a Week." Canynge's grandfather was mayor of Bristol six times, his father twice, and himself five times.

in the same year, which had for its object the encouragement of home manufactures, prohibited foreigners from buying or shipping wool from either England or Wales; and ordained, adopting the permissive principles of a former Act, that no English merchant should ship any goods, outward or homeward, in foreign vessels unless sufficient space could not be found in English shipping.[1] In the following year the importation of corn, except the produce of Wales, Ireland, or of the islands belonging to England, was prohibited whenever wheat did not exceed 6*s.* 8*d.*, rye, 4*s.*, and barley 3*s.* per quarter.

First "sliding scale," applied to the importation of corn.

Nor did these prohibitory and protective laws end here. Another law[2] enacts, on the faith of "representations made by the male and female artificers of London, and of other cities, towns, and villages of England and Wales," that as certain foreign articles were of inferior quality, their importation be limited for a time by the king's pleasure; while the sale of woollen caps or cloths, ribands, fringes of silk or thread, saddles, stirrups, harness, spurs, fire-tongs, dripping-pans, dice, tennis-balls, purses, gloves, and innumerable other articles, were entirely prohibited. It soon, however, became apparent that the articles of foreign manufacture, which had been thus prohibited, were far superior in quality to similar articles produced in England; so that the change of the law, while greatly increasing their cost, to the benefit, it is true, of the manufacturer, entailed a corresponding loss upon those who were his customers.

The Scottish Parliament, following the example of

[1] Act 3 Edward IV. c. i.

[2] Act 3 Edw. IV. c. 4.

England, passed several Acts of a similar character, all, no doubt, intended for the advancement, but most of them probably operating for the obstruction, of commerce. Experience soon proved to even the framers of these prohibitory laws that considerable relaxation must be made. Indeed, towards the close of the very year on which the most stringent of them were passed, a treaty of alliance between England and Denmark allowed the merchants of both countries free access to the ports of the other; while a treaty between Edward and the Duke of Bretagne permitted the subjects of both princes a mutual liberty of trade in all merchandise not specially prohibited.[1]

Relaxation of the laws by means of treaties, A.D. 1467.

Various similar treaties appear to have been made in the fifth year of Edward's reign. Desirous of fortifying himself against the rival house of Lancaster by the friendship of continental sovereigns, he entered into treaties of offensive and defensive alliance with as many of the neighbouring nations as possible, including the king of Castile, so that the merchants of each country might, reciprocally, buy and sell whatever merchandise they required, and be treated, in all respects, the same as his own subjects.[2] Moreover, the English people themselves soon perceived the evil effects of a prohibitory system, so that, at their instigation, Edward, in the sixth year of his reign, concluded a treaty with the Netherlands, whereby he and the Duke of Burgundy agreed that, for thirty years, the subjects of both countries were to have free access by land or water, with liberty to buy and sell all kinds of merchandise, except warlike stores, on paying the same

[1] Fœdera, xi. p. 567.

[2] Ibid. xi. pp. 534–569, 572, 583.

duties as were established when formerly commerce had free course between the two countries.[1] Soon afterwards similar commercial treaties were made with France, the towns of Flanders, and the people of Zealand; and in the fourteenth year of his reign, Edward granted to the Hanse merchants the absolute property of the Steelyard in London, with certain other privileges, which they may be said to have enjoyed, through various changes and vicissitudes, almost to our own time.[2] He also favoured the merchants of Italy with an exemption from most of the additional duties which had been imposed upon them during his own and former reigns.[3] A.D. 1471.

Treaties of reciprocity.

Extension of distant maritime commerce, A.D. 1485.

These treaties of reciprocity greatly encouraged the ship-owners of England in embarking on more distant voyages. Hitherto, their ships had been confined almost exclusively to a coasting trade with the Baltic and with the Spanish Peninsula. A few only of the more wealthy and enterprising traders had ventured through the Straits of Gibraltar to the Mediterranean ports; nor, indeed, had even they been able to compete on equal terms with the larger vessels of the north of Europe or with the still superior vessels of the Italian republics which, throughout the middle ages, monopolised the most important and most lucrative branches of the over-sea carrying trade. In the reign, however, of Richard III., English merchants had increased their distant operations to an extent sufficient to justify

[1] Fœdera, xi. p. 591. It is clear, also, from several notices in the "Fœdera," that Edward IV. was himself a considerable owner of merchant vessels.

[2] Ibid. pp. 544–793.

[3] Rymer's MS. Records, Edw. IV. vol. iii, p. 55.

an application for the appointment of an English consul at Pisa, who should have the power of hearing and of summarily determining all disputes between English subjects resident in Italy or belonging to ships frequenting the ports of that country. Lorenzo Strozzi, a merchant of Florence, was, consequently, at the request of the English merchants then in Italy, appointed the first commercial representative of the English nation in the ports of the Mediterranean.[1]

First English consul in the Mediterranean, A.D. 1490.

From this time the trade of England with the Mediterranean, conducted in her own ships, steadily, though slowly, increased. Five years afterwards, a treaty with Florence enabled the English to resort freely to all her territories, and carry thither any kind of lawful merchandise, whether the produce of England or of other countries, not even excepting those countries which might be at war with Florence. On the other hand, the Florentines agreed not to admit any wool produced in the English dominions, if imported in any vessels but those belonging to subjects of England; while the English bound themselves to carry every year to Pisa, the appointed staple port, as much wool as used to be imported annually, on an average of former years, to all the states of Italy, except Venice, unless circumstances, of which the king should be judge, rendered this impracticable. Privileges, similar to those which had been granted to the merchants of the Steelyard, were also then allowed to an association of English

The advantages derived from reciprocal intercourse.

[1] Fœd., xii. p. 270. Roscoe states that this Strozzi was still alive so late as A.D. 1538 (Life of Lorenzo de' Medici, c. 10). Henry VII. appointed another English merchant, Christopher Spene, as consul at Pisa (Fœd., xii. p. 314).

traders in Italy. In some respects, indeed, these were even more liberal. Besides having the privilege of forming themselves into a corporate body at Pisa, with power to frame their own regulations and to appoint their own officers, they had placed at their disposal a suitable edifice or a site on which to build one, and were to be independent of the jurisdiction of the city, while enjoying all the advantages of its citizens or those of Florence.[1]

From this period the business of the ship-owner may be considered as distinct from that of the merchant, although, to the present day, many of the latter are still owners of ships. For the first time English ships were engaged in the trade between England and Italy as carriers alone, deriving their remuneration entirely from the amount of freight they earned. About this time, also, the spirit for discovery in far distant and then unknown regions began to open up new and vast fields of employment for merchant shipping, from which England, in after years, derived greater advantages than any other nation.

[1] Fœd., xii. p. 389.

CHAPTER XIV.

Early efforts of France to restore the civilization of Europe—Charlemagne, A.D. 771–814—Protection against pirates—Efforts of Venice to suppress piracy—Rise of Marseilles—Monopoly in shipping trade—Customs on shipping—Spain; its early commercial importance—Superior influence of the Venetians, which was invariably used to their own advantage—Participation of Genoa and Pisa in the profits derived from the Crusades—Venice claims the dominion of the Adriatic, A.D. 1159—Annual ceremony of espousing the Adriatic—Bucentaur state barge—Form of espousal—The progress and commercial policy of Venice—Variable character of her laws, A.D. 1272; which were protective generally, especially as regards her ships—Official exposition of the trade of Venice—Her ships and dockyards—Merchant galleys—Their greatest size—Contract for the construction of vessels—Great variety of classes—The Gondola—The Tarida—The Zelander—The Huissier—The Cat—The Saitie—The Galliot, &c.—The Galeass—The Galleon—The Buzo—Government merchant galleys—How engaged, equipped, and manned—Nobles' sons taken on board—Capacity of these vessels—Crew, and regulations on board—Value of their cargoes—Despatch boats—Consuls; their establishment, duties and emoluments—Ancient ships' consuls; their duties—The Cartel—Conditions of the contract—Restraints upon seamen—Extraordinary display on the departure of any important expedition—The reception of the commander, and his plan of inspection—Signal to depart—Adaptation of merchant vessels to the purposes of war—Regulations at sea—Stringent rules to regulate the loading of vessels.

Early efforts of France to restore the civilization of Europe.

FRANCE may be ranked among the earliest nations which emerged from the darkness and inactivity into which Europe had fallen, after the invasion of the barbarous tribes of the north; her Merovingian princes, who were highly civilized compared with even the best of the marauders who had overrun the Roman provinces, having devoted themselves to agricultural and other industrial pursuits, and having thus paved the way for the revival of maritime commerce. As the barbarians had divided what Rome had united, and Europe was broken up into innumerable communities with no interest in common, navigation could not be otherwise than dangerous in seas infested by pirates, while strangers could not count on friendly reception at ports occupied by semi-civilized nations: the French princes, however, by the suppression of the Visigoths, obtained possession of Marseilles, then, with the exception of Constantinople, the most important commercial city in Europe, and thus caused their civilizing influence to be felt along the shores of the Levant. About A.D. 500.

But Amalfi, Pisa, Genoa, and Venice, at this period slowly succeeded in rivalling, if not in superseding, the great maritime city of the French. The practice of piracy, however, unfortunately continued long after civilization had again dawned on the shores of the Levant; nor, indeed, as we have seen, did Amalfi, though the first to do so, become really worthy of note as a commercial entrepôt till the close of the eighth century, and even then its maritime commerce was comparatively insignificant and of little importance, until a more enlightened ruler removed a yet further portion of the dark cloud still hanging over the fairest portions of the continent of Europe.

The extensive conquests of Charlemagne, unlike those of but too many of more ancient times, tended Charlemagne, A.D. 771–814.

to spread far and wide the benign influence of civilization, and to secure by all possible means the peaceful operations of trade. The security of property once re-established, the enterprise and cupidity of mankind discovered with alacrity cheap and expeditious modes for exchanging the products of labour with distant as well as with neighbouring nations. To encourage the people under his rule to enter upon commercial transactions, Charlemagne concluded treaties of commerce with various foreign princes, including the Saxon kings of the Heptarchy, to which reference has been already made. He repaired the lighthouse built by Caligula at Boulogne, erecting fresh ones at those points where the greatest danger was to be apprehended, provided effectual means of defence against the pirates and the Saracens, and encouraged those of his people who were willing to embark in over-sea occupations.

Protection against pirates.

This new commercial energy, which first showed itself under the kings of Lombardy, rapidly bore fruit, when Charlemagne resolved that the trading rights of Amalfi, Venice, Marseilles, and of other cities should be rigorously respected. His son, Louis le Débonnaire, followed the bright example of his illustrious father; but the destruction of Marseilles by the Saracens shortly after his death put an end for a while to the progress of commerce in the south of France. Nor, indeed, was Charles the Bold successful in recovering the losses sustained by the capture of Marseilles, while the invasion and piracies of the Normans on the north side of France, and the repeated attacks of the Saracens on the south, well nigh destroyed the seeds of progress sown

A.D. 838.

by Charlemagne, so that the preservation of any form of civilization for some time seemed almost hopeless.

Efforts of Venice to suppress piracy.

But the exiles from other nations, who had, three centuries before, planted their future homes on a few barren isles in the Adriatic, now, A.D. 997, raised a fleet to suppress the Istrians and Dalmatians, who had made descents upon their city by sea as well as by land. Sailing in pursuit of their enemies, they destroyed or captured many of their vessels, compelling them to sue for peace, by these means proving to the neighbouring nations that they were strong enough to vindicate their rights and to protect their commerce. From that period the power and influence of Venice steadily advanced. The natural advantages of the city, in point of security, more than counterbalanced the inconveniences attending her situation; while the character of her constitution and laws afforded a guarantee that industrious and intelligent citizens would reap the full reward of their labour. Gradually rising by her industry, daring,[1] frugality, and above all by her prudence in keeping aloof from the dissensions of other peoples, and confining herself as much as possible to commerce, she obtained extensive privileges from the Greek emperors, and became not only the commercial emporium of Italy but also of Greece.

Rise of Marseilles.

We have already referred to the extensive trade carried on by Marseilles at a very early period, and

[1] One of the most remarkable deeds of daring in the early history of Venice was the carrying away the body of St. Mark from his previous resting-place at Alexandria. This robbery is said to have been committed by the crews of ten Venetian galleys in the year A.D. 827. See Smedley, "Sketches of Venet. Hist." i. p. 15.

pointed out the many advantages which the situation of that port conferred upon its possessors with regard to the trade of the Mediterranean; advantages which might now be extended and materially developed by the passage for large vessels across the Isthmus of Suez, if the rulers of France would only adopt a more liberal and enlightened policy. We have likewise attempted to describe the commerce of Marseilles under the Roman Empire, which, so far as can now be traced, must have been of considerable importance; but, like other commercial towns, its early history, in connection with the business of shipping, is shrouded in doubt and in the mystery of romance.

Various writers, however, confirm the prevailing opinion that the shipping belonging to or frequenting Marseilles was very considerable during the dark and early part of the middle ages, as great numbers of pilgrims took their departure from that port to the Holy Land, although it is not until the time of the Crusades that we have any authentic records of the extent of the intercourse between the two places: however, from these records, it is manifest that trade attracted pilgrims to Jerusalem quite as much as devotion, or, at least, that one speculation by no means excluded the other. Though ready to mingle commerce with their devotion, there is no doubt that when the fervour for the Crusades rose to enthusiasm, the people of Marseilles were among the foremost in this infatuation. They not merely conveyed numbers of crusaders and pilgrims in their ships, but the noble families of Marseilles entered freely into these fanatical expeditions, while the city itself advanced large sums of money and was liberal in its presents to the Frank lords who obtained oriental principalities.[1]

Hence, during the domination of the Franks in Syria, the most intimate relations subsisted between them and the city of Marseilles. Thus, in 1163 the Marseillais lent Rodolph, bishop of Bethlehem, two thousand two hundred and eight bezants upon security of his castle and his possessions in the city of Acre. In 1190 they assisted in besieging that city, and obtained, as the price of their services, various commercial advantages. In 1279 they sent corn to the Grand Master of the Order of Jerusalem, by which means their mercantile franchises were confirmed in Palestine: indeed, the history of Marseilles records many services rendered to the potentates of the time, the consideration for which was, however, invariably the concession of some commercial franchise or the confirmation of ancient privileges, so that amidst all their religious enthusiasm they never forgot their own interests.

A.D. 1163.

A.D. 1190.

A.D. 1279.

Monopoly in shipping trade.

The spirit of monopoly soon, however, exhibited itself at Marseilles as in other places. Her viscounts, who were the lords paramount at the time, had permitted ships belonging to the order of the Temple and of St. John of Jerusalem to frequent the port of Marseilles; but when the commonalty of that city were enfranchised from the jurisdiction of the viscounts, they refused to recognize the freedom of

[1] See, for all that is known of the early mediæval commerce of Marseilles, De Ruffi, Hist. de la Ville de Marseille, 2 vols. fol. 1696; and Fabre, Hist. de Marseille, 2 vols. 8vo. 1829. It was owing to the lead which the French took in the early Crusades, that Orientals came to designate first the Western, and then all Christians by the name of "Franks."

2 H 2

the ships of the military orders, and levied upon them vexatious duties. The two orders complained to the constable of the kingdom of Jerusalem, and the vessels of the Marseillais with their other property were about to be seized by force in the port of Acre, but a negotiation set on foot at Marseilles happily prevented a rupture. In 1234 the burgesses, convened together at the Hotel de Ville at Marseilles, gave permission by a solemn act to the two orders of the Temple and of St. John of Jerusalem to send respectively two ships each, annually, to their port, one at Easter and one at Midsummer, to load or unload any goods they pleased under payment of the usual duties. Each vessel might take on board any number of merchant passengers who desired to make the voyage, and fifteen hundred pilgrims. In the event of the Templars and Hospitallers requiring more vessels to carry cargo belonging to their convents, they were permitted to despatch them; but these supplementary vessels were not permitted to embark either merchants, or pilgrims, as passengers.

A.D. 1234.

Customs on shipping.

Although religious differences were professedly not allowed to interfere with foreign commerce; and although in a convention made between the bishop and the commonalty it was stipulated that all Christians, Jews, and Saracens should have the right of frequenting Marseilles with their merchandise, of discharging their ships' cargoes, and of selling and buying unrestrictedly; yet the records of the Customs show, that while the duties were one denier per livre upon numerous imports, the burgesses of Marseilles were exempt from this duty, and that the shipping of the Levant was placed in a different category. Syrian merchandise paid two bezants[1] and a half per livre; from Alexandria, the rate was one bezant and a half; and from the island of Gerbi, upon the coast of Africa, three bezants and a half. There were also other municipal dues. If a foreign ship in the port of Marseilles took on board pilgrims, passengers, or cargo for the Levant, the owner was obliged to pay the commonalty one-third of the freight. It will be seen, therefore, that Marseilles exacted as high differential duties as her republican neighbours of Italy.

Again, while the Christian religious bodies received many privileges as shippers, the Jews throughout the whole of this period were ground down under excessive taxes. In the same spirit, the Venetians shut them out from the Damascus trade; the Spaniards, as far as they could, expelled them from Spain, and they were then universally persecuted, as much, it may be, from popular indignation against

[1] It is almost impossible now to determine the relative values mentioned in records so old as the thirteenth and fourteenth centuries. Moreover, research only shows that there was the greatest confusion both as to the names and as to the values of the weights and measures of that period. The Bezant (or Byzant), taking its name unquestionably from the City of Byzantium, was a common term for gold money in Western Europe from the tenth to the fourteenth century. Thus Dunstan bought Hendon of King Edgar for two hundred Byzants (Camden's "Remains concerning Britain"), and Wyclif, in his translation of the Bible, uses "besauntis" for the ten pieces of money in the parable. These Byzants were not always of the same weight or purity, but it is generally believed that, in the time of Constantine, seventy-two were coined to the pound, and that therefore they were worth about the same as the ducat (with which they are often confounded), viz., 9*s*. (Savile Script. Dec. post Bedam, fol. 76, 6. Ducange Gloss. in voce.) Those of Alex. Comnenus, A.D. 1081–1118, weigh about seventy grains English.

the social evils they were supposed to promote, as from the hatred engendered by religious prejudice. Yet, in spite of the atrocious treatment which the Jews[1] received from the so-called Christians, they were the means of greatly developing the commerce of the middle ages, and have ever since rendered important service in promoting friendly intercourse between nations, and thereby extending civilization. To the Jews, as much as to the Lombard merchants, we are indebted for the introduction of bills of exchange, by which great facilities have been afforded for the development of trade, and a system of the most perfect security established for remittances to the most distant parts of the globe.

The records of Marseilles demonstrate that the French had for many centuries carried on an important trade with all the Mediterranean ports, as also with India by way of Alexandria,[2] but they do not seem to have made voyages to any of the Atlantic ports. Though daring as mariners in the early portion of their commercial career, the French relapsed during the middle ages into idleness, and, with the exception of the inhabitants of Marseilles, were more notorious as wreckers, who plundered any vessel cast on their shores, than as industrious and honest seamen. Those who resided on its western shores had a wide field for their plunder; for in those days, when vessels hugged the land, the wrecks

[1] One of the most atrocious massacres of the Jews on record is that which broke out on the departure of Richard I. (who had protected them) for the Holy Land in A.D. 1190. (William of Newbury, iv. c. 1. Matthew Paris, p. 157.)

[2] See full details of the course of the trade of Marseilles in Pardessus, i. pp. 62–5; ii. p. 6, &c. Ruffi, Hist. de Marseille, 2 vols. fol. 1696; and Fabre, Hist. de Marseille, i. p. 301, &c.

were numerous along that portion of their coast and especially in the Bay of Biscay, which has been proverbial throughout all time for the storms and the heavy seas which roll in upon it from the Atlantic.

Spain; its early commercial importance.

Spain, after having been conquered by a mixed multitude of Orientals, had by the eleventh century reached a position in manufactures, commerce, and science, superior to that of any country of the West, its port of Barcelona[1] being the principal centre of the intercourse with the eastern countries bordering upon the Mediterranean. Relieved too, except in its south-eastern provinces, towards the close of the ninth century from the yoke of the Saracens, her people had slowly but surely increased in influence and power. Intrepid as mariners, and skilled in ship-building, the Catalonians built not merely all the vessels they required for their own trade, but supplied foreigners to a large extent with their galleys and ships of burden. The ship-owners of Barcelona were then largely employed by the merchants of France, Flanders, and other nations, and stood so high in repute that even the nobility of Spain at that time, and for centuries afterwards, did not disdain to be ship-owners. As the Barcelonians lived under neither an oligarchy nor aristocracy, a certain republican equality subsisted among its citizens. A hundred merchants administered the municipal affairs of the city, and sent thirty-two members to the Council. They also exercised the duties of the consulate and regulated the exchange, sending men chosen from their body as representatives to the Cortes of the provinces. The whole of

[1] Pardessus, ii. p. 66. Capmany, "Memorias," vol. ii.

the early history of the trade of Barcelona[1] shows that its inhabitants owed their progress rather to their natural inclinations for the sea, and their rapidity and skill as mariners and ship-builders, than to the peculiar advantage of the port or to any local consideration.

Superior influence of the Venetians,

But the Venetians still kept ahead of all their commercial rivals; and when invited as we have seen to transport the Crusaders to the Holy Land, they were strong enough to stipulate, over and above the exorbitant freight which they had obtained, for the privilege of establishing factories in any place where the arms of the Crescent were replaced by those of the Cross. Nor were these extravagant terms sufficient. In the latter Crusades their exactions were increased. Thus, Venice then demanded and obtained a moiety of whatever the Crusaders acquired by arms or by convention, with the assumption, after the fall of Constantinople, of many special advantages, such as the general lordship over Greece, and of the towns of Heraclea, Adrianople, Gallipoli, Patras, and Durazzo, with the islands of Andros, Naxos, and Zante. These acquisitions materially increased the wealth and influence of the Venetian republic, and left it almost without a rival in the waters of the Levant.

which was invariably used to their own advantage.

It may therefore be assumed that during the long and protracted wars in the Holy Land, Venice was, without doubt, the first maritime power in Christendom, for, as we have shown, there was then no

[1] Barcelona was indebted to the French for ridding it of the Saracen rule, and subsequently to the wise rule of Raymond Berenger. Pardessus, vol. ii.

other power which had ships enough to convey the hosts of fanatics who, from every nation in Europe, were hurrying on to the coasts of Syria;[1] and although Genoa and Pisa also participated in the profits realized from the Crusades, she was by far the greatest gainer. Indeed it has been well said of her people, that while the Christians lavished money on the Crusades without any return, the Venetians turned everything they touched to an incredible profit. Besides furnishing the largest proportion of the transports, she secured many contracts for military stores and provisions; while her ships were the principal storehouses from which the armies were supplied at enormous profits to their owners. "There are charters yet extant," remarks Dr. Robertson, in his History of the Reign of Charles V.,[2] "containing grants to the Venetians, Pisans, and Genoese, of the most extensive immunities in the several settlements which the Christians made in Asia. All the commodities which they imported or exported are thereby exempted from any imposition; the property of entire suburbs in some of the maritime towns, and of large streets in others, is vested in them; and all questions arising among persons settled within their precincts, or who traded

Participation of Genoa and Pisa in the profits derived from the Crusades.

[1] Pardessus observes that in reading the history of the period of the Crusades, any one would suppose that the great maritime cities of the Mediterranean imagined that these expeditions were made merely to promote and extend their commerce. In vol. ii. p. 39, he gives a remarkable list of the various privileges conceded to Marseilles, Genoa, Pisa, and Venice, with the view of securing their aid (or at least their neutrality) during these expeditions. See also Smedley, "Sketches of Venet. Hist.," i. p. 25–45, for details of exactions made by the Venetians from the leaders of the Crusades.

[2] Vol. i. pp. 34–5.

under their protection, are appointed to be tried by their own laws, and by judges of their own appointment."

Nor were the Venetians in all cases satisfied with a moiety of the spoils of war beyond their gains by trade. Historians say [1] that, when Tyre was besieged by the united forces of the republic and of Varemond, bishop of Jerusalem, the Venetians stipulated that on its reduction they should receive two-thirds of the spoil and property captured. Indeed, the troops on shore complained loudly that while all the fatigue, dangers, and hardships of the two months' siege

A.D. 1124. fell upon them, the Venetians lay at ease in their ships, deriving large profits on everything they supplied, and exacting their full portion of the plunder agreed upon before the operations commenced. Thus riches poured into Venice securing for her a position far beyond that of any other republic.

Venice claims the dominion of the Adriatic, A.D. 1159.

Having brought under subjection the people inhabiting the shores of the Adriatic, she claimed its dominion; the declaration of Pope Alexander III. when he visited Venice confirmed her claims; and other nations admitted them when they asked permission to pass their merchandise and ships through the Gulf. But when the Pope exclaimed to the Doge, "That the sea be subject to you, as the spouse is to her husband, since you have acquired it by victory," he had little idea that the Venetians would consider its dominion as more than an honorary title, much less that they would compel

[1] History of Venice, Universal History, xxiii. p. 414, and E. Smedley, "Sketches of Venetian History," i. p. 72.

even the clergy to pay their share of the tax levied for the special defence of the Adriatic.

Annual ceremony of espousing the Adriatic.

On various occasions the Venetians exhibited the greatest punctiliousness lest their rights to the sovereignty of that sea should be infringed. Every year the ceremony of espousing the Adriatic was per-

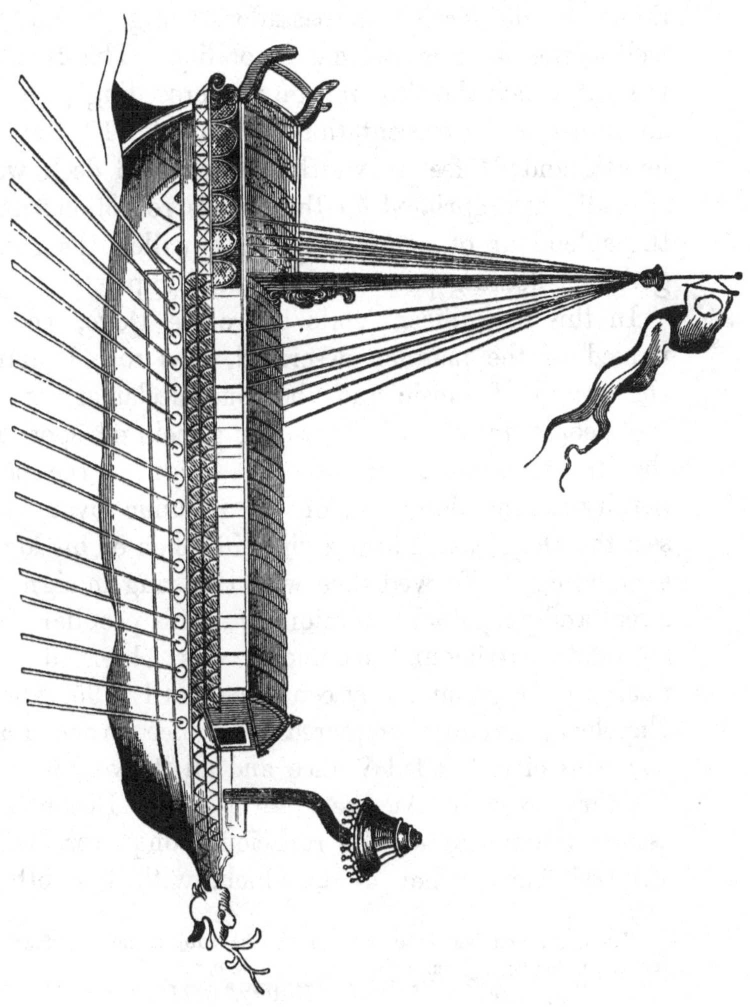

formed with extraordinary magnificence by the Doge. A state galley, celebrated as the Bucentaur,[1] preserved from time immemorial in the Venetian arsenal, carried the Doge and Senate upon these occasions; and everything which could add pomp and splendour to this annual ceremonial was employed, the public functionaries and foreign ambassadors being present as well as the senators and chief nobility. The Bucentaur, of which the drawing on the preceding page is an imperfect representation, measured 110 feet in length, and 21 feet in width. A covered deck was specially appropriated for the Doge's reception; and the splendour of her equipment equalled the most gorgeous floating palaces of ancient Egypt.

Bucentaur state barge.

Form of espousal.

In this magnificent state barge the Doge, accompanied in the manner described, was rowed, amid the sound of music and the loud acclamations of the people, from the city to an appointed spot on the waters of the Adriatic. As a sign of the perpetuity of the dominion of the republic over that sea, the Doge cast into it a ring, in token of his love, exclaiming, "We wed thee with this ring in sign of a real and perpetual dominion!"[2] This peculiar and splendid matrimonial ceremony was observed annually, throughout many centuries, until 1795, when Napoleon, having conquered the once proud and powerful city, handed Venice and all its wealth and territory over to Austria: nor did the Bucentaur escape the notice of the rapacious conqueror, who stripped her of her gold, which, with her other

[1] Though much has been written on the subject, no satisfactory derivation has been given for this remarkable name.

[2] Smedley, "Sketches of Venetian History," p. 74.

valuable contents, he transferred to the treasury of Milan. The hulk afterwards, under the name of the Hydra, became a guard-ship, mounting seven guns, and was anchored to protect the mouth of the Lido, till, in 1824, a decree of the Aulic Council ordered her final demolition. A model of this once magnificent and historical barge, which, in the course of centuries must have been frequently rebuilt, is now preserved in the arsenal of Venice.

The progress and commercial policy of Venice.

Although the Holy Wars gave Venice, Genoa, and Pisa a position which they might never otherwise have attained, other causes contributed to revive the spirit of commerce between different and distant nations. The Italians, by their intercourse and commercial relations with various cities of the Greek empire, and especially with Constantinople, had obtained a knowledge of the valuable trade of the East, and had cultivated a taste for its precious commodities and curious manufactures. They were consequently not slow to embrace and develope direct intercourse with India; hence, in the course of the twelfth century, Venice established a regular commerce with the East through the ports of Egypt, which she maintained during four centuries. Introducing into their own territories manufactories of various kinds, and carrying on these with surprising ingenuity and vigour, the Italians transplanted from warmer climates several new productions which furnished the materials of a lucrative and extended trade. "All these commodities," remarks Dr. Robertson,[1] "whether imported from Asia, or produced by their own skill, they disposed of to great advantage among the other

[1] History of Charles V. i. p. 94.

people of Europe, who began to acquire some taste for an elegance in living unknown to their ancestors, or despised by them. During the twelfth and thirteenth centuries, the commerce of Europe was almost entirely in the hands of the Italians, more commonly known in these ages by the name of Lombards. Companies or societies of Lombard merchants settled in every different kingdom, and were taken under the immediate protection of the several governments, with the enjoyment of extensive privileges and immunities. The operation of the ancient barbarous laws concerning strangers were suspended with respect to them; and they became the carriers, the manufacturers, and the bankers of all Europe."[1]

Variable character of her laws, A.D. 1272; The commercial policy of the Venetian republic frequently varied, and though generally protective and sometimes strictly prohibitory, the most perfect freedom was in many instances allowed to foreign merchants to encourage them to make Venice the chief depôt for the supply of produce and manufactures to the markets of Europe. By the decrees of the Grand Council, during the latter half of the thirteenth century, when Venice had reached the zenith of wealth and splendour, her merchants were allowed to import freely from the Levant, from Marseilles, and from other ports of France, produce and manufactures of every kind, provided they were warehoused in the markets of the republic; while they had equal freedom in the export of their own

[1] Sanuto mentions, so early as A.D. 1171, the establishment of a bank at Venice. On this occasion, the Doge Vitale enforced a loan from the wealthiest citizens, and for this purpose established a "Chamber of Loans" (Camera degl' imprestiti). The contributors to the loan were to receive interest at four per cent. (Vita de' Duchi, p. 502.)

manufactures. This freedom was likewise extended to Flanders. Cloth imported from that country paid no duty. Ship-owners were encouraged by special laws to import iron, tin, and lead, the Senate having in view the policy of concentrating in the city of Venice as many articles of merchandise as possible, so as to attract merchants to that exclusive market, and to secure there a stock of goods for the lading of Venetian merchant ships to the Levant, as also an abundant supply of raw materials for their home manufactures.

In the midst, however, of this liberal policy, the Venetians seem always to have kept clearly before them the interests of their own shipping. In the registers of Venice may be found numerous instances of the anxiety of the merchants to monopolize in their own ships their commercial intercourse with other countries. Thus, in the year 1319 there is a record of one Tomaso Loredano, a merchant of Venice, who had despatched eleven hundred tons of sugar to London, stipulating that the amount arising from its sale should be invested in English wool, to be shipped exclusively in Venetian vessels. Laws were also in force which levied differential duties equivalent to one-half their value upon certain goods imported in foreign vessels; while in some cases the ships of foreign nations were not allowed, under any circumstances, to enter the ports of Venetia.

which were protective generally, especially as regards her ships.

Again, a special law provided that neither German, Hungarian, nor Bohemian traders should have any dealings with Venetian merchants except in Venice itself: these traders were, therefore, compelled to resort thither for the purchase of whatever goods they required, the Venetian merchants being at the same time forbidden to convey them inland, probably to avert any danger of plunder by the barbarians, by whom the interior was too frequently infested. But, perhaps, the most unwisely rigorous portion of this law consisted in the enactment which forbade the Germans, trading with Venetia, from showing their own goods to any foreigner before offering them to the Venetian merchants, and, at the same time, prohibiting those who had brought their goods to Venice to carry back to other places any portion of them that remained unsold. Nevertheless, in spite of such prohibitory laws, a very considerable foreign commerce was carried on with Venetia; the Germans, Armenians, Moors, and Greeks, having each their respective places of resort (*fondas*) in its capital, and the Jews from first to last being its leading bankers.

Official exposition of the trade of Venice, A.D. 1421.

From a speech which the Doge, Tomaso Moncenigo, delivered in the Senate of Venice to Francis Foscari and the Florentine ambassadors, who, in A.D. 1421, sought the aid of the Venetians against the Duke of Milan, some idea may be formed of the extent of the commerce of Venice in the days of her prosperity. "Every week,"[1] remarks the Doge, "there arrive

[1] This remarkable oration, necessarily condensed in the text, is given at great length in Daru. Hist. de la Rép. de Venise, ii. pp. 293-308; cf. also Sanuto, Vita de' Duchi. Ap. Muratori, Antiq. xx. Rendered into English money (reckoning the ducat at 9*s.* 6*d.*), the following amounts are (for the year)—

	Ducats.		Pounds sterling.
1. From the northern towns	1,794,000	=	852,150
2. Imports of cloth	900,000	=	427,500
3. Spices, &c	1,871,000	=	888,725
4. From all sources	28,800,000	=	13,680,000
5 Debt due by Milan	1,600,000	=	850,000

from Milan seventeen to eighteen thousand ducats; from Como, Tortona, Novara, Pavia, Cremona, Palermo, two thousand ducats each; from Bergamo, one thousand and five hundred ducats; and from Monza, Alexandria, and Piacenza, one thousand each . . . . The bankers, also, declare that in every year the Milanese owe us a balance of one million six hundred thousand ducats." "The same and other cities," he adds, "import from us cloths to the value of nine hundred thousand ducats; while France, Lombardy, and other countries receive annually from Venice, pepper, ginger, woods for dyeing, slaves, and soap to the value of one million eight hundred and seventy-one thousand ducats." The entire commercial wealth of Venice the Doge estimated at twenty-eight millions and eight hundred thousand ducats. But he expressly states that he does not include in this the duty on salt, which Filiasi values at one hundred thousand ducats (47,500*l.*), or that derived from conquered districts, which he reckoned (in a subsequent speech) at four hundred and sixty-four thousand (220,400*l.*). "Consider how many ships," exclaims the Doge, "the collection and delivery of these goods maintain in activity; whether to deliver them in Lombardy, whether to seek them in Syria, Roumania, Catalonia, Flanders, Cyprus, or Sicily, and all parts of the world. Venice gains from two and a half to three per cent. on the freight. See how many persons gain a livelihood by this business—brokers, artificers, sailors, thousands of

These amounts, however, do not represent the exact sums which flowed into the Venetian exchequer, as we are ignorant of the relative value of gold and silver at the period.

families, and at last the merchants, whose profits amount, at least, to six hundred thousand ducats. . . . This is the produce of your garden; do you wish to destroy it? Surely not; but we must defend it against all attacks; seeing that you are the only people to whom the land and the sea are equally open; you are the channel through which all riches flow; the whole universe is interested in your prosperity; all the gold and silver in the world come into your hands."

Nor, indeed, though as Count Daru has suggested there may be some inaccuracies in these numbers owing to the errors of copyists, were the words of the old Doge those of merely idle bombast. Besides the revenues recapitulated by him, in the home manufacture of silk, cloth, arras, glass, gold, silver work, and wax, the Venetians, by means of their wealth and skill, assisted in some measure by their system of protection, and by their geographical position, carried on a very extensive and lucrative trade, which, with other branches of their commerce, greatly increased when they obtained the supremacy over their commercial rivals, the Pisans and Genoese. Not the least valuable object of merchandise at that period was the traffic in slaves; for, strange inconsistency! while the Popes rigorously prohibited all commerce with the Infidels, a prohibition to which the Venetians reluctantly submitted, the Church allowed the purchase and sale of slaves without hindrance in the open markets of Europe!

Her ships and dock-yards.

The arsenal of Venice, which included also the dock-yards, had long been the admiration of foreigners; and when that city reached the plenitude of her power, there was nothing of the kind superior to it in the world. Embracing a vast area of land and water, surrounded by walls, and flanked with towers, it presented the appearance of a stupendous fortress. The preparation and equipment of the fleets, destined either for the service of the republic, or for trading purposes, were here effected, as all commercial vessels trading to foreign ports were then, and long afterwards, armed for defence. Some of their galleys employed in distant voyages, such as to Flanders or England, are described as having had two sails only, one on each mast, of very great dimensions, the masts being of extraordinary length.[1]

Merchant galleys.

There is a tradition of a ship built at Venice, shortly before the quarrel between the Venetians and the Emperor Manuel, so large that, when she reached Constantinople, it was remarked that "no vessel of so great a bulk had ever been within that port;" but no historian has furnished posterity with her dimensions. She is merely described as a vessel with three masts and "of immense size,"[2]—a statement which may be one of comparison; and consequently she may not have been greater in her capacity than the larger class merchant ships of the

A.D. 1172.

Their greatest size.

[1] M. Jal has given, in his work on Naval Architecture, a drawing of one of these galleys, but of a much later period—A.D. 1620.

[2] It is stated by Cinnamis (p. 165) in his life of Manuel Comnenus, that this vessel was built by a private Venetian noble, then sold by the builder to his own republic, and then presented to Manuel. Nicetas adds, that this vessel was in the arsenal at Constantinople in 1172, when the emperor tried to imprison all the Venetians there; and that they took it and made their escape in it, in spite of the fire-ships immediately sent after it. M. Jal (ii. pp. 142–152) has given very interesting extracts on the subject of this great vessel from the treatises of Marino and Filiasi. Smedley shows that the Venetians had owned another enormous ship at the siege of Ancona in 1157, which was

present day. One historian[1] describes her as being large enough "to make twenty ships" (coasters ?); another[2] states that being at Constantinople himself, at that time, he found that she was able to shelter from fifteen hundred to two thousand fugitives, whom she conveyed to the Adriatic. Nor, indeed, is there any reason for doubting the existence of such a ship. Vessels employed in the Crusades carried, in various instances, eight hundred persons,[3] and the ships of Marseilles frequently took on board a thousand passengers[4]— (pilgrims ?); wherefore it is not unreasonable to suppose that the Venetians may have built a ship which actually made a somewhat distant voyage, with two thousand persons on board, and such provisions, clothing, and valuables as the fugitives could collect in the emergency. Although furnished with three masts, she does not appear to have carried any sails except the foresail, mainsail, and mizen; nor is there any mention of vessels of any nation, so early as the twelfth century, fitted with topsails; though they occasionally may have carried, in fair weather, triangular sails.

That the wealthy merchants of the Italian republics, and especially of Venice, owned various vessels of considerable dimensions, there can be even

---

called from its magnitude "Il Mondo"—"The World."—Sketches of Venet. Hist. pp. 63, 64.

[1] Dandolo. Chron. Venet.

[2] Cinnam. Vit. Manuel Comnen.

[3] St. Louis returned from the Holy Land in a "Nef," which carried eight hundred persons. See M. Jal, "Mémoire sur les vaisseaux ronds de Saint Louis," ii. pp. 347-446, where all the passages are collected which bear on this subject.

[4] Statut. Marseill. i. c. xxxiv.

less doubt, as there is ample evidence in confirmation of this opinion. Twenty years after the period when the Venetian merchants resident at Constantinople found refuge in the large vessel to which we have just referred, mention is made of five of their ships which returned from Constantinople to Venice,[1] carrying seven thousand men-at-arms; or fourteen hundred men to each, if equally distributed. Although, in this case, the length of the voyage and the class of men are supplied, the mere fact of a ship being able to carry so many persons furnishes, in itself, a very imperfect idea of her dimensions, as they may have consisted of cabin or steerage passengers, troops, or pilgrims, to whom very different extents of space would be allotted. Even at the present day the Muhammedans, in their over-sea pilgrimages to the tomb of Muhammad, are satisfied with one-eighth of the space which the law of England requires for the transport of her meanest subjects; while the amount of space varies in different nations, and materially depends upon the length and character of the voyage.

Contract for the construction of vessels.

The only definite information we possess with regard to the actual dimensions of the vessels built by the Venetians during the periods of their prosperity, is to be found in a contract which their shipbuilders made to furnish the king of France, in 1268, with fifteen ships. Of these vessels M. Jal[2] has furnished a minute description, together with their dimensions, as specified in the contract. The largest, the *Roccaforte*, was 110 feet in length over all, and only 70 feet length of keel, with 40 feet

[1] Ville-Hardouin, p. 154 (ed. 1657). [2] Jal, ii. p. 377.

width of beam, and no less than 39½ feet in depth. The *Saint Mary* and *Saint Nicholas* were respectively 2 and 10 feet shorter, their width and depth being in somewhat similar proportions. The other twelve were smaller, having an extreme length each of 86 feet, with a keel of 58, a beam of 18, and an extreme depth of 29 feet. The two largest had each two decks, 5½ feet in height. Their bows and sterns were somewhat alike, and contained several cabins, with two poops, one above the other, the upper constituting a castle or fighting-deck like the vessels of more ancient times. Their respective crews consisted of 110 seamen; and the contract price for the construction of the largest of these vessels appears to have been fourteen hundred marks, or 933*l.* 6*s.* 8*d.* The smaller craft cost 466*l.* 13*s.* 4*d.*, and they carried 50 men for their working crew.[1]

It is to be regretted that no details are given of the size or number of their masts, yards, sails, rigging, stores, or armament. The contract merely states that the larger vessels are to have two masts and two square sails, the foremast reaching over the bows, and answering the purpose of both mast and bowsprit: but what will strike the nautical reader most in these vessels is their extreme depth and their great width in comparison with their length.

Great variety of classes.

Every account shows that the classes of vessels belonging to the Italian republics were even more numerous and varied than those of our own time.

[1] See, also, "The Ship: its origin and progress," 4to, 1849, by F. Steinitz, p. 94, wherein the engravings and measurements of M. Jal are reproduced.

Besides the galleys we have named, the Venetians had others, which were about one hundred and thirty-five feet long, carrying three sails, very rapid in their movements, and so easily manœuvred, that they were kept almost exclusively for warlike purposes. A third description of galleys, carrying four sails, known by the name of the *Mossane*, were chiefly employed in the commerce of the Levant. Beyond these, the whole of the Italian republics owned a description of ship called coccas, or cocches,[1] of very large capacity, which were also frequently employed in the trade of the Levant. The accompanying drawing of two modern Maltese galleys, running side by side, which exhibits a great resemblance to another plate given by M. Jal from a drawing by an artist of the end of the fourteenth century, no doubt fairly represents the Venetian war galley of that period, and is at the same time not unlike

MALTESE GALLEYS.

[1] This name occurs spelt in various different ways. It is the same as the English "Cog," first noticed in the reign of King John (Spelman *in voce*). Sir H. Nicolas, "Hist. Royal Navy," i. p. 128.

another galley we also give by that author, the original sketch of which is in the famous MS. of Virgil in the Riccardi Library at Venice.

RICCARDI GALLEY, WITH THE EAGLES.

But though varying very much in class, size, and form, as well as in name, ships were then generally distinguished, like the vessels of the ancient Greeks and Phœnicians, as the "long ships" of war, and the "round ships" of the mercantile marine, both being propelled, to a greater or less extent, by oars. The Venetians likewise possessed the Dromond and the Draker, vessels almost exclusively employed on short voyages for the purposes of commerce. They had also a small trading vessel called the Galleon, not unlike the galliot[1] of the present day; and the Pamphyle, which, in the ninth century, was worked with two banks of oars, but, in the fourteenth, had no oars, and during the fifteenth century must have disappeared altogether, as no mention is made of her after that period. Fom time immemorial they have had their gondolas, still to be seen upon the canals of that once gay and beautiful city. Though the following is the representation of the modern gondola, time has made little if any change in its form.

The Gondola.

Beyond the galleys already named, the Italian

[1] Admiral W. H. Smyth describes the galliot as a small Dutch or Flemish merchant vessel.—Sailors' Word-book, p. 332.

republics, especially the Genoese, possessed merchant galleys, which were named Taridas, and were chiefly employed in the trade between the Levant and Constantinople. Marino Torsello recommended the use of

The Tarida.

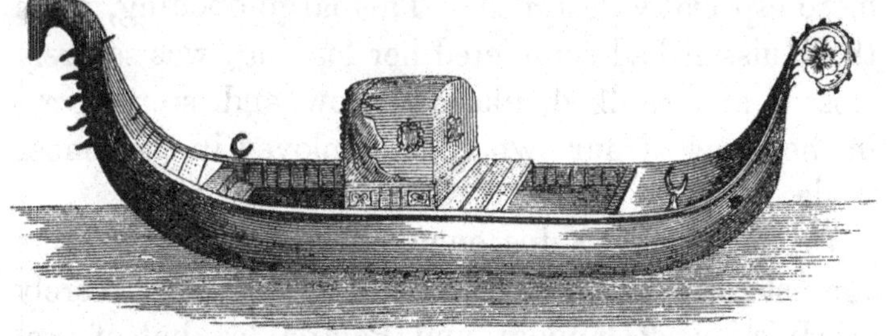

PRESENT GONDOLA.

the Tarida, which had been previously known under the name of Galata, to Pope John XXII. towards the commencement of the fourteenth century.

The Zelander.

During the tenth century the Zelander, or Galander,[1] figures with the Dromond and the Pamphyle; but three centuries afterwards these vessels had discontinued the use of oars and had become sailing vessels under a somewhat similar name. The accounts which have been preserved of the Zelander describe her as a vessel of extraordinary length and great swiftness, having two banks of oars, and a crew of one hundred and fifty men. Contemporary with the Zelander we have the Huissier, a vessel of

The Huissier.

[1] These and the following vessels appear under various spellings, the most correct form of which it is now scarcely possible to determine. Smedley, in his excellent "Sketches of Venetian History," i. p. 87, adopts Palander. *Uissier*, from *Uis*, a door, was a flat-bottomed vessel. Cf. also Gibbon, c. lx. A.D. 1203. For further details of the names of vessels during the Middle Ages, see the works of Mr. Steinitz, M. Jal, and of Sir H. Nicolas.

a peculiar description, and deriving her name from having an opening or large port in her poop, through which horses were shipped, for the conveyance of which these vessels seem to have been more especially designed. This large opening, when the Huissier had completed her loading, was securely closed and caulked, like the bow and stern ports in the ships of our own time employed in the timber trade.

In the list of ships engaged for the expedition against Crete (A.D. 949) mention is made, not merely of Huissiers, Zelanders, and Pamphyles, but of vessels known as Zelander-Huissiers and Zelander-Pamphyles, or of a description embodying the qualities and advantages of both.

The Cat.

"Cats," to which William of Tyre, speaking of an incident in 1121, calls attention, were sharp-beaked ships, larger than galleys, having one hundred oars, each of which was worked by two men, or "double banked" in the phraseology of our own time.

The Saitie.

The Saitie, or Sagette (arrow), was a small, fast-rowing vessel, or barge, propelled by oars, but considerably less than even the smallest class of galleys. In the twelfth century this description of craft had from ten to twelve oars on each side, and was employed during the five succeeding centuries for the same purposes as the Brigantine.

The Galliot, &c.

The Galliot, the Furt, the Brigantine, and the Frigate became in the fifteenth and sixteenth centuries diminutives of the galley, and were known as the Galeass, when large, broad, and heavily armed. The galeass had her oars ranged, either in threes upon a single bank, or had twenty-six oars on each side, in which case, the oar being larger and heavier, from six to seven men, seated upon the same bench, were employed upon it.[1]

The galeass figures among the drawings of other vessels of a similar class in the representation of a naval engagement, of, as is presumed, the fourteenth or fifteenth century. With the exception of the very high poop, she, in nearly all other respects, resembles the galeasses which formed the vanguard of the fleet at the battle of Lepanto (A.D. 1571). Of these a drawing may be seen in Charnock's work on Naval Architecture. The Galeass.

In the tenth century the Saracens possessed large and very heavy ships, which, according to the Emperor Leo, were called Cumbaries, or Gombories. The Venetians adopted this large ship of burden, and Sagarino, the chancellor, says that they, by whom they were called Galleons, built and armed thirty-three of these vessels. Charnock furnishes a drawing of a Galleon of the sixteenth century, A.D. 1564. The Galleon.

These vessels were built with round sides, and broad throughout; short, high out of the water, and of considerable draught when laden. The Venetians had also a merchant vessel called the Buzo, or Busse, which was not unlike the galleon, with the sides bulging out and sitting well upon the water, capable of carrying very large and heavy cargoes. According to Matthew Paris, Richard I. had several busses in the fleet which he took to the Holy Land. Although they had three masts, they were, he says, "scantily provided with sails." It is not known precisely in what manner the ships (nefs) differed The Buzo.

[1] Napier gives the names of most of these vessels, with some remarks on their proportions and uses.—Hist. of Florence, iv. pp. 36–38.

from the busses, but the Italians mark the union of the two ships in their buzo-navi. A Venetian statute of 1255 makes mention of these, together with the busses and the nefs or nés, each class being distinctly specified. Like the nefs, and the common busses, the buzo-navi had two masts, and carried lateen sails.[1]

Perhaps, however, the sketch on the opposite page (p. 493) furnishes a better idea of the ordinary and smaller class of vessels of the Italian republics between the tenth and sixteenth centuries than any other which has been preserved. It appeared for the first time in a little book, published by M. Lanetti,[2] and was copied by him from an old painting by Vittore Carpacci, which, he says, he had often seen and admired in the chapel of St. Ursula by the side of the church of San Giovanni and Paolo at Venice.

Government merchant galleys.

Among the Italian republics, but more especially in Venice during the plenitude of her power, the construction, equipment, and armament of galleys for mercantile purposes constituted a very important branch of the business of the government. Vessels thus built were put up to auction for freightage only, and the privilege of employing them on the "long voyage" was sold by the government. No other merchants of Venice were permitted to send

[1] The words Nefs and Nés occur in many of the Norman descriptions of the marine of those days. "La Blanche Nef" was the name of the ship in which Prince William, the son of Henry I., was drowned, in Nov. A.D. 1120, while crossing from Normandy to England.

[2] An Italian who, in 1758, wrote a small book on certain arts in use amongst the ancient Venetians, which was republished in 1841.

their ships to those ports to which the privileged galleys were consigned.[1]

SMALL GALLEY.

When the mercantile vessels thus engaged were completed and armed, the public crier announced throughout the streets and highways of Venice that a certain number of galeasses were ready for the annual expeditions to Egypt and other countries. This proclamation, issued under the authority of the Doge and the senate, while it allotted the vessels to the highest bidders, required that the charterers should submit to a severe examination, with the object of ascertaining whether those who offered to incur the responsibility of navigating the vessels,

How engaged, equipped, and manned.

[1] A practice somewhat similar was adopted in later times by the East India Company.

possessed the necessary capital and qualifications. Once satisfied in this respect, the government handed over the ships all ready for the voyage to their commanders. For some centuries a singular law, or rather an ancient custom having the authority of law, prevailed among the Venetians. With the object of assisting the families of the indigent nobility, each of these hired galeasses, whatever might be the voyage undertaken, were required to receive on board eight sons of poor nobles, who were allowed the pay of seventy pieces of gold for the expedition, with a mess suitable to their rank. These young nobles had likewise the privilege of carrying four hundred quintals of specie or an equivalent, free of freight, to defray their expenses at the ports they visited, or they might turn the money to account in trade so as to improve their condition.[1]

Nobles' sons taken on board.

Each of these vessels are said to have carried, on an average, five hundred tons of cargo under hatches, besides a large quantity of cargo upon their decks, a ton then consisting of only a thousand weight. Their crews consisted of no less than two hundred men, of whom one hundred and fifty were necessary to work the oars and sails. Twelve of the smartest men of the crew were selected to attend to the duty of steering the vessel under the order of the pilots, of whom there were two in each vessel. These twelve men, on whom the more important duties devolved, were required to take the lead in the work of seamanship, especially in going aloft to furl sails: they bore the name of "gallants," whence, no doubt, the word

Capacity of these vessels.

Crew, and regulations on board.

[1] A similar custom is mentioned at Florence, sub an. 1422. See Napier's "Flor. Hist." iii. p. 56.

top-gallant sails. Although the master assumed the command, the crew were under charge of the leading pilot, who had a chief mate, whose station, as now, was invariably at the bow of the vessel. There were likewise on board a carpenter, smith, archer, and armourer, and their assistants, furnished from the government arsenal. Besides several cooks, there was a storekeeper, and four inspectors, who kept an active watch over everything shipped and delivered, under the direction of a clerk or super-cargo, to whom all the merchandise was entrusted.

Value of their cargoes.

The value of the cargoes brought back in the galeasses, especially from Egypt and Syria, amounted on an average to about two hundred thousand ducats, and consisted to a considerable extent of precious stones, spices, perfumes of Arabia, with everything tending to administer to the luxuries and pleasures of the wealthy Venetians. Large quantities of medicinal drugs were also imported, the greater portion of which were afterwards distributed over the markets of Europe. This eastern trade was a source of immense profit, alike to the merchants and government. Paul Morosini, in a letter to the syndic at Nuremburg,[1] says that in his time the republic had twenty-four large galleys, divided into squadrons, with settled periods of departure for the East, carrying the mails, or rather the despatches of the government, with letters from private individuals. Besides these, the government had in their service numerous despatch boats, known as "geippers," which served in war as scouts, and, during peace, for any service requiring unusual speed.

Despatch boats.

[1] MS. quoted by Filiasi, Memorie Storiche de Venet.

Consuls; their establishment, duties, and emoluments.

In all the commercial places of importance throughout the Mediterranean, where sovereignty was not exercised by the Venetians, they established consuls, investing them with considerable power, so as to ensure the respect of foreigners. Each consulate had a chaplain, a notary, and a physician. The establishment was allowed to levy a duty of two per cent. on all Venetian imports and exports, a percentage which is said to have yielded the consuls of Syria and Alexandria an annual income of no less than 25,000 ducats. The Venetian consuls were not merely the advocates of their countrymen in any wrongs they might suffer, but they had also judicial authority in cases of controversy, and sometimes even decided disputes among the native population.

Ancient ships' consuls; their duties.

Ships' consuls appear to have existed at a very remote period in all the ports of the Mediterranean.[1] Their duty was to watch over the interests of the vessels of the nations they represented, to see that no frauds were committed, and especially that the persons who provisioned them used honest weights, and "mixed no water with the wine" they sold. They were allowed a half share in all penalties imposed, and were entitled to a present of a "carpet," a curious gift, for every enemy's ship captured: should, however, the consul connive at any of the frauds committed against the ships or crews it was their duty to watch over, they were liable to lose their office,

[1] The whole history of these consuls, with their duties, &c., has been published by Pardessus, ii. pp. 49–420, under the title of "Droit maritime connu sur le nom de Consulat de la Mer." Capmany has published the same as "Codigo de las costumbras maritimas."

and even to be branded on the forehead as rogues and outcasts. The same ordinance ordained, that "any person who shall wilfully cut the cable of a ship should be impaled alive."

The Cartel.

It was a general rule at all the Mediterranean ports to engage by "cartel," or proclamation, such ships as were required for special purposes. In those of Aragon and at Marseilles the cartel was usually inscribed upon a board of wood, and affixed to the point of a spear or lance. This cartel stated the number of ships required, and the object and character of the expedition. The ceremony was one of a formal and somewhat attractive description. Garlands of green leaves and ribbons of the most conspicuous colours ornamented the cartel board. The royal banner, or that of the prince who required the ships, floated by the side of the cartel, and a herald repeated in a loud voice the conditions of the charter, formal contracts being executed in the presence of a notary. These contracts were very minute in their details, and specified not only the size of each ship, the number of the crew, the extent of space to be allotted to the passengers, or for the conveyance of horses, but even the size of the rigging, with an inventory of almost every article which had been shipped for the use of the vessel and crew.

Conditions of the contract.

Like the contracts or charter-parties of our own time the conditions varied. Sometimes the charter-commissioners were left to engage for the whole ship, or at a stated rate for each passenger; such rates varying, as now, with the nature of the accommodation afforded, and ranging from the "paradise"[1] and

[1] Commentators have not settled where the "paradise" cabins were

other cabins, where the passengers had the greatest convenience, down to the berths in the lower hold, where they were exposed to stifling heat or offensive smells. In the case of three-decked vessels, or more likely of those with lofty towers or poops, the cost of passage from Marseilles to Syria averaged about four livres tournois in the "paradises" or best parts of the vessel, sixty sous tournois[2] on the main-deck, and forty sous tournois on the lower deck. It is not stated whether the rates of passage included provisions and other necessaries, but these were probably provided by the passengers themselves. The conditions of the charters made at Venice and at Genoa were similar to those entered into at Marseilles.

Restraints upon seamen.

It is a remarkable fact, that the seamen were occasionally obliged to pay for their berths. Besides having a limited space in the hold allowed for their clothes, they had a space on deck allotted to them for sleeping; but if the mattress of any one of them exceeded, in however small a degree, the regulated weight of fifteen pounds, or, if placed upon a bed, the seaman was called upon to pay not only for the excess, but for the total weight of his mattress, according to the rate at which passengers were charged for their accommodation. The law, indeed, provided sleeping places for the seamen; but the owners seem

situated, but they, no doubt, occupied the best part of what is known as the poop in modern vessels.

[2] It is not possible now to determine how much these sums amount to in present English money, the more so that the denier is sometimes used for gold coin. The denier tournois was one-fourth less than the denier Parisis.—Le Blanc, "Monnoies de France, d. 1690. See also Fabre, "Hist. de Marseille," vol. i.

to have expected them to spread their mattresses upon the sails or coils of rope, or at least in places passengers would not occupy, and it is certain that those who insisted on their legal rights were thus punished whenever they in the slightest degree infringed them.

Extraordinary display on the departure of any important expedition.

In the case of vessels of war, or rather those vessels whose services were more required for warlike than for commercial purposes, even greater formalities were made use of when they took their departure for a distant voyage or for an important expedition. When the hour for departure arrived the commander came on board, preceded by trumpeters, and followed by the officers of his staff. The most perfect silence prevailed on board, and every man was at his post ready to answer any question the commander might be pleased to put to him. The account, in Joinville[1] of the scene on board of the galley of the Count de Japhe describes what probably often took place. "This count," he says, "had disembarked in a most grand manner, for his galley was all painted within side and without with escutcheons of his arms, which were a cross *pattée gules* on a field *or*. There were full three hundred sailors on board the galley, each bearing a target of his arms, and on each target was a small flag with his arms likewise of beaten gold. It was a sight worthy to be viewed when he went to sea on account of the noise which these flags made, as well as the sounds of the drums, horns, and Saracen nacaires (tymbals or tambourines) which he had in his galley." The captain, seated in his state chair, having received the homage of his officers,

The reception of the commander,

and his plan of inspection.

[1] Chronicles of the Crusades, p. 391, Bohn's edition.

commenced his tour of inspection of every part of the ship, ascertaining for himself that every oar was sound and in its place, and the rowers on each bench thoroughly well trained and effective. He then as carefully examined the men at arms, crossbowmen, steersmen, and sailors, testing their various accoutrements and appointments to see that everything was in order; the different departments of the ship were then minutely gone over, including his own cabin, which was generally in the lower range of the poop or under the upper deck.

Signal to depart.

Everything being now ready for departure, the rowers, at the sound of a trumpet, simultaneously moved their oars; but if the wind was fair, the oars, at a given signal, were as simultaneously thrown upwards, the sails set, and the vessel under full pressure of canvas proceeded on her voyage. A general holiday usually accompanied the departure of a fleet. In Venice, these rejoicings were celebrated with even greater pomp and magnificence than that which characterized almost every public solemnity of the middle ages. The Doge, with the dazzling pageantry of his court and council; hundreds of gay gondolas covering the placid waters, which flowed from the Adriatic among the numerous islets upon which the proud city had been erected; senators in their scarlet robes, and the *élite* of the Venetian dames, famed for their grace and beauty, and arrayed in the gorgeous dress of the period, constituted a display of wealth and grandeur never since surpassed. But a dark cloud overshadowed those gay and glittering scenes. The galley slaves, with their hideous misery, or reckless daring, formed a saddening contrast to the haughty bearing of the Doge and the splendour of his court, and still more so, when we remember how much that court owed to the daring and unwearied toil of these slaves who were the chief instruments of its wealth.

Adaptation of merchant vessels to the purposes of war.

Throughout the middle ages, the nations of the Mediterranean depended for the constitution of a navy on their merchant shipping almost as much as England. The sovereigns of Europe and the Italian republics had each, no doubt, some ships of their own, though generally these were too few for carrying on war with rival nations of any maritime position. The great barons also, during the feudal system, owned vessels as well as castles; and those especially who lived on the sea-shore possessed one or more ships, which they employed for war or commerce, in accordance with their tastes or ambition. During the period, too, of the Crusades, many noblemen who had no connection with the sea, and whose estates were far away from it, built vessels for themselves, which were always available for warlike purposes. When the time for action arrived these ships were ranged under the flag of an admiral chosen by their owners, generally though not always with the approval of the sovereign. Nor was there much difficulty in converting their trading vessels into ships of war, as most of them were already armed, and every sailor being trained to war, an extra number of men, with a few machines for throwing stones or arrows, were sufficient for the purpose.

Regulations at sea.

In the management of their ships, and in almost everything relating to maritime affairs, the Italian republics were in a great measure guided by the ancient Rhodian laws.[1] These alike regulated the conduct of merchants and masters. When a merchant sailed in a ship which he had chartered on his own account, he was almost supreme on board. If several merchants embarked, and shipped goods, having hired the vessel among them, the majority decided upon the general management of the ship. When bad weather supervened, and it was a question of shortening sail, or when it became necessary to go out of the direct course to avoid pirates, the master invariably consulted the charterers. But if the merchants gave directions that the ship, for safety, or any other purpose, should enter a certain harbour, in disregard of the master's advice, he was no longer responsible for any event or accident arising from such a proceeding; on the other hand, if the master did anything from which fatal consequences ensued, he was liable to heavy punishment, and held responsible for all damages. In case of danger, either by tempest or an enemy, every person on board, including merchants and passengers, was bound to use his utmost endeavours for the protection of the ship and cargo; and merchants, passengers, master, pilots, steersmen, and sailors, all became soldiers whenever a suspicious craft appeared. The trade of a ship-owner, even under the best conditions one of a precarious and speculative character, was doubtless then full of danger from the number of pirates in every sea, and especially in the Mediterranean.

[1] The actual laws of the states were founded on a remembrance of the codex of Justinian, previously to its re-discovery at Amalfi. This codex embodied much of the previous Roman law, and with this whatever the Roman jurists had borrowed from the Rhodians. The whole of this question has been fully and carefully examined by Pardessus.

Stringent rules to regulate the loading of vessels.

Every merchant ship, by the laws in force among the Italian republics, was subject to prescribed rules to prevent them from being overladen. When launched, two experienced inspectors measured the ship's capacity, and, in conformity, marked upon her sides a line which it was forbidden to submerge. At Venice this mark consisted of a cross painted or carved, or formed with two plates of iron. The ships of Genoa had a triple mark of three small plates of iron fastened upon a particular line on each side of the hull, indicating a limit in depth which was not to be exceeded; while, in Sardinia, the centre of a painted ring marked the extent of the immersion allowed by law. The laws, also, prescribed many other details in the loading of the ship and in the stowage of her cargo, which, during the whole period of the middle ages, were enforced with the utmost rigour.

CHAPTER XV.

Prohibition to trade with infidels—Its futility—Commercial policy of the Italian republics—Genoa—Genoese fleets and treaties with the Venetians—The Genoese restore the Greek dynasty, and secure a more permanent footing at Constantinople—Galata—Kaffa—Genoese vessels—Details of contract with the ship-builders—Its inaccuracies—Napier's description of a large Genoese ship of the fifteenth century—Evident mistakes in the account—First great improvement in the Genoese ships—Genoese carrack—Their corsairs and pirates—The most daring of the pirates; their terrible fate—Corsairs—Bologna and Ancona—Importance of Pisa—Her trade with the Saracens, about A.D. 1100; and ships—Her first great misfortune—Mode of conducting her trade—Florence—The Florentines ship goods from a port of Pisa—Sale and transfer of Leghorn, A.D. 1421—First expeditions to Egypt, Constantinople, and Majorca—Freedom of commercial intercourse amongst the Florentines—Their frugality, contrasted with their magnificent public displays—Duties and powers of the board of the "six consuls of the sea"—Their public vessels, and trade in which they were employed—Consular agents—Extent of the Florentine commerce, and cause of its decline—The smaller states—Decorations and traditionary emblems of ships—Signals—Manners and customs of seamen—Their legends—Punishments for gambling and swearing—Superstitions—Manners and morals, A.D. 1420—General severity of punishments—Impaling, flogging, &c.—Branding.

Prohibition to trade with infidels.

WHILE the Popes favoured the trade and influence of the Italian republics in places beyond the seas, with a view to the extension of the authority of the Church, they prohibited all dealings with the Muhammedans. The Bull of Alexander III. even went so far as to confiscate the property, and condemn to slavery every person who furnished the Saracens with arms, iron, or timber for shipping. But though the powers of the Church often struck down remorselessly those who dared to resist the edicts of the successor of St. Peter, the desire of gain and the daring character of the maritime nations often counteracted the most dreadful anathemas of the Vatican. Venice was by far the greatest delinquent; her proud and rapacious merchants, on various occasions, openly resented this interference with their commercial pursuits, and evaded whenever it suited their purpose the observance of the Bulls. The trade with the Levant was too valuable to be relinquished on threats of temporal or even of eternal punishment, and this, too, when urged by an authority often too weak to carry into effect its threats. Hence, while other and weaker nations had occasionally to submit, the Venetians, conscious of their power, resisted with such success the Papal edicts that they at last obtained licences to trade with whomsoever they pleased, and even with the hated followers of Muhammed.

Its futility.

It is curious now to reflect upon the bitter animosity which prevailed among the Christians against the followers of the Crescent, and on the extreme though vain measures adopted to prevent commercial intercourse with them. When, in 1288, the famous Raymund Lully propounded his scheme for the reduction of the Holy Land, he insisted on a prohibition of all dealings with Egypt, and asserted that in six years only of such abstention from trade the Egyptians would become so impoverished as to be easily vanquished; he also urged the expediency of direct journeys to Baghdad and India, to obtain thence the productions of the East instead of from Alexandria. But abstract philosophy, however supported by fanaticism and hatred, will not prevail against material profit; and Lully failed to make converts of merchants and ship-owners to doctrines which would have impoverished them quite as much as the enemies of their faith.

Nor did the efforts of other enthusiasts, with the view of stopping the slave trade and of cutting off the supply of Mamluks for the Sultan's army, prove more successful; nor did even the project of maintaining a Christian fleet in the Mediterranean to prevent all intercourse with Egypt answer the plan of its proposers. Where one country produces articles which cannot be obtained elsewhere, nothing but an absolute blockade of the ports of trans-shipment can prevent their exportation; and, even then, though the price may be greatly enhanced, such articles will find their way by circuitous routes to those who are willing to purchase them regardless of the cost. The consumer invariably suffers by all such attempts at prohibition; but the producer is rarely injured. As the trade in Indian goods was the most profitable of all, neither spiritual authority nor philosophical reasoning availed to restrain the merchants of Europe from joining in it; moreover, the religious prejudices of the age did not demand a total abstinence from Eastern luxuries. The Venetians, indeed, on more than one occasion, boldly defied the terrors of the Inquisition, and maintained that the offence of trafficking in distant seas was only cognizable by the civil tribunals.

The stern, selfish policy of the Venetian republic and its conflicting measures of protection and of freedom are to this day marvels of success. During many centuries a small isolated community held their own amid the revolutions of surrounding nations, and maintained their high position till the discovery of the route to India by the Cape of Good Hope gave the first serious blow to their commercial supremacy. Venice, however, in her rise and progress had some powerful competitors, and, of these, the Genoese were the most conspicuous.

Commercial policy of the Italian republics.

Situated on the western, or opposite shore of Italy to Venice, the Genoese had long beheld with envy the superior wealth and power of Venice, and had resolved, if possible, to acquire such strength as would enable them to compete at sea with the Venetians whenever a favourable opportunity might arise for the trial of their strength. Hence, Genoa was early alive to the importance of securing a fleet which would be at least sufficient to protect her own distant trade. Indeed, before Venice rose to great power, Genoa had had commercial establishments in the Levant, with factories along the coasts of Asia and Africa, requiring from their great importance a protecting fleet. Cruisers, under Venetian colours, too frequently molested her traders with those settlements. But the Genoese had also their marauders; and, strange to say, the hostilities between the rival republics commenced with the capture of a celebrated Genoese pirate who had for a considerable space of time infested the Mediterranean. The attack and defeat of the first regular fleet of the Genoese quickly followed, and the island of Candia (Crete)

Genoa.

A.D. 1206.

was captured by the superior forces of the Venetians. To the rivalry between the Genoese and the Venetians in the market of Constantinople, and to the long wars thence ensuing, we have already referred.

Genoese fleets and treaties with the Venetians.

But Genoa, though defeated, persevered in her determination to curtail, if she could not grasp, the whole maritime commerce of her rival, and while protecting her own vessels, to secure a portion of those branches of trade the merchants of Venice had long monopolised. In the bloody war for the possession of Chioggia in the Adriatic, Genoa put to sea with eighty-four galleys, thirteen large ships, and one hundred and thirteen transports; and in 1293 equipped one hundred and twenty galleys, each manned by two hundred and twenty combatants. Hence, a commercial treaty in 1298 was made between the two republics, by which it was stipulated that, during thirteen years, no Venetian vessel should navigate the Black Sea or pass beyond Constantinople. The Genoese, however, though supported by a treaty with the emperor which secured to them the monopoly of the Black Sea, were not able to maintain that with Venice for the stipulated period. Repeated quarrels arose; and the Genoese, continued for more than a century the most powerful commercial rivals of the Venetians in all parts of the East. Being masters of Galata, they interrupted the landing of the Venetian ships at Constantinople, and forced the Venetian *podesta* resident in that city to seek another anchorage for the merchant traders of his city. But not content with this aggressive policy, they resolved to overthrow the throne of the Latins;

to reinstate the Greek dynasty, then fugitive at Nicæa in Asia; and to demand as their reward the entire command of the commerce of the empire, with an exclusive monopoly of the trade of the Black Sea. Nothing could well have surpassed the audacity of this enterprise. If Genoa failed, her commerce in Greece, at least, would be extinguished; while if she succeeded, she was certain to bring down upon herself the thunders of the Latin Church, the hatred of the Franks, and the vengeance of the Venetians. But the Genoese only thought of humiliating Venice, and of securing for themselves fresh monopolies; and they were for a time completely successful. Their navy brought back the Greek dynasty to Constantinople, and they themselves, armed with an imperial diploma, converted the suburbs of that city into a fortress for their own protection.

The Genoese restore the Greek dynasty,

and secure a more permanent footing at Constantinople.

Having made Galata (now Pera) a place of great strength, their port soon became the entrepôt of commerce with the North and East. With vessels especially adapted for the navigation of the Black Sea, the Genoese, unlike the Greeks, did not intermit their voyages during even the most inclement months of winter; and Kaffa, through their enterprise and influence, thus became a place of great commercial importance as the factory for the receipt of the productions of the north of Persia and of India, which came thither by way of Astracan and the Caspian Sea. The Genoese, however, like the Venetians, were but too frequently harsh and imperious masters, forbidding foreigners to make purchases or sales among themselves, and requiring that every transaction should pass through the hands of their own

Galata.

Kaffa.

people. These restrictive laws necessarily diminished the value of their trade.

Genoese vessels.

Although there are no drawings extant of the vessels of the Genoese during the thirteenth century on which any reliance can be placed, they were as skilful and even more daring in the management of them than the Venetians; and that they were equally conversant with the art of ship-building is certain, from the fact that, in 1268, when Louis IX. king of France contracted with the Venetians for some ships, he also contracted with the Genoese for some others. Of these, two are thus described by Mr. F. Steinitz, from the contracts given at length in the work of M. Jal.[1] "These," he says, "were alike." They were each, by the condition of the contract, "to have thirty-one cubits of keel, and fifty cubits of extreme length, with 40½ palms of beam. The depth of the hold was 17½ palms; of the first deck, nine; of the second, eight; and of the parisade, five palms. Each ship had a large boat, two barges, and a gondola, or small boat, and two rudders (one on each side), nine palms long; the fore-mast was fifty-one cubits in length, and 12¾ palms in circumference. The main-mast was forty-seven cubits long, and 11¾ palms in circumference. The fore-yard, which was made of three pieces of different lengths, seems to have exceeded one hundred cubits; and the main-yard, which was made of two pieces, to have been four cubits shorter. There was also a separate yard, of the same length as the main-yard, for the 'velon,' a large sail, the nature of which has not been exactly ascertained; but as it had a separate yard, it may

Details of contract, with the ship-builders.

[1] F. Steinitz, "The Ship: its origin and progress," p. 101.

have been used when going before the wind as an additional sail. It seems to have been hoisted only on the fore-mast. Four thousand ells of spun hemp to supply cordage, &c., was allowed to every ship, and they had six cotton sails of the following dimensions: viz., for the foresail, sixty-six cubits; for the 'terrasole,' sixty-one cubits; another sail of fifty-six cubits, and another of fifty-two cubits. The mainsail was fifty-eight cubits, and another sail was fifty-two cubits. Two of these sails, namely, a 'terrasole' for the fore-mast, and a 'velon,' also for the fore-mast, were to be made of Marseilles cotton. Each ship had twenty-six iron anchors, twenty of which weighed eight cantares, and the other ten cantares each, and casks for two thousand 'mencaroles' of water. The two ships were to be furnished with stabling to carry one hundred horses between them; and they had fourteen hawsers for fastenings, or moorings in port. The cost of these two ships, with all their stores, was fourteen thousand livres tournois."

The other ship, the *Paradise*, seems to have cost only three thousand seven hundred and fifty livres tournois, and consequently must have been smaller. Her dimensions are not given, but her fore-mast is described as being fifty cubits in length, and 12½ palms in circumference, and her main-mast somewhat smaller. She had seven sails, some of which were, no doubt, duplicate or spare sails; twenty-five anchors, twelve of which had buoys; three cables, thirty-one hawsers, and "four mooring ropes at the bows." She had a barge of fifty-two oars, and two anchors; a boat of thirty-two, another of thirty-four, and a gondola of twelve oars, the smallest of which could hardly have been carried on her deck, and must, with the others, have followed her at sea and attended upon her in harbour. In the contract, the most minute details are given of her stores, in which are comprised a sounding lead, three grapnels with chains, six lanterns, one being of glass, hatchets, nails, hammers, scales, pitch kettles, and so forth.

Its inaccuracies.

There must, however, be various extraordinary inaccuracies in the dimensions of these vessels, as supplied by Steinitz and other historians. The cubit, as known to the Romans and Greeks, was about a foot and a half. It was divided by the Romans into six breadths, or palms, of three inches each; and such were, no doubt, the dimensions of the cubit and palm as known to the Italian republics, and as understood in our own time. If this be so, it follows that each of the larger vessels was seventy-five feet extreme length, and only ten feet beam; four and a half feet depth of hold, with a fore-mast seventy-seven feet in length, of three feet in circumference, and a yard no less than one hundred and fifty feet long. No doubt the yards of the vessels of that period were of enormous length, as may be seen in the "lateen" rigged craft of the present day, and far in excess of the yards of modern ships as compared to the size and length of these vessels; but it would be absurd to suppose that a vessel of only ten feet in width, and under five feet deep, could carry a mast seventy-seven feet long, much less a yard of double that length; nor could a vessel of the dimensions supplied have stabling for fifty horses, or room to hold the spare spars, sails, etc., named in the inventory. Nor is the matter mended if we suppose the palm to have been nine inches ; for then the mast would be *nine* feet in circumference, or equal to that of a first-class modern line-of-battle ship.

However imperfect the drawings which have been preserved, the reader will by these form a more accurate idea of what the vessels were than can be obtained from the few records we have of their dimensions. If, therefore, the following representations, given by M. Jal, from the MS. Virgil in the Riccardi library are examined, and an allowance

made for imperfection of the drawings, we may form a tolerable idea of the ships of that period.

Throughout the whole of the middle ages, and even until the seventeenth century, every vessel was provided with trumpets and bugles, which were played

during fêtes and battles or used in foggy weather as signals: such instruments are very distinctly represented on the Corporation seal of Dover.

Nor, indeed, do writers of nautical experience, who describe the vessels of the Genoese even so late as the fifteenth century, supply information on which reliance can be placed. For instance, Napier, in his "Florentine History," furnishes[1] the following description of one of the largest vessels of the period. "The vessels built during this century for commercial purposes," he remarks, "were large in size, but it would be difficult to ascertain their exact capacity; and by the description of one belonging to the Genoese family of Doria, which anchored at Porto Pisano in 1452, this was quite unequal to their

Napier's description of a large Genoese ship of the fifteenth century.

[1] Napier's "Florentine History," vol. iv. book ii. p. 36.

outward dimensions. Her burden was said to be three hundred "botti," or about two hundred and seventy English tons[1]; her length, on the upper deck, one hundred and seventy-nine feet; the mast, *thirty-eight feet in circumference* at the lowest and thickest part, and one hundred and eighty-four feet high; the height of her poop from the keel, seventy-seven feet nearly, without the after-castle; that of her bow nearly sixty-one, independent of the forecastle; her sail, and she seems to have carried but one, was more than a hundred and fifty-three feet broad, and ninety-six high. She was heavily rigged with so many shrouds, says Cambi, that they alone were worth a treasure; her anchors were numerous, and weighed about twenty-five hundred-weight each; she had seventy cabins; her cables were twenty-three inches round, and eighty fathoms long; she was fitted with ovens, cisterns, and stalls for horses; her *long boat* carried nearly seventy-two tons, and six hundred souls were embarked in her. This was the largest vessel that had been seen in a Florentine port for a long time, and no ordinary seamanship must have been necessary to manage so unwieldy a sail as she seems to have carried."

Evident mistakes in the accounts.

We should rather have expected a Post-Captain in the British Navy to have remarked that no such sail could have been carried on the vessel he names, for its spread would have been equal to close upon fifteen thousand square feet of canvas; dimensions, compared with which the largest sail in the *Great*

[1] "This," remarks Captain Napier, "is probably a mistake in copying the MS., or a typographical error, and is more likely to be three thousand botti (to judge from her great dimensions), unless the 'botti' signified more in ship measurement than in the markets."

Eastern, of somewhere about twenty-four thousand tons register, would be insignificant, and whose main-mast is a walking stick in comparison with the mast of one hundred and eighty-four feet high, and *thirty-eight feet in circumference*, of which Captain Napier has furnished a description. Nor are we disposed to place any more confidence in the account of her height which he furnishes; and we are sure that he would not have considered it safe to have commanded in rough weather a ship of the height he describes in proportion to her length (the breadth is not given), much less would he have attempted to hoist upon her deck a "long boat" which carried "nearly seventy-two tons."

There is no way of accounting for these numerous palpable mistakes than by supposing that they arose "from a mistake in copying the MSS., or from typographical errors;" but how they should have arisen in so many cases is perplexing. Moreover, it is wholly unaccountable why historians, especially men with the experience and practical knowledge of Napier, should not have directed special attention to errors so glaring.

It may, however, from all the information we have been able to collect, be affirmed that, previously to the fifteenth century, practical or professed writers upon shipping were unknown; while those who incidentally refer to it are so inaccurate, that their works have little, if any, real value. Almost everything relating to shipping, and especially to merchant shipping, before that time is, therefore, in a great degree matter for conjecture. Nay, we are even inclined to think that, on the whole, we possess more accurate accounts of the ships of antiquity.

First great improvement in the Genoese ships.

Various causes and circumstances rendered the middle of the fifteenth century a remarkable epoch in the annals of marine architecture, and not the least of these was the competition for maritime supremacy between the great Italian republics. But when Genoa and Venice wisely gave up quarrelling, there was a still more marked improvement in the form and equipment of their vessels. The rivalry of commerce took the place of those foolish contentions which invariably resulted in war. Each nation then strove to produce, not the best fighting ship, but the one most suited to yield remunerative returns. From that period the improvement steadily increased, until vessels not unlike those of our own time were constructed towards the middle of the sixteenth century.

Genoese carrack.

The Genoese, though inferior in, perhaps, all other respects to the Venetians, then surpassed them in the art of ship-building; and they were, so far as can now be traced, the first to construct a ship approaching to the modern form and rig, of which any account and drawing has been preserved. The following, copied from Charnock,[1] affords an excellent and, we believe, accurate illustration of the large Genoese merchant carrack of the first half of the sixteenth century,[2] some of which are said to have been of no less than from fifteen hundred to two thousand tons burden.

The Genoese, more especially in the early part of their history, had, as we have seen, their lawless

[1] Vol. ii. p. 7.

[2] The original drawing is said to have been made at Genoa in 1542; but M. Jal thinks it later, and that Charnock has misread 1542 for 1642.—Arch. Nas. ii. p. 215.

Their corsairs and pirates.

cruisers as well as their peaceable traders. But her corsairs, once so renowned, must not be confounded with her pirates. The former resembled in many respects the privateers of our own time; while their pirates

A GENOESE CARRACK, 1542.

The most daring of the pirates,

were chiefly under the control of men who had been banished from the republic either for some delinquency against the laws or for political offences. A number of these political exiles, belonging to what was known as the "Guelph faction," having been banished from the republic in 1323, fitted out ten galleys armed as cruisers and infested the Mediterranean, pillaging indiscriminately the ships and the coasts of Genoa as well as those of other nations. In one cruise alone they took booty estimated at three hundred thousand golden florins. Their success, however, proved the means of their destruction. Pursued by a squadron of Genoese ships of war as far as the Black Sea, they sought shelter in Sinope, then under a Turcoman ruler, who, quickly learning the wealth they had on board their vessels, took short and effective means to secure it for himself. Inviting the pirate chiefs with their crews to a banquet, he surrounded them in the height of their revelry with his troops and massacred nearly all of them. No fewer than fifteen hundred persons, among whom were forty nobles, perished by this one deed of treachery, and only three galleys succeeded in making good their escape.

Their terrible fate.

The corsairs, on the other hand, were armed as privateers, if not with the express approbation, at least with the tacit acquiescence of the government, and professed to wage war only with the enemies of their own republic. The corsairs also performed the duties of the men-of-war of more modern times, by searching the vessels of neutral and friendly powers to ascertain if they had on board provisions, arms, or merchandise destined for the enemy. The booty thus acquired was divided among the commanders and cruisers, in conformity with the ancient maritime regulations preserved in the "*Consulado de la Mer*."[1]

Corsairs.

The successful resistance of Genoa to the growing

[1] See Pardessus, vol. ii.

power of Venice had, however, another result, in that it encouraged other states inferior in power to either of them to resist as far as they could the commands of these imperious masters. Bologna and Ancona,[1] the first to make the attempt, signally failed; nor did the latter meet with better success when she joined the Istrians in their revolt against Venice, though her ships had the audacity to commit various depredations on the commerce of that state, while she refused to pay the duty required by the Venetians from all vessels which entered that part of the Adriatic acknowledged to be within their dominion.

Bologna and Ancona.

Importance of Pisa.

Amalfi, long before Venice or Genoa, the possessor, as we have seen, of a large and valuable commerce with the East, had now passed away as a place of commercial importance; but Pisa, one of the most ancient cities of Tuscany and the chief pillager of Amalfi,[2] still maintained a high position, and proved, in some respects, a formidable rival to the Venetian and Genoese traders. Despising, in their commercial operations, the narrow dictates of religious bigotry, the Pisans, in frequent voyages to Palermo about the middle of the eleventh century, successfully traded with the Saracen inhabitants. They also traded to the coast of Africa, and, on one occasion, in revenge for a supposed injury, captured and held the royal city of Tunis until they obtained redress. They now played a leading and brilliant part in the maritime commerce of the Mediterranean. Pisa, in the twelfth century, contained two hundred thousand inhabitants,

Her trade with the Saracens, about A.D. 1100;

[1] For details of the war with Ancona about A.D. 1167, see Smedley, "Sketches," vol. i. p. 67, &c.

[2] Amalfi was taken by the Pisans A.D. 1137.—Sismondi, vol. i. p. 203.

and many beautiful monuments still attest its former greatness and splendour.[1] Among the most conspicuous may still be seen its leaning tower, from which has been copied the following representation of one of its ships, sculptured so far back as the year 1178. and ships.

Besides different sorts of merchant vessels bearing a common resemblance to those of the Venetians, the Pisans constructed ships of war with towers of wood, and machines for attacking an enemy, which they managed with a skill that rendered them most formidable opponents. Their expeditions against the Moors of the Balearic Islands, and their conquests in Corsica and Sardinia conferred on them a high military as well as naval reputation. But the Pisans were not without their share of the calamities of the times. In the year 1120, their city was almost laid in ashes and their islands of Sardinia and Corsica

Her first great misfortune.

[1] Pisa contributed the aid of its ships to the first and third Crusades, but, like Genoa, declined to join in the fourth. (Gibbon, ch. lx.) Its trade with Alexandria is mentioned as early as A.D. 823 by Muratori, Ant. v.

taken from them by the Saracens.[1] They, however, assisted by the Genoese, soon after recovered these islands; but the division of the conquest, and probably the exasperation created by commercial jealousy, immediately kindled a war between the allies, in which the Genoese, with a fleet of eighty galleys and four great ships, carrying warlike engines, besieged their harbour, and obliged the Pisans to submit to their pleasure respecting Corsica. The peace that followed was again soon broken; and a sanguinary war, frequently interrupted by insincere pacifications or truces, continued to distress the two neighbouring and rival republics for almost two centuries.

Mode of conducting her trade.

The Pisans seem to have carried on their trade in a great measure by companies, half laymen, half monastic, not altogether unlike some still existing in the ports of Italy. By such means, also, the commerce with their settlements at Tyre, Tripoli, Antioch, and St. Jean d'Acre, was chiefly conducted; and when, in 1171, they gained a position at Constantinople, owing to the quarrel between the Emperor Manuel and the Venetians, they profited greatly by the working of their commercial associations.[2] In less than a hundred years from this time, they had become so powerful that the Venetians found it prudent to enter into amicable arrangements with them, granting, among other favours to the Pisan

[1] The sack of Pisa was no doubt in return for the aid they had given to the Crusaders, from whom they had themselves derived great advantages, with many privileges and charters from the princes of Antioch and kings of Jerusalem. See original Charters ap. Muratori Ant. v., and Stellæ Chronic. ibid.

[2] Brev. Hist. Pis. ap. Muratori V. vi. col. 186. In 1249 Pisan sailors were in the fleet of Louis IX. at Damietta.—Matth. Paris, p. 793.

merchants, the privilege of trading to all their ports of the Levant, Adriatic, and Archipelago, on the payment of only one-fourth of the ordinary customs on the merchandise in which they dealt.

Florence. A.D. 1250.

By this time Tuscany had become one of the most distinguished commercial states of Italy, the merchants of Florence having established relations or branch-houses in other parts of Italy, and even in distant foreign countries; while many of them, who had accumulated larger capital than could be conveniently employed in trade, became dealers in money by exchange. By borrowing and lending on interest at home, and by working their spare capital by means of their *podestas*, or agents abroad, they for a time, in some measure, monopolized the business of foreign exchange, realising immense fortunes to themselves, while rendering a vast boon to every person who had dealings with distant nations. The merchants of the other cities of Italy soon followed the example of the Florentines (who, it may be remarked, had risen from obscurity during the maritime wars of Pisa, their neighbouring city) in dealing in money as well as merchandise. The Florentines also established houses in France and in England, though, as we have seen, Henry III. passed a law[1] forbidding his people to borrow money from any foreign merchants. Having, together with the Lombards,[2] establishments throughout Europe, they became very useful to the Popes, who constantly employed them to receive and remit

[1] 29 Hen. III. c. 6.

[2] The chief cities were in Lombardy, as Milan, Piacenza, Siena, Lucca. Stow states that Lombard Street in London had acquired its name, as the chief residence of these foreign merchants, so early as A.D. 1318.—Survey, p. 376.

the large sums they extracted from different nations in virtue of their ecclesiastical supremacy. They were also doubtless useful in lending on interest the vast fortunes the Popes then possessed—"sowing their money to make it profitable," as is happily expressed by one of the most quaint and intelligent writers of the period.[1]

The Florentines ship goods from a port of Pisa.

During one of those intervals of peace and goodwill of such rare occurrence among these great commercial rivals in Italy, the Florentines obtained permission to deposit and ship their goods from a port of Pisa; but this good understanding proved of short duration. The Pisans repented having made any concessions to their enterprising and industrious neighbours, and soon afterwards the Florentines were obliged to withdraw from Pisa. Further bickerings took place between them, till at length, after holding for a short time an insignificant port belonging to the people of Siena, Pisa had to mourn the success of her rival, who purchased from Genoa the port of Leghorn, for one hundred thousand florins.[2]

Sale and transfer of Leghorn, A.D. 1421.

The acquisition of so convenient and valuable a port rendered Florence, already a city of great wealth and influence, one of the richest of Italy. Aspiring to possess a navy, she created a board known as the "Six consuls of the sea," to manage her naval affairs; but the Florentine genius was more banking and

[1] Matthew Paris, pp. 419–823, &c. It appears further that, in A.D. 1329, the whole of the customs of England were farmed to the great commercial house of the Bardi at Florence, at a rate of twenty pounds per diem (Rot. Pat. 4 Edw. III.); while the frequent notice of the importation of horses into England from Lombardy (as well as Spain), shows that there was a brisk trade between the two countries.—Rymer, Fœd. V. iii. p. 124, &c.

[2] Napier's "Florentine History," vol. iii. p. 53.

commercial than maritime, and her navy, even under the care of the Medicean princes and knights of Stefano, never rose to much importance. She, however, soon obtained merchant vessels sufficient to carry on her trade with the Muhammedans, and to restore the factories which Pisa had formerly established in the East. Her request to obtain, as successor to the Pisans, the advantages they had formerly enjoyed, having been granted by the Sultan of Egypt, the despatch of their first commercial galley to Alexandria was a day of extraordinary exultation. That day inaugurated a new era in the commerce of the now flourishing republic; a new outlet had been opened for Florentine industry and enterprise; a new maritime power had unfurled its flag on the blue waters of the Mediterranean, and it was fitting that so auspicious an event should be opened with great public rejoicings and solemn religious processions.[1]

First expeditions to Egypt, Constantinople, and Majorca.

Nor is it surprising that this day should have been one of exceeding joy to the people of Florence. Though rivalling all other states in the excellence of her manufactures and of her system of banking, she had hitherto failed in establishing a maritime commerce, having, in her earnest endeavours to gain such a position, been on all occasions almost as strenuously opposed by the Venetians and Genoese as by her more immediate neighbours, the Pisans. These obstacles had now been overcome. The departure, therefore, of her own ships from her own port was a matter to call forth something more than the ordinary tokens of joy. The Florentine

[1] See full details of these exultations in Napier, vol. iii.

Argo destined to re-open the valuable trade with Egypt and the far East contained, among its crew of two hundred and fifty persons, twelve young men of the principal families of Florence,[1] sent on board to acquire a knowledge of the trade of the Levant and of maritime affairs. To facilitate, also, commercial intercourse, knowing how difficult it is to reconcile people to a strange coinage and reckoning, the Florentines coined golden florins of the same value as those of Venice, called the "Galley florins," which they sent in large quantities with the expedition to secure an easy currency at the foreign ports and to facilitate their commercial transactions.[2]

Ambassadors were at the same time despatched to Egypt, with full powers to treat on all commercial affairs; a second embassy obtained mercantile concessions in Syria, Constantinople, and the Morea; while a third proceeded to Majorca, to make the Florentine flag known and respected in that part of the Mediterranean.

From this time the commerce of Florence increased so as to rival, if not surpass that of Venice. Her merchants were indeed princes. The trade with the East, opened in a measure by Cosimo de Medici, was greatly extended and improved by his grandson Lorenzo. So highly was this illustrious merchant esteemed by the Sultan of Egypt, that he sent an

[1] A similar practice has been noticed in the case of Venice.

[2] The "Fiorino largo di Galea," or "Broad Galley-piece," was struck of the exact size and weight of the Venetian ducat, A.D. 1422. See Napier, "Flor. Hist." iii. p. 56, and further details of the "Metallic Currency of Florence," vol. iv. p. 9. It may be added that the gold coin—at first so unpopular in England—struck by Edward III. in A.D. 1344, is generally believed to have been made to facilitate trade with Florence.—Cf. Rymer, Fœd. V. v. p. 403, &c.

embassy to him (a mark of respect seldom bestowed by Muhammedan princes even on the most powerful Christian sovereigns) with magnificent presents, including fine cotton cloths of various kinds, and other rich Oriental manufactures, large vases of beautiful porcelain, balsams and spices, and an Arabian horse of great value and beauty.[1] Under this princely merchant, and heartily co-operating with him in his wise administration, Florence reached the zenith of her prosperity. Relieved from wars and tumults, the inhabitants exerted their active spirit in commerce and manufactures. Besides developing the intercourse with India, by way of Egypt, to an extent unknown since the best days of the Roman empire, Florence opened up a large trade with Spain and England, and became the chief buyer of their wools for the supply of her vast manufactures. It was then that the English were allowed to resort freely to the territories of Florence, and to carry thither every kind of merchandise, whether the produce of their own or other countries, not even excepting countries which were at war with the republic. They might there buy and sell, with the Florentines or any other people, all goods not already prohibited, or might carry even prohibited goods through the Florentine territories to any country, whether friendly or hostile, so that the policy of Florence, in her desire to make all nations her merchants, and to centre within herself, as far as possible, the trade of the world, resembled in many respects that of Tyre, and was far more liberal than Venice.[2]

Freedom of commercial intercourse among the Florentines.

[1] Roscoe's "Life of Lorenzo," vol. ii. p. 60.

[2] Fœd. V. xii. p. 389.

The fleets of Florence, though small compared to those of Venice, were equipped and navigated under regulations similar to those of the proud city of the Adriatic. Her state galleys, destined for the long voyages, were in like manner conceded to the highest bidders. With the intention of securing an abundant supply of raw materials for her manufactures, Florence established agencies in Flanders and in France, under arrangements akin to those she had opened in Spain and in England. Her great commerce, numerous manufactures, and wide-spread banking, created a large and constant flow of specie into the capital; and, in the public and private buildings, of the architecture of the fifteenth and sixteenth centuries, which still adorn that beautiful city, may be seen abundant proofs of the then enormous wealth of Florence.

Their frugality,

But while no means were omitted by the Florentines to encourage commerce and manufactures, they were themselves frugal in their habits and discouraged all extravagance and wasteful luxury. The whole force of the state was directed to keeping the market abundantly supplied with food and to preventing its export in order that the manufacturing population should live cheap, and the merchants, in consequence, be able to undersell, with a profit to themselves, all other nations.

Warned by the example of Rome, the Florentines, while they spared no expense in public works, carried their frugality to such an extent, that laws were passed to prevent excess in personal indulgences. The ornaments permitted and forbidden were defined and described by law, and the quality of woollen cloth (the use of silk stuffs being prohibited) was minutely specified. Statutory enactments even regulated the fashion of dress for both sexes, the expense of nuptials, and the number and quality of the viands allowed on such occasions, "in order to avoid any appearance of luxury and extravagance in a people depending on their own industry alone for their national greatness and prosperity;" indeed, the enactments went so far as to forbid retail dealings in some of the more costly descriptions of cloth, in order to prevent their being worn by the citizens.[1]

contrasted with their magnificent public displays.

Duties and powers of the board of the "Six consuls of the sea."

The influential and important board of the "Six consuls of the sea," which regulated the naval affairs of Florence, made all the commercial agreements with foreign states, fixed the quantity and quality of merchandise to be embarked in the public galleys destined for any new and direct trade with the Levant, and kept minute accounts of these voyages. Its members were responsible for their economical management. With them also rested the appointment of the consuls in foreign states; a general superintendence of commerce, with exclusive jurisdiction in maritime causes; and the care of the woods, buildings, chases, and fisheries, besides various other duties totally unconnected with either ships or commerce. Nor did their multifarious duties, as multifarious as those of a modern English Board of Trade, end here. They had power to impose on certain classes of foreign goods and manufactures high and, in some cases, prohibitory duties, "for the encouragement of native industry in those spots where local circumstances, and the natural bent of the people, promised successful competition."[2]

[1] Napier's "Florentine History," vol iv. p. 16. [2] Ibid. p. 26.

Their public vessels and trade in which they were employed.

The public navy of Florence, consisting originally of only two galleys, had been now increased to eleven, besides fifteen "Fuste," or smaller vessels.[1] Though manned and armed as ships of war, they were principally employed in the conveyance of merchandise to all places beyond Rome on the one side, and Genoa on the other, trading eastward with Constantinople, Kaffa, Trebizond, Alexandria, Tunis, Tripoli, and Sicily; and westward with Minorca, Majorca, Bona, and the western coast of Barbary, as well as with Catalonia, England, and Flanders. These voyages were timed so as not to interfere with each other. When there were no private bidders for the public galleys put up to auction for hire, which seldom happened, the voyage was made on account of the government. The sea-consuls settled the number of the crew and the armament of each galley, and nominated the captain, supercargo, and other officers, none of whom were allowed to be in any way connected with the consuls, or to own any part of the cargo: the consuls, too, were not permitted to share in this trade, except when the vessels were freighted on account of the government. The galleys bound westward sailed in September, and those for the Levant in February.

"On the day of sailing," remarks Napier,[2] "the various ports at which the galleys were to touch,

[1] Napier considers the "Fuste" to have been "a lighter species of war-galley," iv. p. 24. M. Jal gives elaborate details on the subject of the names of mediæval ships, in which he differs very much from writers who have gone before him. He, however, invariably gives the authorities on whom he relies, which other writers have too frequently omitted (see "Arch. Nav." ii. p. 3, &c.).

[2] Napier's "Flor. Hist." iv. p. 29.

the period of their stay at each, their ultimate destination, the rates of freight, the names of the officers, and the number of the crews were duly published, except for the voyages to Catalonia and Sicily, which were kept secret for fear of pirates, by whom these coasts were particularly infested. A loan of seven thousand five hundred florins was advanced to the conductor for his expenses, but on good security; and the hire of a galley for the Levant, in 1458, amounted to one thousand four hundred and fifty-eight florins, all charges being paid by the conductor. A hundred and thirty men formed the crew and combatants of one galley, and the conductors of those in the Levant trade were bound to present a carpet, worth not less than fifteen florins, to the seignory on their return, also to carry public ambassadors, and those young men who were sent abroad to learn the art of trading."

Under the rule, however, of the enlightened Lorenzo, the privileges conferred on these public galleys in their trading operations were entirely abolished, and the public permitted to build, freight, and sail such vessels as they pleased. Under his rule, also, the commercial relations with England were firmly established, and fresh treaties, more liberal in their character than even those of 1385, were made in 1490 and 1491.

Consular agents.

So far back as 1339, the Consulates of Florence, established in various European countries, are mentioned as old and widely-extended institutions. The appointment of the consul was for three years only; and he had to see that treaties were strictly observed, to administer justice, maintain order and reputable conduct amongst the merchants, and, besides other miscellaneous duties, to prevent "gambling and swearing." Every Eastern consul was allowed a secretary at four florins a month, two attendants, three horses, and a dragoman, with an annual salary of four thousand aspers.[1] He was strictly prohibited from carrying on trade of any kind on his own account, and was not allowed, under a heavy penalty, to act as consul for other nations or advocate the cause of strangers.

In London, the Florentine consul received by way of remuneration one-twelfth of a penny for every pound sterling of exchange; a penny and half-penny on every pound sterling value of merchandize bought and sold; a penny and half-farthing on every pound sterling of securities; and ten pounds sterling on the cargo of any Florentine galley that arrived in England, on board of which the merchants were compelled to embark their goods, or were subject to the freight if they did not do so.[2] Similar privileges were granted to the consuls at Lyons and in Flanders: in Bruges they were even more specially favoured, as there the Florentine establishments, as we have seen, had flourished since the commencement of the thirteenth century, and her merchants were the most wealthy, and probably also the most numerous and influential in the city. Indeed, so powerful had the Florentine merchants and bankers become in foreign ports that, during the fourteenth and fifteenth centu

Extent of the Florentine commerce.

[1] As previously stated, it is not possible to reduce these sums with accuracy to the modern English value. The asper seems to have varied much in value, and is now superseded, as a money of account, by the piastre.

[2] Napier's "Florentine History," vol. iv. p. 32.

ries, they held a large portion of the trade of Europe in their hands. The whole of the banking of France was then monopolised by them, and a considerable part of her commerce. Spain, Portugal, Flanders, England, and even Venice, her proud competitor, were full of them. The Medici alone had at one time no fewer than sixteen banking establishments in different parts of Europe; and such was the extent and consequent credit of the Florentines, that many of the European mints, towards the close of the thirteenth century, including that of Edward I. of England, were mainly under their control.

and cause of its decline.

Although the western nations, towards the close of the fifteenth century, resolved to direct more attention than they had hitherto done to commercial and maritime pursuits, their opposition would have produced little effect in depriving the Italian republics of those valuable branches of trade, of which they had long held almost an exclusive monopoly, had not the discoveries of the Portuguese, and the consequent alteration of the route of the trade with India, given to them an advantage, against which the Italians, with all their wealth, skill, and knowledge were unable to compete.

Nor were there wanting other causes beyond the discovery of a new route to India to bring about the decline and, at last, the annihilation of the once great republics of Italy. In spite of legislative enactments in favour of frugality, the Florentines, as they increased in wealth, became proud and haughty. There seems, indeed, to be a point in the career of nations as well as of prosperous individuals, when every move is attended with danger. Wealth, though a source of power, is fraught with evil. It as often makes men as nations, vain, presumptuous, and arrogant. Wealth is then no longer an instrument for its increase by the development of new sources of trade and commerce, or of the natural resources of a nation, but is made subservient to individual vanity in the erection of magnificent houses, in luxurious entertainments, or in other modes of extravagance prejudicial to the interests of the state.

Purse-proud men consider wealth essential to their greatness, and its lavish expenditure necessary to the maintenance of their position. They vie with each other in their houses, equipages, dress, dinners, and fêtes of every kind. As it is with individuals so it is with nations; and such was essentially the case with the Italian republics in their career after the fifteenth century. Each of the great cities then claimed for herself the honour of being the foremost in wealth, in power, and in splendour. Independent of each other, they became rivals, not merely for ascendancy, but in empty show. Trifling matters of etiquette were too frequently magnified into national insults. The most frivolous individual complaints were dealt with as matters requiring the serious consideration of the respective states. These petty animosities, the offsprings of overgrown wealth, and of its too frequent accompaniments, arrogance and vanity, imperceptibly increased in time into national jealousies and into a political rivalry, of a character dangerous to the well-being of all the republics. Their differences, craftily fermented by their more military neighbours, made them at last an easy prey to the despotism of an overwhelming German potentate, under whom the people of that rich and sunny land were held in subjection until the sympathies of the free states of Europe and the arms of a near and powerful nation were able in our own time to restore Italy to independence.

The smaller states.

Reference has already been made to Amalfi,[1] Bologna, and Ancona, and to the part they took during the Middle Ages in the commerce of the Mediterranean. Though their trade, and that of Naples, Sicily, and Milan, was insignificant when compared to the trade of Venice, Pisa, Genoa, or Florence, it contributed essentially to the employment of merchant shipping. Naples and Sicily, for instance, furnished large quantities of grain, oil, cotton, sugar, and wines, requiring export to distant parts where they were in demand. Bologna was famous for its cloths and silks; Florence received a considerable portion of its Indian produce through Ancona; and Milan, towards the close of the Middle Ages, was an inland entrepôt of no mean commercial importance. Before the close of the fifteenth century the maritime commerce of Spain and Portugal had risen to a position second only to that of Venice, which was destined soon to be eclipsed by the still greater maritime discoveries of that period. But before taking a glance at the progress of these nations during the Middle Ages, or referring to those interesting episodes in their history, whereby they became the instruments of discovering America, and

[1] Liutprand, bishop of Cremona, gives the fullest account of the trade of Amalfi in the tenth century (Muratori, "Script." V. ii. p. 487 "Antiq." v. ii. p. 884). The merchants of Amalfi built in A.D. 1020 two hospitals at Jerusalem, one dedicated to St. John, which gave the title to the famous Knights Hospitallers, afterwards of Rhodes and Malta ("W. of Tyre," xviii. c. 4; Brencman, "De Republ. Amalf." c. 8).

of establishing a fresh route to India, events which changed the seats and centres of commerce and gave an astounding impetus to shipping, it may be desirable to furnish an outline of the character of the seafaring population at the period to which we now refer, their customs and superstitions, and their love for display in the decoration of their vessels.

Decorations and traditionary emblems of ships.

To cover the unsightly appearance of the resin and pitch necessary to render their vessels tight and to preserve them from decay, pigments were used of various colours, among which white, red lead, and vermilion were long in the highest favour. Green, from its resemblance to sea water, was adopted by piratical cruisers and explorers, to avoid observation. Princes, and other opulent personages, frequently decorated their ships in purple, richly gilt, with highly ornamented poops and sterns, and figure-heads of the most beautiful devices their artists could conceive. In these decorations the taste of the Middle Ages appears to have adhered to the traditionary emblems of the ancients. About the middle of the thirteenth century the Genoese, who, in their encounters with the Pisans, had previously painted their vessels green, assumed the colour of white, dotted with vermilion crosses—the cross gules upon a silver ground being the shield of St. George, the knight both of England and Genoa. In the sixteenth century, red had become the prevailing colour, though frequently black and white were intermingled in foliage, in varied lines or in capricious zigzags; and, sometimes, the ground was entirely black, the ornaments alone being of a dazzling vermilion. Except, however, on special occasions, the colour of mourning, unrelieved by any other, seldom shed its saddening influence over the vessels of the Middle Ages, as it does almost invariably over those of our own time. Then its use was almost exclusively confined to the bearers of death or of other disastrous news. The galleys which conveyed to Manfred the intelligence of the death of his brother Conrad were painted black, and their sails and pendants of a similar colour. In 1525, when Francis I. was captured at the battle of Pavia and carried captive to Barcelona, the six galleys which conveyed the captive monarch and his suite were painted in that sombre colour, from the topmasts down to the water-lines. The sails, banners, pendants, awnings, and oars were all black, and the knights of St. Stephen adopted the same colour when one of their captains was made prisoner by the Turks, vowing never to wear any other until victory should restore him to their country.

Although the ships of the ancients were frequently adorned with purple and gold beyond the decorations to the hull already described, they were surpassed in display by those of the Middle Ages, and, especially, by the ships of the nobles of the Italian republics. Ornaments, emblems, devices, and allegorical subjects with armorial bearings were lavishly engraved or painted on the hulls; while alternate stripes or squares of variegated colours decorated the sails. In the case of the more ordinary vessels of the merchant or of the fisherman, the image of a saint, of the Virgin Mary, or of some sacramental or cabalistic charm, were common devices to ward off malignant influences.

Signals were made by means of figured and painted sails, streamers, or flags, and by the use of the ensigns. Signals.

Indeed, nothing was wanting that could render a ship "magnificent," according to the prevailing tastes of the period.

Manners and customs of seamen.

Having clung to the ancient mythological taste in the decorations of the exterior of their vessels for so many ages, the ship-owners now carried their pious zeal to the extremity of saintly image-worship, which continued until the Reformation, then in its turn relapsing again into pagan heresies. But the manners and habits of the seamen continued almost unchanged. Throughout the whole of the Middle Ages they were the same superstitious mortals, and as much addicted to the marvellous as ever they had been. Prior to the Reformation, they, like the rest of Europe, were of one catholic faith. They believed in God, adored the Virgin Mary, and prayed to every saint in heaven supposed to have any connection with the sea. They had, however, a great fear of a priest, chiefly on account of his black gown; and in bad weather, if peradventure any priest were on board, he would have risked being pitched into the sea, if the master, as was often the case, happened to be as superstitious and ignorant as his crew.

Fantastic shapes and beings of another world, while they awed, pleased their imagination, for they, too, had their sirens, of which their poets sang. Nor were they without their sea-serpent. More marvellous and tantalizing than even that of modern times, which matter-of-fact men are always disputing, the sea-serpent of the dark ages was adorned with a mitre on its head and had a dalmatic robe across its shoulders. Indeed, many of the credulous world on shore believed as firmly in the bishop-fish monster as the sailors themselves, especially since a learned Jesuit confirmed the actual existence of this prodigy of the ocean. But the sea monsters of the Middle Ages, unlike those of our own day, were happily at times instruments of good. One of them, and the statement is attested by a whole boat's crew of seamen, actually swallowed an unbelieving sailor who had been playing at dice, and who, while at play, had wickedly defied the Virgin Mary. So thoroughly were the authorities convinced that this marvellous story was a fact, that to prevent any more sailors from being thus summarily disposed of, the playing of dice was afterwards strictly forbidden on board ship. This happy change appears to have extended to the ships of England, for when Richard I. repaired to the Holy Land he enforced a regulation, that if any seaman played at dice, or any other game of a similar character, without licence, he should be plunged into the sea three mornings successively by way of punishment.

Their legends.

Punishments for gambling,

Seamen of all ages would seem to have been grievously addicted to swearing;[1] and, although the Church and State of every nation have endeavoured to control this wicked and foolish practice, it still prevails to a large extent on board of merchant ships, and is only now curtailed or stifled in ships of war by the strict discipline maintained in them. It was almost universal in the Middle Ages. The French and Mediterranean sailor swore by his bread, by his wine, and by his salt, in the same way that King Richard[2]

and swearing.

[1] The laws of Alençon and of La Roche inflicted the punishment of cutting out the tongue of the sailor who offended for the second time. Jal, "Arch. Nav." ii. p. 109. The laws of Richard do not allude to this habit.

[2] Chronic. Jocelyn. de Brakelond, p. 31-34.

swore by the "very eyes of God." The Church of Rome reproved in the strongest terms the sailor's oath, alleging that, under an apparently simple expression, it covered one decidedly sinful. In the opinion of the Holy Father, bread, wine, and salt were the bases of their daily food; they were also the sacramental elements; they were the symbols of life itself here and hereafter; to swear, therefore, by bread, wine, and salt, was to commit indirectly, in their judgment, an act of horrible atrocity. Accordingly, by a decree of 1543, the most severe penalties are inflicted upon this most "damnable custom;" and these are renewed in a later decree of 1582.[1]

Sailors have ever been a cosmopolitan race. As citizens of the world, they have had almost a common language as well as a common religion. The song which they still sing in lifting the anchor or in hoisting the sails, of "Ye-ho, cheerily, men!" or some such words, for we have never seen them in print, is the song, or at least the same tune sung a thousand years ago by the Venetian sailors, and resembling, we dare say, that lively and invigorating air re-echoed along the shores of Syria from the ships of the ancient Phœnicians as they manned their oars or spread their sails for sea.

Super-stitions. Their superstitions were universal. These may have varied in name and form, but from a very early period even until now sailors have considered Friday to be an unlucky day, and one on which no vessel

[1] The punishment of death for swearing was enjoined by John of Austria just before the battle of Lepanto in A.D. 1571; and similar laws were promulgated by Colbert, the Czar Peter I., and others (Jal, "Arch. Nav." ibid.).

ought to take her departure from a safe harbour. In the Middle Ages it was dreaded by seamen as the day of all days of ill-omen or misfortune: again, salt being spilt horrified them, and knives placed across were, in their opinion, the prognostications of calamity. Divination, sorcery, witchcraft, and necromancy, were then practised by even "thinking minds." What, then, could have been expected from the thoughtless sailor, who, to obtain a fair wind, invariably had recourse to prayers and incantations? In the midst of the gale he invoked a return of fair weather by various superstitious practices. The Greeks of the Mediterranean during a storm threw small loaves into the sea, which they called the loaves of "St. Nicholas." The Russians, to appease the evil spirit which stirs up the boiling waves, and charms the mountain which the sea cannot pass, offered in humility a cake made of flour and butter. The Portuguese, when in imminent peril, fixed to the mast of the ship an image of St. Anthony, and to this idol prayed until the wind changed to his liking.

Nor were these superstitions confined to the sailors of Europe. Some of the Indians, when in danger on the ocean, supplicated the protection of their prince of evil spirits, who was one of their gods, and drank the blood of a cock, swallowing with it a small piece of burning coal, the heat of which they did not feel in the excitement of their insane delirium. When a waterspout was discovered ahead of the ship, the practice prevailed, especially in the Mediterranean, for a sailor to pull out his knife and make the sign of the cross or triple triangle in the air, as representing the Trinity, uttering in his despair some mystical or cabalistic words. If the handle of his knife turned black the water spirit would not reach the ship, and they were safe; but if the danger increased, two sailors resorted to a more powerful charm, a practice which in some measure still prevails in the Levant. They drew their swords and struck them against each other, taking especial care that the weapons formed the figure of a cross every time they clashed. This remedy, in their judgment, was sure to succeed. Some misbelieving sailors would fire a gun against the waterspout in order to disperse it, but these practical fellows, who had no faith in necromancy, deserved to be drowned.

The sailors of the latter portion of the Middle Ages were, however, though superstitious enough, not so superstitious as some of their forefathers had been. They no longer believed that to cut their nails or their hair during fine weather was unlucky, and that such necessary and homely operations inevitably brought on a gale; but they thought, as many sailors still do, that to whistle in a calm would bring wind, and that to continue whistling when the wind came would arouse the anger of the gods and create a storm. They rejected as an idle fable the notion, that if a sailor heard a sneezing from the left hand when going on board ship, it was a fatal omen to which he ought to yield obedience; or, on the contrary, that the voyage would be propitious if the sneezing sound came from the right. But they still implicitly believed it to be a most unlucky sign if, at the moment when they were shipping provisions, the vessel gave a list to starboard. They believed devoutly in a goblin, and considered it a very mischievous imp, which delighted in tormenting sailors during the night by opening their knives, tangling their hair, tearing their bedding, and which, in some of its freaks, would be bold enough to attack the ship herself, tying the ropes into knots so that they would not run through the blocks, carrying away the anchors in a calm, and tearing holes in the sails when they were closely reefed.

Manners and morals, A.D. 1420.

The laws regulating the manners and morals of seamen were frequently very severe. Moncenigo,[1] in 1420, punished with flogging every man guilty of blasphemy, or even of swearing, and inflicted a penalty of one hundred sous on any sailor of the poop, any steersman, officer, or gentleman, who was guilty of the like offence. The Norman code ordered the sailor guilty of robbery to have his head shaved, and then to be tarred and feathered. In this state he was made to pass through the crew ranged in two files, and each man struck him a blow with a stick or a stone, after which he was dismissed the ship.

General severity of punishments.

In conformity with the earlier laws, Peter III., of Aragon, passed in 1354 an ordinance condemning every man to run the gauntlet who gambled with his effects. In certain cases the admiral of a fleet could cut the delinquent's ears off for a similar offence ; and he had even the power also to cut out his tongue, if, for example, any unhappy culprit should insult or menace the master or captain. In the commencement of the fourteenth century, the Catalonian law inflicted the punishment of chopping off the hand of any man who cut the cable of the ship malignantly. In 1397, at Ancona, any sailor who abandoned a ship

[1] Jal, "Arch. Nav." ii. p. 107 *et seq.*, who gives all the punishments mentioned in the text, with reference to the authorities for his statements.

when wrecked, before she was stranded, lost his right hand.

But when the mutilation of members was found to be injudicious, for "afterwards a man was good for nothing," this punishment was removed from the law of Catalonia passed in the year 1354. The ordinance, however, inflicting the loss of the tongue and the ears, and running the gauntlet of sticks and stones along the deck, was not abrogated for some centuries, whilst hanging a man at the yard-arm was for the first time introduced. The laws of the North, terribly severe in the case of a sailor who struck with a knife at the master of a ship, or who merely raised any arms against him, enacted that the offender should have his hand fastened to the mast with the knife which he had used, so that he could only liberate himself by tearing away his own hand by main force, leaving a portion of the member adhering to the mast. Any quarrels among the sailors at Genoa which led to loss of life were rigorously punished, and almost invariably with death. Pilots were most severely dealt with. If any one of them had engaged to carry a vessel into a harbour on the penalty of losing his head, he was decapitated if he failed to do so; in the case of shipwreck he was liable to a similar punishment, unless, indeed, he was rich enough to pay for the loss occasioned by his ignorance and carelessness. Sometimes a man, who cut the cable maliciously so as to cause the loss of the ship confided to his care, was punished by being impaled.[1]

Impaling, flogging, &c.

But the pale, the whip, the cat-o'-nine tails, the mutilation of members, the cutting out the tongue,

[1] Cf. also Pardessus. v. p. 400.

the death by the axe or by a punishment like the gibbet, were not the only chastisements inflicted on mariners who were guilty of crime. Immersion in the water, repeated three times successively, was one more commonly inflicted than any other; and when, in the twelfth century, it was first used by the English, it received the name of keel-hauling; and *cale* (keel) by the French, who inflicted it upon any sailor who used his knife in an assault. At Marseilles three sailors were punished with keel-hauling, who, in a joke, swore by the name of God or by that of any of the saints.[1] Wreckers were punished with great severity by most, if not all, the Mediterranean nations during the Middle Ages. If any person, instead of aiding a ship in peril on a coast, endeavoured to plunder her, and killed or wounded any one on board with a view to robbery, the offenders were upon discovery hurled into the sea, and when taken out half dead were stoned to death, "just as a wolf should be stoned to death."

Branding.

The brand was one of the most ignominious punishments which Venice applied in the thirteenth century. By an enactment of 1232, any seaman who had received advances on any part of his wages whatever by anticipation, and did not fulfil his engagement, was enjoined forthwith to reimburse twice the amount he had received, and was liable to be flogged and branded on his forehead; while a law of the Hanseatic League, renewed in 1418, 1447, and 1597, inflicted the punishment of slitting the ears of any

[1] Keel-hauling seems to have been the common punishment for swearing at Marseilles (see Stat. Mars. Lib. I. and Du Cange).

sailor who deserted the master of his ship in time of danger.[1]

The penal statutes of the Christian countries of the Mediterranean forbade, as already explained, any sale of arms or of ships to the Saracens. Persons who violated this enactment were sometimes "hung by the throat," in the terms of the law of Jerusalem. The most lenient punishment, the dispossession of everything the delinquent had in the world and his exposure on the staircase of the tribunal to the public execration,[2] allowed for selling a ship to the infidels, and thereby "wronging the republics two-fold," was by the statute of Venice of 1232 adopted in principle, if not in all its details, by other Christian countries. But in spite of these stringent laws the Venetians, as already shown, if they did not sell ships or arms to the Saracens, traded with them in other merchandise whenever it suited their purpose. A similar humiliating exposure was inflicted on any pilot or steersman, who, through negligence, had caused the ship under his charge to be boarded, and thus to sustain serious damage or loss. In this case, however, instead of being exposed upon the staircase of the tribunal, the unfortunate offender was obliged, after the confiscation of his property, to sit for six hours upon a cask in a public thoroughfare, in the short dress worn by culprits, with his feet naked, and holding in his hands a helm, amidst the laughter and scorn of the populace.

[1] The Hanseatic law also ordered the branding of the ears.

[2] Marino Faliero was thus exposed. This law would seem to have been general, and not applicable to those only who sold their ships to the infidels.

CHAPTER XVI.

Spain and Portugal—Importance of their commerce in ancient times, and its decline during the Middle Ages—Trade with the coasts of Africa—The maritime discoveries of the Portuguese—Expeditions along the west coast of Africa by order of Prince Henry—Discovery of Madeira, A.D. 1418—Capes Boyador and Blanco, A.D. 1441—Cape Verde Islands, A.D. 1446, and Azores, A.D. 1449—Equator crossed, A.D. 1471—John II. of Portugal—First attempt to reach India by the Cape of Good Hope, A.D. 1487—Ancient dread of the Atlantic —Christopher Columbus—His ideas of the form of the earth, and love for maritime discovery—His visit to Lisbon, and treatment by the Portuguese—His formal proposal in 1480 to the crown of Portugal, which is referred to a learned junto who ridicule his idea —He leaves Lisbon, A.D. 1484; and visits Spain, A.D. 1485—His kind reception by the prior of the convent of La Rabida—First interview with the sovereigns of Spain—Its result—The ridicule he endured—Evidences of an inhabited country to the West of Europe —Orders given by Ferdinand to provide Columbus with the vessels and stores necessary for his voyage to the West—Conditions signed 17th April, 1492—Vessels at last provided for the expedition—Their size and character—Smallness of the expedition—Its departure, 3rd August, 1492—Arrival at the Canary Islands—Great fear and discontent among the crews—Matters become serious—Contemplated mutiny—Land discovered 12th October, A.D. 1492—Columbus takes possession of the island of Guanahani in the name of Spain—The first impressions of the natives on Columbus.

A BRIEF outline has already been furnished of the maritime commerce of Spain during the time of the Phœnicians and Carthaginians, and of her trade with Britain, Western Africa, Asia Minor, and the shores

Spain and Portugal.

Importance of their commerce in ancient times; and its decline during the Middle Ages.

of the Mediterranean. Notice has also been taken of the course adopted by the Romans to secure for themselves the commerce formerly in the hands of the Carthaginians, and of the great value of the trade which Rome ultimately carried on with Spain during the first four centuries of the Christian era. We have also endeavoured to show that when the Vandals wrested Spain from the Romans, the maritime trade of the Peninsula was grievously neglected, and that it did not improve under the semi-
A.D. 711. barbarous rule of the Visigoths. Three hundred years afterwards, when the Saracens established themselves at Cordova, somewhat more attention was paid to mercantile pursuits; but, throughout the whole period of the Saracenic rule, the sea-borne commerce of Spain was insignificant when compared with that of the leading Italian republics. It is true that the invaders so long as they held Seville kept up some commercial relations with the East; but the
A.D. 1340. native population of the country can hardly be said to have done anything worthy of note in maritime matters, till the alliance by marriage of Ferdinand II. of Aragon with Isabella of Castile brought nearly the whole Christian dominion of Spain under one monarchy, and gave renewed life and energy to its trade with other and distant nations.

Trade with the coasts of Africa.

From the commencement of the fourteenth century,[1] the trade between the kingdom of Aragon and the

[1] Barcelona, in 1068, led the way by the creation of an *al-fondech* (Latin, fundicus), or exchange (Capmany v. i. 26). This was greatly aided by the privileges given to it by James, king of Aragon, in 1265, by Pedro III. in 1283, by Peter IV. in 1343, and by many protections from English sovereigns, such as Edward III. in 1353 (Rymer, "Fœd." V. v. p. 762).

coast of Africa had been slowly but surely advancing, as, in spite of their religious differences, the Christians of the West and the Muhammedans had throughout all time mutually conceded to each other the same advantages in their commercial conventions. Thus the Tunisians were allowed to trade as freely at Barcelona as the Catalans did at Tunis, and the corsairs of each country found safe refuge in the harbours of both nations. International arrangements of an intimate character enabled the ship-owners of Catalonia and Sardinia to enter into many profitable joint adventures with those of Barbary and Marocco, especially in the coral and other fisheries, and in the trade of corn, of which Spain obtained, at a price fixed by treaty, large supplies from the coasts of Africa.[1] By this time, too, Portugal had become alive to the advantages to be derived from the discovery of other and distant lands.

The maritime discoveries of the Portuguese.

But though the travels of Marco Polo had more than a century before shown to the nations of Europe the vast extent of the continent of Asia, and had furnished the means of obtaining clearer ideas of its unspeakable riches than had hitherto prevailed, the merchants of the Mediterranean were too desirous of retaining in their own hands the monopoly of the Indian trade to encourage expeditions which had for their object merely the extension of geographical knowledge; the merchants and seamen, who were the chief travellers, having been induced to restrict their knowledge and experience to their own classes.

[1] The original archives of Barcelona give many details of its large ships about the year 1331 (Capmany V. i. p. 46). In one instance, thirteen citizens built a "cog" of three decks, called the San Clemento, which captured several Genoese and Pisan vessels.

Indeed, such commerce as they advocated was essentially practical, and adventurers who proposed novel channels of trade were considered visionaries. It is, however, to an enlightened Portuguese prince that the civilized world is indebted for first setting in motion those expeditions of discovery, which, throughout the greater portion of the fifteenth century, and especially towards its close, afforded so much delight and astonishment to the nations of Europe.

A.D. 1415. Soon after the conquest of Ceuta by Dom John I., king of Portugal, his fifth son Prince Henry, who had been appointed governor of the conquered Moorish province, directed his attention to an exploration of the western coast of Africa. Imbued with a spirit for maritime discovery, this intelligent and accomplished prince was incessant in his efforts to increase the geographical knowledge of the time. From his boyhood he had made mathematics and navigation a continual study. To facilitate his long-meditated voyages of discovery he had fixed his abode in the kingdom of Algarve on the most elevated point of Cape St. Vincent, a spot he considered more favourable than any other on the coast of Spain for his astronomical observations, and where he founded the town of Sagres.[1] The first expedition undertaken in 1417 with two very indifferent vessels proved unsuccessful, having only proceeded five degrees south from its point of departure, the currents at the mouth of the Mediterranean being alleged as unsurmount-

Expeditions along the west coast of Africa, by order of Prince Henry.

[1] See full details of these subjects very carefully worked out in an admirable "Life of Prince Henry the Navigator," by R. H. Major, F.S.A., M.R.S.L., and Keeper of the Department of Maps, British Museum. Lond. 1868.

able obstacles. In the following year, however, João Gonçalvez Zarco, and Tristão Vaz, two gentlemen of rank, annoyed at the difficulties which the Portuguese mariners raised against any further progress southward, and anxious to forward the views of their enlightened prince, volunteered to double Cape Boyador, and to prosecute their voyage to the south. A gale of wind drove them far away from the coast, and by this accident they became acquainted with the position of the island of Madeira, of which they took possession in the name of their sovereign. According to a well-known tradition this island had, however, been previously discovered by an Englishman named Machin, moreover had probably been seen by Hanno or by some of the earlier Phœnician voyagers. Mr. Major has quite recently shown[1] that there is good reason to believe in the truth of the story of Machin. The merit, however, of this important discovery is for all practical purposes due to the Portuguese, who, thus encouraged, renewed their exertions and obtained a grant from Martin V. of the dominion over all territories which might thenceforward be discovered from Cape Boyador to the Indies; but it was only in 1441 that Cape Blanco was reached. The discovery of gold dust and the capture of some slaves still further stimulated a spirit for adventure which had been originally roused by loftier motives. Various Portuguese merchants of Lagos combined and equipped six caravels, with which they sailed to the coast of Guinea. By them the Cape Verde Islands were discovered in 1446; and another somewhat similar expedition discovered the Azores in 1449. In 1471 the Equator

Discovery of Madeira, A.D. 1418.

Capes Boyador and Blanco, A.D. 1441.

Cape Verde Islands, A.D. 1446, and Azores, A.D. 1449.

[1] Life of Prince Henry, p 72.

Equator crossed, A.D. 1471.

was first passed, and ten years afterwards the Portuguese founded a fort and established a trading station on the coast of Guinea for the purpose of maintaining a permanent commercial intercourse with the natives.

From this commercial alliance the Portuguese derived large profits, while the crown received a considerable revenue from the ivory and gold the natives offered in abundance in exchange for trinkets and baubles of European manufacture. The greatest precautions were necessary to preserve in their own hands the valuable trade they had discovered, as other nations had indistinctly heard of the enormous profits the Portuguese were deriving from their commercial intercourse with some distant and hitherto unknown lands. They were, however, successful in keeping this secret for a good many years.[1]

John II. of Portugal.

The reign of Dom John II.[2] was likewise conspicuous for the still wider extension of this spirit of maritime enterprise. Second only to Prince Henry, this monarch displayed the greatest anxiety to foster discoveries by sea. He had been taught to believe that, by coasting along the African continent, a passage to the East Indies might be discovered; and he not only equipped two small squadrons expressly for this purpose, but despatched two of his subjects into India and Abyssinia to find out the route to and between these vast regions, and to ascertain what advantages the trade of his country might derive from the knowledge thus acquired. These researches ulti-

First attempt to reach India by the Cape of Good Hope, A.D. 1487.

[1] The famous motto of Prince Henry, which his life illustrated so fully, was "Talent de bien faire." It is carved on his tomb at Batalha, of which Mr. Major gives a good engraving, p. 305.

[2] Major, pp. 322–391.

mately led to the discovery of the Cape of Good Hope, in 1487, by Bartholomew Dias. The rude winds and mountainous waves which assailed that now well-known promontory led Dias to call it the Cape of Storms; but the king, sanguine that beyond its rugged shores there would be found the rich lands of India, gave it the name it now bears. Dias ventured only a short distance beyond the promontory,[1] and ten years more elapsed before it was doubled by Vasco de Gama, another still more celebrated Portuguese navigator.

While the Portuguese were striving to reach India by the eastern route, another navigator, greater than any the world had hitherto produced, was maturing his plans for endeavouring to reach that cherished land by a voyage to the West. Hitherto the Atlantic Ocean had been regarded with wonder and awe. It seemed to bound the then known world with an impenetrable chaos, a chaos into which the most daring adventurers had feared to penetrate. "No one," says Edrisi, an Arabian writer, whose countrymen for many ages had been the boldest of navigators, "has been able to verify anything concerning it (the Atlantic Ocean), on account of its difficult and perilous navigation, its great obscurity, its profound depth, and frequent tempests; through fear of its mighty fishes and its haughty winds; yet there are many islands in it, some peopled, others uninhabited. There is no mariner who dares to enter into its deep waters; or if any have done so, they have merely kept along its coasts, fearful of departing from them.

Ancient dread of the Atlantic.

[1] Dias reached a river beyond Algoa Bay, now known as the great Fish River (Major, p. 345). He discovered the Cape on his return voyage.

The waves of this ocean, although they roll as high as mountains, yet maintain themselves without breaking, for if they broke, it would be impossible for ship to plough them."[1]

One man was, however, at last found bold enough to brave the dangers of the broad Atlantic and to force a passage across its troubled waters. Only a few years before Vasco de Gama started on his voyage of discovery in the East, a greater and better man had set sail to the West, in the hopes of thus reaching the fabled land of "Cathay." Christopher Columbus, a Genoese, who had been trained from boyhood to the sea, had long cherished the idea that if he could only penetrate the mysterious waters of the Atlantic, he would find beyond them and at less distance than was then supposed, the shores of India, whence Europe had been so long supplied with its spices and numerous luxuries. From the translations of the works of Ptolemy, Pliny, and Strabo, then but recently made known, Columbus obtained all the knowledge the ancients possessed of geography, a knowledge which, though happily preserved, had lain buried amid the darkness and tumults of the Middle Ages, and had been only brought again to light on the revival of science and letters during the fifteenth century.

Christopher Columbus.

His ideas of the form of the earth;

Columbus had formed a crude idea of the extent of the waters which covered the earth; and their presumed limited extent and the shortness of the distance westward, as he supposed, between Spain and the Indies, had, no doubt, exercised considerable influence

[1] Condé, "Historia de la dominacion de los Arabes en España, 8vo. Paris, 1840."

over him in his determination to fathom the mystery of the Atlantic Ocean.[1]

From his earliest youth he had evinced a strong inclination for the study of geography as well as geometry and astronomy, of which he had gained a superficial knowledge long before he resolved to push his fortune from the ports of Spain. Trained to the sea at a period when its followers were exposed to more than usual dangers by the piratical habits then prevalent, he had become daring and adventurous, which, combined with his love for geographical discoveries, rendered him peculiarly well adapted for the exploration of unknown seas. Genoa, his native city, was not then, however, in a position to aid his cherished design, for this republic, once so powerful, had been languishing for some time under the embarrassment of a foreign and a foolish war. Falling slowly but surely from her once high estate, her spirit fell with her fortunes, and she had not the inclination, even if she had had the means, to enter upon extensive but doubtful adventures. Columbus had, therefore, to seek aid in other lands. He repaired to Lisbon, where many of his countrymen had settled; and there, in the full vigour of his manhood, he took up his residence about the year 1470, and soon afterwards married a daughter of Bartolomeo de Palestrello, who had been one of the most distinguished navigators under Prince Henry of Portugal and the colonizer and governor of Porto Santo.

and love for maritime discovery.

His visit to Lisbon,

By this marriage he obtained access to his father-in-

[1] "Select Letters of Columbus," edited, with a careful Introduction, by R. H. Major, Esq., F.S.A., for the Hakluyt Society, 2nd ed. 1870 and "Life of Columbus," by Washington Irving. Lond. 12mo. 1830.

and treatment by the Portuguese.

law's journals and charts, while living with his widowed mother-in-law at Porto Santo,[1] and these were treasures to Columbus. From these and other sources he soon made himself conversant with the various distant sea routes then known to the Portuguese, and learnt also their plans and conceptions for other voyages still more distant, having been allowed to sail occasionally with them in their expeditions to the coast of Guinea. On shore he maintained himself and family by the construction of maps and charts, an occupation which brought him into communication with many men of learning and influence, and notably with Pedro Correa, his wife's brother-in-law and a famous navigator, and also with Paulo Toscanelli of Florence, the most learned cosmographer of the period.[2] The times, too, were favourable to his views. The discoveries of the Cape Verde Islands and of the Azores, with the explorations along the coasts of Africa, as far as the Cape of Good Hope, had inflamed the imaginations of men with visions of other lands of greater wealth and beauty yet to be discovered, and had again revived the speculation of the ancients, the imaginary Atlantis of Plato, and the great oceanic island which the Carthaginians were said to have found. Columbus, therefore, applied himself with redoubled zeal to the study of every writer on geography ancient or modern, being himself firmly convinced that the earth was a sphere or globe, which might be travelled round from east to west, and that men stood foot to foot when on its opposite points.

[1] Columbus also resided some time at Funchal in Madeira, where his house was still shown (in 1846).

[2] His correspondence with Toscanelli was in 1474 (Major, p. 350).

Strabo had already expressed his opinion (following the judgments of Homer and of Poseidonius) that an ocean surrounded the earth;[1] and Marco Polo,[2] and perhaps also Sir John Maundeville, had in the thirteenth and fourteenth centuries visited parts of Asia far beyond the regions laid down by Ptolemy: from the narratives of these travellers, Columbus judged that it would not be difficult to sail from Spain to India on the same parallel, and that a voyage to the West of no long duration would bring him to that far-famed but mysterious land. The most eastern part of Asia known to the ancients, he thought, could not be separated from the Azores by more than a third of the circumference of the globe, the intervening space being in all probability filled up by the unknown residue of Asia.[3]

"It is singular," remarks Washington Irving in his interesting history of the Life and Correspondence of Columbus,[4] "how much the success of this great

[1] Strabo, i. c. 3–5; ii. c. 5.

[2] The celebrated travels of Marco Polo have been recently edited by Colonel Yule, C.B., an accomplished Oriental scholar, who has shown much ability in arranging the mass of new material for their illustration which has been discovered during the fifty years since Marsden's edition. Colonel Yule completely confirms the general truthfulness of Polo's narrative, and shows that the occasional credulity of the traveller (like that of Herodotus) is mainly due to the period in which he journeyed. The date of Marco Polo's absence from Venice is from 1271 to 1295 (Yule, Book of Ser Marco Polo, the Venetian, 2 vols. 8vo. 1871).

[3] It seems probable that Columbus was more influenced by what he heard from Toscanelli of the discoveries of Marco Polo than by anything else. Martin Behaim, in 1492, constructed a map in which Zipango (supposed to be Japan) is placed according to Polo's description, and it is believed that Columbus had a similar map with him on his first voyage. A copy of this map, which was nearly, if not quite, the same as Toscanelli's, is given in W. Irving, p. 16 (Murray).

[4] W. Irving, p. 60.

undertaking depended upon two happy errors, the imaginary extent of Asia to the East, and the supposed smallness of the earth, both errors of the most learned and profound philosophers, but without which Columbus would hardly have ventured upon his enterprise. As to the idea of finding land by sailing directly to the West, it is at present so familiar to our minds, as in some measure to diminish the merits of the first conception, and the hardihood of the first attempt; but in those days, as has been well observed, the circumference of the earth was yet unknown; no one could tell whether the ocean was not of immense extent, impossible to be traversed; nor were the laws of specific gravity, and of central gravitation, ascertained, by which, granting the rotundity of the earth, the possibility of making the tour of it would be manifest."

Several years, however, elapsed before Columbus could make any progress towards carrying into effect his favourite project. He was himself too poor to render any pecuniary assistance towards the fitting out of the requisite expedition; and the government of Portugal was then too much engrossed in a war with Spain to engage the services of a foreigner in any peaceful enterprise of an expensive nature. The public mind, also, though elated by the discoveries which had already been made, was not then prepared for so doubtful and perilous an undertaking, while the sailors, who had rarely ventured far out of sight of land, considered the project of a voyage directly westward into a boundless waste of ocean as dangerous as it was extravagant and visionary. But when John II., who had imbibed the passion for discovery from his grand-uncle, Prince Henry, ascended the throne, a fresh impetus was given to voyages of discovery. These, as we have seen, were prosecuted with increased vigour to the south of the Equator and along the shores of Africa, and soon afterwards preparations were made for extending these voyages round the Cape of Good Hope, till at last India was reached by Vasco de Gama, whose celebrated expedition we shall hereafter attempt to describe.

His formal proposal in 1480 to the crown of Portugal

It was not, however, till 1480, when the successful application of the astrolabe[1] to the purposes of navigation removed from the contemplated expedition of Columbus much of its hazardous character, that he formally proposed his great voyage of discovery to the crown of Portugal. He had always felt it to be an enterprise only to be undertaken in the service of some sovereign state which could assume dominion over whatever territories he might discover, and which, with the means of conquest and colonisation at its disposal, would be also able to spread the Christian religion, a desire which seems to have been at all times present in his meditations. In this year Columbus obtained an audience with the king, and, being graciously received, revealed his plans fully to the monarch. Though the king was at the time discouraged from entering upon any new scheme of discovery, by the cost and trouble already incurred in the as yet unsuccessful exploration of the route along the African coast, he nevertheless gave a favourable consideration to the scheme of Columbus,

is referred to a learned junto, who ridicule his idea.

[1] This instrument was certainly used by Vasco de Gama in 1497 (Major, p. 393). It was invented by Behaim about the year 1480, with the aid of two physicians, Roderigo and Josef (Major, "Select Letters of Columbus," Introd p. lvi.).

and referred it to a learned junto, who were charged with all questions of maritime enterprise. This scientific body, however, treated the project as extravagant, an opinion confirmed by a council composed of the prelates and persons of the greatest learning in the kingdom. But the junto, though unwilling to accept the proposal of Columbus, were not slow to profit by the information he had given to them; and while pretending to afford him their best attention, despatched a vessel on their own account to test some of his views. The whole plan failed; the mariners after sailing for some days to the west of the Cape Verde Islands came back in terror at the rough weather they had experienced, and the seemingly vast extent of ocean to be sailed over; and Columbus, justly indignant at the contemptible treatment he had received, at once took his departure from such a court and country, to seek elsewhere a patron surrounded by more honest counsellors.[1]

He leaves Lisbon, A.D. 1484, and visits Spain, A.D. 1485.

Broken-hearted, friendless, and almost penniless, he left Lisbon with his son Diego, then a little boy, towards the close of 1484, and is supposed to have retraced his steps to Genoa, and thence carried his proposal to Venice. Receiving no encouragement at either of these places, he found his way to Spain, in the winter of 1485, and there had the good fortune to make friends at the ancient convent of La Rabida, situated not far from the small seaport of Palos in Andalusia.

His kind reception by the prior of the convent of La Rabida.

At the gate of this convent the discoverer of a new world stopped to ask a little bread and water for his famishing boy, and the prior, Juan Perez

[1] W. Irving, p. 24.

de Marchena, happening to pass at the time, was struck with the dignified, careworn, and poverty-stricken appearance of the stranger, and, entering into conversation with him, soon ascertained the leading incidents of his life, and the object of his visit to Spain. The prior himself, a man of extensive information, who had already paid some attention to geographical and nautical science, detained Columbus as his guest, at the same time sending for a scientific friend, Garcia Fernandez (to whom we are indebted for this account), to converse with him; and, in the end, the prior's first impressions were in some measure confirmed by the ancient mariners of Palos, for they, too, had heard of strange and rich lands beyond the setting sun. The earnest manner of Columbus, and his extensive knowledge made, day by day, an increasing impression on the prior and his friends, till at length in the spring of 1485, when the Spanish court had reached the ancient city of Cordova with the view of prosecuting the war against the Moorish kingdom of Granada, Columbus, furnished with letters of introduction from the worthy prior, determined to lay his grand scheme before Ferdinand and Isabella.

First interview with the sovereigns of Spain.

Nearly a year elapsed, however, before Columbus was enabled to obtain an audience with the sovereigns, and even then his troubles were not overcome. The king referred his project for consideration to a body of "learned men," who met in the Dominican convent of St. Stephen in Salamanca; and although at this convent Columbus was hospitably entertained during the course of the inquiry, his theory was received with incredulity. Nor, indeed, was this surprising. An obscure mariner and a

Its result.

member of no learned institution could hardly hope to convert at once to his theory an erudite assembly, most of whom entertained the impression that he was at the best a mere visionary. "Was it likely," exclaimed one of his learned examiners, in a burst of indignant unbelief, "that there was a part of the world where the feet of the people who inhabited it were opposite to ours; where they walk with their heels upward, and their heads hanging down; where the trees grow with their branches downward; where it rains, hails, and snows upward, and where all things are topsy-turvy?" "Even 'admitting' the earth to be spherical, it was only," they said, "inhabitable in the northern hemisphere, and in that section only was canopied by the heavens, the opposite half being, in their opinion, a chaos, a gulph, or a mere waste of water." One of their objections was indeed amusing: "Should a ship succeed in reaching," they argued, "the extremity of India, she could never get back again, for the rotundity of the globe would present a kind of mountain, up which it would be impossible for her to sail with the most favourable wind."[1]

The ridicule he endured.

The sound reasoning, however, of Columbus made a deep impression on the minds of some of the members of the conference (as especially on Diego De Deza, afterwards Archbishop of Seville), and the seed thus sown grew and in time prospered. In the meanwhile, however, he had much to endure. The affairs of war hurried the court from place to place, so that any question of less importance than the campaign

[1] W. Irving, vol. i. p. 125, where it appears that these learned men relied chiefly on the authority of the Fathers, Lactantius and St. Augustine, holding that the views of Columbus were in opposition to Holy Scripture.

was disregarded. His plans, too, when known, were generally scoffed at and ridiculed as the dreams of one of the wildest of schemers. The very children of the towns were taught to regard him as a visionary madman, and pointed to their foreheads as he passed them; though, amid the sufferings hope long deferred creates, he was, on the whole, generously treated by the court and his expenses paid while attending on it.

But while the learned scoffers at his theory had no valid answer to give to arguments based on facts they could neither refute nor deny, men of more enlightened views were open to conviction, and saw with Columbus that as the gales from the West brought to Madeira trees and canes of an unknown species, there must be some land, and that too not very far distant, where these trees and canes had grown; and further, that as other productions were found, evidently the work of man, the unknown land must be the abode of human beings. Years, however, elapsed before the sovereigns of Spain could be induced to adopt means for solving the great problem of a new world in the West; till, at length, Columbus, wearied with these continued delays, sent his brother Bartholomew to England to endeavour to persuade Henry VII. to afford him the means of carrying out his expedition of discovery. Misfortunes befell Bartholomew on the way. The vessel in which he had taken his passage having been boarded by pirates, who stripped him of everything he possessed, he was compelled to live for a considerable time after he arrived in London in poverty and obscurity, earning a scanty existence by the construction and sale of

Evidences of an inhabited country to the West of Europe.

sailing charts.[1] When his circumstances were somewhat improved he obtained an audience with Henry VII., and presented to his majesty a map of the world, which bears the date of London, February 13, 1488.[2] He was well received, and the English monarch appears to have expressed an interest in the proposals of his brother Christopher, whom he invited to London. But Columbus could not be induced to leave Spain, perhaps from the still-cherished hope that he would at last succeed with Queen Isabella, or from an attachment he had formed with a lady, with whom he had become acquainted at Cordova.

In February, 1489, Ferdinand and Isabella received an embassy from Henry VII., with whom they had formed an alliance. It does not, however, appear that at that time Columbus was in possession of any reply to the application he had made through his brother Bartholomew to the English court. When the Spanish sovereigns returned to Cordova, in May of that year, the proposals of Columbus received their attention, and steps were at once taken to have the long-adjourned investigation resumed.[3] But war and other matters again intervened, so that it was not till the winter of 1491 that Columbus was enabled to obtain another hearing of his case. This time he was successful. Notwithstanding the unfavourable report of the learned junto of Salamanca, an opinion favourable to his enterprise had gradually sprung up at court, and the sovereigns of Spain were unwilling to close the door upon a project which might prove

[1] D. G. Spotomo, "Memoir of Columbus," p. 243.
[2] Ibid. p. 44.
[3] Historia del Almirante, i. cap. 12. Washington Irving, vol. i. p. 137.

highly advantageous to the nation under their rule. Yet even then no definite orders were given to provide the necessary means for the expedition, and Columbus had to submit to another year's delay.

Orders given by Ferdinand to provide Columbus with the vessels and stores necessary for his voyage to the West.

At length, after ten years' waste of time in Portugal, and seven weary years of solicitations at the court of Spain, the conditions on which the voyage of discovery was to be undertaken were drawn out and executed. In virtue of these Columbus was nominated admiral, viceroy, governor and judge of all islands and mainlands he might discover. He was also constituted admiral of the ocean, with many of the prerogatives enjoyed by the admiral of Castile ; and these honours were to pass to his heirs and successors for ever. He was further entitled to reserve for himself one-tenth of all pearls, precious stones, gold, silver, spices, and of every other article of merchandise, in whatever manner found, bought, bartered, or gained within his admiralty, less the cost of production. While he was allowed to contribute one-eighth part of the expenses in fitting out these vessels, and of all vessels which might hereafter engage in trade with any country he might discover, he was also permitted to receive in return an eighth of their profits.[1]

Conditions signed April 17, 1492

These conditions, liberal in themselves, but nothing more than the Portuguese had granted to their discoverers, were signed by Ferdinand and Isabella at the city of Santa Fé, in the plain of Granada, on the 17th of April, 1492, and proclaimed throughout Spain, with the announcement that Columbus and his heirs were authorized to prefix Don to their names. Palos was fixed on as the place where the ships

[1] Memoir of Columbus, p. 49. W. Irving, vol. i. p. 170.

were to be equipped and commissioned, the inhabitants of that place having, for some reason, been condemned by the royal council to serve the crown, for one year, with a certain number of armed caravels.

When the royal decree was issued, requiring the Andalusian shipowners to provide three vessels ready for sea within ten days from the 30th of April, and to sail in whatever direction Columbus might command, they refused to furnish them for what they conceived to be a desperate service; while the boldest of the Andalusian seamen shrunk from a wild and chimerical cruise into the mysterious regions of an unknown and stormy ocean; hence many weeks elapsed ere the royal commands could be carried into effect, nor could the influence of the prior of La Rabida induce the ship-owners and seamen of Palos to comply with the decree of their sovereigns. It was only when absolute and threatening mandates were issued on the 20th of June, ordering the magistrates of the coast of Andalusia to press into the service any Spanish ships or seamen they pleased, backed by the offer of Martin Alonzo Pinzon, a rich and enterprising navigator, to take a large personal share in the expedition, that the requisite vessels and crews were obtained. His example, and that of his brother, likewise a navigator of great courage and ability, and their combined determination to sail with Columbus, induced many of their relations and friends to embark, so that the equipment was completed within a month after they had resolved to risk their lives and fortunes in the expedition.

Three vessels were apparently all that Columbus had requested. Two of them were light barques, called caravels, described, or rather, from the drawings of the period, delineated as open and without deck in the centre, rising to a considerable height at the bow and stern, with forecastles and cabins for the accommodation of the crew. The third vessel, according to the testimony of Peter Martyr, the learned contemporary of Columbus, was decked throughout. The only reason alleged for employing vessels without decks, or open in the waist, on so hazardous a voyage, was, that from their smallness, Columbus might be enabled to run close to the shore, and to enter shallow waters and harbours, advantages which, he thought, overweighed the danger of an ocean navigation, about which he was comparatively careless. More likely they were really chosen because larger vessels could not readily be obtained at Palos.

Vessels at last provided for the expedition.

But though the size and construction of her vessels were thus accommodated to the short and easy voyages along the coast which they were accustomed to perform, Spain possessed many larger. One hundred and fifty years before the time of Columbus, mention is made in an edict issued by Pedro IV. (1354) of Catalonian merchant ships of two and three decks, and from 8,000 to 12,000 quintals burden.[1] Again, in 1419, Alphonso of Aragon hired several merchant ships to transport artillery and horses, &c., from Barcelona to Italy, two of which carried one hundred and twenty horses each. Mention is also made of a Venetian vessel of 700 tons arriving, in 1463, at Barcelona, from England, laden with wheat, and of a Castilian ship which, in 1497, conveyed to that port a cargo of 12,000 quintals burden. In fact, then as now,

Their size and character.

[1] Capmany, vol. v. p. 58.

all the great maritime nations possessed vessels of large dimensions, although the smaller were comparatively far more numerous than in modern times, being better adapted to the nature of the voyages undertaken and the limited extent of maritime commerce.

If therefore Columbus set sail on his expedition with ships the largest of which, as some writers have imagined, was only from 150 to 200 tons burden, this must have been from choice, or for the reason just named; it could not have arisen from ignorance on his part of the kind of vessels best adapted for his purpose, or of the roughness of the sea about to be explored, for he had made various voyages on the Atlantic, had studied with care the logs of the Portuguese navigators in their discoveries, and had himself visited Iceland,[1] and made a voyage to the 73rd degree of north latitude, then a region of the ocean all but unknown. But unfortunately history furnishes no definite account of the vessels placed under his charge, and no authentic delineation of their form. In the abridged edition[2] of Washington Irving's interesting work, there is, indeed, the representation of a Spanish galley from the tomb of Fernando Columbus in the cathedral of Seville. But there is no reason to suppose that this galley is an actual drawing of any one of the three vessels in which Columbus made his ever memorable voyage, though it probably represents the ordinary coasting vessel of the period, or one of those occasionally employed in the trade between Spain and the smaller Mediterranean ports.

[1] It is now certain that Columbus heard in Iceland traditions of the voyages of Icelanders to "Vinland" (Virginia and Carolina) between the 10th and the 13th centuries.—Rafn. Antiq. American. Copenhagen, fol. 1837.

[2] Murray: London, 1830. See frontispiece.

In a small volume consisting only of ten leaves,[1] preserved in the Grenville library, there are two drawings of vessels said to be copies of the caravels of Columbus, but unfortunately no description whatever is given of them; of these, one is given in the edition of Washington Irving's work just referred to,[2] with the statement that it is "the sketch of a galley coasting the island of Hispaniola, from an illustration contained in a letter written by Columbus to Don Gabriel Sanchez, treasurer of the king of Spain;" and that "the original sketch is supposed to have been made with a pen by Columbus." But the sketch does not represent the kind of vessel which an experienced navigator, like Columbus, would have chosen for an Atlantic voyage, when he must have had more suitable vessels at his disposal.

Though the word "caravel" was generally used to designate vessels of a small size, in the Mediterranean it was occasionally given to the largest class of ships of war among the Mussulmans. Thus, in a naval classification made by King Alphonzo, in the middle of the thirteenth century, large ships propelled only by sails are described as Naos;[3] the second class, or smaller vessel, were known as Caraccas, Fustas, Ballenares, Pinazas, and Carabelas; while boats of the smallest size, with sails and oars, were called Galleys, Galliots, Tardantes, and Sactias. To the latter class the vessel said to have been sketched

[1] Mr. Major ("Select Letters of Columbus") has mentioned all the known copies of this very rare tract.—Introd. p. cviii.

[2] W. Irving (Murray). Ibid. p. lxxxvii.

[3] Columbus calls his own ship the Christopher Nao; and M. Jal, who has at great length discussed the size of Columbus's ships on his voyage, states that Nao was the usual title of an admiral's vessel. —Arch. Nav. ii. p. 249.

with a pen by Columbus, and inclosed in his letter[1] to Don Gabriel Sanchez, evidently belongs. The following delineation from a picture of the fifteenth century, in S. Giovanni e Paolo at Venice, fairly represents the ordinary merchant vessel which might, at the

time, have been lying in the harbour of Palos; and her form, not unlike that of a modern Dutch galliot, is well adapted to encounter in safety the large rolling waves of the Atlantic.

[1] The letter is entitled "De Insulis inventis. Epistola Cristoferi Colom . . . ad Magnificum dñm Raphaelem Sanxis . . . 3 Kal. Maii, 1493 (Grenville Collect. No. 6663).

It is surprising how inconsiderable was the equipment for so important an expedition, but Columbus had evidently reduced his requisitions to the narrowest limits, lest the expense should create further impediments in the way of a voyage which had already caused him so much anxious solicitude. Even until the last moment of his departure he had numerous difficulties to overcome. The owners of one of the smaller vessels impressed into the service showed throughout the greatest repugnance to the voyage, and took an active part in creating quarrels and contentions among the people employed in her equipment. Caulkers performed their work in a careless and imperfect manner; the stores were delayed, and when they arrived were either of the wrong description, or improperly packed; the sails did not fit; the masts were not properly rigged; and, in fact, everything had to be effected by the most harsh and arbitrary measures, and in defiance of bitter popular prejudice. Smallness of the expedition.

At length when seamen were found to supply the place of those who, having enlisted willingly, had been persuaded by their friends to desert, this ever memorable expedition took its departure on Friday, the 3rd of August, 1492, Columbus hoisting his flag in the Santa Maria, the largest vessel of the three; while the second, called the Pinta, was commanded by Martin Alonzo Pinzon, accompanied by his brother, Francisco Martin, as pilot; and the third, the Nina, by the third of the brothers, Vicente Yañez Pinzon. There was besides an officer of the crown, a notary, usually sent on government expeditions to keep an official record of all transactions. A physician, Garcia Its departure, 3rd Aug., 1492.

Fernandez, also accompanied the expedition, together with various private adventurers, several servants, and ninety mariners, making in all one hundred and twenty persons.

No pomp and display marked their departure. On the contrary, when Columbus set sail, he and his crew were so impressed with the solemnity of the occasion, that they confessed before their priests, as if they had been doomed men, partook of the communion, and committed themselves to the especial guidance and protection of heaven, while a deep gloom spread over the whole community of Palos.

Columbus is supposed to have taken with him for his guidance a conjectural chart prepared by Toscanelli of what he presumed to be the position of the continent of which he was in search. On this map the coasts of Europe and Africa, from the south of Ireland to the end of Guinea; and opposite to them, on the other side of the Atlantic, the supposed extremity of Asia, or, as it was termed, India, are believed to have been delineated. Marco Polo had, as we have stated, placed the island of Japan (Zipango) fifteen hundred miles distant from the Asiatic coast; and Columbus had somehow advanced this island a thousand leagues further to the East, supposing it to lie in nearly the same position as Florida.[1] With this view he shaped his course from the Canary Islands, where he had called for fresh supplies and remained for three weeks, refitting the Pinta, which had lost her rudder and was otherwise disabled.

Arrival at the Canary Islands.

From the Canaries, Columbus set sail early on the

[1] Irving, p. 60.

morning of the 6th of September, bidding farewell to these frontier islands of the Old World, and striking out into unknown seas to discover a New World which seems destined to eclipse every other nation of ancient or of modern times. For three days he lay becalmed, and it was not until Tuesday, the 9th of September, that he lost sight of land. Then the hearts of the sailors failed them; behind them lay everything dear to them on earth; before them all was mystery, chaos, and peril.

Great fear and discontent amongst the crews.

The cheering hopes held out by Columbus, with the certainty of great rewards when they reached the land of Cathay, where gold and precious stones were said to be found in vast abundance, had no effect on these disconsolate men, many of whom shed tears, while others broke into loud lamentations, refusing to be comforted. Two days after, they had lost sight of the Canaries, and when, about one hundred and fifty leagues to the westward of Ferro, they fell in with the part of a mast, covered with shells and sea-weed, the fears of the trembling crew were increased; till at length, when, on the 13th of September, Columbus, for the first time, noticed that the variation of the needle increased as he advanced to the westward, the great navigator himself became really alarmed, though he did not make known his doubts and fears. But the variation of the compass soon attracted the attention of the pilots and filled them with consternation. The very laws of nature they thought were changing as they proceeded westward. That instrument they felt was about to lose its mysterious virtues, and without it they would, on such a vast and trackless ocean, be lost for ever. Though Columbus was able to give a plausible if not the correct reason for the variation, it sufficed to satisfy the pilots and masters, who had great confidence in his skill and genius, but the ordinary seamen were not so easily pacified, and it was only when they reached the favourable trade winds that their fears were somewhat allayed.

Day by day they became more resigned, and as the fine weather and fair winds continued until they reached the course of the Gulf stream, their spirits rose almost exultingly, under the impression that the numerous weeds floating about betokened a near approach to the rich lands of Cathay. Pilot and seamen alike vied with each other as to who should catch the first sight of land; and though Columbus felt that they must still be a great distance from the Florida of which he was in search, he kept his own counsel. Frequently deceived by the dark clouds which just before the rising or setting sun in these latitudes often exhibit the appearance of distant land, the spirits of the seamen began again to droop. They had advanced farther West than ever man had done before; still they continued leaving home far away, and pressing onwards into an apparently boundless abyss of ocean, through which they felt they should never be able to retrace their course, till at last the fair wind became in itself a source of the greatest alarm, from a notion that it always blew from east to west, and that if they attempted to return, they would never be able to reach the coast of Spain. At last the seaweed, from being a source of joy and hope, became an object of alarm. They considered these weeds as proof that the sea was growing shallower, and then they talked of unseen rocks and shoals or quicksands, on to which they might be drifted, and be for ever lost far from any habitable land and beyond the reach of human aid. Then when Columbus took soundings to appease their fears, and found no bottom with a deep sea lead, the fact of no depth being found in water where the surface was covered with weeds, which they supposed grew only on shore or near land, increased their vague terrors and superstitious fancies; everything differed, they said, in these strange regions from the world to which they had been accustomed, and nothing but a return to their fatherland would abate their terror and discontent.

Matters now became very serious. In proportion as they approached the regions where land should have been found, their impatience and their fears increased. An open mutiny was feared, and plans were even arranged that if Columbus should not meet their demands to return to Spain, they should throw him overboard, and on their arrival at home spread the report that he had fallen into the sea while engaged in surveying the stars and signs of heaven with his astronomical instruments. Though Columbus was not ignorant of these mutinous intentions, he kept perfectly composed, but consulted seriously with his pilots as to their position. In the midst of these consultations they were aroused by a cheering shout from the Pinta of land to the south-west. Every eye was stretched in that direction, and every voice confirmed the sight of land. So impressed was Columbus with the fact, that he threw himself on his knees, and devoutly thanked God for

Matters become serious.

Contemplated mutiny.

guiding him in safety to the long-hoped-for shores. But alas, the morning sun soon put an end to all their hopes. The Cathay of their dreams was but another evening cloud.

The weather continued delightful; dolphins were now seen in great numbers, and flying fish in every quarter; these for a time diverted the attention, and amused the crew, but only for a time; loud murmurs and menaces were again too frequently heard, until at last Columbus and his crew were at open defiance and his situation became really desperate. Matters could not remain much longer as they were; but fortunately, ere a mutiny actually broke out, the vicinity to land became so manifest as no longer to admit of doubt. Quantities of fresh weeds, such as grow in rivers, made their appearance; a few green fish, found only in the neighbourhood of rocks, were caught; then a branch of thorn, with berries on it, floated past the ship; and at last a staff, artificially carved, was picked up, which more than anything else suggested their vicinity to some inhabited country.[1] The spirits of the crew revived. Columbus felt certain that land must now be close at hand. Appearances now authorized the precaution that they should not sail after midnight. At sunset of the day on which he had issued this precautionary order, the ships were running rapidly before a strong easterly wind. When night approached, Columbus took his station on the highest portion of the castle or poop of his own vessel; hardly an

[1] Many of the documents published by Navarette, are preserved in the great collection at Simancas, from which Mr. Froude has drawn so large a portion of the documents for his history.—Journal of Columbus, Navarette Collection, book i. p. 19.

eye in either vessel closed that night. About ten o'clock he thought he saw a light glimmering in the distance, but it soon disappeared. Again it appeared in a sudden and passing gleam. Others saw it as well as himself; it looked like the torch of some fishing boat, rising and falling with the roll of the ocean. Steadily they proceeded on their course till midnight. Soon afterwards the loom of land could be faintly traced. With feelings of the most intense anxiety they waited for the dawn. As the first rays of the morning light broke slowly through the clouds and haze which hung about the horizon, the land became clearly visible. The life-inspiring cry of "Land" now rang from ship to ship, till at last there was no deception: the land lay not more than two leagues distant. On the morning of Friday, 12th of October, 1492, the great navigator first beheld one of the many islands which lie contiguous to a new and now mighty world.

Land discovered, 12th Oct. 1492.

The land thus discovered proved to be Guanahani, one of the south-eastern of the great cluster of the Lucayos or Bahama Islands,[1] which stretch south-east and north-west from the coast of Florida to Hispaniola, covering the northern coast of Cuba. There are few islands more naturally rich or beautiful. The verdure everywhere is green and luxuriant, and the whole island from the sea looks like a highly cultivated garden. Well might every one on board

[1] Mr. Major, in an able article in the Journ. of the Roy. Geograph. Soc. for 1871, entitled "The Landfall of Columbus," has examined the whole question as to the island on which he first landed on October 12, 1492, and has shown that Humboldt, Washington Irving, and himself (in his edition for the Hakluyt Society of the "Select Letters of Columbus") have been in error, and that the island called by the Indians Guanahani is unquestionably that now called "Watling Island."

of the expedition feel grateful to Columbus. After all their trials and dangers, they had at last reached, they thought, the fabled land of Cathay. We well know how pleasing are our sensations when we again see green fields and luxuriant trees after a long sea voyage, and therefore we can conceive the exquisite sense of enjoyment and delight of Columbus and his crew, when they cast anchor in the roadstead and surveyed the island they had, at length, reached. It was thickly inhabited. The natives knew not what to make of the strangers who had come among them, richly attired, while they were in a state of perfect nudity. From their attitudes and gestures, as they timidly issued from the woods, and approached the shore, they were apparently lost in wonder. The ships they had intently watched from the earliest dawn of day were supposed to be huge monsters of the sea and their crews supernatural beings. When the boats landed, they fled in great trepidation; but by means of friendly signs, and other tokens of goodwill, a few of the boldest of them were induced to draw near Columbus and his captains when he unfurled the standard of Spain, and took formal and solemn possession of the island in the name of the Castilian sovereigns.

Columbus takes possession of the island of Guanahani, in the name of Spain.

Columbus, from his commanding height, authoritative manner, and splendid dress, attracted more especially the admiration of the natives, who frequently prostrated themselves on the earth before him with signs of adoration. Nor were his men who, only a few days before, had concocted schemes for massacring him, less subservient. They thronged around him before he left the ship in their overflowing zeal, some embracing him, others kissing his hands. Abject spirits, who had outraged him by their insolence, now crouched at his feet; and those who had been the most mutinous during the voyage were now as humble and as ready to lick the dust from his feet as the most terrified of the natives. The natives soon recovered from their terror, as no attempt was made to pursue or molest them. Extremely artless and simple in themselves, the slightest acts of kindness were received with gratitude, and the toys and trinkets presented for their acceptance were accepted as gifts from heaven. Beyond cotton yarn, which they possessed in abundance, and parrots, which were domesticated in great numbers among them, they had little or nothing to give in return. Their boats consisted entirely of canoes, formed and hollowed, like those of the earliest on record, from a single tree, and capable of carrying from one to fifty persons. Columbus mentions that he saw one which could have contained one hundred and fifty persons, yet made from the trunk of a single tree.[1]

The first impressions of the natives on Columbus.

The state in which Columbus found the natives is nowhere so well described as in his own language. Writing to the treasurer of Ferdinand and Isabella an account of his first voyage[2]—"As soon," says he, "as they saw our near approach, they would flee with such precipitation, that a father would not even stop to protect his son; and this not because any harm had been done to any of them, for, from the first, wherever I went and got speech with them, I gave

[1] Journal of Columbus, Navarrete Coll.

[2] Major, "Select Letters of Columbus," p. 7.

them of all that I had, such as cloth, and many other things, without receiving anything in return; but they are, as I have described, incurably timid. It is true that when they are reassured, and have thrown off this fear, they are guileless, and so liberal of all they have, that no one would believe it who had not seen it. They never refuse anything that they possess when it is asked of them; on the contrary, they offer it themselves, and they exhibit so much loving-kindness that they would even give their hearts; and, whether it be something of value or of little worth that is offered to them, they are satisfied.

"I forbade that worthless things, such as pieces of broken glass, and ends of straps, should be given to them; although, when they succeeded in obtaining them, they thought they possessed the finest jewel in the world. . . . They took even bits of the broken hoops of the wine barrels, and gave, like fools, all that they possessed in exchange, insomuch that I thought it was wrong, and forbade it. I gave away a thousand good and pretty articles which I had brought with me, in order to win their affections, and that they might be led to become Christians and be well inclined to love and serve their Highnesses and the whole Spanish nation, and that they might aid us by giving us things of which we stand in need, and which they possess in abundance.

"They are not acquainted with any form of worship, and are not idolaters, but believe that all power and, indeed, all good things, are in heaven; and they are firmly convinced that I, with my vessels and crews, came from heaven, and with this belief received me at every place at which I touched, after they had overcome their apprehension. And this does not spring from ignorance, for they are very intelligent, and navigate all these seas, and relate everything to us, so that it is astonishing what a good account they are able to give of everything; but they have never seen men with clothes on, nor vessels like ours."

Such was the character of the natives whom Columbus found in the islands of the numerous Archipelago off the south coast of Cuba, and in those of St. Catharine and Hispaniola, all of which he visited in his first great voyage of discovery, and claimed as the property of his sovereigns. In these formal proclamations and in the erection of the fort, which was afterwards raised on the island of Hispaniola, the innocent natives took an active part, rendering every assistance in their power, little dreaming that these acts were the forerunners of bondage, and of that horrible system of slavery which so long prevailed in those islands, and still contaminates the soil of the largest of them all, the only one that now remains in the possession of the crown of Spain.

CHAPTER XVII.

The state of the West India Islands when discovered—Wreck of one of the vessels of the expedition—A colony established—Columbus sets sail for Spain, 4th January, 1493—Arrives at St. Mary's, 18th February, and in the Tagus a few days afterwards—Re-enters, with his ship, the harbour of Palos, 15th March—Great rejoicings—He proceeds to Seville and Barcelona—Orders for a fresh expedition—Its extent, and departure, 25th Sept., 1493—Reaches Dominica, 2nd Nov., 1493, and Santa Cruz, 14th Nov.—Arrives at Hayti, 22nd Nov. —Founds a fresh colony at Hispaniola or Hayti—Sufferings of the colonists, and disappointment of Columbus—His sanguine expectations for the future—Threatened mutiny among the colonists—Columbus proceeds on further explorations—Discovery of the island of Jamaica—Surveys Cuba, and returns to Isabella—Arrival of Bartholomew Columbus—Intrigues at home—Commission of inquiry despatched to Hayti—Columbus sets sail for Europe, 10th March, 1496—Arrives at Cadiz, 11th June, 1496—Re-visits the West, May, 1498—Reaches Trinidad, 31st July—Discovers Tobago, Granada, and other islands, reaching Hispaniola, 19th August—Finds everything in disorder—Makes a tour of inspection, but is arrested, and sent a prisoner to Spain—Arrives at Cadiz, Nov. 1500, and is restored to the royal favour—A fleet sails for the colony with Ovando, Feb. 1502, and two months afterwards (9th May) Columbus follows, and reaches St. Domingo, 29th June—Discovers the island of Guanaga 30th July —Trading canoe—Her cargo—Prosecutes his researches to the South —Reaches Cape Honduras—Discovers and explores the Mosquito coast — Puerto Bello — Forms a settlement on the river Belem, 6th Feb., 1503—Anchors at Jamaica, June 1503, and Dominica, 13th August of that year—Sails for Spain, 12th September, which he reaches 7th Nov., 1504—His sufferings and death, 20th May, 1506.

PHILOSOPHERS and philanthropists may ask with some show of reason when they read the history of the West Indies during the last three hundred years, and compare the state of its inhabitants with that in which Columbus found them, if civilization has in all cases increased the happiness of the human race. "Their habitations," remarks Washington Irving, referring to the aborigines, "were very simple, being in the form of a pavilion, or high circular tent, constructed of branches of trees, of reeds, and palm They were kept very clean and neat, and sheltered under beautiful and spreading trees. For beds they had nets of cotton extended from two parts, which they called *hamacs*, a name since adopted into universal use among seamen."[1] Their groves were more beautiful than ever Columbus had anywhere else beheld; and the whole country, according to his description of it, was as fresh and green as the richest and most verdant valleys of Andalusia during the month of May, when the peninsula is adorned in its gayest colours. Amply supplied with springs and streams of cool and sweet water, and fruits of the richest description; with abundance of herbs of various kind; with animal food reared on the land where they lived, and abundant fish in the seas with which they were surrounded, what more could the original inhabitants of the West India Islands desire? "Here," says Columbus in his journal, "are large lakes, with groves about them marvellous in beauty and in richness. The singing of the birds is such, that it seems as if one would never desire to depart hence. There are flocks of parrots which obscure the sun, and other birds large and small, of so many kinds, and so different from ours, that it is wonderful; and besides,

The state of the West India Islands when discovered.

[1] Voyages of Columbus, vol i. p. 258.

there are trees of a thousand species, each having its particular fruit, and all of marvellous flavour." These pictures may have been in some respects over-coloured by Columbus and his crew, after their arduous and weary voyage: but contemporary writers confirm the original beauty of the West India Islands; nor are there to this day many islands which look more beautiful from the sea than those which were first made known to the world by Christopher Columbus.[1] But even if the descriptions of the happiness of the natives is in some respects overdrawn, their position, under the patriarchal rule of their native *caciques*, with few wants and little of fear or care, compares favourably with the state of these islands at any period since they came under the rule of the highly civilized nations of Europe. Nor were these poor people, though living in a state of nature, without some of the consolations of religion. "They confess," remarks Peter Martyr, "the soul to be immortal, and having put off the bodily clothing, they imagine it goeth forth to the woods and the mountains, and that it liveth there perpetually in caves."

Throughout the whole time Columbus was engaged in discovering and surveying these islands, he was under the conviction—a conviction which he carried to his grave—that they formed part of Asia, or rather of India, the name by which the greater part of that continent was then known, and that they were the islands spoken of by Marco Polo, as lying opposite Cathay in the Chinese Sea. Indeed, the great navigator construed everything he saw in harmony

[1] See "Letters from the Tropics," by the Rev. C. Kingsley in "Good Words" for 1870.

with the accounts of those opulent regions. When the natives spoke of enemies to the north-west, he concluded these to be people from the mainland of Asia, the subjects of the great Khan of Tatary, who, the Venetian traveller stated, were wont to make war on the islands and to enslave their inhabitants. When they described the country to the south as abounding in gold, he felt convinced that this must refer to the famous island of Zipango, of the magnificent capital of which Marco Polo had given such a glowing description. The fine gold trinkets the natives possessed confirmed their reports and his own impressions, whetted the avarice of the Spaniards, and made a search for the great Khan and his golden islands the chief results of his expedition.

Indeed the main purpose of Columbus, like that of Vasco de Gama—though the former was a man of far loftier character than the latter—was to find an opulent and civilized country in the East, with whom he might establish commercial relations, carrying home gold, spices, drugs, and Oriental merchandise. He hoped, too, that he would thus have the means of establishing the Christian religion in heathen lands, and from the profits of the undertaking to rescue the Holy Sepulchre at Jerusalem from the power of the Infidels. Such an enterprise had been the dream of his early manhood; nor indeed was it forgotten when his own earthly pilgrimage came to a close, for by his will he directs his son to appropriate certain sums of money to that sacred cause.

Wreck of one of the vessels of the expedition.

While cruising among the islands, Columbus had the misfortune to lose one of the three vessels of his expedition. She was swept during a calm by the strong current and through the carelessness of the crew on a sandbank, where she became a total wreck. Fortunately the weather continued calm, so that the lives of the crew, as well as everything on board, were saved. All the stores, with the assistance of the natives, were carefully stowed away in huts on shore. Nor was there the slightest disposition on their part to take the smallest advantage of the strangers who had come among them. Not one article was pilfered; not a "hawk's bell," nor a bead—to them objects of envy and delight—was taken away; nor were the most trifling articles appropriated while removing them in their canoes from the wreck to the shore. "So loving, so tractable, so peaceable are these people," says Columbus in his journal, "that I swear to your Majesties, there is not in the world a better nation, nor a better land. They love their neighbours as themselves."[1] What an example the uncivilized savage here presents to the civilization of our own age, of which we so often make such vaunted boasts!

A colony established.

As most of the shipwrecked crew, besides some other persons belonging to the expedition, expressed a desire to be left behind, and as the two vessels would have been overcrowded with the three crews, their wishes suggested to Columbus the idea of constituting them the germ of a future colony. The wreck of the caravel provided abundant material for the fortress he had resolved to build. Her guns and ammunition were ready for its protection; and with his crews so reduced in number, he could spare provisions for the year, by the end of which he hoped

[1] W. Irving, p. 92.

to return. Having completed his arrangements, Columbus and the remaining caravels set sail for home on the 4th of January, 1493.

Columbus sets sail for Spain 4th Jan., 1493.

After suffering severely from a storm, and a long and wearisome struggle with the trade-winds, the nature and character of which was then unknown, Columbus reached the island of St. Mary's on the 18th of February following, where he was detained for two or three days,[1] and was afterwards obliged, through stress of weather and scarcity of provisions, to put into the Tagus.

Arrives at St. Mary's 18th Feb., and in the Tagus a few days afterwards.

When the tidings reached Lisbon that a Spanish barque lay anchored in the Tagus, freighted with the people and productions of a newly discovered world, the effect was electrical. For nearly a century that city had derived its chief glory from its maritime discoveries; but here was an achievement which eclipsed them all. The ship of a neighbouring and friendly, though rival, nation had, by sailing to the West, discovered the fabled land of Cathay, and had come from Zipango (Japan), and the extremity of India, laden with its treasures. Curiosity and envy combined could hardly have been more excited and aroused had Columbus brought with him the produce of another planet. For several days the once active but now lifeless though still beautiful Tagus was covered with boats and barges of every kind, all winding their way to the caravel. Visitors of every kind, from officers of the crown and cavaliers of high distinction down to the humblest of the people, thronged around the ship, eager to go on board and to see the strange human beings, plants, and animals from

[1] Select Letters of Columbus. Introd. p. lxiv.

the new-found world, and to learn from the crew, if not from Columbus himself, the events of this remarkable voyage. Messengers came from King John with professions of congratulation on the great discovery, and an invitation to the palace, which Columbus accepted with reluctance, and only because the weather continued so stormy that he was unable to leave with his vessel for Spain. The king and the principal cavaliers of his household received him with much courtesy and pomp, though with jealous envy of his success and with many expressions of distrust and doubt.

Columbus re-enters, with his ship, the harbour of Palos 15th March.

Having satisfied the curiosity of the Portuguese court and people, Columbus set sail from the Tagus on the 13th of March, and two days afterwards entered the small harbour of Palos, having been seven months and a half absent on the most important maritime expedition recorded in history. Palos that day was the scene of extraordinary excitement and rejoicings, not unmingled, however, with doubts. Almost every family in the place had some relative or friend among the navigators. Great anxiety prevailed as to the safety of the crew of the wrecked caravel, who had remained to form the settlement at Hispaniola; and of the Pinta, which had been separated from Columbus in a storm the expedition had encountered before it reached St. Mary's. But the fears for the safety of the Pinta were soon removed. In the afternoon of the same day on which Columbus arrived, and while the church and convent bells were still pealing forth a welcome to the great discoverer, Martin Alonzo Pinzon entered the river with his ship.

Great rejoicings.

Slavish, indeed, was the welcome offered by the people to the great navigator, whose plans they had so recently rejected as mischievous and idle dreams. The whole population joined him at their principal church in offering thanks to God for a discovery, in the way of which they had themselves thrown innumerable difficulties. Wherever Columbus passed, the streets resounded with acclamations; and in that same place where he first came, a poor wanderer, craving water and bread at the gate of their convent for his famishing child, and where afterwards he had been hooted and despised, he was welcomed with honours rarely rendered to even monarchy itself.

He proceeds to Seville and Barcelona.

Columbus, having despatched a letter to the king and queen, then at Barcelona, proceeded to Seville to await their orders, taking with him six of the natives whom he had brought to Spain. The letter announcing his discovery had produced an extraordinary sensation, not merely at the Spanish court, but in every part of Europe whither the news had spread. To Spain, then approaching the plenitude of her power, this discovery, following so closely on the conquest of Granada, was considered to be a special mark of Divine favour to the nation which had subdued the Moors and extended the Christian faith. Throughout the whole country it was hailed with the most enthusiastic delight, and the journey of Columbus from Seville to Barcelona was one continued triumph. Every preparation had been made at the latter city to give him a solemn and magnificent reception. Surrounded by a brilliant cavalcade of courtiers and Spanish chivalry, and followed by a long retinue, of which the Indians formed a part, Columbus marched in procession through streets crowded with people, and lined by houses gaily decorated, to the chief square of the city, where the sovereigns, under a rich canopy, awaited his arrival. The principal nobility of Castile, Valentia, Catalonia, and Aragon, were there with Ferdinand and Isabella, impatient to behold and welcome the great discoverer, whose majestic and venerable appearance enhanced their admiration and enthusiasm. When he approached, the sovereigns rose as if receiving a person of the highest rank. Briefly delivering an account of his voyage, Columbus displayed the strange Indians, animals, and plants, with a few specimens of native gold, and some barbaric ornaments he had brought from the new found country; and prayers were then offered by the whole of that brilliant assembly, in which the king and queen on their knees solemnly joined.

A discovery so great and astounding soon spread far and wide, and embassies and travelling merchants diffused the tidings in every land. Sebastian Cabot describes the first receipt of the news in London, and the talk and admiration created in the court of Henry VII., as if it was "a thing more divine than human."[1] Indeed, the whole civilized world, filled with wonder and delight, rejoiced in an event which opened out a new and unbounded field for inquiry and enterprise, although no one had an idea of the real importance of the discovery, nor that it was an entirely new and distinct portion of the globe which had been discovered. Nor, indeed, was any time lost in securing to the crown of Spain these valuable

[1] Hakluyt, "Col. Voyages," p. 7.

acquisitions. Arrangements were at once made to fit out a fleet on an extensive scale, and the royal injunctions, though highly arbitrary, were now obeyed with the utmost alacrity. A fleet of seventeen vessels, large and small, were soon ready. The best pilots were chosen for the service, while skilled husbandmen, miners, and other mechanics, were engaged for the colonies it was intended to found. Horses for military purposes and for stocking the country, together with cattle and domestic animals of various kinds, were likewise provided, as well as seeds of almost every description, and plants, including vines and sugar canes; nor was there wanting an abundant supply of trinkets, beads, hawks'-bells, looking-glasses, and other showy trifles, to induce traffic among the natives. The most exaggerated accounts spread of the fabulous wealth of the territories, and adventurers of every kind, from the highest to the very lowest, were equally eager to join in the expedition. Some were doubtless inflamed with the mere hope and lust of wealth, while others less selfish in their motives pictured to themselves a wide field for the display of their military genius and skill, in what did not seem impossible to them, the actual conquest of the grand Khan and the capture of the fabled land of Cathay.

Orders for a fresh expedition.

The number of persons permitted to embark in the expedition had been originally limited to one thousand, but the applications from volunteers were so numerous that fifteen hundred persons were eventually enrolled; and early on the morning of the 25th of September, 1493, they sailed from the bay of Cadiz in three large vessels and fourteen caravels. No accounts of the size of any of these vessels have been transmitted

Its extent, and departure, 25th Sept., 1493.

to posterity except the brief statement made in a note by Washington Irving,[1] from the writings of Peter Martyr, who says that they "were carracks (a large species of merchant vessel, principally used in the coasting trade), of 100 tons." But the carracks of the commercial marine of the Venetians and Genoese of those days were of very considerable dimensions, in some few instances from 1500 to 2000 tons, and were employed on the most distant voyages then known. Of one of these, Charnock,[2] as we have seen, has given a drawing; she is a full-rigged ship, well equipped, and evidently not less than 1500 tons register, taken from a painting at Genoa, dated 1542, so that it may be fairly presumed that in his second voyage the largest of the vessels of Columbus was far beyond 100 tons. Considering that he had with him fifteen hundred persons, some of them members of the best families of Spain, with large quantities of stores and merchandise, it may be safely assumed that the "three large vessels" were carracks of from 400 to 600 tons; while the fourteen caravels may have been craft ranging from 250 down to 70 tons, as Columbus on more than one occasion had urged the necessity of having small vessels, of light draft of water, adapted for the survey of the coasts, or for river navigation.

The incidents of this voyage have been pleasantly related by one Dr. Chanca, who was physician to the fleet, in a letter addressed by him to the chapter of Seville.[3] Starting with a fair wind and fine weather,

[1] Voyages of Columbus, vol. ii. p. 1.

[2] Vol. ii. p. 7.

[3] Select Letters of Columbus, p. 19, *et seq.*

Columbus, in six days, reached the great Canary Island, where he anchored, and remained for a day to repair a leaky vessel of his flotilla, after which they set sail for Gomera, which they were "four or five days" in reaching, and thence, after another day's rest, during which they took in a fresh supply of wood, beef, and other provisions and replenished their stock of water, they reached in twenty days the island of Ferro; thence with a fair wind, and fine weather, they were other twenty days in sighting land, which "should have been done in fourteen or fifteen days, if the ship *Capitana* had been as good a sailer as the other vessels." This land, which they made on the evening of Saturday, the 2nd of November, proved to be a lofty island, to which Columbus gave the name of Dominica, and "offered fervent prayers to heaven" for their prosperous voyage. The island appeared to be wholly uninhabited.

Reaches Dominica, 2nd Nov., 1493,

Proceeding to the island of Guadeloupe, they visited a village near the shore; but the inhabitants at their approach fled in great trepidation, leaving some of their children, around whose necks and arms the Spaniards placed hawks'-bells, and other trinkets, soothing them at the same time with their caresses, as the most sure means of winning the confidence of their parents. Here provisions were found in abundance, besides parrots of the most variegated plumage, as large as household fowls, and many geese domesticated like those of Europe.

After cruising among the other islands of the group of the Antilles, the expedition anchored on the 14th of November off an island, to which Columbus gave the name of Santa Cruz, which, like all the and Santa Cruz, 14th Nov.

others, was inhabited by Caribs. Thence pursuing his voyage, he shortly afterwards came in sight of a cluster of small islands of various shapes and appearances, some of them covered with forests, but the greater portion naked and sterile, and all apparently uninhabited. To the largest of these he gave the name of Sta. Ursula. Proceeding onwards he soon arrived in sight of the large island, now known as Porto Rico, covered with beautiful forests, and indented with fine havens, the inhabitants of which, who appear to have been peaceful and populous, were much troubled by the ravages of their implacable enemies, the Caribs. Having remained here for two days, Columbus set sail for Hispaniola, where

Arrives at Hayti, 22nd Nov.,

the fleet anchored on the 22nd of November, and having coasted round to La Navidad, where he had formed the settlement on the first voyage, he was greatly grieved to learn the disasters which in the short interval of a year had befallen the Spaniards whom he had left behind. Several of them had died of sickness; others had fallen in a quarrel which had occurred among themselves, and the remainder, it was said, had removed to other parts of the island, where they had taken to themselves native wives. Such was the end of the first European colonists in the New World.

Founds a fresh colony at Hispaniola, or Hayti

Arrangements were, however, made for the establishment of another colony, though not on the same spot, the land in the vicinity being low, moist, and unhealthy, and destitute of stone suitable for the erection of a fortress and of other necessary buildings. After a thorough search around the coast and up various rivers for a suitable site, Columbus decided to settle upon the shores of an excellent and capacious harbour, about ten leagues east of Monte Christo, and disembarking his troops, labourers, and artificers, commenced erecting a city on a well-devised plan, with streets, squares, church, public storehouse, and residence for the admiral built of stone. To this, the first permanent city in the Western world, Columbus gave the name of Isabella, in honour of that enlightened sovereign, without whose aid these islands would probably not have been discovered till many years afterwards.

But the new colony had a severe ordeal to pass through before it was successfully established. Maladies of various kinds broke out among the settlers. Many who had suffered severely from the sea voyage, and from the salt provisions to which they had been reduced, soon fell a prey to the exhalations of the hot climate, and to the humid vapours from the rivers and undrained land; while others, accustomed to highly-cultivated countries with the comforts of a superior home, suffered severely from the stagnant air of the dense forests around them. Most, too, of the settlers were grievously disappointed, that they had not yet discovered the golden regions of Cathay and Zipango, nor even a region of Indian luxury, or wide fields for chivalrous enterprises. Gold, they soon found, could only be obtained in small quantities, chiefly through the medium of barter with the natives: even Columbus was disappointed. When the ships had discharged their cargoes, and it was necessary to send the greater part of them back to Spain, there was neither "gold nor precious merchandise" ready for shipment, which he expected

Sufferings of the colonists,

and disappointment of Columbus.

the Spaniards, whom he had left behind on his previous voyage, would have collected. All these hopes had been rudely dispelled. The most extravagant expectations having been entertained in Spain, Columbus pictured to himself the disappointment of his sovereigns and of the nation when his fleet returned empty, and conveyed to an expectant and excited people the intelligence of the disasters which had befallen the first colonists in a country of such fabled wealth and unbounded resources.

However, in the twelve ships which were despatched to Spain, the remaining five having been retained for his own purposes and for those of the newly-established colony, Columbus sent home some specimens of gold, and such fruits or plants as appeared to be either curious or valuable, expressing his own confident and sanguine anticipations of soon being able to make valuable shipments of precious metals, drugs, and spices. "Without penetrating into the interior of the country," he remarks,[1] "we have found spots showing so many indications of various spices, as naturally to suggest the hope of the best results for the future. The same holds good with respect to the gold mines; for two parties only who were sent out in different directions to discover them, and who, because they had few people with them, remained out but a short time, found, nevertheless, a great number of rivers, whose sands contained this precious metal in such quantity, that each man took

[1] Memorial addressed by Columbus to Antonio de Torres, for Ferdinand and Isabella, from the city of Isabella, dated Jan. 30th, 1494, in "Select Letters of Columbus," p. 73, *et seq.*

up a sample of it in his hand; so that our two messengers returned so joyous, and boasted so much of the abundance of gold, that I feel a hesitation in speaking and writing of it to their highnesses."

His sanguine expectations for the future.

So sanguine, indeed, was Columbus that gold would be found in great abundance that, in the same memorial,[1] he adds, "I will undertake to go in search of these rivers; either proceeding hence by land and looking out for the best expedients that may offer, or else by sea, rounding the island, until we come to the place which is described as being only six or seven leagues from where these rivers that I speak of are situated; so that we may collect the gold in safety, and put it in security against all attacks in some stronghold or tower, which may be quickly built for that purpose; and thus, when the two caravels shall return thither, the gold may be taken away, and finally sent home in safety at the first favourable season for making the voyage."

Few, however, of the thousand colonists who had settled at Isabella were disposed to wait patiently for the happy time Columbus had shadowed forth. Disappointed in their expectations of immediate wealth, disgusted with the labours imposed upon them by which alone they were enabled to erect their houses, and to obtain the necessary means of existence, and appalled by the maladies prevalent throughout the community, they began to look with horror on their situation: and when the last sail disappeared which was destined for Spain, they felt as if severed for ever from their homes, and that the strange land where they had settled seemed destined to be their grave. To

[1] Memorial, p. 79.

Threatened mutiny among the colonists.

return to Spain soon became their ruling idea. Discontent daily increased; and at last the most daring spirits among them proposed that they should seize upon one or all of the five ships then in harbour, and return home. The mutiny was, however, checked for a time by the condign punishment of the ringleaders.

When order had been somewhat restored Columbus made an expedition into the interior, and on his return, on the 29th of March, 1494, he was gratified to find that many of his expectations, in regard to the future prosperity of the colony, were likely to be speedily realised. The plants and fruits of the Old World gave promise of rapid increase; the seeds had produced young plants; the sugar-cane had prospered beyond his most sanguine anticipations; ears of corn made their appearance from seed only sown in January; while cuttings from European vines already began to form their clusters. Amid all his anxieties and troubles, it was gratifying to find that the rich plains of Andalusia were not to be compared to the virgin soil of the new-found world, which, moistened by the rivers, and stimulated by an ardent sun, possessed principles of fecundity unknown in any part of Europe. The town of Isabella, however, proved to have been built on an unhealthy situation, and in after years fell to ruins.

Columbus proceeds on further explorations.

Having left his brother, Don Diego, in charge of the colony, Columbus set forth again, on the 24th of April, on a further voyage of discovery, and steering to the westward, resolved to revisit the coast of Cuba, at the point he had left it on his first voyage, and thence to explore it on the southern side, under the conviction that he must eventually arrive at Cathay. Though charmed beyond measure with everything he saw, nothing indicated the lands Marco Polo had described. A verdant soil, and coasts adorned by stately trees, watered by navigable rivers, and indented by commodious harbours, spoke of riches to come; while a fertile and populous country lay before him, with peaceful and industrious inhabitants, who brought him food, and fruits, and fish, in great abundance. There were however no mines of gold, or palaces covered with that precious metal; but there was everything that might encourage habits of industry, with little or nothing to satisfy the cupidity of the settlers, or to lead them to suppose they had discovered a land where man could live otherwise than by the sweat of his brow.

Discovery of the island of Jamaica.

At Santiago de Cuba Columbus was overwhelmed by the simple hospitality of the natives; but as he approached the island of Jamaica he was met by seventy or eighty canoes, filled with savages, gaily painted, and decorated with feathers, advancing in warlike array, uttering loud yells, and brandishing lances of pointed wood. An explanation, however, from the interpreter, and a few presents to the crew of one of the canoes who had ventured nearer than the rest, soothed the caciques of the other canoes, some of which measured upwards of ninety feet in length, and eight feet in breadth, and were hollowed out of one magnificent tree. From Jamaica, Columbus proceeded to Cuba, and having devoted many months to the survey of the whole of that portion of its coast which he could reach, he set sail for Isabella, where he arrived suffering in health, and

Surveys Cuba, and returns to Isabella.

with his ships greatly in need of repair, on the 4th of September, 1494.

Arrival of Bartholomew Columbus.

Here he was greatly rejoiced to meet his brother Bartholomew, whom he had not seen since he had commissioned him to lay his project of discovery before Henry VII.; and who, on his return to Spain, with the consent from that monarch, had learned that Christopher had made his great voyage of discovery to the new world. The sight of his brother was an inexpressible relief to Columbus, who, alone among strangers, greatly needed the assistance of a man whose prompt action and fearless spirit soon reduced the discontented colonists to a sense of their duty. Anxious to relieve himself from the pressure of public business, Columbus immediately invested his brother Bartholomew with the title and authority of lieutenant-governor, in place of Diego, whose mild and peaceable disposition rendered him little capable of managing the concerns of a factious colony.

By his powerful assistance, and the timely receipt of fresh supplies of stores from Spain, the reign of disorder which had so long prevailed, especially during the absence of Columbus, was brought, in a great measure, to an end; but the conduct of the Europeans had been such that the native tribes turned against them, and for a time threatened the entire annihilation of the colony.

Intrigues at home.

While however the restoration of order and the future security of the colonists occupied the attention of Columbus and of his brother Bartholomew, his enemies were undermining him at home. Reports were circulated that the whole colony was in a state of anarchy, and that Columbus was abusing his power, and neglecting its interests. Loud and long were the complaints against him; and at last they were carried to such an extent, that Ferdinand fitted out a fleet of caravels, which he placed under charge of Diego Carillo, a commander of a military order, giving him instructions that should Columbus be absent, he was to take upon himself the government of the island and inquire into the alleged evils and abuses, at the same time vesting him with power to remedy such as should appear to him really in existence. A proclamation was also issued, granting permission for any native-born Spanish subject to settle in the island of Hispaniola and to undertake private voyages of trade and discovery in the New World. Those who embarked at their own expense were to have caravels assigned to them, and to be provided with a supply of provisions sufficient for the first year, with a right to hold certain lands and any houses they might erect upon them. They likewise were to be allowed to retain one-third of whatever gold they might collect, but the remaining two-thirds were to be handed over to the crown of Spain, which was also to receive one-tenth of all the other produce of the island; while one-tenth of the tonnage capacity of any ship engaged in the trade of the New World was to be at the service of the crown, free of charge.

Commission of inquiry despatched to Hayti.

But a few days before the departure of this expedition, the ships which had carried out fresh supplies to Isabella returned to Spain, with intelligence of the safe arrival of Columbus in Hispaniola, from his long voyage along the southern coasts of Cuba, and bringing with them specimens of the gold and of various animal and vegetable curiosities he had collected. These news so far restored the great navigator to the confidence of his sovereigns, that Juan Aguado, who had some time before returned to Spain, highly recommended by the admiral, was appointed to the command of the fleet about to sail, instead of Diego Carillo, who was known to be personally hostile to Columbus.

When Aguado, with the four caravels under his command, well freighted with supplies of every kind, arrived at Port Isabella in the month of October, Columbus was absent in the interior, being at the time fully occupied in re-establishing the tranquillity of the colony. Finding Bartholomew in command, and conceiving that his commission authorized him to supersede everyone except the admiral, he paid no respect to his brother and ordered various persons to be arrested. Weak in himself and puffed up with a little temporary power, Aguado lost sight alike of the respect and gratitude due to Columbus, and of the nature and extent of his own commission. The more discontented among the colonists at once spread the report that the downfall of Columbus and of his family was at hand, and that an ambassador had arrived from the sovereigns of Spain empowered to hear and redress their grievances. Culprits and offenders of every sort held high revel and were loud in their clamours against the oppression of the admiral, ascribing every misfortune to his mal-administration. To these clamours a weak and vain man, like Aguado, lent but too ready an ear and daily became more arrogant. When the news of his arrival and insolent conduct reached Columbus, he hastened to

Isabella, and received Aguado with the most grave and punctilious courtesy, assuring him of his readiness to acquiesce in whatever might be the pleasure of his sovereigns; but resolving in his own mind to return as soon as practicable to Spain, and to ascertain for himself the reason why this commission of inquiry had been appointed.

Columbus sets sail for Europe, 10th Mar. 1496.

Columbus was, however, detained longer than he wished. When his arrangements were made for returning, a violent hurricane[1] destroyed not merely the four caravels Aguado had brought out with him, but all his own vessels, except the *Nina*, and she was left to him in a very shattered condition. But she was soon repaired, and from the wreck of the others he built a second vessel, which he named the *Santa Cruz*, and set sail for Cadiz on the 10th of March, 1496, he embarking in one of the vessels, and Aguado in the other, leaving his brother Bartholomew in command of Hispaniola. Both caravels were loaded with two hundred and fifty of the most discontented and profligate of the colonists, as also with the sick and others who desired to return to Spain. The voyage proved extremely tedious and toilsome, and it was not until the 11th of June that they anchored in the Bay of Cadiz.

Arrives at Cadiz, 11th June, 1496.

The enemies of Columbus had been only too successful in undermining his popularity. The first excitement of a newly discovered world had died away. Western India had not yielded the gold and spices and wealth anticipated; and the means it really afforded for producing far greater wealth than the

[1] This word is said to be derived from the Indian name for this tempest, Urican.—W. Irving, p. 201.

fabled lands of Ophir or of the mines of Peru have ever produced were then neither appreciated nor understood. The richness which lay in its soil required time and industry to develope; and the adventurous and enthusiastic Spaniards, who had interested themselves in the New World, had neither studied the art of patience, nor accustomed themselves to toil. But the sovereigns of Spain still received Columbus with favour; and, the mission of the ungrateful and arrogant Aguado not having accomplished at court all the injury he had feared, Ferdinand and Isabella were still ready to meet the wishes of the discoverer, and grant him ships for a third expedition

It was not, however, until the spring of 1497, that any further attention was given to the wishes of Columbus, and the affairs of the New World. Although attractive and flattering to the pride of Spain, the previous expeditions to the West had unquestionably fallen far short of meeting the heavy expenses incurred upon them. No large and immediate profits could at once be realized, such as those the Portuguese reaped a few years afterwards from the discoveries of Vasco de Gama. Hence there was great delay in fitting out this fresh expedition, while the changes to be made in the future management of the Indies of the West tended to increase the delay. At length, on the 30th of May, 1498, Columbus set sail from the port of San Lucar de Barrameda, with a squadron of six vessels.

Re-visits the West, May 1489.

On this voyage he resolved to shape a course more to the southward than he had done on either of the two previous ones. After taking his departure from the Cape Verde Islands, he purposed sailing to the south-west until he reached the equinoctial line, and then steering directly west, until he arrived at land or in the longitude of Hispaniola. Having taken his departure from the Cape Verde on the 5th of July, he by pursuing this course found himself, on the 13th of that month, according to his observations, in the fifth degree of north latitude, in the midst of calms, and under a bright and burning sun. Continuing to steer to the west for some days, until he supposed himself to be in the longitude of the Caribbee Islands, he shaped a course for them to the northwards, intending to touch among them for refreshments and repairs; but, being somewhat out of his reckoning, he for the first time beheld, on the 31st of July, a large and fruitful island, which he named La Trinidad.

Reaches Trinidad, 31st July;

Columbus had expected, from the heat of the sun, to find the land, as he approached, parched and sterile; but Trinidad presented a very different appearance. Stately groves of palm-trees and luxuriant forests lined the shores, while the softness and purity of the climate, and the balmy breeze from the land, reminded him of early spring in the beautiful province of Valentia. While coasting along the island in search of suitable anchorage, he descried land to the south, which proved to be that low tract of coast intersected by the numerous branches of the great River Orinoco, though he little suspected that it was the vast continent of America. Remaining at the island, where he found the natives peaceably disposed, and as usual, extravagantly delighted with hawks'-bells and other trifling trinkets, Columbus shaped his course for the coast of Paria, presuming it to be an island, but, though delighted with the beauty of the country, which was cultivated in many places, highly populous, and adorned with magnificent vegetation, he was greatly astonished to find the water fresh, and that it grew more and more so the further he proceeded. He had reached the broad Gulf of Paria at the season of the year when the rivers which empty themselves into it are swollen by rains, and pour forth such quantities of fresh water as to conquer the saltness of the ocean. Here the natives were of a superior class to any he had hitherto seen. Their canoes were large and light, with a cabin in the centre for the accommodation of the owner and his family. Many of the men wore collars and burnished plates about their necks, of an inferior description of gold, while some of the women had strings of pearls round their arms, which they intimated, by signs, were procured on the northern side of their sea-coast. Here, again, Columbus was treated with profound reverence, as if he and his crews were beings descended from heaven. The honour of a banquet of bread and of various fruits of excellent flavour, together with different kinds of beverage, prepared for him in the house of the cacique, was greatly enhanced by the intelligent demeanour and martial frankness of the people, who seemed every way worthy of the beautiful country they inhabited.

Imagining the coast of Paria to be an island, he resolved to circumnavigate it, and, with that object, left the place where he had received so much kindness, on the 10th of August, and continued coasting westward within the gulf, in the vain search of an outlet to the north. But, as his own vessel was too large for the purpose of navigating these narrow waters, and as the stores of all his ships were nearly exhausted, many of them having been entirely destroyed in the tropics, whilst his own health was in a very precarious state, he felt compelled to shorten his voyage, and hasten for Hispaniola.

Discovering on his way the islands of Tobago and Granada, as also the islands of Margarita and Cubagua, afterwards famous for their pearl fisheries, he made the island of Hispaniola on the 19th August, about fifty leagues to the westward of the river Osema, the place of his destination; and having, on the following morning, anchored under the little island of Beata, he sent a boat on shore to procure an Indian messenger, to take a letter to his brother Bartholomew, who, during his absence, had formed a new settlement at Dominica. On his arrival he found that between fresh wars with the natives, and seditions among the colonists combined with their own indolence, everything had again been thrown into a state of confusion and poverty, saved only from utter annihilation by the tact and ability of Bartholomew. Too idle to labour, and destitute of those resources prevalent at home as a means of killing time, the colonists had quarrelled among themselves, mutinied against their rulers, wasted their time in alternate riot and despondency, while their evil passions, which had inflicted great calamities on the once pure and innocent natives, had likewise ensured a merited return of suffering to themselves. Confirming, by proclamation, the measures of his brother, and denouncing the leaders of the conspiracies which had been the cause of so

Discovers Tobago, Granada, and other islands, reaching Hispaniola 19th Aug.

Finds everything in disorder.

much misery and ruin during his absence, Columbus hoped to restore confidence and order. But the ringleaders continued to be a source of trouble to him, and, unfortunately, their hands were too frequently strengthened by the arrival of numerous adventurers, who, taking advantage of the encouragement which the government of Spain had afforded to any persons who desired to emigrate to the New World, flocked there in thousands. The insolence of the rebels against his brother's authority during his absence, though for a time subdued by his presence, had so greatly increased by the accession of numbers of well-armed and desperate confederates, that Columbus felt he required powers greater than he possessed to ensure the fidelity of the well-disposed against the intrigues of the discontented and lawless. He therefore made arrangements for returning to Spain.

Aware that many of the most worthless settlers desired to return home, he issued, on the 12th of September, a proclamation, offering free passage and provisions for the voyage to all who wished to return to Spain, hoping thus to relieve the colony of the idle and disaffected, and to weaken the power of the leaders of revolt, until he could carry into effect the necessary measures for their entire discomfiture and subjection. A large portion of the more lawless of the early colonists accepted the offer; and having sent full advices to his sovereigns, by the vessels in which they sailed on the 18th October, of what was going on in the island, Columbus entered into arrangements which he hoped would tend to restore order before he himself returned to Spain. Having been enabled to settle matters somewhat to his own satisfaction at Dominica, he left his brother, Don Diego, in temporary command of that place, and joined Bartholomew on a tour to visit the various stations, and to restore, if possible, order throughout the whole of the island.

Makes a tour of inspection

The tour of inspection and restoration required much more time than Columbus had anticipated. Everything had fallen into confusion during the late troubles. Farms lay neglected, mines were abandoned, the flocks and herds were scattered or destroyed, the caciques had ceased to pay their tribute, and the natives no longer cultivated their allotted tracts of land. In the midst of these perplexities, and while making herculean exertions to restore order, Columbus received a reply from Spain to his communication, which, though furnishing him with increased power, coldly stated that another investigation would shortly be made into the state of affairs. He was greatly troubled in mind by its tone, naturally feeling that his complaints had little weight with the government, and that the misrepresentations of his enemies were prejudicing him with his sovereigns; nevertheless, his zeal for their cause never flagged, and his labour to restore order was incessant. At length he triumphed; faction was subdued; the Spaniards renewed their labour on the land; the fields which had lain waste were again cultivated; and the natives, like their employers, seeing the folly of resistance, and the loss they themselves sustained by it, submitted patiently to the terms which Columbus had laid down and eventually enforced.

But all these reforms had been brought about by a course which had greatly increased the number of his enemies. Every worthless fellow whom he had sent home or punished became his implacable foe and intrigued for his downfall; and too many of them had influence at court, which, in the absence of Columbus, produced its effect. At last he was superseded; and, to the disgrace of Ferdinand and Isabella, who lent too ready an ear to the calumnious reports spread against him, this great and good man was arrested, and he and his two brothers sent in chains back to the country to which he had given a new and a now mighty world.

but is arrested, and sent a prisoner to Spain.

Arrives at Cadiz, Nov. 1500.

Thus humiliated, Christopher Columbus landed at Cadiz towards the close of the year 1500. The fact of the ignominy to which he had been subjected spoke with the voice of thunder to the feelings of the people. They neither cared for nor inquired into the cause of his great humiliation. It was sufficient for them to know that this noble-minded man had been brought home in chains from the world he had discovered, and the sensation thus produced was almost as great as the reception which had awaited him on his triumphant return from the first discovery of America, in March 1493.

His own feelings of the wrongs he had sustained at the hands of his worthless enemies are nowhere so well described as in the letter he addressed, immediately on his return to Spain, to a lady who was in immediate attendance on the queen, and stood high in her favour.[1] "I have now reached that point,"

[1] Letter of Columbus to Doña Juana de la Torres, in "Select Letters of Columbus," pp. 153 and 158.

he remarks, "that there is no man so vile but thinks it his right to insult me. The day will come when the world will reckon it a virtue to him who has not given his consent to their abuse. If I had plundered the Indies, even to the country where is the fabled altar of St. Peter's, and had given them all to the Moors, they could not have shown towards me more bitter enmity than they have done in Spain. Who would believe such things of a country where there has always been so much nobility? I should much like to clear myself of this affair, if only it were consistent with etiquette to do so, face to face with my queen.... The slanders of worthless men," he continues, "have done me more injury than all my services have profited me. . . . I have had so strange a character given to me that if I were to build hospitals and churches, they would call them caves for robbers."

This letter, combined with other representations of the real facts of the case, and with the unmistakeable expression of public opinion, made a great impression on the mind of Isabella, and had at once the effect of relieving Columbus and his brothers from their ignoble imprisonment. He was invited to the court, then at Grenada, where he appeared on the 17th of December, not in a prison dress, and in the degraded position in which he had landed at Cadiz, but in rich attire, and attended by an honourable retinue. When the Queen saw the venerable navigator approach, she was moved to tears at sufferings to which she and Ferdinand had been the unwilling or unknowing parties—in so far that they had superseded him and given to his successor power to inflict grievous wrong on one of the noblest of men. When the brave old seaman saw how his queen was affected, his spirit, which had endured with lofty scorn the injuries and insults of ignoble men, gave way; he threw himself upon his knees, and wept like a child. His sovereigns had found that he was still as worthy as ever of their confidence, and *that* thought was a sufficient solace for all he had suffered. Columbus was soon reinstated in all his privileges and dignities, and those who had injured him were degraded and disgraced. Everything was done which it was in the power of Isabella to do, to vindicate herself to the world from the charge of ingratitude towards the great navigator.

And is restored to the royal favour.

A considerable time, however, elapsed before any steps were taken to fit out another expedition in which Columbus could return to Dominica and there resume in triumph the viceroyalty of the colony. Many events prevented the immediate despatch of another fleet, some of which were in a measure beyond the control of the sovereigns of Spain. The delay was, however, a grievous disappointment to Columbus. Though Bobadilla, by whom he had been superseded and insulted, was dismissed, Ferdinand, whose professions of friendship were far from being as sincere as those of the queen, deemed it desirable to refill his place for two years by some prudent and able officer, who could put a stop to all remaining faction in the colony, and thus prepare the way for Columbus to enjoy the rights and dignities of his government, both peacefully and beneficially to the crown. But there were other reasons which induced Ferdinand to appoint one

Nicholas de Ovando as governor, for a time, to the new found colony. Listening too readily to the calumnies of the many enemies at court of Columbus, he had imbibed some vague idea that the great navigator might set up an independent sovereignty, or deliver his discoveries into the hands of the Genoese, or of some other European power: he may also have felt that Columbus was no longer indispensable to him, as the throne was daily besieged by applicants to be allowed to fit out expeditions at their own expense, and to share with the crown the profits upon them.

Hence it was that the interests of Columbus were for a time overlooked. Ovando, however, received orders to examine all his accounts; to ascertain the damages he had sustained by his imprisonment, by the interruption of his privileges, and by the confiscation of his effects. His property, which Bobadilla had seized, was to be restored, and to be made good if it had been sold. Equal care was also to be taken to indemnify his brothers for their arrest and for the losses they had sustained. The arrears of the revenue due to Columbus were to be paid to him, and their punctual payment secured for the future. Such were among the instructions given to Ovando, who, on the 13th of February, 1502, sailed in the largest fleet which had previously left for the new colony.

A fleet sails for the colony with Ovando, Feb. 1502.

Washington Irving, quoting from Las Casas, who, however, he states, gives the figures from memory,[1] says "that this fleet consisted of thirty sail, five of them from ninety to one hundred and fifty tons burden; twenty-four caravels, from thirty to ninety, and one

[1] Voyages of Columbus, vol. iii. p. 164.

bark of twenty-five tons. The number of souls," he continues, " embarked in this fleet, was about twenty-five hundred, many of them persons of rank and distinction, with their families." But as the smaller craft were not adapted for a voyage across the Atlantic, and as the number of persons embarked would give eighty-three, on an average, to each vessel, which is a greater number than even the largest vessels could conveniently carry with their luggage, and the requisite stores of provisions and water for such a voyage, there is no doubt some error in the figures of Las Casas. It is more likely, especially as the vessels conveyed many persons of rank and distinction, that the smallest was one hundred, and the largest somewhere about three hundred tons burthen. This fleet, it would appear, did not arrive at Dominica until the 15th of April; and in a violent storm, which it encountered soon after leaving Spain, lost, according to the same authority, one of its number, with " one hundred and twenty persons" on board.

and two months afterwards (9th May) Columbus follows,

Age and care were rapidly reducing the otherwise strong frame of Columbus, when, on the 9th of May, 1502, he set sail from Cadiz in four small caravels on his fourth and last voyage of discovery. He was then about sixty-six years of age; but from the hardships he had encountered, and the mental sufferings he had undergone, his constitution was so much impaired, that he was more infirm than many men who were ten years his senior. In his brother, Don Bartholomew, and in his younger son, Fernando, he however found wise counsellors and able assistants, combined with sincere and affectionate sympathisers.

Arriving at the Grand Canary, on the 20th of May, he took in a fresh supply of wood and water, and five days afterwards sailed for the Caribbee Islands, which he reached without shifting sail on the 15th of June, having had a fair wind and beautiful weather the whole way. On the 29th of that month he arrived at Dominica, where matters were still in so unsettled a state that he did not land, but proceeded to Port Hermoso, to the west of that island, to effect some necessary repairs to his vessels. Thence he sailed on his voyage of research, calling at Port Brazil for shelter from a gale, and leaving that port on the 14th of July, discovering, sixteen days afterwards, a small island within a few leagues of the coast of Honduras, still known by the Indian name of Guanaga or Bonacca. Here Columbus was struck with the contents of a large trading canoe which lay in the harbour, supposed to have come from the province of Yucatan, about forty leagues distant. This canoe, "eight feet wide, and as long as a galley, formed from the trunk of a single tree," was filled with multifarious articles, the manufacture and natural production of the adjacent countries. She was rowed by twenty-five Indians; and under an awning, or cabin of palm leaves, in form resembling that of the gondolas of Venice, sat a cacique, with his wives and children, who, displaying no fear whatever of the Spaniards, seemed to indicate that their ancestors had held intercourse with the people of civilized nations; while the articles of commerce which the canoe contained tended to confirm this impression. Washington Irving adds, that, besides various Indian products Columbus had met with before, this canoe had also in

and reaches Dominica, 29th June.

Discovers the island of Guanaga, 30th July.

Trading canoe.

her, hatchets of copper, wooden swords with sharp flints inserted, and made fast by lines of fish intestines, several copper bells and a rude kind of crucible—with various utensils in clay, marble, and hard wood. It also contained quantities of cacao, a substance not then known to the Spaniards, and which the Indians used both for food and as a species of currency. The Indians made use of a beverage resembling beer, and made from maize; and their women wore mantles, like those of the Moorish women at Granada. From some intelligent natives who were on board this vessel Columbus learned that they came from a rich and luxuriant country in the West, towards which they strongly advised the admiral to steer; and had he acted on this advice, he must have reached Yucatan in a day or two, and added to his previous discoveries that also of Mexico.

Prosecutes his researches to the South.

The discovery of the other opulent countries of New Spain would have necessarily followed; while the disclosure of the Southern Ocean would have revealed to him the true form of that interesting portion of the world, and, affording a succession of splendid discoveries, would have shed fresh renown on his declining years. But Columbus was intent on discovering the imaginary strait which would lead him to the land of Cathay, and the spice islands of India, which Marco Polo had so glowingly described.[1] Consequently on leaving the island of Guanagá, he stood southerly till he discovered the land now known as Cape Honduras, where he again encountered heavy storms, by which his vessel suffered much damage. "I have seen many storms," said Colum-

Reaches Cape Honduras.

[1] Letter of Columbus from Jamaica, "Select Letters," p. 204.

bus, "but none so violent or of such long duration." Against these he struggled for forty days, having advanced in that time only about seventy leagues, to another headland, to which he gave the name of Gracias a Dios (Thanks to God): here the coast turned directly south, and he obtained for his further course a fair wind for his leaky and tempest-tost caravels.

Discovers and explores the Mosquito coast.

Steering along the shore now known as the Mosquito coast, Columbus passed a cluster of twelve small islands, which he named the Limanares, and continuing south for about sixty-two leagues, reached, on the 16th of September, a copious river, where one of his boats, during an expedition to obtain a supply of wood and fresh water, was totally lost with her crew. Thence he proceeded to Cariavi, which he left, on the 5th of October, for a cruise along the coast of Costa Rica until he reached a large bay, called by the natives Carabaro, where he anchored. Here the Spaniards met with specimens of pure gold, and many indications of a higher state of cultivation if not of civilization than they had hitherto seen; signs in the opinion of Columbus of his approach to the territory of the Grand Khan. Pursuing his course, the squadron, on the 2nd of November, anchored in a spacious and commodious harbour, to which he gave the name of Puerto Bello, by which the town and harbour are still known. Here they were detained for seven days by heavy rain and stormy weather. Sailing hence on the 9th of November, the squadron proceeded eight leagues to the eastward, to the point since known as Nombre de Dios, where after visiting other places on the coast,

Puerto Bello.

he determined to relinquish the further prosecution of the voyage to the eastward, and return to the coast of Veragua. But the wind suddenly veered to the west, directly adverse to the new course he had adopted, accompanied by a succession of heavy gales, in which he and his crew endured great sufferings. It was not until the 6th of February, 1503, that Columbus reached the river Belem, where he formed a settlement, under the impression that he had at last discovered one of the richest parts of the Asiatic continent where gold abounded, and (strange hallucination!) the part from whence King Solomon had drawn most of his unbounded wealth.

Forms a settlement on the River Belem, 6th Feb., 1503.

At this favoured spot his brother Bartholomew arranged to remain with eighty men, while Columbus himself returned to Spain. No sooner, however, had they commenced to erect houses, and form the colony, than they were attacked by the Indians. Numerous encounters ensued, with much loss of life and suffering. Unable to maintain their position, the settlement was soon abandoned, and the squadron in a disabled state made the best of its way to Hispaniola. On the 10th of May Columbus sighted the north-west coast of that island, but again encountering boisterous weather and adverse winds, he was unable to reach the port of Dominica, and therefore steered for Jamaica, where he anchored. From thence he despatched a message by canoe to Ovando, the governor of Dominica, requesting that a vessel might be sent to his relief, his own being unseaworthy.

Anchors at Jamaica, June 1503.

More than eight months elapsed before Columbus received an answer of any kind from Ovando; and when a boat at last came with a messenger, it was only to leave a few trifling presents, and say that the necessary vessels would be provided as soon as possible. These at length arrived, and enabled him on the 28th of June, 1504, to leave his unseaworthy vessels behind him, and to set sail for Dominica, which he reached on the 13th of August after a very stormy passage. Ovando and the leading inhabitants gave him a show of welcome, and their conduct was courteous towards him; but there were too deep causes of jealousy and distrust for their intercourse to be cordial; nor was his sojourn at Dominica calculated to restore confidence. The state of things in the colony were far from satisfactory, and his own immediate concerns in great confusion. His rents and dues were either uncollected, or he could not obtain a satisfactory account of them; and the little he did collect was entirely consumed in fitting out the two vessels which were to convey himself and his crews to Spain. On the 12th of September he set sail, and having experienced tempestuous weather throughout the passage, did not arrive in the harbour of St. Lucar until the 7th of November, whence he had himself conveyed, broken down in health and spirits, to Seville, where he hoped to enjoy rest after the many hardships and anxieties he had encountered.

And Dominica, 13th August of that year.

Sails for Spain 12th Sept., which he reaches 7th Nov, 1504.

But there was no rest for the great navigator. Care and sorrow were destined in his latter days to follow him by sea and land. All his affairs were in confusion. Exhausted and infirm he was unable to seek an audience of his sovereigns; the letters he addressed to them, pleading for his rights, and asking

His sufferings,

simple justice at their hands, remained unanswered; and the discoverer of a New World, who had adorned the crown of Spain with by far its brightest jewels, broken down by infirmities, lay despised and impoverished in the city of Seville. This extraordinary conduct on the part of the sovereigns of Spain is, however, in some measure accounted for by the fact that Isabella lay dangerously ill, of an illness from which she never recovered; while the cold-hearted Ferdinand, instigated no doubt by the enemies of Columbus, treated all his applications, if he ever read them, with indifference.

During the remainder of the winter, and a part of the spring, Columbus was detained by painful illness at Seville, and when in May, 1505, he was able to be removed to Segovia, where the court then sat, Ferdinand had lost sight of all his past services, in what appeared to him the inconvenience of his present demands, though receiving the once courted navigator with many professions of kindness. Months were however spent in unavailing attendance upon the court. In the meantime his cares and sorrows were fast drawing to a close. He had for some time felt that he was dying, and having arranged as best he could his worldly affairs, he resigned himself into the hands of that great God whom he had worshipped with the same sincerity in his hours of triumph as he had done in the time of his deep adversity. On the day of Ascension, the 20th of May, 1506, being about seventy years of age, Christopher Columbus, who had done so much without reward, and suffered so much without upbraiding, passed silently away to, I doubt not, a better and a happier world.

and death, 20th May, A.D. 1506.

MERCHANT SHIPPING

VOL. I.

APPENDIX.

CONTENTS OF APPENDIX.

APPENDICES.

APPENDIX No. 1.

Note by Rev. J. O. W. Haweis on the rowing of ancient Galleys.

On a fine summer evening, when the author was seated beneath the tall elm-trees which overshadow his residence at Shepperton, on the banks of the Thames, he had the pleasure of a visit, accompanied by the Rector of the parish, from the Rev. J. O. W. Haweis, of Colwood, Crawley, in the county of Sussex. The author at the moment was in the midst of various calculations, endeavouring to solve the vexed problem of how the galleys of the ancients were rowed. As Mr. Haweis took an interest in scientific pursuits, he handed to him for consideration the notes he had made on the subject of rowing galleys, calling his attention to the fact that all ancient authors had spoken of the operation as being accompanied by the sound of music. Curious to know how a gentleman of his turn of mind would deal with the question, the author requested to be favoured with Mr. Haweis's views on the subject under consideration. The following notes and illustrations are the result. Though he does not think they solve the problem, or would be applicable to the various descriptions of ancient galleys of which accounts have been preserved, they are sufficiently novel and ingenious as to be worthy of preservation.

"I merely propose," remarks Mr. Haweis, "a possible quinquereme, which I imagine might be practically navigated. I am well aware that there is no reason to suppose it the actual plan of any ancient galley. The two sketches will explain themselves.

"I assume the interior breadth as from 27 to 30 feet at the largest part.

"The highest rowlock as 9 feet, the lowest 3 feet from water-line.

"The interior fittings waterproof to the height of 6 feet.

"The lower and second rowlocks, closeable at will by the rower drawing a plug from without, as the rising sea makes them useless.

"The disposition of rowlocks would thus be, for a set:—

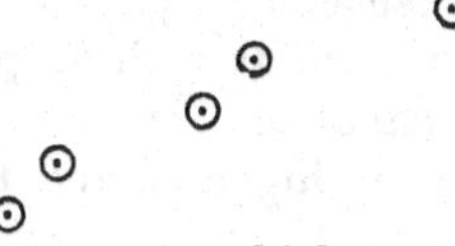

I cannot find any other way in which to avoid collisions.

"The oars are 9 feet, 13 feet, 18 feet, 24 feet 6 inches, and 35 feet. The long oars have handles thus:—

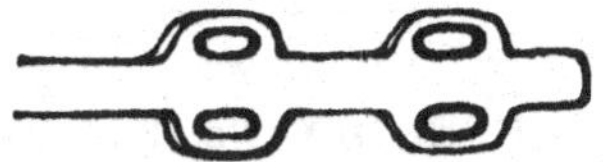

and feather in reverse, by the pusher dropping his hands, and so helping to recover the puller.

"Any two of these oars might be pulled in time with that next above or below it without much inconvenience, but the loss of power in thus working 1 and 5 would be enormous.

"Let 5 and 4 pull together to beat of drum; four strokes and returns to eight beats—

"Let 3 pull two strokes and returns—

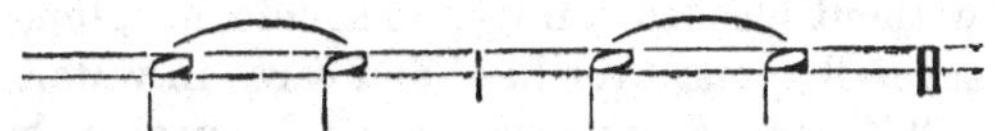

"Let 2 keep time with 3, the men advancing and retreating two steps.

"Let 1 take four steps forward in the two bars, and return in the same time.

"Thus all commence the stroke together; 2 and 3 renew the impulse at the bar; 4 and 5 do the same at half-bar.

"The beat of drum would be accented thus:—

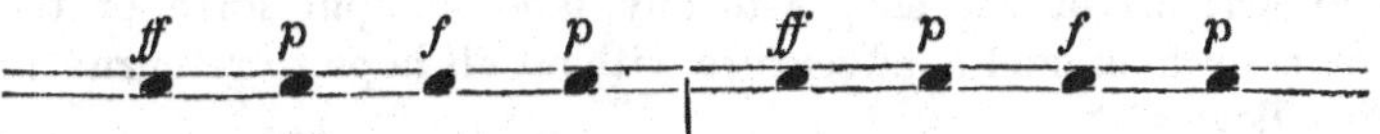

"Thus all would work together, and each man have the beginning of his stroke marked.

"There might be also a deck or gangway on each side for the protection of the men from sun and rain.

"Very large sweeps were exhibited as in actual use in the Exhibition of 1851, if I remember right.

"From some rude experiments with fir poles, I think 35-feet oars could be efficiently handled.

"The lower tiers would ship first, and the hands assist the upper.

"These are mere notions; but if they should be new to you, I shall be glad I entertained them."

APPENDIX No. 2.

Ordinances made by King Richard to be observed among seafaring men, A.D. 1190, *in the second year of his reign.*

Sleigers of men.

'FIRSTE, that if any man chanced to slea another on the Shipbord he should be bound to the deed body and soe throwen into the sea.

Secondly, if he killed him on land he should yett be bound to him as before,and soe buryed quicke, together.

Brauling.

"Thirdly, if any man should be convicted by lawfull witnesse that he drewe any weapon to strike any other, or chanced, by striking of any man, to drawe blood of him that was smitten, he should loose his hand.

The punishment for blood dwrajing.

"Fourthly, if he give but a blowe with his fist, without bloodsheddinge, he should be plunged three severall tymes over head and eares in water.

Revilers.

"Fiftly, if any man reviled another he should for every tyme soe missusinge himselfe forfeit an ounce of silver.

Thefte and Pickerry.

"Sixtely, if any man were taken with thefte or pickerye, and thereof konuicted, he should have his head poolled and hot pitche powred upon bis pate and upon that the feathers of some pillowe or cushione shaken aloft, that he might thereby be knowne for a theefe, and at the next arrivall of the shipps to any land, be put forth of the Company to seeke his adventure without all hope to retourne to his fellowes."*

* MS. Harleian, 158, fol. 2 b. A nearly similar statement is given in MS sloane, 43, fol. 12.

APPENDIX No. 3.

A Mandate for the King of Norway, in favour of his ship the Cogge.

"Anno Domini 1229, 13th year of Henry III.

"WEE will and command all bailliffes of Portes att the which the Cogge of Norway (wherein certain of the King of Norway, his souldiers, and çertayne Marchants of Saxonie, are cominge for England) shall touche, that when the forsaid Cogge shall chance to arrive att any of there hauens, they doe permitt the said Cogge safely to remayne in ther said hauens, soe long as need shall require, and without impedimente alsoe freely to deperte thence whensoever the governair of the said Shipp shall thinke it expediente.

"Witnesse the Kinge."*

APPENDIX No. 4.

New Charter of the Liberties of the Cinque Ports, confirmed in the time of King Edward, son of King Henry (EDWARD I., A.D. 1272–1307).

"EDWARD, by the grace of God, King of England, Lord of Ireland, and Duke of Aquitaine, to the Archbishops, Bishops, Abbots, Priors, Earls, Barons, Justiciaries, Sheriffs, Provosts, Officers, and all Bailiffs and his lieges health, Know ye that we, for the faithful service which our Barons of the Cinque Ports have rendered heretofore to our predecessors Kings of England and to us lately in our army of Wales, and for the service to us and our heirs Kings of England faithfully to be continued for the future, have granted and by this our Charter have confirmed for us and our heirs to the same our Barons and their heirs all their liberties and quittances, so that they may be quit of all duty [thelonium] and from all custom, viz.: from all lastage, tallage, passage, cayage, rivage, sponsage, and from all wrekke, and from all their selling, buying, and redeeming [rechato] through all our land and dominion with soc and sac and thol and theam;

* MS. Harl. 293, fol. 80. See also a long letter from Henry III. to Eric, King of Norway. Cotton. Nero, iii. p. 31, dated A.D. 1218, November 28; and a letter from Haco, King of Norway, promising to meet any complaints brought against his subjects. Rymer, "Fœd." vol. i., sub A.D. 1216–18.

and that they may have infangenethef; and that they may be Wrekfri and Wytefri and lastagefri and lovetopfri; and that they may have Den and stronde at Gernemuthe, according as it is contained in an ordinance by us made to that end, and to be observed perpetually; and moreover that they may be quit from shires and hundreds, so that if any shall wish to plead against them, they may not answer nor plead otherwise than they were wont to plead in the time of the Lord Henry the King, our great-grandsire; and that they may have their findings in sea and on land; and that they may be quit of all their property and of all their markets like as our free men; and that they may have their honours in our court and their liberties through all our land whithersoever they shall have come; and that for all their lands which they possessed in the time of the Lord Henry the King, our father, namely, in the year of his reign the forty-fourth, they may be quit for ever of common summonses before our Justiciaries for whatever pleas itinerant in whatever counties of this land they may be; so that the same may not be bound to come before the Justiciaries aforesaid unless any of the same Barons should implead any one or be impleaded by any one; and that they may not plead elsewhere except where they ought and where they were wont, namely, at Shypwey; and that they may have the liberties and quittances aforesaid for the future as they themselves and their predecessors have ever held them better more fully and more honourably in the times of the Kings of England—Edward, William the First, and Second, King Henry, our great-grandsire, and in the times of King Richard and King John, our grandsire, and of the Lord Henry the King, our father, by Charters of the same, like as those Charters, which the same our Barons have to that effect, and which we have inspected, reasonably testify. And we prohibit that any should unjustly disturb them or their market on pain of forfeiture of ten pounds; so however that when the same Barons shall have failed in doing and receiving justice, our Warden, and the Warden of our heirs of the Cinque ports for the time being, may enter their ports and liberties in their default for the purpose of doing full justice therein; so also that the said Barons and their heirs do to us and our heirs, Kings of England, by the year their full service of fifty and seven ships at their own cost for fifteen days at the summons of us and our heirs. We have granted moreover to the same of our special grace that they may have outfangenethef in their lands within the ports aforesaid in the same manner as the Archbishops, Bishops, Abbots, Earls, and Barons have in their manors in the county of Kent; and that they be not put in assizes of juries or in any recognitions by reason of their forinsec tenure against their will; and that concerning their own wines, in which they traffic, they may be quit of our right prise [*recta prisa*], viz., one cask of wine before the mast and another behind the mast. We have granted moreover to the same our Barons for ourselves and our heirs that they may have for ever this liberty, namely, that neither we nor our heirs shall have wardship or marriages of their heirs by reason of their lands which they hold within the liberties and ports aforesaid, for which they do their service aforesaid, and of which neither we nor our predecessors have had wardship or marriages in times past. The aforesaid our confirmation however of liberties and quittances aforesaid, and other our grants following, we have caused to be made to them anew of our special grace, saving always in all things our Royal dignity, and saving to us and our heirs the pleas of our crown of life and limbs. Wherefore we will and firmly command for ourselves and our heirs that the aforesaid Barons and their heirs have for ever all the liberties and quittances aforesaid, as the Charters aforesaid reasonably testify; and that of our special grace they have utfangenethef in their lands within the ports aforesaid in the same manner as the Archbishops, Bishops, Abbots, Earls, and Barons have in their manors in the county of Kent; and that they be not put in assizes of juries or in any recognitions by reason of their forinsec tenure against their will; and that concerning their own wines, in which they traffic, they may be quit of our right prise, viz., one cask of wine before the mast and another behind the mast; and that in like manner they have for ever the liberty aforesaid, viz., that neither we nor our heirs have wardship or marriage of their heirs by reason of their lands which they hold within the liberties and ports aforesaid, for which they do their service aforesaid, and of which neither we nor our predecessors have had wardship or marriages in times past. The aforesaid our confirmation however of the liberties and quittances aforesaid and other our grants following we have caused to be made to them anew of our special grace saving always in all things our Royal dignity, and saving to us and our heirs the pleas of the crown of life and limbs, as is aforesaid. These being Witnesses, the Venerable Father Robert [Kilwarby], Bishop of Porto, Cardinal of the Holy Roman

Church, William de Valentia [Valence], our uncle, brother William de Southampton, Prior provincial of Friars Preachers in England, Roger de Mortuomari [Mortimer], Roger de Clifford, Master Walter Scamel, Dean of Sarum, Master Robert de Scardeburg, Archdeacon of the East Riding, Bartholomew de Suthleye, Thomas de Weylond, Walter de Hopton, Thomas de Normanville, Stephen de Penecestre, Francis de Bouene, John de Louetot, John de Metyngham, and others. Given by our hand at Westminster the seventeenth day of June in the sixth year of our reign [1278]."*

APPENDIX No. 5.

Account of the Freights and of the Wages of the Sailors of the ships of Edward I. in divers fleets at divers ports, assembled as well for the passage of the King to Flanders as also for the Duchess of Brabant, &c.

	£	*s.*	*d.*
To Ralph de Aldeburgh, Master of the ship called "The Rose," of Lenna (Lynn?), loading in the same ship of his own for Gascony for the assistance of the king's army there, viz., as far as Burgh-on-the-sea, 428½ quarters of wheat from the port of Herewich, and for the freight of the same ship by way of expenses for it and the crew of the same ship, going and returning, paid into his own hands at Herewich, 30th December	15	0	0
To William Helmyn, Master of "La Mariola," of Lenna, freighted in the same manner, from Herewich to Burgh-on-the-sea with 428½ quarters, &c.	15	0	0
To William Brum, Master of the "Virly," of Ipswich, one constable, 48 crew, for wages from Jan. 12 to Feb. 2, 22 days inclusive .	14	6	0
To Walter de Fordham, Master of the Galley of Lenna, two constables, and 87 crew, for wages from Dec. 30, when they set sail from Lenna for Herewich [Harwich], to Feb. 2, 25 days inclusive; the Master and each constable 6*d.*, each sailor 3*d.* per *diem*	40	13	9

Ships carrying wheat to Gascony.

Ipswich.

The galley of Lenna.

* Cotton. Galba, E iv. f. 22.

To the same Walter for the payment of a Lodman [pilot], hired to conduct the same galley to Brabant . . . . £. s. d. 13 4

The principal places of embarcation are Gernemuth (Yarmouth), Bautreseie, Gippewicus (Ipswich), Haveford (Haverfordwest), Herewicus (Harwich), Schottele, Everwarton, Colneseie, Brithlingesei, Meresei (Mersey), Lim (Lyme ?), Loo in Cornwall, Portesmuth, Sandwich, La Stroude, Saltcote, London, Hardeburgh.

f. 89 *b.* A lantern bought. To Robert Le Horner for one large Lantern bought of the same, to hang in the ship assigned to the Duchess of Brabant for her passage to Brabant by precept of the king, that the other ships may be able to follow her in the sea at night . . . . 10*s.* 0*d.*

Pilot for the king's body.

To John Jolif of Sandwich, Pilot (Lodman), leading the ship called "The Coga of St. Edward," in which the body of the king passed over from Winchelsey to La Swyne, in his fleet for Flanders, paid into his own hands at Bruges on the 3rd of September . 26*s.* 8*d.*

Then follows a long list of the ships carrying victuals to Gascony and Flanders, with their names, quantities carried, masters and crews' names, &c.; as for example:

To John de Barewe, Master of the "Alice," carrying 12 barrels flour, 209½ quarters of oats, 23 carcases of beef, wages for himself and six men for 14 days 28*s.*

The names of the ships are interesting as:—La Messagere, La Plente, La Mariole, La Godyer, La Seefare, La Stoule, La Blithe, Le Lionu, La Grace Dieu, La Fankonu of Carmarthen, La Sauueye, La Johanette, Coga St. Thomas, La Mariote, La Furmente, La Viryly, the Hulks of the Blessed Mary, La Constance; many names of Sts., Andrew, Peter, Catherine, Mary, the Trinity, St. Cross, &c., &c.

f. 96. A long account of the passage of the ships at Plymouth for Gascony, arranged under the following ports:—Warham, Weymuth, Exemuth, Tegnemuth, Dertemuth, Loo, Fowy, Briggewater, Bristoll', Houue, Seford, Shorham, Portesmuth, Southhampton and Hamele, Lemyngton, Yaremuth, Pole, Warham, Weymuth, Lym (Lyme Regis), Sidemuth, Exemuth, Tenemuth, Dertemuth, Plymuth, Loo, Fowy, Kermerdyn, (Carmarthen), Briggewater, Chepstowe, Hertelpol, Ireland, Scardeburgh, Lenne, Blakeneye, Scotesmuth, Holan, Thornham, Jernemuth, Donewycus (Dunwich), Oreford, Goseford, Gippewycus (Ipswich), Herewycus (Harwich), Orewell, Colecestre, Sandwycus, Dovorria, Faversham, Folkstan, Heth', Romenale, Rye, Winchelsey, Hastinges, Pevenese, Seford, Baiona (Bayonne), Weymuth, Tegnemuth, Dertemuth.

f. 103. Wages of the sailors at Sandwich in the same year for the fleet of ships for the passage of Robert Fitz-Payn, and his countess to Flanders, arranged under ports with similar names to the above. These additional ones also occur: Gravelinges, Karnarvan (Carnarvon).

Sum total of the wages of the Sailors, £5586 19*s.* 3*d.*

APPENDIX No. 6.

Ships of Edward III. at Calais.

MS. Harl. 246, f. 12*b*.

The number of Shippes and maryners that served Kinge Edw. 3 in these warres.

THE SOWTHE FLEETE.

	Shippes.	Maryners.
The Kinge	25	419
London	25	662
Ayleforde	2	24
Hoo	2	24
Maydestone	2	51
Hope	2	59
Margate	15	160
Nonehethe	5	49
Montormont	2	23
Feversham	2	53
Sandwiche	22	504
Dover	16	334
Wighte	13	220
Wynchelsey	21	396
Waymouthe	15	263
Lyme	4	62
Seton	2	25
Sydmowthe	3	62
Exmowthe	10	193
Tegmouthe	7	120
Dertmowthe	32	756
Portesmowthe	5	96

MS. Harl. 3968, f. 130.

The rolle of the huge ffleete of E. 3 before Callice to be seene in the Kinges great Gardrobe in London, whereby appeareth the wonderfull strengthe of England by sea in those dayes.

THE SOUTHE FLEET.

	Shippes.	Marryners.
The King's	25	419
London	25	662
Ailford	2	24
Hoo *alias* Morne	2	24
Maidston	2	51
Sandwich	22	504
Dover	16	336
Wighte	13	220
Winchelsey	21	596
Waymouth	15	263
Lyme	4	62
Seton	2	25
Sidmouth	3	62
Hope	2	59
Newhith	5	49
Margat	15	160
Morne vel Morne	2	22
Feversham	2	25
Exmouth	10	293
Tegmouth	7	120
Dartmouth	31	757

	Shippes.	Maryners.
Plymowthe	26	603
Loo	20	315
Yalme	2	47
Fowey	47	770
Brystoll	22	608
Tenmowthe.	2	25
Haltinge	5	96
Romner.	4	65

MS. Harl. 246, f. 13.

Rye	9	156
Hythe	6	122
Shoram	20	329
Soforde	5	80
Newmowthe	2	18
Hannilhoke.	7	117
Hoke	11	208
Sowthampton	21	576
Leymingeton	9	159
Poole	4	94
Warham	3	59
Swansey	1	29
Ilfrecombe	6	79
Poterikstowe	2	27
Polerwan	1	60
Wadworthe.	1	14
Kerdiffe	1	51
Bridgewater	1	15
Carmarthen	1	16
Colechesworth	1	12
Mulbroke	1	12

Some of the Sowthe Fleete:

Shippes	473
Maryners	9307

MS. Harl. 246, f. 13b.

THE NORTHE FLEET.

Bamburghe . . .	1	9
Newcaster	27	314
Wolriche	1	12
Hertilpoole	5	145
Hulle	16	466
Yorke	1	9
Ravenser	1	27
Wodhowse	1	12
Storkehithe	1	10
Barton	3	30
Swynfleete	1	11
Saltfleete	2	49
Grymsbye	11	171
Portsmouth	5	96

	Shippes.	Maryners.
Plymouth	26	603
Loo	20	315
Yalme	2	47
Fowey	47	770
Bristoll	22	608
Tenmouth	2	25
Hastinge	5	96
Romney.	4	65

MS. Harl. 3968, f. 130*b*.

Rye	9	156
Hithe	6	122
Shoreham	20	39
Soforde *alias* Seforde .	5	80
Newmouthe	2	18
Hamowlhook	7	117
Hoke	11	208
Southampton	21	576
Lemyngton	9	159
Poole	4	94
Warham	3	59
Swanzey	1	29
Ilfrecoombe	6	79
Padstowe *alias* Patrickstowe . .	2	27
Polerwan	1	60
Wadworth	1	14
Kardiffe	1	51
Bridgwater	1	15
Caermarthen	1	16
Cailchworth	1	12
Mulbrook	1	12

Shippes:

The totall of the Shippes of the South Fleet are . . .	467

Maryners:

The totall of the Maryners of the same South Fleet are	9205

MS. Harl. 3968, f. 131.

THE NORTH FLEET.

Bamburgh	1	9
Walerich	1	12
Hartilpoole	5	145
Hull.	16	466
Ravenser	1	27
Yorke	1	9
Woodhouse	1	22
Stockhith	1	10
Barton	3	30
Swyneflete	1	11
Saltfleete	2	49
Grymesby	11	171
Waynfleet	2	49
Waynefleete	2	49
Wrangle	1	8

	Shippes.	Maryners.
Lemyce	19	382
Blackney	2	38
Scarborowghe	1	19
Yarmowthe	43	1950
Dornewiche	6	102
Orforde	13	303
Ipswiche	3	62
Merrye	13	303
Brightelensey	14	283
Colchester	12	239
Whibanes	1	6
Derwen	5	90
Boston	17	361
Swynhomber	2	32
Malden	2	32
Barton	5	61

Somma totalis of the Northe Fleete:

Shippes	234
Maryners	5624

Somma totalis of all the Englishe Fleete:

Shippes	707
Maryners	14931

Shippes and Maryners of Forrayne Countreyes:

Bayon	15	439
Spayne	7	184
Irelande	1	184
Flaunders	14	133
Gelderlande	1	24

Somma totalis of all the Strangers:

Shippes	38
Maryners	964

	Shippes.	Maryners.
Newcastle	17	314
Yermouth	43	1075 or 1950
Donwiche	6	102
Orford	3	62
Goford	13	303
Herwich	14	383
Ipswich	12	239
Mersey	1	6
Brightlingsey	5	61
Colchester	5	90
Whitbanes	1	17
Malden	2	32
Derwen	1	15
Wrangle	1	8
Lynne	16	382
Blackney	2	38
Scarborough	1	19
Boston	17	361
Swynhumber	1	32
Barton	5	91
The whole totall of the Shippes of the North Fleete	215	4383 or 5258

The somme totall of all the Englishe Ffleete:

Shipps	682
Maryners	13588 or 14463

MS. Harl. 3968, f. 131*b*.

The Shippes and Maryners of Strangers in this Ayde:

Bayon	15	439
Spayne	7	184
Irland	1	25
Flanders	14	133
Gelderland	1	24

The full nomber of the said Strangers Shippes and Maryners: [1]

Shipps	38
Maryners	805

APPENDIX No. 7.

Abstract of some of the more remarkable items in the repairs of the galleys and spinaces of King Edward III. at Bayonne.

	£	*s.*	*d.*	*f.*
Tuesday, 25 *Feb.*—To Dominic of St. Domyngo for xxj. lbs. of *Thomenk'* [? tow] at ij. *d.* halfpenny a pound		iiij.	iiij.	*ob.*
To John de Speruent for one pound of oil, bought for the use of the *calefetores* [? caulkers]				

[1] As the figures differ in the different records, it has been thought best simply to add the sum of the figures given in the text.

	£	s.	d.	f.
To the same for j. quintal xxxvj. lbs. of *gemma* [? tar], bought for the work of caulking the great galley, at per quintal		xv.	vij.	
To Peter Arñ for carriage of the said *gemma* from the house of the said John to the bridge . . .			*ob.*	iij.
To Peter Arñ Daufereyn for j. skin of a sheep for caulking the said galley .			vj.	
To Riudo Berñ for vj. faggots of brushwood bought for the caulking, and for their carriage to the bridge . .			iiij.	*ob. qr.*
To Peter de Mouhay and his three fellows drawing water from the great galley, for one day . . .		iiij.	vj.	
To Dominic of St. Domyngo, caulker, and his fellow; to the said Dominic xvj. *d.* per diem, to the other xij. *d.* .		ij.	iiij.	

Total of the day xxviij. *s.* vj. *d.* q[r]. m[a].

	£	s.	d.	f.
Wednesday, 26 *Feb.*—To John de Ville for v. boards bought for the repair of the galleys, price of each board, ij. *s.* .				
To Joan de Tyrons for l. nails bought for the work of the galleys, price				
To William Faber for j. gymbelette bought for the work of the galleys				
To Forcius de Lesgo and his fellow, carpenters, to the said Forcius xv. *d.* wages per diem, to the other xx. *d.* .		ij.	xi.	
To Dominic of St. Domyngo, caulker, and a certain servant; to the said Dominic xvj. *d.* wages per diem, to the other ix. *d.*		ij.	j.	
To the same Dominic for xvj. lbs. of Thomenk', price per lb. ij. *d. ob.* .		iij.	iiij.	
To Pelegrinus de Lesgo for j. jar, iij. saucers, in which the oil was placed, and for scrapers				
To Gerard Darbent for ij. *corbatons* at vj. *d.* each.				

Total of the day xx. *s.* j. *d.* *ob.* m[a].

	£	s.	d.	f.
27 *Feb.*—To John de Tyrons for c. nails of *rym*		iiij.		
28 *Feb.*—To John de Tyrons for xij. nails of *cauym*			v.	
To Peter Johannis for xij. faggots of wood for heating the *gemma*, and for the carriage of the same . .			ix.	*ob.*
3 *Mar.*—To John de Speruent for one lb. of oil for mixing with the *gemma*				
4 *Mar.*—To Peter Johannis for one ell of *tela* [? woven stuff] for the work of the caulkers			xij.	
7 *Mar.*—To Joan de Tyrons for c. nails of *Tylat*			xj.	
13 *Mar.*—To Dominic the caulker for his expenses from Bourdeaux to Bayonne .		iiij.	vj.	
15 *Mar.*—To Thomas of Sandwich, for carriage of the Serpent and Bygord' from the bridge to the house of the painter .			ij.	
To William Mustard for bread and drink during three days given to the workmen			iiij.	*ob.*
16 *Mar.*—To John de Tyrons for xij. nails of *cauym*			v.	
To John de Castete and his companion for scraping the old painting of the great galley, each per diem xv. .		ij.	vj.	
To the same John for a *calypp̃*, hired for this work			i.	*ob.*
To Forcius de Lesgo, and his four companions, carpenters, working upon the masts and yards, each per diem xvj. *d.*		vj.	viij.	
18 *Mar.*—To John de Castete for hire of a *calipp̃*; and for carrying sea-sand for the galleys			i.	*ob.*
To Adam of Northampton and his two companions, for carrying the said sand and drawing water for the small and the large galley . . .		ij.	ij.	
To the same Adam for three *tribul'* for throwing the sand from the *calipp'* to the galley			i.	*ob.*

	£	s.	d.	f.
20 *Mar.*—To John de Seyntmartre for two anchors bought of him for the great galley	ix.	x.		
To William Martini for carriage of the same from the house of the said John to the smith's, and from the smith's house to the bridge . . .			xvij.	
To Arn. Johannis de Lesgo for *issues* and ij. *plomas* of the said anchors . .		ij.	vj.	
22 *Mar.*—To William Rudi de Mamysan for the repair of two anchors . .		xij.		
To John de Lussy for iiij. *gemell'* of the masts		x.		
To William Rudi de Mamysan for liiij. great nails made for the *gemell'* .		ix.		
28 *Mar.*—To Forcius de Lesgo and his two companions for repairing the seats of the galleys, each per diem xvj. *d.* .		iiij.		
To Joan de Tyrons for cccc. nails of Tylat at xj. *d.* per hundred . .		iij.	viij.	
To the same for ccc. nails of Solira, at vj. *d.* per hundred			xviij.	
To the same for xlviij. nails of Cauym at v. *d.* per dozen			xx.	
29 *Mar.*—To John de Lussye for *furtanes* which were wanting in the said galleys .			x.	
To William Mustard . . . for bread and *pomadr'* for all the workmen for iiij. days		iij.	vj.	
ult. Mar.—To Joan de Tyrons for xxiiij. nails of Cauym for the repair of the hinder part of the great galley . . .			x.	
To Forcius de Lesgo for ij. *corbatons* for the work on the great galley, price .			xij.	
To the same Forcius for v. ells of board bought for repairing the *Bygorus* .			xxij.	
To Arn. Gerardi for ij. *ligna* (*timbers*) for *loffis* and *bousprete*		ij.	vj.	*ob.*
To William Rudi de Mamysau for j. anchor purchased of him for the great galley	iiij.	x.		

&c. &c. &c.

	£	s.	d.	f.
f. 5 *b.* ***Friday*, 14 *March*.**—Ryndo de la Fyte for xxij. lbs. "folii albi de extinctu" for the work of painting the galleys, at xviij. *d.* per lb.		xxxiij.		
To the same for vj. lbs. of Orpiment at xvj. *d.*		viij.		
,, ,, ij. lbs. of Ind. at ix. *s.*		xviij.		
,, ,, viij. lbs. of blankett at viij. *d.*		v.	iiij.	
,, ,, viij. lbs. of Certown at viij. *d.*		v.	iiij.	
,, ,, ix. lbs. of vernyz at xx *d.*		xv.		
,, ,, iiij. lbs. of oil for mixing with the colours, at ix. *d.* per lb. .		iij.		
,, ,, iij. lbs. "picturæ deauratæ" (? gold paint) at ij. *s.* . . .		vj.		
To Petronilla la Mercadere for xij. lbs. of vermylon at ij. *s.*		xxiiij.		
To John de London for xxxv. lbs. and a half of "Cole" at v. *d.*		xiij.	ix.	*ob.*
,, ,, for ij. lbs. of "Sedes de porc̄" at iiij. *s.*		viij.		
To Master John de Troia for waters for mixing with the colours . .			xij.	
,, ,, for a quintal of "Craye" (chalk ?)		iij.		
,, ,, for 1 lb. of wax		ii.	vj.	
,, ,, for eggs for mixing with the colours . .		iii.		
To Master John the painter, commencing the painting of the great galley, *per diem*		iij.		
,, ,, for Thomas the painter			xx.	
To Mark the painter and his companion, each *per diem* xij. *d.*		ij.		
2 *April*.—To Master John de Troia for verdeter			xviij.	

Expenses of the galley of W. Baydn de Furno.

To Benedicto de Pynak' for 1 timber

	£	s.	d.	f.
called the Braunc' bought for the galiot			vj.	
To John de Gys for two timbers called Tymon (rudder?)		iij.		
To Saubatus de Laste for iiij. timbers called Juillate			xii.	
To Garsia Arñ de Castere for xviij. tostes		iij.		

And many similar entries, mentioning ij. band'. ij. latons xxviiij. lattes (laths). Estaunzons (staunchions). xviij. boards of Byerñ for scanull nails of Tylate, Rym, and tasse. a *virga* (or yard). Cavill' and Coynz. Tymon (rudder?). breo albo. x pipes for *cisera* at iij. *s.* ix. *d.* each. nails of Solira, and of Tilat iiij. Corbatouns. Chastereux of the yard. repairing a broken anchor.

	£	s.	d.
To John Garsia de Baeryz (Biarritz) for his spinace hired of him for seeking and carrying the victuals for the mariners of the two galleys of our lord the King, and of one galeot, and for other necessary carriages by sea from Capebretoñ to England whenever necessary		xlv.	vj.
Wages of the mariners conducting the galley "St. George" from Bayonne to England	xxxv.	xviij.	iij.
		sterling.	
Wages &c. "St. Edward" . . .	xxij.	x.	viij.
		sterling.	
Wages &c. the galiot	xvij.	iij.	ix.

Sum total of all the expenses incurred ccc. iiij^{xx}. j. *l.* xviij. *s.* viij. *d.* money equivalent to c. j. *l.* xvj. *s.* viij. *d.* *sterling* ij. *d.* money.*

* Add. MSS. 17364.

APPENDIX No. 8.

The following condensed syllabus from Rymer's "Fœdera," to which great work repeated reference has been made in the foregoing pages, will serve to indicate the course of commerce between England and various states of the Continent between A.D. 1190 and A.D. 1460, and to exhibit, by the number of safe-conducts demanded and granted, the degrees in which it was interrupted by the disputes between the different monarchs of the period, or by acts of piracy. Ample illustration is also therein given of the custom of the day of pressing into the king's service any vessel or vessels he might want for any purpose.

The names of all the states with which England was at war or at peace have been preserved, and a few incidental notices with reference to the course of trade, or of manners and customs. It will be observed that, during the reign of Edward the Third, the impressment of ships for the king's war service descended as low as vessels of twenty tons; and that in one instance, at least, the defence of the sea was specially laid as a duty on the mercantile community. Special forms of safe-conduct, and for the arrest of ships and mariners, are added in illustration from MSS. in the British Museum.

Extracts relating to Maritime affairs from Sir T. Duffus Hardy's "Syllabus of the Documents . . . contained in Rymer's 'Fœdera.'"

RICH. I. 1190.—Ordinances by the king for the punishment of crimes committed on shipboard during the voyage to Jerusalem.

1191, 27 *March.*—The king confirms to the men of Rye and Winchelsea their privileges as under Henry II., they finding two ships to complete the twenty ships of Hastings.

JOHN. 1208, 8 *April.*—The king requests his mariners and merchants to aid the barons of the Cinque Ports in arresting all ships found on the seas, and conveying them to England.

1213, 3 *March.*—The king orders the whole shipping from every port in England to be at Portsmouth by mid-Lent.

JOHN. 1216, 2 *June.*—The king requests the jurats of Bayonne to employ their galleys in annoying his enemies.

HEN. III. 1217, 10 *Oct.*—The king to the king of Norway; will gladly promote commercial intercourse with that realm.

1236, 26 *May.*—Proclamation respecting the goods of persons escaping from shipwreck on the coasts of England, Poitou, Gascony, and Oleron.

1242, 8 *June.*—The king to the barons of the Cinque Ports and the men of Dunwich, to fit out shipping to ravage the coasts of France.

„ 7 *July.*—The king directs that the galleys of Bristol and all the galleys of Ireland shall harass the coasts of France.

1243, 12 *July.*—Men of the Cinque Ports to make reprisals upon John, duke of Brittany.

1259, *July.*—The king permits Henry of Castile to engage ships at Bordeaux and Bayonne for his expedition into Africa.

EDW. I. 1275, 23 *Sept.*—The king instructs Stephen de Penecastre, constable of Dover, relative to the contentions between the merchants of London and Seland (Zealand).

1280, 17 *July.*—Writ of protection for the merchants of Seiland trading with England.

1285, 15 *May.*—Regulations by the king and his council as to the compulsory unloading of ships in the Cinque Ports in time of danger.

1298, 14 *Feb.*—The king orders shipping (100 vessels) to be provided at Sluys for his return into England from Flanders.

1301, 14 *Feb.*—The king orders the bailiffs of Yarmouth and forty-one other ports in England and Wales and six in Ireland to supply him with shipping for the expedition against Scotland.

„ 4 *Oct.*—Proclamation to be made cautioning masters of ships and other sailors to be on their guard in their voyage towards Gascony and other ports of France.

1302, 7 *Nov.*—The king informs the warden of the Cinque Ports that instead of fifty-seven ships (which the barons of those ports are bound to

EDW. I. furnish) he will be satisfied with twenty-five for the Scottish war.

EDW. II. 1307, 26 *Sept.*—The king to Dionysius, king of Portugal, respecting the restitution of an English ship recovered by the Portuguese from some pirates.

„ 25 *Nov.*—The king orders the mayor and sheriffs of London to provide a ship for the conveyance of his tents [into France].

1308, 20 *March.*—The king orders Robert de Kendale, warden of the Cinque Ports, to take care that the merchants of France have liberty to trade in England.

1309, 12 *May.*—The king complains to Robert, count of Flanders, that an English ship had been plundered off Portsmouth by Flemish pirates.

1312, 28 *July.*—The king orders the keepers of the passages of the port of Dover to permit the abbots of seventeen houses of the Cistercian order to cross on their way to Citeaux.

1313, 15 *Feb.*—The king asks Robert, count of Flanders, to prevent the export of victuals, arms, &c., from Flanders into Scotland.

„ 22 *May.*—The king asks the pope to send to him certain Florentine merchants arrested at his suit in the papal court for having defrauded the English revenue.

1314, 1 *April.*—The king orders the barons of the Cinque Ports to send to him for the Scottish war the service of ships which they are bound to provide.

„ 26 *July.*—Robert, count of Flanders, asks the king to permit his subjects to trade with Flanders, and to consent to the establishment of a staple at Bruges.

1315, 13 *April.*—Robert, count of Flanders, complains to the king of the pillage of a Flemish ship in the port of Orwelle.

1315, 18 *Sept.*—The king orders the captains of his fleet to do all possible injury to the Flemish shipping.

1316, 18 *June.*—The king complains to the city of Genoa that the Genoese furnish the Scotch with ships and arms.

Edw. II. 1316, 28 *July*.—Haco, king of Norway, informs the king of England that he will meet any complaint brought against his subjects respecting the arrest of a ship in the port of Selay.

„ 9 *Aug*.—Haco, king of Norway, narrates to the king of England the facts of the complaints of the merchants of Berwick.

1318, 28 *Jan*.—Philip, king of France, complains to the king of England of the illegal detention in London of the goods of some French merchants.

„ 22 *Nov*.—General summons of citizens and merchants to a conference to discuss the establishment of a staple in Flanders.

1322, 6 *June*.—The king orders that the goods and merchandise of the subjects of John, duke of Brabant, shall not be arrested.

1323, 10 *April*.—Notification of the settlement of all disputes between the captains of five galleys of Venice and the town of Southampton.

„ 16 *April*.—The king having pardoned the misconduct of the five Venetian galleys at Southampton, the Venetians may therefore trade with England in safety.

1324, 28 *Jan*.—The king orders that all ships belonging to the subjects of the count of Zealand be arrested.

„ 10 *May*.—The king being about to vindicate his rights in Aquitaine, orders the mayor of Southampton and twelve other ports to provide him with shipping.

„ 10 *May*.—The king orders that the said ships shall be ready upon three days' notice.

„ 18 *Sept*.—The king of England assures Sanctius, king of Majorca, that he is ready to do justice in the matter of his ships, which are said to have been plundered by English pirates.

„ 18 *Dec*.—The king orders that search may be made at various ports for letters from abroad which may be prejudicial to the crown.

1325, 18 *Feb*.—The king of England to James, king of Aragon, respecting the seizure of the galleys of the king of Majorca.

EDW. II. 1325, 7 *May.*—The king of England asks Alphonso, king of Portugal, and his mother Isabella, to permit provisions to be conveyed into Gascony.

" 10 *May.*—The town of Bruges appoints proctors to treat with the king respecting commercial intercourse between Flanders and England.

EDW. III. 1326, 18 *Feb.*—The king orders inquiry to be made respecting a whale cast ashore upon the manor of Walton, belonging to the church of St. Paul's London.

" 3 *Dec.*—Writ for the payment of £10 to certain sailors of Bayonne who had aided Queen Isabella in coming into England from abroad.

1327, 30 *April.*—The king to the burgomasters of Bruges, offering to make reparation for the capture near Boulogne of a ship of Nieuport by men of Sandwich and Winchelsea.

1331, 5 *Feb.*—The king orders the sheriffs of Gloucester and Somersetshire to allow William de Clyvedon and two others to export 600 quarters of corn to Ireland, where there is great scarcity.

" 14 *Oct.*—William de Clynton, constable of Dover Castle and warden of the Cinque Ports, is commanded to allow fishermen to be paid for their goods in English money, notwithstanding the act against taking money out of the realm.

1333, 6 *Oct.*—The king requests Alphonso, king of Aragon, to withdraw the letters of marque granted to Berenger de la Tone.

1335, 16 *May.*—Power to William de la Pole and others to treat with Louis, count of Flanders, and the commonalties of Bruges, Ghent, and Ypres, about the piracies, &c., committed on both sides.

" 26 *May.*—The king requests John, duke of Brittany, earl of Richmond, to make redress for four anchors taken by his subjects from the ship of John Perbroun, of Great Yarmouth, wrecked on the coast of Garound in Brittany.

1335, 26 *Aug.*—The mayor and sheriffs of London are commanded to send to the king the ships arrested in the port of London, and to pay 60 marks

EDW. III. of the 500 marks granted by them in lieu of men.

1335, 20 *Sept.*—The king orders William de Clynton, warden of the Cinque Ports, to provide ships for the return home of certain knights in the company of the count of Juliers.

1336, 15 *March.*—The king orders the mayor and bailiffs of Bristol to take sureties from all masters of ships of the Cinque Ports which come to Bristol, that they will return to their proper ports to be equipped for the defence of the realm.

„ 3 *May.*—The exportation of timber or boards fit for ship-building forbidden.

„ 6 *May.*—The king orders John de Cobham, John de Segrave, and John de Wyndesore to pay 100 marks to Alexander Hurtyn, of Dover, deputy of William de Clynton, warden of the Cinque Ports, as part payment of £87 10*s.* which he has spent on the passage of the count of Juliers.

„ 28 *June.*—The king, having heard that the crews of the ships arrested in North Wales refuse to serve without being prepaid their wages, orders Richard, earl of Arundel, justiciary of North Wales, to survey the ships and give the crews a reward. Similar letter to the justiciary of South Wales.

„ 4 *July.*—The king releases the commonalty of Genoa from the payment of customs, to the amount of 8,000 marks, in recompense for a ship of Yoan Lucian taken by Hugh le Despenser.

„ 5 *Aug.*—The king orders John de Norwich, admiral of the fleet, from the Thames northward, who is searching for hostile galleys, consisting of ships of Great Yarmouth, to hold no communication with the men of the Cinque Ports, in consequence of the dissensions between them and the men of Yarmouth. Similar letter to Geoffrey de Say, admiral of the fleet south of the Thames.

1336, 2 *Oct.*—The king thanks Robert, king of Jerusalem and Sicily, for having stcpped the equipment of

EDW. III. ships which, under colour of assisting the Holy Land, were intended to be used against England; and desires credence for Nicolin Flisco of Genoa.

1336, 2 *Oct.*—The king thanks the Genoese for having burnt certain galleys which were being prepared against him; and desires credence for Nicolin Flisco.

„ 2 *Oct.*—Power to Nicolin de Flasco [sic], called "Cardinal of Genoa," to hire galleys for the king's service.

1337, 28 *Jan.*—The sheriffs of London are ordered to deliver to Thomas de Sapleford, overseer of the works in the Tower, 5000 (?) of iron, 200 Eastland boards, and 100 qrs. of sea-coal, for making anchors for the *Cristoffre* and the *Cogge Edward*, and for other works.

„ 1 *Aug.*—The king orders William Fraunk and Reginald de Donyngton to deliver a ship to William de la Pole, of Kingston-on-Hull, and Reginald de Conductu, for the purpose of exporting 30,000 sacks of wool. Similar letter to the mayor and sheriffs of London.

1338, 20 *May.*—The king has been petitioned by Peter de Puyane, admiral of the fleet at Bayonne, to grant him the rent of £6 on every whale caught at Biarritz, and other rents and dues in Bedured, in the bailiwick of Goes; and desires the seneschal of Gascony and the constable of Bordeaux to report as to their value.

1343, 20 *May.*—The king orders Richard de Aldeburgh and four others, to make inquisition concerning the carrying of two whales and two sturgeons, worth £3000, from the Manor of Hoveden; the bishop of Durham having wrecks of the sea and the right to the royal fish.

1346, 20 *Nov.*—Thomas de Drayton and two others are commissioned to provide twenty fishing smacks and ten boats for the siege of Calais. Similar commission for thirty vessels to Thomas Spigurnel and Philip de Whitton.

1348, 1 *Oct.*—Writs to the sheriffs of London, and the

Edw. III. mayors and bailiff of seventeen seaports, to unload merchant ships and send them to join the fleet.

1354, 8 *July.*—The king informs the captain and council of Genoa, that he has assigned the duty on 1000 sacks of wool for the redress of injuries to Genoa ships.

1355, 27 *April.*—Richard de Cortenhall and Robert de Baildon are appointed to arrest ships of twenty tons and upwards from the Thames to Lynn, and bring them to Southampton by June 11 for the conveyance of Edward, Prince of Wales, to Gascony.

1360, 24 *March.*—John Beech, master of the sloop *La Cogg Johan*, of Sandwich, is ordered to unload his ship and prepare it for war. Similar orders to six other masters.

1362, 22 *Feb.*—Commission to Hugh de Courtenaye, earl of Devon, and two others, to inquire into the plunder of a ship called *Tarrit* (*Tarida?*), and other ships wrecked at Plymouth.

Hen. IV. 1406, 6 *April.*—The king orders the mayor and sheriffs of London, and the mayors and bailiffs of Necastle-upon-Tyne, and nineteen other towns, to arrange for the fulfilment of the covenant made in parliament for committing the custody of the sea to merchants.

" 20 *Oct.*—The king forbids the collectors of subsidies and customs in London, and fourteen other towns to pay the sums assigned to the merchants for the custody of the sea, as they have failed in their engagement.

1410, 18 *Nov.*—The king orders Henry prince of Wales, constable of Dover Castle, and warden of the Cinque Ports, to make restitution to John Dirdolf and others of Berflet in Flanders, whose ships have been taken by Sir John Prendergest.

1411, 25 *June.*—Licence to John Ferkyn to send the two small guns which he made for a ship, in the ship of Spain in which the king is sending his great guns to Spain.

" 9 *Sept.*—The king informs the council of North

HEN. VI. Berve, in Norway, of his forbidding the Hanse merchants leaving England in consequence of the injuries done to English merchants, and of the licence given to nine merchants at St. Botolph to leave England.

1436, 5 *July*.—Proclamations to be made by the sheriffs of London, Kent, and three others, forbidding armourers and victuallers increasing their prices in consequence of the assembly of the duke of Gloucester's troops; and ordering merchants to send goods to Calais.

1438, 29 *Jan*.—Licence to John, bishop of Skalholt, in Iceland, to take a ship to Iceland and send it back with merchandise for the payment of his creditors.

„ 18 *Feb*.—Similar licence to John, bishop of Holar.

1440, 26 *Feb*.—Licence to John Secheford and John Candeler to export corn and other victuals to Iceland for the use of the bishop of Scalhelte, confessor of the king of Denmark.

1449, 22 *Dec*.—Licence to John Taverner, of Hull, to export goods to Italy through the straits of Marrot (Marocco), in his new ship or carrack, called the *Grace Dieu*.

1458, 8 *June*.—Licence to George Morsleyn, merchant of Cracow, to bring a ruby weighing 214 carats, for sale to England.

1460, 9 *May*.—Safe-conduct for a ship laden with Caen stone for the repairs of Westminster Abbey.

APPENDIX No. 9.

Form of "Safe-Conduct." (38 HEN. VI., A.D. 1459–60.)

Concerning safe-conduct.

THE king by his letters patent, having force for one year, of his special favour took into his safe and sure conduct, and into his special protection, keeping, and defence, Robert le Forrester, Roger le Clerk, Leonard Banche, and John de Cormeilles, merchants of Normandy, and each of them and the factors, attorneys, and servants of them and of each of them, with liberty to travel into the realms of the king of England, and through other the domains, possessions, and territories of the king whatsoever or whithersoever else it shall seem good to them, with one ship called the *Grace Dieu*, of Rouen, of the burthen of seventy casks or under, of which John Gognes, Nandin le Bastier, Martin Handry, John le Blanc, John Masse, or William Emery is master, with goods and merchandise of any kind whatsoever, and with twenty mariners and one mate (*pagesto*) as steersman of the same ship, together with the accoutrements, furniture, and other fittings of any kind whatsoever, that may be necessary for their own persons and for the defence of the said ship and of themselves, to be taken and borne with them conjointly or separately, as well by land as by sea, either on horseback or on foot, in journeying to the same place, tarrying, sojourning, abiding, and transacting business as merchants; and in unloading the aforesaid ship and reloading her with other goods and articles of merchandise, of whatsoever kind they may be, not belonging to the staple of Calais, in passing out of and returning into the same kingdom, domains, possessions, and territories of the aforesaid king, with the aforesaid ship reloaded, and with the master, mariners, and mate, with their accoutrements, furniture, and fittings aforesaid, safely and securely to foreign parts, so often as it shall seem good to them during the continuance of the present safe-conduct of the king, freely, without any let, disturbance, or hindrance whatsoever, notwithstanding any marque, counter-marque, or reprisal granted or to be granted, or any other cause or matter whatsoever. And therefore, etc., provided always that good security be given to the king for the customs, aids, and other moneys due to the king on account of the aforesaid goods and merchandise, as is equitable. Provided also, that the aforesaid Robert, Roger, Leonard, and John de Cormeilles, their factors, attorneys, servants, master, mariners, and mate, and those who accompany them, bear and conduct themselves properly and honestly towards the king and his subjects, and do not attempt, or anyone of them attempt, or dare to attempt, or any one of them dare to attempt anything which may turn out to the contempt or injury, the loss or inconvenience of the said king or of the subjects of the said king in any way whatsoever. And that they, nor any one of them shall by any means enter into any camp, fortress, or fortified town belonging to the king unless they shall first show, or some one of them shall show, to the commandants, mayors, or governors, there present, royal letters of safe-conduct. And if it shall chance that any one of the aforesaid Robert, Roger, Leonard, John de Cormeilles, their factors, attorneys, servants, master, mariners, and mate, or any of those who accompany them, does not wish to invalidate the present safe-conduct of the king, and yet to others who do not invalidate it, any damage or inconvenience should accrue, but he desires in the case of any individual or individuals who thus invalidate it, that their persons and property should be safe, then let them bring with them this *vidimus*, or a transcript or translation of these presents, executed in conformity with the king's genuine seal of obedience, to which implicit belief is to be yielded as it would be to the original. Witness, the king at Westminster, the 9th day of April.*

By the king himself verbally
Conformable with original
(Signed) WILLIAM RILEY.

APPENDIX No. 10.

Form for the Arrest of Ships.

Concerning the arrest of ships.

THE king to his well beloved John Accleve and John Scadlock, greeting. Know ye that having full confidence in your fidelity and prudence we have appointed you to arrest all and singular the ships and other vessels both of our kingdom of England and of foreign parts of the burthen of twenty casks and upwards lying in our port of London, and to cause them to be conveyed with all possible speed to the port of our town of Southampton, to serve on our present voyage for our moneys reasonably to be expended in this part. Wherefore we command you that you give due heed to these instructions and carry them out in the form aforesaid. Moreover, we charge all and singular the sheriffs, mayors, constables, bailiffs, ministers, and others concerned by the tenor of these presents, and strictly enjoin them that they should assist you in the execution of these presents, both by advice and by active support as it is fitting. In witness whereof, &c. Witness the king at Southampton the 27th July. By the king himself. Pat. 3 Hen. part i. M. 25 b.†

* MSS. Harl. 4819, fol. 123.

† Add. MSS. 4500, fol. 148.

APPENDIX No. 11.

Form for the Arrest of Mariners.

Concerning the arrest of mariners.

THE king to his beloved Haukin Pytman, master of a certain ship called the *Weathercock of the Tower*, (?) greeting. Know that we having full confidence in your fidelity and prudence have appointed you to arrest and seize so many mariners and servants as may be necessary for the management of the said ship as well within the liberties as without, and to place them and cause them to be placed in the aforesaid ship, under our security for their reasonable wages to be paid through your hands. Wherefore we enjoin you to give good heed in the matter of these premises and carry them out in the form aforesaid. Moreover, we charge all and singular the sheriffs, mayors, bailiffs, constables, ministers, and others our lieges and subjects within and without the liberties by the tenor of these presents, and strictly command that they afford you aid in the execution of these presents, both by their advice and by active assistance as is fitting. In witness whereof, &c. Witness the king at Westminster the 2nd day of January. Patent 3 Henry, 5, part i. M. 12 b.*

APPENDIX No. 12.

Register of Grants.

"A BOOK in fol. formerly belonging (as it is said) to the Lord Treasurer Burleigh, but lately bought of Mr. Strype; being a register of the grants, &c., passing the privy seal, royal signet, or sign manual during the reigns of King Edward V. and King Richard III., with some other entries made upon other occasions or in other reigns."

Among them are the following entries:

1592.—Licence to Loys de Grymaldes, Merchaunt of the parties of Jeane (Genoa), to bring into this realme Dyamount and other Gemmys or preciouse stones; to th' entent, that if they be for the king's pleasure, he may have the sale (*i.e.*, the pre-emption) thereof before alle other. Yeoven at London the 9th day of Decembre, a°. primo. f. 130.

* Add. MSS. 4500, fol. 149.

1636.—Commission to the Magistrates, &c., of the Port Towns, to man out their small Vessels and help the English Fleet in case they shall see them engaged with the Fleet of the Bretons, now lieng in Flaunders. Yeven the 20th day of Dec., an°. primo. f. 136.

1749.—Letter to the Owners, Maisters, &c., of the Naveye of the Counties of Norff. & Suff. entending to departe unto the parties of Islande (Iceland): requiring them not to depart towards the said parties of Islande without the king's licence: But to assemble themselves well harneyshed & apparelled for their owne suretie; and soo to departe alle togidere towarde Humbre, to attend there upon the King's Shippes of Hulle, as their Waughters (*i.e.*, Waiters, or Convoy) for the suertie of them alle. Yeven the 23rd day of February, a°. primo. f. 159. b.

2065.—Letters given to Gregory Walder, Maister of the Ship Marie-Lewe, of Lebyke (Lubeck), for his discharge touching the said ship, which being a stranger and dryven into Dertmouthe was (according to the olde uses and custumes of Englande by the Royall prerogatyve) reteyned for the King's use and bought at his reasonable price. Yeven at London 21 Jan., a°. 2do. f. 203.*

APPENDIX No. 13.

Ancient Form of Procedure for the restitution of Goods unlawfully seized.

Endorsed in French. On the 15th day of June in the 13th year [of King Richard II.], there being present at Westminster the Chancellor, the Treasurer, the bishop of Lo[ndon], the bishop of Sarum, the bishop of Hereford, Monsr. Richard Lescrop̃, Monsr. William Lescrop, this examination was read, and the advice of the above persons and of the Guardian of the Privy seal, that restitution be made of the xiiij. tuns of wine.

Original in Latin.

The following examination was made on the 29th day of Novr., in the 13th year of King Richard II. [A.D. 1389], by Master Edmund Stafford, keeper of the Privy seal, and Edward Dalingrug̃g̃, and Richard

* MSS. Harl. 433.

Stury, knts., for the time being of the king's council, by the same council especially appointed for this affair, upon that, namely, that from a certain ship of a certain Commendator of Germany, with certain casks of wine and other divers merchandises of the goods of Valascus Vincentius and Gunsalous Johannes, Merchants of Portugal, laden, and taken at sea by Englishmen of Sandwich against the will of the said merchants, and taken into the port of Sandwich, Robert de Assh'ton, while he lived, Constable of Dover Castle, had, as is said, 14 casks of wine, applied to his own uses, for which satisfaction had not yet been made, as is said, although the same Robert while he lived had been frequently applied to for it.

Thomas Elys, forty years of age and upwards, sworn, and examined, and diligently required respecting the said matter, says that about 7 years ago at Sandwich 14 casks of wine were taken from the aforesaid ship on the part of Robert Assh'ton for his own uses, as he then heard of public rumour, going about those parts. And of the other casks of wine taken in the same ship restitution was made, as he says, by command of the Council of the Lord King, as he heard from many persons, and he believes truly, as he says, that satisfaction had not yet been given to the said merchants for the 14 casks of wine under consideration.

John Godard, sworn, &c.: had heard from the relation of many, that such a ship had been taken with wine upon Palm Sunday about 7 years ago, &c. &c.

John Conduyt, sworn, &c.: Peter Conduyt, sworn, &c.: knew that such a ship had been taken by his father with wine, and saw the same ship, &c.

Hugh atteWelle, sworn, &c.: heard of, and saw such a ship at Sandwich, &c.; heard by common report that about the time of the last earthquake restitution had been made, &c.

Robert Sandewych', sworn, &c.: says that such a ship was taken and carried into Sandewych, and the wine was sold to the knowledge of this witness, who had charge of the *cista* (chest) which held the money received for this wine, and after that that party came from Portugal with letters of the king of Portugal, by command of the Council of the king of England restitution was made to them of that money for 100 casks of wine, exclusive of that for 14 casks which Robert Assh'ton had for his own uses.

And this deponent says that for a sum of money between 100 shillings and 5 marks each of these casks were sold. This deponent also says that he with those merchants stood security for Robert Assh'ton for payment of the 14 casks; and the same Robert, to the knowledge and hearing of this deponent, acknowledged his debt and said that he was willing to pay for the same, but had made frequent delay in the matter; and this deponent never heard of payment having been made in the matter. The deponent also states that he was present at the sale of the casks of wine, as is aforesaid.

And all the aforesaid witnesses, examined singly, said that they estimate each of these casks at the value of six marks, after that the said 14 casks had been taken out and selected by Robert Assh'ton as being the best.*

* MS. Cott. Nero, B i. f. 18.

INDEX.

END OF VOL. I.

LONDON: PRINTED BY WILLIAM CLOWES AND SONS,
STAMFORD STREET AND CHARING CROSS.

Printed in the United States
By Bookmasters